Readings in Multicultural Practice

Readings in Multicultural Practice

Glenn C. Gamst
University of La Verne
Aghop Der-Karabetian
University of La Verne
Richard H. Dana
Regional Research Institute for Human Services, Portland State University

For information:

SAGE Publications, Inc.
2455 Teller Road
Thousand Oaks, California 91320
E-mail: order@sagepub.com

SAGE Publications Ltd.
1 Oliver's Yard
55 City Road
London EC1Y 1SP
United Kingdom

SAGE Publications India Pvt. Ltd.
B 1/I 1 Mohan Cooperative Industrial Area
Mathura Road, New Delhi 110 044
India

SAGE Publications Asia-Pacific Pte. Ltd.
33 Pekin Street #02-01
Far East Square
Singapore 048763

Printed in the United States of America

Library of Congress Cataloging-in-Publication Data

Readings in multicultural practice/Glenn C. Gamst, Aghop Der-Karabetian, Richard H. Dana [editors].
p. cm.
Includes bibliographical references and index.
ISBN 978-1-4129-6517-0 (pbk. : alk. paper)
1. Cross-cultural counseling—United States. 2. Social work with minorities—United States. 3. Multiculturalism—United States. I. Gamst, Glenn. II. Der-Karabetian, Aghop. III. Dana, Richard H. (Richard Henry), 1927-

BF636.7.C76R42 2008
361′.06—dc22 2008001216

Printed on acid-free paper

08 09 10 11 12 10 9 8 7 6 5 4 3 2 1

Acquiring Editor: Kassie Graves
Editorial Assistant: Veronica Novak
Production Editor: Sarah K. Quesenberry
Copy Editor: Linda Gray
Typesetter: C&M Digitals (P) Ltd.
Proofreader: Jenifer Kooiman
Indexer: Will Ragsdale
Cover Designer: Ravi Balasuriya
Marketing Manager: Carmel Schrire

Contents

Introduction

The purpose of the *Readings in Multicultural Practice* is to provide instructors and students with a readable, current, and fairly comprehensive introduction to the multicultural literature. As a segue into this comprehensive literature, we used the conceptual framework, or four-subscale configuration, that we discovered in the development of the California Brief Multicultural Competence Scale (CBMCS) instrument. (See Article 1 in this reader.) That is, the 29 articles and chapters reprinted in this Reader roughly correspond to the four subscales of the CBMCS instrument and its subsequent four modules of the CBMCS Multicultural Training Program: Module 1—Multicultural Knowledge; Module 2—Awareness of Cultural Barriers; Module 3—Sensitivity and Responsiveness to Consumers; and Module 4—Sociocultural Diversities (Dana, Gamst, & Der-Karabetian, 2008).

One of the many challenges we experienced compiling this Reader was the determination of what to include. The multicultural literature has been growing exponentially over the last decade, making our decision-making process very difficult. A number of suitable candidates emerged during the course of our literature review. Our final selection criteria emphasized manuscript readability, module content relevancy and saliency, and timeliness of the contribution.

This Reader can be used as a main or supplementary text for many undergraduate or graduate course offerings in multicultural psychology, counseling, social work, nursing, or medical science.

We hope this Reader enlightens, motivates, and helps to facilitate multicultural practice.

Reference

Dana, R., Gamst, G., & Der-Karabetian, A. (2008). *CBMCS multicultural training program.* Thousand Oaks, CA: Sage.

PART I

MULTICULTURAL KNOWLEDGE

Each part of the Reader is organized to amplify and accentuate important topics and concepts related to each of the four CBMCS subscales. Part I addresses the general issue of multicultural knowledge and consists of eight research articles and book chapters.

In the first article, Gamst et al. (2004) describe the development of the 21-item California Brief Multicultural Competence Scale (CBMCS). The CBMCS was derived from principal component analysis; its item content was validated by a panel of experts and with confirmatory factor analysis. This article lays the empirical foundation or scaffolding for the subsequent CBMCS Multicultural Training Program and the present Reader.

The second manuscript, from the U.S. Department of Health and Human Services (2001), is the Executive Summary to the *Supplement to Mental Health: A Report to the Surgeon General.* This groundbreaking document underscores the following important findings: (a) Mental illnesses are real and affect all populations, (b) striking disparities in mental health care are common for U.S. racial and ethnic minorities, and (c) these disparities impose a greater disability burden on minorities. This report sounds a clarion call to action that includes an expansion of the ethnic science base, improvement in access to treatment, reduction in barriers to mental health care, and the improvement of quality of mental health services and their expansion.

In the third article, Lam and Sue (2001) review the client-therapist matching literature on various client demographics, such as gender, race/ethnicity, sexual orientation, and social class, on clinical outcomes. Due to a paucity of research in this area, coupled with methodological problems, a clear picture has failed to emerge. But the question of who should do what to whom in the community mental health field still prevails.

The fourth manuscript by Costantino, Dana, and Malgady (2007) explores the various facets of a mental health service delivery model—the multicultural assessment intervention process (MAIP) model. The MAIP model predicts that the match between (a) a client and a mental health provider and (b) the client's ethnic/racial identity and acculturation status are mediated by the provider's self-perceived cultural competence, which in turn influences the client's clinical outcome. The MAIP is one of a few comprehensive frameworks that attempt to model the complex and dynamic multicultural factors shaping community mental health client outcomes.

The fifth article by Abreu, Gim Chung, and Atkinson (2000) provides a succinct review of the multicultural counseling training literature. Following a brief historical overview, several models of multicultural counseling training are described and a model that integrates multiculturalism into the entire training program curriculum is advocated.

Constantine and Sue (2005), in the sixth article, offer a helpful review and synthesis of the American Psychological Association's multicultural guidelines that encourage an infusion of multicultural initiatives into the field of psychology. These initiatives include culturally sensitive education, training, research, practice, and organizational development.

The seventh article, by Arrendondo and Arciniega (2001) reviews useful pedagogical strategies and techniques that stem from the multicultural counseling competencies developed by the Association of Multicultural Counseling and Development. The authors apply these competencies to three critical training domains: awareness of provider cultural values and biases, awareness of client worldview, and culturally appropriate intervention strategies.

The last manuscript in Part I provides a useful introduction and overview of the construct of acculturation, including its measurement and relevancy to multicultural populations. Cuéllar, Siles, and Bracamontes (2004) explore some of the early literature on acculturation, particularly as it pertains to Latino/a Americans and its relationship as a moderator variable to mental health outcomes.

1

Cultural Competency Revised

The California Brief Multicultural Competence Scale

Glenn Gamst

Richard H. Dana

Aghop Der-Karabetian

Myriam Aragon

Leticia Arellano

Gloria Morrow

Luann Martenson

How adequately have training programs prepared professional psychologists to work with culturally diverse populations? This question has been a focus of multicultural competence research for 3 decades. In 1973, the American Psychological Association (APA) endorsed multicultural training recommended by the National Conference on Levels and Patterns of Professional Training (Korman, 1976). The American Counseling Association compiled guidelines for standard test usage with multicultural populations (Prediger, 1994). Early and more recent comprehensive APA guidelines on multicultural education, training, research, practice, and organizational change addressed the centrality of cultural issues for all psychologists (APA, 1993, 2003). However, implementation in professional

Authors' Note: This research was supported in part by the California Department of Mental Health, Fiscal Year Allocation Grant (4440-101-0001 [c]) awarded to the first author. The authors thank Anita Chico, Terry Kramer, Keith Harris, A. J. Guarino, and Larry Meyers for their help in various stages of this article. A California Brief Multicultural Competence Scale user's guide is available on request from the first author.

psychology has been meager except in Counseling Psychology programs (LaFromboise & Foster, 1992; Mio & Morris, 1990), and the characteristics of multicultural competence training have remained elusive (e.g., Murphy, Wright, & Bellamy, 1995; Quintana & Bernal, 1995).

A national examination of multicultural training suggested a model for quality multicultural training (Ponterotto, 1997, 1998), although sensitivity rather than proficiency has apparently resulted from additional training. Each area of professional psychology has reported survey data suggesting limited efficacy for available training (for a review, see Ponterotto & Alexander, 1996). Psychologists in most professional programs report inadequate formal training and supervised experience to prepare them for practice with multicultural clients (Allison, Crawford, Echemendia, Robinson, & Knepp, 1994). Adequacy of self-perceived awareness and skills as reported in a more recent survey of multicultural competencies (Holcomb-McCoy & Myers, 1999). In these two surveys, differences among participants in training, ethnicity, program affiliation, and graduation year may account for differences in findings. Other studies (e.g., Pope-Davis, Reynolds, Dings, & Nielson, 1995) also found that greater self-perceived multicultural competencies among students of color and ethnic minority status per se can provide in vivo cultural knowledge and personal experience with discrimination (Lee & Richardson, 1991; Ponterotto, Casas, Suzuki, & Alexander, 2001; Robinson & Ginter, 1999).

Multicultural Counseling Competency Model

The Cross-Cultural Counseling Competency Model (for a review, see Ponterotto, Fuertes, & Chen, 2000) contained in a Division 17 position paper (Sue et al., 1982) specified 11 competencies in three broad areas, including attitudes/beliefs, knowledge, and skills. Preserving these three superordinate areas, this model was subsequently expanded to 31 specific competencies (Sue, Arredondo, & McDavis, 1992). Operationalization of these competencies by 119 explanatory statements, within an American Counseling Association training context (Arredondo et al., 1996), led to an even more comprehensive formulation by Divisions 17 and 45 (Sue et al., 1998) with a further expansion to 34 competencies.

Multicultural Competency Instrumentation

A number of instruments have been developed to measure multicultural competencies as conceptualized in the Cross-Cultural Counseling Competency Model including the Cross-Cultural Counseling Inventory—Revised (CCCI-R; LaFromboise et al., 1991), the Multicultural Awareness, Knowledge, Skills Survey (MAKSS; D'Andrea et al., 1991), the Multicultural Counseling Awareness Scale-Form B (MCAS-B; Ponterotto & Alexander, 1996) the Multicultural Counseling Knowledge and Awareness Scale (MCKAS; Ponterotto, Gretchen, Utsey, Rieger, & Austin, 2002), the Multicultural Counseling Inventory (MCI; Sodowsky et al., 1994; Sodowsky et al., 1998), and the Multicultural Competency and Training Survey (MCCTS; Holcomb-McCoy, 2000). (The MCAS-B was used in the present study because the new version [MCKAS] was not available during the initial phases of our research.)

Several aspects of the development of these instruments and validation of scores from the instruments are relevant for purposes of comparison and for evaluating the adequacy of construct delineation. Evidence for psychometric properties (i.e., origin of items, scale development, scoring procedures, reliability, validation evidence, subscale development and clarity of subscale interpretation, and factor labels) have been examined for scores from each of the aforementioned instruments (Ponterotto & Alexander, 1996; Pope-Davis & Dings, 1995). Although the items in these instruments had a common source in the multicultural competency model, each instrument implemented somewhat different methods, and several versions of the model were used to create an item pool. Scale development procedures differed, numbers of items varied across instruments, and scoring procedures either added or averaged items. Internal consistency reliabilities were, in general, adequate. There was low to moderate subscale score consistency within instruments, but less than desirable subscale score consistency across instruments, while validation enterprises differed in kind and adequacy across instruments.

All instruments used exploratory factor analyses, although the MCI, MCAS-B, and MCKAS used confirmatory factor analyses as well. These factor analyses yielded one, three, or four factors with a variety of labels reflecting the structure coefficients obtained. The triad of original constructs was augmented by factors for Relationship in the MCI and Racial Identity Development and Multicultural Terminology in the MCCTS. The CCCI-R is uniquely a unidimensional measure, based on supervisor ratings, rather than a performance self-assessment by clinicians. Recent studies (i.e., Constantine et al., 2002; Ponterotto et al., 2002) delineated two consistent factors corresponding to self-perceived multicultural counseling skills and multicultural attitudes/beliefs.

A number of critical reviews from 1985 to 2001 provided evaluations of the multicultural competence construct (e.g., Constantine & Ladany, 2001; Ponterotto & Alexander, 1996; Ponterotto, Fuertes, et al., 2000; Ponterotto & Furlong, 1985; Ponterotto, Rieger, Barrett, & Sparks, 1994; Pope-Davis & Dings, 1995; Pope-Davis et al., 2001; Pope-Davis & Nielson, 1996). These reviews convey only limited support for the three-factor model. These instruments measure beliefs about services rather than attitudes, and caution is advised in using these instruments for the measurement of multicultural competence per se (Constantine et al., 2002).

Pope-Davis and colleagues (2001) examined consequences of omitting consumer perspectives on multicultural competency skills that included expectations and experiences. Research has been affected by inadequate empirical data and sociopolitical attitudes. Legitimate questions have been raised concerning multicultural competencies with systems larger than one individual client or with noncounseling interventions (Constantine & Ladany, 2001; Ladany, Inman, Constantine, & Hofheinz, 1997).

Research using these multicultural competency instruments provided promising correlational and regression analysis relationships to demographic and training variables; case conceptualization skills; and hypothesized, linked constructs (Ponterotto, Fuertes, et al., 2000). In summary, these authors suggested that the findings contributed to an enlarged intercultural perspective with a nonracist personal stance, enhanced worldview, awareness of oppression, and racial identity development. Statistical examination of social desirability influence has been recommended (Worthington, Mobley, Franks, & Tan, 2000). Sodowsky et al. (1998) reiterated this caveat using a new multicultural-specific social desirability scale with the MCI.

The sheer numbers and quality of thoughtful criticisms focused on these instruments suggest their perceived importance for professional training in counseling and psychology. However, there are substantive limitations to all instruments when they are used as diagnostic precursors to specific multicultural competence training objectives or as optimal pre-post measures of the effectiveness of such training. Discrepancies in historical findings may be attributed to the use of several independent instruments developed to measure the same constructs. It has been concluded that the "collective group of instruments is still only in their infancy" (Ponterotto, Fuertes, et al., 2000, p. 646), and continued factor analytic research on a larger scale with all instruments has been recommended (Ponterotto & Alexander, 1996). A single instrument, developed from available instruments, could potentially resolve some of the reported critical issues and shortcomings.

A Rationale for Research on Multicultural Competency Instruments

Multicultural competency instruments were constructed and evaluated primarily in the context of counseling training programs. These programs endorse the centrality of cultural issues, the coextensive nature of multicultural and clinical competencies, and the primacy of culture as a proximal variable in research. Because an acknowledged limitation of multicultural competency instruments is measurement of self-efficacy beliefs rather than skills, objective relationships between these beliefs and demonstrated ability to provide effective mental health services to culturally diverse clients are ultimately necessary (Lent, Brown, & Larkin, 1986). The research history of these instruments endorses their continued use; nonetheless, the lack of uniformity in what they measure suggests that their use to evaluate provider competencies is premature. There has been a call for more valid multicultural counseling instruments to replace the original measures (Atkinson & Israel, 2003), because their item contents were derived from committee consensus rather than empirical identification. It is also necessary to make the most responsible and efficacious use of these existing measures to ensure their continued presence as progenitors of more adequate training that can be evaluated by subsequent clinical outcomes. The potential utility of these existing measures may be simply diagnostic in the sense of legitimizing in-service training as an intervening step prior to evaluation of clinician skills with clients.

The primary objective of this research is to improve multicultural competence instrumentation as a precursor to consistent and replicable multicultural competence training for clinicians within a comprehensive system of mental health care. A secondary objective is to embed competence assessment and training within a quality-of-care model for ethnic minority populations. Ponterotto, Gretchen, and Chauhan (2000) described a number of relevant models, including the Multicultural Assessment-Intervention Process model (MAIP; see Dana, 1993, 1998, 2000) that provides a system of care context in which the present research is a major component. MAIP treats culture as a proximal variable with successive steps for adequate mental health care that include service delivery style, client acculturation or racial identity status, client-clinician matching, multicultural competence training, and use of cultural components in interventions within a format of pre-post client evaluation.

Construction and Development of the California Brief Multicultural Competence Scale (CBMCS)

This research was designed to create a single, brief instrument from items in several multicultural counseling competency measures predicated on responses from direct-service community mental health providers. The development of this new instrument responds to the call for continued scrutiny of the multicultural competency model itself and the operationalization of these beliefs concerning self-perceived competencies (Ponterotto et al., 2002).

This article presents the results of four studies. Study 1 examines items from subscales in the self-report instruments for social desirability. Subsequently, using these instruments, data from a relatively large sample of mental health practitioners were obtained. Thus, in Study 2 (which is subsequently trichotomized into Studies 2a, 2b, and 2c), a short form version of the CBMCS was developed from four instruments (CCCI-R, MAKSS, MCAS-B, MCCTS), factor analyzed, scrutinized by a panel of experts for content validation, and further verified by means of a confirmatory factor analysis. Study 3 provided an additional check for social desirability bias within the CBMCS subscales. Study 4 provided further support of the CBMCS with an additional confirmatory factor analysis on an independent sample. This brief instrument (the CBMCS) can be used as an empirical basis for the development of training programs that can be evaluated for efficacy in treatment settings.

Study 1: Social Desirability Check

This study related the Marlowe-Crowne Social Desirability Scale (SDS; Crowne & Marlowe, 1960) to each of the individual items in a comprehensive item pool representing four measures in order to eliminate those items correlating with the SDS from subsequent analyses.

Method

Participants. The Study 1 participants constituted a convenience sample of 54 mental health service providers at a Southern California community mental health agency. The mean age for the sample was 28.9 (SD = 14.79, Mdn = 30.0). Sixty percent of the sample was female. Sample ethnicity was as follows: White American (37%), Latino American (32%), African American (15%), Asian American (7%), Native American Indian (2%), and other (7%). Education levels for the sample were master's degree (46%), bachelor's degree (30%), high school diploma (23%), and doctoral degree (1%). Approximately 41% of the sample was bilingual, primarily bilingual Spanish. The mean years worked in the mental health field was 5.70 (SD = 5.22), and the mean years this sample worked with multicultural clients was 7.35 (SD = 5.36). The percentage of this sample trained in multicultural counseling programs was 46%, approximately 69% had received multicultural course work, and 67% had taken a multicultural workshop or seminar.

Questionnaire and procedure. Participants were given a consent form and a brief explanation of the goals of the project. The questionnaire consisted of a page of demographic items (13), followed by 157 Likert-type questions compiled from the four cultural competency scales, all on a 4-point scale (4 = *strongly agree*, 1 = *strongly disagree*). Some of the items were slightly reworked to conform to an agree–disagree response format. The 33-item (true or false) SDS (Crowne & Marlowe, 1960) was completed immediately after the 157 cultural competency items.

Results and Discussion

The SDS scores did not correlate appreciably with any of the multicultural competence subscale scores, with the exception of one moderate negative correlation. Because of the interest other researchers are likely to have in this topic, we report these correlations as follows: MCI-Skills (–.18), MCI-Awareness/Experience (.02), MCI-Relationship (.18), MCI-Knowledge (–.04), CCCI-R Skills (–.17), CCCI-R-Awareness (–.07), CCCI-R-Sensitivity (–.09), MAKSS-Awareness (–.11), MAKSS-Knowledge (.09), MAKSS-Skills (–.13), MCAS-B-Knowledge/Skills (–.06), MCAS-B-Awareness (–.37; $p < .01$), MCAS-B-Social Desirability (.04; $p < .01$), MCCTS-Knowledge (–.06; $p < .01$), MCCTS-Awareness (–.20; $p < .01$), MCCTS-Definitions (–.22; $p < .01$), MCCTS-Racial Identity (.10; $p < .01$), and MCCTS-Skills (–.18; $p < .01$). What is impressive about these coefficients, when scrutinized as a whole, is the fairly consistent apparent lack of social desirability contamination among the scores of these subscales. These low correlations appear to contradict some earlier studies that used self-report cultural competence scales, which may be a function of the mental health practitioner sample used in Study 1.

All 157 individual Likert-type questions that composed the four self-report multicultural competency measures were correlated with the SDS. The goal was to identify questions that correlated significantly with the SDS for possible elimination from the Study 2 item pool. The SDS instrument was not used in Study 2 in order to reduce questionnaire length and possible respondent fatigue.

All correlations were evaluated at alpha = .01, even though a Bonferroni adjustment (.05/157) suggests a more stringent alpha level of $p < .0003$. Use of a less stringent alpha (i.e., a more conservative appraisal) coincides with our primary objective of item reduction. Only 13 of the 157 items (from three of the four scales) correlated significantly ($p < .01$) with the SDS. The MAKSS (D'Andrea et al., 1991) had three items that had significant correlations: Question 7, $r = .35$; Question 13, $r = -.33$; and Question 15, $r = -.28$. The MCAS-B (Ponterotto et al., 1996) produced the largest number of items (8) that correlated with the SDS: Question 2, $r = -.29$; Question 6, $r = -.30$; Question 14, $r = -.30$; Question 15, $r = -.37$; Question 17, $r = -.29$; Question 28, $r = -.27$; Question 43, $r = -.31$; and Question 44, $r = .30$. The MCCTS (Holcomb-McCoy, 2000) yielded two significant correlations: Question 3, $r = -.31$, and Question 17, $r = -.28$. The CCCI-R measure (LaFromboise et al., 1991) produced no significant correlation between its items and the SDS. Because item reduction is one of the major purposes of this investigation, the 13 items that were found to correlate with the SDS were eliminated from the item pool in Study 2, along with three MCAS-B specialized social desirability items. Hence, 16 items were identified for future elimination.

Study 2: Scale Development

The purpose of Study 2 was to collect self-report cultural competency data on a relatively large sample of California mental health practitioners. Toward this end, a similar questionnaire and consent form, as in Study 1, contained basic demographic and descriptive information with five self-report cultural competency instruments (i.e., the MCI, CCCI-R, MAKSS, MCAS-B, and the MCCTS). The SDS was not included in order to reduce questionnaire length. The goal of Study 2 was to create a large item pool of questions from four of the original cultural competency instruments (i.e., the CCCI-R, MAKSS, MCAS-B, and MCCTS) and, through factor analytic analyses, to create a short form version, subsequently called the CBMCS. Because we did not receive permission from the author of the MCI (Sodowsky et al., 1994) to use her individual items in our item pool, we used the MCI for validation purposes instead. Subsequent analyses compared the subscale scores of the CBMCS with the MCI scores for a criterion-related validation check. Permissions were obtained from the authors of the CCCI-R, MAKSS, MCAS-B, and MCCTS to use their items in our study.

Study 2: Analysis Strategy

Because of the relatively large Study 2 sample size (*N* = 1,244), we decided to trichotomize the sample into three equal random subsamples in order to conduct two exploratory factor analyses and one confirmatory factor analysis. Thus, Study 2a (*N* = 415) consisted of an initial exploratory factor analysis with strict exclusion criteria using the entire item pool (less the 16 items identified for elimination in Study 1), and Study 2b (*N* = 415) incorporated feedback on the factor solution in Study 2a from a panel of multicultural experts. A final exploratory factor analysis was conducted based on both the initial (Study 2a) factor analysis and the expert opinions. Study 2c (*N* = 414) reports a confirmatory factor analysis to determine if the factor model developed in Study 2b can reproduce the observed item covariances.

A generic Method section follows delineating characteristics of the participants and procedures used in Studies 2a, 2b, and 2c. Separate Results and Discussion sections for each study follow the Method section.

Method

Participants

A convenience sample of 1,244 California public mental health workers completed the questionnaire, and the sample's demographics/characteristics can be seen in Table 1. Nearly two thirds of the sample was female. The average age was 37.31 years (*SD* = 16.77). Nearly half (52%) of the sample was White/European American, followed by Latino American (14%), African American (11%), Asian American/Pacific Islander (9%), and Native American Indian (1%). The modal degree among the participants was a master's degree (45%). Bilingual abilities were found among 31% of the sample. Forty-eight percent of the sample was trained in a multicultural counseling program, and 66% indicated taking multicultural course work. Seventy-five percent participated in a multicultural workshop. The average number of years working in the mental health field was 10.51 (*SD* = 8.83) for the sample. The average number of years the sample reported working with multicultural clients was 12.07 (*SD* = 9.56). Twelve counties, representing mental health agencies across California (northern counties = 18%, southern counties = 82%), participated in this study. The sample closely resembles recent statewide demographic profiles of practitioner ethnicity and bilingual ability among the 12 targeted counties. The separate random subsamples of equal size were generated from the original sample of 1,244 mental health practitioners to provide the constituents for Studies 2a–2c. (A complete demographic assessment of mental health practitioner demographics for California does not exist. However, the California Department of Mental Health, Office of Multicultural Services, was able to provide ethnicity and bilingual ability counts for the 12 counties sampled in our study. The 12-county statewide average for ethnicity was as follows: White American [54%], African American [19%], Latino American [14%], Asian American/Pacific Islander [9%], Native American Indian [1%], and other [3%]. Bilingual ability was English only [76%] and bilingual [24%]. These percentages align very closely with our convenience sample and demonstrate the representativeness of the sample to the target population.)

Procedure

County community mental health agencies were contacted by the fourth author for possible participation in this study. The 12 counties that made up the final sample represented more than 140 separate departments or organizations. Staff who volunteered to complete the questionnaire did so during normal working hours. The average amount of time to complete the questionnaire varied from 30 to 60 minutes. The present sample reflects our goal of developing a brief self-report instrument for measuring cultural competency in the community mental health arena.

Study 2a: Results and Discussion

Item Analysis

For Study 2a, the 40-item MCI was eliminated from the potential item pool, thus enabling this instrument to be used in conjunction with the subsequent CBMCS for the purposes of criterion-related validity checks. On the basis of the social desirability results of Study 1, 16 of the 157 items were eliminated (13 due to possible social desirability contamination and 3 items from the MCAS-B Social Desirability subscale) from the item pool. For the remaining 141-item pool (representing the CCCI-R, MAKSS, MCAS-B, and MCCTS), the following criteria were followed for eliminating items (see Ponterotto et al., 1996; Serling & Betz, 1990). The remaining Study 2a items were omitted from the pool if (a) the corrected item-total correlation was below .20 or if elimination of the item caused the alpha to increase, (b) a reduced range of responses was observed (i.e., fewer than all four Likert-type response options were used), and (c) item means were found to be extreme (e.g., over 3.34 or below 1.66).

Application of these criteria eliminated 25 items: 20 items were eliminated because of a corrected item-total correlation of less than .20, and 5 items were eliminated due to distribution skewness. This procedure resulted in a reduced item-pool of 116 items (Cronbach's $\alpha = .98$), which became the ingredients for our subsequent factor analytic work.

CBMCS Factor Structure

Principal component analysis resulted in an initial 25-factor solution with eigenvalues greater than 1.0. Scree tests plus a comparison of the residual correlation matrices of a 3-, 4-, and 5-factor solution suggested that four factors would clearly represent the data set (see Meyers, Gamst, & Guarino, in press; Ponterotto et al., 2002; Tabachnik & Fidell, 2001). A four-factor principal component analysis was run with a Varimax rotation. Because the primary purpose of this factor analysis was item-pool reduction, fairly stringent item-elimination criteria were used: An item was eliminated if it did not produce a high structure coefficient (.55 or greater) on one factor and low structure coefficient (less than .35) on all other factors or if it had a low extraction communality (less than .50).

The four-factor solution that provided the best fit for the present data set accounted for 44.2% of the total variance and yielded a 27-item scale (i.e., 91 items were eliminated for not meeting the item-inclusion criteria). The factor structure took the following form: Factor 1, Sensitivity to Consumers (eigenvalue = 35.4), had 3 items; Factor 2, Nonethnic Ability (eigenvalue = 6.8), had 7 items; Factor 3, Awareness of Cultural Barriers (eigenvalue = 5.6), had 8 items; and Factor 4, Multicultural Knowledge (eigenvalue = 8.4), had 9 items. The rationale we used for naming these four factors was guided, in part, by the recommendations of Comrey and Lee (1992)

Table 1 Demographics/Characteristics of Study 2 Participants (N = 1,244)

Characteristic	*Sample*	
	N	*%*
Gender		
Male	397	32
Female	795	64
Unknown	52	4
Age group		
65+ years	17	2
55–64	142	11
45–54	307	25
35–44	293	24
25–34	299	24
24 and under	43	4
Unknown	143	10
Ethnicity		
White/European American	642	52
Latino American	178	14
African American	139	11
Asian American/ Pacific Islanders	107	9
Native American Indian	15	1
Other	109	9
Unknown	54	4
Highest earned degree		
Doctorate	145	12
Master's	553	45
Bachelor's	226	18
High school	82	6
Other	221	18
Unknown	17	1
Language		
English only	846	69
Bilingual	377	31
Multicultural training (trained in multicultural counseling program)		
Yes	594	48
No	484	39
Unknown	166	13
Received multicultural course work		
Yes	819	66
No	289	23
Unknown	136	11
Received multicultural counseling workshops		
Yes	929	75
No	220	18
Unknown	95	7
Years of mental health experience		
3 years or fewer	319	26
4–7	268	22
8–11	209	17
12–15	153	12
16 or more	295	23
Years working with multicultural clients		
3 years or fewer	238	19
4–7	263	21
8–11	223	18
12–15	153	12
16 or more	367	30
County		
Contra Costa	51	4
Los Angeles	258	21
Mendocino	3	0.2
Merced	12	1
Riverside	36	3
Sacramento	32	3
San Bernardino	559	45
San Diego	162	13
San Luis Obispo	1	0.1
Santa Barbara	14	1
Solano	100	8
Tehama	7	0.3
Unknown	9	0.4

and Rummel (1970), in which sorted factor structure coefficients in excess of .65 were used to "drive" the process of labeling and interpreting each factor. The four-factor model was deemed the best solution because it addressed our overarching goal of a brief scale development and because of its conceptual clarity and ease of interpretability (see Ponterotto et al., 1996).

Study 2b: Results and Discussion

With the basic factor structure in place from Study 2a, one final item-elimination criterion on the 27-item four-factor solution was imposed. A regional expert panel (from the California Department of Mental Health, Cultural Competence Advisory Committee, and from the California Institute for Mental Health, Center for Cultural Competence Advisory Committee) was recruited (with the assistance of the Chief Office of Multicultural Services, California Department of Mental Health) for the purpose of providing content validation from a community mental health perspective. These experts were not part of Study 1 or Study 2a. Experts were included in the panel if they had at least 5 years of experience working with community mental health multicultural populations and were currently active members of their respective advisory committees. The 20 experts from the two committees were sent a questionnaire that asked them to rate the "appropriateness" of each item (i.e., the suitability or goodness of a statement to be an indicator of multicultural competence in a mental health service delivery setting). Each of the 27 items was evaluated on a 4-point Likert-type scale (1 = *inappropriate* and 4 = *very appropriate*). Characteristics of the experts who responded yielded M = 16.9 years of multicultural mental health experience. Expert ethnicity was as follows: Asian American (30%), Latino American (25%), White American (25%), African American (15%), and Native American Indian (5%). An item was eliminated if more than half of the expert sample indicated some degree of ambiguity about the "appropriateness" of the item. Based on this criterion, 6 additional items were eliminated (4 from the Multicultural Knowledge subscale and 2 from the Awareness of Cultural Barriers subscale), yielding a four-factor 21-item scale.

CBMCS Final Factor Structure

A final factor structure of the remaining 21 self-report items was realized with an exploratory factor analysis using a principal component extraction method and a Varimax rotation. Using the Kaiser-Guttman retention criterion of eigenvalues greater than 1.0, a four-factor solution (similar to the solution in Study 2a) provided the clearest extraction. Table 2 presents the 21 items, the original scale and subscale they came from, their factor structure coefficients, communality estimates, and item-total correlations. Communalities were fairly high for each of the 21 items, with a range of .51 to .71. These results reinforce and refine the factor structure we originally delineated in Study 2a: Four underlying factors (that account for 59% of the total variance) depict or best fit the variability found among the 21 multicultural self-report items.

Factor 1, Nonethnic Ability (eigenvalue = 6.50), accounted for 31% of the variance and had 7 items; Factor 2, Awareness of Cultural Barriers (eigenvalue = 2.55), accounted for 12.1 % of the variance and had 6 items; Factor 3, Multicultural Knowledge (eigenvalue = 2.10), accounted for 10% of the variance and had 5 items; and Factor 4, Sensitivity to Consumers (eigenvalue = 1.21), accounted for 5.8% of the variance and had 3 items.

Table 3 presents a matrix of intercorrelations of the CBMCS and the MCI with their respective subscales, key demographic items, and measures of internal consistency (Cronbach's α) for the scores of each subscale. Criterion validity was examined by comparing the CBMCS subscale scores with the MCI subscale scores.

Cronbach's coefficient alpha for the scores of the 21-item CBMCS was .89. The alphas for the scores of the four subscales were Nonethnic Ability = .90, Awareness of Cultural Barriers = .78, Multicultural Knowledge = .80, and Sensitivity to Consumers = .75. Coefficient alpha for the scores of the MCI-Total scale score was .84. The scores of the MCI subscales produced the following alphas: Skills = .78, Awareness = .80, Relationship = .27, and Knowledge = .57.

The pattern of intercorrelations showed that the CBMCS subscales all had low positive intercorrelations. (We do not report the pattern of intercorrelations among the five self-report scales [i.e., MCI, CCCI-R, MAKSS, MCAS-B, and MCCTS] because the main purpose of this article is to demonstrate the validity and reliability of the CBMCS). Low moderate correlations were observed between the CBMCS and MCI subscales (ranging from –.01 to .62, with a mean correlation of .31), with the exception of the MCI-Relationship subscale (ranging from –.01 to .08, with a mean of .02), which is difficult to interpret due to the unreliability of the scores of this subscale. Taken as a whole, these correlations provide some evidence of criterion-related validity for the scores of the CBMCS.

We also examined the correlation of the two same-named subscales in the CBMCS and the MCI (i.e., the Multicultural Knowledge and Awareness of Cultural Barriers subscales). The CBMCS and MCI Knowledge subscales yielded a low positive correlation of $r = .21$. The correlation between the CBMCS Awareness of Cultural Barriers and MCI Awareness subscales was $r = .45$, indicating a moderate positive relationship. This pattern of correlation among the same-named subscales provides some support of recent findings by Kocarek, Talbot, Batka, and Anderson (2001), who reported a "lack of consistency between same-named subscales" (p. 494), that is, low intercorrelations for the same construct. A much larger sample size in the present study than in the Kocarek et al. study provides additional credence to their concerns.

Criterion-Related Validity

Criterion-related validity was explored by examining CBMCS subscale score differences among key demographic subgroups within the Study 2b random sample. These demographic variables were selected because of their importance in previous studies (e.g., Ponterotto et al., 1996). Four one-way multivariate analyses of variance (MANOVAs) were computed on the four CBMCS dependent variables: Multicultural Knowledge, Awareness of Cultural Barriers, Sensitivity to Consumers, and Nonethnic Ability. The four independent variables were gender, age group (five levels), ethnicity (five levels), and education (five levels). To reduce the possibility of Type I error, the alpha level for all analyses was set at .01.

A one-way MANOVA compared CBMCS subscales by gender and indicated a significant multivariate effect, Wilks's lambda $F(4,374) = 3.07$, $p < .01, \eta^2 = .03$. Univariate F tests yielded significant effects for the Multicultural Knowledge, $F(1,377) = 4.60, p <.01, \eta^2 = .01$, and Awareness of Cultural Barriers subscales, $F(1, 377) = 4.44$, $p < .01, \eta^2 = .01$. These univariate analyses indicated that male mental health practitioners had significantly higher Multicultural Knowledge subscale scores ($M = 2.49, SD = .58$) than female practitioners ($M = 2.37$, $SD = .55$) had. Conversely, female practitioners had significantly higher Awareness of Cultural Barriers scores ($M = 3.11$, $SD = .45$) than male practitioners had ($M = 3.00$, $SD = .45$).

A significant multivariate practitioner education effect was also found, Wilks's lambda $F(4, 394) = 3.52, p <.01, \eta^2 = .03$. Univariate F tests indicated significant Awareness of Cultural Barriers, $F(4, 397) = 10.14, p < .01, \eta^2 = .09$, and Nonethnic Ability subscales, $F(4, 397) = 5.53, p < .01, \eta^2 = .05$. Least significant difference multiple comparison tests ($p < .01$) were conducted for both subscales. The comparison for the Awareness of Cultural Barriers subscale indicated that doctorate-level ($M = 3.22, SD = .45$) and master's-level practitioners ($M = 3.17, SD = .38$) scored significantly higher than all other groups: bachelor's level ($M = 3.02, SD = .43$), high school level ($M = 2.76, SD = .55$), and others ($M = 2.89, SD = .52$). For the Nonethnic Ability subscale, high school-level practitioners ($M = 2.39, SD = .55$) had significantly lower subscale scores than all other groups: doctorate level ($M = 2.84, SD = .45$), master's level ($M = 2.88, SD = .46$), bachelor's level ($M = 2.77, SD = .57$), and others ($M = 2.70, SD = .64$). Two of the four MANOVAs (age group and ethnicity) were not significant ($p > .01$), indicating comparable scores on the four dependent measures for these two independent variables.

Table 2 Summary of Items and Structure Coefficients From Principal Component Analysis With Varimax Rotation Study 2b ($N = 415$)

	Structure Coefficients					
Scale and Subscale	*Factor 1*	*Factor 2*	*Factor 3*	*Factor 4*	η^2	*CITC*
MAKSS						
Skills						
1. I have an excellent ability to assess accurately the mental health needs of gay men.	.83	–.02	.15	–.07	.71	.55
2. I have an excellent ability to assess accurately the mental health needs of lesbians.	.80	–.01	–.09	.14	.67	.55
3. I have an excellent ability to assess accurately the mental health needs of persons with disabilities.	.78	–.02	.23	–.06	.67	.56
4. I have an excellent ability to assess accurately the mental health needs of older adults.	.74	.09	.09	.09	.58	.53
5. I have an excellent ability to assess accurately the mental health needs of men.	.73	.19	.13	.14	.60	.61
6. I have an excellent ability to assess accurately the mental health needs of persons who come from very poor socioeconomic backgrounds.	.71	.26	.28	.11	.66	.70
7. I have an excellent ability to assess accurately the mental health needs of women.	.68	.31	.06	.19	.60	.62
MCAS-B						
Knowledge/Skills						
8. I am aware that counselors frequently impose their own cultural values on minority clients.	.05	.78	.09	.05	.62	.41

Scale and Subscale	Structure Coefficients					
	Factor 1	Factor 2	Factor 3	Factor 4	η^2	CITC
Awareness						
9. I am aware that being born a White person in this society carries with it certain advantages.	.01	.72	.04	.05	.52	.33
Knowledge/Skills						
10. I am aware of institutional barriers which may inhibit minorities from using mental health services.	.15	.69	.15	.17	.56	.50
Awareness						
11. I am aware that being born a minority in this society brings with it certain challenges that White people do not have to face.	–.05	.67	.04	.26	.52	.35
MCCTS						
Awareness						
12. I am aware of how my cultural background and experiences have influenced my attitudes about psychological processes.	.26	.57	.09	.18	.43	.48
Skills						
13. I can identity my reactions that are based on stereotypical beliefs about different ethnic groups.	.33	.53	.14	.07	.41	.49
14. I have an excellent ability to critique multicultural research.	.16	–.03	.80	.11	.68	.45
MAKSS						
Skills						
15. I have an excellent ability to identify the strengths and weaknesses of psychological tests in terms of their use with persons with different cultural/racial/ethnic backgrounds.	.17	–.03	.71	.12	.55	.41
Knowledge						
16. I can discuss within-group differences among ethnic groups (e.g., low socioeconomic status [SES] Puerto Rican client vs. high SES Puerto Rican client).	.13	.16	.71	–.02	.55	.43
MCCTS						
Knowledge						
17. I can discuss research regarding mental health issues and culturally different populations.	.09	.15	.71	.01	.53	.41

(Continued)

Table 2 (Continued)

Scale and Subscale	*Structure Coefficients* Factor 1	Factor 2	Factor 3	Factor 4	η^2	*CITC*
MCAS-B						
Knowledge/Skills						
18. I am knowledgeable of acculturation models for various minority groups.	.17	.25	.69	−.02	.56	.49
CCCI-R						
Skills						
19. My communication is appropriate for my clients.	.27	.07	.02	.77	.67	.41
Cultural Sensitivity						
20. I am aware of institutional barriers that affect the client.	.09	.30	.11	.75	.68	.44
Socio-Political Awareness						
21. I am aware of how my own values might affect my client.	.18	.24	.03	.72	.61	.42
Eigenvalues	6.50	2.55	2.10	1.21		
% of variance	30.95	12.13	10.00	5.78		
Coefficient α	0.90	0.78	0.80	0.75		

Note: Factor 1 = Nonethnic Ability; Factor 2 = Awareness of Cultural Barriers; Factor 3 = Multicultural Knowledge; Factor 4 = Sensitivity to Consumers; CITC = corrected item-total correlation. MAKSS = Multicultural Awareness, Knowledge, Skills Survey; MCAS-B = Multicultural Counseling Awareness Scale-Form B; MCCTS = Multicultural Competency and Training Survey; CCCI-R = Cross-Cultural Counseling Inventory-Revised. Boldfaced values indicate highest factor loadings.

Study 2c: Results and Discussion

The purpose of Study 2c was to obtain empirical evidence through the use of confirmatory maximum likelihood factor analysis of the construct validity of the four-factor CBMCS elucidated in Studies 2a and 2b. The sample size of $N = 414$ was deemed adequate for the purpose of conducting a confirmatory factor analysis (CFA; Quintana & Maxwell, 1999).

Construct validity was assessed through a series of CFAs. CFA is a technique that assesses the degree to which an expected or hypothesized factor model can effectively reproduce the observed or sample item covariances. CFA begins with an a priori hypothesized model and deductively ascertains its feasibility by offering more definitive empirical evidence of the underlying factor structure of a scale than an exploratory factor analysis (Meyers et al., in press; Tabachnick & Fidell, 2001). Missing data were estimated through a full information maximum likelihood imputation.

The models were tested in the following order: (a) a single-factor model in which all items were free to load on only one common factor, (b) a correlated three-factor model in which each factor was correlated with each other, (c) a correlated four-factor model in

Table 3 Study 2b Correlation Coefficients, Means, Standard Deviations, Alpha Coefficients for California Brief Multicultural Competence Scale (CBMCS) and Multicultural Counseling Inventory (MCI) Subscales, and Demographics

Scale	*1*	*2*	*3*	*4*	*5*	*6*	*7*	*8*	*9*	*10*	*11*	*12*	*13*	*14*	*15*	*16*	*M*	*SD*	*α*
1. CBMCS-Knowledge	—	.28*	.22*	.40*	.25*	.41*	.08	.21*	.11*	−.10*	−.05	−.12*	.07	.20*	.21*	.18*	2.43	0.58	.80
2. CBMCS-Awareness		—	.36*	.32*	.35*	.45*	−.01	.40*	−.01	.09	−.02	−.08	.29*	.26*	.33*	.28*	3.06	0.47	.78
3. CBMCS-Sensitivity			—	.37*	.62*	.50*	−.02	.46*	−.02	.02	−.04	−.01	.11*	.18*	.21*	.15*	3.25	0.50	.75
4. CBMCS-Nonethnic Ability				—	.50*	.42*	.04	.28*	.01	.01	.02	.02	.17*	.22*	.17*	.10*	2.79	0.54	.90
5. MCI-Skills					—	.57*	.03	.56*	.04	.01	.04	.06	.15*	.17*	.24*	.17*	3.06	0.35	.78
6. MCI-Awareness						—	.09	.50*	−.10	.04	−.02	.01	.14*	.26*	.30*	.30*	2.94	0.45	.80
7. MCI-Relationship							—	−.05	−.07	−.03	−.06	−.03	.10*	.03	−.03	.02	2.65	0.31	.27
8. MCI-Knowledge								—	−.07	−.03	−.06	−.03	.32*	.21*	.30*	.29*	2.92	0.32	.57
9. Age									—	−.24*	.38*	.38*	.10*	.01	.04	.06	37.5	16.0	
10. Gender										—	−.23*	−.20*	.07	.03	.14*	.01	1.65	0.48	
11. Years in mental health											—	.79*	.13*	.04	−.07	.11*	2.82	1.53	
12. Years with multicultural clients												—	.05	.06	−.05	.11*	3.15	1.50	
13. Education													—	.28*	.35*	.36*	2.91	1.32	
14. Multicultural counseling														—	.54*	.37*	1.57	0.50	
15. Multicultural course work															—	.49*	1.73	0.45	
16. Multicultural workshops																—	1.80	0.40	

*$p < .01$.

which each factor was correlated with each other, and (d) a nonorthogonal four-factor model in which one factor is a second-order hierarchical factor loading on four first-order factors. Conceptually, each item was viewed as an indicator of one of the first-order factors; then the first-order factors were considered to be indicators of the higher order factor. These models were developed to address whether the CBMCS is unitary, multidimensional, or influenced by a higher order factor.

The models were assessed by AMOS version (4.0) maximum likelihood factor analysis (Arbuckle, 1999). The models were evaluated by a variety of fit measures that are classified as absolute, relative, parsimonious, and population discrepancy. Absolute fit measures assess how well the proposed interrelationships among the variables match the interrelationships among the actual interrelationships. The chi-square test was the measure of absolute fit used in this study because AMOS does not provide other absolute measures when missing data are estimated with the full information maximum likelihood imputation procedure. Jöreskog and Sörbom (1989) and Bentler (1992), however, advised against the sole use of the chi-square value in assessing the fit of the model because of the sensitivity of the chi-square to sample size. Measures of relative fit compare the hypothesized model with the null model. The relative fit measures used in this study were the comparative fit index (Bentler, 1990) and the Tucker-Lewis index (Bentler & Bonett, 1980; Tucker & Lewis, 1973). Hu and Bentler (1999) suggested cutoff values close to .95 as acceptable for model fit. Measures of parsimonious fit determine if the overall fit of the model has been accomplished by overfitting the data (Byrne, 1999). The parsimonious fit measures in this study were the chi-square divided by the degrees of freedom and the incremental fit index. Bollen (1989) reported that there is no consensus on the value of the chi-square divided by the degrees of freedom ratio for an adequate fit because values range from 5, 3, 2, or less. The incremental fit index was developed by Bollen to address the issues of parsimony and sample size with values close to .95, which is indicative of an acceptable fit (Hu & Bentler, 1999). Finally, population discrepancy measures are estimates between the sample coefficients and the population coefficients. The population discrepancy measure in this study was the root mean square error of approximation, with suggested values of less than .05 (as indicative of a good fit) and values as high as .08 (representing reasonable errors of approximation in the population; Browne & Cudeck, 1993).

Those models achieving an acceptable fit were then compared by examining differences in values of chi-square to identify statistically significant variations among the models, the expected cross-validation index (ECVI; Browne & Cudeck, 1993), and the Akaike's information criterion (AIC; Akaike, 1987). Both the ECVI and the AIC are used in the comparison of models, with smaller values representing a better fit of the hypothesized model (Hu & Bentler, 1995).

The responses of a holdout sample of 414 participants from the initial study were subjected to a series of CFA. All three comparison indices (the chi-square difference test, the ECVI, and the AIC) indicated that the four-factor correlated model demonstrated statistically significant structure coefficients to their assigned factor. The fit indices for the four models are presented in Table 4.

These results suggest that the scores of the CBMCS achieved construct validity (i.e., the items were shown to measure their respective hypothetical constructs). Furthermore, the psychometric properties of the final 21-item CBMCS indicated acceptable alpha coefficients for the four subscales, and their intercorrelations demonstrated discriminant validity.

Table 4 Fit Indices for Four Models in Study 2c ($N = 414$) and Study 4 ($N = 414$)

Model		*df*	*x^2/df*	*IFI*	*CFI*	*TLI*	*RMSEA*	*90% CI*	*ECVI*	*AIC*
					Study 2c					
Single-factor	1,785.09	190	9.39	.945	.945	.933	.140	.134–.146	4.48	1,909.1
Three-factor correlated	955.90	186	5.14	.974	.974	.967	.099	.092–.105	2.55	1,087.9
Four-factor correlated	757.58	183	4.14	.980	.980	.975	.086	.080–.092	2.10	895.6
Second order	774.57	185	4.18	.980	.980	.975	.086	.080–.093	2.13	908.5
					Study 4					
Single-factor	1,361.67	190	7.16	.954	.953	.943	.130	.125–. 137	4.07	1,485.6
Three-factor correlated	677.17	186	3.64	.981	.981	.976	.085	.078–.092	2.21	809.2
Four-factor correlated	665.28	183	3.63	.981	.981	.976	.085	.078–.092	2.20	803.2
Second order	758.17	185	4.10	.977	.977	.972	.092	.084–.099	2.44	892.2

Note: IFI = incremental fit index; CFI = comparative fit index; TLI = Tucker-Lewis index; RMSEA = root-mean-square error of approximation; 90% CI = 90% confidence interval; ECVI = expected cross-validation index; AIC = Akaike's information criterion. *p < .05.The results of the chi-square test for differences, the AIC, and the ECVI reveal that the correlated four-factor model is superior to the other models. The correlated four-factor model yielded acceptably high goodness of fit indices (i.e., > .97) for both the comparative fit index and the Tucker-Lewis index. The root mean square error of approximation achieved a value of .086, indicating an acceptable fit of the model in relation to the degrees of freedom (Browne & Cudeck, 1993). The correlations among the four factors are presented in Table 5. The intercorrelations among the factors were all less than .9, indicating that the five factors demonstrated discriminant validity. Table 6 shows that all measured variables correlated significantly with their respective factors.

Table 5 Correlations Among the Four Factors

Factor	*1*	*2*	*3*	*4*
1. Nonethnic Ability	.91			
2. Sensitivity to Consumers	.426	.72		
3. Multicultural Knowledge	.485	.287	.97	
4. Awareness of Cultural Barriers	.366	.500	.350	.78

Note: Cronbach's alpha on the diagonal. *$p < .05$.

Because this is a recently developed scale, additional studies are needed to further test CBMCS scores' validity and reliability.

Study 3: Social Desirability Check Revisited

This study reassessed the possibility of CBMCS social desirability contamination, first discussed in Study 1, by relating the SDS to the subscales of the final 21-item CBMCS with a new sample of respondents.

Participants and Procedure

Participants consisted of beginning marriage and family therapy graduate students from two Southern California universities, enrolled in introductory multicultural or research methods courses (*N* = 33 of 44 students), 79% female, with a mean age of 32.19. Student ethnicity was as follows: White American (57.6%), Latino American (24.2%), Asian American (6.1%), and other (12.1 %). Education levels were bachelor's degree (78.8%), master's degree (15.2%), and other (6.0%). Student language ability yielded 63.6% English only and 36.4% bilingual ability. Students completed a consent form, the CBMCS, and the SDS, followed by a debriefing. Participation was voluntary and anonymous.

Results and Discussion

To examine the possibility of social desirability contamination of the CBMCS, we computed Pearson correlations between the SDS and the four CBMCS subscale scores. All correlations were not statistically significant ($p > .05$). The specific correlations between the CBMCS and SDS scores were as follows: Multicultural Knowledge ($r = .18$), Awareness of Cultural Barriers ($r = -.04$), Sensitivity to Consumers ($r = -.09$), and Nonethnic Ability ($r = -.03$). These results suggest that the CBMCS subscales were probably not contaminated by social desirability effects.

Study 4: CFA of the 21-Item CBMCS

Although the CFA of Study 2c provided support for the initial four-factor model explicated in Study 2b, a possible confound exists that needs to be addressed. This potential confound deals with the fact that all 1,244 respondents in Studies 2a, 2b, and 2c were exposed to all the items on the five cultural competence self-report inventories, and the respondents may have been biased inadvertently through this exposure. To overcome this potential confound, an additional CFA was conducted on a new, sufficiently large sample of community mental health providers exposed to only the 21-item CBMCS.

Participants and Procedure

Participants (*N* = 366) were community mental health providers conveniently sampled from several Southern California community mental health agencies. About 62.6% of the sample was female. The average age was 45.92 years (*SD* = 11.17). Over half the sample was White American (54.6%), followed by Latino American (13.7%), African American (11.5%), Asian American/Pacific Islander (11.5%), Native American Indian (1.4%), and other (7.3%). The modal degree observed among these providers was a master's degree (52.8%). Bilingual abilities were found among 30.1 % of the sample. Respondents reported an average of 13.67 years (*SD* =10.00) working in the mental health field and 16.41 years (*SD* = 9.83) working with multicultural clients.

County staff members were contacted by the fourth author for possible participation in this study. Staff who volunteered to complete the questionnaire did so during normal working hours. The average amount of time to complete the CBMCS and the demographic information sheet was about 15 minutes.

Results and Discussion

A new sample of mental health providers (*N* = 366), exposed only to the 21-item CBMCS, was used to see if the four-factor correlated model was the superior model. Again, all three comparison indices (the chi-square difference test, the ECVI, and the AIC) indicated that the four-factor correlated model achieved a better fit of the data than did the other three models. Additionally, all measured variables demonstrated statistically significant structure/pattern coefficients to their assigned factor. Thus, the

Table 6 Factor Pattern Coefficients of the California Brief Multicutural Competence Scale (Study 2c)

Item	*Nonethnic Ability*	*Knowledge*	*Awareness*	*Sensitivity*
Q18	.81			
Q5	.79			
Q3	.78			
Q21	.75			
Q13	.72			
Q6	.71			
Q20	.67			
Q12		.74		
Q7		.68		
Q19		.66		
Q15		.63		
Q17		.63		
Q14			.71	
Q8			.71	
Q1			.61	
Q10			.60	
Q11			.56	
Q16			.50	
Q4				.76
Q2				.73
Q9				.66

Note: Knowledge = Multicultural Knowledge; Awareness = Awareness of Cultural Barriers; Sensitivity = Sensitivity to Consumers.

Study 4 sample supports the construct validity of the four-factor correlated model observed in Study 2c. The fit indices for the four models are presented in Table 4.

General Discussion

Results from these studies suggest that the CBMCS is an efficient and effective tool for examining self-reported mental health practitioner cultural competency. This 21-item scale, specifically developed to measure self-reported multicultural competencies of mental health practitioners, is a promising measure. The new scale has advantages in comparison with other self-report measures: (a) shorter length; (b) development from a strong theoretical foundation; and (c) utilization of a large number of practitioners from various ethnic backgrounds, educational levels, ages, and experience.

Our findings demonstrate adequate CBMCS psychometric properties. For example, reliability, as measured by Cronbach's alpha, for the scores of the CBMCS subscales ranged from .75 to .90. Social desirability effects (e.g., Crowne & Marlowe, 1960) are minimal due to careful item screening prior to final scale development. Predictable correlations of the scores of the MCI subscales and the scores of the CBMCS subscales provided criterion-related validity.

Exploratory factor analyses of the CBMCS yielded four subscales (Nonethnic Ability, Awareness of Cultural Barriers, Multicultural Knowledge, and Sensitivity to Consumers) that were subsequently supported by two CFAs. Three of these factors—Multicultural Knowledge, Awareness of Cultural Barriers, and Sensitivity to Consumers—coincide roughly with the three competencies (i.e., tools) delineated by Sue (1991)—Beliefs/Attitudes, Knowledge, and Skills. This tripartite definition of multicultural competence is emphasized in most scales (Constantine & Ladany, 2001). However, Sodowsky et al. (1994) expanded this domain to include a fourth factor, Multicultural Counseling Relationship. Holcomb-McCoy and Myers (1999) also found that multicultural competencies comprise more than three dimensions and include racial identity and multicultural terminology.

An additional factor, Nonethnic Ability, appears to tap a relatively unique dimension of competence that may require an expansion of focus and broadening of the conceptualization of "multicultural competency." Previous multicultural competence self-report measures have emphasized competence in dealing with people/clients of color (Constantine & Ladany, 2000).

More recent conceptualizations required that "to sufficiently assess a broad range of multicultural issues, various approaches will need to be developed to measure counselors' abilities or competencies regarding working with other cultural groups (e.g., women, men, the impoverished, and persons with disabilities)" (Constantine & Ladany, 2001, p. 486). The Nonethnic Ability factor appears to address this need, and the facets within this subscale explore issues related to people with disabilities or low socioeconomic status, lesbians and gay men, and seniors, as well as heterosexual men and women.

The CBMCS subscale scores achieved low-to-moderate positive correlations with the MCI subscales, with one important exception: The MCI relationship subscale did not correlate with the CBMCS subscales, which is probably due to the unreliability of scores on the MCI Relationship subscale in the present study.

The present study also examined the relationship of a variety of demographic variables to the CBMCS. MANOVA analyses indicated a significant gender effect, with male providers having higher CBMCS—Multicultural Knowledge subscale scores than female providers: Women were found to self-report higher Awareness of Cultural Barriers scores than men were. Graduate-level providers achieved higher CBMCS—Awareness of Cultural Barriers subscale scores than bachelor's or high school-level providers did. Nonethnic Ability scores were lower for high school-level providers than for all other educational groupings. Multivariate effects of provider ethnicity and age were not observed.

Limitations

Several limitations are present in this study. First, although the sample is large and does not include college students or academic practitioners, it is still a convenience sample and may not generalize to all mental health service providers. Additional research with this scale is needed to demonstrate replicability of the present findings with other populations. Second, the present study is based on self-report data from practitioners. Third, the underlying three-factor conceptual framework from which the original cultural competency self-report scales were derived may be inadequate (see Constantine et al. 2002). Fourth, some investigators (Constantine & Ladany, 2001; Worthington et al., 2000) have reported weak relationships between self-reported cultural competence and observer ratings of cultural competence. Fifth, there is no consumer perspective on staff cultural competency as recommended in recent literature (Fuertes, Bartolomeo, & Nichols, 2001; Pope-Davis et al., 2001). Sixth, although efforts were made to statistically control for social desirability, the CBMCS remains vulnerable to possible self-evaluations by counselors who anticipated outcomes instead of documenting actual competency outcomes that resulted from their interventions (Constantine & Ladany, 2001; Fuertes et al., 2001; Ponterotto & Alexander, 1996; Pope-Davis & Dings, 1995; Ridley, Mendoza, Kanitz, Angermeier, & Zenk, 1994). Seventh, omission of the MCI from the item pool considered by Pope-Davis and Dings (1995) to have the best overall validity evidence was unfortunate and may have affected the CBMCS items and factors. Eighth, although the overall goal of this study was to develop a brief, self-report cultural competence instrument, it should be noted that our subscales are very short (ranging from three to seven items each) and may not adequately address all of the facets found within each of the four constructs.

Implications

The current scale allows for the assessment of competencies with nonethnic groups previously unexamined by existing scales. The finding of four primary factors may imply a limitation in current multicultural training because this training has focused historically on three general multicultural counseling competency domains: awareness, knowledge, and skills. Consequently, the expansion of these three domains to include nonethnic ability challenges the existing array of constructs believed to underlie multicultural competence. As a consequence of these findings, educators and trainers should address all multicultural competence domains and encourage development of courses and training experiences specifically pertaining to other cultural groups (Holcomb-McCoy & Myers, 1999) in a variety of venues in addition to mental health, including rehabilitation (Dana, 2001), geriatrics, and health care. Ethnic differences are equally salient and relevant among persons with disabilities; older adults; persons who are indigent; and in gay, lesbian, bisexual, and transgendered populations.

The use of a large sample of mental health providers rather than graduate students increases professional counselors' and researchers' understanding of multicultural competencies among service providers currently employed in mental health settings. As noted by Constantine and Ladany (2001), longitudinal studies are needed to examine the effects of multicultural counseling competencies. Such studies also provide the opportunity to gather much-needed baseline data regarding these competencies and aid our understanding of how competencies are further developed and refined. The question remains, do multicultural competencies remain stable, or do they change over time? The use of longitudinal data would allow educators to examine the impact of training on multicultural competencies, particularly because multicultural competencies of graduate students and counseling and psychology interns are frequently evaluated.

The use of qualitative approaches can also contribute to an understanding of how multicultural competencies evolve (Holcomb-McCoy & Myers, 1999) as a result of increased exposure to culturally diverse clients or of postdegree training. For instance, follow-up interviews to examine outcomes of a multicultural training course reported the participants' need for additional training to develop personal and professional culture self-awareness and self-knowledge (Tomlinson-Clarke, 2000). Qualitative approaches are also useful in allowing clients to identify and describe multicultural competencies in their own language, independently of language established by the counseling profession (Pope-Davis et al., 2001). Qualitative approaches provide valuable information anchored in the subjective experience of clients, thus providing insight into other salient variables affecting the therapeutic process that are infrequently captured in quantitative research (Fuertes et al., 2001; Pope-Davis et al., 2001). Integrating clients in the research process can facilitate the development of future theories of multicultural counseling competencies. Clients may or may not concur with the counseling profession in their perceptions of these competencies.

The CBMCS was neither conceived nor constructed to be simply another multicultural competence assessment instrument. Rather, the purpose of this new instrument is to provide an empirical resource for the design of in-service staff training using the CBMCS to identify staff competencies and limitations in areas delineated by each of the 21 items (see also Manese, Wu, & Nepomuceno, 2001). A user guide contains psychometric properties, scoring directions, transformation tables, and a profile sheet

(Der-Karabetian et al., 2002). The CBMCS items were then used to develop a preliminary training manual (Dana, 2002) that was subsequently operationalized into syllabi for training purposes that contain modules representative of each factor (Arellano, Huff-Musgrove, & Morrow, 2003).

Multicultural competence assessment that leads to training of service providers is one important component of a system of quality care. The present CBMCS research embedded in the MAIP model provides an example of how services for multicultural populations can be improved and ultimately evaluated. Continued collaboration and joint efforts by professional counselors and psychologists toward increased understanding of these complex and dynamic constructs are sorely needed as contributions to appropriate and effective care for culturally diverse clients (Constantine & Ladany, 2000, 2001). This research is consistent with a continuing emphasis on assessment of multicultural competence in professional counseling and psychology (e.g., Pope-Davis, Coleman, Liu, & Toporek, 2003) and provides an additional avenue for delineation of in-service training that can be monitored and evaluated with public agencies.

References

Akaike, H. (1987). Factor analysis and AIC. *Psychometrika, 52,* 317–332.

Allison, K. W., Crawford, I., Echemendia, R., Robinson, W. L., & Knepp, D. (1994). Human diversity and professional competence: Training in clinical and counseling psychology revisited. *American Psychologist, 49,* 792–796.

American Psychological Association. (1993). Guidelines for providers of psychological services to ethnic, linguistic, and culturally diverse populations. *American Psychologist, 48,* 45–48.

American Psychological Association. (2003). Guidelines on multicultural education, training, research, and practice, and organizational change for psychologists. *American Psychologist, 58,* 377–402.

Arbuckle, J. L. (1999). Amos 4.0 [Software]. Chicago: Small Waters Corporation.

Arellano, L., Huff-Musgrove, R., & Morrow, G. (2003). *Tri-City Mental Health Center Multicultural Competency Training Program.* Unpublished manuscript.

Arredondo, P., Toporek, R., Brown, S. P., Jones, J., Locke, D. C., Sanchez, J., et al. (1996). Operationalization of the multicultural counseling competencies. *Journal of Multicultural Counseling and Development, 24,* 42–78.

Atkinson, D. R., & Israel, T. (2003). The future of multicultural counseling competence. In D. B. Pope-Davis, H. L. K. Coleman, W. M. Liu, & R. L. Toporek (Eds.), *Handbook of multicultural competencies in counseling and psychology* (pp. 591–606). Thousand Oaks, CA: Sage.

Bentler, P. M. (1990). Comparative fit indexes in structural models. *Psychological Bulletin, 107,* 238–246.

Bentler, P. M. (1992). On the fit of models to covariances and methodology. *Psychological Bulletin, 112,* 400–404.

Bentler, P. M. & Bonett, D. G. (1980). Significance tests and goodness of fit in the analysis of covariance structures. *Psychological Bulletin, 88,* 588–606.

Bollen, K. (1989). *Structural equations with latent variables.* New York: Wiley.

Browne, M. W., & Cudeck, R. (1993). Alternative ways of assessing model fit. In K. A. Bollen & J. S. Long (Eds.), *Testing structural equation models* (pp. 136–162). Newbury Park, CA: Sage.

Byrne, B. M. (1999). *Structural equation modeling with EQS and EQS/S Windows: Basic concepts, applications, and programming.* Thousand Oaks, CA: Sage.

Comrey, A. L., & Lee, H. B. (1992), *A first course in factor analysis* (2nd ed.). Hillsdale, NJ: Erlbaum.

Constantine, M. G., Gloria, A. M., & Ladany, N. (2002). The factor structure underlying three self-report multicultural counseling competence scales. *Cultural Diversity and Ethnic Minority Psychology, 8,* 334–345.

Constantine, M. G. & Ladany, N. (2000). Self-report multicultural counseling competence scales: The irrelation to social desirability attitudes and multicultural case conceptualization ability. *Journal of Counseling Psychology, 47,* 155–164.

Constantine, M. G., & Ladany, N. (2001). New visions for defining and assessing multicultural counseling competence. In J. G. Ponterotto, J. M. Casas, L. A. Suzuki, & C. M. Alexander (Eds.), *Handbook of multicultural counseling* (2nd ed., pp. 482–498). Thousand Oaks, CA: Sage.

Crowne, D. P., & Marlowe, D. (1960). A new scale of social desirability independent of psychopathology. *Journal of Consulting Psychology, 24,* 349–354.

Dana, R. H. (1993). *Multicultural assessment perspectives for professional psychology.* Boston: Allyn & Bacon.

Dana, R. H. (1998): *Understanding cultural identity in intervention and assessment.* Thousand Oaks, CA: Sage.

Dana, R. H. (Ed.). (2000). An assessment-intervention model for research and practice with multicultural populations. In R. H. Dana (Ed.), *Handbook of cross-cultural and multicultural personality assessment* (pp. 6–16). Mahwah, NJ: Erlbaum.

Dana, R. H. (2001). Multicultural issues in rehabilitation assessment. In B. Bolton (Ed.), *Handbook of measurement and evaluation in rehabilitation* (3rd ed., pp. 449–469). Gaithersburg, MD: Aspen.

Dana, R. H. (2002). Manual for multicultural competence training: Preliminary version. Unpublished manuscript.

D'Andrea, M. Daniels, J., & Heck, R. (1991). Evaluating the impact of multicultural counselor training. *Journal of Counseling & Development, 70,* 143–150.

Der-Karabetian, A., Gamst, G., Dana, R. H., Aragon, M., Arellano, L., Morrow, G., et al. (2002). *California Brief Multicultural Competence Scale (CBMCS) user guide.* Unpublished manuscript.

Fuertes, J. N., Bartolomeo, M., & Nichols, C. M. (2001). Future research directions in the study of counselor multicultural competency. *Journal of Multicultural Counseling and Development, 29,* 3–13.

Holcomb-McCoy, C. C. (2000). Multicultural counseling competencies: An exploratory factor analysis. *Journal of Multicultural Counseling and Development, 28,* 83–97.

Holcomb-McCoy, C. C, & Myers, J. E. (1999). Multicultural competence and counselor training: A national survey. *Journal of Counseling & Development, 77,* 294–302.

Hu, L.-T., & Bentler, P. M. (1995). Evaluating model fit. In R. H. Hoyle (Ed.), *Structural equation modeling: Concepts, issues, and applications* (pp. 76–99). Thousand Oaks, CA: Sage.

Hu, L.-T., & Bentler, P. M. (1999). Cutoff criteria for fit indexes in covariance structure analysis: Conventional criteria versus new alternatives. *Structural Equation Modeling: A Multidisciplinary Journal, 6,* 1–55.

Jöreskog, K. G., & Sörbom, D. (1989). *LISREL-7 user's reference guide.* Mooreville, IN: Scientific Software.

Kocarek, C. E., Talbot, D. M., Batka, J. C, & Anderson, M. Z. (2001). Reliability and validity of three measures of multicultural competency. *Journal of Counseling & Development, 79,* 486–496.

Korman, M. (Ed.). (1976). *Levels and patterns of professional training in psychology.* Washington, DC: American Psychological Association.

Ladany, N., Inman, A. G., Constantine, M. G., & Hofheinz, E. W. (1997). Supervisee multicultural case conceptualization ability and self-reported multicultural competence as functions of supervisee racial identity and supervisor focus. *Journal of Counseling Psychology, 44,* 284–293.

LaFromboise, T. D., Coleman, H. L. K., & Hernandez, A. (1991). Development and factor structure of the Cross-Cultural Counseling Inventory-Revised. *Professional Psychology: Research and Practice, 22,* 380–388.

LaFromboise, T. D., & Foster, S. L. (1992). Cross-cultural training: Scientist-practitioner model and methods. *The Counseling Psychologist, 20,* 472–489.

Lee, C. C., & Richardson, B. I. (1991). Promise and pitfalls of multicultural counseling. In C. C., Lee & B. I. Richardson (Eds.), *Multicultural issues in counseling: New approaches to diversity* (pp. 3–9). Alexandria, VA: The American Association for Counseling and Development.

Lent, R. W., Brown, S. D., & Larkin, K. C. (1986). Self-efficacy in the prediction of academic performance and perceived career options. *Journal of Counseling Psychology, 33,* 265–269.

Manese, J. E., Wu, J. T., & Nepomuceno, C. A. (2001). The effect of training on multicultural counseling competencies: An exploratory study over a ten-year period. *Journal of Multicultural Counseling and Development, 29,* 31–41.

Meyers, L. S., Gamst, G., &. Guarino, A. J. (in press). *Applied multivariate research: Design and interpretation.* Thousand Oaks, CA: Sage.

Mio, J. S., & Morris, D. R. (1990). Cross-cultural issues in psychology training programs: An invitation for discussion. *Professional Psychology: Research and Practice, 7,* 434–441.

Murphy, M. C., Wright, B. V., & Bellamy, D. E. (1995). Multicultural training in university counseling center predoctoral psychology internship programs: A survey. *Journal of Multicultural Counseling and Development, 23,* 170–180.

Ponterotto, J. G. (1997). Multicultural counselor training: A competency model and national survey. In D. B. Pope-Davis & H. L. K. Coleman (Eds.), *Multicultural counseling competencies: Assessment, education, training, and supervision* (pp. 111–130). Thousand Oaks, CA: Sage.

Ponterotto, J. G. (1998). Charting a course for research in multicultural counseling training. *The Counseling Psychologist, 16,* 43–68.

Ponterotto, J. G., & Alexander, C. M. (1996). Assessing the multicultural competence of counselors and clinicians. In L. A. Suzuki, P. J. Meller, & J. G. Ponterotto (Eds.), *Handbook of multicultural assessment: Clinical, psychological, and educational applications* (2nd ed., pp. 651–672). San Francisco: Jossey-Bass.

Ponterotto, J. G., Casas, J. M., Suzuki, L. A., & Alexander, C. M. (2001). *Handbook of multicultural counseling* (2nd ed.). Thousand Oaks, CA: Sage.

Ponterotto, J. G, Fuertes, J. N., & Chen, E. C. (2000). Models of multicultural counseling. In S. D. Brown & R. W. Lent (Eds.), *Handbook of counseling psychology* (3rd ed., pp. 639–669). New York: Wiley.

Ponterotto, J. G., & Furlong, M. J. (1985). Evaluating counselor effectiveness: A critical review of rating scale instruments. *Journal of Counseling Psychology, 32,* 597–616.

Ponterotto, J. G., Gretchen, D., & Chauhan. R. V. (2000). Cultural identity and multicultural assessment: Quantitative and qualitative tools for the clinician. In L. A. Suzuki, J. G. Ponterotto, & P. J. Meller (Eds.), *Handbook of multicultural assessment: Clinical, psychological, and educational applications* (2nd ed., pp. 67–100). San Francisco: Jossey-Bass.

Ponterotto, J. G., Gretchen, D., Utsey, S. O., Rieger, B. P., &. Austin, R. (2002). A revision of the Multicultural Counseling Awareness Scale. *Journal of Multicultural Counseling and Development. 30,* 153–180.

Ponterotto, J. G., Rieger, B. P., Barren, A., Harris, G., Sparks, R., Sanchez, C. M., et al. (1996). Development and initial validation of the Multicultural Counseling Awareness Scale. In G. R. Sodowsky & J. C. Impara (Eds.), *Multicultural assessment in counseling and clinical psychology* (pp. 247–282). Lincoln, NE: Buros Institute of Mental Measurements.

Ponterotto, J. G., Rieger, B. P., Barrett, A., & Sparks, R. (1994). Assessing multicultural counseling competence: A review of instrumentation.

Journal of Counseling & Development, 72, 316–322.

Pope-Davis, D. B., Coleman, H. L. K., Liu, W. M., & Toporek, R. L. (2003). *Handbook of multicultural competencies in counseling and psychology.* Thousands Oaks, CA: Sage.

Pope-Davis, D. B., & Dings, J. G. (1995). The assessment of multicultural counseling competencies. In J. G. Ponterotto, J. M. Casas, L. A. Suzuki, & C. M. Alexander (Eds.), *Handbook of multicultural counseling* (pp. 287–311). Thousand Oaks, CA: Sage.

Pope-Davis, D. B., Liu, W. M., Toporek, R. L., & Brittan-Powell, C. S. (2001). What's missing from multicultural competency research: Review, introspection, and recommendations. *Cultural Diversity and Ethnic Minority Psychology,* 7, 121–138.

Pope-Davis, D. B., & Nielson, D. (1996). Assessing multicultural counseling competencies using the Multicultural Counseling Inventory: A review of the research. In G. R. Sodowsky & J. C. Impara (Eds.), *Multicultural assessment in counseling and clinical psychology* (pp. 325–343). Lincoln, NE: Buros Institute of Mental Measurements.

Pope-Davis, D. B., Reynolds, A. L., Dings, J. G., & Nielson, D. (1995). Examining multicultural competencies of graduate students in psychology. *Professional Psychology: Research and Practice, 26,* 322–329.

Prediger, D. K. (1994). Multicultural assessment standards: A compilation for counselors. *Measurement and Evaluation in Counseling and Development, 27,* 68–73.

Quintana, S. M., & Bernal, M. E. (1995). Ethnic minority training in counseling psychology: Comparisons with clinical and proposed standards. *The Counseling Psychologist, 23,* 102–121.

Quintana, S. M., & Maxwell, S. E. (1999). Implications of recent developments in structural equation modeling for counseling psychology. *The Counseling Psychologist, 27,* 485–527.

Ridley, C. R., Mendoza, D. W., Kanitz, B. E., Angermeier, L., & Zenk, R. (1994). Cultural sensitivity in multicultural counseling: A perceptual schema model. *Journal of Counseling Psychology, 41,* 125–136.

Robinson, T. L., & Ginter, E. J. (1999). Introduction to the *Journal of Counseling & Development*'s special issue on racism. *Journal of Counseling & Development,* 77, 3.

Rummel, R. J. (1970). *Applied factor analysis.* Evanston, IL: Northwestern University Press.

Serling, D. A., & Betz, N. E. (1990). Development and evaluation of a measure of fear of commitment. *Journal of Counseling Psychology, 37,* 91–97.

Sodowsky, G R., Kuo-Jackson, P. Y., Richardson, M. F., & Corey, A. T. (1998). Correlates of self-reported multicultural competencies: Counselor multicultural social desirability, race, social inadequacy, locus of control, racial ideology, and multicultural training. *Journal of Counseling Psychology, 45,* 256–264.

Sodowsky, G. R., Taffe, R. C., Gutkin, T. B., & Wise, S. L. (1994). Development of the Multicultural Counseling Inventory: A self-report measure of multicultural competencies. *Journal of Counseling Psychology, 41,*137–148.

Sue, D. W. (1991). A conceptual model for cultural diversity training. *Journal of Counseling & Development, 70,* 99–105.

Sue, D. W., Arredondo, P., & McDavis, R. J. (1992). Multicultural counseling competencies: A call to the profession. *Journal of Multicultural Counseling and Development, 20,* 64–88.

Sue, D. W., Bernier, J. E., Durran, A., Feinberg, L., Pedersen, P., Smith, E. J., et al. (1982). Position paper: Cross-cultural counseling competencies. *The Counseling Psychologist, 10,* 45–52.

Sue, D. W., Carter, R. T., Casas. J. M., Fouad, N. A., Ivey, A. E., Jensen, M., et al. (1998). *Multicultural counseling competencies: Individual and organizational development.* Thousand Oaks, CA: Sage.

Tabachnick, B. G., & Fidell, L. S. (2001). *Using multivariate statistics* (4th ed.). Needham Heights, MA: Allyn & Bacon.

Tomlinson-Clarke, S. (2000). Assessing outcomes in a multicultural training course: A qualitative study. *Counseling Psychology Quarterly, 13,* 221–231.

Tucker, L. R., & Lewis, C. (1973). A reliability coefficient for maximum likelihood factor analysis. *Psychometrika, 38,* 1–10.

Worthington, R. L., Mobley, M., Franks, R. P., & Tan, J. A. (2000). Multicultural counseling competencies: Verbal content, counselor attributions and social desirability. *Journal of Counseling Psychology, 47,* 460–468.

2

Mental Health: Culture, Race, and Ethnicity

A Supplement to Mental Health: A Report of the Surgeon General

U.S. Department of Health and Human Services

Message From Tommy G. Thompson, Secretary of Health and Human Services

As a nation, we have only begun to come to terms with the reality and impact of mental illnesses on the health and well-being of the American people. This groundbreaking publication makes clear that the tragic and devastating effects of mental illnesses touch people of all ages, colors, and cultures. And though *Mental Health: A Report of the Surgeon General* informed us that there are effective treatments available for most disorders, Americans do not share equally in the best that science has to offer. Through the process of conducting his comprehensive scientific review for this Supplement, and with recognition that mental illnesses are real, disabling conditions affecting all populations regardless of race or ethnicity, the Surgeon General has determined that disparities in mental health services exist for racial and ethnic minorities, and thus, mental illnesses exact a greater toll on their overall health and productivity.

Diversity is inherent to the American way of life, and so is equal opportunity. Ensuring that all Americans have equal access to high quality health care, including mental health care, is a primary goal of the Department of Health and Human Services. By identifying the many barriers to quality care faced by racial and ethnic minorities, this Supplement provides an important road map for Federal, State, and local leaders to follow in eliminating disparities in the availability, accessibility, and utilization of mental health services.

An exemplary feature of this Supplement is its consideration of the relevance of history and culture to our understanding of mental health, mental illness, and disparities in services. In particular, the national prevention agenda can be informed by understanding how the strengths of different groups' cultural and historical experiences might be drawn upon to help prevent the emergence of mental health problems or reduce the effects of mental illness when it strikes. This Supplement takes a promising first step in this direction.

One of the profound responsibilities of any government is to provide for its most vulnerable citizens. It is now incumbent upon the public health community to set in motion a plan for eliminating racial and ethnic disparities in mental health. To achieve this goal, we must first better understand the roles of culture, race, and ethnicity, and overcome obstacles that would keep anyone with mental health problems from seeking or receiving effective treatment. We must also endeavor to reduce variability in diagnostic and treatment procedures by encouraging the consistent use of evidence-based, state-of-the-art medications and psychotherapies throughout the mental health system. At the same time, research must continue to aid clinicians in understanding how to appropriately tailor interventions to the needs of the individual based on factors such as age, gender, race, culture, or ethnicity.

To ensure that the messages outlined by the Surgeon General in this document reach the American people, the Department of Health and Human Services encourages its State and local partners to engage communities and listen to their needs. We must understand how local leaders and communities, including schools, families, and faith organizations, can become vital allies in the battle against disparities. Together, we can develop a shared vision of equal access to effective mental health services, identify the opportunities and incentives for collaborative problem solving, and then seize them. From a commitment to health and mental health for all Americans, communities will benefit. States will benefit. The Nation will benefit.

Foreword

As was the case when *Mental Health: A Report of the Surgeon General* was released in 1999, *Mental Health: Culture, Race, and Ethnicity* provides cause for both celebration and concern for those of us at the Substance Abuse and Mental Health Services Administration (SAMHSA) and its Center for Mental Health Services (CMHS). We celebrate the Supplement's comprehensive coverage of issues relevant to the mental health of racial and ethnic minorities, its providing a historical and cultural context within which minority mental health may be better understood, and its appreciation of the hardships endured and the strength, energy, and optimism of racial and ethnic minorities in their quest for good mental health. The Supplement causes us concern because of its finding that very serious disparities do exist regarding the mental health services delivered to racial and ethnic minorities. We must eliminate these disparities.

SAMHSA and CMHS envision a Nation where all persons, regardless of their culture, race, or ethnicity, enjoy the benefits of effective mental health preventive and treatment services. To achieve this goal, cultural and historical context must be accounted for in designing, adapting, and implementing services and service delivery systems. Communities must ensure that prevention and treatment services are relevant, attractive, and effective for minority populations. As the field learns more about the meaning and effect of cultural competence, we will enrich our commitment to the delivery of evidence-based treatment, tailored to the cultural needs of consumers and families. This Supplement, and the activities it will inspire, represents both a Surgeon General and a Department striving to improve communication among stakeholders through a shared appreciation of science, culture, history, and social context.

Not only does this Supplement provide us with a framework for better understanding scientific evidence and its implications for eliminating disparities, it also reinforces a major finding of *Mental Health: A Report of the Surgeon General.* That is, it shows how stigma and shame deter many Americans, including racial and ethnic minorities, from seeking treatment. SAMHSA and CMHS have long been leaders in the fight to reduce the stigma of mental illness. We pledge to carry on our efforts in this fight.

SAMHSA and CMHS are proud to have developed this Supplement in consultation with the National Institute of Mental Health (NIMH) in the National Institutes of Health. NIMH has contributed to this Supplement in innumerable ways, and many of the future directions reflected herein, especially those related to the need for more research, can be addressed adequately only through NIMH's leadership. We are grateful that this leadership and the commitment to eliminating mental health disparities are well established at NIMH.

We again celebrate the publication of this Supplement, and we trust that you will see it as we do—as a platform upon which to build positive change in our mental health system for racial and ethnic minorities, and indeed, for our Nation as a whole.

Joseph H. Autry III, M.D.
Acting Administrator
Substance Abuse and
Mental Health Services Administration

Bernard S. Arons, M.D.
Director
Center for Mental Health Services

Preface

From the Surgeon General
U.S. Public Health Service

Mental health is fundamental to health, according to *Mental Health: A Report of the Surgeon General,* the first Surgeon General's report ever to focus exclusively on mental health. That report of two years ago urged Americans to view mental health as paramount to personal well-being, family relationships, and successful contributions to society. It documented the disabling nature of mental illnesses, showcased the strong science base behind effective treatments, and recommended that people seek help for mental health problems or disorders.

The first mental health report also acknowledged that all Americans do not share equally in the hope for recovery from mental illnesses. This is especially true of members of racial and ethnic minority groups. That awareness galvanized me to ask for a supplemental report on the nature and extent of disparities in mental health care for racial and ethnic minorities and on promising directions for the elimination of these disparities. This Supplement documents that the science base on racial and ethnic minority mental health is inadequate; the best available research, however, indicates that these groups have less access to and availability of care, and tend to receive poorer quality mental health services. These disparities leave minority communities with a greater disability burden from unmet mental health needs.

A hallmark of this Supplement is its emphasis on the role that cultural factors play in mental health. The cultures from which people hail affect all aspects of mental health and illness, including the types of stresses they confront, whether they seek help, what types of help they seek, what symptoms and concerns they bring to clinical attention, and what types of coping styles and social supports they possess. Likewise, the cultures of clinicians and service systems influence the nature of mental health services.

Just as health disparities are a cause for public concern, so is our diversity a national asset. This Supplement carries with it a call to the people of the United States to understand and appreciate our many cultures and then impact on the mental health of all Americans. The main message of this Supplement—that culture counts—should echo through the corridors and communities of this Nation. In today's multicultural reality, distinct cultures and then relationship to the broader society are not just important for mental health and the mental health system, but for the broader health care system as well.

This Supplement encourages racial and ethnic minorities to seek help for mental health problems and mental illnesses. For this advice to be meaningful, it is essential that our Nation continues on the load toward eliminating racial and ethnic disparities in the accessibility, availability, and quality of mental health services. Researchers are working to fill gaps in the scientific literature regarding the exact roles of race, culture, and ethnicity in mental health, but much is already known. The mental health system must take advantage of the direction and insight offered by the research presented in this Supplement. Because State and local governments have primary oversight of public mental health spending, they have a clear and important role in assuring equal access to high quality mental health services for racial and ethnic minorities. Just as important, we need to redouble our efforts to support communities, especially consumers, families, and community leaders, in welcoming and demanding effective treatment for all. When it is easy for minorities to seek and use treatment, our vision of eliminating mental health disparities becomes a reality.

Finally, as noted in the previous report, it is inherently better to prevent an illness from occurring in the first place than to need to treat it once it develops. Just as other areas of medicine have promoted healthy lifestyles and thereby have reduced the incidence of conditions such as heart disease and some cancers, so now is the time for mental health providers, researchers, and policy makers to focus more on promoting mental health and preventing mental and behavioral disorders. Following this course will yield incalculable benefits, not only in terms of societal costs, but also in the significant decrease of human suffering.

David Satcher, M.D., Ph.D.
Surgeon General

Executive Summary

America is home to a boundless array of cultures, races, and ethnicities. With this diversity comes incalculable energy and optimism. Diversity has enriched our Nation by bringing global ideas, perspectives, and innovations to all areas of contemporary life. The enduring contributions of minorities, like those of all Americans, rest on a foundation of mental health.

Mental health is fundamental to overall health and productivity. It is the basis for successful participation in family, community, and society. Throughout the lifespan, mental health is the wellspring of thinking and communication skills, learning, resilience, and self-esteem. It is all too easy to dismiss the value of mental health until problems appear. Mental health problems and illnesses are *real* and *disabling* conditions that are experienced by one in five Americans. Left untreated, mental illnesses can result in disability and despair for families, schools, communities, and the workplace. This toll is more than any society can afford.

This report is a Supplement to the first ever Surgeon General's Report on Mental Health, *Mental Health: A Report of the Surgeon General* (U.S. Department of Health and Human Services [DHHS], 1999). That report provided extensive documentation of the scientific advances illuminating our understanding of mental illness and its treatment. It found a range of effective treatments for most mental disorders. The efficacy of mental health treatment is so well documented that the Surgeon General made this single, explicit recommendation for all people: *Seek help if you have a mental health problem. Or think you have symptoms of a mental disorder.*

The recommendation to seek help is particularly vital, considering *the majority of people with diagnosable disorders, regardless of race or ethnicity, do not receive treatment.* The stigma surrounding mental illness is a powerful barrier to reaching treatment. People with mental illness feel shame and fear of discrimination about a condition that is as real and disabling as any other serious health condition.

Overall, the earlier Surgeon General's report provided hope for people with mental disorders by laying out the evidence for what can be done to prevent and treat them. It strove to dispel the myths and stigma that surround mental illness. It underscored several overarching points about mental health and mental illness (see box). Above all, it furnished hope for recovery from mental illness.

But in the Preface to the earlier report, the Surgeon General pointed out that all Americans do not share equally in the hope for recovery from mental illness:

"Even more than other areas of health and medicine, the mental health field is plagued by disparities in the availability of and access to its services. These disparities are viewed readily through the lenses of racial and cultural diversity, age, and gender" (DHHS, 1999, p. vi).

This Supplement was undertaken to probe more deeply into mental health disparities affecting racial and ethnic minorities. Drawing on scientific evidence from a wide-ranging body of empirical research, this Supplement has three purposes:

- To understand better the nature and extent of mental health disparities;
- To present the evidence on the need for mental health services and the provision of services to meet those needs; and
- To document promising directions toward the elimination of mental health disparities and the promotion of mental health.

This Supplement covers the four most recognized racial and ethnic minority groups in the United States. According to Federal classifications, African Americans (blacks), American Indians and Alaska Natives, Asian Americans and Pacific Islanders, and white Americans (whites) are races. Hispanic American (Latino) is an ethnicity and may apply to a person of any

Mental Health: A Report of the Surgeon General

Themes of the Report

- Mental health and mental illness require the broad focus of a public health approach.
- Mental disorders are disabling conditions.
- Mental health and mental illness are points on a continuum.
- Mind and body are inseparable.
- Stigma is a major obstacle preventing people from getting help.

Messages From the Surgeon General

- Mental health is fundamental to health.
- Mental illnesses are real health conditions.
- The efficacy of mental health treatments is well documented.
- A range of treatments exists for most mental disorders.

race (U.S. Office of Management and Budget [OMB], 1978). For example, many people from the Dominican Republic identify their ethnicity as Hispanic or Latino and their race as black.

The Federal Government created these broad racial and ethnic categories in the 1970s for collecting census and other types of demographic information.[1] Within each of the broad categories, including white Americans, are many distinct ethnic subgroups. Asian Americans and Pacific Islanders, for example, include 43 ethnic groups speaking over 100 languages and dialects. For American Indians and Alaska Natives, the Bureau of Indian Affairs currently recognizes 561 tribes. African Americans are also becoming more diverse, especially with the influx of refugees and immigrants from many countries of Africa and the Caribbean. White Americans, too, are a profoundly diverse group, covering the span of immigration from the 1400s to the 21st century, and including innumerable cultural, ethnic, and social subgroups.

Each ethnic subgroup, by definition, has a common heritage, values, rituals, and traditions, but there is no such thing as a homogeneous racial or ethnic group (white or nonwhite). Though the data presented in this Supplement are often in the form of group averages, or sample means (standard scientific practice for illustrating group differences and health disparities), it should be well noted that each racial or ethnic group contains the full range of variation on almost every social, psychological, and biological dimension presented. One of the goals of the Surgeon General is that no one will come away from reading this Supplement without an appreciation for the intrinsic diversity within each of the recognized racial or ethnic groups and the implications of that diversity for mental health.

Clearly, the four racial and ethnic minority groups that are the focus of this supplement are by no means the only populations that encounter disparities in mental health services. However, assessing disparities for groups such as people who are gay, lesbian, bisexual, and transgender or people with co-occurring physical and mental illnesses is beyond the scope of this Supplement. Nevertheless, many of the conclusions of this Supplement could apply to these and other groups currently experiencing mental health disparities.

Main Findings

Mental Illnesses Are Real, Disabling Conditions Affecting All Populations, Regardless of Race or Ethnicity

Major mental disorders like schizophrenia, bipolar disorder, depression, and panic disorder are found worldwide, across all racial and ethnic groups. They have been found across the globe, wherever researchers have surveyed. In the United States, the overall annual prevalence of mental disorders is about 21 percent of adults and children (DHHS, 1999). This Supplement finds that, based on the available evidence, the prevalence of mental disorders for racial and ethnic minorities in the United States is similar to that for whites.

This general finding about similarities in overall prevalence applies to minorities living in the community.[2] It does not apply to those individuals in vulnerable, high-need subgroups such as persons who are homeless, incarcerated, or institutionalized. People in these groups have higher rates of mental disorders (Koegel et al., 1988; Vernez et al., 1988; Breakey et al., 1989; Teplin, 1990). Further, the rates of mental disorders are not sufficiently studied in many smaller racial and ethnic groups—most notably American Indians, Alaska Natives, Asian Americans, and Pacific Islander groups—to permit firm conclusions about overall prevalence within those populations.

This Supplement pays special attention to vulnerable, high-need populations in which minorities are overrepresented. Although individuals in these groups are known to have a high need for mental health care, they often do not receive adequate services. This represents a critical public health concern, and this Supplement identifies as a course of action the need for earlier identification and care for these individuals within a coordinated and comprehensive service delivery system.

Striking Disparities in Mental Health Care Are Found for Racial and Ethnic Minorities

This Supplement documents the existence of several disparities affecting mental health care of racial and ethnic minorities compared with whites:

- Minorities have less access to, and availability of, mental health services.
- Minorities are less likely to receive needed mental health services.
- Minorities in treatment often receive a poorer quality of mental health care.
- Minorities are underrepresented in mental health research.

The recognition of these disparities brings hope that they can be seriously addressed and remedied. This Supplement offers guidance on future courses of action to eliminate these disparities and to ensure equality in access, utilization, and outcomes of mental health care.

More is known about the disparities than the reasons behind them. A constellation of barriers deters minority treatment. Many of these barriers operate for all Americans: cost, fragmentation of services, lack of availability of services, and societal stigma toward mental illness (DHHS, 1999). But additional barriers deter racial and ethnic minorities; mistrust and fear of treatment, racism and discrimination, and differences in language and communication. The ability for consumers[3] and providers to communicate with one another is essential for all aspects of health care, yet it carries special significance in the area of mental health because mental disorders affect thoughts, moods, and the highest integrative aspects of behavior. The diagnosis and treatment of mental disorders greatly depend on verbal communication and trust between patient and clinician. More broadly, mental health care disparities may also stem from minorities' historical and present day struggles with racism and discrimination, which affect their mental health and contribute to their lower economic, social, and political status. The cumulative weight and interplay of all barriers to care, not any single one alone, is likely responsible for mental health disparities.

Disparities Impose a Greater Disability Burden on Minorities

This Supplement finds that racial and ethnic minorities collectively experience a greater disability burden from mental illness than do whites. This higher level of burden stems from minorities receiving less care and poorer quality of care, rather than from their illnesses being inherently more severe or prevalent in the community.

This finding draws on several lines of evidence. First, mental disorders are highly disabling for all the world's populations (Murray & Lopez, 1996; Druss et al., 2000). Second, minorities are less likely than whites to receive needed services and more likely to receive poor quality of care. By not receiving effective treatment, they have greater levels of disability in terms of lost workdays and limitations in daily activities. Further, minorities are overrepresented among the Nation's most vulnerable populations, which have higher rates of mental disorders and more barriers to care. Taken together, these disparate lines of evidence support the finding that minorities suffer a disproportionately high disability burden from unmet mental health needs.

The greater disability burden is of grave concern to public health, and it has very real consequences. Ethnic and racial minorities do not yet completely share in the hope afforded by remarkable scientific advances in understanding and treating mental disorders. Because of disparities in mental health services, a disproportionate number of minorities with mental illnesses do not fully benefit from, or contribute to, the opportunities and prosperity of our society. This preventable disability from mental illness exacts a high societal toll and affects all Americans. Most troubling of all, the burden for minorities is growing. They are becoming more populous, all the while experiencing continuing inequality of income and economic opportunity. Racial and ethnic minorities in the United States face a social and economic environment of inequality that includes greater exposure to racism and discrimination, violence, and poverty, all of which take a toll on mental health.

Main Message: Culture Counts

Culture and society play pivotal roles in mental health, mental illness, and mental health services. Understanding the wide-ranging roles of culture and society enables the mental health field to design and deliver services that are more responsive to the needs of racial and ethnic minorities.

Culture is broadly defined as a common heritage or set of beliefs, norms, and values (DHHS, 1999). It refers to the shared attributes of one group. Anthropologists often describe culture as a system of shared meanings. The term "culture" is as applicable to whites as it is to racial and ethnic minorities. The dominant culture for much of United States history focused on the beliefs, norms, and values of European Americans. But today's America is unmistakably multicultural. And because there are a variety of ways to define a cultural group (e.g., by ethnicity, religion, geographic region, age group, sexual orientation, or profession), many people consider themselves as having multiple cultural identities.

With a seemingly endless range of cultural subgroups and individual variations, culture is important because it bears upon what *all* people bring to the clinical setting. It can account for variations in how consumers communicate their symptoms and which ones they report. Some aspects of culture may also underlie *culture-bound syndromes*—sets of symptoms much more common in some societies than in others. More often, culture bears upon whether people even seek help in the first place, what types of help they seek, what coping styles and social supports they have, and how much stigma they attach to mental illness. All cultures also feature strengths, such as resilience and adaptive ways of coping, which may buffer some people from developing certain disorders. Consumers of mental health services naturally carry this cultural diversity directly into the treatment setting.

Culture is a concept not limited to patients. It also applies to the professionals who treat them. Every group of professionals embodies a "culture" in the sense that they too have a shared set of beliefs, norms, and values. This is as true for health professionals as it is for other professional groups such as engineers and teachers. Any professional group's culture can be gleaned from the jargon they use, the orientation and emphasis in their textbooks, and from their mindset or way of looking at the world.

Health professionals in the United States and the institutions in which they train and practice are rooted in Western medicine, which emphasizes the primacy of the human body in disease and the acquisition of knowledge through scientific and empirical methods. Through objective methods, Western medicine strives to uncover universal truths about disease: its causation, diagnosis, and treatment. Its achievements have become the cornerstone of medicine worldwide.

To say that physicians or mental health professionals have their own culture does not detract from the universal truths discovered by their fields. Rather, it means that most clinicians share a worldview about the interrelationship between body, mind, and environment informed by knowledge acquired through the scientific method. It also means that clinicians view symptoms, diagnoses, and treatments in ways that sometimes diverge from their clients' views, especially when the cultural backgrounds of the consumer and provider are dissimilar. This divergence of viewpoints can create barriers to effective care.

The culture of the clinician and the larger health care system govern the societal response to a patient with mental illness. They influence many aspects of the delivery of care, including diagnosis, treatments, and the organization and reimbursement of services. Clinicians and service systems, naturally immersed in their own cultures, have been ill-equipped to meet the needs of patients from different backgrounds and, in some cases, have displayed bias in the delivery of care.

The main message of this Supplement is that "culture counts." The cultures that patients come from shape their mental health and affect the types of mental health services they use. Likewise, the cultures of the clinician and the service system affect diagnosis, treatment, and the organization and financing of services. Cultural and social influences are not the only influences on mental health and service delivery, but they have been historically underestimated—*and they do count.* Cultural differences must be accounted for to ensure that minorities, like all Americans, receive mental health care tailored to their needs.

Personal Health Recommendation: Seek Help

The efficacy of treatment is well documented, according to the main finding of *Mental Health: A Report of the Surgeon General.* There is evidence, described in this Supplement, that racial and ethnic minorities benefit from mental health treatment. And it is abundantly clear that good treatment is preferable to no treatment at all. Untreated mental disorders can have dire consequences—distress, disability, and, in some cases, suicide. Therefore, this Supplement underscores the personal health recommendation of the earlier report: *Every person, regardless of race or ethnicity, should seek help if they have a mental health problem or symptoms of a mental disorder.*

Individuals are encouraged to seek help from any source in which they have confidence. If they do not improve with the help received from the first source, they are encouraged to keep trying. At present, members of minority groups may experience limited availability of, and access to, culturally sensitive treatments. With time, access to these services should improve as a result of awareness of this problem and the courses of action identified in this Supplement. In the meantime, anyone who needs help must hear a simple, yet resounding, message of hope: *Treatment works and recovery is possible.*

Organization of Supplement and Major Topics Covered

The first chapter reviews the core messages of the original Surgeon General's Report on Mental

Health. It also covers scope and terminology, the overall public health approach, and the science base for this Supplement. Chapter 2 lays the foundations for understanding the relationships among culture, society, mental health, mental illness, and mental health services. Chapters 3–6 provide information about each of the four major racial and ethnic minority groups, and Chapter 7 concludes with promising courses of action to reduce disparities and improve the mental health of racial and ethnic minorities.

Each chapter concerning a racial or ethnic minority group follows a common format. The chapter begins with the group's history in the United States, which is central to understanding contemporary ethnic identities, adaptive traditions, and health. Similarly, each chapter describes the group's demographic patterns, including their family structure, income and education, and health status. These patterns reflect the group's history, and they are relevant for understanding that group's needs for mental health services. The chapter then reviews the available scientific evidence regarding the need for mental health services (as measured by prevalence), the availability, accessibility, and utilization of services, and the appropriateness and outcomes of mental health services.

Chapter Summaries and Conclusions

Chapter 2: Culture Counts

The cultures of racial and ethnic minorities influence many aspects of mental illness, including how patients from a given culture communicate and manifest their symptoms, their style of coping, their family and community supports, and their willingness to seek treatment. Likewise, the cultures of the clinician and the service system influence diagnosis, treatment, and service delivery. Cultural and social influences are not the only determinants of mental illness and patterns of service use, but they do play important roles.

- Cultural and social factors contribute to the causation of mental illness, yet that contribution varies by disorder. Mental illness is considered the product of a complex interaction among biological, psychological, social, and cultural factors. The role of any of these major factors can be stronger or weaker depending on the specific disorder.

- Ethnic and racial minorities in the United States face a social and economic environment of inequality that includes greater exposure to racism, discrimination, violence, and poverty. Living in poverty has the most measurable effect on the rates of mental illness. People in the lowest strata of income, education, and occupation (known as socioeconomic status) are about two to three times more likely than those in the highest strata to have a mental disorder.

- Racism and discrimination are stressful events that adversely affect health and mental health. They place minorities at risk for mental disorders such as depression and anxiety. Whether racism and discrimination can by themselves cause these disorders is less clear, yet deserves research attention.

- Mistrust of mental health services is an important reason deterring minorities from seeking treatment. Their concerns are reinforced by evidence, both direct and indirect, of clinician bias and stereotyping.

- The cultures of racial and ethnic minorities alter the types of mental health services they use. Clinical environments that do not respect, or are incompatible with, the cultures of the people they serve may deter minorities from using services and receiving appropriate care.

Chapter 3: African Americans

The overwhelming majority of today's African American population traces its ancestry to the slave trade from Africa. The legacy of slavery, racism, and discrimination continues to influence the social and economic standing of this group. Almost one quarter of African Americans are poor, and their per capita income is much lower than that of whites. They bear a disproportionate burden of health problems and higher mortality rates from disease. Nevertheless, African Americans are a diverse group, experiencing a range of challenges as well as successes in measures of education, income, and other indices of social well-being. Their steady improvement in social standing is significant and serves as testimony to the resilience and adaptive traditions of the African American community.

- *Need for Services:* For African Americans who live in the community, rates of mental illness appear to be similar to those for whites. In one study, this similarity was found *before,* and in another study, *after* controlling for differences in income, education, and marital status. But African Americans are overrepresented in vulnerable, high-need populations because of homelessness, incarceration, and, for children, placement in foster care. The rates of mental illness in high-need populations are much higher.

- *Availability of Services:* "Safety net" providers furnish a disproportionate share of mental health care to African Americans. The financial viability of such providers is threatened as a result of the national transformation in financing of health care over the past two decades. A jeopardized safety net reduces availability of care to African Americans. Further, there are very few African American mental health specialists for those who prefer specialists of their own race or ethnicity.

- *Access to Services:* African Americans have less access to mental health services than do whites. Less access results, in part, from lack of health insurance, especially for working poor who do not qualify for public coverage and who work in jobs that do not provide private health coverage. About 25 percent of African Americans are uninsured. Yet better insurance coverage by itself is not sufficient to eliminate disparities in access because many African Americans with adequate private coverage still are less inclined to use services.

- *Utilization of Services:* African Americans with mental health needs are less likely than whites to receive treatment. If treated, they are likely to have sought help in primary care, as opposed to mental health specialty care. They frequently receive mental health care in emergency rooms and in psychiatric hospitals. They are overrepresented in these settings partly because they delay seeking treatment until their symptoms are more severe.

- *Appropriateness and Outcomes of Services:* For certain disorders (e.g., schizophrenia and mood disorders), errors in diagnosis are made more often for African Americans than for whites. The limited body of research suggests that, when receiving care for appropriate diagnoses, African Americans respond as favorably as do whites. Increasing evidence suggests that, in clinical settings, African Americans are less likely than whites to receive evidence-based care in accordance with professional treatment guidelines.

Chapter 4: American Indians and Alaska Natives

American Indians and Alaska Natives (AI/ANs) flourished in North America for thousands of years before Europeans colonized the continent. As Europeans migrated westward through the 19th century, the conquest of Indian lands reduced the population to 5 percent of its original size. Movement to reservations and other Federal policies have had enduring social and economic effects, as AI/ANs are the most impoverished of today's minority groups. Over one quarter live in poverty, compared to 8 percent of whites. A heterogeneous grouping of more than 500 Federally recognized tribes, the AI/AN population experiences a range of health and mental health outcomes. While AI/ANs are, on average, five times more likely to die of alcohol-related causes than are whites, they are less likely to die from cancer and heart disease. The Indian Health Service, established in 1955, is the Federal agency with primary responsibility for delivering health and mental health care to AI/ANs. Traditional healing practices and spirituality figure prominently in the lives of AI/ANs—yet they complement, rather than compete with, Western medicine.

- *Need for Services:* Research on AI/ANs is limited by the small size of this population and by its heterogeneity. Nevertheless, existing studies suggest that youth and adults suffer a disproportionate burden of mental health problems and disorders. As one indication of distress, the suicide rate is 50 percent higher than the national rate. The groups within the AI/AN population with the greatest need for services are people who are homeless, incarcerated, or victims of trauma.

- *Availability of Services:* The availability of mental health services is severely limited by the rural, isolated location of many AI/AN communities. Clinics and hospitals of the Indian Health Service are located on reservations, yet the majority of American Indians no longer live on them. Moreover, there are fewer mental health providers, especially child and adolescent specialists, in rural communities than elsewhere.

- *Access to Services:* About 20 percent of AI/ANs do not have health insurance, compared to 14 percent of whites.

- *Utilization of Services:* An understanding of the nature and the extent to which AI/ANs use mental health services is limited by the lack of research. Traditional healing is used by a majority of AI/ANs.

- *Appropriateness and Outcomes of Services:* The appropriateness and outcomes of mental health care for AI/ANs have yet to be examined, but are critical for planning treatment and prevention programs.

Chapter 5: Asian Americans and Pacific Islanders

Asian Americans and Pacific Islanders (AA/PIs) are highly diverse, consisting of at least 43 separate ethnic groups. The AA/PI population in the United States is increasing rapidly; in 2001, about 60 percent were born overseas. Most Pacific Islanders are not immigrants; their ancestors were original inhabitants of land taken over by the United States a century ago. While the per capita income of AA/PIs is almost as high as that for whites, there is great variability both between and within subgroups. For example, there are many successful Southeast Asian and Pacific Islander Americans; however, overall poverty rates for these two groups are much higher than the national average. AA/PIs collectively exhibit a wide range of strengths—family cohesion, educational achievements, and motivation for upward mobility—and risk factors for mental illness such as preimmigration trauma from harsh social conditions.

Diversity within this population and other hurdles make research on AA/PIs difficult to carry out.

- *Need for Services:* Available research, while limited, suggests that the overall prevalence of mental health problems and disorders among AA/PIs does not significantly differ from prevalence rates for other Americans. Thus, contrary to popular stereotypes, AA/PIs are not, as a group, "mentally healthier" than other groups. Refugees from Southeast Asian countries are at risk for posttraumatic stress disorder as a result of the trauma and tenor preceding their immigration.

• *Availability of Services:* Nearly half of AA/PIs have problems with availability of mental health services because of limited English proficiency and lack of providers who have appropriate language skills.

• *Access to Services:* About 21 percent of AA/PIs lack health insurance, but again there is much variability. The rate of public health insurance for AA/PIs with low income, who are likely to qualify for Medicaid, is well below that of whites from the same income bracket.

• *Utilization of Services:* AA/PIs have lower rates of utilization compared to whites. This underrepresentation in care is characteristic of most AA/PI groups, regardless of gender, age, and geographic location. Among those who use services, the severity of their condition is high, suggesting that they delay using services until problems become very serious. Stigma and shame are major deterrents to their utilization of services.

• *Appropriateness and Outcomes of Services:* There is very limited evidence regarding treatment outcomes for AA/PIs. Because of differences in their rates of drug metabolism, some AA/PIs may require lower doses of certain drugs than those prescribed for whites. Ethnic matching of therapists with AA/PI clients, especially those who are less acculturated, has increased their use of mental health services.

Chapter 6: Hispanic Americans

The Spanish language and culture forge common bonds for many Hispanic Americans, regardless of whether they trace their ancestry to Africa, Asia, Europe, or the Americas. Hispanic Americans are now the largest and fastest growing minority group in the United States.

Their per capita income is among the lowest of the minority groups covered by this Supplement. Yet there is great diversity among individuals and groups, depending on factors such as level of education, generation, and country of origin. For example, 27 percent of Mexican Americans live in poverty, compared to 14 percent of Cuban Americans. Despite their lower average economic and social standing, which place many at risk for mental health problems and illness, Hispanic Americans display resilience and coping styles that promote mental health.

• *Need for Services:* Hispanic Americans have overall rates of mental illness similar to those for whites, yet there is wide variation. Rates are lowest for Hispanic immigrants born in Mexico or living in Puerto Rico, compared to Hispanic Americans born in the United States. Hispanic American youth are at significantly higher risk for poor mental health than white youth are by virtue of higher rates of depressive and anxiety symptoms, as well as higher rates of suicidal ideation and suicide attempts.

• *Availability of Services:* About 40 percent of Hispanic Americans in the 1990 census reported that they did not speak English very well. Very few providers identify themselves as Hispanic or Spanish-speaking. The result is that most Hispanic Americans have limited access to ethnically or linguistically similar providers.

• *Access to Services:* Of all ethnic groups in the United States, Hispanic Americans are the least likely to have health insurance (public or private). Their rate of uninsurance, at 37 percent, is twice that for whites.

• *Utilization of Services:* Hispanic Americans, both adults and children, are less likely than whites to receive needed mental health care. Those who seek care are more likely to go to primary health providers than to mental health specialists.

• *Appropriateness and Outcomes of Services:* The degree to which Hispanic Americans receive appropriate diagnoses is not known because of limited research. Research on outcomes, while similarly sparse, indicates that Hispanic Americans can benefit from mental health treatment. Increasing evidence suggests that Hispanic Americans are less likely in clinical settings to receive evidence-based care in accordance with professional treatment guidelines.

Chapter 7: A Vision for the Future

This Supplement has identified striking disparities in knowledge, access, utilization, and quality of mental health care for racial and ethnic minorities. Reducing or eliminating these disparities requires a steadfast commitment by all sectors of American society. Changing systems of mental health care must bring together the public and private sectors, health service providers, universities and researchers, foundations, mental health advocates, consumers, families, and communities. Overcoming mental health disparities and promoting mental health for all Americans underscores the Nation's commitment to public health and to equality. This chapter highlights promising courses of action for reducing barriers and promoting equal access to quality mental health services for all people who need them.

1. Continue to expand the science base.

Good science is an essential underpinning of the public health approach to mental health and mental illness. The science base regarding racial and ethnic minority mental health is limited but growing. Since 1994, the National Institutes of Health (NIH) has required inclusion of ethnic minorities in all NIH-funded research (NIH Guidelines, 1994, p. 14509). Several large epidemiological studies that include significant samples of racial and ethnic minorities have recently been initiated or completed. These surveys, when combined with smaller, ethnic-specific epidemiological surveys, may help resolve some of the uncertainties about the extent of mental illness among racial and ethnic groups.

These studies also will facilitate a better understanding of how factors such as acculturation, help-seeking behaviors, stigma, ethnic identity, racism, and spirituality provide protection from, or risk for, mental illness in racial and ethnic minority populations. The researchers have collaborated on a set of core questions that will enable them to compare how factors such as socioeconomic status, wealth, education, neighborhood context, social support, religiosity, and spirituality relate to mental illness. Similarly, it will be possible to assess how acculturation, ethnic identity, and perceived discrimination affect mental health outcomes for these groups. With these ground-breaking studies, the mental health field will gain crucial insight into how social and cultural factors operate across race and ethnicity to affect mental illness in diverse communities.

A major aspect of the vision for an adequate knowledge base includes research that confirms the efficacy of guideline- or other evidence-based treatments for racial and ethnic minorities. A special analysis performed for this Supplement reveals that the researchers who conducted the clinical trials used to generate treatment guidelines for several major mental disorders did not conduct specific analyses for any minority group. While the lack of ethnic-specific analyses does not mean that current treatment guidelines are ineffective for racial or ethnic minorities, it does highlight a gap in knowledge. Nevertheless, these guidelines, extrapolated from largely majority populations, are clearly the best available treatments for major mental disorders affecting all Americans.

As a matter of public health prudence, existing treatment guidelines should continue to be used as research proceeds to identify ways in which service delivery systems can better serve the needs of racial and ethnic minorities.

The science base of the future will also determine the efficacy of ethnic- or culture-specific interventions for minority populations and their effectiveness in clinical practice settings. In the area of psychopharmacology, research is needed to determine the extent to which the variability in people's response to medications is accounted for by factors related to race, ethnicity, age, gender, family history, and/or lifestyle.

This Supplement documents the fact that minorities tend to receive less accurate diagnoses than whites. While further study is needed on how to address issues such as clinician bias and diagnostic accuracy, the fifth edition of the *Diagnostic and Statistical Manual of Mental Disorders,* now under development, will extend and elaborate the "Glossary of Culture-Bound Syndromes," the "Outline for Cultural Formulation," and other concepts introduced in DSM-IV regarding the diagnostic process.

In terms of the promotion of mental health and the prevention of mental and behavioral disorders, important opportunities exist for researchers to study cultural differences in stress, coping, and resilience as part of the complex of factors that influence mental health. Such work will lay the groundwork for developing new prevention and treatment strategies—building upon community strengths to foster mental health and ameliorate negative health outcomes.

2. Improve access to treatment.

Simply put, the Nation's health systems must work to bring mental health services to where the people are. Many racial and ethnic minorities live in areas where general health care and specialty mental health care are in short supply. One major course of action is to *improve geographic availability of mental health services.* Innovative strategies for training providers, delivering services, creating incentives for providers to work in underserved areas, and strengthening the public health safety net promise to provide greater geographic access to mental health services for those in need.

Another step toward better access to care is to *integrate mental health care and primary care.* Primary care is where many minority individuals prefer to receive mental health care and where most people who need treatment are first recognized and diagnosed. A variety of research and demonstration programs have been or will be created to strengthen the capacity of these providers to meet the demand for mental health services and to encourage the delivery of integrated primary health and mental health services that match the needs of the diverse communities they serve.

Another major step in improving access to mental health services is to *improve language access.* Improving communication between clinicians and patients is essential to mental health care. Service providers receiving Federal financial assistance have an obligation under the 1964 Civil Rights Act to ensure that people with limited English proficiency have meaningful and equal access to services (DHHS, 2000).

Finally, a major way to improve access to mental health services is to *coordinate care to vulnerable, high-need groups.* People from all backgrounds may experience disparities in prevalence of illness, access to services, and quality of services if they are in underserved or vulnerable populations such as people who are incarcerated or homeless and children living in out-of-home placements. As noted earlier, racial and ethnic minorities are overrepresented in these groups. To prevent individuals from entering these vulnerable groups, early intervention is an important component to systems of care, though research is needed to determine which interventions work best at prevention. For individuals already in underserved or high-need groups, mental health services, delivered in a comprehensive and coordinated manner, are essential. It is not enough to deliver effective mental health treatments: Mental health and substance abuse treatments must be incorporated into effective service delivery systems, which include supported housing, supported employment, and other social services (DHHS, 1999).

3. Reduce barriers to mental health care.

The foremost barriers that deter racial and ethnic minorities from reaching treatment are the cost of services, the fragmented organization of these services, and societal stigma toward mental illness. These obstacles are intimidating for all Americans, yet they may be even more formidable for racial and ethnic minorities. The Nation must strive to dismantle these barriers to care.

Mental Health: A Report of the Surgeon General spotlighted the importance of overcoming stigma, facilitating entry into treatment, and reducing financial barriers to treatment (DHHS, 1999). This Supplement brings urgency to these goals. It aims to make services more accessible and appropriate to racial and ethnic minorities, it encourages mental health coverage for the millions of Americans who are uninsured, and it maintains that parity, or equivalence, between mental health coverage and other health coverage is an affordable and effective strategy for reducing racial and ethnic disparities.

4. Improve quality of mental health services.

Above all, improving the quality of mental health care is a vital goal for the Nation. Persons with mental illness who receive quality care are more likely to stay in treatment and to have better outcomes. This result is critical, as many treatments require at least four to six weeks to show a clear benefit to the patient. Through relief of distress and disability, consumers can begin to recover from mental illness. They can become more productive and make more fulfilling contributions to family and community.

Quality care conforms to professional guidelines that carry the highest standards of scientific rigor. *To improve the quality of care for minorities, this Supplement encourages providers to deliver effective treatments based on evidence-based professional guidelines.* Treatments with the strongest evidence of efficacy have been incorporated into treatment guidelines issued by organizations of mental health professionals and by government agencies.

A major priority for the Nation is to transform mental health services by tailoring them to meet the needs of all Americans, including racial and ethnic minorities. To be most effective, *treatments always need to be individualized in the clinical setting according to each patient's age, gender, race, ethnicity, and culture* (DHHS, 1999). No simple blueprint exists for how to accomplish this transformation, but there are many promising courses of action for the Nation to pursue.

At the same time, research is needed on several fronts, such as how to adapt evidence-based treatments to maximize their appeal and effectiveness for racial and ethnic minorities. While "ethnic-specific" and "culturally competent" service models take into account the cultures of racial and ethnic groups, including their languages, histories, traditions, beliefs, and values, these approaches to service delivery have thus far been promoted on the basis of humanistic values rather than rigorous empirical evidence. Further study may reveal how these models build an important, yet intangible, aspect of treatment: trust and rapport between patients and service providers.

5. Support capacity development.

This Supplement encourages all mental health professionals to develop their skills in tailoring treatment to age, gender, race, ethnicity, and culture. In addition, because minorities are dramatically underrepresented among mental health providers, researchers, administrators, policy makers, and consumer and family organizations, racial and ethnic minorities are encouraged to enter the mental health field. Training programs and funding sources also need to work toward equitable racial and ethnic minority representation in all these groups.

Another way to support capacity development and maximize systems of care is to promote leadership from within the community in which a mental health system is located. Issues of race, culture, and ethnicity may be addressed while engaging consumers, families, and communities in the design, planning, and implementation of their own mental health service systems. To reduce disparities in knowledge, and the availability, utilization, and quality of mental health services for racial and ethnic minority consumers, mental health educational, research, and service programs must develop a climate that conveys an appreciation of diverse cultures and an understanding of the impact of these cultures on mental health and mental illness. Doing so will help systems better meet the needs of all consumers and families, including racial and ethnic minorities.

6. Promote mental health.

Mental health promotion and mental illness prevention can improve the health of a community and the Nation. Because mental health is adversely affected by chronic social conditions such as poverty, community violence, racism, and discrimination, the reduction of these adverse conditions is quite likely to be vital to improving the mental health of racial and ethnic minorities. Efforts to prevent mental illness and promote mental health should build on intrinsic community strengths such as spirituality, positive ethnic identity, traditional values, educational attainment, and local leadership. Programs founded on individual, family, and community strengths have the potential to both ameliorate risk and foster resilience.

Families are the primary source of care and support for the majority of adults and children with mental problems or disorders. Efforts to promote mental health for racial and ethnic minorities must include strategies to strengthen families to function at their fullest potential and to mitigate the stressful effects of caring for a relative with a mental illness or a serious emotional disturbance.

Notes

1. The Office of Management and Budget has recently separated Asian Americans from Native Hawaiians and other Pacific Islanders (OMB, 2000).
2. Most epidemiological studies using disorder-based definitions of mental illness are conducted in community household surveys. They fail to include nonhousehold members, such as persons without homes or persons residing in institutions such as residential treatment centers, jails, shelters and hospitals.
3. Although a number of terms identify people who use or have used mental health services (e.g., mental health consumer, survivor, ex-patient, client), the terms "consumer" and "patient" will be used interchangeably throughout this Supplement.

Source: U.S. Department of Health and Human Services. (2001). *Mental health: Culture, race, and ethnicity. A supplement to mental health: A report of the Surgeon General.* 2001. Rockville, MD: Author.

References

Breakey, W. R., Fischer, P. J., Kramer, M., Nestadt, G., Romanoski, A. J., Ross, A., Royall, R. M., & Stine, O. (1989). Health and mental health problems of homeless men and women in Baltimore. *Journal of the American Medical Association, 262,* 1352–1357.

Druss, B. G., Marcus, S. C., Rosenheck, R. A., Olfson, M., Tanielian, T., & Pincus, H. A. (2000). Understanding disability in mental and general medical conditions. *American Journal of Psychiatry, 157,* 1485–1491.

Koegel, P. M., Burnam, A., & Farr, R. K. (1988). The prevalence of specific psychiatric disorders among homeless individuals in the inner city of Los Angeles. *Archives of General Psychiatry, 45,* 1085–1093.

Murray, C. J. L., & Lopez, A. D. (Eds.). (1996). *The global burden of disease. A comprehensive assessment of mortality and disability from diseases, injuries, and risk factors in 1990 and projected to 2020.* Cambridge, MA: Harvard School of Public Health.

Teplin, L. A. (1990). The prevalence of severe mental disorder among male urban jail detainees: Comparison with the Epidemiologic Catchment Area program. *American Journal of Public Health, 80,* 663–669.

U.S. Department of Health and Human Services. (1999). *Mental health: A report of the Surgeon General.* Rockville, MD: Author.

U.S. Department of Health and Human Services. (2000). *Policy guidance on the Title VI prohibition against national origin discrimination as it affects persons with limited English proficiency.* Rockville, MD: Author.

U.S. Office of Management and Budget. (1978). *Directive No. 15: Race and ethnic standards for Federal statistics and administrative reporting.* Washington, DC: Author.

U.S. Office of Management and Budget. (2000). *Guidance on aggregation and allocation of data on race for use in civil right monitoring and enforcement* (OMB Bulletin No. 00–02). Retrieved July 20, 2001, from http://www.whitehouse.gov/omb/bulleting:/b00-02.html.

Vernez, G. M., Burnam, M. A., McGlynn, E. A., Trude, S., & Mittman, B. (1988). *Review of California's program for the homeless mentally ill disabled* (Report No. R3631-CDMH). Santa Monica, CA: RAND.

3

Client Diversity

Amy G. Lam

Stanley Sue

The purpose of this article is to examine the empirical support for customizing the therapeutic relationship for women, ethnic minorities, gay, lesbian, and bisexual individuals, and individuals from lower social classes. At first glance, the grouping of such diverse populations may seem inappropriate and even insulting, a ventable wastepaper basket of diverse groups. However, these groups share several important elements in common. Specifically, they are considered oppressed groups in society, have been subjected to detrimental stereotypes, have not been targeted for much psychological research, and are often underserved or inappropriately served in the mental health system.

Nevertheless, three considerations are important to keep in mind. First, care must be taken not to infer that the groups are too similar. Second, there are significant within-group differences that must be acknowledged. Third, individuals have multiple group memberships and identities, and it is presently difficult to address the effects of these identities simultaneously.

Our review addresses several different questions for each population: First, is there evidence that these diverse populations fare less well in treatment than mainstream populations? Second, does matching of therapists with clients in terms of gender, ethnicity, sexual orientation, and social class improve outcomes? Third, are treatment outcomes better when population-specific strategies are used with members of these diverse populations? These questions are important to address because they underlie most of the existing guidelines. We review the research for the four groups and then offer suggestions for therapeutic practices. In the analysis, direct outcomes (e.g., symptom reduction, functioning, or improvement) are distinguished from indirect outcomes (e.g., dropping out of treatment, treatment duration).

Authors' Note: This study was supported in part by the National Research Center on Asian American Mental Health (National Institute of Mental Health Grant MH59616). This article is adapted from "Cultural and Demographic Diversity" in J. C. Norcross (Ed.), *Psychotherapy relationships that work.*

The authors gratefully acknowledge the assistance of Yuko Onodera and Melinda Tran.

Gender

Effectiveness of Therapy With Women

According to research reviews concerning gender and psychotherapy outcomes, gender is not a significant main effect in psychotherapy outcome studies (Beutler, Crago, & Arizmendi, 1986; Brodsky & Hare-Mustin, 1980; Garfield, 1994; Orlinsky & Howard, 1980). One of the more recent and rigorous studies on this topic was conducted by Thase and colleagues (Thase et al., 1994). Specifically, they compared how depressed men and women responded to 16 weeks of cognitive-behavioral therapy. Results indicated that neither gender nor the interaction between gender and length of treatment were significantly related to these outcome measures. While a few empirical studies were found that showed a gender effect favoring women (Kirshner, Genack, & Hauser, 1978; Mintz, Luborsky, & Auerbach, 1971; Seeman, 1954; Talley, Butcher, Maguire, & Pinkerton, 1992), two of these studies had small sample sizes, limiting the interpretability of the results (Mintz et al., 1971; Seeman, 1954). In sum, the majority of studies comparing women and men in psychotherapy have found that improvement in therapy is independent of client gender.

Client and Therapist Match

The limited research on client-therapist gender match suggests that match is related to indirect outcomes. Most recently, Zlotnick, Elkin, and Shea (1998) examined whether same-gender match and mixed-gender match were related to psychotherapy processes and outcomes. Results indicated that the type of therapist seen (i.e., same-gender or mixed-gender match) was not related to attrition rates, depression ratings after treatment, or client perceptions of therapist empathy. Furthermore, clients' beliefs about who would be more helpful (i.e., a male or female therapist) and their match or mismatch with this expectation was not related to therapeutic outcomes. These findings are in contrast to other studies conducted by Jones and his colleagues (Jones, Krupnick, & Kerig, 1987; Jones & Zoppel, 1982), which have suggested that gender match is related to improved symptom outcome and more satisfaction with therapy. Moreover, some studies on gender match have found interaction effects between gender and other client characteristics such as age, ethnicity, marital status, and diagnosis, as well as therapist experience, on client satisfaction and treatment duration (Fujino, Okazaki, & Young, 1994; Hill, 1975; Orlinsky & Howard, 1976). In sum, while gender match is related to indirect outcomes, less is known about the relationship between gender match and direct outcomes.

Feminist Therapies

We were able to locate only four studies assessing the effectiveness of feminist therapies. Two studies on gender-awareness therapy found therapy to be helpful in (a) bringing awareness to clients of how gender influenced their illness and (b) improving levels of self-esteem and sexual knowledge (Alyn & Becker, 1984; Sirkin, Maxey, Ryan, French, & Clements, 1988). However, these studies had relatively small sample sizes and one study did not have a control group. One study examining the effectiveness of consciousness-raising as a therapy in decreasing depression indicated that participants attributed psychological benefits (i.e., direct and indirect outcomes) to the consciousness-raising group (Weitz, 1982). However, the study did not include a control group. Finally, Rinfret-Raynor and Cantin (1997) examined the impact of feminist therapy on battered women. While therapy, in general, was found to be helpful, there were no differences among the feminist group therapy, feminist individual therapy, and standard individual treatment. This study was limited by the lack of random assignment of participants, as well as by the potential similarity between the comparison standard treatment and feminist treatments with regard to actual approaches to therapy.

The results of the four empirical studies on feminist therapies have not provided definitive results. Specifically, two of these studies did not have comparison control groups. Moreover, one comparative study did not find differences between feminist and standard therapy.

Ethnic Minorities

Effectiveness of Therapy

The limited studies examining the effectiveness of therapy with ethnic minorities indicate that minorities tend to exhibit either similar or worse outcomes than Whites in psychotherapy. For African Americans, three studies found no ethnic differences (Jones, 1978, 1982; Lerner, 1972), while three other studies found that African Americans do worse in therapy (Brown, Joe, & Thompson, 1985; Markowitz, Spielman, Sullivan, & Fishman, 2000; Sue, Fujino, Hu, Takeuchi, & Zane, 1991). For American Indians, the sole empirical study on treatment effectiveness found that American Indians did not benefit from treatment as much as White Americans (Query, 1985). While no differences on psychological functioning between Asians and Whites have been reported (Sue et al., 1991; Zane & Hatanaka, 1988), differences on client satisfaction variables may exist, with Asians reporting less satisfaction with treatment and progress in therapy than Whites (Less & Mixson, 1993; Zane, 1983). Studies with Latino clients, however, seem to suggest that Latinos do improve after psychotherapy treatment (Cortese, 1979; Navarro, 1993; Rosenthal, 2000; Sue et al., 1991).

Client and Therapist Match

Empirical studies on ethnic match seem to indicate that match may be important for indirect treatment outcomes. Studies with African Americans indicate that while match was not related to direct outcomes (Jones, 1978, 1982; Lerner, 1972), match was related to greater number of therapy sessions (Rosenheck, Fontana, & Cottrol, 1995; Sue et al., 1991). For both Asian Americans (Flaskerad & Hu, 1994; Fujino et al., 1994; Gamst, Dana, Der-Karabetian, & Kramer, 2001; Lau & Zane, 2000; Sue et al., 1991; Takeuchi, Sue, & Yen, 1995) and Latinos (Flaskerud, 1986; Gamst, Dana, Der-Karabetian, & Kramer, 2000; Sue et al., 1991; Takeuchi et al., 1995), match is associated with less likelihood of dropout and increased length of therapy. Moreover, it appears that ethnic and language match may be especially important for treatment outcomes with limited-English-speaking clients (Sue et al., 1991). Unfortunately, studies with American Indians are limited to preference studies.

In contrast to these studies, Gamst et al. (2000) found that among African Americans at one mental health center, match was associated with fewer treatment sessions as well as lower scores on Global Assessment of Functioning (GAP). It is not clear whether the findings from Gamst and his colleagues are confined to one institution or have greater generalizability. Thus, the bulk of studies point to the benefit of match for indirect outcomes, but not direct outcomes.

Ethnic-Specific Therapies

While there is theoretical and clinical literature that discusses ethnic-specific modifications of therapy for African Americans and Asian Americans, we could not locate empirical studies that tested the therapeutic outcomes of psychotherapy advocated in the theoretical literature for these two populations.

For American Indians, traditional methods of healing, including sweat lodges and talking circles, are increasingly being incorporated into mental health treatments. Gutierres and colleagues (Gutierres, Russo, & Urbanski, 1994; Gutierres & Todd, 1997) found that, compared to control groups, a culturally-enhanced substance abuse program is related to increased treatment completion as well as lowered levels of depression for American Indians. However, they offered no reports as to how the program worked to decrease substance abuse.

For Latinos, two therapies that have some empirical support are cuento therapy (Costantino, Malgady, & Rogler, 1986; Malgady, Rogler, & Costantino, 1990a, 1990b) and family therapy (Szapocznik et al., 1989). Cuento therapy was created to provide a culturally sensitive method of modeling adaptive behavior for Puerto Rican children through folktales and qualifies as a probably efficacious therapy for Puerto Rican children (Costantino et al., 1986; Malgady et al., 1990a, 1990b). Family therapy has been shown to be potentially useful with Latino clients. Szapocznik et al. (1989) found in a sample of Latino boys that both structural family therapy and individual psychodynamic child therapy were more effective than a control condition with regard to treatment duration and premature dropout. Moreover, followup data indicated that boys in the family therapy condition continued to improve in family functioning, compared to boys in the individual therapy.

Sexual Orientation

Effectiveness of Therapy With Lesbian, Gay, and Bisexual (LGB) Individuals

Dunkle (1994) conducted one of the few reviews of treatment outcome studies with gay male clients. Only six studies were found from the period of 1975 to 1993. While the studies indicated that treatment was effective, because of the nonexperimental nature of the majority of these studies, Dunkle (1994) stated that conclusive statements regarding the effectiveness of certain therapies for gay male clients could not be made.

Since this review, three studies on the effectiveness of HIV risk-reduction programs (e.g., Choi et al., 1996; Peterson et al., 1996; Roffman et al., 1997), one study on a bereavement support group (Goodkin et al., 1999), and two studies examining treatment for depression (e.g., Lee, Cohen, Hadley, & Goodwin, 1999; Markowitz et al., 1998) with gay clients have been conducted. The three studies examining the effectiveness of HIV risk-reduction interventions indicate that these programs are effective for gay men. Choi et al. (1996) examined a brief group counseling program for Asian American and Pacific Islander men who have sex with men and found significant treatment effects for number of partners but not for frequency of unprotected anal intercourse. Peterson et al. (1996) indicated a significant treatment effect on unprotected anal intercourse among a group of African American homosexual and bisexual men. Roffman et al. (1997) found that counseling had different effects on gay and bisexual men. Exclusively gay counseling participants were almost four-and-a-half times more likely to be successful in reducing HIV risk than gay men in the control condition. For bisexual men, there were no significant differences on risk reduction between the treatment and control groups.

The one study examining a bereavement support group for gay men found the intervention to be effective in reducing the composite grief and distress index for both HIV-I-seropositive and -seronegative participants (Goodkin et al., 1999). Therapy also seems to be effective in treating depression in HIV-positive individuals. Lee et al. (1999) found that a group cognitive-behavioral therapy showed a high retention rate and significantly reduced depressive symptomatology in 15 gay men with AIDS or symptomatic HIV infection. A more rigorous study by Markowitz et al. (1998) examined the effectiveness of different types of therapy (i.e., interpersonal psychotherapy, cognitive-behavioral therapy, supportive therapy, and imipramine plus supportive therapy) among HIV-positive clients (mostly male and gay). Results indicated that while depressive symptomatology decreased across all groups over time, differential benefits were found, with HIV-positive clients in the interpersonal psychotherapy and supportive psychotherapy with imipramine groups having significantly greater improvements on depression measures than those in the cognitive-behavioral or supportive therapy groups.

These findings provide evidence that psychotherapy interventions are effective for gay men. Unfortunately, at this time, there is little empirical research on the effectiveness of treatments for lesbians and bisexuals.

Client and Therapist Match

To date, there are only three published empirical studies on the effects of client-therapist match on sexual orientation, and they provide partial support for the importance of match. Liljestrand, Gerling, and Saliba's (1978) study indicated that client-therapist match on sexual orientation was important for sexual orientation. Brooks (1981) and Liddle (1996) found a significant difference in gay and lesbian client perceptions of helpfulness of heterosexual male therapists and all other therapists (i.e., heterosexual female, lesbian, gay, or bisexual therapists). The finding that heterosexual female therapists were no less helpful than gay, lesbian, and bisexual therapists suggests that heterosexual therapists can be effective with the lesbian and gay population (Liddle, 1996). Taken together, these studies point to the possibility that match may be important for lesbian and gay clients, especially when dealing with sexual orientation. Moreover, sexual orientation match is partially supported as females of both orientations have not been shown to produce differential effects on clients, whereas heterosexual males are thought to have a negative influence on lesbian and gay clients. It should be noted, however, that the outcome measures were limited to client ratings.

Gay Affirmative Therapies

While there has been recent literature discussing the potential benefit of gay affirmative therapy, we could locate no empirical research on the effectiveness of this therapy in treating LGB individuals.

Social Class

Effectiveness of Therapy With Low-Socioeconomic Status (SES) Individuals

Several reviews of the relationship between social class and direct therapy outcomes have found no relationship between these variables. Luborsky, Chandler, Auerback, Cohen, and Bachrach (1971) reviewed five studies and found no SES effect in therapy. Lorion's 1973 review concluded that social class was related to treatment assignment and duration, but not to direct treatment outcomes.

Three empirical studies provide preliminary evidence for the use of active, directive therapy for low-SES clients. Two less rigorous studies (Organista, Munoz, & Gonzalez, 1994; Satterfield,

1998) found treatment effects with cognitive-behavioral therapy for low-SES clients. A more rigorous study conducted by Goin, Yamamoto, and Silverman (1965) compared active, directive therapy to insight-oriented therapy. They found that while there was a trend that clients in the active advice group were more satisfied with therapy, because of the small sample size, there was no statistical difference in the percentage of satisfaction between the two groups. No significant differences between the groups were found in terms of length of treatment (Goin et al., 1965).

In conclusion, there is preliminary evidence suggesting that directive therapies may be beneficial for low-SES clients. However, given the absence of more rigorous studies, definitive statements cannot be made about the effectiveness of these therapies for low-SES clients.

Client and Therapist Match

While one potential way of reducing premature termination may be to match clients with therapists in terms of social class (Mitchell & Namenek, 1970), we could not find any systematic research on the relationship of SES matching with therapy outcomes.

Population-Specific Therapies

Specific alternative forms of therapy have not been identified for clients of low-SES backgrounds. However, several studies have examined social class effects with regard to different existing therapies (Lorion & Felner, 1986). Two studies have examined the benefits of time-limited therapies. While Stone and Crowthers (1972) found their short-term therapy program to have dropout rates of less than 3%, Koegler and Brill's (1967) more rigorous study found no significant differences in symptom reduction between brief contact therapy and insight-oriented therapy. Therefore, these limited studies do not wholly support the benefit of brief therapy over insight therapy.

Despite the dearth of research on social class and outcomes research, several studies have suggested that social class is related to psychotherapy dropout. There is a greater likelihood of premature termination for clients of lower SES (Garfield, 1994; Reis & Brown, 1999).

Limitations of the Research

From our review, we identify several limitations in terms of the quantity and quality of psychotherapy research on these diverse populations. First, there is a disappointing paucity of research on treatment outcomes, especially for ethnic minority groups, lesbian, gay, and bisexual persons, and members of lower social classes. Psychotherapy appears to be effective, but findings also suggest that outcomes are sometimes not as positive for these groups (e.g., ethnic minorities) as for mainstream groups (e.g., European Americans). Second, much of the available research has methodological limitations, such as the lack of comparison groups, random assignment of clients to treatments, and adequate sample sizes. Third, most studies involving ethnic minorities and individuals from a lower social class deal with effectiveness rather than efficacy. Fourth, widely argued conditions for improving treatment outcomes—such as matching of therapists and clients and population-specific treatments—are mostly based on theoretical orientation, clinical observations, and social-political-ethical considerations rather than research. While these are good reasons to use such strategies, many of these strategies have not been subjected to rigorous research tests. Perhaps one of the highest priorities in mental health efforts should be to conduct systematic research on these groups.

Therapeutic Practices

Match of Therapist and Client Under Appropriate Conditions

Advocates from diverse groups have argued the importance of match, as clients may feel more comfortable, understood, and be more self-disclosing with therapists who are similar. The existing empirical evidence for the benefits of match is mostly found in client satisfaction variables and indirect outcomes. This is not surprising because match in gender, ethnicity, sexual orientation, or social class is only one of many characteristics that may be matched. Matches in demographic characteristics may be moderator variables because beneficial effects may be dependent on the interaction of match and client characteristics. Further, sociodemographic matches may not result in cultural matches. For example, a highly acculturated, non-Chinese-speaking Chinese American therapist may have tremendous difficulties working with a recent Chinese immigrant with limited English proficiency. Thus, match appears to be important in certain, but not all conditions. A final issue to consider is freedom of choice. Some clients do have preferences for these therapist characteristics, and preferences should be honored in almost all situations.

Population-Specific Strategies of Therapy

A number of suggestions have been made concerning therapeutic strategies to use when working with clients of diverse backgrounds. However, research findings on the use of group-specific tactics are mixed, with some studies showing the tactics to be effective and other studies not demonstrating their superiority. The value of population-specific treatments appears to be well supported in the case of Latino clients. Again, it is highly likely that such strategies are better suited for some, but not all, members of the group. For example, feminist therapy may be more beneficial with women who are dealing with oppression, status differences, and domestic violence. As in the case of therapist and client match, the effectiveness of population-specific strategies may largely depend on the type of client.

In summary, the current state of the field suggests there is a dearth of research on treatment outcomes with diverse populations. As such, the empirically supported therapeutic practices that we have provided are not definitive and should not be seen as opposed to current guidelines. Rather, our review underscores the need for more rigorous research regarding psychotherapy outcomes with diverse clients, in order to inform guidelines for these populations.

References

Alyn, J. H., & Becker, L. A. (1984). Feminist therapy with chronically and profoundly disturbed women. *Journal of Counseling Psychology, 31,* 202–208.

Beutler, L. E., Crago, M., & Arizmendi, T. G. (1986). Therapist variables in psychotherapy process and outcome. In S. L. Garfield & A. E. Bergin (Eds.), *Handbook of psychotherapy and behavior change* (3rd ed., pp. 257–310). New York: Wiley.

Brodsky, A. M., & Hare-Mustin, R. T. (1980). Psychotherapy and women: Priorities for research. In A. M. Brodsky & R. T. Hare-Mustin (Eds.), *Women and psychotherapy: An assessment of research and practice* (pp. 385–409). New York: Guilford.

Brooks, V. R. (1981). Sex and sexual orientation as variables in therapists' biases and therapy outcomes. *Clinical Social Work Journal, 9,* 198–210.

Brown, B. S., Joe, G. W., & Thompson, P. (1985). Minority group status and treatment retention. *International Journal of the Addictions, 20,* 319–335.

Choi, K. H., Lew, S., Vittinghoff, E., Catania, J. A., Barrett, D. C, & Coates, T. J. (1996). The efficacy of brief group counseling in HIV risk reduction among homosexual Asian and Pacific Islander men. *AIDS, 10,* 81–87.

Cortese, M. (1979). Intervention research with Hispanic Americans: A review. *Hispanic Journal of Behavioral Sciences, 1,* 4–20.

Costantino, G., Malgady, R.G., & Rogler, L. H. (1986). Cuento therapy: A culturally sensitive modality for Puerto Rican children. *Journal of Counseling and Clinical Psychology, 54,* 639–645.

Dunkle, J. H. (1994). Counseling gay male clients: A review of treatment efficacy research: 1975-present. *Journal of Gay and Lesbian Psychotherapy, 2,* 1–19.

Flaskerud, J. H. (1986). The effects of culture-compatible intervention on the utilization of mental health services by minority clients. *Community Mental Health Journal, 22,* 127–141.

Flaskerud, J. H., & Hu, L. (1994). Participation in and outcome of treatment for major depression among low income Asian-Americans. *Psychiatry Research, 53,* 289–300.

Fujino, D. C., Okazaki, S., & Young, K. (1994). Asian-American women in the mental health system: An examination of ethnic and gender match between therapist and client. *Journal of Community Psychology, 22,* 164–176.

Gamst, G., Dana, R. H., Der-Karabetian, A., & Kramer, T. (2000). Ethnic match and client ethnicity effects on global assessment and visitation. *Journal of Community Psychology, 28,* 547–564.

Gamst, G., Dana, R. H., Der-Karabetian, A., & Kramer, T. (2001). Asian American mental health clients: Effects of ethnic match and age on global assessment and visitation. *Journal of Mental Health Counseling, 23,* 57–71.

Garfield, S. L. (1994). Research on client variables in psychotherapy. In A. E. Bergin & S. L. Garfield (Eds.), *Handbook of psychotherapy and behavior change* (4th ed., pp. 193–228). New York: Wiley.

Goin, M. K., Yamamoto, J., & Silverman, J. (1965). Therapy congruent with class-linked expectations. *Archives of General Psychiatry, 13,* 133–137.

Goodkin, K., Blaney, N. T., Feaster, D. J., Baldewicz, T., Burkhalter, J. E., & Leeds, B. (1999). A randomized controlled clinical trial of a bereavement support group intervention in human immunodeficiency virus type I-seropositive and -seronegative homosexual men. *Archives of General Psychiatry, 56,* 52–59.

Gutierres, S. E., Russo, N. F., & Urbanski, L. (1994). Sociocultural and psychological factors in American Indian drug use: Implications for treatment. *International Journal of the Addictions, 29,* 1761–1786.

Gutierres, S. E., & Todd, M. (1997). The impact of childhood abuse on treatment outcomes of substance users. *Professional Psychology: Research and Practice, 28,* 348–354.

Hill, C. E. (1975). Sex of client and sex and experience level of counselor. *Journal of Counseling Psychology, 22,* 6–11.

Jones, E. E. (1978). Effects of race on psychotherapy process and outcome: An exploratory investigation. *Psychotherapy: Theory, Research and Practice, 15,* 226–236.

Jones, E. E. (1982). Psychotherapists' impressions of treatment outcome as a function of race. *Journal of Clinical Psychology, 38,* 722–731.

Jones, E. E., Krupnick, J. L., & Kerig, P. K. (1987). Some gender effects in a brief psychotherapy. *Psychotherapy, 24,* 336–352.

Jones, E. E., & Zoppel, C. L. (1982). Impact of client and therapist gender on psychotherapy process and outcome. *Journal of Consulting and Clinical Psychology, 50,* 259–272.

Kirshner, L. A., Genack, A., & Hauser, S. T. (1978). Effects of gender on short-term psychotherapy. *Psychotherapy: Theory, Research and Practice, 15,* 158–167.

Koegler, R. R., & Brill, N. Q. (1967). *Treatment of psychiatric outpatients.* Norwalk, CT: Appleton-Century-Crofts.

Lau, A., & Zane, N. W. S. (2000). Examining the effects of ethnic-specific services: An analysis of cost-utilization and treatment outcome for Asian American clients. *Journal of Community Psychology, 28,* 63–77.

Lee, M. R., Cohen, L., Hadley, S. W., & Goodwin, F. K. (1999). Cognitive-behavioral group therapy with medication for depressed gay men with AIDS or symptomatic HIV infection. *Psychiatric Services, 50,* 948–952.

Lee, W. M. L., & Mixson, R. J. (1995). Asian and Caucasian client perceptions of the effectiveness of counseling. *Journal of Multicultural Counseling and Development, 23,* 48–56.

Lerner, B. (1972). *Therapy in the ghetto: Political impotence and personal disintegration.* Baltimore: Johns Hopkins University Press.

Liddle, B. J. (1996). Therapist sexual orientation, gender, and counseling practices as they relate to ratings on helpfulness by gay and lesbian clients. *Journal of Counseling Psychology, 43,* 394–401.

Liijestrand, P., Gerling, E., & Saliba, P. A. (1978). The effects of social sex-role stereotypes and sexual orientation on psychotherapeutic outcomes. *Journal of Homosexuality, 3,* 361–372.

Lorion, R. P. (1973). Socioeconomic status and traditional treatment approaches reconsidered. *Psychological Bulletin, 79,* 263–270.

Lorion, R. P., & Felner, R. D. (1986). Research on psychotherapy with the disadvantaged. In A. E. Bergin & S. L. Garfield (Eds.), *Handbook of psychotherapy and behavior change* (3rd ed., pp. 739–776). New York: Wiley.

Luborsky, L., Chandler, M., Auerback, A. H., Cohen, J., & Bachrach, J. M. (1971). Factors influencing the outcome of psychotherapy: A review of quantitative research. *Psychological Bulletin, 75,* 145–185.

Malgady, R. G., Rogler, L. H., & Costantino, G. (1990a). Hero/heroine modeling for Puerto Rican adolescents: A preventive mental health intervention. *Journal of Counseling and Clinical Psychology, 58,* 469–474.

Malgady, R. G., Rogler, L. H., & Costantino, G. (1990b). Culturally sensitive psychotherapy for Puerto Rican children and adolescents: A program of treatment outcome research. *Journal of Counseling and Clinical Psychology, 58,* 704–712.

Markowitz, J. C., Kocsis, J. H., Fishman, B., Spielman, L. A., Jacobsberg, L. B., Frances, A. J., Klerman, G. L., & Perry, S. W. (1998). Treatment of depressive symptoms in Human Immunodeficiency Virus-positive patients. *Archives of General Psychiatry, 55,* 452–457.

Markowitz, J. C., Splelman, L. A., Sullivan, M., &. Fishman, B. (2000). An exploratory study of ethnicity and psychotherapy outcome among HIV-positive patients with depressive symptoms. *Journal of Psychotherapy Practice and Research, 9,* 226–231.

Mintz, J., Luborsky, L., & Auerbach, A. H. (1971). Dimensions of psychotherapy: A factor-analytic study of ratings of psychotherapy sessions. *Journal of Consulting and Clinical Psychology, 36,* 106–120.

Mitchell, K. M., & Namenek, T. M. (1970). A comparison of therapist and client social class. *Professional Psychology: Research and Practice, 1,* 225–230.

Navarro, A. M. (1993). Efectividad de las psicoterapias con Latinos en los Estados Unidos: Una revision meta-analitica. *Revista Interamericana de Psicologia, 27,* 131–146.

Organista, K. C., Munoz, R. F., & Gonzalez, G. (1994). Cognitive behavioral therapy for depression in low-income and minority medical outpatients: Description of a program and exploratory analyses. *Cognitive Therapy and Research, 18,* 241–259.

Orlinsky, D. E., & Howard, K. I. (1976). The effects of sex of therapist on the therapeutic experiences of women. *Psychotherapy: Theory, Research and Practice, 13,* 82–88.

Orlinsky, D. E., & Howard, K. I. (1980). Gender and psychotherapeutic outcome. In A. M. Brodsky & R. T. Hare-Mustin (Eds.), *Women and psychotherapy: An assessment of research and practice* (pp. 3–34). New York: Guilford.

Peterson, J. L., Coates, T. J., Catania, J., Hauck, W. W., Acree, M., Daigle, D., Hillard, B., Middleton, L., & Hearst, N. (1996). Evaluation of an HIV risk reduction intervention among African-American homosexual and bisexual men. *AIDS, 10,* 319–325.

Query, J. N. (1985). Comparative admission and follow-up study of American Indians and Whites in a youth chemical dependency unit on the North Central Plains. *International Journal of the Addictions, 20,* 489–502.

Reis, B. F., & Brown, L. G. (1999). Reducing psychotherapy dropouts: Maximizing perspective convergence in the psychotherapy dyad. *Psychotherapy, 36,* 123–136.

Rinfret-Raynor, M., & Cantin, S. (1997). Feminist therapy for battered women: An assessment. In G. K. Kantor & J. L. Jasinski (Eds.), *Out of darkness: Contemporary perspectives on family violence* (pp. 219–234). Thousand Oaks, CA: Sage.

Roffman, R. A., Downey, L., Beadnell, B., Gordon, J. R., Craver, J. N., & Stephens, R. S. (1997). Cognitive-behavioral group counseling to prevent HIV transmission in gay and bisexual men: Factors contributing to successful risk reduction. *Research on Social Work Practice, 7,* 165–186.

Rosenheck, R., Fontana, A., & Cottrol, C. (1995). Effect of clinician-veteran racial pairing in the treatment of post-traumatic stress disorder. *American Journal of Psychiatry, 152,* 555–563.

Rosenthal, C. (2000). Latino practice outcome research: A review of the literature. *Smith College Studies in Social Work, 70,* 217–238.

Satterfield, J. M. (1998). Cognitive behavioral group therapy for depressed, low-income minority clients: Retention and treatment enhancement. *Cognitive and Behavioral Practice, 25,* 65–80.

Seeman, J. (1954). Counselor judgments of therapeutic process and outcome. In C. Rogers & R. F. Dymond (Eds.), *Psychotherapy and personality change* (pp. 99–108). Chicago: University of Chicago Press.

Sirkin, M., Maxey, J., Ryan, M., French, C., & Clements, O. (1988). Gender awareness group therapy: Exploring gender-related issues in a day-treatment population. *International Journal of Partial Hospitalization, 5,* 263–272.

Stone, J. L., & Crowthers, V. (1972). Innovations in program and funding of mental health services for blue-collar families. *American Journal of Psychiatry, 128,* 1375–1380.

Sue, S., Fujino, D. C., Hu, L. T., Takeuchi, D. T., & Zane, N. W. S. (1991). Community mental health services for ethnic minority groups: A test of the cultural responsiveness hypothesis. *Journal of Consulting and Clinical Psychology, 59,* 533–540.

Szapocznik, J., Rio, A., Murray, E., Cohen, R., Scopetta, M., Rivas-Vazquez, A., Hervis, O., Posada, V., & Kurtines, W. (1989). Structural family versus psychodynamic child therapy for problematic Hispanic boys. *Journal of Counseling and Clinical Psychology, 57,* 571–578.

Takeuchi, D. T., Sue, S., & Yeh, M. (1995). Return rates and outcomes from ethnicity-specific mental health programs in Los Angeles. *American Journal of Public Health, 85,* 638–643.

Talley, J. E., Butcher, T., Maguire, M. A., & Pinkerton, R. S. (1992). The effects of very brief psychotherapy on symptoms of dysphoria. In J. E. Talley (Ed.), *The predictors of successful very brief psychotherapy: A study of differences by gender, age, and treatment variables* (pp. 12–45). Springfield, IL: Charles C. Thomas.

Thase, M. E., Reynolds, C. F., Frank, E., Simons, A. D., McGeary, J., Fasiczka, A. L., Garamoni, G. G., Jennings, R., & Kupfer, D. J. (1994). Do depressed men and women respond similarly to cognitive behavior therapy? *American Journal of Psychiatry, 151,* 500–505.

Weitz, R. (1982). Feminist consciousness raising, self-concept, and depression. *Sex Roles, 8,* 231–241

Zane, N. (1983, August). *Evaluation of outpatient psychotherapy for Asian and non-Asian American clients.* Paper presented at the American Psychological Association conference, Anaheim, CA.

Zane, N., & Hatanaka, H. (1988, October). *Utilization and evaluation of a parallel service delivery model for ethnic minority clients.* Paper presented at Recent Trends and New Approaches to the Treatment of Mental Illness and Substance Abuse, Oklahoma Mental Health Research Institute, OK.

Zlotnick, C., Elkin, I., & Shea, M. T. (1998) Does the gender of a patient or the gender of a therapist affect the treatment of patients with major depression? *Journal of Consulting and Clinical Psychology, 66,* 655–659.

4

TEMAS (Tell-Me-A-Story) Assessment in Multicultural Societies

Giuseppe Costantino

Richard H. Dana

Robert G. Malgady

The Multicultural Assessment-Intervention Process (MAIP) model described in this chapter includes the CBMCS Training Program, published originally in Costantino, Dana, and Malgady, 2007, Chapter 1, Child/Adolescent Mental Health Needs and Services, pp. 31–48. This chapter is presented in the Reader to summarize the history and development of the CBMCS as a component of the MAIP model. This model was designed to acknowledge and incorporate individual, racial/cultural, and social class difference among consumers in all phases of public sector behavioral health services.

MAIP Assessment Service Delivery Model

The MAIP model emerged from a variety of sources including a social justice ideology, multicultural competence training in counseling psychology, multicultural assessment, and culturally sensitive research (e.g., Dana, 1993, 1997, 1998b; 2000a, 2002a, 2005a, 2005b). Originally developed to provide a context for culturally sensitive assessment of psychopathology and personality, this model examines the assessment-intervention process at five points employing a series of questions to clarify cultural orientation (acculturation/racial identity status), instrument usage, need for cultural formulations or conceptualizations, and interventions (standard or modified). These questions refer to particular times during the assessment-intervention process when cultural issues embedded in the mental health service delivery process can signal the potential usefulness of additional information resources (Figure 1):

1. Availability of a universal instrument for all clients?
2. Cultural orientation status?

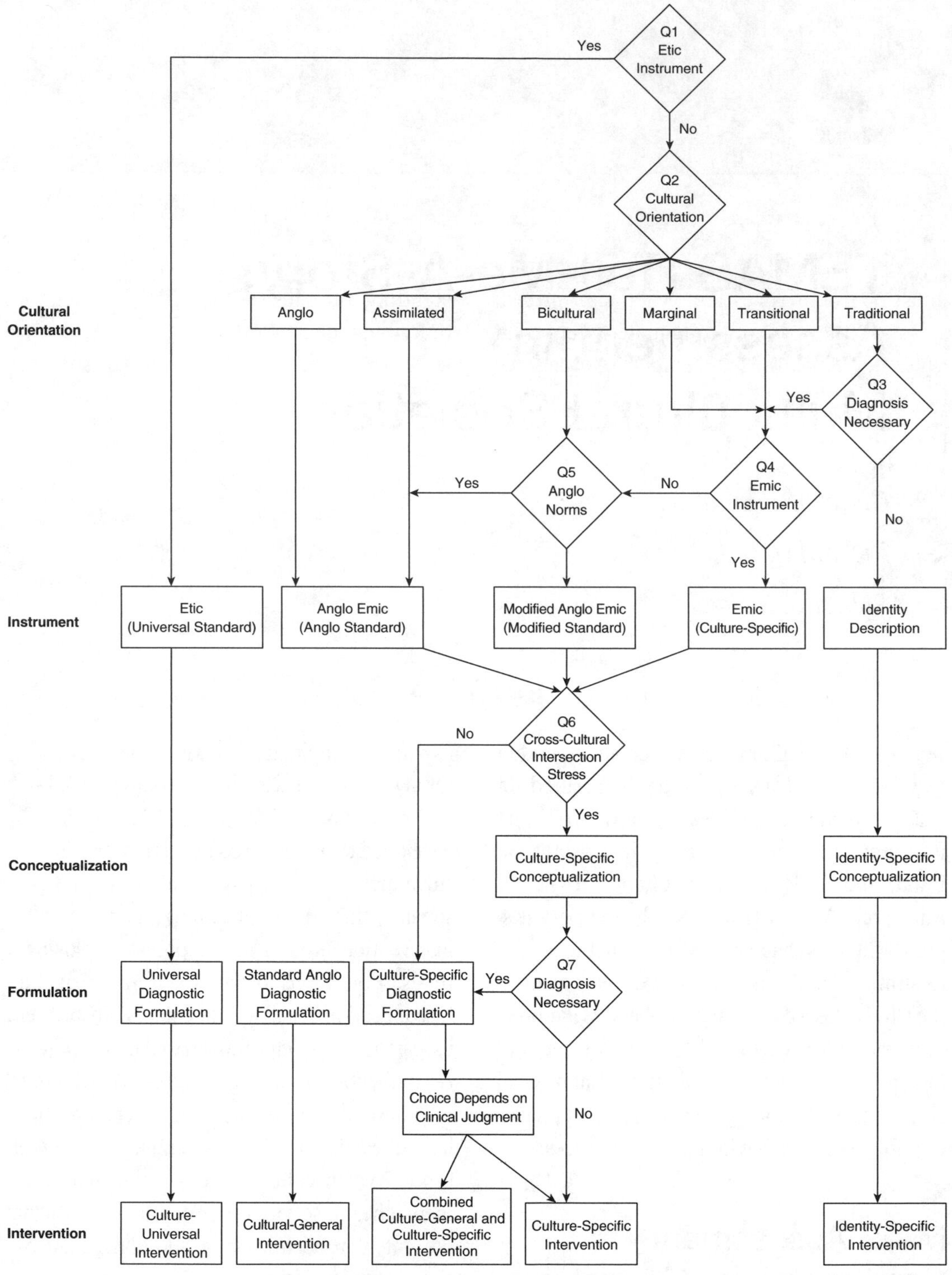

Figure 1 Multicultural Assessment-Intervention Process Model

Source: From *Handbook of Cross-Cultural and Multicultural Personality Assessment* (p. 7), by R. H. Dana, 2000c, Mahwah, NJ: Lawrence Erlbaum Associates, Inc. Copyright 2000 by Lawrence Erlbaum Associates, Inc. Adapted with permission.

3. Diagnosis necessary?
4. Culture-specific instruments?
5. Anglo-American norms?
6. Cross-cultural interaction stress?
7. Diagnosis necessary?

With regard to Question 1, although ostensibly universal instruments are available, they must be used with extreme caution at present because they do not adequately represent culture-specific traits and employ international samples similar to Western samples (Triandis & Suh, 2002). The existence of global or universal traits remains controversial in the absence of convincing demonstrations of cross-cultural construct equivalence (Dana, 2000b, 2005a). There is also compelling evidence that depression as well as other personality characteristics and their identified symptom constellations have few or many culture-specific descriptors and are clustered and identified differently across countries (e.g., Brandt & Boucher, 1986).

The etic instruments in Question 1 are more accurately described as imposed etics rather than genuine etics (Lonner, 1985). These imposed etic instruments have been used in the United States with ethnic minority populations and exported internationally as if they were genuine etics with identical meanings in nonoriginating cultures. However, before describing these instruments as genuine etics, it is mandatory to establish their cultural equivalence (see Allen & Dana, 2004). MAIP explicitly acknowledges the necessity for proper labeling of etic instruments as imposed etic instruments with the present limitations on cultural equivalence interpretations.

Cultural equivalence is demonstrated by cross-cultural translation (also referred to as item or linguistic equivalence) as well as construct/concept, metric/scalar (Brislin, 1993), and functional equivalence (Berry, 1980). Translation is a necessary first step toward establishing cultural equivalence, but it is never sufficient to report only translation equivalence without commensurate research attention to the full range of necessary equivalencies (Dana, 2000b). In the absence of construct and metric equivalence demonstrations for standard instruments, caution in multicultural/cross-cultural interpretation is mandatory (Dana, 2005a).

Question 2 requires identification and understanding of cultural orientation categories describing the relationship between an original cultural identification and assimilation to a host culture for major cultural groups. Four of these modes of acculturation—Assimilation, Separation, Marginalization, and Integration—were originally developed by Berry (1989) and correspond with MAIP cultural orientations of Anglo/Assimilated, Traditional, Marginal, and Bicultural. The Anglo and Assimilated orientations, characteristic of many mainstream individuals in the United States, are consistent with ignoring and disengaging from cultures of origin. Traditional clients maintain original cultural identities and value systems while rejecting the cultural norms of the dominant culture. Marginal clients selectively reject aspects of both mainstream culture and their culture of origin. A Transitional cultural orientation status describes bilingual Native Americans/Alaska Natives who question traditional values and religion (LaFromboise, Trimble, & Mohatt, 1990). Cultural orientation status may be determined by interview questions or established moderators for the four major cultural/racial groups in the United States (e.g., Dana, 1993, 2005a; Lin & Kelsey, 2000; Van de Vijver & Phalet, 2004).

Cultural orientation and racial identity status (CRI) describe an individual balance between original and acquired cultural/racial identities. Cultural orientation status measures are available for all groups, including African Americans (Dana, 1993, 2005a). These measures should be distinguished from African American racial identity developmental measures (Burlew, Bellow, & Lovett, 2000). CRI statuses markedly affect score elevations on standard objective assessment instruments. For example, measured acculturation my be confounded with psychopathology on the MMPI/MMPI-2 as well as other instruments not explicitly constructed for ethnic minority populations (Dana, 1993, 2005a). Racial identity developmental status may also be confounded with psychopathology for African Americans on the MMPI (Whatley, Allen, & Dana, 2003).

CRI information is often necessary for differentiating between diagnosis of psychopathology and description of personality on standard assessment instruments when these instruments are used for subsequent treatment planning decisions and specific interventions. For example, traditional individuals, as well as some marginal individuals, have historically underutilized or failed to benefit from standard ethnic-general mental health interventions. These interventions may lack credibility because majority cultural professional service delivery etiquette was not employed or can be simply inappropriate for culturally relevant problems requiring culture-specific interventions, contain culturally relevant elements, or necessitate culturally informed clinicians for responsible service delivery.

Question 3 calls attention to a potential psychopathology-culture or psychopathology-racial identity confound whenever standard tests/methods are used as imposed emics with traditional, transitional, or marginal individuals, and the effects of these instruments with bicultural individuals are not known. When the MAIP was developed, there were very few emic instruments, although the handbook of African American instruments now provides numerous examples of emic measures for this population (Jones, 1996). These emics provide useful information to document the necessity for subsequent conceptualization suggesting the usefulness of culture-specific or identity-specific interventions whenever a DSM diagnosis may not be relevant or appropriate.

Question 4 helps the clinician decide whether or not to rely on standard Anglo emic/imposed etic instruments. These standard instruments may require adaptations for applications with specific cultural populations or use of emic instruments developed for these cultural populations. Emic instruments provide useful information not only concerning the relevance, accuracy, and usefulness of DSM diagnosis but are necessary for developing culture-specific or identity-specific conceptualizations as well as for understanding the cultural self (Dana, 1998c).

Question 5 raises issues concerning the adequacy of using the normative data available for mainstream tests/methods with ethnic minority populations. Standard assessment erroneously assumes that these available norms are sufficient regardless of the numbers, representativeness, or matching criteria for ethnic minority and mainstream participants. One solution to the dilemma of inappropriate norms is to employ acculturation/racial identity status norms to correct standard objective tests such as the MMPI/MMPI-2 (Dana, 2000b). Acculturation/racial identity status delineation identifies the need for relevant diagnostic formulations/conceptualizations as well as for the availability of culturally sensitive treatment alternatives. The continuing presences of these unresolved issues suggest that MAIP model applications in the public sector may benefit from a non-normative comparative approach to consumer ethnicity.

Question 6 provides an opportunity to evaluate relevant life history information from individuals who are at risk for misdiagnosis because they experience stress in their cross-cultural interactions. Whenever standard interventions are employed with ethnic minority clients, their personality characteristics are vulnerable to distortion and/or misunderstanding. Reactivity to racist events may also lead to realistic paranoia and erroneous pathology diagnoses for these individuals. Because racist events may orchestrate potentially dysfunctional behaviors, or predispose individuals to situation-specific behaviors misconstrued as psychopathology, differentiating these stress-related interactions from psychopathology per se is aided by formulations and conceptualizations. These formulations and conceptualizations are required preparation for interventions dealing with interpersonal interactions involving discrimination and racism. As a consequence, either treatment or alternative culturally sensitive psychological interventions may be necessary.

Question 7 reiterates the necessity for diagnosis by changing the context from an imposed etic or emic assessment instrument recommendation to a recommendation for culture-general, culture-specific, or combined intervention options. This strategy forces attention to the potential availability and usefulness of nonmedical-psychiatric interventions for problems-in-living conducted by culturally competent clinicians in both private and public sector settings. The MAIP classifies these treatments/interventions as ethnic-general or culture-general (i.e., suitable for majority culture, assimilated, and acculturated individuals, as well as for self-selected bicultural, marginal, and transitional individuals) or culturally sensitive interventions including various combined culture-general/culture-specific as well as culture-specific interventions (for review by ethnic/racial group, see Dana, 1998a).

MAIP Research

Research with this model provides studies on the effects of matching or not matching certain factors believed to be important in the therapeutic relationship. These factors include clinician-client ethnicity, language preference, and gender. A number of studies report conflicting effects of matching on clinical outcomes (e.g., Gamst, Dana, Der-Karabetian, & Kramer, 2000, 2001, 2004; Gamst, Dana, Der-Karabetian, Aragon, Arellano, & Kramer, 2002; Jerrell, 1995, 1998; Maramba & Hall, 2002; Russell, Fujino, Sue, Cheung, & Snowden, 1996; Shin et al., 2005).

Despite the lack of clear-cut, consistent, consensual findings of these studies, some limited conclusions require emphasis:

1. Beneficial match findings were clearer for Latinos and Asians Americans than for African Americans and White Americans (Gamst et al., 2000, 2004b).
2. Match was much more important for ethnic minority consumers (Maramba & Hall, 2002), although match per se may be of less predictive significance than provider cultural competency (Martin, 1995).
3. Match should not be considered independently of ethnic-specific services (e.g., service delivery style, combined culture-general + culture-specific, or culture-specific interventions) for Asian Americans (Lau & Zane, 2001).
4. Part of the variability found among studies reporting statistically significant matching effects may be attributed to undocumented language matching rather than specifically due to ethnic or racial matching per se (Shin et al., 2005).
5. Variability in the published literature on ethnic matching may be due to lack of clarity concerning the service providers' professional identities as well as inconsistency and insufficient descriptive detail in reporting this information.

Gamst et al. (2002) observed the practical and research relevance of the fact that mental health clients are typically seen by a variety of providers (e.g., psychiatrist, psychologist, marriage and family therapist, case manager, etc.). The mental health service provider who had the most frequent contact with a particular client during a specific time frame as determined by billing records was subsequently operationalized by the concept of *modal provider/modal therapist.*

Public Sector MAIP Model

Managed care service delivery systems have insufficiently acknowledged individual, cultural, and social class differences among their consumers (Dana, 1998d; Dana, Conner, & Allen, 1996). Policy decisions for cost containment prioritized health care and emphasized human similarities rather than differences. These decisions minimized the range of available assessment and treatment options and eschewed responsibility for inclusion of medical-offset approaches, adequate opportunities for preventive services, and sufficient long-term care. A multicultural research and practice agenda requires careful planning, coordination, training of staff, elicitation of feedback from consumers, and meticulous tracking of all assessments and dispositional decisions by supervisory staff under the aegis of the concerned and participant multicultural communities and agency clients. In managed care agencies, this agenda provides a tradeoff between implementation costs of staff time and resources and anticipated benefits of higher consumer satisfaction with services, clinical outcomes, and lower dropout rates that drive up mental health care costs. A managed-care focus on language and interpreter services to satisfy cultural competency may be tempered by the necessity to serve all populations, which overlooks embedding issues throughout services.

MAIP Model Essentials

History

The MAIP model was introduced and applied over a period of years in the Tri-City Community Mental Health Center (Dana, Aragon, & Kramer, 2002). This application began with employment of the Agency Cultural Competence Checklist (ACCC; Dana, Behn, & Gonwa, 1992), continued with development of a research management process for tracking and managing data (Gamst & Dana, 2005) that facilitated the completion of the empirical studies described in an earlier section of this chapter, and was terminated with the demise of the agency in 2005.

Foundations for Public Sector Application

This section describes the status of five essential MAIP components providing the foundations for public sector applications: (a) performance measurement design; (b) disposition coordination; (c) dedicated computerized tracking system; (d) statistical model for simultaneous assessment of practice parameters; and (e) in-service provider cultural competency training. The materials in this section and MAIP summary section were developed from a series of published and unpublished papers documenting MAIP history and application (Dana, 2002c; 2005b; Dana, Aragon, & Kramer, 2002; Gamst & Dana, 2005).

Performance Measurement Design

The necessity of embedding cultural competency in mental health services and the MAIP components for achieving this objective are congruent with public sector performance measurement design currently under consideration by the California Department of Mental Health (2005). In the public domain, performance is measured at client, program, and community levels-of-analysis. The MAIP model provides an effective way to operationalize objective cultural competency indicators at the client and program levels and is consistent with the necessity for mental health services to function with community-level oversight.

At the individual-level collection of client outcome data, 15 indicators are recommended (i.e., housing, crime, employment, education, hospitalization, income, family preservation, symptoms, suicide, functioning, substance use, quality of life, illness self-management, individual goals, and physical health). MAIP employment would also include client-level data assessing ethnic identity as well as acculturation and racial identity status.

The second level provides the "mental health system accountability" data necessary for monitoring programs and systems, quality assurance and multistakeholder coordination. In this level the focus is on client satisfaction scales with adult clients and completed by parents/caregivers for their children. In addition, the MAIP model tracks and assesses cultural factors affecting clinical outcomes (e.g., client-provider match preferences). Staff cultural competence is also examined at this level to facilitate assignment of clients to providers and to determine future training needs.

At the community level, performance measurement emphasizes community outreach, education, prevention, and public relations and thus provides a forum for community aegis on services for community members. For example, what are the most successful ways of conducting mental health outreach in each cultural community? What special strategies need to be employed to overcome mental health service stigma for each racial/ethnic group? How can mental health practitioners tap strengths, resiliencies, and capacity for positive growth within various ethnic communities? A tripartite levels-of-analysis measurement and evaluation system (i.e., client, agency, community) serving the interests of all consumers can be realized using the MAIP model.

Disposition Coordination

The MAIP model systematically mobilizes, allocates, and channels agency resources to meet each client's needs. Following the initial intake interview and clinical/cultural assessment, clients are connected to appropriate modal providers and culturally generic or specific programs on a case-by-case basis. This "disposition" process occurs on a weekly or more frequent basis with a midlevel clinical staff team. The MAIP disposition process encourages an agency to consistently attempt to accommodate client-requested preferences for a specific gender, language, or ethnic match. Whenever feasible, the disposition team funnels unacculturated clients to culturally competent staff or programs best equipped to meet client needs. Acculturated clients with no specific matching preferences can be routed to less culturally competent or sophisticated staff and/or ethnic-general treatment programs.

Computerized Tracking System

The MAIP model was predicated on the simultaneous coordination of multiple factors. Such a complex mix of strategic variables required a dedicated tracking system, typically available at community health agencies to assist in billing and other business-side activities. A prototype tracking form, the Consumer Outcome Profile (COP), was routinely generated for each client after the initial intake processing and completed during discharge/termination or annual review. The COP example provides pertinent demographic and descriptive information about the client, together with any outcome data and a description of the modal therapist characteristics.

The COP example, presented in Figure 2, indicates the client was a Latina, English-speaking mental health consumer with a mood disorder diagnosis. She was referred from a nonpsychiatric private hospital and indicated no particular cultural or language preferences. The client had a tenth-grade education and was living alone in a house or apartment. Her intake GAF score was 50 and increased to 75 at termination. Her modal therapist was also a Latina; hence both gender and ethnic match occurred without a specific request by the client. The client's Time 2 Brief Psychiatric Rating Scale (BPRS; Overall & Gorham, 1988) total score (and subscale scores) were well within the "not severe" range. Client service satisfaction was also consistently high for the various Consumer Survey scales associated with a Mental Health Report Card prepared for the Mental Health Statistics Improvement Program (Teague et al., 1997). At the end of treatment, a "disconnect" between the client's objective and subjective quality of life self-appraisals was observed. Objective quality of life (e.g., number of friends, family contacts, financial resources) was perceived to be low while subjective quality of life (e.g., happiness with current life situation) was relatively high.

Simultaneous Assessment of MAIP Model Parameters

In multicultural mental health research, key variables are seldom examined in their relationship to each other. A statistical model is necessary to assess the simultaneous effects of key MAIP variables of ethnic match, client acculturation status, client ethnic identity, provider cultural competence, client therapeutic intervention (ethnic-general, ethnic-specific), and their relationship to prediction of client outcome measures. A structural equation modeling (SEM) application for the MAIP model, described in Meyers, Gamst, and Guarino (2006), was subsequently used to obtain evidence of the invariance of the MAIP model for successful therapeutic outcomes among four ethnic minority mental health consumers. Four latent variable pathways predicted by theory or supported by previous research—Client Racial Identity, Acculturation Status, Client Matching, and Therapist Cultural Competence—were hypothesized to have a direct effect on Successful Therapeutic Outcomes. In addition, Racial Identity, Acculturation Status, and Client Matching have an indirect effect on Successful Therapeutic Outcomes mediated by Therapist Cultural Competency. Employment of SEM provided substantive empirical MAIP evidence for successful therapeutic outcomes among African American, Latino, Asian, and Caucasian mental health consumers in the public sector (Dana, Gamst, Meyers, & Guarino, 2005; Gamst et al., in preparation).

In-Service Cultural Competency Training

While the MAIP empirical studies described earlier were in process, Rachel Guerrero, Chief, Office of Multicultural Services, California Department of Mental Health, provided support and an interface between this research program and the cultural competency training objectives of her department. This interest was shared, facilitated, and sponsored jointly with the California Institute for Mental Health, the University of La Verne, and the Eli Lilly Company.

In-service cultural competency training was initiated by the availability of the California Brief Multicultural Competence Scale (CBMCS), a composite of earlier competency instruments identified as a major component of the MAIP model (Gamst et al., 2004a). The CBMCS was developed from the item contents of these

Tri-City Mental Health Center Consumer Outcome Profile

Consumer Information: 5/14/03

Gender: F	Diagnosis Type: MOOD D/O	Culture Preference: Doesn't matter
Ethnicity: Latino	Trauma Code:	Gender Preference: Doesn't matter
Language: English	Program: 160	Language preference: English only
Education: 10th grade	NONPAYCH PRIV HOSP GAFTI: 50	
	GAF T2: 75	

Living: Lives alone Home/Apt

Modal Staff Information: Last Activity Date 4/10/03

3 - Gender: F	Ethnicity: LATINO	Degree: N/A	Language: ENG

Outcome Measures:

BPRS

Anxious/Depression 5 (00-21)	Not Severe
Hostile/Suspiciousness 3 (00-21)	Not Severe
Thinking Disturbance 4(00(???)21)	Not Severe
Withdrawal/Retardation (???) (00-14)	Not Severe
Total Score 18	

MHSIP

Access 4.67(00(???)05)	High
Appropriateness 5.00 (00-05)	High
Outcomes 5.00(00(???)05)	High
Satisfaction 4.67 (00(???)05)	High
Total Score 4.88	

QL-SF OBJECTIVE 0.92 (00-05) Low

QL-SF-SUBJECTIVE 5.22 (00 05) High

Figure 2 Tri-City Mental Health Center Consumer Outcome Profile

earlier instruments, with 1,244 California public mental health workers using a principal components analysis, expert panel item content evaluations, and confirmatory factor analysis (Gamst et al., 2004a). CBMCS factors include awareness of culture, sensitivity to consumers, multicultural knowledge, and sociocultural diversities. The CBMCS provided a standard, open-ended, psychometrically adequate instrument for measurement of cultural knowledge and abilities organized by these four relevant training areas. The CBMCS provided for assessment of training needs within a context of continuous monitoring and evaluation of the effects of training on outcomes of mental health services for clients in community settings.

These CBMCS objectives were implemented by a structured, organized training curriculum, the California Multicultural Competency Training Program (Dana, Gamst, & Der-Karabetian, 2006). Evaluation of a CBMCS training program pilot was completed by 38 experienced, sophisticated, and ethnically diverse community mental health practitioners representing 15 California counties during 6 days of training in 2004 (Gamst & Der-Karabetian, 2004).

PowerPoint presentations, small-group activities, and handouts were employed during this training. Program participants completed the CBMCS before and after the training and responded to open-ended and Likert scale questions for each module and on a separate readiness questionnaire at the conclusion of training. This questionnaire, together with ongoing written and oral commentary on the modules and feedback from focus groups, tapped their readiness to train others using this program. Participants significantly improved their pre-post total CBMCS scores and sociocultural diversity scale scores. The four modules were considered effective by 75% of participants, slightly over 50% expressed confidence in training others, and nearly 60% wanted to be considered as a pilot training-site cadre helping to improve the program.

Summary: Application Steps, Components, and Objectives

MAIP application steps (i.e., Intake, Training, Diagnosis/No Diagnosis, Intervention, Outcome) are dovetailed with their component processes and activities for salient objectives within public sector mental health facilities (Table 1). These steps all embed cultural issues in mental health services, but Intake, structured by Initial Contact and Initial Interview, is of overarching importance for Access and subsequent utilization of services. These early steps afford opportunities for clients to decide the potential usefulness of these services for themselves and/or their children and whether or not the agency and/or service providers are capable of assistance in a credible and acceptable manner. Thus, there is much to be accomplished in the process, particularly for ethnic minorities, by communicating to them that safe, comfortable, respectful, and culturally competent access is indeed feasible.

Intake

Table 1 separates Access into a number of components. Initial Contact, Intake Interview, Psychosocial Assessment, Pretest Outcome Measures, and Parent/Child assessments for child consumers.

A variety of means are used to schedule an intake interview. The quality, content, and the social etiquette employed during the initial contact often determines whether or not a client will return for services. During initial contact, basic demographic and other descriptive information is obtained. In the interval between contact and intake, critical questions still require empirical work. For example, what percent of clients fail to show for this appointment? How long is the average delay interval between initial contact and intake? Are appropriate language services available? Is the agency conducting effective and appropriate outreach for members of all groups in the community? These questions can be explored within an agency by using the ACCC for self-study.

The intake interview provides an opportunity for the provider to obtain presenting problem and case history information on client functioning and culture and to provide a Global Assessment of Functioning (GAF) rating, a DSM-IV diagnosis, and clinical formulations, as well as cultural and identity formulations as needed for diagnosis and treatment. In addition, the intake interview is a second opportunity to practice credible service delivery social etiquette to continue the process of developing a therapeutic relationship while serving to guide selection of agency treatment strategies and allocation of human resources.

Table 1 Steps, Components, and Objectives in Public Sector MAIP Model Applications

Step	*Component*	*Objective*
Intake	*Initial Contact*	First opportunity for credible social etiquette to facilitate establishing professional relationship
	Intake Interview: Presenting problem Case history, GAF (pre) DSM-IV	Establish/consolidate relationship, Screening information, Describe community functioning, Clinical diagnosis, Cultural Formulation, Cultural/Identity Conceptualizations
	Agency information/Consumer goals	Information-processing dialogue with consumer
	Psychosocial Assessment: Ethnic identity/gender, Acculturation/racial identity status for adults and/children and parent/child assessments	Comprehensive intake questionnaire to establish provider-consumer match preferences/requirements or employ various measuring instruments
	Pretest Outcome Measures: Clinical outcome measures, Multicultural assessment (e.g., ARSMA, MEIM, SMAS)	Cost-effective performance assessment to capture consumer functioning + cultural information for resource allocation, Multicultural clinical intake snapshot as benchmark for client functioning and guide for selecting treatment strategies
Training	*Cultural competence (modal provider)*	CBMCS description is basis for in-service cultural competence training (32 hours or determined by CBMCS factor scores)
Diagnosis/ No Diagnosis	*Cultural formulation* *Non-DSM conceptualization*	Confirm DSM-IV diagnosis, Prepare Cultural Conceptualization, Prepare Identity Conceptualization
Intervention	*Ethnic-general* *Ethnic-specific*	Distinction recognizes current research limitations for describing ethnic-specific interventions
Outcome	*Disposition coordination* *Discharge/Annual Review* *Outcome Evaluation*	COP summary, post GAF, clinical outcome and consumer satisfaction measures

Psychosocial assessment permits use of a questionnaire or instruments to establish preferences for provider-consumer gender, ethnic, and racial identity, or acculturation status matches for children and adults. In the California mental health center conducting the MAIP research, match assignments were requested by approximately 20% of consumers. Multicultural assessment measures examined for use with the MAIP model include (a) the Acculturation Rating Scale for Mexican Americans (ARSMA—II; Cuéllar, Arnold, & Maldonado, 1995); (b) the Multigroup Ethnic Identity Measure (MEIM), Phinney, 1992); the Stephenson Multigroup Acculturation Scale (SMAS; Stephenson, 2000); the Twenty Statements Test (Dana, 2005a), and the Self-Categorization Test and Ethnic Identification Scale (Van de Vijver & Phalet, 2004).

Acceptable cost-effective client-level pretest outcome measures in managed care organizations must be seamless in design and nonintrusivesive for providers and consumers. Moreover, these measures must be linked to empirically identified evaluation outcomes of services and employed with flexible tracking of service delivery and services. The California-mandated measures enumerated earlier, clinical outcome measures (American Psychiatric Association, 2000), and MAIP-relevant multicultural assessment measures and devices (Dana, 1993, 1998a, 2000c), are employed as needed.

A multicultural clinical intake snapshot is prepared to summarize the available information. Preparation requires knowledge provider skills, training levels, and cultural competency for consumer-provider matching for ethnicity, gender, or language on the basis of preference or prior local research findings. This initial information is part of a tracking form, the Consumer Outcome Profile (COP; Gamst & Dana, 2005). Figure 1 contains a COP example. Table 1 indicates the use of COP in a MAIP model public sector application.

Training

All providers need in-service cultural competency assessment and subsequent training predicated on CBMCS-measured cultural competency. Cultural competency in the initial contact, the intake interview, and all subsequent services can only be assured by adequate in-service training for all providers. The effectiveness of this training must be demonstrated by routine agency monitoring of client outcomes, with feedback to providers using a computerized tracking system. The modal provider concept recognizes that services often require several different providers for research and evaluation purposes, although the tracking system provides individual provider accountability as a basis for cultural competency assessment and evaluation of in-service training requirements.

Diagnosis/No Diagnosis

The MAIP recognizes that a universal diagnostic formulation is not available at present (see Figure 1). A standard Anglo diagnostic formulation prevails except when a cultural formulation is employed. Cultural formulations for ethnic minority individuals who are immigrants, or first generation, as well as for some second-generation individuals, are frequently necessary. Many of these individuals present culture-bound disorders, and epidemiological studies suggest these diagnoses occur with much greater frequency in traditional individuals than hitherto anticipated by psychiatrists (e.g., Dana, 2002b). Presenting problems-in-living rather than psychopathologies may suggest non-DSM cultural and identity conceptualizations as more descriptive of reactions to prejudice/discrimination or personal identity issues. Table 1 simplifies Figure 1 by recognizing only Diagnosis and No Diagnosis categories. This is done because a cultural formulation may lead to a diagnosis of a culture-bound disorder as well as a DSM-IV disorder. The No Diagnosis category recognizes that cultural and identity conceptualizations lead to interventions for problems-in-living.

Interventions

The original MAIP specified five categories of interventions (Figure 1): culture-universal, culture-general, combined culture-general/culture-specific, culture-specific, and identity-specific. As culture-universal interventions are not yet available, consumers with identified psychopathology also require interventions that are either standard ethnic-general or culturally sensitive and ethnic-specific (Table 1). Culturally sensitive interventions were defined in the original MAIP (Figure 1) as interventions containing components representing both culture-general and culture-specific interventions or exclusively culture-specific components (Dana, 1998a). However, the efficacy studies providing the evidence base for treatments do not adequately include ethnic minorities, although evidence-based treatment for depression does improve outcome for Latinos and African Americans, and established psychosocial care may be beneficial for Asians (Miranda et al., 2005). Thus, although there are cogent and compelling examples of successful adaptation of interventions for ethnic minorities, it is premature to rely on the original MAIP categorizations. Table 1 thus recognizes the necessity for both ethnic-general and ethnic-specific interventions that are susceptible to evaluation within the model.

Outcome

Outcomes are described in Table 1 by the COP summaries amplified by post-GAF, consumer satisfaction, and a variety of outcome measures. These summaries, including disposition coordination, discharge or annual review, posttest outcome assessment, computerized tracking system, and the simultaneous of MAIP model parameters. Although there is no consensus on outcome measures (Hoagwood, Jensen, Petti, & Burns, 1996; Jensen, Hoagwood, & Petti, 1996), the GAF Axis 5 rating of the Diagnostic and Statistical Manual IV (DSM-IV; American Psychological Association, 1994) is widely used in practice and research.

Clients terminating therapy on their own volition, discharged by the agency after successful treatment, or reaching 6-month or annual review for chronic disorders are all given the same set of outcome measures they received at intake except for cultural assessment instruments. Adult outcome/satisfaction measures used with the MAIP include the Brief Psychiatric Rating Scale (BRPS; Overall & Gorham, 1988), the Mental Health Statistics Improvement Program (MHSIP; Teague et al., 1997), and the Quality of Life Scale (QL-SF; Lehman, 1988). For children and adolescent clients, the Ohio Scales (Ogles, Melendez, Davis, & Lunnen, 2001) and the Columbia Impairment Scale (CIS; Bird, Schwab-Stone, Andrews, Goodman, & Duncan, 1996) were used. Service satisfaction has been assessed using the Youth Services Survey (YSS; Brunk, 2001) and the Youth Services Survey for Families (YSS-F; Brunk, 2001) with children and parents/caregivers, respectively. Multicultural assessment consonant with the MAIP model include the MEIM (Phinney, 1992), ARSMA-II (Cuéllar et al, 1995), and the Stephenson Multigroup Acculturation Scale (Stephenson, 2000).

At the mental health systems accountability level, the focus is on monitoring systems and programs, quality assurance, and multistakeholder coordination. Client service satisfaction inventories are completed by parents/caregivers and children, and MAIP cultural factors affect clinical outcomes at the program/system accountability level. For example, client-therapist match preferences could be assessed at this level and tracked (e.g., ethnic/racial match, gender match, language match). Staff cultural competence assessment would determine future training needs and the assignment of clients to mental health providers.

TEMAS-MAIP Adaptations

Extending the adult-oriented MAIP model to children/adolescents requires adaptation in each step or component. Intake becomes more complicated by inclusion of family members. CRI differences between parents and children affect intergenerational relationships. Conflicts with parents often result from increasing child biculturality and dual language skills. These conflicts exacerbate differences between parental and peer cultures in values pertinent to family cohesion, discipline, and child behaviors.

The assessment necessary to determine goodness-of-fit between an ethnic minority child/adolescent and a particular intervention thus may differ substantially in content, breadth, and depth from adult measures. This aspect of the assessment-intervention relationship has not been carefully considered in the public sector due to the increased time required for comprehensive assessment of children and adolescents.

Nonetheless the short-form TEMAS can be completed during intake within a two-hour assessment time allocation (Camara et al., 2000). TEMAS is particularly useful in agency settings because diagnostic information is available within the context of a broader range of information relevant for development of consensual eligibility criteria for any recommended interventions for all children/adolescents. As subsequent chapters with TEMAS examples indicate, the substantial increase in relevant test information also provides increased knowledge for parents and adult nonprofessional caregivers and contributes to informed decision making. TEMAS findings can also be useful to positively affect communication and contribute to joint decision-making responsibility by parents and professional providers. A role for TEMAS in cultural formulations or cultural and identity conceptualizations is feasible, but research is necessary for this suggested usage.

The MAIP model is also congruent with common characteristics of 23 successful programs (Roberts, 1994). These programs focus on the ecology of the child in family, peer, school, and community, require strong leadership to reduce barriers to access, provide collaborative efforts across agencies, and employ clearly defined, comprehensive, and versatile services. These services should be accountable and have demonstrated effectiveness that can be replicated and adapted.

References

Allen, J., & Dana, R. H. (2004). Methodological issues in cross-cultural and multicultural Rorschach research. *Journal of Personality Assessment, 82,* 189–206.

American Psychiatric Association. (1994). *Diagnostic and statistical manual of mental disorders* (4th ed.). Washington, DC: Author.

American Psychiatric Association. (2000). *Handbook of psychiatric measures.* Washington, DC: Author.

Angold, A., Costello, E. J., Farmer, E. M. Z., Burns, B. J., & Erkanli, A. (1999). Impaired but undiagnosed. *Journal of the American Academy of Child and Adolescent Psychiatry, 38,* 129–137.

Berry, J. W. (1980). Introduction to methodology. In H. C. Triandis & J. W. Berry (Eds.), *Handbook of cross-cultural psychology* (Vol. 2, pp. 1–28). Boston: Allyn & Bacon.

Berry, J. W. (1989). Psychology of acculturation. *Nebraska Symposium on Motivation, 21,* 257–277.

Bird, H., Schwab-Stone, M., Andrews, H., Goodman, S., Dulcan, M. et al. (1996). Global measures of impairment for epidemiologic and clinical use with children and adolescents. *Journal of Methods in Psychiatric Research, 6,* 295–308.

Brandt, M. E., & Boucher, J. D. (1986). Concepts of depression in emotion lexicons of eight cultures. *International Journal of Intercultural Relations, 10,* 321–346.

Brislin, R. W. (1993). *Understanding culture's influence on behavior.* New York: Harcourt Brace.

Brunk, M. (2001, October). *Youth Services Surveys.* Paper presented at the meeting of the Mental Health Data Infrastructure Grant Annual meeting, Washington, DC.

Burlew, A. K., Bellow, S., & Lovett, M. (2000). Racial identity measures: A review and classification system. In R. H. Dana (Ed.), *Handbook of cross-cultural and multicultural personality assessment* (pp. 173–196). Mahwah, NJ: Lawrence Erlbaum Associates.

California Department of Mental Health (2005). *Preliminary discussion of the performance measurement design for the California Mental Health Services Act.* Department of Mental Health, Sacramento, CA.

Cuéllar, I., Arnold, B., & Maldonado, R. (1995). An Acculturation Rating Scale for Mexican Americans-II (ARSMA-II): A revision of the original ARSMA scale. *Hispanic Journal of Behavioral Sciences, 17,* 275–304.

Dana, R. H. (1993). *Multicultural assessment perspectives for professional psychology.* Boston: Allyn & Bacon.

Dana, R. H. (1997). Multicultural assessment and cultural identity: An assessment-intervention model. *World Psychology, 3(1–2),* 121–141.

Dana, R. H. (1998a). *Understanding cultural identity in intervention and assessment.* Thousand Oaks, CA: Sage.

Dana, R. H. (1998b). Multicultural assessment in the United States: Still art, not yet science, and controversial. *European Journal of Personality Assessment, 14,* 62–70.

Dana, R. H. (1998c). Personality assessment and the cultural self: Emic and etic contexts as learning resources. In L. Handler & M. Hilsenroth (Eds.), *Teaching and learning personality assessment* (pp. 325–345). Hillsdale, NJ: Lawrence Erlbaum Associates.

Dana, R. H. (1998d). Problems with managed mental health care for multicultural populations. *Psychological Reports, 83,* 283–294.

Dana, R. H. (2000a). Multicultural assessment of child and adolescent personality and psychopathology. In A. L. Comunian & U. Gielen (Eds.), *International perspectives on human development.* Lengerich, Germany: Pabst Science Publishers.

Dana, R. H. (2000b). Culture and methodology in personality assessment. In I. Cuéllar & F. Paniagua (Eds.), *Handbook of multicultural mental health: Assessment and treatment of diverse groups* (pp. 97–120). San Diego, CA: Academic Press.

Dana, R. H. (Ed.) (2000c). *Handbook of cross-cultural and multicultural personality assessment.* Mahwah, NJ: Lawrence Erlbaum Associates.

Dana, R. H. (2002a). Mental health services for African Americans: A cultural/racial perspective. *Cultural Diversity and Ethnic Minority Psychology, 8,* 3–18.

Dana, R. H. (2002b). Examining the usefulness of DSM-IV. In K. Kurasaki, S. Okazaki, & S. Sue (Eds.), *Asian American mental health: Assessment, theories, and methods* (pp. 29–46). New York: Kluwer Academic/Plenum Publishers.

Dana, R. H. (2002c). The development of cultural competence in California public sector mental health services. In S. Lurie (Chair), *International innovations in community mental health I.* Symposium conducted at the XXVIIth International Congress of Law and Mental Health, Amsterdam, The Netherlands.

Dana, R. H. (2005a). *Multicultural assessment principles, applications, and examples.* Mahwah, NJ: Lawrence Erlbaum Associates.

Dana, R. H. (2005b). *The Multicultural Assessment-Intervention Process Model (MAIP).* Unpublished paper.

Dana, R. H., Aragon, M., & Kramer, T. (2002). Public sector mental health services for multicultural populations: Bridging the gap from research to clinical practice. In M. N. Smyth (Ed.), *Health care in transition* (Vol. 1, pp. 1–13). Hauppauge, NY: Nova Science Publishers.

Dana, R. H., Behn, J. D., & Gonwa, T (1992). A checklist for examination of cultural competence in social service agencies. *Research in Social Work Practice, 2,* 220–233.

Dana, R. H., Conner, M. G., & Allen, J. (1996). Cost containment and quality in managed mental health care: Policy, education, research, advocacy. *Psychological Reports, 79,* 1395–1422.

Dana, R. H., Gamst, G., & Der-Karabetian, A. (2006). *The California Brief Multicultural Competence Scale-Based Training Program: A manual for trainers.* La Verne, CA: University of La Verne.

Dana, R. H., Gamst, G., Meyers, L., & Guarino, A. J. (2005). *Assessing the invariance of the Multicultural Assessment-Intervention Process model (MAIP) among African-American, Latino, Asian, and Caucasian mental health consumers.* Unpublished paper.

Der-Karabetian, A., Gamst, G., Dana, R. H., Aragon, M., Arellano, L., Morrow, G., et al. (2004). *California Brief Multicultural Competence Scale (CBMCS): User guide.* La Verne, CA: University of La Verne.

Gamst, G., & Dana, R. H. (2005). *Testing the MAIP model: A proposed method for assessing culturally sensitive mental health service delivery for adults and children.* Unpublished paper.

Gamst, G., Dana, R. H., Der-Karabetian, A., Aragon, M., Arellano, L., & Kramer, T. (2002). Effects of Latino acculturation and ethnic identity on mental health outcomes. *Hispanic Journal of Behavioral Sciences, 24,* 479–505.

Gamst, G., Dana, R. H., Der-Karabetian, A., Aragon, M., Arellano, L., Morrow, G., et al. (2004a). Cultural competency revised: The California Brief Multicultural Competence Scale. *Measurement and Evaluation in Counseling and Development, 37,* 163–183.

Gamst, G., Dana, R. H., Der-Karabetian, A., & Kramer, T. (2000). Ethnic match and client ethnicity effects on global assessment and visitation. *Journal of Community Psychology, 28,* 547–564.

Gamst, G., Dana, R. H., Der-Karabetian, A., & Kramer, T. (2001). Asian American mental health clients: Cultural responsiveness and global assessment. *Journal of Mental Health Counseling, 23,* 57–71.

Gamst, G., Dana, R. H., Der-Karabetian, A., & Kramer, T. (2004b). Ethnic match and treatment outcomes for child and adolescent mental health center clients. *Journal of Counseling and Development, 82,* 457–465.

Gamst, G., Dana, R. H., Der-Karabetian, A., Meyers, L., & Guarino, A. J. (2006). *Assessing the validity of the Multicultural Assessment Intervention Process (MAIP) model for mental health consumers.* Manuscript submitted for publication.

Gamst, G., & Der-Karabetian, A. (2004). *Preliminary evaluation of the California Brief Multicultural Competency Training Program.* La Verne, CA: University of La Verne.

Hoagwood, K., Jensen, P. S., Petti, T., & Burns, B. J. (1996). Outcomes of mental health care for children and adolescents: I. A comprehensive conceptual model. *Journal of the American Academy of Child and Adolescent Psychiatry, 35,* 1055–1063.

Jensen, P. S., Hoagwood, K., & Petti, T. (1996). Outcomes of mental health care for children and adolescents: II. Literature review and application of a comprehensive model. *Journal of the American Academy of Child and Adolescent Psychiatry, 35,* 1064–1077.

Jerrell, J. M. (1995). The effects of client-counselor match on service use and costs. *Administration and Policy in Mental Health, 23,* 119–126.

Jerrell, J. M. (1998). Effect of ethnic matching of young children and mental health staff. *Cultural Diversity and Mental Health, 4,* 297–302.

LaFromboise, T. D., Trimble, J. E., & Mohatt, G. V. (1990). Counseling intervention and American Indian tradition: An integrative approach. *The Counseling Psychologist, 18,* 628–654.

Lau, A., & Zane, N. (2001). Examining the effects of ethnic-specific services: An analysis of cost-utilization and treatment outcome for Asian American clients. *Journal of Community Psychology, 28,* 63–67.

Lehman, A. F. (1988). A Quality of Life Interview for the chronically mentally ill. *Evaluation and Program Planning, 11,* 51–62.

Lin, S. S., & Kelsey, J. L. (2000). Use of race and ethnicity in epidemiological research. *Epidemiologic Reviews, 22,* 187–202.

Lonner, W. J. (1985). Issues in testing and assessment in cross-cultural counseling. *The Counseling Psychologist, 13,* 599–614.

Maramba, G. G., & Hall, G. C. (2002). Meta-analyses of ethnic match as a predictor of dropout, utilization, and level of functioning. *Cultural Diversity and Ethnic Minority Psychology, 8,* 290–297.

Martin, T. W. (1995). Community mental health services for ethnic minority adolescents: A test of the cultural responsiveness hypothesis. *Dissertation Abstracts International, 55(7–B),* 3018 (Abstract only).

Meyers, L., Gamst, G., & Guarino, A. J. (2005). *Applied multivariate research: Design and interpretation.* Thousand Oaks, CA: Sage.

Miranda, J., Bernal, G., Lay, A., Kohn, L., Hwang, W-C, & LaFromboise, T. (2005). State of the science on psychosocial interventions for ethnic minorities. *Annual Review of Clinical Psychology, 1,* 113–142.

Ogles, B. M., Melendez, G., Davis, D. C., & Lunnen, K. M. (2001). The Ohio Scales: Practical outcome assessment. *Journal of Child and Family Studies, 10,* 199–212.

Overall, J. E., & Gorham, D. R. (1988). The Brief Psychiatric Rating Scale (BRPS): Recent developments in ascertainment and scaling. *Psychopharmacological Bulletin, 24,* 97–99.

Phinney, J. S. (1992). The Multigroup Ethnic Identity Measure: A new scale for use with diverse groups. *Journal of Adolescent Research, 7,* 156–176.

Roberts, M. C. (1994). Models for service delivery in children's mental health: Common characteristics. *Journal of Clinical Child Psychology, 23,* 212–219.

Russell, G. L., Fujino, D. C., Sue, S., Cheung, M-K., & Snowden, L. R. (1996). The effects of counselor-client ethnic match on assessment of mental health functioning. *Journal of Cross-Cultural Psychology, 27,* 598–615.

Shin, S. M., Chow, D., Camacho-Gonsalves, T., Levy, R. J., Allen, I. I., & Leff, H. S. (2005). A meta-analytic review of racial/ethnic matching for African American and Caucasian American clients and clinicians. *Journal of Counseling Psychology, 52,* 45–56.

Stephenson, M. (2000). Development and validation of the Stephenson Multigroup Acculturation Scale (SMAS). *Psychological Assessment, 12,* 77–88.

Teague, G. B., Hornik, J., Ganju, V., Johnson, J. R., & McKinney, J. (1997). The MHSIP Mental Health Report Card: A consumer-oriented approach to monitoring the quality of health plans. *Evaluation Review, 21(3),* 330–341.

Triandis, H. C., & Suh, E. M. (2002). Cultural influences on personality. *Annual Review of Psychology, 53,* 133–160.

Van de Vijver, F. J. R., & Phalet, K. (2004). Assessment of multicultural groups: The role of acculturation. *Applied Psychology: An International Review, 53,* 215–236.

Whatley, R., Allen, J., & Dana, R. H. (2003). Racial identity and the MMPI in African American male college students. *Cultural Diversity and Ethnic Minority Psychology, 9,* 344–352.

5

Multicultural Counseling Training

Past, Present, and Future Directions

José M. Abreu

Ruth H. Gim Chung

Donald R. Atkinson

The growing number of ethnic minorities in the United States represents a challenge to counselors and other mental health practitioners trained to implement therapeutic interventions designed primarily for European Americans. Whereas 73% of our nation is currently composed of European Americans, by the year 2050 this figure is expected to decline to 53%, with the remainder composed of Latinos and Latinas (25%), African Americans (14%), Asian Pacific Americans (8%), and American Indians (1%) (U.S. Bureau of the Census, 1990).

Utilization statistics show that minority populations underuse mental health services and that those who do enter therapy tend to drop out prematurely (Cheung & Snowden, 1990; Sue & Sue, 1999). During the past three decades, this reality has resulted in a call upon the profession to be more responsive to and inclusive of racial-ethnic minority concerns, resulting in what Pedersen (1991) declared as the "fourth force" in psychology. The challenge has been to determine exactly what it means to be culturally competent, how to facilitate development of said competence, and how to determine when this has occurred.

In keeping with rituals that mark significant moments in time and the passage of time, it is appropriate to pause at the beginning of the new millennium to reflect on the training of counseling psychologists. Within the broader context of this major contribution, the purpose of this article is to selectively review the training literature to identify critical issues for the present and future of multicultural counseling training (MCT). The first section briefly describes the history of multicultural counseling (MCC). The second section presents the various models of MCT. In the third section, training objectives tied to specific MCC skills are described. The fourth and final section covers the MCT research literature. Interested readers on the topic might wish to consult the following sources for additional details: Pope-Davis and Coleman (1997); Ridley, Mendoza, and Kanitz (1994); Ponterotto, Puentes, and Chen (2000).

The Rise of MCC

Sue et al. (1982) defined cross-cultural counseling as "any counseling relationship in which two or more of the participants differ with respect to cultural background, values, and lifestyle" (p. 47; see also Pedersen, 1991). Although differences between clients and counselors have included cultural dimensions tied to gender, socioeconomic status, sexual orientation, and physical or mental ability, the term *multicultural counseling*—now often used interchangeably with *cross-cultural counseling*—is most commonly identified as a distinct specialty area that focuses on counseling relationships that cross racial and ethnic boundaries (Ivey, Fouad, Arredondo, & D'Andrea, 2000; Sue, Arredondo, & McDavis, 1992). The focus of this article is limited to this narrower definition of MCC.

M. Jackson (1995) traced the history of the MCC movement back to five articles published during the 1950s in the *Personnel and Guidance Journal* that addressed the counseling needs of Black Americans. In the 1960s, the civil rights movement and the increase of racial and ethnic diversity among counselors and psychologists began to make the helping professions more responsive to minority populations. During the late 1960s and early 1970s, groups of racial and ethnic minority psychologists began to push the American Psychological Association (APA) into actively endorsing their interests. To this end, representatives of these groups established the Association of Black Psychologists (1968), the Association of Psychologists Por La Raza (1970), the Asian American Psychological Association (1972), and the Society of Indian Psychologists (1975).

Early recognition by APA of the need to address cultural diversity in the training of psychologists dates back to the Vail conference of 1973. In the summary statement resulting from this conference, Korman (1973) defined cultural competence as a matter of ethical practice and recommended that issues of cultural diversity be included in the education and training of psychologists. Continued pressure on the APA led to the establishment of the Office of Ethnic Minority Affairs (OEMA) in 1979, followed by the Board of Ethnic Minority Affairs (BEMA) in 1981 and the Division of Ethnic Minority Affairs (Division 45) in 1986. In turn, these APA entities served as catalysts to the development of specific mandates that promote MCT (readers interested in a more comprehensive account of APA involvement in diversity issues are referred to Heppner, Casas, Carter, & Stone, 2000).

Mandates promoting MCT have been codified in APA's *Accreditation Handbook* (APA, 1986), *Guidelines for Providers of Psychological Services to Ethnic, Linguistic, and Culturally Diverse Populations* (APA, 1993), and *Guidelines and Principles for Accreditation of Programs in Professional Psychology* (APA, 1996a). Consistently, these publications highlight the increasing need to prepare mental health practitioners to work effectively with culturally diverse populations. Notice, for example, how the APA (1996a) guidelines define a training program that satisfies accreditations standards.

> The program has and implements a thoughtful and coherent plan to provide students with relevant knowledge and experiences about the role of cultural and individual diversity in psychological phenomena as they relate to the science and practice of professional psychology. The avenues by which these goals are achieved are to be developed by the program. (APA, 1996a, pp. 9, 10)

Counseling programs accredited by the Council for Accreditation of Counseling and Related Educational Programs (CACREP) must take into account (a) "current knowledge . . . concerning the counseling and human development needs of a multicultural society" and (b) "the present and projected needs of a multicultural society for which specialized counseling and human development activities have been developed" (*Accreditation Procedures Manual and Application,* 1988, p. 25).

There is some evidence suggesting that these mandates, increases in program faculty and students of color, and a growing recognition of the need for MCT have affected clinical training in the desired direction. In the 1970s, only a few training programs offered courses in MCC (APA, 1982). By 1980, an estimated 41% of clinical psychology training programs offered diversity-related courses, but only 9% of the programs required completion of the course for graduation (Bernal & Castro, 1994). A decade later, the proportion of clinical psychology programs offering and requiring multicultural course work had increased to 62% and 26%, respectively (Bernal & Castro, 1994). A similar survey limited to APA-approved counseling psychology programs revealed that 87% offered at least one diversity course and that 59% required students to take at least one multicultural class (Hills & Strozier, 1992). By the late 1990s, Ponterotto (1997) found that almost all of the doctoral programs in counseling psychology and counselor education programs surveyed (8%) professed to have a multicultural course requirement (see also Rogers, Hoffman, & Wade, 1998).

MCT Models

Professional directives to implement diversity training have initiated a variety of instructional models designed to increase the cultural competency of counselors in training (e.g., Copeland, 1982; LaFramboise & Foster, 1992; Ridley, Mendoza, & Kanitz, 1992, 1994). Ridley, Mendoza, and Kanitz's (1994) Multicultural Program Development Pyramid (MPDP) represents the most comprehensive MCT model to date. Although the MPDP has been available for more than 5 years, we believe its full potential to guide MCT has yet to be realized and that it can offer counseling programs a good measure of direction in the new century. We provide a brief summary of the program design component of this model and encourage interested readers to consult the original work, published in this journal as a major contribution.

Ridley, Mendoza, and Kanitz (1992, 1994) identified six MCT models or schemes that have been employed by counseling programs: (a) traditional program, (b) workshop design, (c) separate course, (d) interdisciplinary cognate, (e) subspecialty cognate, and (f) integrated program. In the order given, these approaches represent increasing adherence to the training mandates imposed by APA and CACREP.

The traditional approach assumes that psychological treatments designed for European Americans are also appropriate for non-White clients and that no modification to theory or technique is necessary. This approach represents a "business as usual" attitude toward diversity. Any difficulty in applying existing counseling techniques to ethnic minority clients is ascribed to the pathology of the latter rather than to the soundness of the former. Like the traditional program, the workshop design requires no changes to existing training curriculum and is considered an extension of the traditional approach. Trainees are simply encouraged to attend diversity workshops or in-service events that are not integral to the training program. Singly or in tandem, these two approaches are considered inadequate, as they seem to evade rather than endorse program commitment to a multicultural training perspective.

In the separate course model, one or two course offerings are added to a program's training curriculum. These courses are designed to promote trainee competence in cross-cultural counseling. They typically cover the socio-political histories of oppressed minority groups; the role of culture in the development of self-concept and worldview; self-awareness of racist, sexist, and homophobic attitudes or beliefs; and counseling techniques particularly well suited for diverse clients. The interdisciplinary and subspecialty cognate designs are extensions of the separate course design because they are based on the notion that multicultural competency cannot be simply packaged into one or two courses. In the interdisciplinary model, counseling trainees interested in diversity issues are directed by a faculty advisor to take a series of relevant courses offered by departments such as sociology, anthropology, ethnic studies, and linguistics. In the subspecialty design, a series of courses are developed that emphasize different multicultural clinical skills or areas of knowledge, such as testing and assessment, family systems interventions, supervision, and practicum. Given its dependence on the availability and development of a variety of courses, the subspecialty approach requires substantial program commitment to diversity training.

The integrated program is the most holistic multicultural training approach. This model requires the integration of multiculturalism into the entire body of course work offered by a training program. It is worth noting that adoption of the model does not necessarily mean dropping other program efforts to enhance trainee competence in MCC; programs already offering an MCC course, for example, could next work on integrating multicultural material into other courses. Advantages of the integration model are manifold, including consistent trainee exposure to multicultural training across all courses and practica. Copeland (1982), LaFramboise and Foster (1992), and Ridley, Mendoza, and Kanitz (1992, 1994) all promote the integration model as ideal. Unfortunately, there is little evidence that training programs are responding accordingly.

We noted in the previous section how the proportion of training programs offering and requiring MCC courses is slowly increasing. However, the way these data were reported (i.e., proportion of programs that require at least one course) indicated that the most popular approach to diversity training is the addition of only one or two multicultural courses to a program's curriculum—the separate course model (Ridley, Espelage, & Rubenstein, 1997). Although this is laudable, we believe it is simply not enough, as we feel that multiculturalism needs to be infused into a program's entire curriculum. At the same time, we realize the difficulty of this objective, because it involves coordination and cooperation of an entire faculty. Programs interested in working toward multicultural integration may find the Multicultural Competency Checklist (Ponterotto, 1997; Ponterotto, Alexander, & Grieger, 1995) to be a useful tool.

The Multicultural Competency Checklist involves a series of checks indicating whether the program under evaluation has met or not met each of 22 competencies. The competencies cover (a) minority representation, (b) curriculum issues, (c) practicum and/or supervision, (d) research considerations, (e) student and faculty competency evaluation, and (f) physical environment. *Minority representation* refers to percentage of minority and bilingual faculty, students, and staff; a 30% minority representation is considered the "critical mass" to create an environment supportive of multiculturalism. Curriculum issues address the number of multicultural courses offered and required, whether multicultural issues are integrated into the syllabi of other courses, and whether diverse teaching strategies and student evaluations have been implemented. Practicum and supervision focus on the percentage of minority clients seen by students, whether multicultural issues are considered an important component of clinical supervision, and whether the program has an active committee of faculty and students to provide leadership and support to MCT. Checklist items related to research considerations assess whether there is a multicultural research presence in the program. Student and faculty evaluation items tap into program mechanisms that ensure multicultural competency, such as formal evaluations of professors and comprehensive examinations completed by students. Physical environment, the sixth and last area of evaluation, is composed of two items that deal with the display of artwork reflecting appreciation for diversity and presence of a multicultural resource center that minority and interested White students can call home.

Given that very few (if any) counseling programs are likely to meet all checklist criteria, training directors and other faculty are encouraged to rank the relative importance of the competencies that are checked "not met." Working together, program faculty can then proceed to articulate and prioritize a realistic long-range plan of action steps needed to actualize a fully integrated MCT program. As racial and/or ethnic minority populations continue to grow, it is not unrealistic for the integration model of MCT to become the standard rather than the exception. In fact, perhaps it is time for both professional organizations (e.g., APA) and individual programs to take a more active role in promoting the integration model of MCT as one of the new 21st century accreditation mandates.

MCT Objectives: Promotion of MCC Competencies

Much of the MCT literature has focused on the promotion of specific counseling skills tied to various models of MCC (for a recent review of this literature, see Ponterotto et al., 2000). A model of MCC identifies and describes the components and processes needed for the successful cross-cultural interventions (Arredondo et al., 1996; Atkinson, Thompson & Grant, 1993; Carney & Kahn, 1984; Helms, 1995; Ridley, Mendoza, Kanitz, Angermeier, & Zenk, 1994; Sue et al., 1982). Of the models cited, Sue et al.'s (1982) is considered the most influential, published in this journal as a position article containing the first articulation of specific MCC competencies. In this document, the characteristics of culturally skilled counseling psychologists were defined in three general areas: (a) awareness of personal beliefs and/or attitudes toward culturally diverse clients, (b) knowledge about diverse cultures, and (c) abilities to use intervention skills or techniques that are culturally appropriate (Sue et al., 1982). These competencies were refined by Sue et al. (1992) and later operationalized in Arredondo et al. (1996).

Arredondo et al.'s (1996) MCC model is perhaps the most relevant to MCT because it specifies the training objectives needed to achieve multicultural competence in counseling. In meticulous fashion, Arredondo et al. lay out the behavioral manifestations of the awareness, knowledge, and skills competencies. Competent counselors in the area of self awareness "can identify social and cultural influences on their cognitive development and current information processing style" (p. 60) and "can recognize their stereotyped reactions to people different from themselves . . . consciously attend to examples that contradict stereotypes . . . [and] give specific examples of how their stereotypes . . . can affect the counselor-client relationship" (p. 63). Competent counselors in the cultural knowledge area "can discuss recent research addressing issues of racism, White identity development, antiracism, and so forth" (p. 60) and "can describe at least two different models of minority identity development and their implications for counseling"

(p. 64). In the area of technical skills, competent counselors "can give examples of how they may modify a technique or intervention or what alternative intervention they may use to more effectively meet the needs of a client" (p. 71), and "can describe concrete examples of situations in which it is appropriate and possibly necessary for a counselor to exercise institutional intervention skills on behalf of a client" (p. 71).

One long-standing impediment to MCT objectives is trainee resistance to multicultural material. In describing personal experiences as a multicultural trainer, Ponterotto (1998) classified trainee reactions to MCT along a "zealot-defensive" continuum, wherein some become very zealous and involved in fostering a multicultural perspective, whereas others become withdrawn and passive recipients of training activities. Ten years later, a survey of trainees enrolled in an APA-approved program of counseling psychology (Steward, Morales, Bartell, Miller, & Weeks, 1998) asked participants to indicate whether their overall reaction to MCT addressed in departmental courses was positive or negative. One third (33.3%) indicated they had a negative experience and that MCT was meaningless and unnecessary.

Consequently, training strategies targeting counseling trainee apathy and negative reactions to multiculturalism have begun to appear in the MCT literature (Abreu, in press; Jackson, 1999; Kiselica, 1998; Locke & Kiselica, 1999; Reynolds, 1995; Tomlinson-Clarke, 1999; Tomlinson-Clarke & Ota-Wang, 1999). For example, Tomlinson-Clarke (1999) suggested that multicultural training may be more effective when experiential and/or affective training is preceded by didactic and/or cognitive instruction. Tomlinson-Clarke and Ota-Wang (1999) assert that

> discussion of race and racism often result in the 'conspiracy of silence about racism' . . . emotionally powerful feelings, potentially explosive situations, and feelings of guilt from members of racial groups who have intentionally or unintentionally benefited from who they are (e.g., White privilege) have often fueled this conspiracy of silence. (p. 160)

Their premise for a didactic component preceding experiential activities is intuitively appealing. It may reduce preliminary nervousness and defensiveness among counseling trainees and facilitate emotional readiness for affective exercises as well as other multicultural teaching. A recent qualitative study that examined the outcomes of a multicultural training course provides preliminary empirical support for this premise (Tomlinson-Clarke, 1999).

Tomlinson-Clarke (1999) directed counseling psychology students to provide written evaluations immediately upon completing a multicultural training course, then again at a 4-month follow-up. Among her many findings, Tomlinson-Clarke reported that didactic, cognitively based aspects of training apparently helped students feel more comfortable with and eager to learn from other training components. She concluded that

> the recognition of the need for further cultural self-awareness and self-knowledge is critical in viewing multicultural competence as a process in which professionals and trainees continue to challenge deeply embedded cultural assumptions and increase understanding of oneself as a racial-cultural being. (p. 16)

In a similar effort to manage negative trainee reactions to MCT, Abreu (in press) proposed a didactic approach based on selected theory and research on stereotyping. Intended to promote the cultural self-awareness competency, this approach makes use of the existing scientific evidence clearly indicating that perceptual processes taking place outside the conscious awareness give rise to biased perceptions involving racial or ethnic categories. The objective of this strategy is to impress upon counseling trainees the importance of coming to terms with racial prejudice and biases often hidden from conscious scrutiny.

Apathy toward MCT may also reflect lack of integration between course work and counseling applications, a problem that can be addressed by extending MCT into practicum and fieldwork settings by way of supervision (Carlson, Brack, Laygo, Cohen, & Kirkscey, 1998). Publications that address supervision from a multicultural perspective at the conceptual level are beginning to appear in the literature (e.g., Daniels, D'Andrea, & Kim, 1999; Pope-Davis & Coleman, 1997). However, the effects of cross-cultural clinical supervision on trainees and their clients have not been well researched. Goodyear and Guzzardo's (2000) recent review of this literature identified only eight empirical studies that addressed racial and ethnic differences in supervision (e.g., Duan, Roehlke, & Matchisky, 1998; Ladany, Brittan-Powell, & Pannu, 1997). One of the most consistent findings reported in this scant literature is that trainee appreciation for supervision is heavily dependent on whether supervisors are willing to initiate discussion of diversity issues. Duan et al. (1998) also reported that feeling respected by supervisors was the most frequent response associated with minority trainee satisfaction in cross-cultural supervision. A study that examined the effects of supervisor race (White, non-White) and level of racial identity (high, low) on trainee scores of cross-cultural competence reported higher ratings of competence among trainees supervised by a person of color than those assigned to a White supervisor. In addition, level of trainee and supervisor racial identity development was positively correlated with ratings indicating the amount of strength in working alliances (Ladany et al., 1997).

Although more research is needed to define and establish multicultural approaches to clinical supervision, the available findings strongly suggest that cultural differences between supervisors, trainees, and clients are important factors that merit increased attention. With regard to the improvement of courses designed to promote specific MCC skills, we suggest that instructors pay more attention to how they put together their curricula, such as balancing didactic and experiential components in ways that minimize trainee resistance. We encourage instructors to approach this balancing act as researchers so their successes (or failures) can be documented in the literature for others to emulate (or avoid).

MCT Research

In their recent literature review, Ponterotto et al. (2000) identified two MCC foundational models—Sue et al.'s (1982) MCC competencies model and Helms's (1995) interaction model based on racial identity theory—that have been subjected to a fair amount of empirical research (for other relevant reviews, see Kiselica, Maben, & Locke, 1999; Ponterotto, 1998). This research typically examines the effectiveness of MCT by tracking changes in trainee racial identity development (e.g., Brown, Parham, & Yonker, 1996) or scores reflecting trainee levels of acquired MCC competence (e.g., Neville et al., 1996).

Brown et al. (1996), for example, examined the effects of the MCT course on the racial identity attitudes of participating White counseling students. We make reference to how this study was developed because we feel it is generally representative of MCT research design and implementation. Brown et al.'s 16-week course was divided into three phases: (a) personal beliefs and/or self-awareness, (b) knowledge of five ethnocultural populations, and (c) development of preliminary skills to counsel diverse clients. Phase 1 was composed of experiential activities designed to raise consciousness of prejudicial biases and oppressive behaviors. These activities included participation in a mock version of Jane Elliott's blue-eyed-brown-eyed experience, actual interviews with individuals racially or ethnically different from the interviewer (e.g., a White student interviewing a Latino classmate), and other such experiences to promote group bonding and ways of relating to racially different clients. In Phase 2, several speakers representing each of five ethnocultural groups were invited to join the class and present didactic and experiential material on issues, histories, and dynamics of the guests' racial-ethnic heritages. Phase 3 involved skills training such as identification and interpretation of verbal and nonverbal communication, stages of racial identity development for Whites and people of color, and awareness of biased assumptions inherent in traditional counseling theories and techniques. In discussing the relevant findings, Brown et al. concluded that their course effectively enhanced students' psychological acceptance of racial differences, increased appreciation of the potential impact of racial attitudes on people of color, and decreased exhibition of racist behavior.

Brown et al.'s (1996) findings were based on pretest-posttest comparisons using the White Racial Identity Scale (WRIAS) (Helms & Carter, 1990) scores as the dependent data. Neville et al. (1996) also used the WRIAS to examine the effectiveness of an MCT course and obtained similar results. In addition, Neville et al. reported pretest-to-posttest and pretest-to-follow-up increases of MCC competencies as measured by the Multicultural Awareness-Knowledge-Skills Survey (MAKSS) (D'Andrea, Daniels, & Heck, 1991). The MAKSS and three other instruments used in MCT research were specifically developed to measure MCC skills, as specified in Sue et al. (1982). The other three measures are the Cross-Cultural Counseling Inventory-Revised (CCCI-R) (LaFramboise, Coleman, & Hernandez, 1991), the Multicultural Counseling Awareness Scale-Form B (MCAS-B) (Ponterotto, Sanchez, & Magids, 1991), and the Multicultural Counseling Inventory (MCI) (Sodowsky, Taff, Gutkin, & Wise, 1994).

One notable deficit in the extant research examining MCT effectiveness is the lack of more up-to-date measures of MCC skills. For example, all four measures noted above are based on Sue et al.'s (1982) awareness, knowledge, and skills competencies. We stated previously that Arredondo et al.'s (1996) operationalizations of Sue et al.'s (1982) competencies have been useful for the development of MCT course work. Why not develop new instruments (or update existing ones) that also conform to Arredondo et al.'s operationalizations? Also, three of these measures rely on trainee self-ratings of competence (only the CCCI-R is based on objective ratings), which are vulnerable to social desirability confounds (Sowdowsky, Kuo-Jackson, Richardson, & Corey, 1998). Perhaps new measures of cultural competence based on achievement may prove more impervious to demand characteristics. For example, instead of asking counseling trainees to state whether they are familiar with a specific model of acculturation, they can be directed to identify this model of acculturation (or some other fundamental component of MCT). Futhermore, the reliability and validity of Black (Helms, 1990) and White (Helms & Carter, 1990) Racial Identity Scales (BRIAS and WRIAS) used in MCT research have been questioned (Behrens, 1997; Yanico, Swanson, & Tokar, 1994), and more advanced methods of validation are needed (Helms, 1999). We also encourage 21st century multicultural writers and researchers to move forward with the development of more sophisticated definitions of cultural competence.

Another notable deficit is the lack of data connecting MCT to actual treatment processes or outcome. This is understandable to some extent. Ridley, Mendoza, and Kanitz (1994) suggested that treatment outcome provides only limited information about the particular MCT components that determine intervention success or failure. A year later, Yutrzenka (1995) noted that limitations of research connecting MCT to treatment outcomes is not unique to this field but common to professional training research in general. Nevertheless, attempts to confirm the training-outcome link are promising. Lefley and colleagues (Lefley, 1985a, 1985b; Lefley & Bestman, 1991), for example, found significant short-term and long-term benefits of MCT in promoting desired effects in the form of increased utilization rates and decreased dropout rates among ethnic minorities. We maintain that more research examining the relationship between MCT and treatment outcome is sorely needed. Indeed, one of the catalysts for the advent of multiculturalism in professional psychology is low mental health utilization by ethnic minorities, presumably reflecting the irrelevancy of existing therapeutic interventions designed primarily for European Americans but ill-suited for non-Whites.

Before concluding this article, we would also like to briefly highlight the need to increase the number of ethnic minority academics who, in turn, tend to promote MCT research. Atkinson, Neville, and Casas (1991) surveyed a group of ethnic minority psychologists regarding past mentoring experiences and came to the conclusion that in light of ethnic minority underrepresentation in psychology, more European American professors need to step forward and take on an active role in mentoring and guiding minority students interested in research. This is consistent with the findings of a recent panel commissioned by the APA (1996b) to evaluate program efforts to recruit and retain ethnic minority students and faculty in professional psychology. The panel noted that few minority students are encouraged, by way of mentoring, to pursue an academic career track, and that those who enter academia often experience stresses unique to their minority status, such as pressure to join multiple committees to present cultural diversity interests. It is encouraging, however, that some training programs have begun to take specific steps to ensure that ethnic minority students receive adequate mentoring. For example, Hill, Castillo, Ngu, and Pepion (1999) described the Western Interstate Commission of Higher Education Doctoral Scholars Program (WICHE), a mentoring program embraced by the counseling psychology program at the University of Utah that provides external funding and other structural strategies that encourage faculty-student mentoring. Hill et al. provide enough detailed description for interested readers to identify and tap into possible WICHE financial resources or mentoring strategies. Senior faculty who take upon themselves the task of mentoring ethnic minority psychologists can expect to derive considerable benefit from this process (Atkinson, Casas, & Neville, 1994).

Conclusion

In reviewing the development of MCT, we noted the birth of several professional entities and mandates in the field of psychology with the explicit charge of promoting multiculturalism. Existing models of MCT were described, and development toward an integration model of training in which multiculturalism is infused into a program's entire curriculum was encouraged. Approaches that balance experiential and didactic components and extend training into practicum and fieldwork settings were discussed as possible strategies to enhance training and to manage trainee resistance to MCT. With respect to MCT research, we noted the need to further test and develop measures of MCC competence as well as research that examines the relationship between MCT and actual treatment processes and outcome.

References

Abreu, J. M. (in press). Theory and research on stereotypes and perceptual bias: A didactic resource for multicultural counseling trainers. *The Counseling Psychologist.*

Accreditation procedures manual and application. (1988). Alexandria, VA: Council for Accreditation of Counseling and Related Educational Programs.

American Psychological Association. (1982). *Survey of graduate departments of psychology.* Washington, DC: Author.

American Psychological Association. (1986). *Accreditation handbook.* Washington, DC: Author.

American Psychological Association. (1993). Guidelines for providers of psychological services to ethnic, linguistic, and culturally diverse populations. *American Psychologist, 48,* 45–48.

American Psychological Association. (1996a). *Guidelines and principles for accreditation of programs in professional psychology.* Washington, DC: Author.

American Psychological Association. (1996b, June). Minority faculty are still low in numbers. *American Psychological Association Monitor,* p. 40. Washington, DC: Author.

Arredondo, P., Toporek, R., Brown, S. P., Jones, J., Locke, D. C., Sanchez, J., & Stadler, H. (1996). Operationalization of the multicultural counseling competencies. *Journal of Multicultural Counseling and Development, 24,* 37–48.

Atkinson, D. R., Casas, A., & Neville, H. (1994). Ethnic minority psychologists: Whom they mentor and benefits derived from the process. *Journal of Multicultural Counseling and Development, 22,* 37–48.

Atkinson, D. R., Neville, H., & Casas, A. (1991). The mentorship of ethnic minorities in psychology. *Professional Psychology: Research and Practice, 22,* 257–277.

Atkinson, D. R., Thompson, C. E., & Grant, S. K. (1993). A three-dimension model for counseling racial/ethnic minorities. *The Counseling Psychologist, 21,* 257–277.

Behrens, J. T. (1997). Does the White Racial Identity Attitude Scale measure racial identity? *Journal of Counseling Psychology, 44,* 3–12.

Bernal, M. E., & Castro, F. G. (1994). Are clinical psychologists prepared for service and research with ethnic minorities? Report of a decade of progress. *American Psychologist, 49,* 797–805.

Brown, S. P., Parham, T. A., & Yonker, R. (1996). Influence of a cross-cultural training course on racial identity attitudes of White women and men: Preliminary perspectives. *Journal of Counseling and Development, 74,* 510–516.

Carlson, M. H., Brack, C. J., Laygo, R., Cohen, R., & Kirkscey, M. (1998). An exploratory study of multicultural competence of counselors in training: Support for experiential skills building. *Clinical Supervisor, 17,* 75–87.

Carney, C. G., & Kahn, K. B. (1984). Building competencies for effective cross-cultural counseling: A developmental view. *The Counseling Psychologist, 12,* 111–119.

Cheung, F. K., & Snowden, L. R. (1990). Community mental health and ethnic minority populations. *Community Mental Health Journal, 26,* 277–291.

Copeland, E. J. (1982). Minority populations and traditional counseling programs: Some alternatives. *Counselor Education and Supervision, 21,* 187–193.

D'Andrea, M., Daniels, J., & Heck, R. (1991). Evaluating the impact of multicultural counseling training. *Journal of Counseling and Development, 70,* 143–150.

Daniels, J., D'Andrea, M., & Kim, B. S. K. (1999). Assessing the barriers and changes of cross-cultural supervision: A case study. *Counselor Education and Supervision, 38,* 191–204.

Duan, C., Roehlke, H., & Matchisky, D. J. (1998, August). *National survey of cross-cultural supervision: When the supervisor and the supervisee are different in race.* Paper presented at the annual meeting of the American Psychological Association, San Francisco, California.

Goodyear, R. K., & Guzzardo, G. R. (2000). Psychotherapy supervision and training. In S. D. Brown & R. W. Lent (Eds.), *Handbook of counseling psychology* (pp. 83–108). New York: John Wiley.

Helms, J. E. (1990). *Black and White racial identity: Theory, research, and practice.* Westport, CT: Greenwood.

Helms, J. E. (1995). An update of Helm's White and people of color racial identity models. In J. G. Ponterotto, J. M. Casas, L. A. Suzuki, and C. M. Alexander (Eds.), *Handbook of multicultural housing* (pp. 181–198). Thousand Oaks, CA: Sage.

Helms, J. E. (1999, February). *Using personal-level analysis to study racial identity.* Workshop presented at the annual meeting of the Winter Roundtable on Cross-Cultural Psychology and Education, New York.

Helms, J. E., & Carter, R. T. (1990). Development of the White racial identity inventory. In J. E. Helms (Ed.), *Black and White racial identity: Theory, research, and practice* (pp. 67–80). Westport, CT: Greenwood.

Heppner, P. P., Casas, J. M., Carter, J., & Stone, G. L. (2000). The maturation of counseling psychology: Multifaceted perspectives 1978–1998. In S. D. Brown & R. W. Lent (Eds.), *Handbook of counseling psychology* (pp. 3–49). New York: John Wiley.

Hill, R. D., Castillo, L. G., Ngu, L. Q., & Pepiou, K. (1999). Mentoring ethnic minority students in academia: The WICHE Doctoral Scholars Program. *The Counseling Psychologist, 27,* 827–845.

Hills, H. I., & Strozier, A. L. (1992). Multicultural training in APA-approved counseling psychology programs: A survey. *Professional Psychology: Research and Practice, 23,* 43–51.

Ivey, A. E., Fouad, N. A., Arredondo, P., & D'Andrea, M. (2000). *Guidelines for multicultural counseling competencies: Implications for practice, training and research.* Unpublished manuscript.

Jackson, L. C. (1999). Ethnocultural resistance to multicultural training: Students and faculty. *Cultural Diversity and Ethnic Minority Psychology, 5,* 27–36.

Kiselica, M. S. (1998). Preparing Anglos for the challenges and joys of multiculturalism. *The Counseling Psychologist, 26,* 5–21.

Kiselica, M. S., Maben, P., & Locke, D. C. (1999). Do multicultural education and diversity appreciation training reduce prejudice among counseling trainees? *Journal of Mental Health Counseling, 21,* 240–254.

Korman, M. (1973). *Levels and patterns of professional training in psychology.* Paper presented at the annual meeting of the American Psychological Association, Washington, DC.

Ladany, N, Brittan-Powell, C. S., & Pannu, R. K. (1997). The influence of supervisory racial identity interaction and racial matching on the supervisory working alliance and supervisee multicultural competence. *Counselor Education and Supervision, 36,* 284–304.

LaFramboise, T. D., Coleman, H. L. K., & Hernandez, A. (1991). Developmental and factor structure of the Cross-Cultural Counseling Inventory-Revised. *Professional Psychology: Research and Practice, 22,* 380–388.

LaFramboise, T. D., & Foster, S. L. (1992). Cross-cultural training: Scientist-practitioner model and methods. *The Counseling Psychologist, 20,* 472–489.

Lefley, H. P. (1985a). Impact of cross-cultural training on Black and White mental health professionals. *International Journal of Intercultural Relations, 9,* 305–318.

Lefley, H. P. (1985b). Mental-health training across cultures. In P. B. Pedersen (Ed.)., *Handbook of cross-cultural counseling and therapy* (pp. 259–273). Westport, CT: Greenwood.

Lefley, H. P., & Bestman, E. W. (1991). Public-academic linkages for culturally sensitive mental health. *Community Mental Health Journal, 27,* 473–488.

Locke, D. C., & Kiselica, M. S. (1999). Pedagogy of possibilities: Teaching about racism in multicultural counseling courses. *Journal of Counseling and Development, 77,* 80–86.

Neville, H. A., Heppner, M. J., Louie, C. E., Thomson, C. E., Brooks, L., & Baker, C. E. (1996). The impact of multicultural training on White racial identity attitudes and therapy competencies. *Professional Psychology: Research & Practice, 27,* 83–89.

Pedersen, P. B. (1991). Multiculturalism as a generic approach to counseling. *Journal of Counseling and Development, 70,* 7–12.

Ponterotto, J. G. (1988). Racial consciousness development among White counselor trainees: A stage model. *Journal of Counseling and Development, 16,* 146–156.

Ponterotto, J. G. (1997). Multicultural counseling training: A competency model and national survey. In D. B. Pope-Davis & H. L. K. Coleman. (Vol. Eds.), *Multicultural aspects of counseling series: Vol. 7. Multicultural counseling competencies: Assessment, education and training, and supervision* (pp. 111–130). Thousand Oaks, CA: Sage.

Ponterotto, J. G. (1998). Charting a course for research in multicultural counseling training. *The Counseling Psychologist, 26,* 43–68.

Ponterotto, J. G., Alexander, C. M., & Grieger, I. (1995). A multicultural competency checklist for counseling training programs. *Journal of Multicultural Counseling and Development, 23,* 11–20.

Ponterotto, J. G., Puentes, J. N., & Chen, E. C. (2000). Models of multicultural counseling. In S. D Brown & R. W. Lent (eds.), *Handbook of counseling psychology* (pp. 639–669). New York: John Wiley.

Ponterotto, J. G., Sanchez, C. M., & Magids, D. M. (1991, August). *Initial development and validation of the Multicultural Counseling Awareness Scale (MCAS).* Paper presented at the annual meeting of the American Psychological Association, San Francisco, California.

Pope-Davis, D. B, & Coleman, H. L. K. (1997). *Multicultural counseling competencies: Assessment, education and training, and supervision.* Thousand Oaks, CA: Sage.

Reynolds, A. L. (1995). Challenges and strategies for teaching multicultural counseling courses. In J. G. Ponterotto, J. M Casas, L. A. Suzuki, & C. M. Alexander (Eds.), *Handbook of multicultural counseling* (pp. 263–286). Thousand Oaks, CA: Sage.

Ridley, C. R., Espelage, D. L, & Rubenstein, K. J. (1997). Course development in multicultural counseling. In D. B. Pope-Davis, H. L. K. Coleman (Vol. Eds.), *Multicultural aspects of counseling series: Vol. 7. Multicultural counseling competencies: Assessment, education and training, and supervision* (pp. 131–158). Thousand Oaks, CA: Sage.

Ridley, C. R., Mendoza, D. W., & Kanitz, B. E. (1992). Program designs for multicultural training. *Journal of Psychology and Christianity, 11,* 326–333.

Ridley, C. R., Mendoza, D. W., & Kanitz, B. E. (1994). Multicultural training: Reexamination, operationalization, and integration. *The Counseling Psychologist, 22,* 227–289.

Ridley, C. R., Mendoza, D. W., Kanitz, B. E., Angermeier, L., & Zenk, R. (1994). Cultural sensitivity in multicultural counseling: A perceptual schema model. *Journal of Counseling Psychology, 41,* 125–136.

Rogers, M. R., Hoffman, M. A., & Wade, J. (1998). Notable multicultural training in APA-approved counseling psychology and school psychology programs. *Cultural Diversity & Ethnic Minority Psychology, 4,* 212–226.

Sodowsky, G. R., Kuo-Jackson, P. Y., Richardson, M. F., & Corey, A. T. (1998). Correlates of self-reported multicultural competencies: Counselor multicultural social desirability, race, social inadequacy, locus of control, racial ideology, and multicultural training. *Journal of Counseling Psychology, 45,* 256–264.

Sodowsky, G. R., Taffe, R. C., Gutkin, T. B., & Wise, S. L. (1994). Development of the Multicultural Counseling Inventory: A self-report measure of multicultural competencies. *Journal of Counseling Psychology, 41,* 137–148.

Steward, R. J., Morales, P. C., Bartell, P. A., Miller, M., & Weeks, D. (1998). The multiculturally responsive versus the multiculturally reactive: A study of perceptions of counselor trainees. *Journal of Multicultural Counseling and Development, 26,* 13–7.

Sue, D. W., Arredondo, P., & McDavis, R. J. (1992). Multicultural counseling competencies/standards: A call to the profession. *Journal of Multicultural Counseling and Development, 20,* 64–88.

Sue, D. W., Bernier, J. E., Durran, A., Feinberg, L., Pedersen, P., Smith, E. J., & Vasquez-Nuttal, E. (1982). Position paper: Cross-cultural counseling competencies. *The Counseling Psychologist, 10,* 45–52.

Sue, D. W., & Sue, D. (1999). *Counseling the culturally different* (3rd ed.). New York: John Wiley.

Tomlinson-Clarke, S. (1999). *A qualitative study assessing outcomes in a multicultural training course.* Manuscript submitted for publication.

Tomlinson-Clarke, S., & Ota-Wang, V. (1999). A paradigm for racial-cultural training in the development of counselor cultural competencies. In M. S. Kiselica (Ed.), *Confronting prejudice and racism during multicultural training.* Alexandria, VA: American Counseling Association.

U.S. Bureau of the Census. (1990). *Statistical abstract of the United States: 1990* (110th ed.). Washington, DC: Government Printing Office.

Yanico, B. J., Swanson, J. L., & Tokar, D. M. (1994). A psychometric investigation of the Black Racial Identity Attitude Scale–Form B. *Journal of Vocational Behavior, 44,* 218–234.

Yutrzenka, B. A. (1995). Making a case for training in ethnic and cultural diversity in increasing treatment efficacy. *Journal of Counseling and Clinical Psychology, 63,* 197–206.

6

The American Psychological Association's Guidelines on Multicultural Education, Training, Research, Practice, and Organizational Psychology

Initial Development and Summary

Madonna G. Constantine

Derald Wing Sue

People of color, including those of multiracial and multiethnic heritage, represent an increasing proportion of the U.S. population (Jones & Smith, 2001; U.S. Census Bureau, 2003). According to the 2000 U.S. Census (U.S. Census Bureau, 2003), approximately 40% of the nation's population consists of people of color (Jones & Smith, 2001). The landscape of racial and ethnic diversity across the United States indicates particularly high cultural diversity in coastal and border states, especially California, Texas, Arizona, New Mexico, Washington, Florida, New York, and Louisiana, and a general growth in cultural diversity in the midwestern, northwestern, and southern regions of the United States (U.S. Census Bureau, 2003) These demographic statistics underscore the need for professional psychologists to have a vested interest in addressing cultural diversity issues as practitioners, educators, researchers, and policymakers. Thus, it behooves psychologists and the larger field of psychology to reflect on potential monocultural biases to foster cultural relevance in research, practice, education, and training (Sue, 2001)

Recently, the American Psychological Association (APA) as a professional organization has responded to the increased diversification of the United States, in part, with explicit statements endorsing the importance of cultural competence for psychologists. Specifically, the "Guidelines on Multicultural Education, Training, Research, Practice, and Organizational Change for Psychologists" (APA, 2003), herein referred to as the APA Multicultural Guidelines, is a compilation of six prescriptive statements that reflect the evolution of the psychology profession with regard to recognizing that cultural competence is necessary in meeting the varied needs of individuals belonging to diverse cultural groups or historically marginalized groups. These multicultural competencies reflect a response to several APA divisions' calls for recognition and integration of multicultural initiatives within the larger psychological community, as well as the exponentially growing representation of people of color in the United States (Sue, Bingham, Porche-Burke, & Vasquez, 1999). As a living document, this set of competencies was designed to be expanded alongside future empirical and conceptual psychological contributions and as broader social movements influence public interests.

Relevant Background

The APA Multicultural Guidelines (APA, 2003) were published with the goal of affecting current and future psychological practice, training, education, and research and had been preceded by nearly 40 years of attention to multicultural issues in certain subfields of applied psychology. Social movements such as the Civil Rights Movement in the 1950s and 1960s represented forums for political action and subsequent public policy initiatives that addressed explicit differential access to human rights and power based on race and ethnicity. In the social context of change, structural and functional changes occurred within the psychology profession that affected the development of organizational bodies focused on cultural diversity issues. Specifically, momentum from the sociopolitical activism in the late 1960s created an atmosphere in which leading African American psychologists mobilized to increase representation of Black people in psychology and in leadership roles in professional psychological organizations, eliminate racially biased research from professional journals, and establish training programs in which cultural issues were included (Robinson & Morris, 2000). This kind of activism marked the beginning of the Association of Black Psychologists (ABP); other subgroups of psychologists of color, such as the Asian American Psychological Association (AAPA), were formed in the early 1970s.

Greater visibility of psychologists of color in the profession facilitated the development and disbursement of research related to people of color (APA, 2003). For example, in 1971, the National Institute of Mental Health (NIMH) established an Office of Minority Research; NIMH reorganized 15 years later to support research that included populations of color in all research. With financial and instrumental support from NIMH, organizations such as ABPsi and AAPA were able to support and publish research pertinent to populations of color. Additionally, interfacing with NIMH gave psychologists of color the opportunity to represent and increase visibility for multicultural issues within the profession.

Significant contributions to the multicultural psychology literature emerged from several counseling psychologists' commitment to enhancing mental health professionals' competence in working with clients of color (Constantine, 2002; Robinson & Morris, 2000). Sue and his colleagues' seminal work and development of a tripartite model of multicultural counseling competence (i.e., Sue et al., 1982) has laid the foundation for much of the existing literature on multicultural counseling (Constantine & Ladany, 2001). Sue and his colleagues defined the tripartite model in terms of counselors' (1) recognizing their personal attitudes and values around race and ethnicity, (2) developing their knowledge of diverse cultural worldviews and experiences, and (3) identifying effective skills in working with clients of color.

Ten years later, under the leadership of Dr. Thomas Parham, members of the Professional Standards Committee of the Association for Multicultural Counseling and Development (i.e., Sue, Arredondo, & McDavis, 1992) expanded the tripartite model to include three desired characteristics of multiculturally competent counselors: awareness of personal assumptions, values, and biases; understanding the worldviews of culturally diverse clients; and developing abilities to use and create culturally appropriate intervention strategies. The three counselor characteristics were crossed with the three dimensions of competence from the first iteration of the tripartite model to yield nine competency areas in which 31 total statements were offered. Arredondo and her colleagues (1996) produced a supplement to Sue et al.'s competencies that served to formally define constructs and competencies that had been hard to implement in the previous version.

The third major revision of the multicultural competencies (Sue et al., 1998) reflected major empirical and theoretical emphases in the literature, namely, research in racial and ethnic identity models (see Helms & Cook, 1999), and expanded the range of professional helping roles, such as social change agent and advocate (Atkinson, Thompson, & Grant, 1993). This was evident in the inclusion of three new competencies under the skills dimension, two of which speak to racial and cultural identity models and the third to adopting helping roles other than those of counselor or psychotherapist. Further, characteristics of multiculturally competent organizations were described and operationalized (Sue et al., 1998). Eleven operationalization statements concerning multiculturally inclusive organizations stressed commitment to diversity in all levels of personnel (including formal and informal mentorship), mission statements, and action plans. These competencies promoted the inclusion of diversity agendas in all facets of organizational management such that culture was now regarded as central rather than peripheral in multicultural organizational settings. The third iteration of the tripartite model of multicultural counseling competence also underscored the role of psychologists in addressing the effects of interpersonal and institutional racism from mesocosmic levels, including therapy and the classroom, to systemic levels that include the field of psychology itself (Sue et al., 1998).

Foundational Principles of the Multicultural Guidelines

The APA Multicultural Guidelines are grounded in six principles that "articulate respect and inclusiveness for the national heritage of all groups, recognition of cultural contexts as defining forces for individuals' and groups' lived experiences, and the role of external forces such as historical, economic, and socio-political events" (APA, 2003, p. 382). In their philosophical underpinnings, the principles of the APA Multicultural Guidelines encourage psychologists to see themselves as potential leaders of social justice in teaching, research, and clinical capacities and as active advocates of multiculturalism against the deleterious effects of racism, discrimination, and oppression. The principles are designed to influence the planning and actualization of education, research, practice, and organizational change informed by multiculturalism. Although all of the principles encourage psychologists to reflect on their own professional stances, Principles 5 and 6 specifically address organizational and social change roles that psychologists may engage to benefit clients, students, trainees, and the broader society.

Principle 1: Ethical conduct of psychologists is enhanced by knowledge of differences in beliefs and practices that emerge from socialization through racial and ethnic group affiliation and membership and how those beliefs and practices will necessarily affect the education, training, research, and practice of psychology.

In accordance with ethical principles related to respecting all individuals (APA, 1992: Principle D; APA, 2002: Principle E) and social responsibility (APA, 1992: Principle E; APA, 2002: Principle D) it is clear that greater knowledge of cultural differences will guide psychologists' understanding of their roles as teachers, trainers, researchers, and practitioners, such that their behavior in these capacities would reflect multicultural sensitivity. In particular, psychologists who engage social justice work that derives from knowledge of contextual influences on a group of marginalized individuals may exhibit appreciation and respect for others' broader social and cultural conditions.

Principle 2: Understanding and recognizing the interface between individuals' socialization experiences based on ethnic and racial heritage can enhance the quality of education, training, practice, and research in the field of psychology.

Psychologists should be aware of how their own cultural identities might affect interpersonal dynamics in practice, teaching, training, and research contexts. Additionally, psychologists' understanding of collective experiences based in race and ethnicity may contribute to greater sensitivity to intra- and intercultural group dynamics.

Principle 3: Recognition of the ways in which the intersection of racial and ethnic group membership with other dimensions of identity (e.g., gender, age, sexual orientation, disability, religion/spiritual orientation, educational attainment/experiences, and socioeconomic status) enhances the understanding and treatment of all people.

An appreciation of how cultural identities interface, in addition to recognition of within-group differences along varied dimensions of identity, can inform research, treatment, and organizational interventions for given cultural groups. The integration of various dimensions of identity may lead to richer understandings of individuals' experiences and contribute to complex and innovative research in psychology.

Principle 4: Knowledge of historically derived approaches that have viewed cultural differences as deficits and have not valued certain social identities helps psychologists to understand the underrepresentation of ethnic minorities in the profession and affirms and values the role of ethnicity and race in developing personal identity.

Historical knowledge of the institutional uses of psychology to promote oppressive systems, such as academic segregation, institutionalization in mental illness facilities, slavery, and immigration restrictions, may lead psychologists to reflect on the systemic implications of research treatment, conceptualization, and education models. Additionally, recognizing that traditional models of psychology and psychotherapy were derived in specific social contexts that may not have validated the humanity of people of color can allow psychologists to adopt or create novel approaches to psychology that may better suit clients' concerns.

Principle 5: Psychologists are uniquely able to promote racial equity and social justice. This is aided by their awareness of their impact on others and the influence of their personal and professional roles in society.

Sensitivity to racism, oppression, and mechanisms of social injustice related to race and ethnicity affords psychologists opportunities to address inequality at individual, group, and political levels. For example, at the individual level, psychologists may work with clients in naming certain experiences as discriminatory and finding personal advocacy resources. Psychologists may be able to address injustices at the group level through encouraging collegial faculty members to recruit prospective graduate students of color into majority-White graduate programs. At the political level, psychologists may develop research programs that address psychological and academic benefits of affirmative action and use this research to promote public policy and law.

Principle 6: Psychologists' knowledge about the roles of organizations, including employers and professional psychological associations, are potential sources of behavioral practices that encourage discourse, education and training, institutional change, and research and policy development that reflect rather than neglect cultural differences. Psychologists recognize that organizations can be gatekeepers or agents of the status quo, rather than leaders in a changing society with respect to multiculturalism.

Psychologists may be able to utilize their connections to organizations, specifically professional psychological associations, to promote multicultural initiatives and contribute to ongoing pushes for integrating multiculturalism. For example, groups of psychologists may become involved as consultants with secondary school educational boards to increase retention, graduation, and college enrollment rates of students of color. Further, psychologists may be involved in psychological organizations, such as the Society for the Psychological Study of Ethnic Minority Issues (APA, Division 45), to develop professional strategies that explicitly target enrollment, retention, and graduation rates of students of color at secondary and postsecondary educational levels.

The Multicultural Guidelines

Guideline 1: Psychologists are encouraged to recognize that, as cultural beings, they may hold attitudes and beliefs that can detrimentally influence their perceptions of and interactions with individuals who are ethnically and racially different from themselves.

The APA Multicultural Guidelines state that interactions between any two people are multicultural in that individuals' cultural perspectives shape perceptions of life experiences (Arredondo et al., 1996; Sue & Sue, 2003). Knowledge of cultural influences on worldview orientations may inform psychologists' understanding of how their norms and values may contrast with those of clients, trainees, and research participants. Additionally, primary awareness of personal race-based stereotypes may allow psychologists the opportunity to reflect on the origin and reinforcement of these stereotypes on social and psychological levels, addressing how, when, and to whom stereotypes are conjured; this may be a critical step in developing cultural sensitivity. Psychologists are not immune from tendencies to differentiate in-groups from out-groups; however, it is when power is distributed unequally, favoring psychologists, that psychology may be a medium for exploitation, insult, and ignorance. Mental health professionals may de-emphasize racial and ethnic group membership through the adoption of color-blind approaches or the focus on universal aspects of human behavior over racial or ethnic differences. Values endorsing assimilation with the White majority group may be masked by a color-blind approach, though psychologists may be unaware of pernicious effects of color blindness, including maintaining a harmful status quo and ignoring potentially salient race-related factors (Ridley, 1995). Once aware of attitudes and values related to race, ethnicity, and culture, psychologists may process and reduce their biases through various strategies, including building a "we" conceptualization of human interaction from an "us versus them" conceptualization (Gaertner & Dovidio, 2000) or increasing contact with people of color to foster connection and empathy.

Guideline 2: Psychologists are encouraged to recognize the importance of multicultural sensitivity/responsiveness to, knowledge of, and understanding about ethnically and racially different individuals.

Cultural empathy for the experiences of people of color may foster psychologists' understandings of clients,' students,' and research participants' worldviews and perspectives. In particular, appreciation of others' perceptions of psychologists as cultural beings may facilitate their understanding of others' willingness to seek help and their level of trust (Terrell & Terrell, 1981). Knowledge of racial identity (e.g., Atkinson, Morten, & Sue, 1998; Cross, 1971; Helms, 1984; Root, 1998), ethnic identity (e.g., Phinney, 1990, 1992), and spiritual identity (e.g., Myers et al., 1991) models may provide insight into the psychological experiences of people of color. Additionally, psychologists are encouraged to research the history of and legislative attention to culturally diverse populations to build contextual knowledge of potential experiences of clients, students, and research participants of color. The development of a cultural knowledge base in concert with cultural self-awareness may in turn facilitate crosscultural communication between psychologists and clients, peers, students, research participants, and organizations.

Guideline 3: As educators, psychologists are encouraged to employ the constructs of multiculturalism and diversity in psychological education.

Psychologists as educators may not adequately address multiculturalism and diversity in psychological education out of fear of perpetuating stereotypes of portraying themselves as racist (Ridley, 1995), discomfort with multiculturalism (Helms & Cook, 1999; Sue & Sue, 2003), or the belief that multiculturalism is not a legitimate area of psychological study. Psychologists who operate from these beliefs may take a color-blind approach to race and culture, exhibit ethnocentric monoculturalism, or willfully omit the role of culture in psychological development and theory, respectively. Because multicultural training has been associated with the development of multicultural competence (e.g., Constantine & Gainor, 2001; Constantine, Juby, & Liang, 2001), trainees' competence in working with culturally diverse people may be compromised when educators do not address multicultural issues in psychology. Although training programs in applied fields of psychology increasingly have included multiculturalism in their curricula (Bernal & Castro, 1994; Hills & Strozier, 1992; Suarez-Balcazar, Durlak, & Smith, 1994), psychology educators may take steps toward comprehensive integration of multiculturalism in the classroom.

Support for multiculturalism and diversity in psychological education may be exhibited through the process, as well as the content, of education. Model programs of minority retention efforts can encourage psychologists to develop strategies to increase enrollment and retention of students of color in training programs. Psychology educators may include explicit statements valuing multiculturalism and diversity in the syllabi, offer experiential opportunities related to cultural diversity, and employ various modalities of teaching to reach students' varied learning styles. Last, psychology educators may participate in faculty committee searches for prospective faculty of color.

Guideline 4: Culturally sensitive psychological researchers are encouraged to recognize the importance of conducting culture-centered and ethical psychological research among persons from ethnic, linguistic, and racial minority backgrounds.

Psychologists are encouraged to pursue and respect research that is relevant to national demographic changes. Populations that are increasing rapidly include bilingual individuals and non-English speakers, aging people of color, and multiracial individuals (U.S. Census Bureau, 2003). However, limitations to multicultural research include the omission of culture as a nuisance variable, predominance of White participants or overuse of culturally diverse convenience samples, and the ignorance of within-group differences among populations of color (Quintana et al., 2001). To address these limitations, psychologists are encouraged to be mindful of potential culture-boundness in research design, assessment procedures, and interpretation of data (Quintana et al., 2001). Culture-centered researchers are encouraged to ground research design in theories that complement the worldview and experiences of the population of study. Additionally, culture-centered researchers use assessment strategies with specific cultural populations for which sound psychometric evidence is available and have knowledge of linguistic, conceptual, and functional equivalence of measurement constructs across diverse cultures (Rogler, 1999). Moreover, culture-centered researchers are encouraged to incorporate relevant cultural value-based hypotheses into interpretations of research results (Quintana et al., 2001). Last, culture-centered researchers report the racial, gender, and age characteristics of their sample and address possible limitations to the generalizability of their results based on sample characteristics.

Guideline 5: Psychologists are encouraged to apply culturally appropriate skills in clinical and other applied psychological practices.

Cultural self-awareness and knowledge about worldview variables and experiences of people of color predicate the application of culturally appropriate skills in psychological practice (Sue et al., 1992; Sue et al., 1998). Although formulaic skill sets specific to cultural groups may be counterproductive (Helms & Cook, 1999; Sue & Sue, 2003), the development of a multiculturally informed skill set may facilitate psychologists' adaptations of traditional interventions to suit clients' needs more appropriately. Eager practitioners who are motivated to implement culture-specific interventions might find that a certain dimension of cultural identity is not necessarily salient for their clients in a certain therapeutic context. Similarly, visible group membership (e.g., race or ethnicity) may overshadow within-group variations (e.g., racial identity status) that may require further psychological processing. Moreover, psychological literature may not provide detailed intervention strategies for specific cultural populations, such as multiracial individuals or aging people of color. Psychologists are thus encouraged to adopt holistic and ecological perspectives of their clients, with reference to cultural and sociopolitical factors such as gender, generational status, language ability, parental migration histories, neighborhood of origin, educational attainment, and availability of community resources (Root, 1998) when considering potential intervention strategies. Additionally, it may be valuable for psychologists to include indigenous healers and community support networks, such as herbalists, religious groups, and respected elders, in intervention strategies (Atkinson et al., 1993).

Guideline 6: Psychologists are encouraged to use organizational change processes to support culturally informed organizational (policy) development and practices.

The parameters of psychologists' roles may shift in accordance with the interests of the diversifying population of the United States. Psychological services that are constrained to an office setting might not adequately meet the mental health needs of individuals who are unfamiliar with social institutions (including mental health services), have limited English proficiency, or have experienced systematic discrimination or oppression in social institutions (Atkinson et al., 1993; Sue et al., 1998). Evidenced in the history of the multicultural movement in particular (Arredondo & Perez, 2003), psychologists have been instrumental in the development of professional and public policy changes related to experiences of people of color through their involvement in professional organizations. Culture-centered psychologists are encouraged to participate in local, state, and national legislative efforts devoted to promoting equality across dimensions of identity (Vera & Speight, 2003). However, despite the availability of models of multicultural organizational development (e.g., Sue, 2001; Sue et al., 1998), many psychologists have limited experience and training in social justice and organizational development issues (Prilleltensky & Prilleltensky, 2003). The APA Multicultural Guidelines provide examples of "best practice" approaches to organizational change, although the reflection of such approaches in organizational settings may be gradual.

Conclusion

The APA Multicultural Guidelines represent a hallmark in the movement toward including multicultural initiatives in the field of psychology. These Multicultural Guidelines imply that all psychologists should engage in culturally relevant education, training, research, practice, and organizational development. Therefore, psychologists who traditionally had not endorsed these practices may experience direct or indirect pressure to do so; in other words, psychologists who endorse more traditional models of training, research, and practice may be taken out of their comfort zones. Training institutions also might need to employ multicultural consultants to address potential professional resistance. Further, it behooves psychologists to become more adept at understanding how to impact large organizational bodies with regard to multicultural organizational issues.

References

American Psychological Association. (1992). *Ethical principles of psychologists and code of conduct.* Retrieved June 23, 2003, from http://www.apa.org/ethics/code1992.html.

American Psychological Association. (2002). *Ethical principles of psychologists and code of conduct.* Washington, DC: Author.

American Psychological Association. (2003). Guidelines on multicultural education, training, research, practice, and organizational change for psychologists. *American Psychologist, 58,* 377–402.

Arredondo, P., & Perez, P. (2003). Expanding multicultural competence through social justice leadership. *Counseling Psychologist, 31,* 282–289.

Arredondo, P., Toporek, R., Brown, S. P., Jones, J., Locke, D. C., Sanchez, J., et al. (1996). Operationalization of the multicultural counseling competencies. *Journal of Multicultural Counseling and Development, 24,* 42–78.

Atkinson, D. R., Morten, G., & Sue, D. W. (1998). *Counseling American minorities* (5th ed.). New York: McGraw-Hill.

Atkinson, D. R., Thompson, C. E., & Grant, S. K. (1993). A three-dimensional model for counseling racial/ethnic minorities. *Counseling Psychologist, 21,* 257–277.

Bernal, M. E., & Castro, F. G. (1994). Are clinical psychologists prepared for service and research with ethnic minorities? Report of a decade of progress. *American Psychologist. 49,* 797–805.

Constantine, M. G. (2002). Predictors of satisfaction with counseling: Racial and ethnic minority clients' attitudes toward counseling and ratings of their counselors' general and multicultural counseling competence. *Journal of Counseling Psychology, 49,* 255–263.

Constantine, M. G., & Gainor, K. A. (2001). Emotional intelligence and empathy: Their relation to school counselors' multicultural counseling knowledge and awareness. *Professional School Counseling, 5,* 131–137.

Constantine, M. G., Juby, H. L., & Liang, J. J.-C. (2001). Examining multicultural counseling competence and race-related attitudes among White marital and family therapists. *Journal of Marital and Family Therapy, 27,* 353–362.

Constantine, M. G., & Ladany, N. (2001). New visions for defining and assessing multicultural counseling competence. In J. G. Ponterotto, J. M. Casas, L. A. Suzuki, & C. M. Alexander (Eds.), *Handbook of multicultural counseling* (2nd ed., pp. 482–498). Thousand Oaks, CA: Sage.

Cross, W. E. (1971). The Negro-to-Black conversion experience: Toward a psychology of Black liberation. *Black World, 20,* 13–27.

Gaertner, S. L., & Dovidio, J. F. (2000). *Reducing intergroup bias: The common ingroup identity model.* Philadelphia: Brunner/Mazel.

Helms, J. E. (1984). Toward a theoretical explanation of the effect of race on counseling: A Black and White Model. *Counseling Psychologist, 12,* 153–165.

Helms, J. E., & Cook, D. A. (1999). Using race and culture in counseling and psychotherapy: Theory and process. Boston: Allyn & Bacon.

Hills, H. I., & Strozier, A. L. (1992). Multicultural training in APA-approved counseling psychology programs: A survey. *Professional Psychology: Research and Practice, 23,* 43–51.

Jones, N. A., & Smith, A. S. (2001). *Census 2000 brief: Two or more races.* U.S. Census Bureau. Retrieved May 30, 2003, from http://www.census.gov/prod /2001 pubs/c2kbr01-6.pdf.

Myers, L. J., Speight, S. L., Highlen, P. S., Cox, C. I., Reynolds, A. L., Adams, E. M., et al. (1991). Identity development and worldview: Toward an optimal conceptualization. *Journal of Counseling and Development, 70,* 54–63.

Phinney, J. S. (1990). Ethnic identity in adolescents and adults: Review of research. *Psychological Bulletin, 198,* 499–514.

Phinney, J. S. (1992). The Multigroup Ethnic Identity Measure: A new scale for use with diverse groups. *Journal of Adolescent Research, 7,* 156–176.

Prilleltensky, I., & Prilleltensky, O. (2003). Synergies for wellness and liberation in counseling psychology. *Counseling Psychologist, 31,* 273–281.

Quintana, S. M., Troyano, N., & Taylor, G. (2001). Cultural validity and inherent challenges in quantitative methods for multicultural research. In J. G. Ponterotto, J. M. Casas, L. A. Suzuki, & C. M. Alexander (Eds.), *Handbook of multicultural counseling* (2nd ed., pp. 604–630). Thousand Oaks, CA: Sage.

Ridley, C. R. (1995). *Overcoming unintentional racism in counseling and therapy: A practitioner's guide to intentional intervention.* Thousand Oaks, CA: Sage.

Robinson, D. T., & Morris, J. R. (2000). Multicultural counseling: Historical contexts and current training considerations. *Western Journal of Black Studies, 29,* 235–249.

Rogler, L. H. (1999). Methodological sources of cultural insensitivity in mental health research. *American Psychologist, 54,* 424–433.

Root, M. P. P. (1998). Resolving "other" status: Identity development of biracial individuals. In P. B. Organista, K. M. Chun, & G. Marin (Eds.), *Readings in ethnic psychology* (pp. 100–122). New York: Routledge.

Suarez-Balcazar, Y., Durlak, J. A., & Smith, C. (1994). Multicultural training practices in community psychology programs. *American Journal of Community Psychology, 22,* 785–798.

Sue, D. W. (2001). Multidimensional facets of cultural competence. *Counseling Psychologist, 29,* 790–821.

Sue, D. W., Arredondo, P., & McDavis, R. J. (1992). Multicultural counseling competencies and standards: A call to the profession. *Journal of Multicultural Counseling and Development, 20,* 64–88.

Sue, D. W., Bernier, J. B., Durran, M., Feinberg, L., Pedersen, P., Smith, E., et al. (1982). Position paper: Cross-cultural counseling competencies. *Counseling Psychologist, 10,* 45–52.

Sue, D. W., Bingham, R. P., Porche-Burke, L., & Vasquez, M. (1999). The diversification of psychology: A multicultural revolution. *American Psychologist, 54,* 1061–1069.

Sue, D. W., Carter, R. T, Casas, J. M., Fouad, N. A., Ivey, A. E., Jensen, M., et al. (1998). *Multicultural counseling competencies: Individual and organizational development.* Thousand Oaks, CA: Sage.

Sue, D. W., & Sue, D. (2003). *Counseling the culturally diverse* (4th ed.). Hoboken, NJ: Wiley.

Jerrell, F., & Terrell, S. L. (1981). An inventory to measure cultural mistrust among Blacks. *Western Journal of Black Studies, 5,* 180–184.

United States Census Bureau. (2003). National population estimates: Characteristics. Retrieved June 28, 2003, from http://eire.census.gov/popest/data/national/tables/asro/NAEST2002-ASRO-.04.php.

Vera, E. M., & Speight, S. L. (2003). Multicultural competence, social justice, and counseling psychology: Expanding our roles. *Counseling Psychologist, 31,* 253–272.

7

Strategies and Techniques for Counselor Training Based on the Multicultural Counseling Competencies

Patricia Arredondo

G. Miguel Arciniega

To begin a commentary about strategies and techniques based on the Multicultural Counseling Competencies (Arredondo et al., 1996; Sue, Arredondo, & McDavis, 1992), developed by the Association of Multicultural Counseling and Development (AMCD), requires (a) defining the scope of the discussion, (b) stating a rationale for recommending a competency-based framework for teaching, and (c) establishing premises about counseling programs as learning organizations. On the basis of these goals, we make recommendations specifically to counselor educators and program administrators about the use of multicultural competencies for revising curricula. Our intent is not to infringe on academic freedom nor to suggest that there is only one approach to focusing on multicultural counseling in counselor education. Rather, we wish to share what we know has worked in curricula in which an infusion approach has been used.

Defining the scope for the application of multicultural counseling competencies means acknowledging the changing landscape in the profession. Each year, there is more literature, research, conferences, and other forms of communication that promote multicultural and culture-specific perspectives in counseling. In 1999, several divisions of the American Psychological Association cosponsored a national multicultural summit; a second summit was held January 2001, and a third is scheduled for January 2003. Since 1995, there have been monthly columns in *Counseling Today,* the official newspaper of the American Counseling Association (ACA), promoting different applications and interventions "to promote dignity and development through diversity." Almost every journal published for ACA divisions has included articles that have a multicultural and diversity focus. In particular, the *Journal for Multicultural*

Counseling and Development has become a forum for reporting groundbreaking multidisciplinary research and model development. The Association for Counselor Education and Supervision has endorsed the Multicultural Counseling Competencies (MCCs) as have six other divisions of the ACA (Sue & Sue, 1999). What does this mean for counselor preparation?

A national survey on multicultural competence and counselor training (Holcomb-McCoy & Myers, 1999) revealed that "there was no significant difference in self-perceived multicultural competence between graduates of Council for Accreditation of Counseling and Related Educational Programs (CACREP) accredited and non-accredited programs" (Holcomb-McCoy & Myers, 1999, p. 294). The only significant difference reported was between ethnicity as it relates to "higher levels of perceived multicultural competence" (Holcomb-McCoy & Myers, 1999, p. 294). The survey also probed the graduates' perceptions about the adequacy of training in the area of multicultural competence. Once again, there were no significant differences, except in the domain of knowledge, regarding adequacy of training by the two types of respondents.

Another national study (Steward, Morales, Bartell, Miller, & Weeks, 1998) investigated whether counselor trainees' perceptions were multiculturally responsive or multiculturally reactive. Findings suggested that trainees in programs that infused multicultural content in all courses in addition to providing multicultural-specific course work did not necessarily embrace the multicultural literature nor were they any clearer on what multicultural competence is. It is unfair to draw hasty conclusions, particularly when an infusion approach is one that is recommended in this article. However, particular questions do surface about the types of factors that might contribute to these outcomes.

In this article, we describe two grounding principles that provide a rationale for systemic use of the AMCD's MCCs and briefly define the MCCs. Our goal is to examine the relationship between a learning organization, competency-based teaching, and instruction for practical counseling interventions at interpersonal and organizational levels.

Grounding Principles for the Systemic Use of MCCs

Principle 1: The Learning Organization

The first principle in creating a framework of change is that of the *learning organization.* Popularized by the book *The Fifth Discipline* (Senge, 1990) and used in different workplace environments and industries, this concept and its principles seem most appropriate for reframing counseling programs. A *learning organization* is characterized as one that "develops an ability to question, challenge and change operating norms and assumptions" (Morgan, 1997, p. 90). This represents both a mind-set change and a skill-development process, as the learning organization looks out to the environment to notice shifting patterns and trends. A parallel can be drawn to counselor training programs, which are directly affected by environmental changes of many types, such as legislation that affects licensure or the rights of linguistic minority individuals, global migration from war-torn countries, the role of managed health care, or funding cutbacks that affect education.

Two outcomes of the forces of change are longer training programs with more requirements and a focus on accreditation. In addition to CACREP guidelines, some training programs are following the Comprehensive Competency-Based Guidance model ("The ASCA Counselor," 1997). This model promotes counselor training in one of three specialty domains: career, academic, and personal/social.

A second compelling argument for a learning organization comes from the forces of multiculturalism and diversity that are taking center stage in the counseling profession. Ironically, there is still a gap in the deliberate attention to multicultural competencies in counselor training programs even though there has been an increase in leadership training at national conferences and even more doctoral research in this area. Essentially, we mean that teaching one course in multicultural counseling is not evidence of a learning organization nor does it demonstrate that training programs and their faculty are being responsive to the forces of change that have been described thus far (Reynolds, 1995). Applying the principles of a learning organization to counselor training requires systematic self-reflection and evaluation of existing practices as a preliminary step to revising curricula.

Principle 2: A Competency Rationale

For some time, the counseling profession has struggled to endorse a focus on multiculturalism and diversity. Endorsement of the MCCs by ACA divisions and two divisions of the American Psychological Association points to an increasing recognition that competencies are needed to reframe and redesign ethnocentric monocultural counselor preparation (Sue & Sue, 1999) and that the MCCs can be the basis for new lines of research to better inform more effective and ethical practices (Pedersen & Ivey, 1993; Pope-Davis & Coleman, 1997; Reynolds, 1995).

We invite counselor educators to consider the following premises about competency-based teaching and practice: (a) A competence approach is contrasted with deficit-based, remedial, or pathological models that suggest something or someone needs to be fixed; (b) Competencies (knowledge, skills, and attitudes) "lead to having adaptive payoffs in significant environments" (Sundberg, Snowden, & Reynolds, 1978, p. 196); and (c) "Individuals' self-perceptions and expectations must be continually fed by a lifelong acquisition of adaptive behaviors, cognitions, and relations" (Masterpasqua, 1989, p. 1366), In summary, a competency-based approach to teaching provides guidelines and developmental benchmarks for adaptive cognitive, emotional, and behavioral attributes. Contemporary counselor educators can consider using competency-based teaching in the area of multiculturalism and diversity as well as in other course work.

The MCCs' Framework

The AMCD competencies heretofore referred to outline general and specific competency domains at three levels: Counselor Awareness of Own Cultural Values and Biases, Counselor Awareness of Client's Worldview, and Culturally Appropriate Intervention Strategies. Within each domain are three interdependent competency areas: (a) Beliefs and Attitudes, (b) Knowledge, and (c) Skills. The article "Operationalization of the Multicultural Counseling Competencies" (Arredondo et al., 1996) was based on an earlier article (Sue et al., 1992) that presented 31 MCCs. With the expansion by Arredondo et al., 117 behavioral, outcome-based explanatory statements were added. The latter have become tools for planning course objectives, establishing individual learning goals, and creating research agendas to determine the efficacy of the competencies.

Arredondo et al. (1996) added two new features to the multicultural competencies: Multicultural groups were defined as African Americans, American Indians, Asian Americans,

White/Caucasian Americans, and Latinos/Hispanics, and the Dimensions of Personal Identity Model (Arredondo & Glauner, 1992) was introduced, providing an integrative approach to the concepts of multiculturalism and the A, B, and C dimensions of human diversity. In short, the model provides flexibility for discussing multiple identities in both sociopolitical and historical contexts.

The philosophy underlying the MCCs is as follows: All counseling is multicultural in nature; sociopolitical and historical forces influence the culture of counseling beliefs, values, and practices and the worldview of clients and counselors; and ethnicity, culture, race, language, and other dimensions of diversity need to be factored into counselor preparation and practice.

From Principles to Practice Through Cultural Competency-Based Strategies and Techniques

This article is geared toward counselor educators in particular. We have, in a sense, "deconstructed" the competencies to demonstrate their flexibility and applicability to a variety of counseling courses. Instructors might establish a competency-based curriculum, as we have, by using the format detailed in the 1996 competencies (Arredondo et al., 1996). The following outline first presents one of the three major areas (i.e., Counselor Awareness of Own Cultural Values and Biases, Counselor Awareness of Client's Worldview, and Culturally Appropriate Intervention Strategies), followed by the general competency domain; a behavioral/explanatory competency; course objectives, strategies, and techniques; and outcome statements. Because only a few examples are offered, we recommend that the reader refer to the original article (Arredondo et al., 1996) to identify other explanatory statements.

Domain 1: Counselor Awareness of Own Cultural Values and Biases

General Competency: Attitudes and Beliefs

Behavioral/explanatory competency. A2a. Culturally skilled counselors "can identify the history of their culture in relation to educational opportunities and its impact on their current worldview." (Arredondo et al., 1996, p. 57).

Course objectives—Career counseling. To develop awareness and knowledge about the role of cultural background and dimensions of human diversity, for example, gender, physical disability, race, and other contextual forces, including history and sociopolitical conditions, on education and career opportunities and access.

Strategy and technique: The autobiography. Through a structured written exercise, students are asked to investigate educational experiences that have historically been available or not available to members of their cultural group. They are asked to analyze how the legacy of the presence or absence of these experiences has affected group and individual behavior. Students comment on self-expectations and expectations of others based on this legacy. Class discussion can be used to generate an exchange of perspectives based on unchecked assumptions, individual and cultural group experiences, worldviews as they relate to occupational and career status, and the role of privilege and oppression in attaining educational opportunities.

Outcome. Role taking and perspective taking heighten awareness and knowledge building. These skills lead to an identification of biases and assumptions about educational orientation, institutional barriers, preferences about careers and jobs, and the meaning of work held by one's primary reference group as well the meaning held by other cultural groups.

General Competency: Knowledge, Example 1

Behavioral/explanatory competency. B1b. Culturally skilled counselors "can recognize and discuss their family's and culture's perspectives of acceptable (normal) codes of conduct and what are unacceptable (abnormal) codes of conduct and how this may or may not vary from those of other cultures and families" (Arredondo et al., 1996, p. 59).

Course objectives—Family and relationships, multicultural, practicum, and community counseling. To develop awareness, knowledge, and cognitive and socioemotional skill development in the context of learning about cross-cultural family roles and norms, indigenous and community-based modes of helping, and historical information.

Strategy and technique. Use video clips from Issues in Cross-Cultural Counseling (Microtraining Associates, 1981), Specifics of Practice for Counseling with Latina/os (Microtraining Associates, 1995), and Culturally-Competent Counseling & Therapy: Live Demonstrations of Innovative Approaches (Microtraining Associates, 2000). The simulated counseling vignettes on these tapes provide case study material that can be analyzed from various points of view, for example the influence of the culture of counseling on the counselor's style and approach, the client's sense of "right and wrong" based on a collectivist worldview, socialization differences based on gender, the range of emotions expressed by both counselors and clients, and the exploration of historical factors.

Outcome. There is increased awareness and knowledge about (a) family rules and norms that become internalized; (b) the application of these norms based on gender, age, and other dimensions of human diversity; and (c) the thinking process that clients and counselors from similar and different backgrounds bring to a counseling session. Attention can be given to the roles of emotions (countertransference, in particular), language, and metaphors that might affect the relationship.

General Competency: Knowledge, Example 2

Behavioral/explanatory competency, B3. Culturally skilled counselors "possess knowledge about their social impact on others. They are knowledgeable about communication style differences, how their style may clash with or foster the counseling process with persons of color and others different from themselves based on the A, B, and C Dimensions (of human diversity), and how to anticipate the impact it may have on others" (Arredondo et al., 1996, p. 60).

Course objectives—Introduction to counseling, practicum, supervision, and multicultural counseling. To heighten awareness about interpersonal comfort and discomfort with respect to different styles of communication, expression of emotions, and contact in general with persons perceived as different from oneself on different dimensions of human diversity.

Strategy and technique. Use the film *The Color of Fear* (Wah, 1994), which features a multicultural group of 10 men discussing their ethnic/racial identity and how it has affected their life experiences. Students can role-play and discuss the film from the perspective of different characters as well as from their own personal experiences. Another training tool is the *Triad Model* video developed by Pedersen (Pedersen & Ivey, 1993).

Outcome. Emotional competence is tapped through video viewing and discussion. Students must acknowledge their "hot buttons" about racism, privilege, and oppression, either as recipients or beneficiaries. This is excellent practice that encourages students to engage in difficult dialogues with fellow students about race-related issues, interactions that many students often avoid.

Domain 2: Counselor Awareness of Client's Worldview

General Competency: Attitudes and Beliefs

Behavioral/explanatory competency. A1a. Culturally skilled counselors "identify their common emotional reactions about individuals and groups different from themselves and observe their own reactions in encounters" (Arredondo et al., 1996, p. 62).

Course objectives—Introduction to counseling skills, career counseling, multicultural counseling, and practicum. To recognize and acknowledge personal emotional reactions based on oppression, loss, and other negative experiences that affect human dignity.

Strategy and technique. (a) Use the video *True Colors* (Lukasiewicz & Harvey, 1991), which introduces two professional men who are treated differently on the basis of the color of their skin (black & white) in job seeking, car purchasing, apartment hunting, and many public behaviors in which adults might engage and (b) Enact the "party experience," which requires students to speak to others about fundraising for a particular charity. On their foreheads, participants wear a label that denotes a particular identity that is not known to them, (e.g., teenage mother, HIV patient). Debriefing begins with the following questions: How did you experience others' reactions to you? How did you respond to the different labels? How did stereotypes engender different emotional reactions? With whom were you most comfortable or uncomfortable? How do institutions reinforce labels?

Outcome. These assignments require the student to role-play to understand how a societally "labeled" person might experience oppression, marginalization, or loss. Institutional practices that perpetuate exclusionary practices toward marginalized groups are also examined.

General Competency: Knowledge

Behavioral/explanatory competency. B1c. Culturally skilled counselors "understand and can explain the historical point of contact with dominant society for various ethnic groups and the impact of the types of contact (enslaved, refugee, seeking economic opportunities, conquest, and so forth) on current issues in society" (Arredondo et al., 1996, p. 64).

Course objectives—Counseling theory and multicultural counseling. To recognize the historical and political contexts that have affected and continue to affect different cultural groups in the United States and the processes that many immigrants and refugees experience.

Strategy and technique. These can include guided imagery or the journey of an immigrant or refugee. Instructors must be skilled in leading guided imagery exercises. Each participant is given a "foreign" destination as a site for advanced counseling study. They are guided through the different phases of the immigrant's journey: premigration, migration-specific, and postmigration (Arredondo-Dowd, 1981). Another highly recommended resource is a videotaped presentation by Susan Cameron (American Association for Counseling and Development, 1994) on the history of American Indians, contemporary life stressors and concerns, and the implications for contemporary counseling practice.

Outcome. There is heightened awareness about historical and current immigrant experiences, increased knowledge about historical incidents that have left a negative legacy on today's American Indian, and new insights about the worldviews of American Indians with respect to counseling as it is traditionally taught and practiced.

General Competency: Skills

Behavioral/explanatory competency. C1a. Culturally skilled counselors "can discuss recent research regarding such topics as mental health, career decision making, education and learning that focuses on issues related to different cultural populations as represented in A and B Dimensions" (Arredondo et al., 1996, p. 66).

Course objectives—Research planning; psychological testing; and career, school, and multicultural counseling. To become critical consumers of research that involves different ethnic minority groups, women, and other underrepresented groups and to engage in difficult dialogues about these practices.

Strategy and technique. This assignment requires a review of 8 to 10 articles that present critical analyses of research findings from the perspectives of multiculturalism and diversity. Suggested readings include the special issue of the *Journal of Counseling & Development* on racism (Robinson & Ginter, 1999), *Even the Rat Was White* (Guthrie, 1997), and other new research published in the *Journal of Multicultural Counseling and Development,* Questions for analysis include the following: Are mere norms for the instrument used that apply to all participants in the study? How was language equivalency ensured? Were all relevant variables (e.g., socioeconomic status, length of residence in the country) considered?

Outcome. This technique allows students to become better informed consumers of research and literature that include studies on ethnic and racial minority groups.

Domain 3: Culturally Appropriate Intervention Strategies

General Competency: Knowledge

Behavioral/explanatory competence. B1a. Culturally skilled counselors "can articulate the historical, cultural, and racial context in which traditional theories and interventions have been developed" (Arredondo et al., 1996, p. 68).

Course objectives—Prepracticum and family counseling. Students will be able to discuss three major counseling theories and identify the major assumptions of each in terms of their historical, cultural, and racial context.

Strategy and technique. Assigned readings from Helms (1990), Katz (1985), LaFromboise and Low (1989), and Sue and Sue (1999) will assist students in identifying mainstream theoretical issues and inherent assumptions about the four main minority racial/ethnic groups that might present barriers and cultural misunderstanding in counseling.

Outcome. Through role-playing and refraining of other worldview perspectives, students' will become more aware of how traditional counseling approaches are rooted in historical Euro American assumptions.

General Competency: Skills

Behavioral/explanatory competency. C2a. Culturally skilled counselors "can recognize and discuss examples in which racism or bias may actually be embedded in an institutional system or in society" (Arredondo et al., 1996, p. 71).

Course objectives—Multicultural counseling and practicum. To be able to identify, conceptually and behaviorally, examples of institutional racism or bias. To be able to process how a counselor may provide the client with information about institutional racism and how this may affect clients.

Strategy and techniques. Review literature concerning institutional racism and White identity development and develop a critical written analysis of how these can be a part of a client's ability to articulate a problem (Helms, 1990; Katz, 1985; Sue & Sue, 1999). Role-play participant perspectives from *The Color of Fear* (Wah, 1994) and require students to critique each other's role-playing.

Outcome. As a result of the strategies, students will be able to discuss how institutionalized racism against White and racial/ethnic groups operates in individual's lives. They will also be able to generalize these concepts to sexism, ageism, and homophobia.

Other Strategies, Techniques, and Resources

The examples cited in the previous section are a few of the many existing exercises, videos, and readings available for use in courses on multiculturalism. One video that is often used is *A Class Divided* (William, 1984). A review by Williams (1999) described different applications of this video in counselor training. Assessment tools have been reviewed by Pope-Davis and Coleman (1997) and should be considered by program administrators to determine the multicultural competency level of students entering and exiting a counselor training program.

Implications for Counseling Program Administrators and Educators

According to Sue and Sue (1999), "In order to be culturally competent, mental health professionals must be able to free themselves from the cultural conditioning of their personal and professional training, to understand and accept the legitimacy of alternative worldviews, and to begin the process of developing culturally appropriate intervention strategies in working with a diverse clientele" (p. ix).

By applying the principles of a learning organization to counselor training, counselor educators are in a better position to self-reflect and to evaluate existing practices as a preliminary step to revising curricula. Although there is little agreement about the most effective strategies and approaches to teaching about multiculturalism and diversity (D'Andrea, Daniels, & Heck, 1992), the fact remains that educators must begin to implement competency-based teaching.

Now is the time for change. Our relevance as professional counselors is at stake. In marketing, it is essential that one is knowledgeable and ready to meet the needs of his or her internal and external consumers. In counselor education, students are the internal consumers and clients; communities, legislators, and similar groups are some of our external consumers. The call for curriculum revision is now.

References

American Association of Counseling and Development. (1994). *Multicultural counseling summit: A town meeting.* Alexandria, VA: American Counseling Association.

Arredondo-Dowd, P. (1981). Personal loss and grief as a result of immigration. *Guidance Journal, 59,* 376–378.

Arredondo, P. (1998). Integrating multicultural counseling competencies and universal helping conditions in culture-specific contexts. *The Counseling Psychologist, 26,* 592–601.

Arredondo, P., & Glauner, T. (1992). *Personal dimensions of identity model.* Boston: Empowerment Workshops.

Arredondo, P., Toporek, R., Brown, S. B., Jones, J., Locke, D. C., Sanchez, J., & Stadler, H. (1996). Operationalization of the multicultural counseling competencies. *Journal of Multicultural Counseling and Development, 24,* 42–78.

The ASCA Counselor. (1997). *The ASCX Counselor, 35,* 1, 7.

D'Andrea, M., Daniels, J., & Heck, R. (1992). Evaluating the impact of multicultural counseling training. *Journal of Counseling & Development, 70,* 143–150.

Guthrie, R. V. (1997). *Even the rat was white: A historical view of psychology* (2nd ed.). New York: Harper & Row.

Helms, J. E. (1990). *Black and White racial identity: Theory, research, and practice.* New York: Greenwood Press.

Holcomb-McCoy, C. C., & Myers, J. E. (1999). Multicultural competence and counselor training: A national survey. *Journal of Counseling & Development,* 77, 294–302.

Katz, J. (1985). The sociopolitical nature of counseling. *The Counseling Psychologist, 73,* 615–624.

LaFromboise, T., & Low, K. (1989). American Indian adolescents. In J. Gibbs & L. Hwang (Eds.), *Children of color* (pp. 114–147). San Francisco: Jossey-Bass.

Lukasiewicz, M., & Harvey, E. (Producers). (1991, September 26). *True colors on 20/20: Primetime live.* [Television broadcast]. New York: American Broadcasting Corporation.

Masterpasqua, F. (1989). A competence paradigm for psychological practice. *American Psychologist, 44,* 1366–1371.

Microtraining Associates, Inc. (Producer). (1981). *Issues in cross-cultural counseling.* [Film]. (Available from Microtraining and Multicultural Development, PO Box 9641), North Amherst, MA 01059–9641)

Microtraining Associates, Inc. (Producer). (1995). *Specifics of practice with Latina/os.* [Film]. (Available from Microtraining and Multicultural Development, PO Box 9641, North Amherst, MA 01059–9641)

Microtraining Associates, Inc., & The Society for the Psychological Study of Ethnic Minority Issues, Division 45 of the American Psychological Association (Producers and sponsors). (2000). *Culturally-competent counseling and therapy: Live demonstrations of innovative approaches.* [Film]. (Available from Microtraining Associates, Inc., PO Box 9641, North Amherst, MA 01059-9641)

Morgan, G. (1997). *Images of organization* (2nd ed.). Thousand Oaks, CA: Sage.

Pedersen, P., & Ivey, A. E. (1993). *Culture-centered counseling and interviewing skills.* Westport, CT: Greenwood.

Pope-Davis, D. B., & Coleman, H. L. K. (1997). *Multicultural counseling competencies: Assessment, education and training, and supervision.* Thousand Oaks, CA: Sage.

Reynolds, A. L. (1995). Challenges and strategies for teaching multicultural counseling courses. In J. G. Ponterotto, J. M. Casas, L. A. Suzuki, & C. M. Alexander (Eds.), *Handbook of multicultural counseling* (pp. 312–330). Thousand Oaks, CA: Sage.

Reynolds, T. L., & Ginter, E. J. (Eds.). (1999). Racism: Healing its effects [Special Issue]. *Journal of Counseling & Development, 77*(1).

Senge, P. (1990). *The fifth discipline.* New York: Doubleday.

Steward, R. J., Morales, P. C., Bartell, P. A., Miller, M., & Weeks, D. (1998). The multiculturally responsive versus the multiculturally reactive: A study of perceptions of counselor trainees. *Journal of Multicultural Counseling and Development, 26,* 13–27.

Sue, D. W., Arredondo, P., & McDavis, R. J. (1992). Multicultural counseling competencies and standards: A call to the profession. *Journal of Counseling & Development, 70,* 477–483.

Sue, D. W., & Sue, D. (1999). *Counseling the culturally different* (3rd ed.). New York: Wiley.

Sundberg, N. A., Snowden, L. R., & Reynolds, W. M. (1978). Toward assessment of personal competence and incompetence in life situations. *Annual Review of Psychology, 29,* 179–221.

Wah, Lee Mun. (Director). (1994). *The color of fear.* [Film]. (Available from Stir-Fry Productions, 470 3rd St., Oakland, CA 94607)

William, P. (Producer, Director). (1984). *A class divided.* [Film]. Boston: Public Broadcasting Service.

Williams, C. B. (1999). The color of fear and blue-eyed: Tools for multicultural counselor training. *Counselor Education and Supervision, 39,* 76–79.

8

Acculturation

A Psychological Construct of Continuing Relevance for Chicana/o Psychology

Israel Cuéllar

Roxana I. Siles

Erika Bracamontes

Introduction

This chapter reviews the construct of acculturation, its measurement, and its relevance not just to the psychology of Chicana/os, but also to that of all persons who live and develop in multicultural or pluralistic environments. It is well understood that there are many complex and interesting changes resulting from different cultures coming into continuous contact with each other. Historically, great centers of trade, growth, and prosperity resulted from this convergence as well as long-lasting and, unfortunately, apparently irresolvable conflicts. Chicana/os are caught between two cultures (the cultures of Mexico and of the United States). They experience different degrees of exposure to these two large complex cultural systems over time and integrate different aspects of these cultures throughout their lifespan. There are no fixed outcomes from acculturation processes: They are interdependent, transactional, and ecological and depend on numerous types of variables, including but not limited to environmental and contextual, individual personality, status, sociocultural, and political. Acculturation outcomes at the individual level are very much like personality characteristics: They are difficult to define, occur along continuous dimensions or degrees, are generally multidimensional in nature, and are influenced by both genetic and cultural factors. Chicana/o social scientists, including psychologists, have played an important role in understanding acculturation processes, their influences, measurement, and importance with respect to psychological well-being and development.

Definition and History

Acculturation began as an anthropological construct, evolving out of a body of literature on culture change and culture contact that was popular at the turn of the century. One publication was an article on Yaqui and Apache Indians as they moved through four theoretical linear stages of acculturation: Savagery, Barbarism, Civilization, and finally Enlightenment (McGee, 1898), another the changing roles of females in the Antler Indian culture through contact with Whites (Mead, 1932). This literature was largely qualitative and ethnographic. Anthropologists struggled with a definition of acculturation as its conceptual definition became increasingly all encompassing. The Social Science Research Council appointed a team of experts to clarify the definition of what was included in the construct of acculturation. According to their published report in the *American Anthropologist*, "acculturation comprehends those phenomena which result when groups of individuals having different cultures come into continuous first-hand contact, with subsequent changes in the original cultural patterns of either or both groups" (Redfield, Linton, & Herskovitz, 1936, p. 149). This definition, as noted, included macro- to micro-level changes and phenomena; it was not exclusionary and it also included all that might change as a result of people from different cultures coming into contact. This distinction was important because anthropologists and psychologists soon followed by making it clear that psychological processes were a part of acculturation phenomena. Robert C. Pierce (a research psychologist) along with M. Margaret Clark and Christie W. Kiefer (both anthropologists) laid the groundwork for the first empirical measure of acculturation at the individual psychological level (Pierce, Clark, & Kiefer, 1972). Prior to their research, others had made serious efforts to measure cognitive ideologies relevant to acculturation. For example, Levinson and Huffman (1955) developed the Traditional Family Ideologies Scale, and Kluckholm and Strodtbeck (1961) created the Values Orientation Scale. These cognitive references of acculturation were not identified as "acculturation measures" per se but were, nonetheless, examples of measures that assessed cultural changes at the psychological level.

Several works by Chicana/o psychologists in the late 1970s were instrumental in focusing research on Chicana/os in the developing field of psychological acculturation. The first was the introduction of the Measure of Acculturation for Chicano Adolescents (Olmedo, Martinez, & Martinez, 1978; Olmedo & Padilla, 1978), the second was the *American Psychologist* article entitled "Acculturation: A psychometric perspective" by Olmedo (1979), and the third was the book entitled *Acculturation: Theory, Models, and Some New Findings* (Padilla, 1980). This book contained several important chapters, including contributions from Padilla (1980), which had very seminal theoretical and applied influences such as the idea of acculturative typologies. These three publications led to a proliferation of measures and research on acculturation, not only on Chicana/os, but through paradigmatic measures on acculturation in any two ethnic-cultural groups. (For a selected listing of trends and a chronology of acculturation and various ethnicity measures between 1955 and 1995, see Cuéllar, 2000c, and Roysircar-Sodowsky & Maestas, 2000.)

Ethnic identity as a concept and construct was growing in parallel to the concept of acculturation. How ethnic identity and acculturation relate to each other was, and continues to be, of much theoretical interest. Clark, Kaufman, and Pierce (1976), Cohen (1978), and Padilla (1980) argued that ethnic identity was a part of acculturation phenomena or, as Cohen noted, ethnicity arises from a situation of contact between different cultural groups. Ethnic identity is often discussed in terms of what determines what. Ethnic identity models and their measurement became the focus of acculturation research in the 1980s and 1990s. Some of the representative ethnic identity models developed were Phinney's Ethnic Identity Development Model (Phinney, 1989), Cross' (1991) Psychological Nigrescence Model, Helms' (1990) Racial Identity Model, and Knight-Bernal's Social Cognitive Model of Ethnic Identity Development (Knight, Bernal, Garza, & Cota, 1993). (Examples of ethnic identity measures were the Multigroup Ethnic Identity Measure or MEIM, Phinney, 1992, and the Ethnic Identity Questionnaire, Bernal, Knight, Ocampo, Garza, & Cota, 1993.)

A very significant methodological and theoretical contribution in the assessment of acculturation was made with what has been labeled variously as the "Two-Culture Matrix Model" (McFee, 1968; Ruiz, Casas, & Padilla, 1977; see also Keefe & Padilla, 1987), the "Orthogonal Model" (Oetting & Beauvais, 1991), or the "Two-Dimensional Model" (Buriel, 1993). In these models, each culture is conceived as a separate axis and their interaction as forming a matrix. Each person undergoing acculturation may vary independently in his or her exposure, acceptance, rejection, or adaptation with respect to each of the two cultures. This methodological advancement led to the psychometric assessment of bicultural adaptations including forms of integration and marginalization for the first time.

Among the contributions of acculturation research, both on and by Chicana/os and others in the field of acculturation, was the notion that the cultural context in which individuals grow up determines who they are, how they identify themselves, their psychological characteristics, and their sense of well-being. Berry (1994), a world-renowned giant in the field of acculturation, noted that acculturation processes, defined as those processes that allow one "to move toward a culture," change people in various ways and are commonly associated with some form of stress. In order to comprehend the influences of acculturation on the self, an ecological construction of culture and the individual is required (Cuéllar, 2000a).

Brief Review of Literature on Chicana/os and Latina/os and Acculturation

A review conducted by the authors of this chapter of published articles on MEDLINE and PsycINFO searches using "Acculturation and Hispanics" as keywords over the period of 1966 to 2001 found 996 ($n = 743$ unduplicated) articles. The largest category (40% or 401 hits) was that of health, followed by alcohol use (10.6% or 106 hits). Mental health represented 9.4% or 94 hits. A total of 56% (564) of the hits were found on MEDLINE and 44% (432) on the PsycINFO database. When other ethnic groups were included, the number of hits was truly incredible ($n = 4{,}122$) given the very limited interest in the subject of acculturation by psychologists prior to 1970.

Culture, Acculturation, and Mental Health

The concept of illness is far broader than that of disease and includes psychosocial and sociocultural influences, not traditionally thought of as being part of a disease (Kleinman, 1988). The lack of understanding of this difference hampered the understanding of the role of culture on health for many years. Culture has a profound impact on illness as well as disease, although not as directly on the latter. With the introduction of the biopsychosocial model

(Engel, 1977), a formal understanding of the role of psychosocial-cultural variables became more generally accepted. The influences of culture on mental health and its treatment have now been well documented (National Institute of Mental Health [NIMH], 1995; Cuéllar & Paniagua, 2000). Cultural influences have been found to be associated with numerous symptoms of well-being and adjustment and have etiological influence on many mental disorders as noted in the *Diagnostic and Statistical Manual of Mental Disorders-IV* (American Psychological Association, 1994). Clearly the role of culture and pathology extends far beyond specific culture-bound syndromes.

The relationship of acculturation to mental health has been increasingly researched and reviewed (Berry & Kim, 1988; Negy & Woods, 1992b; NIMH, 1995; Rogler, Cortes, & Malgady, 1991). The experience of living simultaneously within more than one cultural context has led to much speculation about coping with present, as well as potential cultural conflicts, particularly for members of racial, cultural, and ethnic minority groups. Speculation about the relation of acculturation to mental health can be traced to Stonequist's hypothesis (1935, 1937), which stipulated that being caught between two cultural groups, particularly with regard to "the system of mores," leads to mental tension and possible changes in self-concept or ethnic identity. Stonequist believed that psychologically marginalized individuals were at greater risk for, and experienced more, mental health related problems. Accommodations reached during acculturation processes can also have positive effects, including forms of biculturalism that lessen experiences of conflict (NIMH, p. 103). Very little is known about accommodations to acculturation with respect to their relative distribution, how they come about, or how they increase or decrease risk and vulnerability to health and mental health problems.

Mental Health and Acculturation of Latina/o Hispanics

There are increasing amounts of data pertaining to the effects of acculturation on Latina/o mental health. In fact, this area of research comprises the second largest number of hits when the words "acculturation," "Hispanic," and "mental health" are entered using the MEDLINE and PsycINFO databases. In the field of mental health, the three most common areas of research are depression, alienation and stress, and overall mental status. Not only have studies on these topics increased in number, variety, and complexity, but they have also become more intense as they elucidate either unequivocal or conflicting trends in this area of research.

Stemming from this extensive field of research are important trends that provide a better understanding of the overall mental status of Latina/os. For example, Mexican-born immigrants have consistently better mental health profiles than U.S.-born Mexican Americans when socioeconomic variables are controlled for (Escobar et al., 1988; Escobar, Hoyos-Nervi, & Gara, 2000). Among Mexican-born persons living in the U.S., less acculturated Mexican Americans have healthier psychological profiles than more acculturated Mexican Americans. A second consistent trend in this field is that "biculturalism," or an intermediate level of acculturation among Latina/os, is "the least detrimental to Latina/os' mental health" (Miranda & Umhoefer, 1998, p. 159). Another publication by Miranda supports previous work on the subject suggesting that "bicultural" Latina/os have better mental health profiles than both less and more acculturated Latina/os (Miranda, 1995). These studies emerge from the idea that depression increases and social interest decreases with increasing levels of acculturation (Miranda, Miranda, & Umhoefer, 1998).

Depression is probably the most commonly studied and conflicting aspect of Latina/o mental health. For example, Zamarian et al. (1992) pointed to a strong inverse relationship between acculturation and depression: They explain that apparent retention of Mexican culture without concomitant attempts to incorporate aspects of the dominant culture results in the most vulnerable position to depression. Recent work in this area by Gonzalez, Haan, and Hinton (2001) supports the idea that less acculturated Mexican Americans have a higher risk of depression than their highly acculturated counterparts. Along the same line, however, the evidence suggests that depression does not directly correlate with acculturation (Griffith, 1983). In fact, Griffith stated that socioeconomic status can best explain mental conditions such as anxiety among Latina/os. In accordance with this finding, subsequent research by Canabal and Quiles (1995) demonstrates that socioeconomic variables, including education, age, and employment, have a significantly stronger correlation than acculturation with depression among Latina/os. Interestingly, a dissertational study by Duran (1995) suggests that more acculturated Latinas exhibit a higher degree of somatization of depressive symptoms than less acculturated Latinas. The same study then explains that somatization is a cultural modality to elicit support and, consequently, is not associated with depression among less acculturated individuals.

Data on "alienation" and its effects on stress among Latina/os offer a complex and confounding view of the effects of alienation among Latina/os. For example, one study by Kaplan and Marks (1990) suggested that distress symptoms increase significantly with higher levels of acculturation among young adults, but not among older adults. The same study then asserted that higher levels of acculturation are directly correlated with more feelings of alienation and discrimination among young Latina/os. On the contrary, Negy and Woods (1992b) showed that feelings of alienation have an inverse relationship with increasing levels of acculturation.

Immigration and Mental Health

The Immigrant Paradigm of Acculturation has as its subject an adult immigrant living in the U.S. who acquires characteristics of the host culture in order to adapt, function, and prosper in the new culture (cf. Cuéllar, 2000b). For many second-, third-, and fourth-generation minority group members, acculturation experiences are bicultural and the Immigrant Paradigm does not apply, but the Minority Paradigm of Acculturation does. In the Minority Paradigm of Acculturation, the minority individual is "acculturating" and "enculturating" with regards to at least two cultures throughout his or her lifespan. The Minority Paradigm emphasizes biculturalism and bicognitive adaptation and subjects are required to acculturate simultaneously, but in varying degrees, to both their ethnic traditional culture and mainstream American culture.

A subject of growing interest in acculturation research is the effect of American culture on the immigrant who is undergoing acculturation based on the Immigrant Paradigm of Acculturation. Suarez-Orozco (1997) noted that an increasing number of studies show that the new immigrant from Mexico displays better mental health and a healthier attitude toward wanting to do well in school and graduate from college than third-generation U.S.-born Chicana/os.

Suarez-Orozco (1997) was not the only investigator to note that new immigrants sometimes have better mental health than more acculturated Chicana/os. Vega et al. (1998) compared adjusted lifetime prevalence rates for various mental disorders using the Composite International Diagnostic Inventory (CIDI) of Mexican immigrants with native-born Mexican Americans. The results show that the native-born lifetime prevalence rate for any disorder (48.1%) is twice that of the immigrants (24.9%). Vega et al. also concluded that short-term-stay immigrants (< 13 years) have almost half the lifetime prevalence rates for any disorder than long-term immigrants, those having lived in the U.S. for more than 13 years. In comparing the lifetime prevalence rates for Mexicans in Mexico City with short-term immigrants, long-term immigrants, and native-born Mexican-origin populations, they found that prevalence rates increase with increased acculturation to the U.S. culture. Additionally, they discovered that individuals of Mexican origin who were born and raised in the U.S. or who had lived the longest there had higher prevalence rates of depression, affective disorders, and psychiatric disorders than those who were born in Mexico or who had lived the longest in Mexico.

Obesity and Related Diseases and Acculturation in Latina/o Hispanics

An important health concern affecting the increasing mortality rates of the Hispanic population is the upsurge of hypertension and diabetes. Despite the significance of diabetes and cardiovascular-related diseases for Latina/os, these problems are not heavily represented in current research.

The current literature findings on nutrition and acculturation appears to demonstrate a positive correlation between acculturation towards the U.S. culture and better nutrition. For example, Woodruff, Zaslow, Candelaria, and Elder (1997) showed that Hispanics who identified themselves as being highly acculturated were more likely to avoid fat, cholesterol, and high-calorie foods in their diet. Those Latina/os who fell under the less acculturated group were more likely to eat fruits, rice, beans, meat, and fried foods and to drink whole milk than more acculturated Latina/os (Otero-Sabogal, Sabogal, Perez-Stable, & Hiatt, 1995).

In addition to healthier food consumption, the highly acculturated Latina/os exhibited more knowledge about nutrition. Vega, Sallis, Patterson, Atkins, and Nader (1987) showed that Hispanic children with high parental acculturation levels have an increased awareness of health behavior knowledge and are likely to be more knowledgeable about the importance of exercise.

Given their lack of awareness about a healthy lifestyle, it should follow that less acculturated Latina/os are more obese than those in the highly acculturated group, but some of the literature on obesity appears to contradict this hypothesis (Hazuda, Haffner, Stem, & Eifler, 1988). In Hispanic males and females obesity and acculturation are inversely related. In a related study, Khan, Sobal, and Martorell (1997) found that Latinas with a greater preference for speaking English (highly acculturated group) have a reduced Body Mass Index in comparison to the less acculturated group.

Interestingly enough, Sundquist and Winkleby's (2001) findings were conflicting. They used an individual's waist circumference to monitor obesity and found that acculturation status was positively associated with waist circumference and abdominal obesity: subjects in the most highly acculturated group had the largest waist circumference. In addition to being more obese, this study found that the highly acculturated group was more likely to suffer from non-insulin-dependent diabetes, hypertension, or high fat and cholesterol levels.

In terms of diseases, most studies found that acculturation led to higher rates of hypertension and that it was a greater predictor of hypertension than socioeconomic status (Espino & Maldonado, 1990). Markides, Lee, and Ray (1993) suggested that middle-aged Latino men in the moderate acculturated group had higher rates of hypertension than men in the less acculturated group.

The influence of acculturation and diabetes proves to be inconclusive. Stern et al. (1991) pointed out that the prevalence of Type II diabetes declines with acculturation toward the values, attitudes, and behaviors of American society. Other evidence suggests that greater acculturation, higher educational attainment, and higher diabetes prevalence are associated (Weller et al., 1999).

From these contradictory findings, one can see that more research is needed in this area. Because cardiovascular disease is the leading cause of mortality for Latina/os, researchers must strive to find valid conclusions regarding the effects of acculturation on heart-related diseases such as hypertension and diabetes.

In addition to more research, there is also a need for the development of better scales for acculturation. Once again, the general trend of acculturation measurements seems to be the preferred language spoken. This type of scale proves to be inefficient for measuring the full realm of acculturation. In order to obtain a full scope of the Hispanic community, more work must focus on the health and development of this growing population within the American culture.

Substance Abuse and Acculturation in Chicana/o Hispanics

There are three major areas of interest in the study of Latino acculturation and substance abuse: alcohol use, tobacco use, and use of other drugs such as marijuana and crack cocaine. Current research shows an overwhelmingly large disparity between acculturation and the practices of substance use as well as an increase of substance abuse within the Latina population.

Research links an increase in the use and abuse of alcohol with a higher degree of acculturation. A common finding suggests that acculturation is positively correlated with the frequency of alcohol consumption as well as the probability of being a drinker (Black & Markides, 1993). In a study by Cherpitel (1992), Latinos with a higher level of acculturation were more likely to have an alcohol-related injury resulting in the need for hospital emergency care.

Studies have found that highly acculturated Latinos share drinking behaviors with the non-Hispanic White subjects, who tend to have a more liberal view of alcohol and its consumption (Marin, 1996). In research done by Neff, Hoppe, and Perea (1987), less acculturated Mexican Americans consumed alcohol less frequently but in higher quantities than Whites. This suggests that less acculturated Mexican Americans consume higher amounts of alcohol, but less habitually than the more acculturated Mexican Americans.

Motivation behind drinking also varies for the acculturated groups. In the least acculturated group, expectations of emotional and behavioral impairment as well as an increase in social extroversion were found to motivate alcohol consumption (Marin, Posner, & Kinyon, 1993). Like non-Hispanic Whites, the more highly acculturated groups were not as likely to be motivated by social extroversion or ideas of escape, which led Neff et al. (1987) to conclude that less acculturated Latina/os are at higher risk for heavy, problem drinking.

Acculturation plays a further role in the differences of alcohol-related behaviors. Results of a study done by Hines and Caetano (1998) linked excessive alcohol consumption with risky sexual behavior: Less acculturated men engage in heavy drinking and are more likely to employ risky sexual behaviors than the highly acculturated group. This study also showed that less acculturated women engaged in riskier sexual behavior even though the highly acculturated group of Hispanic women consumed more alcohol.

The influence of American cultural values affects alcohol use more for acculturated females than for males. Evidence shows that acculturated females have more drinks in their lifetime, and more acculturated males and females are more likely to binge drink in the last 30 days than the less acculturated group

(Lovato, Litrownik, Elder, & Nunez-Liriano, 1994). Findings suggest that there is more open-mindedness and validation for alcohol consumption with the more acculturated group of Latinas, leading to an increase in alcohol use.

Acculturation is also influential in tobacco use. Sabogal et al. (1989) found that more acculturated Hispanics have higher levels of nicotine addiction and smoke more cigarettes and that, among the highly acculturated Hispanics, the self-efficacy to avoid smoking and lower levels of addiction show that Hispanics as a whole are more likely to quit smoking and avoid relapse compared to non-Hispanic Whites.

Gender is another determining factor for smoking. Epstein, Botvin, and Diaz (1998) showed that adolescent Hispanic females smoke more frequently than adolescent males and that acculturation is an associated factor of smoking. In addition, smoking during pregnancy, low birth weight, and preterm delivery are associated with Latinas with a moderate level of acculturation more than less acculturated women (Wolff & Portis, 1996),

It has been found that the higher the level of acculturation, the lower the level of drug use (Garcia, 1999). Wagner-Echeagaray, Schuetz, Chilcoat, and Anthony (1994) pointed out that, among Mexican Americans, the higher the degree of acculturation, the less likely the subjects were to have used crack cocaine. In the case of marijuana use, however, the results differ: Adolescents who were more acculturated smoked marijuana more frequently than those who were less acculturated (Epstein, Botvin, & Diaz, 2001).

Many of the researchers dealing with acculturation and substance abuse failed to include the tools used to measure acculturation within their reports. The scales that were included were generally described as some form of linguistic acculturation, meaning that they rated acculturation based on whether the subject was interviewed in Spanish or English or if the subject spoke Spanish to his or her parents (Epstein et al., 2001). Other researchers, such as Lessenger (1997), used the Acculturation Rating Scale for Mexican Americans-II (ARSMA-II) to study the relation between acculturation and substance abuse.

Measuring acculturation based on language falls short of truly capturing a Latina/o's adoption of American culture, especially considering the current trend of code switching, where Latina/os combine English and Spanish in their speech. Thus, new research should focus on the development of new and legitimate methods to measure acculturation so that the various levels of acculturation can be taken into consideration.

As an overall trend, research demonstrates that acculturation may have negative effects on the Latino population. The increased use of substances, both legal and illegal, in association with the increased acculturation of Latinos presents a problem. Although we know that there is an increase in substance abuse, we do not know the reason why. Is it a result of stress? Is it an attempt to belong to the predominant culture? Now that research points out a disparity between the acculturated groups of Latina/os, it needs to search for the reasons why such changes occur in the adoption of American cultural values. With these answers in hand, more effective means of promoting drug awareness and successful treatment programs can be developed to prevent Latina/os from falling victim to substance abuse.

HIV and AIDS and Acculturation in Latina/o Hispanics

The relatively high number of HIV and AIDS cases among racial minorities indicates a need for the modification and improvement of campaign prevention efforts within these groups. In response to the epidemiological trends pertaining to HIV and AIDS and Latina/os, research has focused on the effects of acculturation and

HIV and AIDS, especially during the 1990s. The published work concentrates on acculturation and its effects on high-risk behaviors and knowledge about the disease. For example, Marin and Marin (1990) indicated that less acculturated Latina/os had more erroneous beliefs about "casual" transmission and were less aware that someone can be infected without being ill. In accordance with this finding, Dawson (1995) concluded that acculturation serves as a predictor of AIDS-related beliefs of moralism, blame, and perceived control over contracting AIDS. Based on these data, one would then expect to see an inverse relationship between acculturation and high-risk behavior, but the literature suggests that this is not the case. According to some researchers, higher levels of acculturation augment risk behaviors for AIDS (Peragallo, 1996; Rapkin & Erickson, 1990) as well as the likelihood of being engaged in unsafe sexual practices (Marks, Cantero, & Simoni, 1998; Rapkin & Erickson).

An important characteristic of the studies found on the MEDLINE and PsycINFO databases is that they vary widely in methodology (e.g., sample size, age and gender of the subjects, type of surveys). Although this contributes to the diversity of research on the subject, it unfortunately confounds the results. The research on HIV and AIDS focuses largely on the need to target interventions in a culturally appropriate manner, but it also strives to improve the effectiveness of campaigns aimed at lowering the incidence of HIV transmission among Latina/os. One drawback is that, outside the realm of Latina/o knowledge and popular beliefs about HIV and AIDS, present research on trends pertaining to specific behavioral practices (e.g., condom use, sharing needles) is lacking.

A significant number of these studies, however, do not follow a standard form of measurement for the acculturation variable. Most published materials see acculturation in terms of language use and language preference, thereby minimizing the effects of other cultural components (e.g., customs and beliefs) on HIV and AIDS knowledge and risk behavior. They also hinder the cross-analysis of published materials among investigators. Accordingly, researchers are encouraged to continue their efforts to better understand the effects of acculturation on HIV and AIDS and to incorporate the use of standard measures or scales of acculturation.

Acculturation and Women's Health

The most commonly researched aspect of women's health is reproductive health, particularly breast and cervical cancer. In fact, most of the research materials found using the MEDLINE and PsycINFO search engines and the words "acculturation," "Hispanic," and "cancer" retrieved information relevant to pap smear and mammogram screening practices. Investigations in this area suggest that less acculturated women, especially Spanish-speaking women, have less knowledge about pap smear examinations and fewer cervical cancer screenings (Harmon, Castro, & Coe, 1996; O'Malley, Kerner, Johnson, & Mandelblatt, 1999; Peragallo, Fox, & Alba, 2000; Suarez, 1994; Suarez & Pulley, 1995). Ruiz, Marks, and Richardson (1992) studied the effects of acculturation on exposure to health information found in reading materials, television, and radio. They suggested that understanding and preference for the English language is positively correlated with exposure to "media-based health information," which, in turn, increases the knowledge and use of cancer screening practices among Latinas.

A second important trend in Latina women's health is that women with stronger traditional Mexican attitudes toward their family have increased rates of mammogram screenings (Suarez, 1994; Suarez & Pulley, 1995). Other studies state that access to health care (i.e., health insurance) and prior screening practices are more strongly associated with reproductive health screening among Latinas than accultural factors (Zambrana, Breen, Fox, & Gutierrez-Mohamed, 1999). These findings have important implications for planning and designing effective programs to increase the utilization of breast and cervical cancer screening among Latinas in the U.S.

Like acculturation research on HIV and AIDS, the available literature on women's health uses various types of sample groups with respect to recruitment for participation, socioeconomic and demographic variables, and sample sizes. Although most of the materials relative to women's health emphasize the utilization of cancer screening programs, there are data that focus on other aspects of women's health and, more recently, on children's health. These include acculturation research on desired family size (Marin, Marin, & Padilla, 1981), attitudes about sex-role behavior (Kranau, Green, & Valencia-Weber, 1982), beliefs about breastfeeding (Thiel de Bocanegra, 1998), beliefs about immunization (Prislin, Suarez, Simpson, & Dyer, 1998), and low birth weight (Scribner & Dwyer, 1989). It is noteworthy that a significant number of these published studies rely on information obtained from the Hispanic Health and Nutrition Examination Survey (HHANES) for data analysis.

Unlike acculturation studies that focus on HIV and AIDS, studies on cancer screening practices among Latinas use a variety of measures for acculturation. For example, Suarez and Pulley (1995) compared two different acculturation scales, namely, an abbreviated version of Cuéllar's Acculturation Rating Scale for Mexican Americans (ARSMA) and the Hazuda scale, in order to study cancer screening practices among older Mexican American women. Another study, Suarez (1994), used five different subscales, including: English use, English proficiency, value placed on culture, traditional family attitudes, and social interaction, as measures of acculturation. Despite the increasing use of acculturation scales, however, the most common determinant for acculturation in women's health research is use of the English language. Moreover, no studies with a focus on women's health found on the MEDLINE or PsycINFO search engines used the Orthogonal Model (Oetting & Beauvais, 1991) or the "Two-Dimensional Model" (Buriel, 1993) as standard measures for acculturation.

Another significant limitation of previous research is the lack of information about the screening practices for other types of cancers, such as prostate cancer in men. Although there are data available on acculturation and its effects on diet and tobacco use, there are hardly any studies that focus directly on acculturation and colon cancer or lung cancer among Latina/os. The results of these studies would provide information for health practitioners, researchers, and campaign coordinators about health belief models and cancer screening practices for the Latino population.

Issues in Acculturation Measurement and Research

The number one issue in acculturation measurement is still: How does one measure culture when culture is a construct whose very definition is unclear? The answer to this question is complicated by numerous factors, including the fact that there is no such thing as a pure culture. Rather, culture is an amorphous entity, neither static nor unidimensional. Although the components of culture (food, language, music, customs, beliefs, values, behaviors, gender roles, ideologies, beliefs, practices, etc.) are not definable as concrete entities with set parameters and descriptions, there are definable differences between and among cultures and their respective components.

Culture is a complex concept, much like personality and intelligence, difficult to define yet clearly important and useful as a psychological construct. A serious problem with the acculturation construct is that it can be misused or misdefined, leading to simplistic and erroneous assumptions about it and its influences. The myths surrounding culture abound and can be very problematic (Cuéllar & Glazer, 1996; Mumford, 1981). The development of acculturation scales exemplifies the misconstruction of culture. The very first scales had items like "Who was Pedro Infante?" measuring Mexican culture, which is comparable to "Who was Louis Armstrong?" on an American intelligence test. These items relating to education and history can become outdated very easily. The item "Who was Pedro Infante?" relates to cultural heritage, but not necessarily cultural identity. Likewise, language items may assess only one component of acculturation. Like the construct of intelligence, the construct of acculturation is composed of multiple factors, in which people demonstrate varying degrees of strengths, weaknesses, capacities, and abilities. There is no single test that assesses all the components of acculturation. Cognitions, emotions, and behaviors play a role in the processes of acculturation. Acculturation, like the construct of stress, is both an exogenous and an endogenous construct, that is, its influences can be external factors or variables that include macrochanges in the world around us. Acculturation can also be an endogenous concept in that it represents learned behavior, feelings, or thought processes (internalized referents of what has transpired in our outside world, of which we are a part). The internal referents of acculturation are the same as the psychological correlates that result from acquiring aspects of the culture(s) to which one is exposed. Verbal abilities appear to be particularly important in assessing both learning and acculturation, but nonverbal behaviors can be just as important.

One of the simplest and earliest definitions of culture was one proposed by Linton (1936): "learned behavior passed on from one generation to the next." Intelligence also once had a simple definition, provided by Binet and Simon (1905): "Intelligence is our capacity to make adaptations" to our environment. Likewise, personality was described as a "variety of characteristics whose unique organization define an individual" (Domino, 2000, p. 69). Although enormously complex and difficult to define and measure, the construct of acculturation, like the constructs of intelligence and personality, continues to have considerable construct validity and can be measured both reliably and validly when operationally defined.

New Directions in Acculturation

Acculturative Typologies and Psychological Functioning

There have been few studies demonstrating the validity of typologies generated from orthogonal measurement, but this should soon change. The lead author of the present chapter has been involved in an ongoing program of acculturation research that demonstrates significant psychological differences in individuals representing various acculturative typologies. Two of these studies are briefly described here.

Study 1. This study was carried out on a sample of 1,865 freshmen students in southern Texas. These young adults, 95% of whom were of Mexican origin, were administered the ARSMA-II (Scale 1) and various other tests including measures of ethnic identity, self-esteem, loneliness, stress, and depression. These subjects were categorized into four acculturative typologies using the cutting scores defined by Cuéllar, Arnold, and Maldonado (1995). Only 46.2% ($n =$ 865) were classified based on the four-way classification schema. The numbers and percentages classified were: traditional 12.5% ($n = 235$), marginal 8.9% ($n = 167$), highly integrated bicultural 19.6% ($n = 368$), and assimilated 5.1% ($n =$ 368). Stress was measured using an abbreviated and adapted version of the Hispanic Stress inventory (Cervantes, Padilla, & Salgado de Synder, 1991). Self-esteem was measured using an eight-item version of Rosenberg's (1965, 1979) self-esteem scale. Loneliness was measured using the Roberts UCLA Loneliness Scale-8 (RULS-8, Roberts, Lewinsohn, & Seely, 1993). Depression was measured using the DSM Scale for Depression-26 (DSD-26, Cuéllar & Roberts, 1997). The results in Figure 1 show significant differences in patterns for each of the typologies based on psychological functioning. Specifically, significant differences were found for stress, $F(3,757) = 6.09, p = < .0005$; loneliness, $F(3,844) =$ 6.47, $p = < .0005$; and self-esteem, $F(3,860) =$ 5.298, $p = < .0005$. Depression was not found to vary significantly among the groups.

The results from Study 1 show convincingly that each acculturative typology has a distinct psychological profile and mental health risk. The low acculturation or marginal acculturative typology shows the highest risk and the highly integrated bicultural typology shows the lowest risk or best psychological profile.

Study 2. This study involved 2,686 Hispanic adolescents also from the Lower Rio Grande

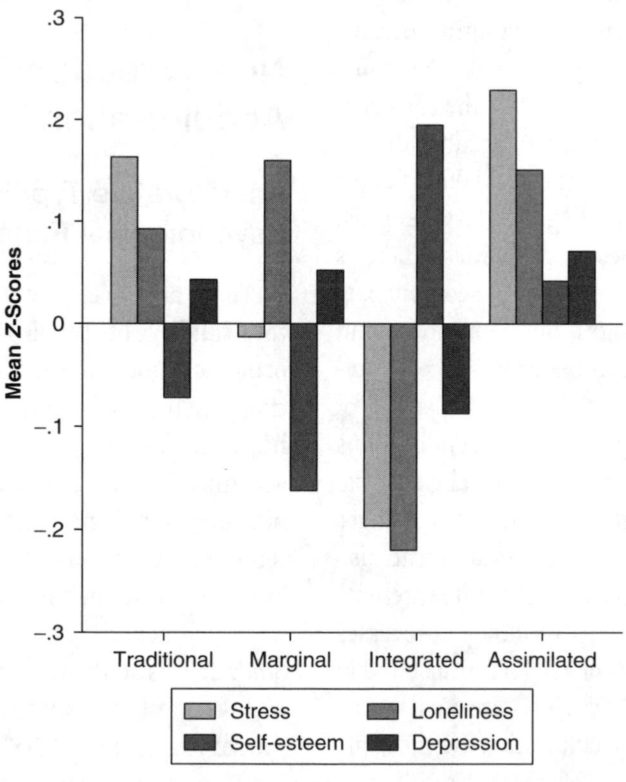

Figure 1 Study 1: Young Chicana/o Latina/o Adults' Acculturative Types and Psychological Scores

Valley of southern Texas along the U.S.-Mexico border. These adolescents were administered an abbreviated 12-item version of Scale 1 of the ARSMA-II, along with several measures of psychosocial functioning including ethnic identity, stress, depression, and family social support. These students were categorized into four acculturative typologies using the same cutting scores defined by Cuéllar, Arnold, and Maldonado (1995). A total of 1,651 subjects were classified, representing 61.5% of the total. Representation by typology was as follows: traditional 8.4% ($n = 226$), marginal 25.8% ($n = 694$), highly integrated bicultural 5.1% ($n = 138$), assimilated 22.1% ($n = 593$). Ethnic identity was measured using the Multigroup Ethnic Identity Measure (MEIM, Phinney, 1992). Self-esteem was measured by the eight-item Abbreviated Rosenberg Scale; stress was measured using a 26-item event scale assessing stressful events related to school, family, friends, and neighborhood. Depression was measured using the DSM Scale for Depression (DSD-26) and social support was measured by the Multidimensional Scale of Perceived Social Support (Zimet, Dahlem, Zimet, & Farley, 1988).

The results are shown in Figure 2. Clear patterns are discernable for the various typologies by psychological functioning with the high bicultural typology showing the most favorable pattern and the marginal typology showing the highest risk pattern. The differences among the four typologies were significant for each of the four dependent measures. One-way ANOVA analyses were as follows: self-esteem, $F(3,1445) = 17.72, p < .0005$; depression, $F(3,1245) = 437, p < .05$; social support, $F(3,1009) = 14.264, p < .0005$; ethnic identity, $F(3,1375) = 17.847, p < .0005$; stress, $F(3,1016) = 3.468, p < .05$.

The results from Study 2 showed that each acculturative typology appears to have a distinct profile with respect to risk for mental health and adjustment problems. However, the findings in Study 1 and Study 2 are not consistent across all dependent measures. The highly biculturals in the adolescent sample represented a much lower percentage of all typologies than at the young adult level. Yet, the highly bicultural typology in both studies stood out as clearly having a better overall profile than the other three typologies. Likewise, the marginal typology appeared to be at greater risk in both samples. Clearly the highly bicultural typology has the better sense of ethnic identity, but an interesting finding is that the highly bicultural group in the adolescent sample reported higher stress and depression despite having higher self-esteem and social support.

A point to consider with respect to both Study 1·and 2 is that linear correlations between acculturation and the various measures used did not reveal other than a few weak significant relations. The point is that the relations of acculturation and mental health are not always linear and the use of orthogonal measures of acculturation is needed in order to fully reveal and understand them.

Acculturation as a Moderator Variable in Clinical Practice

A growing area of interest is the use of acculturation measures to assist in developing or providing culturally appropriate and competent health and mental health care. Because not all Chicana/o Latinos are the same, they should not be stereotyped or treated in the same way. Therefore, it becomes necessary to assess the acculturation characteristics of the client in order to apply the most culturally tailored and appropriate services. Professional assessment practices in psychology mandate providing linguistically and culturally appropriate services to linguistically and culturally diverse populations. Acculturation assessment provides a means to assist in these practices, although the

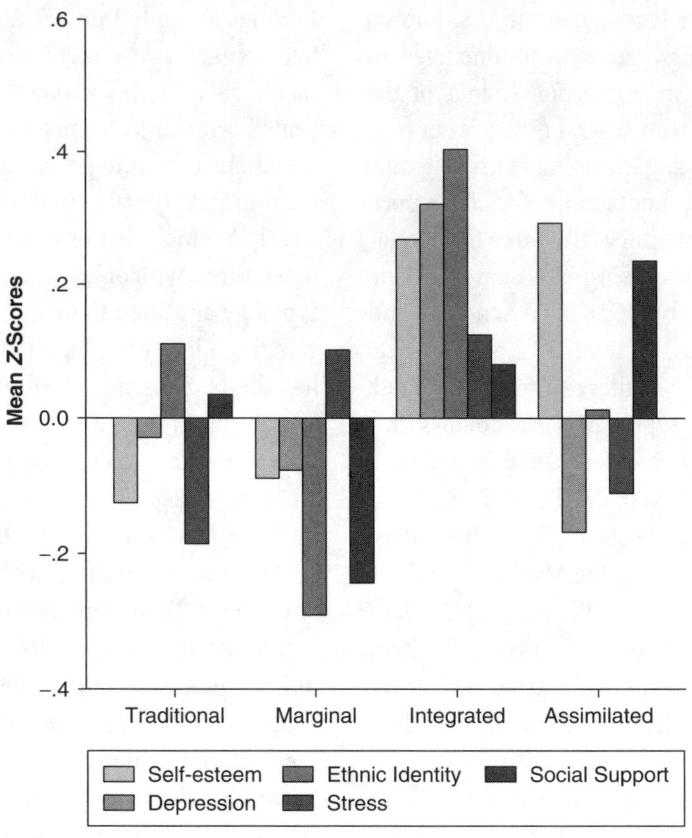

Figure 2 Chicana/o Latina/o Adolescents

methodologies and approaches are still in the developmental stages. Acculturation scores can be used for assigning clinicians to match for understanding, language, culture, and sensitivity. This practice has been going on informally for years and is now becoming more widely practiced as it has some clear benefits in terms of effectiveness of and compliance with treatment.

In order to make assignments to treatment in response to culturally competent practices, acculturation assessment is justifiable and useful. The history of intellectual and personality assessment reveals a gradual increase in understanding of the influence of such variables as gender, socioeconomic status, and ethnicity on the norms, standardization, and psychometrics of psychological tests. One approach has been to eliminate items that reflect bias (differential item functioning) against a particular subgroup; another has been to develop representative standardization for normative reference groups. Other methods have developed separate normative groups using the same instrument, an emic measure of the construct being developed with a specific cultural group, or various combinations of each of these approaches. Although these approaches appear useful, they are very expensive, work intensive, and often very difficult to achieve. An alternate approach suggested by Dana (1993) is to use moderator variables to achieve these aims. Acculturation measurement is used as a gauge to assess the extent to which the person (i.e., Chicana/o) being assessed differs from the normative sample used in the development of a particular instrument (Cuéllar, 1998, 2000c). The scores on the standardized instrument are adjusted or corrected for culture according to the direction and strength of the correlation between acculturation and the psychological construct being assessed. Obviously, this "correction for culture" is an index that requires some empirical foundation in order to perform or calculate. However, this does not prevent clinicians from making a clinical judgment as to the direction and magnitude of such a correction. This clinical judgment can be justified on the basis that the null hypothesis (that there is no effect for culture) is no longer defensible.

The intent of the present chapter has been to provide a brief review of the continuing relevance of the construct of acculturation to both the field of psychology and the subspecialty of Chicana/o psychology. Chicana/o psychology has taken an important lead in the development and construction of acculturation instruments and in furthering the understanding of the role of culture and ethnicity on human development psychological adjustment, mental health, health, and treatment. There has been an explosion in the development of measures of acculturation and ethnic identity in minorities, not just in the U.S., but throughout the world. As the U.S. and other countries experience increased globalization and cultural pluralism, the study of multicultural personality development has gained significance. Of increased concern is how multicultural environments affect human development and functioning. The field of Chicana/o psychology, through its enlightenment of acculturation processes, has played an important role in furthering understanding of cultural influences on such important areas as: appropriate utilization of services, health disparities, folk illness ideologies, appropriate assessment and treatment, stages of ethnic identity, mental health, substance abuse, manifestation of symptoms, culture-bound syndromes, gender roles, and cultural competence, among numerous others. Additionally, acculturation has important ramifications for the fields of cross-cultural, clinical, and community psychology. It is our conclusion that there is strong evidence for the continuing relevance of the construct of acculturation for both psychology and Chicana/o psychology.

References

American Psychiatric Association. (1994). *Diagnostic and statistical manual of mental disorders* (4th ed.). Washington, DC: Author.

Bernal, M. E., Knight, G. P., Ocampo, K. A., Garza, C.A., & Cota, M. K. (1993). Development of Mexican American identity. In M. E. Bernal &. G. P. Knight (Eds.), *Ethnic identity: Formation and transmission among Hispanics and other minorities* (pp. 32–46). Albany: State University of New York Press.

Berry, J. (1994). Acculturative stress. In W. J. Lonner & R. Malpass (Eds.), *Psychology and culture* (pp. 211–215). Needham Heights, MA: Allyn & Bacon.

Berry, J., & Kim, U. (1988). Acculturation and mental health. In P. Dasen, J. W. Berry, & N. Sartorious (Eds.), *Health and cross-cultural psychology: Towards application* (pp. 207–236). London: Sage.

Binet, A., & Simon, T. (1905). Méthodes nouvelles pour le diagnostic du niveau intellectuel des anormaux. *L'Année Psychologique, 11*, 191–244.

Black, S. A., & Markides, K. S. (1993). Acculturation and alcohol consumption in Puerto Rican, Cuban-American, and Mexican American women in the United States. *American Journal of Public Health, 83*, 890–893.

Buriel, R. (1993). Acculturation, respect for cultural differences, and biculturalism among three generations of Mexican American and Euro American school children. *Journal of Genetic Psychology, 154*, 531–543.

Canabal, M. E., & Quiles, J. A. (1995). Acculturation and socioeconomic factors as determinants of depression among Puerto Ricans in the United States. *Social Behavior and Personality, 23,* 235–248.

Cervantes, R. C, Padilla, A. M., & Salgado de Snyder, V. M. (1991). The Hispanic Stress Inventory: A culturally relevant approach to psychosocial assessment. *Psychological Assessment, 3,* 438–447.

Cherpitel, C. J. (1992). Acculturation, alcohol consumption, and casualties among United States Hispanics in the emergency room. *International Journal of the Addictions, 27,* 1067–1077.

Clark, M., Kaufman, S., & Pierce, R. (1976). Explorations of acculturation: Toward a model of ethnic identity. *Human Organization, 35,* 231–238.

Cohen, R. (1978). Ethnicity: Problem and focus in anthropology. *Annual Review of Anthropology, 7,* 379–403.

Cross, W. (1991). *Shades of Black: Diversity in African American identity*. Philadelphia: Temple University Press.

Cuéllar, I. (1998). Cross-cultural clinical psychological assessment of Hispanic Americans. *Journal of Personality Assessment, 70,* 71–86.

Cuéllar, I. (2000a). Acculturation and mental health: Ecological transactional relations of adjustment. In I. Cuéllar & F. A. Paniagua (Eds.), *Handbook of multicultural mental health: Assessment and treatment of diverse populations* (pp. 45–62). San Diego, CA: Academic Press.

Cuéllar, I. (2000b). Acculturation and mental health: Ecological transactional relations of adjustment. In I. Cuéllar & F. A. Paniagua (Eds.), *Multicultural mental health* (pp. 45–62). San Diego, CA: Academic Press.

Cuéllar, I. (2000c). Acculturation as a moderator of personality and psychological assessment. In R. Dana (Ed.), *Handbook of cross-cultural and multicultural personality assessment* (pp. 113–129). Mahwah, NJ: Lawrence Erlbaum Associates.

Cuéllar, I., Arnold, B., & Maldonado, R. (1995). The Acculturation Rating Scale for Mexican Americans-II: A revision of the original ARSMA scale. *Hispanic Journal of Behavioral Sciences, 27*(3), 275–304.

Cuéllar, I., & Glazer, M. (1996). The impact of culture on the family. In M. Harway (Ed.), *Treating the changing family: Handling normative and unusual events* (pp. 17–36). New York: Wiley and Sons.

Cuéllar, I., & Paniagua, F. A. (2000). *Handbook of multicultural mental health: Assessment and treatment of diverse populations*. San Diego, CA: Academic Press.

Cuéllar, I., & Roberts, R. E. (1997). Relations of depression, acculturation, and socioeconomic status in a Latino sample. *Hispanic Journal of Behavioral Sciences, 19*(2), 230–238.

Dana, R. (1993). *Multicultural assessment perspectives for professional psychology*. Boston: Allyn and Bacon.

Dawson, E. J. (1995). Acculturation as a predictor of parents' and children's attitudes and knowledge of HIV/AIDS in a multicultural population. *Sciences and Engineering, 56,* 0564.

Duran, D. G. (1995). The impact of depression, psychological factors, cultural determinants, and the patient/care-provider relationship on somatic complaints of the distressed Latina. *Dissertation Abstracts International, 56*(6A), 2428.

Engel, G. L. (1977). Need for a new medical model—challenge for medicine. *Science, 296*(4286), 129–136.

Epstein, J. A., Botvin, G. J., & Diaz, T. (1998). Linguistic acculturation and gender effects on smoking among Hispanic youth. *Preventative Medicine: An International Journal Devoted to Practice and Theory, 27,* 683–689.

Epstein, J. A., Botvin, G. J., & Diaz, T. (2001). Linguistic acculturation associated with higher marijuana and polydrug use among Hispanic adolescents. *Substance Abuse and Misuse, 36,* 477–499.

Escobar, J. I, Hoyos-Nervi, C, & Gara, M. A. (2000). Immigration and mental health: Mexican

Americans in the United States. *Harvard Review of Psychiatry, 8*, 64–72.

Escobar, J. I., Karno, M., Burnam, A., Hough, R. L., & Golding, J. (1988). Distribution of major mental disorders in an US metropolis. *ACTA Psychiatrica Scandinavica, 78*(Suppl. 344), 45–53.

Espino, D. V., & Maldonado, D. (1990). Hypertension and acculturation in elderly Mexican Americans: Results from 1982–84 Hispanic HANES. *Journal of Gerontology, 45*, 209–213.

Garcia, S. E. (1999). Substance abuse, acculturation, and alienation among Hispanic adolescents. *Dissertation Abstracts International, 60*,3B.

Gonzalez, H. M., Haan, M. N., & Hinton, L. (2001). Acculturation and the prevalence of depression in older Mexican Americans: Baseline results of the Sacramento area Latino study on aging. *Journal of the American Geriatrics Society, 49*, 948–953.

Gowen, L. K., Hayward, C, Killien, J. D., Robinson, T. R, & Taylor, C. B. (1999). Acculturation and eating disorder symptoms in adolescent girls. *Journal of Research on Adolescence, 9*, 67–83.

Griffith, J. (1983). Relationship between acculturation and psychological impairment in adult Mexican Americans. *Hispanic Journal of Behavioral Sciences, 5*, 431–459.

Harmon, M. P., Castro, F. G., & Coe, K. (1996). Acculturation and cervical cancer knowledge, beliefs and behaviors of Hispanic women. *Women and Health, 24*(3), 37–58.

Hazuda, H. P., Haffner, S. M., Stern, M. P., & Eifler, C. W. (1998). Effects of acculturation and socioeconomic status on obesity and diabetes in Mexican Americans. *American Journal of Epidemiology, 128*,1289–1301.

Helms, J. (1990). *Black and White racial identity: Theory, research, and practice*. New York: Oxford University Press.

Hines, A. M., & Caetano, R. (1998). Alcohol and AIDS-related behavior among Hispanics: Acculturation and gender differences. *AIDS Education and Prevention, 10*, 533–547.

Kaplan, M., & Marks, G. (1990). Adverse effects of acculturation: Psychological distress among Mexican American young adults. *Social Science and Medicine, 31*, 1313–1319.

Keefe, S. E., & Padilla, A. M. (1987). *Chicano ethnicity*. Albuquerque: University of New Mexico Press.

Khan, L. K., Sobal, J., & Martorell, R. (1997). Acculturation, socioeconomic status, and obesity in Mexican Americans, Cuban Americans, and Puerto Ricans. *International Journal of Obesity and Related Metabolic Disorders, 21*(2), 91–96.

Kleinman, A. (1988). *The illness narratives: Suffering, healing and the human condition*. New York: Basic Books.

Kluckholm, F. R., & Strodtbeck, F. L. (1961). *Variations in value orientations*. Homewood, IL: Dorsey.

Knight, G., Bernal, M., Garza, C., & Cota, M. K. (1993). A social cognitive model of ethnic identity and ethnically based behaviors. In M. E. Bernal & G. P. Knight (Eds.), *Ethnic identity: Formation and transmission among Hispanics and other minorities* (pp. 213–234). Albany: State University of New York Press.

Kranau, E. J., Green, V., & Valencia-Weber, G. (1982). Acculturation and the Hispanic woman: Attitudes toward women, sex-role attribution, sex-role behavior, and demographics. *Hispanic Journal of Behavioral Sciences, 4*, 21–40.

Lessenger, L. H. (1997). Use of Acculturation Rating Scale for Mexican Americans II with substance abuse patients. *Hispanic Journal of Behavioral Sciences, 19*,387–398.

Levinson, D. J., & Huffman, P. E. (1955). Traditional Family Ideology Scale. *Journal of Personality, 23*, 251–273.

Linton, R. (1936). *The study of man*. New York: Appleton-Century.

Lovato, C. Y, Litrownik, A. J., Elder, J., & Nunez-Liriano, A. (1994). Cigarette and alcohol use among migrant Hispanic adolescents. *Family and Community Health, 16*(4), 18–31.

Marin, B. V., & Marin, G. (1990). Effects of acculturation on knowledge of AIDS and HIV among Hispanics. *Hispanic Journal of Behavioral Sciences, 12*,110–121.

Marin, B. V., Marin, G., & Padilla, A. M. (1981). Attitudes and practices of low-income Hispanic contraceptors. *Spanish Speaking Mental Health Research Center Occasional Papers, 13*, 20.

Marin, G. (1996). Expectancies for drinking and excessive drinking among Mexican Americans and non-Hispanic Whites. *Addictive Behaviors, 21*, 491–507.

Marin, G., Posner, S. E, & Kinyon; J. B. (1993). Alcohol expectancies among Hispanics and non-Hispanic Whites: Role of drinking status and acculturation. *Hispanic Journal of Behavioral Sciences, 15*, 373–381.

Markides, K. S., Lee, D. J., & Ray, L. A. (1993). Acculturation and hypertension in Mexican Americans. *Ethnicity and Disease, 3*, 70–77.

Marks, G., Cantero, P. J., & Sirnoni, J. M. (1998). Is acculturation associated with sexual risk behaviors? An investigation of HIV-positive Latino men and women. *AIDS Care, 10*, 283–295.

McFee, M. (1968). The 150% man: A product of Blackfeet acculturation. *American Anthropologist, 70*,1096–1103.

McGee, W. J. (1898). Piratical acculturation. *American Anthropologist, 11*, 243–249.

Mead, M. (1932). *The changing culture of an Indian tribe.* New York: Columbia University Press.

Miranda, A. O. (1995). Adlerian life styles and acculturation as predictors of the mental health in Hispanic adults. *Dissertation Abstracts International, 55*, 10A.

Miranda, A. O., & Umhoefer, D. L. (1998). Depression and social interest differences between Latinos in dissimilar acculturation stages. *Journal of Mental Health Counseling, 20*, 159–171.

Mumford, E. (1981). Culture: Life perspectives and the social meaning of illness. In R. C. Simon & H. Pardes (Eds.), *Understanding human behavior in health and illness* (pp. 271–280). Baltimore: Williams and Wilkins.

National Institute of Mental Health. (1995). *Basic behavioral science research for mental health: A report of the National Advisory Mental Health Council* (NTH Publication No. 95-3682). Washington, DC: U.S. Government Printing Office.

Neff, J. A., Hoppe, S. K., & Perea, P. (1987). Acculturation and alcohol use: Drinking patterns and problems among Anglo and Mexican American male drinkers. *Hispanic Journal of Behavioral Sciences, 9*, 151–181.

Negy, C., & Woods, D. J. (1992a). Mexican Americans' performance on the Psychological Screening Inventory as a function of acculturation level. *Journal of Clinical Psychology, 48*, 315–319.

Negy, C., & Woods, D. J. (1992b). The importance of acculturation in understanding research with Hispanic-Americans. *Hispanic Journal of Behavioral Sciences, 249*(2), 224–247.

Oetting, E. R., & Beauvais, F. (1991). Orthogonal cultural identification theory: The cultural identification of minority adolescents. *International Journal of the Addictions, 25*, 655–685.

Olmedo, E. L. (1979). Acculturation: A psychometric perspective. *American Psychologist, 34*,1061–1070,

Olmedo, E. L., Martinez, J. L., & Martinez, S. R. (1978). Measure of acculturation for Chicano adolescents. *Psychological Reports, 42*,159–170.

Olmedo, E. L., & Padilla, A. (1978). Empirical and construct validation of a measure of acculturation for Mexican Americans. *Journal of Social Psychology, 105*, 179–187.

O'Malley, A. S., Kerner, J., Johnson, A. E., & Mandelblatt, J. (1999). Acculturation and breast cancer screening among Hispanic women in New York City. *American Journal of Public Health, 89*, 219–227.

Otero-Sabogal, R., Sabogal, E., Perez-Stable, E. J., & Hiatt, R. A. (1995). Dietary practices, alcohol consumption, and smoking behavior: Ethnic, sex, and acculturation differences. *Journal of National Cancer Institute Monographs, 18*, 73–82.

Padilla, A. M. (1930). The role of cultural awareness and ethnic loyalty in acculturation. In

A. M. Padilla (Ed.), *Acculturation: Theory, models and some new findings* (pp. 47–84). Boulder, CO: Westview.

Peragallo, N. (1996). Latino women and AIDS risk. *Public Health Nursing, 13,* 217–222.

Peragallo, N. P., Fox, P. G., & Alba, M. L. (2000). Acculturation and breast self-examination among immigrant Latina women in the USA. *International Nursing Review, 47,* 38–45.

Phinney, J. S. (1989). Stages of ethnic identity development in minority group adolescents. *Journal of Early Adolescence, 9,* 34–49.

Phinney, J. S. (1992). The Multigroup Ethnic Identity Measure: A new scale for use with diverse groups. *Journal of Adolescent Research, 7,* 156–176.

Pierce, R. C, Clark, M. M., & Kiefer, C. W. (1972). A "Bootstrap" Scaling Technique. *Human Organization, 32,* 403–410.

Prislin, R., Suarez, L., Simpson, D. M., & Dyer, J. A. (1998). When acculturation hurts: The case of immunization. *Social Science and Medicine, 47,*1947–1956.

Rapkin, A. J., & Erickson, P. I. (1990). Differences in knowledge of and risk factors for AIDS between Hispanic and non-Hispanic women attending an urban family planning clinic. *AIDS, 4,* 889–899.

Redfield, R., Linton, R., & Herskovitz, M. J. (1936). Memorandum for the study of acculturation: Committee report to the Social Science Council. *American Anthropologist, 38,*149–152.

Roberts, R. E., Lewinsohn, P. M., & Seely, J. R. (1993). A brief measure of loneliness suitable for use with adolescents. *Psychological Reports, 72,* 1379–1391.

Rogler, L. H., Cortes, D. E., & Malgady, R. G. (1991). Acculturation and mental health status among Hispanics. *American Psychologist, 46,* 585–597.

Rosenberg, M. (1965). *Society and the adolescent self-image.* Princeton: Princeton University Press.

Rosenberg, M. (1979). *Conceiving the self.* New York: Basic Books.

Roysircar-Sodowsky, G., & Maestas, M. V. (2000). Acculturation, ethnic identity, and acculturative stress: Evidence and measurement. In R. Dana (Ed.), *Handbook of cross-cultural and multicultural personality assessment* (pp. 131–172). Mahwah, NJ: Lawrence Erlbaum Associates.

Ruiz, M. S., Marks, G., & Richardson, J. L. (1992). Language acculturation and screening practices of elderly Hispanic women: The role of exposure to health-related information from the media. *Journal of Aging and Health, 4,* 268–281.

Ruiz, R. A., Casas, J. M., & Padilla, A. M. (1977). *Culturally relevant behavioristic counseling* (Occasional Paper No. 5). Los Angeles Spanish Speaking Mental Health Research Center, University of California, Los Angeles.

Sabogal, F., Otero-Sabogal, R., Perez-Stable, E. J., Marin, B. V., & Marin, G. (1989). Perceived self-efficacy to avoid cigarette smoking and addiction: Differences between Hispanics and non-Hispanic Whites. *Hispanic Journal of Behavioral Sciences, 11,* 136–147.

Scribner, R., & Dwyer, J. H. (1989). Acculturation and low birth weight among Latinos in the Hispanic HANES. *American Journal of Public Health, 79,* 1263-1267.

Stern, M. P., Knapp, J. A., Hazuda, H. P., Haffner, S. M., Patterson, J. K., & Mitchell, B. D. (1991). Genetic and environmental determinants of type E diabetes in Mexican Americans: Is there a descending limb to the modernization/diabetes relationship? *Diabetes Care, 14,* 649–654.

Stonequist, E. V. (1935). The problem of the marginal man. *American Journal of Sociology, 41,* 1–12.

Stonequist, E. V. (1937). *The marginal man: A study in personality and culture conflict.* New York: Russell and Russell.

Suarez, L. (1994). Pap smear and mammogram screening in Mexican American women: The effects of acculturation. *American Journal of Public Health, 84,* 742–746.

Suarez, L., & Pulley, L. (1995). Comparing acculturation scales and their relationship to cancer screening among older Mexican

American women. *Journal of the National Cancer Institute Monographs, 18*, 41–47.

Suarez-Orozco, M. M. (1997). The cultural psychology of immigration. In A. Ugalde & G. Cardenas (Eds.), *Health and social services among international labor migrants* (pp. 131–149). Austin, TX: The Center for Mexican American Studies.

Sundquist, J., & Winkleby, M. (2001). Country of birth, acculturation status and abdominal obesity in a national sample of Mexican American women and men. *International Journal of Epidemiology, 29*, 470–477.

Thiel de Bocanegra, H. (1998). Breast-feeding in immigrant women: The role of social support and acculturation. *Hispanic Journal of Behavioral Sciences, 20*, 448–467.

Vega, W. A., Kolody, B., Aguilar-Gaxiola, S., Alderete, E., Catalano, R., & Caraveo-Anduaga, J. (1998). Lifetime prevalence of DSD-III-R psychiatric disorders among urban and rural Mexicans. *Archives of General Psychiatry, 55*(9), 771–778.

Vega, W. A., Sallis, J. R, Patterson, T., Atkins, C., & Nader, P. R. (1987). Assessing knowledge of cardiovascular health-related diet and exercise behaviors in Anglo- and Mexican Americans. *Preventive Medicine, 16*(5), 696–709.

Wagner-Echeagaray, F. A., Schuetz, C. G., Chilcoat, H. D., & Anthony, J. C. (1994). Degree of acculturation and the risk of crack cocaine smoking among Hispanic Americans. *American Journal of Public Health, 54*(11), 1825–1827.

Weller, S. C., Baer, R. D., Pachter, L. M., Trotter, R. T., Glazer, M., Garcia, J. E., & Klein, R. E. (1999). Latino beliefs about diabetes. *Diabetes Care, 22*, 722–728.

Wolff, C. B., & Portis, M. (1996). Smoking acculturation and pregnancy outcome among Mexican Americans. *Health Care for Women International, 17*, 563–574.

Woodruff, S. I., Zaslow, K. A., Candelaria, J., & Elder, J. P. (1997). Effects of gender and acculturation on nutrition-related factors among limited-English proficient Hispanic adults. *Ethnicity and Disease, 7*, 121–126.

Zamarian, K., Thackrey, M., Starrett, R. A., Brown, L. G., Lassman, D., & Blanchart, A. (1992). Acculturation and depression in Mexican American elderly. *Clinical Gerontologist, 11*, 109–121.

Zambrana, R. E., Breen, N., Fox, S. A., & Gutierrez-Mohamed, M. L (1999). Use of cancer screening practices by Hispanic women: Analyses by subgroup. *Preventive Medicine, 29*, 466–477.

Zimet, G. D., Dahlem, N. W., Zimet, S, G., & Farley, G. K. (1988). The Multidimensional Scale of Perceived Social Support. *Journal of Personality Assessment, 52*, 30–41.

PART II

Awareness of Cultural Barriers

Part II of this Reader focuses our attention on the human costs of racial discrimination, prejudice, and oppression. Emphasis is placed on exploring the concept of white privilege, ethnic and racial identity, and treatment issues pertaining to Latino/a Americans, African Americans, Native American Indians, and Asian Americans.

The first manuscript in Part II, McIntosh (2000), focuses on the issue of white privilege, which the author asserts provides white Americans (both men and women) with an "invisible package of unearned assets." The 46 examples of common everyday "privileges" that the author provides should provoke meaningful thought and dialogue concerning unacknowledged power differentials between white Americans and people of color.

The second manuscript by Trimble, Helms, and Root (2003) provides an authoritative overview of the ethnic and racial identity literature across the fields of psychology, sociology, and anthropology. Careful attention has been paid to defining key concepts from multiple theoretical perspectives. A special contribution that the authors make to the multicultural arena is an insightful discussion about the relationship of a client's acculturation status and his or her ethnic identity development.

In the third article, Abreu, Consoli, and Cypers (2004) examine treatment issues with Latino/a American clients. Underutilization of mental health services by Latino/a Americans is critically reviewed, and preventive approaches to health concerns (e.g., HIV and diabetes) are covered as well.

The fourth article by Morris (2001) examines clinical practice with African American clients from standard and Afrocentric perspectives. Morris argues that African American underutilization of mental health services is a function of cultural factors, service access barriers, economic constraints, and client-practitioner worldview incongruence. A culturally sensitive assessment and treatment model for African Americans that incorporates ideas from the theoretical work of Richard Dana and Janet Helms is provided.

The fifth manuscript by Weaver (2005) reviews the history of racism, oppression, genocide, and cultural imperialism that Native American peoples have had to endure for centuries.

Weaver eloquently argues that culturally competent direct services, program planning, and policy development can succeed only with an understanding of historical and contemporary struggles, coupled with Native peoples' human strengths and resiliency.

The last manuscript by Zane, Morton, Chu, and Lin (2004) provides a comprehensive overview of treatment issues with Asian American mental health clients. Issues of historical oppression, racism, and discrimination provide context for cultural factors such as acculturation, racial identity, family dynamics, and communication styles that directly and indirectly affect the client-provider relationship.

9

White Privilege and Male Privilege

A Personal Account of Coming to See Correspondences Through Work in Women's Studies

Peggy McIntosh

Through work to bring materials and perspectives from Women's Studies into the rest of the curriculum, I have often noticed men's unwillingness to grant that they are overprivileged in the curriculum, even though they may grant that women are disadvantaged. Denials that amount to taboos surround the subject of advantages that men gain from women's disadvantages. These denials protect male privilege from being fully recognized, acknowledged, lessened, or ended.

Thinking through unacknowledged male privilege as a phenomenon with a life of its own, I realized that since hierarchies in our society are interlocking, there was most likely a phenomenon of white privilege that was similarly denied and protected, but alive and real in its effects. As a white person, I realized I had been taught about racism as something that puts others at a disadvantage, but had been taught not to see one of its corollary aspects, white privilege, which puts me at an advantage.

I think whites are carefully taught not to recognize white privilege, as males are taught not to recognize male privilege. So I have begun in an untutored way to ask what it is like to have white privilege. This paper is a partial record of my personal observations and not a scholarly analysis. It is based on my daily experiences within my particular circumstances.

I have come to see white privilege as an invisible package of unearned assets that I can count on cashing in each day, but about which I was "meant" to remain oblivious. White privilege is like an invisible weightless knapsack of special provisions, assurances, tools, maps, guides, codebooks, passports, visas, clothes, compass, emergency gear, and blank checks.

Since I have had trouble facing white privilege, and describing its results in my life, I saw parallels here with men's reluctance to acknowledge male privilege. Only rarely will a man go beyond acknowledging that women are disadvantaged to acknowledging that men have unearned advantage, or that unearned privilege has not been good for men's development as human beings, or for society's development, or that privilege systems might ever be challenged and changed.

I will review here several types or layers of denial that I see at work protecting, and preventing awareness about, entrenched male privilege. Then I will draw parallels, from my own experience, with the denials that veil the facts of white privilege. Finally, I will list forty-six ordinary and daily ways in which I experience having white privilege, by contrast with my African American colleagues in the same building. This list is not intended to be generalizable. Others can make their own lists from within their own life circumstances.

Writing this paper has been difficult, despite warm receptions for the talks on which it is based.[1] For describing white privilege makes one newly accountable. As we in Women's Studies work reveal male privilege and ask men to give up some of their power, so one who writes about having white privilege must ask, "Having described it, what will I do to lessen or end it?"

The denial of men's overprivileged state takes many forms in discussions of curriculum change work. Some claim that men must be central in the curriculum because they have done most of what is important or distinctive in life or in civilization. Some recognize sexism in the curriculum but deny that it makes male students seem unduly important in life. Others agree that certain individual thinkers are male oriented but deny that there is any systemic tendency in disciplinary frameworks or epistemology to overempower men as a group. Those men who do grant that male privilege takes institutionalized and embedded forms are still likely to deny that male hegemony has opened doors for them personally. Virtually all men deny that male overreward alone can explain men's centrality in all the inner sanctums of our most powerful institutions. Moreover, those few who will acknowledge that male privilege systems have overempowered them usually end up doubting that we could dismantle these privilege systems. They may say they will work to improve women's status, in the society or in the university, but they can't or won't support the idea of lessening men's. In curricular terms, this is the point at which they say that they regret they cannot use any of the interesting new scholarship on women because the syllabus is full. When the talk turns to giving men less cultural room, even the most thoughtful and fair-minded of the men I know will tend to reflect, or fall back on, conservative assumptions about the inevitability of present gender relations and distributions of power, calling on precedent or sociobiology and psychobiology to demonstrate that male domination is natural and follows inevitably from evolutionary pressures. Others resort to arguments from "experience" or religion or social responsibility or wishing and dreaming.

After I realized, through faculty development work in Women's Studies, the extent to which men work from a base of unacknowledged privilege, I understood that much of their oppressiveness was unconscious. Then I remembered the frequent charges from women of color that white women whom they encounter are oppressive. I began to understand why we are justly seen as oppressive, even when we don't see ourselves that way. At the very least, obliviousness of one's privileged state can make a person or group irritating to be with. I began to count the ways in which I enjoy unearned skin privilege and have been conditioned into oblivion about its existence, unable to see that it put me "ahead" in any way, or put my people ahead, overrewarding us and yet also paradoxically damaging us, or that it could or should be changed.

My schooling gave me no training in seeing myself as an oppressor, as an unfairly advantaged person, or as a participant in a damaged culture. I was taught to see myself as an individual whose moral state depended on her individual moral will. At school, we were not taught about slavery in any depth; we were not taught to see slaveholders as damaged people. Slaves were seen as the only group at risk of being dehumanized. My schooling followed the pattern which Elizabeth Minnich has pointed out: whites are taught to think of their lives as morally neutral, normative, and average, and also ideal, so that when we work to benefit others, this is seen as work that will allow "them" to be more like "us." I think many of us know how obnoxious this attitude can be in men.

After frustration with men who would not recognize male privilege, I decided to try to work on myself at least by identifying some of the daily effects of white privilege in my life. It is crude work, at this stage, but I will give here a list of special circumstances and conditions I experience that I did not earn but that I have been made to feel are mine by birth, by citizenship, and by virtue of being a conscientious law-abiding "normal" person of goodwill. I have chosen those conditions that I think in my case attach somewhat more to skin-color privilege than to class, religion, ethnic status, or geographical location, though these other privileging factors are intricately intertwined. As far as I can see, my Afro-American co-workers, friends, and acquaintances with whom I come into daily or frequent contact in this particular time, place, and line of work cannot count on most of these conditions.

1. I can, if I wish, arrange to be in the company of people of my race most of the time.
2. I can avoid spending time with people whom I was trained to mistrust and who have learned to mistrust my kind or me.
3. If I should need to move, I can be pretty sure of renting or purchasing housing in an area which I can afford and in which I would want to live.
4. I can be reasonably sure that my neighbors in such a location will be neutral or pleasant to me.
5. I can go shopping alone most of the time, fairly well assured that I will not be followed or harassed by store detectives.
6. I can turn on the television or open to the front page of the paper and see people of my race widely and positively represented.
7. When I am told about our national heritage or about "civilization" I am shown that people of my color made it what it is.
8. I can be sure that my children will be given curricular materials that testify to the existence of their race.
9. If I want to, I can be pretty sure of finding a publisher for this piece on white privilege.
10. I can be fairly sure of having my voice heard in a group in which I am the only member of my race.
11. I can be casual about whether or not to listen to another woman's voice in a group in which she is the only member of her race.
12. I can go into a book shop and count on finding the writing of my race represented, into a supermarket and find the staple foods that fit with my cultural traditions, into a hairdresser's shop and find someone who can deal with my hair.
13. Whether I use checks, credit cards, or cash, I can count on my skin color not to work against the appearance that I am financially reliable.

14. I could arrange to protect our young children most of the time from people who might not like them.
15. I did not have to educate our children to be aware of systemic racism for their own daily physical protection.
16. I can be pretty sure that my children's teachers and employers will tolerate them if they fit school and workplace norms; my chief worries about them do not concern others' attitudes toward their race.
17. I can talk with my mouth full and not have people put this down to my color.
18. I can swear, or dress in secondhand clothes, or not answer letters, without having people attribute these choices to the bad morals, the poverty, or the illiteracy of my race.
19. I can speak in public to a powerful male group without putting my race on trial.
20. I can do well in a challenging situation without being called a credit to my race.
21. I am never asked to speak for all the people of my racial group.
22. I can remain oblivious to the language and customs of persons of color who constitute the world's majority without feeling in my culture any penalty for such oblivion.
23. I can criticize our government and talk about how much I fear its policies and behavior without being seen as a cultural outsider.
24. I can be reasonably sure that if I ask to talk to "the person in charge," I will be facing a person of my race.
25. If a traffic cop pulls me over or if the IRS audits my tax return, I can be sure I haven't been singled out because of my race.
26. I can easily buy posters, postcards, picture books, greeting cards, dolls, toys, and children's magazines featuring people of my race.
27. I can go home from most meetings of organizations I belong to feeling somewhat tied in, rather than isolated, out of place, outnumbered, unheard, held at a distance, or feared.
28. I can be pretty sure that an argument with a colleague of another race is more likely to jeopardize her chances for advancement than to jeopardize mine.
29. I can be fairly sure that if I argue for the promotion of a person of another race, or a program centering on race, this is not likely to cost me heavily within my present setting, even if my colleagues disagree with me.
30. If I declare there is a racial issue at hand, or there isn't a racial issue at hand, my race will lend me more credibility for either position than a person of color will have.
31. I can choose to ignore developments in minority writing and minority activist programs, or disparage them, or learn from them, but in any case, I can find ways to be more or less protected from negative consequences of any of these choices.
32. My culture gives me little fear about ignoring the perspectives and powers of people of other races.
33. I am not made acutely aware that my shape, bearing, or body odor will be taken as a reflection on my race.
34. I can worry about racism without being seen as self-interested or self-seeking.
35. I can take a job with an affirmative action employer without having my co-workers on the job suspect that I got it because of my race.
36. If my day, week, or year is going badly, I need not ask of each negative episode or situation whether it has racial overtones.
37. I can be pretty sure of finding people who would be willing to talk with me and

advise me about my next steps, professionally.

38. I can think over many options, social, political, imaginative, or professional, without asking whether a person of my race would be accepted or allowed to do what I want to do.
39. I can be late to a meeting without having the lateness reflect on my race.
40. I can choose public accommodation without fearing that people of my race cannot get in or will be mistreated in the places I have chosen.
41. I can be sure that if I need legal or medical help, my race will not work against me.
42. I can arrange my activities so that I will never have to experience feelings of rejection owing to my race.
43. If I have low credibility as a leader, I can be sure that my race is not the problem.
44. I can easily find academic courses and institutions that give attention only to people of my race.
45. I can expect figurative language and imagery in all of the arts to testify to experiences of my race.
46. I can choose blemish cover or bandages in "flesh" color and have them more or less match my skin.

I repeatedly forgot each of the realizations on this list until I wrote it down. For me, white privilege has turned out to be an elusive and fugitive subject. The pressure to avoid it is great, for in facing it I must give up the myth of meritocracy. If these things are true, this is not such a free country; one's life is not what one makes it; many doors open for certain people through no virtues of their own. These perceptions mean also that my moral condition is not what I had been led to believe. The appearance of being a good citizen rather than a troublemaker comes in large part from having all sorts of doors open automatically because of my color.

A further paralysis of nerve comes from literary silence protecting privilege. My clearest memories of finding such analysis are in Lillian Smith's unparalleled *Killers of the Dream* and Margaret Andersen's review of Karen and Mamie Fields' *Lemon Swamp.* Smith, for example, wrote about walking toward black children on the street and knowing they would step into the gutter; Andersen contrasted the pleasure that she, as a white child, took on summer driving trips to the south with Karen Fields' memories of driving in a closed car stocked with all necessities lest, in stopping, her black family should suffer "insult, or worse." Adrienne Rich also recognizes and writes about daily experiences of privilege, but in my observation, white women's writing in this area is far more often on systemic racism than on our daily lives as light-skinned women.[2]

In unpacking this invisible knapsack of white privilege, I have listed conditions of daily experience that I once took for granted, as neutral, normal, and universally available to everybody, just as I once thought of a male-focused curriculum as the neutral or accurate account that can speak for all. Nor did I think of any of these perquisites as bad for the holder. I now think that we need a more finely differentiated taxonomy of privilege, for some of these varieties are only what one would want for everyone in a just society, and others give license to be ignorant, oblivious, arrogant, and destructive. Before proposing some more finely tuned categorization, I will make some observations about the general effects of these conditions on my life and expectations.

In this potpourri of examples, some privileges make me feel at home in the world. Others allow me to escape penalties or dangers that others suffer. Through some, I escape fear, anxiety, insult, injury, or a sense of not being welcome, not being real. Some keep me from having to hide, to be in disguise, to feel sick or crazy, to negotiate each transaction from the position of being an outsider or, within my group, a person who is suspected of having too close links with a dominant culture. Most keep me from having to be angry.

I see a pattern running through the matrix of white privilege, a pattern of assumptions that were passed on to me as a white person. There was one main piece of cultural turf; it was my own turf, and I was among those who could control the turf. I could measure up to the cultural standards and take advantage of the many options I saw around me to make what the culture would call a success of my life. *My skin color was an asset for any move I was educated to want to make.* I could think of myself as "belonging" in major ways and of making social systems work for me. I could freely disparage, fear, neglect, or be oblivious to anything outside of the dominant cultural forms. Being of the main culture, I could also criticize it fairly freely. My life was reflected back to me frequently enough so that I felt, with regard to my race, if not to my sex, like one of the real people.

Whether through the curriculum or in the newspaper, the television, the economic system, or the general look of people in the streets, I received daily signals and indications that my people counted and that others *either didn't exist or must be trying, not very successfully, to be like people of my race.* I was given cultural permission not to hear voices of people of other races or a tepid cultural tolerance for hearing or acting on such voices. I was also raised not to suffer seriously from anything that darker-skinned people might say about my group, "protected," though perhaps I should more accurately say *prohibited,* through the habits of my economic class and social group, from living in racially mixed groups or being reflective about interactions between people of differing races.

In proportion as my racial group was being made confident, comfortable, and oblivious, other groups were likely being made unconfident, uncomfortable, and alienated. Whiteness protected me from many kinds of hostility, distress, and violence, which I was being subtly trained to visit in turn, upon people of color.

For this reason, the word "privilege" now seems to me misleading. Its connotations are too positive to fit the conditions and behaviors which "privilege systems" produce. We usually think of privilege as being a favored state, whether earned, or conferred by birth or luck. School graduates are reminded they are privileged and urged to use their (enviable) assets well. The word "privilege" carries the connotation of being something everyone must want. Yet some of the conditions I have described here work to systemically overempower certain groups. Such privilege simply *confers dominance,* gives permission to control, because of one's race or sex. The kind of privilege that gives license to some people to be, at best, thoughtless and, at worst, murderous should not continue to be referred to as a desirable attribute. Such "privilege" may be widely desired without being in any way beneficial to the whole society.

Moreover, though "privilege" may confer power, it does not confer moral strength. Those who do not depend on conferred dominance have traits and qualities that may never develop in those who do. Just as Women's Studies courses indicate that women survive their political circumstances to lead lives that hold the human race together, so "underprivileged" people of color who are the world's majority have survived their oppression and lived survivors' lives from which the white global minority can and must learn. In some groups, those dominated have actually become strong through *not* having all of these unearned advantages, and this gives them a great deal to teach the others. Members of so-called privileged groups can seem foolish, ridiculous, infantile, or dangerous by contrast.

I want, then, to distinguish between earned strength and unearned power conferred systemically. Power from unearned privilege can look like strength when it is, in fact, permission to escape or to dominate. But not all of the privileges on my list are inevitably damaging. Some, like the expectation that neighbors will be decent to you, or that your race will not count against you in court, should be the norm in a just society and should be considered as the entitlement of everyone. Others, like the privilege not to listen to less powerful people, distort the humanity of the holders as well as the ignored groups. Still others, like finding one's staple foods everywhere, may be a function of being a member of a numerical majority in the population. Others have to do with not having to labor under pervasive negative stereotyping and mythology.

We might at least start by distinguishing between positive advantages that we can work to spread, to the point where they are not advantages at all but simply part of the normal civic and social fabric, and negative types of advantage that unless rejected will always reinforce our present hierarchies. For example, the positive "privilege" of belonging, the feeling that one belongs within the human circle, as Native Americans say, fosters development and should not be seen as privilege for a few. It is, let us say, an entitlement that none of us should have to earn; ideally it is an *unearned entitlement.* At present, since only a few have it, it is an *unearned advantage* for them. The negative "privilege" that gave me cultural permission not to take darker-skinned Others seriously can be seen as arbitrarily conferred dominance and should not be desirable for anyone. This paper results from a process of coming to see that some of the power that I originally saw as attendant on being a human being in the United States consisted in *unearned advantage* and *conferred dominance,* as well as other kinds of special circumstance not universally taken for granted.

In writing this paper I have also realized that white identity and status (as well as class identity and status) give me considerable power to choose whether to broach this subject and its trouble. I can pretty well decide whether to disappear and avoid and not listen and escape the dislike I may engender in other people through this essay, or interrupt, answer, interpret, preach, correct, criticize, and control to some extent what goes on in reaction to it. Being white, I am given considerable power to escape many kinds of danger of penalty as well as to choose which risks I want to take.

There is an analogy here, once again, with Women's Studies. Our male colleagues do not have a great deal to lose in supporting Women's Studies, but they do not have a great deal to lose if they oppose it either. They simply have the power to decide whether to commit themselves to more equitable distributions of power. They will probably feel few penalties whatever choice they make; they do not seem, in any obvious short-term sense, the ones at risk, though they and we are all at risk because of the behaviors that have been rewarded in them.

Through Women's Studies work I have met very few men who are truly distressed about systemic, unearned male advantage and conferred dominance. And so one question for me and others like me is whether we will be like them, or whether we will get truly distressed, even outraged, about unearned race advantage and conferred dominance and if so, what we will do to lessen them. In any case, we need to do more work in identifying how they actually affect our daily lives. We need more down-to-earth writing by people about these taboo subjects. We need more understanding of the ways in which white "privilege" damages white people, for these are not the same ways in which it damages the victimized. Skewed white psyches are an inseparable part of the picture, though I do not want to confuse the kinds of damage done to the holders of special assets and to those who suffer the deficits. Many, perhaps most, of our white students in the United States think that racism doesn't affect them because they are not people of color; they do not see "whiteness" as a racial identity. Many men likewise think that Women's Studies does not bear on their own existences because they are not female; they do not see themselves as having gendered identities. Insisting on the universal "effects" of "privilege" systems, then, becomes one of our chief tasks, and being more explicit about the *particular* effects in particular contexts is another. Men need to join us in this work.

In addition, since race and sex are not the only advantaging systems at work, we need to similarly examine the daily experience of having age advantage, or ethnic advantage, or physical ability, or advantage related to nationality, religion, or sexual orientation. Professor Marnie Evans suggested to me that in many ways the list I made also applies directly to heterosexual privilege. This is a still more taboo subject than race privilege: the daily ways in which heterosexual privilege makes some persons comfortable or powerful, providing supports, assets, approvals, and rewards to those who live or expect to live in heterosexual pairs. Unpacking that content is still more difficult, owing to the deeper imbeddedness of heterosexual advantage and dominance and stricter taboos surrounding these.

But to start such an analysis I would put this observation from my own experience: the fact that I live under the same roof with a man triggers all kinds of societal assumptions about my worth, politics, life, and values and triggers a host of unearned advantages and powers. After recasting many elements from the original list I would add further observations like these:

1. My children do not have to answer questions about why I live with my partner (my husband).
2. I have no difficulty finding neighborhoods where people approve of our household.
3. Our children are given texts and classes that implicitly support our kind of family unit and do not turn them against my choice of domestic partnership.
4. I can travel alone or with my husband without expecting embarrassment or hostility in those who deal with us.
5. Most people I meet will see my marital arrangements as an asset to my life or as a favorable comment on my likability, my competence, or my mental health.
6. I can talk about the social events of a weekend without fearing most listeners' reactions.
7. I will feel welcomed and "normal" in the usual walks of public life, institutional and social.
8. In many contexts, I am seen as "all right" in daily work on women because I do not live chiefly with women.

Difficulties and dangers surrounding the task of finding parallels are many. Since racism, sexism, and heterosexism are not the same, the advantages associated with them should not be seen as the same. In addition, it is hard to isolate aspects of unearned advantage that derive chiefly from social class, economic class, race, religion, region, sex, or ethnic identity. The oppressions are both distinct and interlocking, as the Combahee River Collective statement of 1977 continues to remind us eloquently.[3]

One factor seems clear about all of the interlocking oppressions. They take both active forms that we can see and embedded forms that members of the dominant group are taught not to see. In my class and place, I did not see myself as racist because I was taught to recognize racism only in individual acts of meanness by members of my group, never in invisible systems conferring racial dominance on my group from birth. Likewise, we are taught to think that sexism or heterosexism is carried on only through intentional, individual acts of discrimination, meanness, or cruelty, rather than in invisible systems conferring unsought dominance on certain groups. Disapproving of the systems won't be enough to change them. I was taught to think that racism could end if white individuals changed their attitudes; many men think sexism can be ended by individual changes in daily behavior toward women. But a man's sex provides advantage for him whether or not he approves of the way in which dominance has been conferred on his group. A "white" skin in the United States opens many doors for whites whether or not we approve of the way dominance has been conferred on us. Individual acts can palliate, but cannot end, these problems. To redesign social systems, we need first to acknowledge their colossal unseen dimensions. The silences and denials surrounding privilege are the key political tool here. They keep the thinking about equality or equity incomplete, protecting unearned advantage and conferred dominance by making these taboo subjects. Most talk by whites about equal opportunity seems to me now to be about equal opportunity to try to get into a position of dominance while denying that *systems* of dominance exist.

Obliviousness about white advantage, like obliviousness about male advantage, is kept strongly inculturated in the United States so as to maintain the myth of meritocracy, the myth that democratic choice is equally available to all. Keeping most people unaware that freedom of confident action is there for just a small number of people props up those in power and serves to keep power in the hands of the same groups that have most of it already. Though systemic change takes many decades, there are pressing questions for me and I imagine for some others like me if we raise our daily consciousness on the perquisites of being light-skinned. What will we do with such knowledge? As we know from watching men, it is an open question whether we will choose to use unearned advantage to weaken invisible privilege systems and whether we will use any of our arbitrarily awarded power to try to reconstruct power systems on a broader base.

Notes

1. This paper was presented at the Virginia Women's Studies Association conference in Richmond in April 1986, and the American Educational Research Association conference in Boston in October 1986, and discussed with two groups of participants in the Dodge seminars for Secondary School Teachers in New York and Boston in the spring of 1987.

2. Andersen, Margaret, "Race and the Social Science Curriculum: A Teaching and Learning Discussion." *Radical Teacher,* November 1984, pp. 17–20. Smith, Lillian, *Killers of the Dream,* New York: W. W. Norton, 1949.

3. "A Black Feminist Statement," The Combahee River Collective, pp. 13–22 in G. Hull, P. Scott, B. Smith, Eds., *All the Women Are White, All the Blacks Are Men, But Some of Us Are Brave: Black Women's Studies,* Old Westbury, NY: The Feminist Press, 1982.

Source: Reprinted by permission from Peggy McIntosh, Wellesley College Center for Research on Women, Wellesley, MA 02481-8203, (781) 283-2522, fax (781) 283-2504.

10

Social and Psychological Perspectives on Ethnic and Racial Identity

Joseph E. Trimble
Janet E. Helms
Maria P. P. Root

In September 1931, distinguished anthropologist Margaret Mead ventured from New York City to study the way sex roles are characterized in different cultural groups. After a long journey across the United States and the Pacific Ocean, she and her then husband, Reo Fortune, landed in New Guinea. Her meticulously and carefully conducted ethnographic study provided her with sufficient information to publish in 1935 the now-classic book, *Sex and Temperament in Three Primitive Societies,* where she describes the contrasting personalities of men and women from three New Guinea villages. The first group she contacted and studied lived in the Prince Alexander Mountains located in New Guinea's northwestern corner. In a letter dated April 20, 1932, Mead states, "We still have not decided what to call this mountain people for they have no name for themselves, just friendly little nicknames or names for sections of a community, like man-o-bush or 'poisonous snakes'" (Mead, 2001, p. 125). After much thought, Mead eventually chose to refer to them as the Arapesh or Mountain Arapesh.

Currently, it may be difficult to comprehend the possibility that any society or ethnocultural group does not have an identity or label to use to refer to it in some collective manner. Such a discovery by Margaret Mead challenges conventional beliefs that all collectives, societies, and

Authors' Note: The senior author wants to extend his deepest gratitude to the administration and research staff at the Radcliffe Institute for Advanced Study, Harvard University, for providing him with the time, resources, and support that allowed him to conduct research for the preparation and writing of this chapter. In addition, he wishes to extend his warm appreciation to his Radcliffe research junior partners, Harvard College seniors Peggy Ting Lim and Maiga Miranda, who conducted research and provided him with wonderful, thought-provoking commentary and advice for many topics covered in this chapter.

ethnocultural groups have distinct names for the collective or refer to themselves in some designated manner, such as "people" in their language. The fundamental principle of any identity theory suggests that all groups have a label or name for themselves. Thus, how does an outsider ask whether it is possible that a small remote collective living in New Guinea in the 1920s would not know what to call themselves? Is it possible that identity is an "etic-bound" construct not universally valued and expressed by all societies and cultures? Certainly, additional questions can be phrased concerning Mead's finding, and those are left for further speculation and articulation.

Nonetheless, interest in collective and individual identity theory has generated considerable discussion and research in the past 60 years. Within the past 30 years, specific attention has been devoted to the construct and its relationship to ethnic and racial groups. The following chapter is a summary of the definitions, theories, research findings, speculations, controversies, and challenges presented by the study of the structural, functional, and dynamic characteristics of ethnic and racial identity.

The topic may appear to be limited in scope, but in fact, it is a broad and expansive one. Since 1887, according to the citations found in the PsycINFO electronic database, slightly more than 3,000 articles have been written on the topic of ethnic and racial identity; two thirds of those articles have been written since 1990. Sociological Abstracts indicates that 3,648 articles have been written on the topic since 1963, and an anthropology electronic database indicates that 1,149 were written from that field's perspective, although no specific time frame was provided. The literature search suggests that interest in the topic is multidisciplinary and has accelerated considerably since 1990. The accelerated interest indicates that we must stop and take stock of the topic and its future direction; also, the content and emphasis of publications dedicated to the topic are changing strongly, pointing to the need for a summary of the findings and discussions.

Overview

A plethora of theories and models of ethnic and racial identity exist. Varying in emphasis, they generally define a dynamic, multifaceted construct (cf. Mio, Trimble, Arredondo, Cheatham, & Sue, 1999). Ethnic and racial identity can include personal identity, notions of belonging, knowledge of the reference group, and shared values. Its expression or belonging may change across situations, points in time, and within the same people (Stephan & Stephan, 1989; Trimble, 1988; Trimble & Mahoney, 2002; Waters, 1990). The literature suggests that at least three layers of context influence how these components of ethnic identity manifest time context (history and generation), space (size of community), and place (geography or region). Finally, a reflexive process affected by the continuous impact of events and experiences drives enculturation in part through experiences that range from stressful to traumatic as part of acculturative stress (Bernal & Knight, 1993; Berry, 1975), reflected in our constructs of the process of acculturation and assimilation. Furthermore, cross-culturally, ethnic identification derives from social and political processes (Romanucci-Ross & DeVos, 1995; Roosens, 1989). Despite the challenge to conceptualize ethnic identity, it eludes definitive measurement. At best, measurement presents a partial picture of someone's ethnic identity. Consider the following examples of three people who all identify as Filipino American in some situations.

Example 1. Annabel is second generation, raised in the Virginia Beach area of Virginia. Her mother and father are both college educated, born in the Philippines. They obtained their graduate degrees in the United States in the early 1970s in nursing and dentistry, respectively. They socialize with the significant Filipino community in their area, many of whom are professionals and have immigrated post-1965. Annabel, an attorney, now lives in Washington, D.C., and works in a medium-sized law firm. Except for visits home, she seldom participates in organized Filipino community events.

Example 2. Patrick immigrated with his parents in the early 1980s for safety reasons because of his father's ties with the Marcos government as an attorney. His mother had never worked outside the home prior to fleeing the Philippines. Now, in the United States, both his parents work, his father as a grossly underemployed stock clerk in a grocery store and occasional law clerk, his mother as a janitor in an elementary school. Now a young adult, Patrick lives in Los Angeles and struggles to finish college. He became a citizen at 22 years of age. He is involved with the Filipino immigrant community and still speaks Tagalog some portion of every day.

Example 3. Tony is second generation, born in Seattle. His father worked the field as a migrant worker up and down the West Coast. His mother was also from a Filipino migrant farm family. Tony, now almost 70, has proudly identified as Filipino American. He was part of the first significant generation of American-born Filipinos to forge the meaning of Filipino American. College educated, he was the first in his family to obtain this level of education. He has worked in mainstream university and government institutions, always advancing the agenda of minorities.

Although applied initially to the concept of race, sociologist Robert Parks (1937) observed the complex interactive dimensions of identity. He maintained,

> Race relations, like many if not most other relations among human beings, must be conceived as existing in three dimensions rather than as we ordinarily conceive it, in two . . . between individuals and between groups of individuals. . . . Changes may be, or seem to be, merely fortuitous. At other times, they assume a cyclical or secular form. All three types of change are involved in the processes of growth and all three are more or less involved in what we may describe as the "race relation cycle." . . . At any time and place . . . once initiated, inevitably continues until it terminates in some predestined racial configuration, and one consistent with an established social order of which it is a part. (pp. xiii–xiv)

Ethnicity has both a private and social construction. Ironically, the confusion between race and ethnicity in part stems from social assignments to ethnic groups based on some markers of origins, behavior, and phenotype versus personal identification. When the former are thought to arise from biologically based markers, more mistakes are likely to be made in social assignment as factors of change over time, person, and location are not factored into personal identification processes. Moreover, ethnic and racial identity is a form of self-determination as expressed through a self-declaration. The declaration, however, may not be recognized by others. Thus,

> a person or group of people can suffer real damage, real distortion, if the people of society mirror back to them a confining or demeaning or contemptible picture of themselves. Nonrecognition or misrecognition can inflict harm, can be a form of oppression, imprisoning someone in a false, distorted and reduced mode of being. (Taylor, 1992, p. 25)

Individuals may privately know who they are, but certain social forces and groups can and do deny or limit self-declaration.

Ethnic Gloss

Before the topic of ethnic identity is considered in more detail, attention must be given to the manner in which researchers, among many others, specify and describe ethnic and culturally distinct populations. As one scans the ethnic and racial identity literature, it becomes readily apparent that a number of studies focus on American Indians (or Native Americans), African Americans (Blacks), Asian and Pacific Americans, Mexican Americans and Puerto Ricans, and other ethnic-specific or ethnocultural groups. Occasionally, researchers provide greater specificity concerning their respondents in their titles and abstracts by giving reference to a geographic or geocultural region or city in the United States. Others will distinguish their respondents along urban and rural lines, whereas others, when referring to an American Indian group, will specify the tribe (e.g., Dine, Lakota, Hopi, or one of the Pueblos in New Mexico). Nonetheless, most studies in the ethnic/racial social and behavioral science literature provide descriptions of ethnic and cultural groups that tend to rely on the use of broad "ethnic glosses"—superficial, almost vacuous, categories that serve only to separate one group from another (Trimble, 1991). Use of such "glosses" gives little or no sense of the richness and cultural variation within these groups, much less the existence of numerous subgroups characterized by distinct lifeways *(ethos)* and thoughtways *(eidos)*. Furthermore, the use of broad "ethnic glosses" to describe a cultural or ethnic group in a research venture may be poor science. Apart from the fact that such sweeping references to ethnic groups are gross misrepresentations, their use can violate certain tenets concerning external validity (the ability to generalize findings across subgroups within an ethnic category) and erode any likelihood of an accurate and efficient replication of research results.

In selecting ethnic samples for social and behavioral science studies, researchers almost tacitly assume that the respondents share a common understanding of their own ethnicity and nationalistic identification. It is as though the researcher believes that African Americans, American Indians, Hispanics, and others share some modal characteristic that at one level sets them apart from another comparative sample, such as "Whites" (Trimble, 1988).

Mounting evidence suggests that the assumption may be invalid. Marín and Marín (1982) illustrated how the use of an ethnic category, in this case, Hispanic, can disrupt a well-intended sampling strategy. The researchers were interested in the health records of some 500 patients at a clinic in East Los Angeles, California, an area known for its high concentration of people with Hispanic origins. Because of the location of the clinic, they expected to find mostly Hispanics in their sample. Much to their surprise, they found that some patients with Spanish surnames actually checked the "White" and "other" ethnic category on the medical form. On examining the "other" category, they found that 3% of the patients wrote in specific ethnic identifiers such as "Mexican American" and "Chicano." All in all, some 13% chose to identify themselves in a way that differed from what one might expect from a person with a Spanish surname. Indeed, the use of "Hispanic" as a means to identify a sample is insufficient because the category can mean quite different things to people. Heath (1978) pointedly argued that "categories of people such as those compared under the rubric of 'ethnic groups' are often not really meaningful units in any sociocultural sense" (p. 60). Heath went on to add that "the ways in which people define and maintain the 'social boundaries' between or among self-identified categories are often far more important and revealing of sociocultural dynamics" (p. 60).

Use of broad-brush ethnic categories does have a useful purpose at one level. Researchers and policy planners can use the results to differentiate groups to highlight salient characteristics. In a crude way, it is a good deal easier to discuss differences between ethnic and cultural groups by using the "gloss." As such, planners, legislators, and decision makers find it convenient to balance and present the findings and problems of one or more ethnic groups against other groups. Use of the ethnic gloss at this level is tolerable. Most definitions of ethnic identity rely on an identifiable group to form the basis of the construct. Reliance on a group orientation not only views identity as static but also provides little credence to individual-level variations and influences created by situational or contextual circumstances. In short, psychological and situational characteristics are not found in typical definitions and conceptualizations of ethnic identity.

Definitions of Constructs

A construct such as ethnic identity generates many viewpoints. To understand the complications, one must consider the meanings of race and ethnicity. Feagin (1978) defined a racial group as one in which "persons inside or outside the group have decided what is important to single out as inferior or superior, typically on the basis of real or alleged physical characteristics subjectively selected" (p. 7). An ethnic group, maintained Feagin, is one "which is socially distinguished or set apart, by others and/or by itself, primarily on the basis of cultural or nationality characteristics" (p. 9). Thompson (1989) elaborated on the term *ethnic* and chose to view it as a culturally distinct population that can be set apart from other groups. Such groups, Thompson argued, engage in behaviors "based on cultural or physical criteria in a social context in which these criteria are relevant" (p. 11).

Although there are numerous "White" and "non-White" ethnic groups in the Americas, more often than not, non-White ethnics are designated as minority groups. At one level, the term *minority* implies that a "majority group" exists that assumes a position of dominance within a given country. To an extent, the term *minority group* has racist overtones and implies that a particular group has been and continues to be the victim of collective discrimination. Most notably in North America, an ethnic minority group may be defined as

> (1) subordinate segments of complex state societies; (2) [having] special physical or cultural traits which are held in low esteem by the dominant segments of the society; (3) self-conscious units bound together by the special traits which their members have and by the special disabilities which these bring; (4) [one where] membership is transmitted by a rule of descent which is capable of affiliating succeeding generations even in the absence of readily apparent special cultural or physical traits; and (5) [people who] by choice or necessity tend to marry within the group. (Wayley & Harris, 1958, p. 10)

Ethnic and *racial identity* are overlapping constructs, but their distinctiveness flows from the emphasis placed on the seemingly interchangeable terms. Phinney (2000) defined ethnic identity as a dynamic, multidimensional construct that refers to one's identity, or sense of self, in ethnic terms, that is in terms of a subgroup within a larger context that claims a common ancestry and shares one or more of the following elements: culture, race, religion, language, kinship, or place of origin (p. 254).

Compare her definition of the construct with one offered by Bram (1965). He defined the construct as

> a form of self-conceptualization by a person which may be accepted or rejected by the social world around him. It may be forced on him by coercion and is of limited predictive value for his own ancestry or that of his descendants. It varies in meaning across persons and through history and is interchangeable with national identity. (p. 242)

The definitions are similar, but the emphasis of the source of the identity varies. Helms (1990) maintained that "racial identity" refers to a sense of group or collective identity based on one's perception that he or she shares a common racial heritage with a particular racial group" (p. 3). The terms *ethnic, racial,* and *cultural* all share a common meaning but only from the perspective that people congregate around common core characteristics. The source of the core characteristics can be criteria established and deeply held by the in-group and out-groups, which can also set their own criteria for designating and differentiating one group from another. Thompson (1989) was highly critical of the labeling process and drew attention to theoretical and practical matters befallen "those who have had the fortune or, in most cases, the misfortune of being labeled 'ethnics' in the modern world" (p. 42). Helms (1990) concurred, to an extent, as she found it rather confusing "since one's racial-group designation does not necessarily define one's racial, cultural, or ethnic characteristics" (p. 7). In her work on Black and White identities, Helms preferred to emphasize "race" as an organizing construct. To distinguish one group or individual from another by appealing to race, ethnicity, or culture is an attempt to be distinctive. Labeling a group as a distinct cultural (racial or ethnic) unit, however, tends to promote stereotypes and leads to overgeneralizations, further compounding the complexity of the problem. It is not uncommon for outsiders to believe that identifiable members of a racial group act as a single unitary whole—a group mind—and that they are more homogeneous than heterogeneous. Such labeling leads to blanket-type statements, such as "(fill in the blank) are all the same." Many Americans use similar statements when referring to such nationalistic groups as Japanese, Mexicans, Nigerians, and Saudi Arabians, among many others—many Americans actually use the blanket-type statement to refer to all Asians, often claiming that they cannot differentiate a Japanese from a Korean, Chinese, Laotian, or Indonesian, and so on.

Numerous debates emerging in the literature challenge many of the theories espoused to explain the complex meaning and nature of ethnic identity. Pierre van den Berghe (1981) and Richard Thompson (1989) are two whose perspectives on the topic stir up some controversy. Thompson has taken issue with van den Berghe's "pop sociobiological" view of ethnic and race relations. Van den Berghe has advocated a primordialist position about ethnicity, in which one's sense of attachment and belongingness is tied to an ancestral origin. Unlike sociologist Edward Shils and anthropologist Clifford Geertz, early proponents of the primordialist theory, van den Berghe has held that sociobiological principles and tenets must be used to tighten loose theoretical ends. Thompson has taken on the primordialist position—a viewpoint that is used to explain and justify emerging "ethnic consciousness" movements—by appealing to other, more seemingly social structural perspectives such as assimilationism, capitalism, and neo-Marxism. He is critical of these perspectives, too. Thompson also laid out a sequence of interesting topics that any theory of ethnicity must accommodate: (a) ethnic and racial classifications, (b) ethnic and racial sentiments, and (c) ethnic and racial social organization. Put another way, humans typically develop systems to categorize and classify themselves and others, attach significance and meaning to the classification, and use racial and ethnic classifications for organizational criteria.

Race and ethnicity share histories of constructions of social relations that have served economic, social, and political purposes to separate classes and even castes, often starkly observed in colonial projects (Forbes, 1990; Young, 1995). Rules are invented that must be internalized and tend to be highly illogical. Nevertheless, *race* and *ethnicity* are not synonymous. However, their juxtaposition uses physically visible differences or socially constructed imaginings of character or characteristics as shorthand markers of ethnicity. With racially visible groups other than European-originated persons, race has been used as a biological marker for signaling ethnicity. Whereas ethnic options—and even ethnic divestment—are possible for European-originated persons (Waters, 1990), these choices are constrained for persons who are identified racially as other than White.

Race

Sociologist Pierre van den Berghe (1967) noted that

> the human group that defines itself, and/or is defined by other groups is different by virtue of innate or immutable characteristics. These physical characteristics are in turn assumed to be intrinsically related to moral, intellectual and other non-physical attributes or abilities. A race, therefore, is a group that is socially defined on the basis of physical criteria. (p. 18)

The social construction of race that is embedded in U.S. history is captured formally every 10 years by the formal census. The rules for racial classification over the decades demonstrate the social construction of race. Rules of *hypodescent,* assignment to the race of lower social status or greater social stigma, have prevailed. For example, until 1989, biracial babies with a White parent were assigned to the racial status of the non-White parent; babies of two parents of color were assigned the race of the father. As of 1989, all infants are designated by their mothers' race (Waters, 1994). In 1978, the Federal Office of Management and Budget designated that racial data be collected according to five mutually exclusive racial categories: Black, White, Asian/Pacific Islander, American Indian/Alaska Native, and other. People were to enact the rules of hypodescent by designating themselves as people in their community would identify them. These categories also set the framework for civil rights protections. All of these racial designations assume rules of hypodescent to perpetuate monoracial affiliation that protects Whiteness (Root, 1996). Later, Hispanic was created as an ethnic group, but it actually serves as a pseudo-racial group in daily life because all the other racial groups are also used as "ethnic glosses," which eliminates the possibility of describing their actual ethnicity. By 1990, people were allowed to identify themselves as they personally wanted to be identified. By 2000, racial categories had changed: Asian and Pacific Islander were now two separate categories, and people were allowed to check more than one racial category in response to the race category. Six racial categories now existed, although they were no longer deemed mutually exclusive. With the 2000 census, the racial system was further challenged. Despite the option for multiple checkoffs to the racial question and placing the Hispanic origin question before the race question, 42% of Hispanics still checked "other" for race (U.S. Bureau of the Census, 2001). In addition, more than 4,119,000 individuals chose to mark "American Indian and Alaska Native" along with one or more "race" categories. The "race alone or in combination" count is much higher than the "race alone" count of 2,475,956. The discrepancy raises the question about which count is more accurate or representative of the "true" Indian population (cf. Trimble, 2000). Similar findings occurred for other ethnic and racial groups in the United States.

The racial system in this country has functioned as a caste system to create barriers to protect Whiteness; thus, in this sense, it is a political construction intended initially to serve a few. Although Root (2001) noted that some racially designated groups are now experiencing a shift from caste to class, particularly if they do not live in enclaves but do operate fluidly and skillfully as bicultural, caste remnants remain, particularly for persons of African descent. Caste regulates sexual relations and, subsequently, status, privileges, and social mobility (Montague, 1997). This backdrop for understanding the necessity for racial construction in this country is important for understanding some of the complexity in ethnic identity construction and choice.

Ethnicity

Waters (1990) observed that the common assumption about ethnic identity is that it is inherited versus dynamic, socially constructed, and even chosen. She also observed that a tension exists in the construction of ethnic identity between freedom to choose and constraint based on one's socially ascribed race. Although many persons of European mixed stock can opt for which ethnicity to declare—if any—this freedom does not pertain to persons of other origins who have been constructed as racially non-White in the United States. Waters (1990) further observed that White persons even have the option to divest themselves of an ethnicity and declare themselves American.

On the other hand, some of the declarations of ethnicity by White Americans are only symbolic, with little knowledge or attachment to their grandparents' origins. Waters (1990) described a respondent in her study who wanted a "thick culture" that was flexible. She described this process as resulting in symbolic ethnicity because

> it gives middle-class Americans at least the appearance of both: conformity and individuality; community with social change. And as an added bonus—which almost ensures its appeal to Americans—the element of choice is there also. This partly explains the patterns in the choices [White] people make about their ethnic identities. When given a choice, whites will choose the most "ethnic" of the ancestries in their backgrounds. (p. 154)

The symbolic identity has little social cost or stigmatization and even provides individual satisfaction.

Symbolic identity stands in contrast to non-symbolic ethnicity, the experience of racial minorities. Waters (1990) noted that as persons of European ancestry invoke symbolic ethnicity and equate it with enjoyment and lack of constraint, the understanding of the racially juxtaposed or constrained ethnic options for racial minorities will be less understood.

Seldom discussed is the role of maternal or paternal lineage in determining one's ethnic identity, particularly when one inherits more than one ethnic lineage. Ethnic options may be directed by patrilineal rules when ethnicity is mixed, even if both parents are of European stock. Several large-scale survey studies (e.g., the Census Bureau's Reinterview Study and the Michigan National Election Study) demonstrated people's tendency to choose paternal ancestry over maternal ethnicity when multiple ethnicities were involved (cf. Waters, 1990, pp. 20–22). Furthermore, ethnicities are often traced through surnames, which still are governed by patrilineal rules.

Because intergroup prejudices still pertain in the United States, nonsymbolic identity is tied largely to minority or disenfranchised status by racial group belonging and economic disenfranchisement. The social tensions that further maintain ethnicity as a defining characteristic for many residents of the United States stem from a greater gap in inequality between those who operate the wealth and those who live at poverty lines. Necessarily, individual and group processes combined provide more comprehensive models by which to understand ethnic identity.

Cultural Identity

A little attention also should be given to the term *cultural identity.* It, too, is a complex term and is probably the most difficult to define. There are a number of complications owing to theoretical differences; however, the definition of *culture (cultural)* presents the biggest problem. Anthropologists and cross-cultural psychologists claim that there are more than 165 different definitions of *culture* (Kroeber & Kluckhohn, 1952). In defining *culture,* one must consider not only what exists but also what is desirable. Cultures are not merely an amalgam of specific behaviors because they include, in addition to activities of a standard nature, consistent cognitive, perceptual, motivational, and affective patterns and a distinctive array of artifacts of human alterations of the environment. Cultures also are continuous, cumulative, and progressive (White, 1947).

Thus, culture can be a way of life attributed to a distinct collective of humans who reside in a particular geographic locale, but however broad this definition may be, it is not without flaws. For the sake of brevity, we can appeal to Brown's (1991) definition. He maintained that

> culture consists of the conventional patterns of thought, activity, and artifact that are passed on from generation to generation in a manner that is generally assumed to involve learning rather specific programming. Besides being transmitted "vertically" from generation to generation, culture may also be transmitted "horizontally" between individuals and collectivities. (p. 40)

Primordialists and sociobiologists undoubtedly would have something to say about this concise and somewhat learning-centered version.

Ego and Ethnic Development Theories

Ethnic identity is closely aligned to ego identity and self-esteem. The social status of a group also can influence self-esteem; if an ethnic group has experienced a long, oppressive history of prejudice and discrimination, then group members could experience a devalued sense of self (Tajfel, 1981). The self-image, however, is significantly influenced by one's evaluation of the group—if the evaluation is positive, then commitment is strong, contentment is high, and involvement in ethnic behaviors and practices is significant, therefore allowing one to achieve a strong secure identity with the group (Phinney, 1991). But if the evaluation is negative, then involvement, preferences, contentment, and commitment will be minimal in these instances; multiethnic individuals will seek ways to pass as members of other groups or denigrate the value of the group by forging relations with related subgroups.

Using ego involvement, the group evaluation process, and Eriksen's model (Stevens, 1983) as a foundation, Phinney (1989) developed the Ethnic Identity Development Measure (EIDM). Essentially, individuals (especially adolescents) can experience one of four identities:

1. Diffused identity, in which individuals express little or no interest in their identity;
2. Foreclosed identity, in which a person shows some interest in his or her ethnicity and parental influences have been internalized;
3. Moratorium identity, in which an individual continues to explore his or her ethnic identity but in the process may be experiencing some degree of confusion; and
4. Achieved identity, in which one's identity has been successfully integrated into his or her self-concept.

Individuals' self-esteem is the mainstay of the theory and can be influenced by any one of their developmental stages.

Writing more than 30 years ago, Cross (1971) developed the first of a series of his iterations of Nigrescence theory. Like Phinney's (1989) model, it rests on a developmental sequence composed of five stages:

1. Preencounter, in which the process of identification is formed and directed to a group;
2. Encounter, in which individuals decide they need a change in their sense of ethnic self-awareness that is influenced by significant events;
3. Immersion-Emersion, in which old and new identities create a struggle for the individuals;
4. Internalization, in which the newly adopted identity becomes accepted; and
5. Internalization-Commitment, the ultimate stage in which ethnicity is salient and is an integral part of one's daily life.

Similar to Phinney's (1989) model, levels of self-esteem are related to Cross's (1971) stages, and consequently esteem levels are lowest at the Preencounter stage and change accordingly to a peak positive level at the Internalization-Commitment stage.

Owing to the mounting research on ethnic identity models, especially for Helms's racial identity model (Helms, 1989a, 1990) and the addition of several alternative models, Cross (1991) was compelled to revise his levels. Cross now believes that social situations can act as a moderating variable; one's identity in some situations may be reinforcing and contribute to positive ego functioning, but in other situations, identification with a group may be of little consequence. Cross also learned that identity may not be salient for some individuals; they know they are Black or American Indian or some other group, and they feel no need to explore its meaning. Cross found that self-esteem is not necessarily correlated with one's identity, which is a consistent finding in the field (cf. Bates, Trimble, & Beauvais, 1997; Trimble, 1987, 2000; Trimble & Mahoney, 2002). To accommodate new thoughts and research findings, Cross revised his levels by expanding the meaning of the Preencounter and Internalization levels; the salience of one's identity serves to sharpen the meaning of the two levels. The revised model accounts for those individuals for whom ethnicity is central to their sense of self and for those whose ethnicity is not important to them.

In recent years, a good deal of attention has been devoted to the salience of ethnic identity for Blacks (African Americans), in part stimulated by the works of Cross and Helms. Mays (1986) described in a compelling article the various historical forces that shaped the identity of Blacks. Using a psychological framework, she emphasized the influences that various social and economic forces have had on an ethnic population that was essentially powerless to effect change. Ethnic and group identity among Blacks has been strong and robust. The strength of that identity was supported in the results of a national survey of Black Americans by

Broman, Neighbors, and Jackson (1988), in which the older and least educated Blacks expressed the strongest identity.

The literature on Black identity quite often suggests that some African Americans hold differing opinions about who and what they are. Parham and Helms (1985) and Parham (1989) explored the process of psychological Nigrescence among different Black populations in an effort to support and extend Cross's (1971) model of psychological Nigrescence. In one study, the authors found that pro-White/anti-Black and pro-Black/anti-White student attitudes were associated with personal distress. Awakening Black attitudes were positively associated with the process of self-actualization and negatively associated with inferiority feelings and anxiety levels. Their findings hold some importance for cross-cultural counselors.

Undoubtedly, identity is a major portion of what it means to be an African American in a multicultural society. Aries and Moorehead (1989) found among a sample of Black adolescents that ethnicity was most important in forming an overall identity. In a related finding, Looney (1988) demonstrated that an interesting relationship existed between ego development and Black identity: Individuals with a strong ego will define who and what they are, but those with a weak ego will allow others to define them. White and Burke (1987) supported a similar relationship; that is, identity salience, commitment, and self-esteem are associated with ethnic identity among Black and White youth. In their study, Black respondents who expressed strong ethnic identity also reported a high sense of self-esteem. Identity can also be influenced by the sociocultural context in which one is reared, socialized, and educated. Baldwin, Duncan, and Bell (1987) found that Black identity was higher among Black students who attended a predominantly Black university than Blacks who attended a predominantly White school. Moreover, the researchers found that identity was high among those who attended all-Black elementary schools and were older in years. Therefore, the context in which individuals find themselves reinforces and strengthens their sense of belongingness and their identity. However, there are questions about the extent to which socioeconomic status relates to ethnic identity among African Americans (Carter & Helms, 1988). Finally, it should be noted that the exploration and meaningfulness of ethnic identity appear to be more important for ethnic minority youth than White youth (Phinney & Alipuria, 1990). Related to this conclusion is the likelihood that self-esteem also may be of importance for ethnic minorities, although the findings on this topic are inconclusive (see Trimble, 1987; Trimble & Mahoney, 2002).

Rowe, Bennett, and Atkinson (1994) also proposed an intriguing and compelling ethnic identity model that eventually may prove useful. Their model deserves attention in part because it challenges the other models' oppressive-adaptive orientation, their reliance on attitudes about out-groups, and their dependence on identity formation as a developmental sequence. Rowe, Bennett, and Atkinson lean heavily on Phinney's (1989) stages to form their two-part consciousness levels. The three counseling psychologists constructed their theoretical model to account for White (Euro-American) racial consciousness; however, their status can be generalized to other groups. The model's component elements are (a) unachieved racial consciousness that includes an avoidance, dependent, and dissonant typology and (b) achieved racial consciousness that includes a dominative, conflictive, reactive, and integrative typology. Rowe et al. maintained that the "key element in the process . . . is the role of dissonance," in which "dissonance between previously held attitudes and new attitudes and feelings resulting from some recent, intense, and/or significant life event" can influence movement between the phases (p. 142). The model awaits empirical validation.

Principles of Helms's Racial Identity Model

Racial identity theory addresses the psychological processes that individuals develop in response to societal socialization, in which they are treated as though they belong to mutually exclusive racial groups. Although some theorists (e.g., Phinney, 1996) use *ethnic identity* and *racial identity* synonymously, other theorists argue that ethnic identity pertains to a self-conception based on own-group cultural customs, traditions, and behavioral practices that one learns to function adaptively in one's kinship group(s) (Betancourt & Lopez, 1993; Helms & Talleyrand, 1997). Racial identity, however, refers to the psychological mechanisms that people develop to function effectively in a society where some people enjoy social and political advantage because of their or their ancestors' (presumed) physical appearance, but others suffer disadvantage and lower status for the same reasons. Thus, racial identity is essentially imposed by political and economic forces and typically is based on easily recognizable characteristics, whereas ethnic identity is chosen and may be invisible to people who are not members of the relevant ethnic group.

In U.S. society, racial survival issues differ depending on whether one's ascribed racial group is advantaged or disadvantaged. Traditionally, formal racial identity models have focused on the identity formation of indigenous Black Americans because theorists assumed that they experienced considerable traumatic racial socialization (e.g., racism) but no ethnic cultural socialization at all—especially if they were Black (Cross, 1971; Eriksen, 1968). On the other hand, models of ethnic identity formation and acculturation typically have been used to describe the racial socialization effects for Asian and Pacific Islanders and Latina/Latino Americans, but their experiences of traumatic racial socialization have been disregarded (Alvarez & Helms, 2001; Takaki, 1993).

Moreover, until recently (Helms, 1984, 1989b), the racial identity of White people was an unexplored domain. Instead, when race was discussed with respect to White people, their feelings and attitudes about members of other racial groups rather than their own group or themselves were the focus of most theoretical models pertaining to White people. Thus, many models and measures of White racism exist and continue to be quite influential in the social psychology literature (Dovidio, Kawakami, Johnson, Johnson, & Howard, 1997), but models of White identity are becoming more available (Hardiman, 1982; Helms, 1984, 1990).

Although various models of Black, White, and people of color models of identity are now becoming the focus of research and theory (Hutnik, 1991), in this section, we focus on Helms's models of racial identity. This is because her models were the first to treat racial identity as a construct that could be measured at the individual as well as systemic levels (Cross, Parham, & Helms, 1991). They were also the first to incorporate emic measures of identity. *Emic*, in this case, refers to identity issues that are specific to the racial socialization experiences of members of each group according to the conditions of oppression or advantage in society that characterize their ascribed racial group(s).

Both Helms's people of color and White racial identity models have in common the assumption that the development of a healthy racial self-conception involves transcending the internalized racism inherent in U.S. socialization. For people of color, internalized racism manifests as self- or group-devaluing messages to the effect that oneself and members of one's ascribed racial group are not as good as "pure" White people or members of that group (Takaki, 1993; Zinn, 1980). For White people, internalized racism manifests as internalized socialization messages to the effect that oneself and members of the White group are superior to people of color and, consequently, deserve to have privileged status relative to them. As a consequence, for people of color, development of a healthy "nonracist" identity involves transcending messages intended to communicate inferiority, whereas for Whites, it involves transcending messages intended to communicate superiority and privilege.

Helms (1997) proposed that transcendence for all groups occurs via a developmental process in which, increasingly, more cognitively and emotionally complex schemas for processing racial information potentially become available to the person. She suggested that schemas are the observable or measurable aspects of identity but that statuses are the dynamic or motivational forces that define the schemas. Other theorists use "stages" rather than "statuses" as labels for the motivational forces as Helms formerly did (Helms, 1984, 1990; Phinney, 1990; Sellers, Chavous, & Cooke, 1998). However, regardless of how the processes or their exact content are labeled, most contemporary theories share the following assumptions: (a) identity development is a person-level intrapsychic process that occurs within a particular type of social (racial) context, (b) the developmental process involves efforts to define oneself relative to one's racial group(s), and (c) "better" development occurs as the person acquires the capacity to overcome self-limiting constraints imposed by either one's own group or society more generally. It is probably also the case that most racial identity theories are self-schema theories in that one's self-perceptions relative to one's own group are thought to have broad implications for other aspects of personality development and interpersonal behavior. In this respect, they are similar to other self-schema theories in social psychology (e.g., Iran-Nejad & Winsler, 2000).

In Helms's (1997) people of color racial identity model, the developmental process consists of six statuses and parallel schemas: Conformity, Dissonance, Immersion, Emersion, Internalization, and Integrative Awareness. These processes are assumed to be interrelated and dynamic rather than static. Conformity is characterized by the person's incapacity to perceive the adverse effects of racial socialization on herself or himself and the unthinking internalization of negative socialization messages about those of her or his own racial group(s) that are defined as "not White." The nature of Dissonance is ambivalent awareness of the racial self or one's own group. Immersion is characterized by psychological and (if possible) physical withdrawal into one's own group, idealization of one's group of color, and denigration of the White group(s) and its culture. Internal commitment and interpersonal affiliation with one's group(s) of color and its culture characterize Emersion. Internalization involves ongoing efforts to respond objectively to own-group/White-group racial issues from the perspective of one who is positively committed to his or her own group. Integrative Awareness is the process of integrating various demographic identities (e.g., gender, sexual orientation) into one's self-conception as well as one's conception of others (Helms & Cook, 1999).

Six racial identity statuses and related schemas also define Helms's (1990, 1997) White racial identity model. The statuses are Contact, Disintegration, Reintegration, Pseudo-Independence, Immersion-Emersion, and Autonomy. As is the case with respect to her people of color and Black models of racial identity, the statuses are not disjunctive. Rather, they are conceived as dynamic, interrelated hypothetical processes, which are expressed through observable or measurable schemas. Contact is characterized by a lack of self-awareness with respect to one's own or the White group's privileged racial status in society. The process of Disintegration involves ambivalent identification with the White racial group and confusion about the implications of membership in the group for oneself. Reintegration status is characterized by psychological and physical separation of oneself from all people and things perceived to be "not White" and idealization of the White group. Pseudo-Independence is characterized by an intellectualized understanding of White privilege and oneself as a beneficiary of it. Immersion-Emersion is the process of redefining Whiteness to avoid benefiting from White privilege and attempting to replace "bad" White people with other White people who share a similar racial consciousness. The Autonomy status defines an ongoing process of recognizing racial as well as other forms of oppression and attempting to eradicate them.

The parallel or co-related schemas for racial identity statuses are hypothesized to be multidimensional. In other words, they may be expressed in several ways. For example, for people of color, possible characteristics of the Conformity schema are obliviousness, distortion, and minimization. For White people, possible characteristics of the Contact schema are obliviousness, denial, and avoidance. Both models are summarized in Helms (1997) and Helms and Piper (1994); Helms and Cook (1999) provide real-life examples of each.

Social Interaction Theory

Because schematic behaviors are often visible to other people, the perceived behaviors may become the catalysts for other people's racial reactions. That is, perceived racial identity reactions stimulate the perceiver's racial identity reactions in response to them. Alternatively, people may use the "appearance" of a stimulus person as the catalyst for their racial identity reactions to the person. Helms (1984, 1997; Helms & Cook, 1999) developed racial identity social interaction theory to describe the qualitative dimensions of various types of race-related interpersonal interactions (e.g., groups, dyads).

Racial identity interaction theory is intended to pertain to two or more individuals of either the same or different races. It assumes that the individuals involved in the interaction are of different social statuses because of race or ethnicity, social role (e.g., parent-child, teacher-student), numerical representation, or other characteristics by which society accords different levels of social power to people. The theoretical constructs are described from the viewpoint of the person or persons with the least social power in the interaction. Also, the model assumes that within the context of the interaction, a person may wield a different level of social power than he or she possesses in interactions external to the interaction.

Thus, three types of racial identity social interactions are progressive, regressive, and parallel. Crossed interactions are subcategories of progressive or regressive interactions. Each type of interaction is characterized by specific behavior and emotional themes, which are described in considerable detail in Helms (1990, 1997) and Helms and Cook (1999, chap. 7).

Briefly, parallel interactions are defined as placid, harmonious relations whose nature is determined by the characteristics of the schemas that are being expressed. For example, interactions may be parallel because each participant is using a schema that involves addressing racial issues (e.g., Autonomy–Integrative Awareness, Autonomy-Autonomy). They may also be parallel because each participant is using a schema that involves not addressing racial issues (e.g., Contact-Conformity, Conformity-Conformity).

Progressive interactions potentially occur when the participant with the most social power is able to use more developmentally sophisticated schemas to respond to racial events than the participant with less social power. These interactions typically are invigorating, collaborative, and cooperative.

Regressive interactions occur when the participant with greater social power uses more immature racial identity schemas to respond to perceived racial catalysts than the participant with less social power. These types of interactions typically are combative as each participant struggles for power. If they are also crossed (i.e., the racial identity schemas used by participants are opposites on all dimensions), then the interactions may also be hostile or antagonistic.

Measurement of Racial Identity

Measurement of racial identity constructs provides some as yet unresolved dilemmas at both the individual and interaction levels. Racial identity at the individual level typically is measured via ostensible "attitudinal" measures. Because interaction theory proposes that characteristics of the individuals within any given situation determine the quality of the interaction, individual-level measures typically have been used to study interactions. Therefore, it might be useful to discuss some of the measurement issues that are perhaps unique to racial identity measurement as it involves individuals and interactions.

Individual

Racial identity theories typically describe the race-related developmental issues of individuals. Individuals potentially develop the capacity to process racial information better or differently than they could when their response repertoire was limited to less developmentally mature statuses of development. Thus, for example, when a White person is capable of using Immersion-Emersion (e.g., sensitization) as a primary schema for processing racial information, then, according to Helms's (1996) theory, they cannot also use Contact (e.g., obliviousness) as a primary schema. Various pairs of developmental constructs (e.g., schemas, stages) operate in opposition to each other in Helms's racial identity theories as well as in other theories (e.g., Hutnik, 1991; Phinney, 1990). Use of some schemas involves different kinds of repression or suppression of racial cues (i.e., Contact, Conformity), whereas others involve different kinds of sensitization to such cues (e.g., Reintegration, Immersion-Emersion).

According to racial identity theories, an individual should not use both repressing and sensitizing schemas equivalently. Therefore, scales assessing the use of repressing and sensitizing schemas have to be inversely related at the level of the individual respondent, if they adequately reflect racial identity constructs. Consequently, Helms (1999) pointed out that racial identity theoretical constructs are ipsative. The term *ipsative* typically is used in psychometric theory to refer to measures that yield scale scores that are interdependent at the level of the individual (Hicks, 1970). That is, when a person's score on one scale is high, her or his score on another scale has to be low when a measure is ipsative. Ordinarily, ipsativity is caused by structural properties of measures such as response format (e.g., forced choice) or scoring procedures (e.g., subtracting mean total scores from each individual scale). Ipsativity, in the case of measuring racial identity constructs, does not occur because response format or scoring procedures typically consist of summated Likert-type or bipolar attitudinal scales. However, Helms (1999) pointed out that if developmental racial identity constructs are conceptual opposites, they are ipsative (i.e., interdependent) by definition, regardless of the structure of the measure's items or scoring procedures.

An implication of her observation for assessing individuals is that combinations of scale scores (e.g., profiles) rather than single scales (i.e., highest scores) are necessary to adequately capture their characteristics. However, there are virtually no well accepted psychometric procedures available for evaluating the psychometric properties of measures whose constructs and, therefore, scales are interrelated.

Measurement theory in psychology assesses psychometric characteristics of measures from large samples and makes inferences from these large groups to the individual rather than examining characteristics of individuals per se (Nunnally, 1978). Thus, properties of scale scores such as reliability and validity coefficients typically are summary statistics derived from large groups. Use of traditional psychometric analyses is problematic when a measure is ipsative or partially ipsative for several reasons. Because scale scores must be interrelated to adequately reflect the theory on which they are based, reliability coefficients also must be interrelated such that when the reliability of one scale is high, the reliability of its conceptual opposite has to be low (cf. Tenopyr, 1988). Rather than recognizing this statistical artifact as a spurious effect, researchers have often used such findings as evidence that racial identity scales were not functioning properly and erroneously discarded or revised measures based on such findings (Behrens, 1997; Swanson, Tokar, & Davis, 1994).

If a measure is ipsative, regardless of the reason for its ipsativity (i.e., theory, scoring procedures), then some of its scales will be inversely related to each other for reasons previously discussed. In such cases, if factor analysis is used to study the psychometric properties of the scales, then bipolar factors will be identified. These factors merely indicate that within the sample, some people use one type of racial identity schema whereas others in the sample use the opposite schema.

Several theorists and researchers have recommended statistical procedures that can be used when factor analysis is counterindicated (Cohen & Cohen, 1975; Cornwell & Dunlap, 1994; Guilford, 1952; Johnson, Wood, & Blinkhorn, 1988). Recommended strategies include theory-driven hierarchical regression analyses in which scales are successively entered in an order derived from theoretical principles, Q-type factor analyses, cluster analyses, and configural or profile analyses in which people rather than scales or items are the variables. Although racial identity measures have been the focus of many psychometric studies, researchers typically have used traditional psychometric criteria to evaluate the scales regardless of whether such criteria were appropriate.

Interactions

Assessment of the dynamics of racial identity social interactions has been the least investigated area of racial identity theory. When assessing the racial identity themes of social interactions, measurement problems occur because no measures have been developed to date that assess climates from a racial identity theoretical perspective. Therefore, researchers either study these processes qualitatively or attempt to classify interactions based on scale scores of the individuals involved in the interactions (Ladany, Inmani, Constantine, & Hofheinz, 1997). Yet given that patterns of scores rather than single scores best describe a person, the assessment problem with respect to interactions is how to combine the patterns of individuals to effectively reflect the nature of interactions involving them.

The Measurement of Ethnic Identity

Ethnic groups can be viewed as units of analysis. To identify and discover the ethnic perspective of an ethnocultural group, Berry (1985) suggested that one should first consider compiling an inventory. The investigator should carefully explore the concept of a group's ideas about ethnic identification, which essentially involves a cognitive orientation and values expressions from a cognitive-behavioral orientation. Determining one's ethnicity provides researchers with data that enable them to define clustered homogeneous subgroups. Identifying value orientations, in addition, provides data that reveal the extent to which a respondent endorses traditional indigenous values against those more representative of a dominant culture that serves as the major acculturating agent. Presumably a native-oriented, nonacculturated individual would endorse and act out native-oriented values, and one who expressed the least ethnic identification would espouse values more in line with the group to which he or she affiliates. Once data are accumulated on the two variables, researchers can then proceed to conduct ethnic group-specific and comparative cross-cultural studies by introducing other variables of interest. Furthermore, data on the two variables could extend the measurement procedure to a deeper, more definitive level, assuming a relatively homogeneous sample of members is obtained from a particular subgroup or for a generalized category of the unit as a whole.

Hierarchical Nesting and Identity

A hierarchical nesting respondent identification procedure produces a rather subjective interpretation of one's ethnicity and value orientation. In fact, the method comes close to the main premises of symbolic interactionism, which are

1. Humans act toward things on the basis of the meanings that the things have for them;
2. The meaning of the things is derived from, or arises out of, the social interaction that one has with one's fellows; and
3. The meanings are handled in, and modified through, an interpretative process used by the person in dealing with the things he encounters. (Blumer, 1969, p. 2)

In more specific terms, one's ethnicity and expression of values are centralized meanings particular to the individual and therefore have intrinsic importance in their own right. The main premise of symbolic interactionism closely resembles Triandis's (1972) notion of subjective culture; however, he takes a more collective rather than an individual approach. "By subjective culture," Triandis says, "we mean a cultural group's characteristic way of perceiving its social environment" (p. 3). The variables of the subjective culture approach are essentially attributes of cognitive domains and are analyzed by extracting consistently generated responses, which generates a map outlining the group's characteristics. Use of both perspectives comes close to emergent thinking of the *neoideographic approach, a* term probably first introduced by Zavalloni (1980). The approach actually emphasizes the person element in the Person × Situation schema advocated by the interactional school of personality. The importance of a neoidiographic perspective lies in the manner in which an individual interprets and internalizes lifeways and converts them to thoughtways, both of which become the source of one's identity. Zavalloni emphasized that neoidiographic data take the form of "psychological processes that are idiosyncratic and individual rather than central tendencies in an aggregate" (p. 109). Data, therefore, take the form of "idiosyncratic cognitive productions" such as those elicited by free-association procedures. It can be argued that ethnic identification is a subjective experience designed "to express affiliation, allegiance or oneness" with a preferred group (Casino, 1981, p. 16). Equally important is the notion that ethnic identity is contextual, in that it

> is a product of *social transaction* [italics added] insofar as one assumes an ethnic identity by claiming it and demonstrating the conventional signs of membership. A claimant is always subject to the response of others who may concur with or deny the claim. (Casino, 1981, p. 18)

Efforts at establishing ethnic identity typically occur at an *exonymic* level, where the researcher presents a set of fixed attitude-like statements to the respondents. Often, the ethnic identity scale resembles a pseudo-etic set of items. What emerges is an outsider-produced level of identity, the exonymic, and not the respondent's *autonymic* definition. Ethnic actors indeed embody an ethnic consciousness (Klineberg & Zavalloni, 1969) that is closely aligned with the culturalogical elements of the group with which they affiliate. The ultimate test, of course, is "the 'authentic' union of personal identity (the autonym) with communal identity" (Casino, 1981, p. 17). Therefore, it is logical to assume that a concordance would exist between the autonymic and the exonymic, in which importance is placed on the individual's own categories and intentions for self-identification. Yet it would be foolhardy to assume that one's criteria would not line up with those of the group; often, however, the criteria developed by researchers do not align with the group's criteria and hence may well be conceived as "pseudo-exonymic" or, worse yet, an "ethnic gloss."

Nesting the ethnic identity of an individual from a neoidiographic process and following the symbolic interactionist approach can serve to refine the identification of ethnic group samples. It makes sense, then, that merely identifying respondents on the basis of outward physical appearances and their present residence is hardly an "authentic" representation of the cultural group in question.

Neoidiographic ethnic identification involves more than merely nesting oneself in a hierarchical scheme. More often than not, individuals will use rather "ethnolocal" speech patterns and gestures to promote the authenticity of their claim. If outward physical appearances do not mesh or there is the sense that the other party doubts the identity claim, ethnic actors will tend to exaggerate and give emphasis to mannerisms and speech idiosyncrasies known to be particular (or peculiar) to the group in question. Such emphasis of ethnolocal mannerisms often occurs when people from the same ethnic group gather in geographic areas other than their homelands or communities of common origin. The somewhat stylized ritual can be referred to as *situational ethnicity*, in which ethnic actors take the occasion to reaffirm their ethnicity, often to the dismay and puzzlement of outsiders. Including these ethnic specific mannerisms in a measure of ethnic identification, although a worthy research effort in its own right, would be awkward, time-consuming, and possibly redundant.

Multidimensionality of Measurement

Santiago-Rivera (1999) pointed out that ethnic identity is multidimensional and consists of the following components: self-identification or the label individuals give themselves; knowledge about one's own culture, including language, customs, values, beliefs, and norms; attitudes and feelings about group membership; and language fluency. Note that particularly if a single component is chosen, what is being measured may be very circumscribed and not comparable between studies. Measurement, because it is typically done at a single point in time, attempts to capture a dynamic construct with methods intended for static concepts. For example, given that ethnic identity can be situational and change within a person across time or context, the measurement captures a moment or stage in time and poses a general context within which to answer questions. Nevertheless, several researchers have attempted to develop scales that capture several components of the first four approaches (e.g., Felix-Ortiz, 1994, for Latinos measuring self-identification, knowledge, preferences, and behaviors; Suinn, Ahuna, & Khoo, 1992, for Asians assessing self-identification, preferences, and behaviors; and Phinney, 1992, for any multiple-group identification emphasizing the cognitive and affective components).

The assessment and measurement of ethnic identification must account for people's natal background, subjective preferences, the behavior they are likely to engage in that reflects their ethnic and cultural interests, and the extent to which various situations and contexts influence their pronouncement and enactment of their ethnicity. Use of a single construct such as natality or one's self-declaration is insufficient to capture the full effect that identity has on our lives. In keeping with this position, Trimble (1995) developed a four-part ethnic identity measurement model that includes natal, subjective, behavioral, and situational measurement domains. Use of a subjective label is one small part of the measurement process. The depth of one's identification can be expanded to include measures of acculturative status, ego involvement, value preferences, role models, and preferred reference groups, and participation in cultural and religious activities, among many other variables. Figure 1 shows the interactive nature of the four domains and some variables that might be considered for each one. The situational setting domain presents unusual methodological and measurement challenges as the list of situations that one finds himself or herself in on any given day can vary considerably. Moreover, certain situations may be prescriptive, so one may find it necessary to shift the degree to which he or she identifies with a group to accommodate the unwitting ethnic rules of the setting that consists of members of another ethnic group. Often referred to as situational ethnicity, the possibility that one may shift to accommodate bicultural or multicultural ethnic demands presents extraordinary measurement problems that cannot be captured in a typical survey format.

Ethnic identity can be conveyed by a self label. This self-identification can be symbolic or nonsymbolic. In contrast to early assumptions that such self-labels are absolutely correlated with reference group recognition of an individual, these components are separated. Measurement is simple and occurs by selecting a label from a list, using narrative studies, or having children selecting pictures or dolls to identify themselves.

Affective, attitudinal, and value endorsement constitutes another way of trying to establish ethnic identity. In essence, this conceptual approach to identity attempts to measure similarity to some static notion of ethnicity and a sense of belonging and affiliation. Direct questions about affiliation; questionnaires asking about activities, food preferences, and social affiliations; and questionnaires or scales attempting to measure ethnic pride are characteristic of measurement. Betancourt and Lopez (1993) and Phinney (1996) have emphasized the importance of measuring cultural values rather than having single items to confirm or disconfirm ethnicity.

Intellectual knowledge about the group with whom one identifies constitutes another means of determining the degree of ethnic identity. This cognitive knowledge can be measured through questionnaires and narrative interviews assessing knowledge of history, traditions, and how one has used this information to construct, strengthen, and understand one's ethnicity.

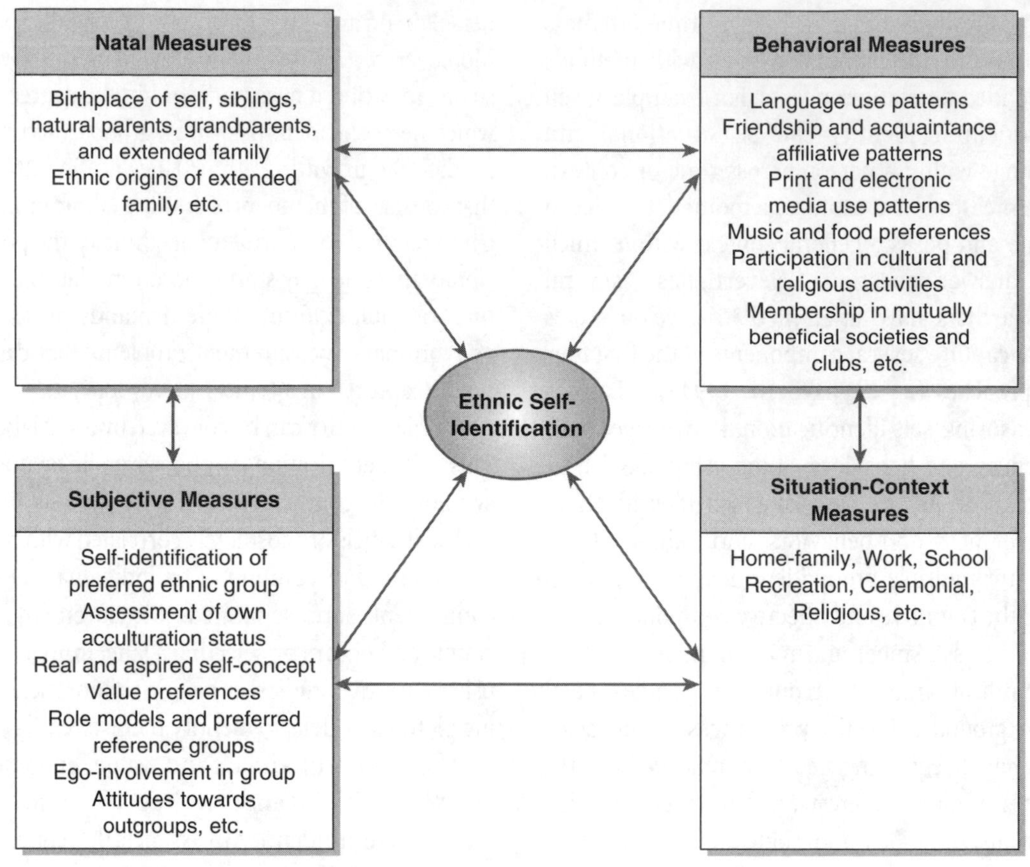

Figure 1 Ethnic Self-Identification Measurement Domains

Worldview and relational orientation of self within and between the reference ethnic community serves as a different approach to understanding ethnic identity. Questionnaires are usually used to assess orientation to the family *(familialism),* individualism, and collectivism. Work in this area suggests that the latter two concepts are very complex and are contextually and class driven. Collectivism, in contrast to individualism, puts the group's well-being and goals above the individual. These orientations have drastic implications for the value a group or individual places on interdependence versus independence, the age and orientation to attachment and separation, and motives for affiliation (Markus & Kitayama, 1991). However, Singelis, Triandis, Bhawuk, and Gelfand (1995) have noted that horizontal and vertical aspects exist within collectivism. Vertical collectivism is class driven. Those with wealth and status in otherwise collectivistic cultures operate very much from day to day with an individualistic orientation determining one's level of identification. Nonetheless, the arguments for using an abridged version of identity structure analysis in the field are compelling (Weinreich & Saunderson, 2002).

Most measures of ethnic identity provide little or no opportunity to assess the variable and fluctuating nature of the concept. One's identification with an ethnic group is not static or immutable. It can and does change over time as a function of varied circumstances and social contexts. In some situations, people tacitly identify with significant others who are associated with the contexts, and then there are other settings where an individual may act quite differently because the ethnic makeup may be quite different. When individuals vary their behavior, they may more or less vary their level of group association from a weak-nominal, almost passive, level to a strong-committed, active one.

Hence, it may be that one's intensity of ethnic identification fluctuates with a particular social context or situation. According to Weinreich (1986), one's ethnic identity is "situated in a specific social context [and] is defined as that part of the totality of one's self construal" (p. 299). Weinreich has been exploring the variable nature of situated identities through the use of identity structure analysis (ISA), a method that permits the operationalization of "a person's conflicted identification with another, so that the relative magnitudes of self's various identification conflicts may be estimated" (p. 300). As a result of his extensive work on the subject, Weinreich strongly suggested that

> (1) individuals can indeed be somewhat different beings according to which ethnic context they cue into; (2) when cued into the one ethnicity, the values characteristics of the "alternative" ethnicity may be emphasized; and (3) in . . . linguistic contexts, the identity structures of individuals are essentially the same kind of complex amalgamation of identification elements across . . . ethnicities. (pp. 305–306)

ISA involves the use of a complex array of measurement items and therefore could be time-consuming. It, too, necessitates dealing with specific situations one encounters to determine one's level of identification. Nonetheless, the arguments for using an abridged version of ISA in the field are compelling (Weinreich & Saunderson, 2002).

Oetting and Beauvais (1991) proposed an orthogonal cultural identification theory and a correspondent measurement tool to assess cultural identity. Their approach is built on the assumption that cultural identity is not a linear phenomenon and follows the four-part ethnic identity measurement model developed by Trimble (1995) (cf. Bates et al., 1997). They argued that cultural dimensions are independent of one another and that an increasing identification with one culture does not produce a decreasing identification with another culture. One could, for example, highly identify with two cultural groups and conversely not identify with any group. Hence, the researchers would argue that an individual could conceivably identify with two, three, and even four cultural groups and not in the least be disoriented or confused about their cultural identification.

Oetting and Beauvais (1991) developed a set of items that allows an individual to "independently express identification or lack of identification" with several cultural groups (p. 663). They claimed that "in large-scale surveys of adults, only two basic items may be needed to assess identification with any one culture reasonably well: (1) Do you live in the . . . way of life? and (2) Are you a success in the . . . way of life?" (p. 664). Other issues can be added to assess such things as family identification and tradition, participation in cultural events, language preferences, and parental identification to expand the scale's measurement domains and its presumed effectiveness.

The Orthogonal Cultural Identity Scale has been used to determine the relationship between cultural identity and drug use. Results have been mixed. Bates et al. (1997) found that a moderately strong identification with American Indian culture among fourth to sixth graders predicted less drug use; however, no relationship was found for adolescents. In another study, Oetting and Beauvais (1990) found that Hispanic adolescent females with high cultural identity were less likely to use drugs, particularly marijuana.

Strengthening our understanding of ethnic minority respondents using measures of identification is no small matter. Smith (1980) reminds us that "(1) ethnicity is a difficult attribute to measure; and (2) ethnic identification does not start with given nationalities, but rather begins with whether a person has an ethnicity to identify with" (p. 92). Indeed, efforts to develop ethnic identity scales tacitly assume that people have an ethnicity that they can call their own. Phinney (1991) presented a model that presents the variable components that define ethnic identity. The model is a continuum with one end representing a high, strong, secure, or achieved level of identity and the other a low, weak, or diffuse identity. The former continuum would describe a person with a strong identity as one who has high self-identification, is involved in ethnic behaviors and practices, evaluates his or her own group positively, is committed to belonging to the group, and is happy with membership. Phinney's model typifies the approach taken by most who develop ethnic identity measures. Weinreich's (1986) work with ISA would be an exception.

What follows is a brief overview of the approaches taken to measure the construct over the years. The literature on the topic is extensive; hence, the following reflects a small portion of what is available.

Language has been used both as indices of core ethnic identity and acculturation (Giles, 1977). However, ties with one's ethnic group of choice may be maintained despite loss of language or fluency. Language is thought to be core because of the way in which it is a lens for a worldview.

Some studies have attempted to assess ethnic identity using multiple components from the previous variable list but examine changes in identity over time with age and life circumstance. These range from large-scale studies to small ones but often involve an interview to illuminate the process of this dynamic aspect of ethnicity.

Socialization experiences of mixed-race and transracial adoptees can influence ethnic identity and awareness of one's own natal culture. McRoy, Zurcher, Lauderdale, and Anderson (1984) found that the degree to which families discussed racial identity issues can affect transracial youths' perception of themselves when compared to members of their own ethnic group; hence, identities varied as a function of the cultural composition of a family's network. In a related finding, McRoy and Freeman (1986) emphasized that racial conception and racial evaluation can influence a child's racial identity and that attention should be given to the two processes in working with racially mixed families. Andujo (1988) also found that socioeconomic factors could influence an adopted child's ethnic identity. To adequately describe and account for the development of racial identity, Poston (1990) argued that the following measurement areas must be considered: personal identity, choice of group categorization, enmeshment/denial, appreciation, and integration.

A number of studies point to a potential relationship between intermarriage and adoption and degrees of ethnic identity both among married partners, offspring, and added family members. Judd (1990) found that in families with parents who have different religious affiliations, material influences can serve to maintain or enhance a youth's religio-ethnic identity, especially if the child follows the mother's religious preference. In a related study, Parsonson (1987) found that children's ethnic identities are stronger when parents come from the same ethnic group.

Immigration and relocation are potent forms of sociocultural change. A few researchers have conducted studies to examine the effects of resettlement on ethnic identity, especially among Asian American populations. Bromley (1988) drew attention to the identity formation problems occurring among Southeast Asian adolescent refugees, especially those who were unaccompanied, to the United States. She pointed out that four distinct conditions have affected identity development among this age group—specifically, exposure to overwhelming tension-producing situations, failure in values, withdrawal from channels that promote identity formation, and inadequate coping mechanisms. Westermeyer, Neider, and Callies's (1989) decade-long study of relocated Hmong in Minnesota supports some of Bromley's contentions. Essential to the maintenance of culture among the refugees was the maintenance of traditional values—a finding that seems to be a consistent theme in the literature (cf. Wooden, Leon, & Toshima, 1988).

Identity formation is especially significant among adolescents. As part of the process, ethnic minorities often are saddled with the additional matter of affirming and internalizing their cultural background into the formation process. Phinney and Tarver (1988) found that more than a third of their eighth grade respondents actively engaged in a search for their ethnic identity; the search was especially evident for Black females. The authors also found that Blacks tended to focus on their own ethnic background, whereas White youth were more concerned about relationships with other groups. Forming a solid identity with one's own ethnic group, however, can be accompanied by some behavioral and personal problems. Grossman, Wirt, and Davids (1985) found among samples of Chicano and Anglo youth that ethnic esteem mediates with self-esteem. Chicano youth expressed strong ethnic esteem but demonstrated low self-esteem and low behavioral adjustment patterns. Gonzalez (1988), in a related study, found that high-achieving Chicano women who expressed strong ethnic esteem tended to be a threat to Chicano males; the threat perception tended to create distress for the women. Maintenance of ethnic identity, therefore, creates a conflict between achievement and the desire to maintain close interpersonal and cultural relations with men. Conflicts among adolescent Hispanic women extend into many spheres and become so overwhelming that suicide may result. Identity and acculturative status problems can be a contributing factor (Zayas, 1987).

Caetano (1986) developed a useful fourfold measure of ethnic identification to assess drinking patterns and alcohol problems among a sizable household sample of Hispanics. Respondents in his survey were asked a series of demographic and ethnic identification questions that focused on (a) ethnicity of family of origin, (b) own or subjective ethnic identification, (c) country of ancestors, and (d) respondent's country of birth. Results from his study show that different ethnic identifiers are useful in assessing levels of alcohol consumption among Hispanics, as there were significant differences among drinking patterns. Caetano commented that "ethnicity of family of origin seems to be the most encompassing definition, followed by national group, and there is a good level of agreement between these two rubrics" (p. 341). However, he cautioned that "the search for a standard definition of Hispanic ethnicity does not seem to be near its end . . . [and that] researchers should consider multiple ways to identify this ethnic group" (p. 342).

Teske and Nelson (1973) developed two scales to assess identity among Mexican Americans. One scale measured identity and consisted of 16 items, and the other assessed interaction with others and contained 19 items. Reliability coefficients for the two scales were quite high, suggesting that the overall combined item pool could be used with confidence. Garcia (1982) extended the notion of identity among Chicanos to include measures of political consciousness along with ones for ethnic consciousness. He found that the two constructs were not highly correlated and suggested that ethnicity may be more related to self-identification.

Elements of cognitive social learning, cognitive development, and self-esteem theories were included in a study of ethnic identity among Mexican American children (Bernal, Knight, Garza, Ocampo, & Cota, 1990). Using a "Who am I?" approach that ties identity with self-concept, Bernal et al. (1990) demonstrated that age-related developmental shifts occurred among Mexican American children. Shifts in changing identities, therefore, may influence the social settings and persons who are likely to have an impact on the child.

Researchers have resorted to the use of less obtrusive measures in an effort to tap ethnic identity. Most researchers are acutely aware of the seminal doll selection technique developed by Clark and Clark (1947). Basically, Black children showed a preference for White dolls, suggesting that the youth identified more with Whites than Blacks. Their work, especially the methodology and conclusions, has been questioned by other researchers (see Katz & Zalk, 1974; Stephan & Rosenfield, 1978). Use of the technique persists. For example, although aware of the flaws, Vaughan (1986) demonstrated that Maori children in New Zealand select pictures and dolls that represent their image of their group within the dominant culture. The article also contains a solid review of the literature on using picture and doll tests. Fine and Bowers (1984) replicated the design and procedure of the Clark and Clark studies. Their findings revealed that young female Blacks were more likely to identify with Black dolls than were young Black males. The socioeconomic and political climate, the authors suggest, may contribute to their findings; such factors must be considered when results from doll selection techniques are used. For instance, Gopaul-McNicol (1988) found that samples of Black preschool youth from New York City and Trinidad preferred the White doll over a Black one. The racial contexts in which the techniques are used also must be considered. Pfeffer (1984) used a Draw-A-Person procedure with Yoruba (Nigerian) children as a measure of ethnic identity. Findings revealed that the Yoruba youth avoided use of dark colors when coloring the skin; results from a comparable Black sample in the United States were quite different.

Acculturation and Ethnic Identity Measures

Ethnicity is learned through a process of enculturation. In this process, an abstract concept of ethnicity must be learned through direct instruction and interaction within the reference group; at a more advanced level, the social and political meaning and construction of ethnicity, like race, is instructed by relations between groups (Bernal & Knight, 1993; Berry, 1975). Unfortunately, as racial identity is constructed in part through a process of stressful and traumatic experience (Root, 2001), ethnic identity is influenced by a process of acculturative stress. Both assimilation and acculturation reflect processes rather than static points. They are processes that reflect tension and intergroup interaction. Trimble (1988, 1996) has proposed an ecological framework to understand the process of ethnic identity development in American Indians that is composed of exogenous variables, person variables, situations, and acculturative patterns filtered through worldviews, cognitive appraisals, and behavioral perceptions.

Acculturation historically referred to relinquishing ethnic group ways and adopting the host culture's way. Thus, to be assimilated, one must acculturate. Whereas acculturation has been discussed as a unidirectional process, the ratio of one group to another may allow for a bidirectional influence. For example, Le Vine and Padilla (1980) suggested that there may be mutual influences in some of the southwest regions due to the large historical and population size of persons of Mexican descent. Similarly, Trimble (1988) noted that mutual influence has a salient impact on groups, influencing identity and acculturation in various contextual settings.

The bulk of the research in psychological acculturation tends to emphasize person characteristics that emerge from contact with and participation in some lifestyle facet of the contact or dominant culture. A selected review of the literature indicates that many of the variable domains included in identity measures can be found in acculturation scales and measures. In compiling a variable domain, a researcher is likely to ask informants to respond to a series of items that assess the number of elements they use or borrow from the dominant culture, those elements of their own culture that they continue to use, and the level of participation in activities found in both cultural contact groups. An example of a contact measure is the 8-variable scale developed by Berry, van de Koppel, et al. (1986) for use in Central Africa. The scale tapped such contact-specific information as number of local languages spoken, property and material ownership, employment status, clothing, and religiosity. Responses to the scale were collapsed to a single score from which an inference about one's acculturative status was derived. Rauch, Bowler, and Schwarzer (1987) developed a 3-item culture contact scale to assess acculturation effects on the self-esteem of three American ethnic minority groups. Although Rauch et al. found significant differences for self-esteem between the groups, they also reported an extremely low correlation between contact and self-esteem ($r = .12$), suggesting that contact may not influence one's sense of self.

Triandis, Kashima, Shimada, and Villareal (1986) used a participatory measure of acculturation to assess the existence of cultural differences among a sample of Hispanic and non-Hispanic navy recruits. Triandis et al. used a 4-item index, including items that assessed length of residence in the United States, media acculturation, number of non-Hispanic coworkers, and number of non-Hispanic friends and romantic partners. Summing the four indices created a single acculturation score. The study's Hispanic participants were grouped according to the single culture index into low-, medium-, and high-acculturation categories. The authors concluded that "one can use indexes of acculturation to establish the existence of cultural differences" (p. 67). Pumariega (1986) also used a 15-item contact and participation acculturation scale to explore the relationship between socioeconomic status (SES) and eating attitudes among Hispanic adolescent girls. His results showed that the more one moves toward a contact culture, the greater is one's vulnerability for developing an eating disorder. Pumariega also found that SES is not correlated with acculturative status, suggesting that one's occupational and educational status may not be useful in understanding the influences of cultural contact and participation.

Hispanic populations, more than any other ethnic group, appear to be the focus of interest among a few acculturation researchers. Franco (1983) developed a 10-item acculturation scale for Mexican American children that is filled out by a child's teacher, counselor, or someone who knows the child well. Franco included items to tap peer associations, ethnic identity, and language preference. Martinez, Norman, and Delaney (1984) also developed a scale for Hispanic children. The acculturation measure contains 23 items and assesses food preferences, Spanish usage among self and significant others, and general cultural exposure. Both scales reportedly have a high reliability. Montgomery and Orozco (1984) cross-validated an acculturation scale developed for use with Mexican Americans by Cuéllar, Harris, and Jasso (1980).

A factor analysis of the items generated four dimensions: language preference, ethnic identity and generation removed from Mexico, ethnicity of friends and associates, and extent of direct contact with Mexico. Their findings tend to support the general item content of related Hispanic acculturation measures. Mainous (1989), however, suggested that self-concept, conceived of as role identity, should be included in Mexican American acculturation scales. His 9-item index yielded three factor dimensions: language, self-definition as an insider, and self-definition as an outsider.

Mendoza (1989) developed an elaborate Cultural Life Style Inventory to assess acculturative status among Mexican American adolescents and adults. The inventory taps five factor dimensions: intrafamily language usage, extrafamily language usage, social affiliations and activities, cultural identification and pride, and cultural resistance, incorporation, and shift. Note again that the scale contents capture much of the same information developed in other scales.

Richman, Gaviria, Flaherty, Birz, and Wintrob (1987) developed a 21-item scale that tapped five dimensions—language (6 items), customs (4 items), ethnic identity (1 item), sociability (4 items), and discrimination (6 items)—for use among Huahuapuquien Indian migrants in Lima, Peru. The multifaceted scale was used to assess the acculturative process within the Peruvian social-structural context. Of importance is the researchers' attempt to assess the effects of discrimination on adaptation.

Suinn, Rickard-Figueroa, Lew, and Vigil (1987) developed an acculturation scale for assessing Asian acculturation; the scale contents were modeled after several scales developed for use with Hispanics. Atkinson and Gim (1989) modified the Suinn-Lew scale and administered it to three different Asian American groups. Results show that most acculturated students were likely (a) to recognize the need for professional psychological help, (b) to be tolerant of the stigma associated with psychological help, and (c) to be open to discussing their problems with a psychologist. Moreover, the researchers were able to validate the Suinn-Lew scale in an applied setting.

Two studies are reported in the literature that draw attention to the development of more generalized acculturation scales that transcend ethnic-specific measures. Oakland and Shermis (1989) analyzed the factor structure of the Sociocultural Scales of the System of Multicultural Pluralistic Assessment. Their analysis supported the existence of four subscales, one of which was urban acculturation. The latter subscale is a measurement domain that heretofore has received little attention in the acculturation field. An American International Relations Scale developed by Sodowsky and Plake (1991) represents the current state of the art in measuring acculturation. The researchers maintain that the following moderator variables influence the acculturation process: (a) generation status, (b) education and income, (c) age, (d) years of residence in the United States, (e) ethnic density of neighborhood, (f) country of birth, and (g) job skills, religion, kinship structures, and purposes of immigration. Their 34-item scale has been expanded to include 43 items and is referred to as the Majority-Minority Relations Survey (Sodowsky, Lai, & Plake, 1991). Results from their early work with the scale are favorable and suggest that a valid, generalizable, and reliable scale has been developed to assess acculturation attitudes of Asian Americans and Hispanics.

Most measures of contact-participation acculturation generate a single average or cumulative score. To some extent, the single unit scales have proven to be reliable and hence useful largely because certain researchers have been able to discriminate between and among cultural groups and predict outcomes such as mental health, alcohol and drug use, and eating disorders. The use of a single score is presumptive because it considers all that fall at or about the unit to be relatively homogeneous. That may not be the case.

Berry, Trimble, and Olmedo (1986) agreed that "not every person in the acculturating group will necessarily enter into the acculturation process in the same way or to the same degree" (p. 296). Not every individual from his or her culture will respond to the elements presented by the dominant culture. Individual variations in the adaptation, adjustment, and internalization of another culture's folkways and mores can be mediated by resistance, fear, anxiety, allegiance to one's own culture, and the level of perceived acceptance in one's own and the dominant culture. Moreover, an individual may make specific accommodations in certain settings and situations but in others cling to and maintain traditional and conventional own-culture behaviors. Consequently, one's adjustments and accommodations, combined with the rejection of acceptable behavioral patterns, generate a good deal of variation in acculturative styles. The process of changing and adapting to another culture is not a unidirectional process in which one progresses "solely from the host groups to the newcomer groups" (Richman et al., 1987, p. 841).

Questions concerning the unidirectional issue and individual variations in acculturative styles, combined with the use of single unit measures of acculturation, are beginning to emerge in the literature. Berry (1990) has taken the position, for example, that acculturation can be viewed as a multilinear phenomenon rather than a single dimension. Building his argument on the assumptions that (a) an individual may prefer to remain culturally as he or she has been and (b) that the same individual may prefer to have variable and selective contact and participation with those of other cultures, Berry developed a framework that identifies four varieties of acculturation—namely, integration, assimilation, separation, and marginalization. Using a Likert-type scale format, Berry developed a series of items that ultimately generate four separate cumulative scores, thus providing a more inclusive understanding of one's attitude toward acculturation and one's position in the process.

Padilla (1980) proposed an acculturation framework that embraces elements of the contact-participation dimension and one's perceived loyalty to his or her own culture. Padilla used 11 dimensions (e.g., language preferences, name preference for children) to measure loyalty and 15 dimensions to assess cultural awareness. Padilla concluded that "cultural awareness is the more general component" and "ethnic loyalty is the more tenuous" (p. 65).

Padilla's (1980) two-factor model formed the basis of a multifactorial acculturation model developed by Richman et al. (1987), who agreed that

> the process of acculturation in Peru is composed of a more complex set of sub-components, each of which may have very different social meanings, covary separately for different social status groups, and have differing consequences for psychological distress or well being. (p. 842)

As a consequence of their observations of the various Peruvian cultural groups, Richman et al. (1987) created an overall acculturation scale containing five subscales, including language use; ethnic customs that encompassed music, food preferences, and dress; ethnic identification; sociability preferences; and perceived discrimination. The scale generates six distinct scores. Scale results are useful in identifying variations across age and generation levels and changes among certain individuals that are bidirectional and characterized by inequality.

The measurement of the acculturation process tends to emphasize person characteristics in which information is compiled to identify one's preferences, tendencies, and elements of another culture that internalize into one's lifestyle orientation. Despite the changes occurring in acculturation measures and concepts, problems abound. Escobar and Vega (2000), for example, forcefully challenged the meaning and measurement of acculturation on the grounds that it has become a "catchall" for anything that has to do with social and individual change involving people from different ethnocultural groups. Similarly, Suarez-Orozco (2001) has pointed out that assimilation and acculturation themes predict that change is "directional, unilinear, nonreversible, and continuous" (p. 8), but that is not what occurs with immigrant populations. Berry, Trimble, and Olmedo (1986) admitted that a good deal of confusion surrounds the measurement of acculturation, owing largely to confusion surrounding the conceptualization of acculturation itself. To achieve a partial remedy to the confusion, Berry suggested that any comprehensive study should approach the topic from a multivariate perspective. From this perspective, researchers should compile information about an acculturating group's general mode of adaptation, experiences with cultural contact and conflict, and the contact and conflict experiences of the individual.

A multivariate perspective as recommended by Berry (1983) and amplified by Olmedo (1979) would indeed provide useful information about the source of influences as the acculturation process is experienced. However, such knowledge would provide us with information only about a person's style, preferences, behavior, and orientation. Ethnographic and case-directed interviews of acculturating individuals generate observations that point to the fact that the context in which acculturation occurs and the situations one encounters often dictate unique behaviors that in themselves are situation specific. Given the observations, it would seem reasonable to propose that more attention should be given to the situations and the contexts in which acculturation occurs.

As individuals experience a new culture, they will undoubtedly encounter new and varied situations. For those interested in the acculturative process, it makes sense to focus on the individuals' perceptions of any situation they encounter, the behavior they choose to evoke, and their cognitive appraisals of the effect the situation holds for them. Interactionists—that is, those who study the person-situation interaction—recognize that individuals often will select the situations they encounter. Many situations may not be selected simply because people do not know what to do or how to react. Individual variations in situation selection may be directly related to acculturative status. Hence, the selection of situations may shed some insights on the types of situations selected and consequently further our understanding of the acculturative process.

The advancement of our understanding of the acculturative process interest should focus on how individuals vary or are similar in the selection of situations. This would include an effort to identify how one selects and organizes situations, the motivations involved in the selection process, the perceived ability to perform, and the general feelings elicited by the situation and the behavioral consequences. Argyle (1978) identified four structural variables that appear useful in investigating the situation selection process: choice of situations, grouping of situations, motivation/emotion, and ability.

Including a situational measurement domain in assessing the acculturative process can serve to uncover a relationship between one's identity and one's choice of situations. Foote (1951) suggested that one's identity can be a function of that person's performance in situations and hence can be motivational. He added that a problematic situation calls for performance of a particular act, in which consummations and consequences are more or less anticipated, thereby releasing the energy appropriate to performing it. Successful encounters with problematic situations, especially those experienced in another culture, can assist in strengthening one's sense of confidence and building a bicultural or multicultural sense of identity.

Some Concluding Thoughts

Studies of ethnicity, racial identity, ethnic consciousness, ethnic self-identification, and the measurement of the constructs are part of a complex, intertwined multidisciplinary process. The complexity is confounded by the increased interest in the constructs across many academic disciplines; the levels of analysis particular to each discipline further complicate matters because the units and methods of inquiry often conflict with one another. Although the definitions of the constructs may resemble one another, ethnic and racial identity theories differ from one another both within and between disciplines. Indeed, the "invention of ethnicity is an interdisciplinary field . . . [as are] attempts to understand the processes that give ethnic debates such a virulent centrality in the modern world" (Sollors, 1989, p. xx).

From all indications, the literature and findings from the 2000 census indicate that Americans are probing deeply into their biological ancestry and cultural backgrounds to identify a source for meaning and structure in their lives. From the discoveries, one constructs a "symbolic identity." "If you wish to understand persons—their development and their relations with significant others," maintained Strauss (1959), "you must be prepared to view them as embedded in historical context" (p. 164). In the course of constructing and maintaining the identity, common historical symbols are identified, shared, and passed along to future generations. The symbols also can serve as a public affirmation of one's ethnic claim. Along with the declaration and discovery, individuals are openly expressing pride and respect for their ancestries and their ethnic orientations.

Many of the literature findings suggest that ethnic and racial declarations are not private acts "but are usually if not predominantly public concerns, problematic situations, and issues of public contention as well as private debate" (Strauss, 1959, p. 26). Identity declarations at some point require external validation, and therefore the judgments of others play a major role in the transaction. Ordinarily, people construct their identities within the context of their biological background and the sociopolitical context in which they are socialized. Many people declare their ethnic and racial heritage to place themselves in the social order and seek out settings and situations for confirmation (Harre, 1989). Quite often, people construct their identity and image to fit preferred sociocultural contexts and, along with self-declaration, construct the situations and contexts to fit the preferred image (Fitzgerald, 1993). The identity process, no matter how conceived and measured, is not static and invariant—people change, and their identities and sense of self-satisfaction change accordingly.

Erik Eriksen (1968) undoubtedly has contributed immensely to the ongoing debate about identity development and formation. He maintained that identity was located in the self or core of the individual, and one's communal culture—self-esteem and one's sense of affiliation and belongingness—is deeply affected by the process. Identity, then, is inextricably linked to self-understanding and therefore can be posited "as the academic metaphor for self-in-context" (Fitzgerald,1993, p. ix). Without a context, identity formation and self-development cannot occur.

To further an understanding of identity, most social and psychological theorists must contend with the concept of self. To approach a modicum of understanding of the self process, one must provide plausible if not reasonable explanations for the following domains: physical traits and characteristics, personal experiences and their memory, personal behaviors, "what belongs to me and what I belong to," the person I believe myself to be, and "who and what others tell me I am" (Cirese, 1985). Explanations for these domains consume volumes; indeed, studies of the personal, social, and situational self present a most challenging and daunting task. Adding ethnicity and racial constructs to the inquiry further complicates the exploration.

Future studies and developments in the field of ethnic and racial identity must continue to examine and advance understanding of developmental and self influences such as those advanced by Cross (1991), Helms (1990), and Phinney (1989). In addition, situational and contextual correlates must be examined because ethnic and racial declarations can be influenced by settings. Referred to as "situational ethnicity," people often will modify or amplify their declarations to fit the settings or contexts where others are perceived as potent sources of self and ethnic validation. People will change their speech patterns, often speaking in a dialect or the language (lingua franca) particular to the setting. Moreover, behavioral mannerisms, gestures, physical positioning of the body relative to others, and clothing styles will be adjusted. The extent to which there are modifications may be a function of an individual's need to be accepted and perceived as a member of the group who has not forgotten his or her heritage and cultural background. Similarly, some people may become "more ethnic or native" in ethnic specific contexts because they are most comfortable with the self-presentation.

There is one final important point that bears attention and recognition. Self-identification and self-declarations are powerful phenomena that strongly influence personality, one's sense of belonging, one's quality of life, and one's sense of connectedness with others who share similar identities. The powerful nature of identity can readily be seen in the civil strife and struggles of nations and ethnic groups in Africa and Eastern Europe, along with the growing preoccupation with ethnic differences in North America, especially in Québec. At the core of these struggles is the assertion that individuals have a right to their identity within the context of a common cultural orientation. On that point, Forbes (1990) argued that people have a right to state who and what they are; hence, we must recognize that there are multiple approaches to achieving and asserting identity. And with this in mind, we "must recognize that all ethnic groups and units can change genes, while yet remaining whole and retaining their identity" (Forbes, 1990, p. 48).

References

Alvarez, A. N., & Helms, J. E. (2001). Racial identity and reflected appraisals as influences on Asian Americans' racial adjustment. *Cultural Diversity and Ethnic Minority Psychology, 7,* 217–231.

Andujo, E. (1988). Ethnic identity of transethnically adopted Hispanic adolescents. *Social Work, 33(6),* 531–535.

Argyle, M. (1978). *The psychology of interpersonal behaviour* (3rd ed.). Harmondsworth, UK: Penguin.

Aries, E., & Moorehead, K. (1989). The importance of ethnicity in the development of identity of Black adolescents. *Psychological Reports, 65(1),* 75–82.

Atkinson, D., & Gim, R. (1989). Asian-American cultural identity and attitudes toward mental health services. *Journal of Counseling Psychology, 36(2),* 209–212.

Baldwin, J., Duncan, J., & Bell, Y. (1987). Assessment of African self-consciousness among Black students from two college environments. *Journal of Black Psychology, 13(2),* 27–41.

Bates, S., Trimble, J., & Beauvais, F. (1997). American Indian alcohol involvement and ethnic identification. *Substance Use and Misuse, 32(14)*, 2013–2031.

Behrens, J. T. (1997). Does the White Racial Identity Attitude Scale measure racial identity? *Journal of Counseling Psychology, 44*, 3–12.

Bernal, M., & Knight, G. (Eds.). (1993). *Ethnic identity: Formation and transmission among Hispanics and other minorities.* Albany: State University of New York Press.

Bernal, M., Knight, G., Garza, C., Ocampo, K., & Cota, M. (1990). The development of ethnic identity in Mexican-American children. *Hispanic Journal of the Behavioral Sciences, 12(1)*, 3–24.

Berry, J. (1975). Ecology, cultural adaptation, and psychological differentiation: Traditional patterning and acculturative stress. In R. Brislin, S. Bochner, & W. Lonner (Eds.), *Cultural perspectives in learning* (pp. 207–228). Beverly Hills, CA: Sage.

Berry, J. (1983). Acculturation: A comparative analysis of alternative forms. In R. Samuda & S. L. Woods (Eds.), *Perspectives in immigrant and minority education* (pp. 65–77). New York: Lanham.

Berry, J. (1985). Cultural psychology and ethnic psychology: A comparative analysis. In I. Lagunes & Y. Poortinga (Eds.), *From a different perspective: Studies of behavior across cultures* (pp. 3–15). Lisse, the Netherlands: Swets & Zeitlinger.

Berry, J. (1990). Psychology of acculturation. In J. Berman (Ed.), *Nebraska symposium on motivation* (Vol. 37, pp. 201–234). Lincoln: University of Nebraska Press.

Berry, J., Trimble, J. E., & Olmedo, E. (1986). Assessment of acculturation. In W. J. Lonner & J. W. Berry (Eds.), *Field methods in cross-cultural research* (pp. 291–324). Newbury Park, CA: Sage.

Berry, J., van de Koppel, J., Senechal, C., Annis, R., Bahuchet, S., Cavalli-Sforza, L., & Witkin, H. (1986). *On the edge of the forest: Cultural adaptation and cognitive development in Central Africa.* Lisse, the Netherlands: Swets & Zeitlinger.

Betancourt, H., & Lopez, S. R. (1993). The study of culture, ethnicity, and race in American psychology. *American Psychologist, 48(6)*, 629–637.

Blumer, H. (1969). *Symbolic interactionism: Perspective and method.* Englewood Cliffs, NJ: Prentice Hall.

Bram, J. (1965). Change and choice in ethnic identification. *Transactions of the New York Academy of Sciences, 28(2)*, 242–248.

Broman, C., Neighbors, H., & Jackson, J. (1988). Racial group identification among Black adults. *Social Forces, 67(1)*, 146–158.

Bromley, M. (1988). Identity as a central adjustment issue for the Southeast Asian unaccompanied refugee minor. *Child and Youth Care Quarterly, 17(2)*, 101–114.

Brown, D. E. (1991). *Human universals.* Philadelphia: Temple University Press. Caetano, R. (1986). Alternative definitions of Hispanics: Consequences in an alcohol survey. *Hispanic Journal of Behavioral Sciences, 8*, 331–344.

Carter, R., & Helms, J. (1988). The relationship between racial identity and social class. *Journal of Negro Education, 57(1)*, 22–30.

Casino, E. (1981). *Introduction to ethnicology: Ways of talking about ethnicity.* Unpublished manuscript, University of Hawai'i at Manoa.

Cirese, S. (1985). *Quest: A search for self.* New York: Holt, Rinehart & Winston.

Clark, K. B., & Clark, M. (1947). Racial identification and preferences in Negro children. In T. M. Newcomb & E. L. Hartley (Eds.), *Readings in social psychology* (pp. 169–178). New York: Holt.

Cohen, J., & Cohen, P. (1975). *Applied multiple regression/correlation analyses for the behavioral sciences.* Hillsdale, NJ: Lawrence Erlbaum.

Cornwell, J. M., & Dunlap, W. P. (1994). On the questionable soundness of factoring ipsative data: A response to Saville & Willson (1991). *Journal of Occupational and Organizational Psychology, 67*, 89–100.

Cross, W. (1991). *Shades of black: Diversity in African American identity.* Philadelphia: Temple University Press.

Cross, W. E., Jr. (1971). The Negro-to-Black conversion experience: Toward a psychology of Black liberation. *Black World, 20(9),* 13–27.

Cross, W. E., Jr., Parham, T. A., & Helms, J. E. (1991). The stages of Black identity development: Nigrescence models. In R. L. Jones (Ed.), *Black psychology* (pp. 319–338). Berkeley, CA: Cobb & Henry.

Cuéllar, I., Harris, L., & Jasso, R. (1980). An acculturation scale for Mexican American normal and clinical populations. *Hispanic Journal of Behavioral Sciences, 2,* 199–217.

Dovidio, J. F., Kawakami, K., Johnson, C., Johnson, B., & Howard, A. (1997). On the nature of prejudice: Automatic and controlled processes. *Journal of Experimental Social Psychology, 33(5),* 510–540.

Eriksen, E. (1968). *Identity, youth, and crisis.* New York: Norton.

Escobar, J., & Vega, W. (2000). Mental health and immigration's AAAs: Where are we and where do we go from here? *Journal of Nervous and Mental Disorders, 188(11),* 736–740.

Feagin, J. R. (1978). *Racial and ethnic relations.* Englewood Cliffs, NJ: Prentice Hall.

Felix-Ortiz, M. (1994). A multidimensional measure of cultural identity for Latino and Latina adolescents. *Hispanic Journal of Behavioral Sciences, 16,* 99–116.

Fine, M., & Bowers, C. (1984). Racial self-identification: The effects of social history and gender. *Journal of Applied Social Psychology, 14(2),* 136–146.

Fitzgerald, T. K. (1993). *Metaphors of identity: A culture-communication dialogue.* Albany: State University of New York Press.

Foote, N. (1951). Identification as the basis for a theory of motivation. *American Sociological Review, 16,* 14–21.

Forbes, J. D. (1990). The manipulation of race, caste and identity: Classifying AfroAmericans, Native Americans and Red-Black people. *Journal of Ethnic Studies, 17,* 1–51.

Franco, J. (1983). An acculturation scale for Mexican-American children. *Journal of General Psychology, 108(2),* 175–181.

Garcia, J. (1982). Ethnicity and Chicanos: Measure of ethnic identification, identity, and consciousness. *Hispanic Journal of Behavioral Sciences, 4(3),* 295–314.

Giles, H. (1977). *Language, ethnicity, and intergroup relations.* London: Academic Press.

Gonzalez, J. (1988). Dilemmas of the high-achieving Chicana: The double-bind factors in male/female relationships. *Sex Roles, 18(7–8),* 367–380.

Gopaul-McNicol, S. (1988). Racial identification and racial preference of Black preschool children in New York and Trinidad. *Journal of Black Psychology, 14(2),* 65–68.

Grossman, B., Wirt, R., & Davids, A. (1985). Self-esteem, ethnic identity and behavioral adjustment among Anglo and Chicano adolescents in west Texas. *Journal of Adolescence, 8(1),* 57–68.

Guilford, J. P. (1952). When not to factor analyze. *Psychological Bulletin, 49,* 26–37.

Hardiman, R. (1982). *White identity development: A process oriented model for describing the racial consciousness of White Americans.* Unpublished doctoral dissertation, University of Massachusetts, Amherst.

Harre, R. (1989). Language games and the texts of identity. In J. Shotter & J. J. Gergen (Eds.), *Texts of identity* (pp. 20–35). Newbury Park, CA: Sage.

Heath, D. B. (1978). The sociocultural model of alcohol use: Problems and prospects. *Journal of Operational Psychiatry, 9,* 55–66.

Helms, J. (1984). Toward a theoretical model for explaining the effects of race on counseling: A Black and White model. *The Counseling Psychologist, 12,* 153–165.

Helms, J. (1989a). Considering some methodological issues in racial identity counseling research. *The Counseling Psychologist, 17(2),* 227–252.

Helms, J. (1989b). Eurocentrism strikes in strange ways and in unusual places. *The Counseling Psychologist, 17(4),* 643–647.

Helms, J. (Ed.). (1990). *Black and White racial identity: Theory, research, and practice.* Westport, CT: Greenwood.

Helms, J. E. (1996). Toward a methodology for measuring and assessing "racial" as distinguished from "ethnic" identity. In G. R. Sodowsky & J. Impara (Eds.), *Multicultural assessment in counseling and clinical psychology* (pp. 143–192). Lincoln, NE: Buros Institute of Mental Measurements.

Helms, J. E. (1997). Implications of Behrens (1997) for the validity of the White Racial Identity Attitude Scale. *Journal of Counseling Psychology, 44(1),* 13–16.

Helms, J. E. *(1999).* Another meta-analysis of the White Racial Identity Attitude Scale's Cronbach alphas: Implications for validity. *Measurement & Evaluation in Counseling & Development, 32(3),* 122–137.

Helms, J. E., & Cook, D. A. *(1999). Using race and culture in counseling and psychotherapy: Theory and process.* Needham, MA: Allyn & Bacon.

Helms, J. E., & Piper, R. E. (1994). Implications of racial identity theory for vocational psychology. *Journal of Vocational Psychology, 44,* 124–138.

Helms, J. E., & Talleyrand, R. M. (1997). Race is not ethnicity. *American Psychologist, 52(11),* 1246–1247.

Hicks, L. (1970). Some properties of ipsative, normative, and forced-choice normative measures. *Psychological Bulletin, 74(3),* 167–184.

Hutnik, N. (1991). *Ethnic minority identity: A social psychological perspective.* Oxford, UK: Oxford University Press.

Iran-Nejad, A., & Winsler, A. (2000). Bartlett's schema theory and modern accounts of learning and remembering. *Journal of Mind and Behavior, 21(1–2),* 5–35.

Johnson, C. E., Wood, R., & Blinkhorn, S. F. (1988). Spuriouser and spuriouser: The use of ipsative personality tests. *Journal of Occupational Psychology, 61,* 153–162.

Judd, E. (1990). Intermarriage and the maintenance of religio-ethnic identity: A case study. *Journal of Comparative Family Studies, 21(2),* 251–268.

Katz, P., & Zalk, S. (1974). Doll preferences: An index of racial attitudes? *Journal of Educational Psychology, 66,* 663–668.

Klineberg, O., & Zavalloni, M. (1969). *Tribalism and nationalism.* The Hague, the Netherlands: Mouton.

Kroeber, A., & Kluckhohn, C. (1952). Culture: A critical review of concepts and definition. *Papers of the Peabody Museum of American Archeology and Ethnology, 47(1).*

Ladany, N., Inmani, A., Constantine, M., & Hofheinz, E. (1997). Supervisee multicultural case conceptualization ability and self-reported multicultural competence as functions of supervisee racial identity and supervisor focus. *Journal of Counseling Psychology, 44,* 284–293.

Le Vine, E., & Padilla, A. (1980). *Crossing cultures in therapy: Pluralistic counseling for the Hispanic.* Belmont, CA: Wadsworth.

Looney, J. (1988). Ego development and Black identity. *Journal of Black Psychology, 15(1),* 41–56.

Mainous, A. (1989). Self-concept as an indicator of acculturation in Mexican Americans. *Hispanic Journal of Behavioral Sciences, 11(2),* 178–189.

Marín, G., & Marín, B. V. (1982). Methodological fallacies when studying Hispanics. In L. Bickman (Ed.), *Applied social psychology annual* (Vol. 3, pp. 99–117). Beverly Hills, CA: Sage.

Markus, H. R., & Kitayama, S. (1991). Culture and the self: Implications for cognition, emotion, and motivation. *Psychological Review, 98(2),* 224–253.

Martinez, R., Norman, R., & Delaney, H. (1984). A Children's Hispanic Background Scale. *Hispanic Journal of Behavioral Sciences, 6(2),* 103–112.

Mays, V. (1986). Identity development of Black Americans: The role of history and the importance of ethnicity. *American Journal of Psychotherapy, 40(4),* 582–593.

McRoy, R., & Freeman, E. (1986). Racial identity issues among mixed-race children. *Social Work in Education, 8(3),* 164–174.

McRoy, R., Zurcher, L., Lauderdale, M., & Anderson, R. (1984). The identity of transracial adoptees. *Social Casework, 65(1),* 34–39.

Mead, M. (1935). *Sex and temperament in three primitive societies.* New York: Morrow.

Mead, M. (2001). *Letters from the field, 1925–1975.* New York: HarperCollins.

Mendoza, R. (1989). An empirical scale to measure type and degree of acculturation in Mexican-American adolescents and adults. *Journal of Cross-Cultural Psychology, 20(4),* 372–385.

Mio, J., Trimble, J., Arredondo, P., Cheatham, H., & Sue, D. (Eds.). (1999). *Keywords in multicultural interventions: A dictionary.* Westport, CT: Greenwood.

Montague, A. (1997). *Man's most dangerous myth: The fallacy of race* (6th ed.). Walnut Creek, CA: AltaMira Press.

Montgomery, G., & Orozco, S. (1984). Validation of a measure of acculturation for Mexican Americans. *Hispanic Journal of Behavioral Sciences, 6(1),* 53–63.

Nunnally, J. C. (1978). *Psychometric theory* (2nd ed.). New York: McGraw-Hill.

Oakland, T., & Shermis, M. (1989). Factor structure of the sociocultural scales. *Journal of Psychoeducational Assessment, 7(4),* 335–342.

Oetting, E. R., & Beauvais, F. (1990). Adolescent drug use: Findings of national and local surveys. *Journal of Consulting and Clinical Psychology, 58(4),* 385–394.

Oetting, E. R., & Beauvais, F. (1991). Orthogonal cultural identification theory: The cultural identification of minority adolescents. *International Journal of Addictions, 25(5A-6A),* 655–685.

Olmedo, E. (1979). Acculturation: A psychometric perspective. *American Psychologist, 34,* 1061–1070.

Padilla, A. (1980). *Acculturation: Theory, models and some new findings.* Boulder, CO: Westview.

Parham, T. (1989). Cycles of psychological Nigrescence. *The Counseling Psychologist, 17(2),* 187–226.

Parham, T., & Helms, J. (1985). Relation of racial identity attitudes to self-actualization and affective states of Black students. *Journal of Counseling Psychology, 32(3),* 432–440.

Parks, G. (1937). Foreword. In R. Adams (Ed.), *Interracial marriage in Hawaii* (pp. i-xvii). New York: Macmillan.

Parsonson, K. (1987). Intermarriages: Effects on the ethnic identity of the offspring. *Journal of Cross-Cultural Psychology, 18(3),* 363–371.

Pfeffer, K. (1984). Interpretation of studies of ethnic identity: Draw-A-Person as a measure of ethnic identity. *Perceptual and Motor Skills, 59(3),* 835–838.

Phinney, J. (1989). Stages of ethnic identity development in minority group adolescents. *Journal of Early Adolescence, 9(1–2),* 34–49.

Phinney, J. (1990). Ethnic identity in adolescents and adults: Review of research. *Psychological Bulletin, 108,* 499–514.

Phinney, J. (1991). Ethnic identity and self esteem: A review and integration. *Hispanic Journal of Behavioral Sciences, 13(2),* 193–208.

Phinney, J. (1992). The multigroup ethnic identity measure: A new scale for use with diverse groups. *Journal of Adolescent Research, 7,* 156–176.

Phinney, J. (1996). When we talk about American ethnic groups, what do we mean? *American Psychologist, 51(9),* 918–927.

Phinney, J. (2000). Ethnic identity. In A. E. Kazdin (Ed.), *Encyclopedia of psychology* (pp. 254–259). New York: Oxford University Press.

Phinney, J., & Alipuria, L. (1990). Ethnic identity in college students from four ethnic groups. *Journal of Adolescence, 13(2),* 171–183.

Phinney, J., & Tarver, S. (1988). Ethnic identity search and commitment in Black and White eighth graders. *Journal of Early Adolescence, 8(3),* 265–277.

Poston, W. (1990). The Biracial Identity Development Model: A needed addition. *Journal of Counseling and Development, 69(2),* 152–155.

Pumariega, A. J. (1986). Acculturation and eating attitudes in adolescent girls: A comparative and correlational study. *Journal of the American Academy of Child Psychiatry, 25(2),* 276–279.

Rauch, S., Bowler, R., & Schwarzer, R. (1987, August). *Acculturation effects on personality characteristics in three minority groups.* Paper presented at the meeting of the American Psychological Association, New York.

Richman, J., Gaviria, M., Flaherty, J., Birz, S., & Wintrob, R. (1987). The process of acculturation: Theoretical perspectives and an empirical investigation in Peru. *Social Science Medicine, 25(7),* 839–847.

Romanucci-Ross, L., & DeVos, G. (1995). *Ethnic identity: Creation, conflict and accommodation.* Walnut Creek, CA: AltaMira Press.

Roosens, E. (1989). *Creating ethnicity.* Newbury Park, CA: Sage.

Root, M. P. P. (1996). The multiracial experience: Racial borders as a significant frontier in race relations. In M. P. P. Root (Ed.), *The multiracial experience: Racial borders as the new frontier* (pp. xiii–xxviii). Thousand Oaks, CA: Sage.

Root, M. P. P. (2001). *Love's revolution: Interracial marriage.* Philadelphia: Temple University Press.

Rowe, W., Bennett, S., & Atkinson, D. (1994). White racial identity models: A critique and alternative proposal. *The Counseling Psychologist, 22(1),* 129–146.

Santiago-Rivera, A. L. *(1999).* Ethnic identity. In J. Mio, J. Trimble, P. Arredondo, H. Cheatham, & D. Sue (Eds.), *Keywords in multicultural interventions: A dictionary* (pp. 107–108). Westport, CT: Greenwood.

Sellers, R. M., Chavous, T. M., & Cooke, D. (1998). Racial ideology and racial centrality as predictors of African American college students' academic performance. *Journal of Black Psychology, 24(1),* 8–27.

Singelis, T. M., Triandis, H. C., Bhawuk, D. P. S., & Gelfand, M. J. (1995). Horizontal and vertical dimensions of individualism and collectivism: A theoretical and measurement refinement. *Cross-Cultural Research, 29(3),* 240–275.

Smith, T. W. (1980). Ethnic measurement and identification. *Ethnicity, 7,* 78–95.

Sodowsky, G., Lai, E., & Plake, B. (1991). Moderating effects of sociocultural variables on acculturation attitudes of Hispanics and Asian Americans. *Journal of Counseling Development, 70,* 194–204.

Sodowsky, G., & Plake, B. (1991). Psychometric properties of the American International Relations Scale. *Educational and Psychological Measurement, 51,* 207–216.

Sollors, W. (Ed.). (1989). *The invention of ethnicity.* New York: Oxford University Press.

Stephan, W., & Rosenfield, D. (1978). Effects of desegregation on racial attitudes. *Journal of Personality and Social Psychology, 36(8),* 795–804.

Stephan, W., & Stephan, W. G. (1989). After intermarriage: Ethnic identity among mixed heritage Japanese-Americans and Hispanics. *Journal of Marriage and the Family, 51,* 505–519.

Stevens, R. (1983). *Erik Eriksen: An introduction.* New York: St. Martin's. Strauss, A. L. (1959). *Mirrors and masks: The search for identity.* Glencoe, IL: Free Press.

Suarez-Orozco, M. (2001). Everything you ever wanted to know about assimilation but were afraid to ask. In R. Shweder, M. Minow, & H. Markus (Eds.), *The free exercise of culture* (pp. 1–30). New York: Russell Sage Foundation.

Suinn, R., Ahuna, C., & Khoo, G. (1992). The Suinn-Lew Asian Self-Identity Acculturation Scale: Concurrent and factorial validation. *Educational and Psychological Measurement, 52,* 1041–1046.

Suinn, R., Rickard-Figueroa, K., Lew, S., & Vigil, P. (1987). The Suinn-Lew Self-Identity Acculturation Scale. *Educational and Psychological Measurement, 47(2),* 401–407.

Swanson, J. L., Tokar, D. M., & Davis, L. E. (1994). Content and construct validity of the White Racial Identity Attitude Scale. *Journal of Vocational Behavior, 44,* 198–217.

Tajfel, H. (1981). *Human groups and social categories.* Cambridge, UK: Cambridge University Press.

Takaki, R. (1993). *A different mirror: A history of multicultural America.* Boston: Little, Brown.

Taylor, C. (1992). *Multiculturalism and "the politics of recognition."* Princeton, NJ: Princeton University Press.

Tenopyr, M. L. (1988). Artifactual reliability of forced-choice scales. *Journal of Applied Psychology, 73,* 749–751.

Teske, R., & Nelson, B. (1973). Two scales for the measurement of Mexican-American identity. *International Review of Modern Sociology, 3(2),* 192–203.

Thompson, R. H. (1989). *Theories of ethnicity: A critical appraisal.* New York: Greenwood.

Triandis, H. (1972). *The analysis of subjective culture.* New York: John Wiley.

Triandis, H., Kashima, Y., Shimada, E., & Villareal, M. (1986). Acculturation indices as a means of confirming cultural differences. *International Journal of Psychology, 21(1),* 43–70.

Trimble, J. (1987). Self-understanding and perceived alienation among American Indians. *Journal of Community Psychology, 15,* 316–333.

Trimble, J. (1988). Multilinearity of acculturation: Person-situation interactions. In D. Keats, D. Munro, & L. Mann (Eds.), *Heterogeneity in cross-cultural psychology* (pp. 173–186). Berwyn, PA: Swets & Zeitlinger.

Trimble, J. (1991). Ethnic specification, validation prospects and future of drug abuse research. *International Journal of the Addictions, 25(2),* 149–169.

Trimble, J. (1995). Toward an understanding of ethnicity and ethnic identification and their relationship with drug use research. In G. Botvin, S. Schinke, & M. Orlandi (Eds.), *Drug abuse prevention with multiethnic youth,* (pp. 3–27). Thousand Oaks, CA: Sage.

Trimble, J. (1996). Acculturation, ethnic identification and the evaluation process. In A. H. Bayer, F. L. Brisbane, & A. Ramirez (Eds.), *Advanced methodological issues in cultural competent evaluation for substance abuse prevention* (Cultural Competence Series 6, Pub. [SMA]96-3110). Washington, DC: Center for Substance Abuse Prevention, Department of Health and Human Services.

Trimble, J. (2000). Social psychological perspectives on changing self-identification among American Indians and Alaska Natives. In R. H. Dana (Ed.), *Handbook of cross-cultural/multicultural personality assessment* (pp. 197–222). Mahwah, NJ: Lawrence Erlbaum.

Trimble, J., & Mahoney, W. (2002). Gender and ethnic differences in adolescent self-esteem: A Rasch measurement model analysis. In P. D. Mail, S. Heurtin-Roberts, S. E. Martin, & J. Howard (Eds.), *Alcohol use among American Indians: Multiple perspectives on a complex problem* (National Institute on Alcohol Abuse and Alcoholism Research Monograph No. 37). Bethesda, MD: National Institute on Alcohol Abuse and Alcoholism.

U.S. Bureau of the Census. (2001). *Census of the population: General population characteristics, 2000.* Washington, DC: Government Printing Office.

van den Berghe, P. (1967). *Race and racism: A comparative perspective.* New York: John Wiley.

van den Berghe, P. (1981). *The ethnic phenomenon.* New York: Elsevier.

Vaughan, G. M. (1986). Social change and racial identity: Issues in the use of picture and doll measures. *Australian Journal of Psychology, 38(3),* 359–370.

Waters, M. C. (1990). *Ethnic options: Choosing identities in America.* Berkeley: University of California Press.

Waters, M. C. (1994, April). *The social construction of race and ethnicity: Some examples from demography.* Paper presented at American Diversity: A Demographic Challenge for the Twenty-First Century, Center for Social and Demographic Analysis Conference, SUNY, Albany, NY.

Wayley, C., & Harris, M. (1958). *Minorities in the new world: Six case studies.* New York: Columbia University Press.

Weinreich, P. (1986). The operationalisation of identity theory in racial and ethnic relations. In J. Rex & D. Mason (Eds.), *Theories of race and ethnic relations* (pp. 299–320). Cambridge, UK: Cambridge University Press.

Weinreich, P., & Saunderson, W. (Eds.). (2002). *Analysing identity: Cross-cultural, societal and clinical contexts.* London: Routledge/Taylor & Francis/Psychology Press.

Westermeyer, J., Neider, J., & Callies, A. (1989). Psychosocial adjustment of Hmong refugees during their first decade in the United States: A longitudinal study. *Journal of Nervous and Mental Disease, 177(3)*, 132–139.

White, C., & Burke, P. (1987). Ethnic role identity among Black and White college students: An interactionist approach. *Sociological Perspectives, 30(3)*, 310–331.

White, L. (1947). Culturological vs. psychological interpretations of human behavior. *American Sociological Review, 12*, 686–698.

Wooden, W., Leon, J., & Toshima, M. (1988). Ethnic identity among Sansei and Yonsei church-affiliated youth in Los Angeles and Honolulu. *Psychological Reports, 62(1)*, 268–270.

Young, R. J. C. (1995). *Colonial desire: Hybridity in theory, culture, and race.* New York: Routledge.

Zavalloni, M. (1980). Values. In H. C. Triandis & R. W. Brislin (Eds.), *Handbook of cross-cultural psychology: Social psychology* (Vol. 5, pp. 73–120). Boston: Allyn & Bacon.

Zayas, L. (1987). Toward an understanding of suicide risks in young Hispanic females. *Journal of Adolescent Research, 2(1)*, 1–11.

Zinn, H. (1980). *A people's history of the United States.* New York: Harper & Row.

11

Treatment Issues With Hispanic Clients

José M. Abreu

Andrés J. Consoli

Scott J. Cypers

Hispanics are the fastest growing minority group in the United States. High rates of fertility and continued immigration within the last decade have produced a dramatic growth rate estimated in the 60% range. Island Puerto Ricans and undocumented residents not included, more than 35 million Hispanics currently live in the United States. This statistic is expected to increase to 100 million or more by 2050. As a group, Hispanics face a multitude of risk factors, including poverty (one third meets poverty criteria) and its related consequences such as homelessness or inadequate housing; unsafe neighborhoods characterized by crime, violence, disease, and pollution; high rates of single-parent homes; high unemployment and underemployment; low educational attainment; lack of health insurance and limited health care access; higher prevalence rates of HIV infection and diabetes; and discrimination and acculturative stress. The purpose of this chapter is to highlight some of the treatment issues affecting Hispanics such as patterns of utilization, acculturation, and counseling approaches.

Mental Health Utilization

There is a sizable, persistent unmet need for treatment in people suffering from mental disorders. Overall, it is estimated that about 50 million adults in the United States need mental health care at any given time, yet only one third to one fifth, or even fewer, receive the needed care (Robins & Regier, 1991). The gap in services holds true even among people who are experiencing substantial distress and impairment and

Authors' Note: Partial work for this chapter was supported by NIMH grant #3 R24 MH61573-01A ISI awarded to the second author. We thank Maria Moore and Enjolie Lafaurie for their assistance in compiling the references for this chapter.

among those who acknowledge needing help (Katz et al., 1997; Wells, Golding, Hough, Burnam, & Karno, 1988). Among ethnic minorities, the proportion receiving the care needed is even lower (Swartz et al., 1998).

Many studies indicate that ethnic minorities are underrepresented among those who use mental health services (Diala et al., 2000; Vega, Kolody, Aguilar-Gaxiola, & Catalano, 1999)—particularly outpatient services such as psychotherapy (Olfson & Pincus, 1994a, 1994b)—and those who seek services drop out of treatment at higher rates than Whites do (Sue, 1977, 1988, 1998) For example, the 1987 National Medical Expenditure Survey indicated that ethnic minorities were dramatically underrepresented among long-term users of psychotherapy (e.g., over 21 sessions), with Caucasians accounting for 93.5% of these users (Olfson & Pincus, 1994b). These findings suggest problems of differential access, effectiveness, or both (Sledge, 1994) Some studies, however, have challenged the belief that ethnic minorities underuse mental health services (Goodman & Siegel, 1978), and others have documented a significant improvement over time (Sue, 1977, contrasted with O'Sullivan, Peterson, Cox, & Kirkeby, 1989).

Patterns of Utilization Among Hispanics

Data addressing the utilization patterns of Hispanics indicate that this topic is a complex one. For example, Padilla, Ruiz, and Alvarez (1975) reported evidence of serious underuse by Hispanics, whereas Karno and Morales (1971) reported overutilization. Investigations focusing specifically on Mexican American utilization of mental health services are also mixed; some report underuse (Jaco, 1960; Karno & Edgerton, 1969; Keefe, Padilla, & Carlos, 1978; Padilla & Ruiz, 1973; Torrey, 1972), and others show use consistent with community representation (Andrulis, 1977; S. López, 1981; Sánchez, Acosta, & Grosser, 1979; Trevino & Bruhn, 1977; Trevino, Bruhn, & Bunce, 1979). Cheung and Snowden (1990) reported that Hispanic utilization rates varied according to type of service available and that Hispanics overutilized community-based facilities. Generally, these conclusions corroborate the results of an earlier study (Sue, 1977). S. López (1981) addressed the inconsistencies in these findings by pointing to methodological problems associated with utilization research, including the basis on which comparisons are made, that is, nationwide versus community-wide ethnic representation, and failure to take into account mental health services needed. In addition, Hispanics have been significantly underrepresented in applied psychology research (Case & Smith, 2000), particularly in psychotherapy studies (see Miranda et al., 1996).

Studies based on large population samples typically provide some evidence indicating low rates of mental health service utilization. For example, in the Los Angeles Epidemiological Catchment Area site, Hough and collaborators (Hough et al., 1987) found that Mexican Americans were only half as likely as non-Hispanic Whites to have made a mental health visit, and the researchers reported a significantly lower number of general medical or mental health visits (approximately three visits by Mexican Americans compared to more than six visits by non-Hispanic Whites). Vega and collaborators (Vega et al., 1999) surveyed a probability sample (N = 3,012) of Fresno County, California, and found that among those diagnosed with a mental disorder, only about one fourth had accessed services. Significant differences in use were found between Mexican immigrants and Mexican Americans born in the United States. The use by the former (15.4%) was two fifths that by the latter (37.5%). Furthermore, the most educated, urban population had the highest utilization of mental health services whereas the least educated, rural population had the highest use of informal care providers. Most recently, Vega and Lopez (2001) argued that total utilization rates of public mental health systems by Hispanics in California point to persistent underutilization. Although Hispanics represent 29% of the population in California, they received 15.4% of inpatient or residential care, 19.7% of outpatient care and 16.9% of partial day care.

Reasons for Underutilization

Several writers have identified acculturation as a critical factor contributing to the probability of mental health service use by Mexican Americans (Sanchez & Atkinson, 1983; Wells et al., 1988). Additionally, some studies have documented that ethnic minorities may be more likely to seek services in the general care sector than in the mental health sector (Cooper-Patrick, Crum, & Ford, 1994; Cooper-Patrick et al., 1999; Ford, Kamerow, & Thompson, 1988; Gallo, Marino, Ford, & Anthony, 1995; Olfson et al., 2000) In fact a significant proportion of mental health care is provided by professionals outside the mental health field, mostly by general medical practitioners followed by human services professionals and voluntary support networks, a state of affairs described as a "de facto mental health system" (Regier et al., 1993, p. 85).

Conflicts between values reflected in counseling theories and practices and Hispanic values comprise another possible reason for underutilization. Simoni and Pérez (1995) and Zea, Quezada, and Belgrave (1994) argue that Hispanic values such as familism, interdependence, family and community centeredness, well-defined gender roles (*machismo/marianismo*) *simpatía* (smooth and pleasant social relationships), power distance (societal support for power differentials leading to obedience and conformity), *personalismo* (personable demeanor), *respeto* (deference based on power differentials such as wealth, age, and prestige), linearity (an emphasis on the role of authority in solving problems), present-time orientation, *dignidad* (dignity, worthiness), *confianza* (trust) spirituality (fatalism), and a collectivistic worldview play a role in attitudes toward mental health services. Indeed, tension between individualism and collectivism seems to be quite prevalent when mental health researchers compare and contrast "traditional" theories of psychotherapy and more contemporary theories, including but not limited to those with a multicultural emphasis.

Other cultural factors may pose further barriers to treatment. Some writers have singled out language or location of services as dimensions that affect treatment utilization (Cheung & Snowden, 1990; Flaskerud, 1986; O'Sullivan & Lasso, 1992). Relatedly, other investigators point to ethnic matching between client and mental health practitioner as a significant factor (Abreu & Gabarain, 2000; Atkinson, Poston, Furlong, & Mercado, 1989; three studies in S. R. López, López, & Fong, 1991). For example, analogue studies examining Mexican American preferences for practitioner ethnicity have reported clear preferences for an ethnic match, that is, a mental health practitioner who is ethnically similar to the client (S. R. López et al., 1991). However, in a subsequent study that examines the role of possible confounds in Mexican American practitioner preference analogue research, Abreu and Gabarain found that social desirability might play a role in the reported findings (expressing a preference for an ethnically dissimilar practitioner is less socially desirable than stating a preference for an ethnically similar practitioner).

Although expressed preference for an ethnically similar mental health practitioner may be partially a function of social desirability, this preference should not be interpreted as evidence that practitioner ethnicity is unimportant to prospective Mexican American or other Hispanic clients. Preference for mental health practitioner ethnicity very likely plays a major role in ethnic minority utilization of mental health services regardless of whether it is based on social desirability or presumptions about the practitioner's cultural values, knowledge, or skills. It may be that prospective clients expect to be better understood by a mental health practitioner who, by virtue of being ethnically similar, may have had comparable life experiences and faced interrelated problems. For example, a Hispanic mental health practitioner may be assumed to have experienced certain culture-specific events, such as speaking Spanish at home and English in school, the influences of *padrinos/madrinas* (godparents), *quinceañeras,* or other such occurrences that foster a sense of affinity toward the practitioner. Or more generally, Hispanic clients may feel better able to identify with and trust a Hispanic mental health practitioner because of the common experiences of surviving and managing a social milieu characterized by prejudice and biases. It is also possible that a client may be better able to express certain feelings in Spanish than English and that the prospect of seeing a Hispanic helper may involve *expectations* that he or she would be better able to understand these expressions. Some empirical evidence supports the speculation that Hispanic preference for a Hispanic practitioner involves a priori expectations.

For example, in a study based on a sample of Mexican American college students, Abreu (2000) found that expectations about mental health practitioners and the counseling process were more positive when the practitioner was Mexican American rather than European American. In discussing his findings, Abreu argued that to the extent that counseling expectations interact with decisions to seek help (Tinsley, Brown, de St-Aubin, & Lucek, 1984), the obtained finding is consistent with reports indicating that Mexican American utilization rates of mental health services vary depending on availability of community-based bilingual and bicultural services (Cheung & Snowden, 1990). This finding is congruent, at least in principle, with Sue and Zane's (1987) proposition that the lack of *ascribed* credibility attributed to nonminority practitioners may be the primary reason for ethnic minority underutilization of mental health services.

Although favorable counseling expectations of an ethnically similar mental health practitioner by Hispanic clients is consistent with strategies that seek to match practitioners and clients on ethnicity, unrealistically high expectations of performance could put some Hispanic practitioners at a disadvantage, and they may need to assess their clients' expectations carefully when formulating treatment goals. By the same token, European American practitioners exceeding relatively low client expectations of performance are likely to be perceived in a positive light by their Hispanic clients. There is some empirical evidence for this phenomenon. Atkinson, Casas, and Abreu (1992), for example, reported higher Mexican American ratings of cross-cultural competence for a European American practitioner portrayed as culturally sensitive than for a Mexican American practitioner also portrayed as culturally sensitive. From a practical standpoint, it would be reasonable to speculate that practitioner behaviors that are responsive to the counseling expectations of Hispanic clients may improve the effectiveness of Hispanic as well as non-Hispanic practitioners assigned to work with this population. This speculation is consistent with Sue and Zane's (1987) position that although ascribed mental health practitioner credibility may be related to initial decisions to seek (or not seek) help, achieved practitioner credibility determines treatment termination or persistence among those minority clients who choose to seek help.

Enabling resources, such as health insurance coverage, are also considered important factors that influence access to mental health services. Some surveys estimate that approximately 35% of Hispanics in the United States lack health insurance. Although health insurance may account for some of the underuse described in this chapter, it does not explain the whole picture. While acknowledging the need to address the role of lack of insurance as a barrier to mental health care for Mexican Americans, Vega, Kolody, and Aguilar-Gaxiola (2001) pointed out that even among those who are insured there is a need for "education and more effective referral from other sectors . . . to encourage use of these services" (p. 133). These findings suggest a strong role for sociological, psychological, and cultural dimensions to influence access beyond enabling resources.

Finally, a number of other barriers to Hispanic use of mental health services have been articulated but have not been empirically supported. Specifically, alternative resources, such as *curanderos* and *herbalistas* (Mexican Americans) and *espiritistas* (Puerto Ricans and Cuban Americans) have been cited as substitutes for conventional mental health services (Atkinson, Abreu, Ortiz-Bush, & Brewer, 1994; Padilla, Carlos, & Keefe, 1976). Additional dimensions as barriers to access and use may include negative attitudes toward the seeking of services (e.g., social stigma or shame) and anti-immigrant policies.

Treatment Issues: Preventive Approach

In defining culturally sensitive mental health services for Hispanics, Rogler, Malgady, Costantino, and Blumenthal (1987) affirm that treatment approaches need to take into account Hispanic norms and values. A sound multicultural perspective honors not only a person's individuality and collectivity but also the centrality of context and circumstances in which any given behavior is embedded. In other words, a person's comportment is rendered comprehensible when a practitioner carefully integrates subjective and personal explanations with intersubjective and interpersonal ones. In this vein, Bohart (2000) identified the client as the most important "common factor," further arguing that a true holistic or integrative approach needs to honor and facilitate the self-healing capacities of clients.

Congruent with these views, the role of the mental health practitioner can be conceived as that of a change agent who seeks to provide the necessary services not only to treat those diagnosed with an illness or disorder but also to proactively engage others in a range of activities destined to promote physical and mental health via the fostering of protective factors and the reduction of risk factors. We believe strongly that much of the potential and actual contributions that mental health practitioners have to offer are not only at the tertiary treatment level but also at the preventive and maintenance level, especially with regard to physical health concerns affecting Hispanics. To underscore our position that counseling activities can respond to a model that focuses on primary as well as secondary and tertiary treatments, we offer the following discussions about HIV and AIDS and diabetes and how they affect Hispanic populations.

HIV and AIDS

Because HIV (and by extension, AIDS) is not partial to the race and ethnicity of its recipients, effective prevention and treatment are clearly behaviorally based. The statistics show that HIV transmission via sexual contact and intravenous substance abuse accounts for most of the AIDS cases reported in the year 2000. In the fight against AIDS, not only has HIV testing proven to be a valuable tool in the effective management of HIV disease, but it has also brought about much-needed public awareness regarding the role of risk behaviors and prevention. Recent research, for example, indicates that people who are tested for HIV tend to respond by reducing their sexual risk behaviors (Alwano-Edyegu & Marum, 1999; Denning, Nakashima, Wortley, & Shas Project Group, 1999). With regard to timely treatment, the International AIDS Society—USA Panel indicated that HIV testing improves the clinical prognosis through early detection and antiretroviral treatment (Carpenter et al., 1998). In addition, Quinn et al. (2000) found that early treatment makes HIV-infected individuals less infectious.

Although previous studies indicated that the lapse of time between HIV infection and testing (which is critical for effective interventions) was much longer for Hispanics than for Whites (Sabogal & Catania, 1996; Scwarcz et al., 1997), a more recent study indicates that this disparity may be narrowing (Fernández, Perrino, Royal, Ghany, & Bowen, 2002). In this survey study, more than 1,000 Hispanic men who trace their origin to one of several Latin American countries were recruited from gay and non-gay venues (i.e., bars, gyms) in south Florida and were interviewed with regard to risk behaviors and HIV testing. Results show that overall testing rates were high (76% compared with 66% for the general U.S. population), especially among those at high risk for HIV infection. Fernández et al. found that men who had a higher number of sexual partners, who had sex with men, and who were worried about sexually transmitted diseases were more likely to be tested (unfortunately, injection drug use as a risk was not assessed); these findings indicate that self-assessment of risk behaviors was a likely motivator for men to seek help. Men who had never been tested were more likely to identify themselves as heterosexual than as men who have sex with men. Consequently, the authors argue that there is a need to examine further the behaviors associated with testing among heterosexual men and to identify their motivating factors. Persuading high-risk heterosexual men to recognize their risk for infection and the importance of HIV testing may be our next challenge (p. 383).

Organized efforts to address the threat of AIDS among Hispanics has taken the form of community planning groups, an outgrowth of the belief that responses to local HIV prevention priorities and needs are best carried out through local participatory planning. To this end, two national conferences (Community Planning Leadership Summit in Houston, Texas, and Capacity Building for HIV prevention in Atlanta, Georgia) and a regional meeting (Enlace: Skills Building for the Latino Community in El Paso, Texas) were held in 2001, at which various topics and themes were raised and discussed. On the basis of their experience in working with Hispanics, participating health officials and staff generated the following suggestions:

- Assist clinical staff to recognize the risk and stigma among Hispanics associated with homosexuality (*rechazo,* or rejection), with having AIDS, or with a nondocumented immigration status
- Get to know the impact of AIDS on Hispanic communities
- Acknowledge interlinked issues of religion, fatalism, *machismo* or gender (e.g., difficulty negotiating condom use), and denial ("AIDS doesn't happen to us!")
- Address barriers to AIDS prevention or treatment program attendance: child care, transportation, cost, multiple jobs, incentives, meeting times, location of meetings
- Avoid generalizations of Hispanics (lack of recognition and awareness of different national backgrounds)

- Generate Spanish-language materials that are culturally targeted to the local Hispanic groups (e.g, Mexican, Puerto Rican, Cuban, Dominican)
- Establish outreach to migrant and seasonal farmworkers, injection drug users, people living with HIV and AIDS, and men who self-identify as non-gay but who have sex with men

Whereas a competent mental health practitioner will help HIV-positive Hispanics process their diagnosis, treatment, and prognosis (tertiary treatment), a culturally competent practitioner will conceptualize and implement culturally relevant strategies such as the ones just listed to redress the spread of HIV (VanOss Marín, 1994).

Diabetes

On the average, Hispanics are nearly twice as likely to have diabetes as Whites are. Mexican Americans are three to five times more likely than Whites to be afflicted by diabetes; in some communities, the prevalence rates are alarmingly high (Brown, Becker, Garcia, Barton, & Hanis, 2002). Health beliefs have long been considered an important component to diabetes management (Given, Given, Gallin, & Condon, 1983). Studies have shown that health beliefs have direct and indirect effects on diabetes metabolic control (Brown & Hedges, 1994), especially beliefs related to a sense of agency or control over the disease (Surgenor, Horn, Hudson, Lunt, & Tennent, 2000). Health beliefs relative to control issues are especially important to members of ethnic minority groups (Fitzgerald et al., 2000). For example, in the Brown et al. (2002) study, which was implemented among the residents of Starr County, Texas (a community that is nearly 100% Hispanic), researchers found that the high prevalence rates of diabetes apparently led to the belief among community residents that one could not control diabetes and that everyone eventually would get the disease.

One of the main goals to any diabetes prevention or treatment program is to encourage individuals to prevent or control diabetes by making healthy food choices. In order to bring this message to Hispanic communities, key organizations (such as the National Council of La Raza and the National Hispanic Council on Aging) could be contacted to help distribute culturally appropriate diabetes education messages through established community channels. Another resource is the National Diabetes Information Clearinghouse, which provides many fact sheets and pamphlets about diabetes and its management in easy-to-read formats in English and Spanish.

Food is an integral part of family gatherings and community celebrations in the Hispanic culture. Diabetes prevention and treatment campaigns need to encourage Hispanic families to consider how much and how often they eat and how they prepare their food. They should not be told that they have to give up favorite foods when making dietary decisions, because this approach has been shown to be ineffective at best (National Coalition of Hispanic Health and Human Services Organizations, 1998). This problem is highlighted by the question raised by a Hispanic woman reacting to written materials that promoted a healthy diet: "*¿Qué es un bagel?*" ("What's a bagel?"). The message should be that people can continue to eat the foods they love and that they simply need to consider making a few small changes in portion sizes and in how favorite dishes are prepared. Cooking with olive oil instead of lard and limiting salt intake by using fresh herbs and spices like cilantro to season foods are just two examples of ways that Hispanics can prepare healthier foods without sacrificing taste. Similar recipe guides can also offer suggestions on how to make other healthy ingredient substitutions and how to alter preparation of traditional foods to preserve flavor but reduce added fat, high-fat meats, and salt. It is also important to disseminate information regarding control issues. That is, individuals, not doctors or nurses, control diabetes prevention and treatment. The message here is that individuals can assume control over their health by making small lifestyle changes (Brown et al., 2002).

General Approach to Address Other Concerns

We would like to suggest the following approaches as a general strategy for mental health practitioners working with Hispanic populations:

- To earn the *confianza* (trust) of a targeted community, find out who is respected in the community. Ask clients, staff, business owners, clergy, members of the media, teachers, and so on to identify the respected leaders and agencies that serve the community's needs. This takes time; be patient.
- Learn (or remember) the value of *personalismo.* Go to local leaders and ask for their opinions about what people in the community need the most. Don't assert your agenda; instead, listen to the community's agenda and assign your priorities based on their needs.
- Develop culturally relevant media and materials to convey your message; target whole families, not individuals. Persons developing such media and materials should be familiar with the literacy level and culture of specific target groups.
- Remember that the purpose of any intervention is to improve health by changing the cultural and environmental factors that support unhealthy behaviors (e.g., tobacco commercials that target young Hispanics).

Treatment Issues: Secondary and Tertiary Approaches

The treatments of Hispanic mental health problems have been conceptualized from a variety of sociological, psychosociological, and psychiatric perspectives. One common denominator across these points of view is the fundamental assumption that acculturation poses a risk for Hispanic health, an assumption with some empirical support (Burnam et al., 1987; Cabrera Strait, 2001; Hovey & Magaña, 2002).

Acculturation, Stress, and Approach to Counseling

Alderete, Vega, Kolody, and Aguilar-Gaxiola (2000) identified four interrelated etiological explanations relative to acculturation processes affecting Hispanic mental health: acculturative stress, social learning or deculturation, social marginality, and identity disintegration. A variant of the general social stress model (Pearlin, Menaghan, Lieberman, & Mullan, 1981), acculturative stress theory is based on the assumption that adaptation (acculturation) to U.S. culture produces social conflict, including intergenerational friction (Gil & Vega, 1996; Rogler, Cortes, & Malgady, 1991). Personal resources such as psychological and emotional coping skills as well as external social networks are taxed, resulting in various forms of mental health concerns. The other side of acculturation is deculturation, that is, as new patterns of U.S. values, behaviors, and customs are learned, native culture might be weakened, and individuals may lose natural protective or coping factors inherent to the indigenous cultural milieu, such as familistic values, cultural traditions, and social support (Rumbaut, 1977; Suarez-Orozco

& Suarez-Orozco, 1995). Increases in drug and alcohol use, interpersonal violence, and lowered expectations of personal attainment are likely outcomes, especially among Hispanic adolescents (Swanson, Linskey, Quintero-Salinas, & Pumariega, 1992). Social marginality refers to Hispanic integration into low-income communities riddled with social pathologies and a long history of discrimination and social neglect. Social marginality may explain why "years of living in U.S." is apparently a risk factor for Hispanic health (Vega et al., 1998). Identity disintegration refers to the destruction of cultural referents that give meaning to self-identity; it has been used as an etiological explanation of psychopathology among Mexican Indians.

Although these four broad categories have been used as a heuristic to conceptualize the effects of acculturative stress on Hispanic psychosocial functioning, as of yet little empirical data validate or tie these categories with outcome or process measures. Nonetheless, we would like to suggest several approaches that are based on the acculturation literature (Comas-Diaz & Minrath, 1987; Rogler et al., 1991; Smart & Smart, 1995; Vargas-Willis & Cervantes, 1987; Padilla, 1980) and that are likely to be effective in the prevention and treatment of this source of psychosocial stress among Hispanics.

Because the sociopolitical factors that catalyze Hispanic immigration to the United States differ from those that affect Asians, Europeans, and other groups, several issues warrant special consideration from mental health practitioners who work with Hispanic clients.

Discrimination and Racial Identity. In Latin American countries, people are used to being around and are accepting of individuals who represent a wide variety of skin color without the pervasive dichotomization of "White" versus "non-White" that is so prevalent in the United States. Although Latin American countries are far from impervious to prejudice and discrimination based on skin color, immigrants adjusting to U.S. culture are likely to become confused in a sociopolitical environment so attuned to race rather than ethnicity. For example, Hispanic immigrants with African ancestry often have to contend with being perceived as African American rather than as immigrants from a Latin American country. In some cases, these individuals or their children may choose to identify as African American. Mental health practitioners working with Hispanics need to be sensitive to these sources of stress by assessing how their clients identify themselves (e.g., by nationality, race, or ethnicity) and whether their clients, through this identification, feel discriminated against. In this vein, one of the objectives of counseling could be to help clients develop a sense of pride about their unique features (skin color, Spanish accent) in spite of prevalent stereotypes that denigrate these characteristics; this approach may be especially helpful for clients suffering from depressive symptoms. Likewise, mental health practitioners can facilitate their clients' sense of empowerment as they become more aware of societal stressors. For example, a practitioner could help a first-generation client articulate the types of social injustices or discrimination experienced in his or her country of origin and then help the client compare and contrast them with experiences of inequality while living in the United States. This approach could help the client foster a sense of empowerment as well as a political and social consciousness within which to make sense of the stress involved in acculturating to U.S. culture (La Roche, 2002).

Discrimination against Hispanics relative to biased treatment in employment, education, housing, and other human services is common (Padilla, 1980), especially for undocumented Hispanics, who live in constant fear of deportation and are often subjected to work exploitation. Mental health practitioners working with undocumented clients need to understand basic immigration laws and develop an appreciation for the acculturative stress (which may be experienced as depression or anxiety) that undocumented status imposes on Hispanic immigrants. More generally, discrimination experienced by Hispanics is a likely precursor to poor psychological functioning. For example, Finch, Hummer, Kolody, and Vega (2001) surveyed a large sample of Mexican Americans (N = 3,012) living in California and found that discrimination was related to poor physical health and depression. Mental health practitioners working with depressed Hispanic clients would do well to explore the possible link between their clients' symptoms and stress caused by discrimination.

Language Use. As U.S. immigrants, Hispanics have demonstrated a remarkable commitment to the Spanish language. Even in cases where second- or third-generation individuals lose the use of Spanish almost completely, certain Spanish words are retained and used in the company of other Hispanics. In fact, many Hispanics speak "Spanglish" with each other, a combination of Spanish and English mingled together. The sociopolitical histories relative to the colonial and Mexican hegemony plus perennial waves of immigration from Latin American countries have left a legacy of Spanish-language culture in U.S. geographical areas such as the West Coast, Southwest, and south Florida. Names of towns and cities, broadcast and printed media, cuisine, and historical sites speak to these legacies. Because language is so central to the counseling process, bilingual services are a must when Spanish is a client's preferred language. Second- (or subsequent) generation clients who may prefer English to Spanish would still benefit from a mental health practitioner who has at least a working knowledge of Spanish. Because Spanish is typically the first language that second-generation Hispanics learn, many early emotions and thoughts are likely encoded in Spanish rather than English. A practitioner who can understand Spanish may facilitate awareness of thoughts and emotions held outside of consciousness, which the client may be able to express more freely in the language in which they were encoded (Santiago-Rivera & Altarriba, 2002).

Spanish *dichos* (used generally in Latin American folklore) or *refranes* (used in Mexican folklore) may also prove helpful to mental health practitioners working with Hispanic, Spanish-speaking clients. *Dichos* and *refranes* are sayings or proverbs that capture folk wisdom relative to various human situations (Zuñiga, 1991). Aviera (1996) facilitated a *dichos* therapy group with hospitalized Spanish-speaking patients and reported that his intervention effectively facilitated rapport building, decreased defensiveness, enhanced motivation, stimulated exploration and articulation of feelings, and improved insight and self-esteem. Similarly, Costantino, Malgady, and Rogler (1986) developed an approach to therapy based on Spanish language folklore. Costantino et al. designed and implemented what they termed *cuento,* or folklore therapy, to assist Puerto Rican second-generation children in a mental health clinic at risk of mental health disorders because of family conflicts involving acculturation differences. The therapy was facilitated by bilingual therapists who read folktales (in Spanish and English) to the children and then led group discussions on the meaning of the stories. In subsequent sessions, the children were asked to role-play the various characters in the *cuentos* and then to discuss the role-playing activities in relation to their own personal problems. The authors report that this intervention successfully reduced level of trait anxiety among participants.

Generation Status and Family Structure. Hispanic families comprised of first- and second-generation individuals experience intergenerational cultural stress, especially adolescent members. Throughout this phase of development, normative conflicts arise between parents and their children, and intergenerational acculturation differences are likely to exacerbate this process. Conflict within Hispanic families can cause a sense of alienation between parents and children, leading the latter to engage in high-risk behaviors such as dropping out of school and using alcohol and drugs.

At a more general level, there is typically a high degree of interdependence between Hispanic parents and their children (Marín & Triandis, 1985). In Hispanic culture, emphasis is placed on social relationships and group goals rather than on individuality. Hispanics learn behavioral expectations for self and others through scripts (cultural scripts are an essential component of the meaning system of any cultural group) passed down from parents to their children (La Roche, 1999). Such scripts include *personalismo* (personal rather than institutional relationships), *familismo* (family orientation), *respeto* (deferential behaviors toward others based on age, sex, and authority), *simpatía* (friendly interpersonal attitude that eschews conflict), and allocentrism (a cultural value predicated on the notion that individuals understand themselves through others). Mental health practitioners working with Hispanic families need to take these cultural factors into account to better understand family dynamics and to develop appropriate treatment plans.

For example, when working with Hispanic families wherein parents speak only Spanish and their children are bilingual, non-Spanish-speaking clinicians who rely on the children to translate need to be careful not to insult parents. For such mental health practitioners, it may seem natural to face the children while speaking to them, then to wait while the children translate to their parents. Because the parents (especially the father when present) may perceive such interaction as lacking *respeto,* it is best for practitioners to face parents and speak to them rather than to the children. Mental health practitioners working with Hispanic adolescents at risk of dropping out of school or engaging in other problem behaviors would benefit from a family approach that takes into account Hispanic family values and intergenerational conflicts caused by acculturation differences.

Assessment

Acculturation is a very salient factor of the Hispanic experience, a process associated with stress and a likely precursor to other psychosocial concerns. Therefore, assessment of acculturation should be one of the first objectives among mental health practitioners working with Hispanic clients (readers interested in Hispanic assessment for DSM-IV diagnostic purposes can see Cuéllar, 1998).

A measurement model frequently cited by researchers of acculturation was developed by John Berry and his colleagues (Berry, 1990, 1994; Berry & Kim, 1988; Berry, Kim, Power, Young, & Bajaki, 1989; Berry, Trimble, & Olmeda, 1986), who proposed four acculturation attitudes (integration, assimilation, separation, and marginalization). These attitudes express the combined level of adherence to host and indigenous cultures, with each culture represented by a separate continuum. *Integration* occurs when an individual sustains an active interest in the indigenous culture while maintaining daily interactions with members of the dominant or host group. Thus, a person with this acculturation attitude desires to become proficient in the culture of the dominant group and yet retains proficiency in the indigenous culture; this attitude represents biculturalism and is believed to be the most adaptive.

Assimilation occurs when an individual maintains daily interactions with members of the host group but has no interest in remaining conversant with the native culture; an assimilated individual absorbs the culture of the dominant group while rejecting the indigenous culture. *Separation* occurs when much value is placed on the culture of origin and its members, but contact with members of the host culture is avoided. An individual with a separation attitude is not interested in learning the culture of the dominant group and only wants to maintain and perpetuate the culture of origin. Finally, *marginalization* represents the attitude of an individual with no interest in maintaining or acquiring proficiency in any culture, native or host. Marginalization is perhaps the most problematic of the four acculturation attitudes because, by definition, a marginalized individual would generally not be expected to relate well to others. To the extent that individuals may not always have the freedom to choose how they want to acculturate and that their choices are inevitably influenced if not constrained by the dominant group, mental health practitioners ought to thoughtfully consider the context in which acculturation choices are made. The terms *pluralism, conformity, segregation,* and *discrimination* may describe the attitudes of a dominant group that, in turn, may influence the individual choices of integration, assimilation, separation, and marginalization, respectively (Berry, 1997).

Mental health practitioners working with Hispanics can choose from a wide variety of tests developed to measure acculturation. Currently, there are at least 23 instruments developed to measure Hispanic acculturation, 8 of which were designed to be used with Hispanics in general, 3 with Cuban Americans, 11 with Mexican Americans, and 1 with Puerto Rican Americans. Although a description of extant instruments tapping Hispanic acculturation is beyond the scope of this chapter (an exhaustive review of acculturation instruments is provided by Kim and Abreu, 2001), we will provide a brief description of one such measure.

The Bidimensional Short Acculturation Scale for Hispanics (BSASH; Marin & Gamba, 1996) is a 24-item instrument derived from an initial set of 60 items (30 for Hispanic domain and 30 for non-Hispanic domain) measuring language use, media preference, participation in cultural activities, and ethnicity of social relations. The final instrument was derived from the results of a factor analysis, and it measures language use, linguistic proficiency, and preferences for electronic media on two subscales, each representing a continuum on the use of Spanish and English. The BSASH has adequate internal consistency for both subscales and evidence of criterion, convergence, and face validity. It follows the acculturation model that was described in this section; high English but low Spanish scale scores are indicative of an assimilation attitude, and the reverse pattern of scores indicates a separation attitude. High scores on both Spanish and English scales represents an integration attitude, whereas low scores on each scale represents marginalization. The Short Acculturation Scale for Hispanic Youth (Barona & Miller, 1994) is a 12-item instrument for children and adolescents that is similar in construction to the BSASH.

Using Alderete et al.'s (2000) model of acculturation as an etiological dimension of Hispanic mental health, practitioners can utilize BSASH scores (or scores from other acculturation measures) to help determine the likely source of acculturation stress that their Hispanic clients are experiencing. Given the importance of *familismo* and allocentrism in Hispanic culture, assessment of acculturation should focus on the members of an entire family unit whenever possible.

Culture-Bound Syndromes

Hispanics use several labels to describe psychological syndromes such as *susto* (fright), *mal de ojo* (evil eye), *nervios* (nerves), and *ataques de nervios* (attack of nerves). Guarnaccia, Canino, Rubio-Stipec, and Bravo (1993) reported that up to 14% of a sample of Puerto Ricans reported having an *ataque*. The concept of *nervios* is also used more generally by Hispanics to describe distress associated with anxiety and depression (Salgado de Snyder, Diaz-Perez, & Ojeda, 2000) and with delusions or hallucinations (Jenkins, 1988). Knowledge of these syndromes should help clinicians working with Hispanics to identify distress and illness in their clients that may be manifested in ways that may not conform to *DSM* nomenclature.

Conclusion

The utilization patterns of Hispanic mental health services are complex, but research data indicate that overall this ethnic group tends not to take advantage of services as readily as European Americans do. The reasons for this apparent underutilization are complicated, and several explanations have been offered: the use of health care professionals outside of mental health; value conflicts between Hispanic culture and conventional psychological principles; acculturation and language issues; lack of Hispanic mental health practitioners; and the difficulties that Hispanics have in accessing care due to lack of insurance and for other structural reasons. Preventive approaches to health concerns of Hispanics, such as diabetes and HIV disease, were discussed as were treatments of mental health concerns that focus on the Hispanic experience in the United States. This focus includes issues generally related to acculturative stress, such as discrimination, language use, generational status, and family structure. Lastly, an assessment approach based on acculturation was presented.

Exercises

1. You have been commissioned by the National Coalition of Hispanic Health and Human Services Organizations to develop and implement culturally sensitive programs that address (1) HIV-AIDS or (2) diabetes prevention and treatment among Hispanics. Based on the information presented in this chapter, provide an outline for the development and implementation of such a program focusing on HIV-AIDS or diabetes (choose one).
2. A mental health agency serving a largely Hispanic clientele hires you to develop and implement a culturally sensitive training program for its mental health staff (e.g., psychologists, counselors, social workers). Based on the information provided in this chapter, provide an outline detailing a training program that incorporates issues and concepts related to "acculturation and stress," "discrimination and racial identity," "language use," "family structure," and "clinical assessment."

References

Abreu, J. M. (2000). Counseling expectations among Mexican American college students: The role of counselor ethnicity. *Journal of Multicultural Counseling and Development, 28,* 130–143.

Abreu, J. M., & Gabarain, G. (2000). Social desirability and Mexican American counselor preferences: Statistical control for a potential confound. *Journal of Counseling Psychology, 47,* 165–176.

Alderete, E., Vega, W. A., Kolody, B., & Aguilar-Gaxiola, S. (2000). Effects of time in the United States and Indian ethnicity on DSM-III-R psychiatric disorders among Mexican Americans in California. *Journal of Nervous and Mental Disease, 188,* 90–100.

Alwano-Edyegu, M. G., & Marum, E. (1999). *Knowledge is power: Voluntary HIV counseling and testing in Uganda.* Geneva: UNAIDS.

Andrulis, D. P. (1977). Ethnicity as a variable in the utilization and referral patterns of a comprehensive mental health center. *Journal of Community Psychology, 5,* 231–237.

Atkinson, D. R., Abreu, J. M., Ortiz-Bush, Y., & Brewer, S. (1994). Mexican American and

European American ratings of four alcoholism treatment programs *Hispanic Journal of Behavioral Sciences, 16,* 265–280.

Atkinson, D. R., Casas, A., & Abreu, J. M. (1992). Mexican-American acculturation, counselor ethnicity and cultural sensitivity, and perceived counselor competence. *Journal of Counseling Psychology. 39,* 515–520.

Atkinson, D. R., Poston, W. C., Furlong, M. J., & Mercado. P. (1989). Ethnic group preferences for counselor characteristics. *Journal of Counseling Psychology, 36,* 68–72.

Aviera, A. (1996). "Dichos" therapy group: A therapeutic use of Spanish language proverbs with hospitalized Spanish-speaking psychiatric patients. *Cultural Diversity and Mental Health, 2,* 73–87.

Barona, A., & Miller, J. A. (1994). Short acculturation scale for Hispanic youth (SASH-Y): A preliminary report. *Hispanic Journal of Behavioral Sciences, 16,* 155–162.

Berry, J. W. (1990). Psychology of acculturation: Understanding individuals moving between cultures. In R. W. Brislin (Ed.), *Applied cross-cultural psychology* (pp. 232–253). Newbury Park, CA: Sage.

Berry, J. W. (1994). Acculturation and psychological adaptation: An overview. In A. Bouvy, F. J. R. van de Vijver, P. Boski, & P. Schmitz (Eds.), *Journeys into cross-cultural psychology* (pp. 129–141). Amsterdam: Swets and Zeitlinger.

Berry, J. W. (1997). Acculturation and health. In S. Kazarian & D. Evans (Eds.), *Cultural clinical psychology* (pp. 39–57). New York: Oxford.

Berry, J. W., & Kim, U. (1988). Acculturation and mental health. In P. R. Dasen, J. W. Berry, & N. Sartorius (Eds.), *Health and cross-cultural psychology: Toward applications* (pp. 207–236). Newbury Park, CA: Sage.

Berry, J. W., Kim, U., Power, S., Young, M., & Bajaki, M. (1989). Acculturation attitudes in plural societies. *Applied Psychology: An International Review, 38,* 185–206.

Berry, J. W., Trimble, J. E., & Olmeda, E. L. (1986). Assessment of acculturation. In W. J. Lonner & J. W. Berry (Eds.), *Field methods in cross-cultural research* (pp. 291–324). Newbury Park, CA: Sage.

Bohart, A. C. (2000). The client as active self-healer: Implications for integration. *Journal of Psychotherapy Integration, 10,* 127–149.

Brown, S. A., Becker, H. A., Garcia, A. A., Barton, S. A., & Hanis, C. L. (2002). Measuring health beliefs in Spanish-speaking Mexican Americans with type 2 diabetes: Adapting an existing instrument. *Research in Nursing and Health, 25,* 145–158.

Brown, S. A., & Hedges, L. V. (1994). Predicting metabolic control in diabetes: A pilot study using meta-analysis to estimate a linear model. *Nursing Research, 43,* 362–368.

Burnam, M. A., Hough, R. L., Karno, M., Escobar, J., & Telles, C. A. (1987). Acculturation and lifetime prevalence of psychiatric disorders among Mexican Americans in Los Angeles. *Journal of Health and Social Behavior, 28,* 89–102.

Cabrera Strait, S. (2001). An examination of the influence of acculturative stress on substance use and related maladaptive behavior among Latino youth. *Dissertation Abstracts International: Section B. The Sciences and Engineering, 62*(5-B), 2532.

Carpenter, C. C., Fishl, M. A., Hammer, S. M., Jacobsen, D. M., Katzenstein, D. A., Montaner, J. S., Richman, D. D., Saag, M. S., Schooley, R. T., Thompson, M. A., Vella, S., Yeni, P. G., & Valberding, P. A. (1998). Antiretroviral therapy for HIV infection in 1998: Updated recommendations of the International AIDS Society-USA panel. *Journal of the American Medical Association, 280,* 78–86.

Case, L., & Smith, T. B. (2000). Ethnic representation in a sample of the literature of applied psychology. *Journal of Consulting and Clinical Psychology, 68,* 1107–1110.

Cheung, F. K., & Snowden, L. R. (1990). Community mental health and ethnic minority populations. *Community Mental Health Journal, 26,* 277–291.

Comas-Diaz, L., & Minrath, M. (1987). Psychotherapy with ethnic minority borderline clients. *Psychotherapy, 225,* 418–426.

Cooper-Patrick, L., Crum, R. M., & Ford, D. E. (1994). Characteristics of patients with major depression who received care in general medical and specialty mental health settings. *Medical Care, 32,* 15–24.

Cooper-Patrick, L., Gallo, J. J., Powe, N. R., Steinwachs, D. S., Eaton, W. W., & Ford, D. E. (1999). Mental health service utilization by African Americans and Whites: The Baltimore Epidemiologic Catchment Area follow-up. *Medical Care, 37,* 1034–1045.

Costantino, G., Malgady, R., & Rogler, L. (1986). Cuento therapy: A culturally sensitive modality for Puerto Rican children. *Journal of Consulting and Clinical Psychology, 54,* 639–645.

Cuéllar, I. (1998). Cross-cultural clinical psychological assessment of Hispanic Americans. *Journal of Personality Assessment, 70,* 71–86.

Denning, P., Nakashima, A., Wortley, C., & Shas Project Group. (1999). *High-risk sexual behaviors among HIV infected adolescents and young adults.* Paper presented at the sixth conference on retroviruses and opportunistic infections, Chicago, IL.

Diala, C., Muntaner, C., Walrath, C., Nickerson, K. J., LaVeist, T. A., & Leaf, P. J. (2000). Racial differences in attitudes toward professional mental health care and in the use of services. *American Journal of Orthopsychiatry, 70,* 455–464.

Fernández, M. I., Perrino, T., Royal, S., Ghany, D., & Bowen, G. S. (2002). To test or not to test: Are Hispanic men at higher risk for HIV getting tested? *Aids Care, 14,* 375–384.

Finch, B. K., Hummer, R. A., Kolody, B., & Vega, W. A. (2001). The role of discrimination and acculturative stress in the physical health of Mexican-origin adults. *Hispanic Journal of Behavioral Sciences, 23,* 399–429.

Fitzgerald, J. T., Gruppen, L. D., Anderson, R. M., Funnell, M. M., Jacober, S. J., Grunberger, G., & Aman, L. C. (2000). The influence of treatment modality and ethnicity on attitudes in type 2 diabetes. *Diabetes Care, 23,* 313–318.

Flaskerud, J. H. (1986). The effects of culture-compatible intervention on the utilization of mental health services by minority clients. *Community Mental Health Journal, 22,* 127–141.

Ford, D. E., Kamerow, B. D., & Thompson, J. W. (1988). Who talks to physicians about mental health and substance abuse problems? *Journal of General and Internal Medicine, 3,* 363–369.

Gallo, J. J., Marino, S., Ford, D., & Anthony, J. C. (1995). Filters on the pathway to mental health care: II. Sociodemographic factors. *Psychological Medicine, 25,* 1149–1160.

Gil, A. G., & Vega, W. A. (1996). Two different worlds: Acculturation stress and adaptation among Cuban and Nicaraguan families. *Journal of Social and Personal Relationships, 13,* 435–456.

Given, C. W., Given, B. A., Gallin, R. S., & Condon, J. W. (1983). Development of scales to measure beliefs of diabetic patients. *Research in Nursing and Health, 6,* 127–141.

Goodman, A. B., & Siegel, C. (1978). Differences in white-nonwhite community mental health center service utilization patterns. *Journal of Evaluation and Program Planning, 1,* 51–63.

Guarnaccia, P. J., Canino, G., Rubio-Stipec, M., & Bravo, M. (1993). The prevalence of ataques de nervios in the Puerto Rico Disaster Study: The role of culture in psychiatric epidemiology. *Journal of Nervous and Mental Disease, 181,* 157–165.

Hough, R. L., Landsverk, J. A., Karno, M., Burnam, A., Timbers, D. M., Escobar, J. I., & Regier, D. A. (1987). Utilization of health and mental health services by Los Angeles Mexican Americans and non-Hispanic whites. *Archives of General Psychiatry, 44,* 702–709.

Hovey, J. D., & Magaña, C. G. (2002). Psychosocial predictors of anxiety among immigrant Mexican migrant farmworkers: Implications for prevention and treatment. *Cultural Diversity and Ethnic Minority Psychology, 8,* 274–289.

Jaco, E. G. (1960). Mental health of the Spanish American in Texas. In M. K. Opler (Ed.), *Culture and mental health: Cross-cultural studies.* New York: Macmillan.

Jenkins, J. H. (1988). Ethnopsychiatric interpretations of schizophrenic illness: The problem of nervios within Mexican-American families. *Culture, Medicine, and Psychiatry, 12,* 301–329.

Karno, M., & Edgerton, R. B. (1969). Perception of mental illness in a Mexican-American community. *Archives of General Psychiatry, 20,* 233–238.

Karno, M., & Morales, A. (1971). A community mental health service for Mexican Americans in a metropolis. *Comprehensive Psychiatry, 12,* 116–121.

Katz, S. J., Kessler, R. C, Frank, R. G., Leaf, P., Lin, E., & Edlund, M. (1997). The use of outpatient mental health services in the United States and Ontario: The impact of mental morbidity and perceived need for care. *American Journal of Public Health, 87,* 1136–1143.

Keefe, S. E., Padilla, A. M., & Carlos, M. L. (1978). Emotional support systems in two cultures: A comparison of Mexican Americans and Anglo Americans. *Spanish Speaking Mental Health Research Center Occasional Paper* (No. 7). Los Angeles: University of California Press.

Kim, B. S. K., & Abreu, J. M. (2001). Acculturation: Theory, measurement, research, and future directions. In J. G. Ponterotto, J. M. Casas, L. A. Suzuki, & C. M. Alexander (Eds.), *Handbook of multicultural counseling* (2nd ed., pp. 394–424). Thousand Oaks, CA: Sage.

La Roche, M. J. (1999). Culture, transference, and countertransference among Latinos. *Psychotherapy, 36,* 389–397.

La Roche, M. J. (2002). Psychotherapeutic considerations in treating Latinos. *Harvard Review Psychiatry, 10,* 115–122.

López, S. (1981). Mexican American usage of mental health facilities: Underutilization considered. In A. Baron, Jr. (Ed.), *Exploration in Chicano psychology.* New York: Praeger.

López, S. R., López, A. A., & Fong, K. T. (1991). Mexican Americans' initial preferences for counselors: The role of ethnic factors. *Journal of Counseling Psychology, 38,* 487–496.

Marín, G., & Gamba, R. J. (1996). A new measurement of acculturation for Hispanics: The bidimensional acculturation scale for Hispanics (BAS). *Hispanic Journal of Behavioral Sciences, 18,* 297–316.

Marín, G., & Triandis, H. C. (1985). Allocentrism as an important behavior of Latin-Americans and Hispanics. In R. Diaz-Guerrero (Ed.), *Cross-cultural and national studies in social psychology.* Amsterdam; New York: North-Holland.

Miranda, J., Azocar, F., Organista, K. C., Muñoz, R. F., & Lieberman, A. (1996). Recruiting and retaining low-income Latinos in psychotherapy research. *Journal of Consulting and Clinical Psychology, 64,* 868–874.

National Coalition of Hispanic Health and Human Services Organizations. (1998). *Delivering preventive health care to Hispanics: A manual for providers.* Washington, DC: Author.

O'Sullivan, M. J., & Lasso, B. (1992). Community mental health services for Hispanics: A test of the culture compatibility hypothesis. *Hispanic Journal of Behavioral Sciences, 14,* 455–468.

O'Sullivan, M. J., Peterson, P. D., Cox, G. B., & Kirkeby, J. (1989). Ethnic populations: Community mental health services ten years later. *American Journal of Community Psychology, 17,* 17–30.

Olfson, M., & Pincus, H. A. (1994a). Outpatient psychotherapy in the United States: I. Volume, costs, and user characteristics. *American Journal of Psychiatry, 151,* 1281–1288.

Olfson, M., & Pincus, H. A. (1994b). Outpatient psychotherapy in the United States: II. Patterns of utilization. *American Journal of Psychiatry, 151,* 1289–1294.

Olfson, M., Shea, S., Feder, A., Fuentes, M., Nomura, Y., Gameroff, M., & Weissman, M. M. (2000). Prevalence of anxiety, depression, and substance use disorders in an urban general medicine practice. *Archives of Family Medicine, 9,* 876–883.

Padilla, A. M. (1980). *Acculturation: Theory, models, and some new findings.* Boulder, CO: Westview.

Padilla, A. M., Carlos, M. L., & Keefe, S. E. (1976). Mental health services utilization by Mexican Americans. In M. Miranda (Ed.), *Psychology for the Spanish Speaking* (Monograph No. 3). Los Angeles: Spanish Speaking Mental Health Research Center.

Padilla, A. M., & Ruiz, R. A. (1973). *Latin mental health: A review of the literature* (DHEW Publication No. HSM 73-9142). Washington, DC: U.S. Government Printing Office.

Padilla, A. M., Ruiz, R. A., & Alvarez, R. (1975). Community mental health services for the Spanish-speaking/surnamed population. *American Psychologist, 30,* 892–905.

Pearlin, L. I., Menaghan, E. G., Lieberman. M. A., & Mullan, J. T. (1981). The stress process. *Journal of Health and Social Behavior, 22,* 337–356.

Quinn, T. C., Wawer, M. J., Sewankambo, N., Serwadda, D., Li, C., Wabwire-Mangen, F., Meehan, M. O., Lutalo, T., & Gray, R. H. (2000). Viral load and heterosexual transmission of HIV type I. *Journal of the American Medical Association, 342,* 921–929.

Regier, D. A., Narrow, W. E., Rae, D. S., Manderscheid, R. W., Locke, B. Z., & Goodwin, F. K. (1993). The de facto U.S. mental and addictive disorders service system: Epidemiologic catchment area prospective 1-year prevalence rates of disorders and services. *Archives of General Psychiatry, 50,* 85–94.

Robins, L. N., & Regier, D. A. (1991). *Psychiatric disorders in America: The epidemiological catchment area study.* New York: Free Press.

Rogler, L. H., Cortes, D. E., & Malgady, R. G. (1991). Acculturation and mental health status among Hispanics. *American Psychologist, 46,* 585–597.

Rogler, L. H., Malgady, R. G., Costantino, G., & Blumenthal, R. (1987). What do culturally sensitive mental health services mean? The case of Hispanics. *American Psychologist, 42,* 565–570.

Rumbaut, R. D. (1977). Life events, change, migration, and depression. In W. E. Fann, I. Karocan, A. D. Pokorny, & R. L. William (Eds.), *Phenomenology and treatment of depression* (pp. 115–126). New York: Spectrum.

Sabogal, F., & Catania, J. A. (1996). HIV risk factors, condom use, and HIV antibody testing among heterosexual Hispanics: The National AIDS Behavioral Survey. *Hispanic Journal of Behavioral Sciences, 18,* 367–391.

Salgado de Snyder, V. N., Diaz-Perez, M. J., & Ojeda, V. D. (2000). The prevalence of nervios and associated symptomatology among inhabitants of Mexican rural communities. *Culture, Medicine, and Psychiatry, 24,* 453–470.

Sánchez, A. R., Acosta, R., & Grosser, R. (1979). *Mental health services to ethnic minorities in Colorado.* Denver: Division of Mental Health, Department of Institutions, State of Colorado.

Sánchez, A. R., & Atkinson, D. R. (1983). Mexican American cultural commitment, preference for counselor ethnicity, and willingness to use counseling. *Journal of Counseling Psychology, 30,* 215–220.

Santiago-Rivera, A. L., & Altarriba, J. (2002). The role of language in therapy with the Spanish-English bilingual client. *Professional Psychology: Research and Practice, 33,* 30–38.

Scwarcz, S. K., Spitters, C., Ginsberg, M. M., Anderson, L., Kellogg, T., & Katz, M. H. (1997). Predictors of HIV counseling and testing among sexually transmitted disease clinic patients. *Sexually Transmitted Diseases, 24,* 347–352.

Simoni, J. M., & Pérez, L. (1995). Latinos and mutual support groups: A case for considering culture. *American Journal of Orthopsychiatry, 65,* 440–445.

Sledge, W. H. (1994). Psychotherapy in the United States: Challenges and opportunities. *American Journal of Psychiatry, 151,* 1267–1270.

Smart, J. F., & Smart, D. W. (1995). Acculturative stress; The experience of the Hispanic immigrant. *The Counseling Psychologist, 23,* 25–42.

Suarez-Orozco, C., & Suarez-Orozco, M. M. (1995). *Transformations: Immigration, family life, and achievement motivation among Latino adolescents.* Stanford, CA: Stanford University Press.

Sue, S. (1977). Community mental health services to minority groups: Some optimism some pessimism. *American Psychologist, 32,* 616–624.

Sue, S. (1988). Psychotherapeutic services for ethnic minorities: Two decades of research findings. *American Psychologist, 43,* 301–308.

Sue, S. (1998). In search of cultural competence in psychotherapy and counseling. *American Psychologist, 53,* 440–448.

Sue, S., & Zane, N. W. S. (1987). The role of culture and cultural techniques in psychotherapy: A critique and reformulation. *American Psychologist 42,* 37–45.

Surgenor, L. J., Horn, J., Hudson, S. M., Lunt, H., & Tennent, J. (2000). Metabolic control and psychological sense of control in women with diabetes mellitus. *Journal of Psychosomatic Research, 49,* 267–273.

Swanson, J. W., Linskey, A O., Quintero Salinas, R., & Pumanega, A. J. (1992). A binational school survey of depressive symptoms, drug use, and suicidal ideation. *Journal of the American Academy of Child and Adolescent Psychiatry, 31,* 669–678.

Swartz, M. S., Wagner, H. R., Swanson, J. W., Burns, B. J., George, L. K., & Padgett, D. K. (1998). Comparing use of public and private mental health services: The enduring barriers of race and age. *Community Mental Health Journal, 34,* 133–144.

Tinsley, H. E., Brown, M. T., de St-Aubin, T. M., & Lucek, J. (1984). Relationship between expectancies for a helping relationship and tendency to seek help from a campus help provider. *Journal of Counseling Psychology, 31,* 149–160.

Torrey, E. F. (1972). *The mind game: Witch doctors and psychiatrists.* New York: Bantam Books.

Trevino, F. M., & Bruhn, J. G. (1977). Incidence of mental illness in a Mexican community. *Psychiatric Annals, 7,* 33–51.

Trevino, F. M., Bruhn, J. G., & Bunce, H. (1979). Utilization of community mental health services in a Texas-Mexico border city. *Social Science and Medicine, 13A,* 331–334.

VanOss Marín, B. (1994). La cultura latina y la sexualidad: Implicaciones para la prevención del VIH/SIDA [The Latin culture and sexuality: Implications for the prevention of HIV and AIDS]. *Revista de Psicologia Social y Personalidad, 10,* 171–183.

Vargas-Wills, G., & Cervantes, R. C. (1987). Consideration of psychological stress in the treatment of the Latina immigrant. *Hispanic Journal of Behavioral Sciences, 9,* 315–329.

Vega, W., Kolody, B., & Aguilar-Gaxiola, S. (2001). Help seeking for mental health problems among Mexican Americans. *Journal of Immigrant Health, 3,* 133–140.

Vega, W. A., Kolody, B., Aguilar-Gaxiola, S., Alderete, E., Catalano, R., & Caraveo-Anduaga, J. B. (1998). Lifetime prevalence of DSM-III-R psychiatric disorders among urban and rural Mexican Americans in California. *Archives of General Psychiatry, 55,* 771–778.

Vega, W., Kolody, B., Aguilar-Gaxiola, S., & Catalano, R. (1999). Gaps in service utilization by Mexican Americans with mental health problems. *American Journal of Psychiatry, 156,* 928–934.

Vega, W. A., & López, S. R. (2001). Priority issues in Latino mental health services research. *Mental Health Services Research, 3,* 189–200.

Wells, K. B., Golding, J. M., Hough, R. L., Burnam, A., & Karno, M. (1988). Factors affecting the probability of use of general and medical health and social/community services for Mexican Americans and non-Hispanic whites. *Medical Care, 26,* 441–452.

Zea, M. C., Quezada, T., & Belgrave, F. Z. (1994). Latino cultural values: Their role in adjustment to disability. *Journal of Social Behavior and Personality, 9,* 185–200.

Zuñiga, M. E. (1991). "Dichos" as metaphorical tools for resistant Latino clients. *Psychotherapy: Theory, Research, Practice, and Training, 28,* 480–483.

12

Clinical Practices With African Americans

Juxtaposition of Standard Clinical Practices and Africentricism

Edward F. Morris

In clinical practices throughout the United States, psychologists are finding that increasingly more clients are from cultural backgrounds different from their own. The majority of service providers are European American with middle-class values and orientations; a sizable portion of diverse client populations are African American and underserved with mixed values and orientations (Carter, 1995). The prevailing therapeutic orientation is cognitive-behavioral; the predominant conceptual orientation is psychodynamic. Most therapy and assessment evaluations are conducted in office settings or in large group practices. Little consideration is given to matching service providers with clients' ethnicity or worldview. Unless required by external sources, little allotment is made for continuous multicultural training (Dana, 1998; Helms, 1984). From the onset, invisible boundaries are established between service providers and African American clients. For the service providers, the ill effects of the invisible boundaries are uncertainty about clients' needs and cultural expectations, projection of problems onto clients, and sociocultural ignorance (Dana, 1998). For the clients, the ill effects are underutilization of services, premature termination, and other undesirable outcomes (S. Sue & Morishima, 1982).

Numerous researchers have shown that race, ethnicity, and acculturation levels are important variables in understanding the prevalence, treatment efficacy, and differential diagnoses of ethnic minorities in the mental health community (Burham, Hough, Karno, Escobar, & Telles, 1987; Geary, Brown, Milburn, Ahmed, & Booth, 1989; McIntosh, 1984; Moscicki, Locke, Rae, & Boyd, 1989; Rumbaut, 1989; Somervell, Leaf, Weissman, Blazer, & Bruce, 1989; D. W. Sue & Sue, 1987). On the basis of the literature, African Americans in particular have historically underutilized mental health services. They attend relatively fewer sessions than European Americans and frequently terminate treatment prematurely (Armstrong, Ishiki, Heiman, Mundt, & Womack, 1984; Goodman & Siegel, 1978; Scheffler & Miller, 1989). In fact, half of the African Americans who do initiate contact with mental health services tend not to return after the first session (S. Sue, 1977). Conversely, European Americans are 4 to 5 times more likely than African Americans to return for continued mental health services (Gallo, Marino, Ford, & Anthony, 1995). Interestingly, when African Americans are in need of mental health services, they are more apt to use inpatient and emergency services, more likely to be rehospitalized after inpatient treatment, and more often admitted involuntarily to mental institutions (Havassy & Hopkin, 1989; Lindsey & Paul, 1989; Scheffler & Miller, 1989; Snowden & Cheung, 1990). On the basis of this utilization of mental health services, for African Americans, there is a preference for emergency services over ongoing treatment services, tertiary prevention over secondary prevention, and crisis mode over preventive mode.

Several explanations for the underutilization of mental health services by African Americans have been offered. On the basis of the literature, the explanations can be grouped into several categories (Dana, 1998; Wells, Goldin, & Hough, 1989). The first category, cultural factors, consists of training deficiencies among therapists and diagnosticians who do not share a similar cultural background with the client, negative stigmas frequently associated with going "outside" of the community for assistance with personal problems, inadequate services, different or unrealistic treatment expectations, and clinically inappropriate or culturally inconsistent services. Service access barriers, the second category, include those economic, job, and resource factors (e.g., transportation, inflexible job schedules, resource knowledge) that preclude African Americans from gaining access to services as often as they may need or desire. The third category, economic constraints, has become increasingly more of an impediment during recent years. With the further marginalization of African Americans by managed care and other insurance companies, access to quality mental health services has become more difficult and costly. Whereas federal and private funds were available 20 years ago for an array of mental health services, those funds and, consequently, services are no longer available (Dana, 1998; Scheffler & Miller, 1989). Those individuals who would have used the services are now confronted with another process barrier that makes access even more difficult. Those individuals whose emotional instability warrants therapeutic intervention now have a legitimate excuse not to seek assistance. Although there is considerable evidence that their need for mental health services is high (Neighbors, 1984; Scheffler & Miller, 1989), the service shortfall precludes access, thereby further exacerbating the emotional strain that is placed on African Americans as individuals and as a cultural group.

At a surface level, cultural factors, service access barriers, and economic constraints could account for most of the reasons that African Americans underutilize mental health services. At a deeper level, however, these impediments provide only a partial explanation. African Americans' history and current experiences in this country provide multiple interactive variables that we as diagnosticians and clinicians are just beginning to understand. Westernized theoretical thinking is inadequate in explaining the psychological mind-set of most

African Americans. European American diagnostic tools are insufficient in providing a character sketch of the intrapersonal and interpersonal processes of African Americans. The current diagnostic system is insensitive to the multitude of cultural variables that could affect the certainty with which clinicians diagnose African Americans who exhibit certain behavioral and emotional patterns. Fortunately, there is increasing recognition in the psychological community of the limited understanding that we currently have of African Americans. In fact, Allison, Crawford, Echemendia, Robinson, and Kemp (1994) concluded that less than half of doctoral-level clinicians felt competent with African Americans despite their training exposure and diverse clientele. Recognizing this dilemma, several scholars have introduced alternative worldviews that are consistent with the cultural heritage of African Americans (Akbar, 1984; Baldwin, 1979, 1980, 1985; Nobles, 1976), diagnostic measures that are sensitive to the unique emotional and behavioral patterns of African Americans (R. Jones, 1996), clinical conceptualizations that are germane to the identity structure of African Americans (Carter, 1995; Helms, 1984, 1990; Helms & Carter, 1991; Parham, 1989; Parham & Helms, 1981), and conceptualization strategies for cross-cultural clients (Dana, 1992, 1993).

Understanding African Americans from a multicultural perspective requires a level of intentionality that goes beyond clinicians' and diagnosticians' usual role and function. First, it requires that they assume that their intimate knowledge of African American clients and culture is inadequate, especially if they are not from this particular cultural group. Adopting this position would help service providers listen more carefully to clients' issues and needs with fewer cultural filters. Because these filters tend to bend and blend their perceptions of the clients' experiences in a way that is more comfortable intellectually and emotionally, there is a high probability of misinterpretation that is prompted by their cultural shortsightedness. Conversely, when clinicians and diagnosticians are in a better "listening" mode with respect to the clients, they can interpret information from within the context of the clients' cultural experiences. Understanding clients from within their cultural context would help service providers be more adaptable in their theoretical orientation, flexible with their skills and strategies, and sensitive to clients' cultural idiosyncrasies. More important, such a position helps service providers to be less ethnocentric in their orientation and interactions with clients. Cultural intentionality not only requires the "given" skills of being a competent clinician or diagnostician but also necessitates flexibility with ever-changing clients who may come from widely varying intracultural and intercultural backgrounds. Not all African Americans come from the same cultural mind-set, not all African Americans have the same worldviews, and not all African Americans are at the same stage of identity development. All African Americans, however, have similar cultural roots and have experienced, to varying degrees, the effects of racism and the divergent impact of Eurocentric thinking on then-psychosocial development. Because clients live within a social context, awareness of African Americans' environment and their surrounding cultural context becomes as important as the individuals themselves.

Development of a therapeutic or conceptual orientation is an ongoing process. Typically, the process begins in graduate school when the prospective clinician learns about various theoretical perspectives in more than a superficial manner. It is also during graduate school that most students start to emulate supervisors or mentors whom they respect. Early in the process, the graduate student memorizes theoretical tenets and testing protocols. With more experience, practice, and supervision, the graduate student becomes better able to synthesize the material and integrate theory with his or her experiences in the field. Eventually, the graduate student becomes a practicing clinician or diagnostician and begins to integrate personal style and idiosyncrasies into activities with clients. Because the clinician or diagnostician is a conglomeration of personal and professional experiences, supervisors' wisdom and intervention, and formal education, it is conceivable that his or her theoretical orientation is influenced by his or her cultural worldview as well as that of his or her supervisors and mentors. If the worldview is Eurocentric, then one set of assumptions will be made about clients and their sociocultural experiences. Similarly, if the worldview is Africentric, then another set of assumptions will be made about clients and their sociocultural experiences.

The categories Africentric and Eurocentric are more than geographic designations. They represent an individual's social, political, and cultural orientation. They consist of the presumptions and assumptions that an individual holds about the makeup of his or her world (Kearney, 1975; D. W. Sue, 1978). Homer and Vanderhuis (1981) said that racial identity is a "culturally based variable that influences the relationship between the helper and the client" (p. 33). Similarly, Dana (1998) noted that one's worldview contains the collective wisdom that a person uses to make sense of life experiences. It is imperative, therefore, that clinicians and diagnosticians understand, or try to understand, clients' presumptions and assumptions. Such knowledge can make a difference for the client between effective intervention and disappointment and dissatisfaction. If the service provider and the client's worldviews coincide, then the person-environment fit will be good. Therapy will most likely progress, and the client will most likely feel satisfied with the treatment. Conversely, if the worldviews clash, then the fit will not be productive. The services, consequently, will become unacceptable or underutilized, with the client feeling frustrated, misunderstood, and defensive (Ibrahim, 1985; S. Sue & Zane, 1987).

Because traditional clinical therapy and practice are grounded in Western assumptions, there is a high probability that many clinicians and diagnosticians are "operating in the dark" when working with African American clients. Because of limited cultural information, there is the potential for service providers to make faulty assumptions, inaccurate diagnoses, incongruous treatment plans, and inappropriate assessment protocols. To avoid these errors, clinicians and diagnosticians need to understand the philosophical premises of African Americans as individuals and as a cultural group. Such an awareness will assist them in developing the skills necessary for effective cross-cultural therapy and assessment evaluations. The Africentric perspective gives service providers a foundation for understanding the philosophical premises of this particular cultural group. Once this particular worldview is understood, then the challenge becomes finding a way to integrate elements of Africentricism with Eurocentricism. Bennett (1986) offered the concept of *ethno-relativism* as a means to reconcile the differences between the two worldviews. He contended that for service providers to be cross-cultural within their professional orientation, they should strive for the following goals: They must accept that different worldviews can coexist, they must adapt their skills and abilities so they are applicable to other cultures, and they must integrate the different worldviews so as to be comfortable in "both worlds" as a therapist or diagnostician.

Several authors (e.g., Baldwin & Hopkins, 1990; Katz, 1985; D. W. Sue & Sue, 1990) have attempted to articulate the differences between Eurocentric values and Africentric values. Such a description provides clinicians and diagnosticians with an empirically based delineation of the predominant values and behavioral indicators of these two worldviews. Table 1 provides a summary of these characteristics.

Africentricism and Eurocentricism, as theoretical worldviews, do not represent monolithic orientations. They can represent a continuum of thoughts within a particular cultural group as well as a variety of racial affiliations. Thus, European Americans can have an Africentric orientation and African Americans can have a Eurocentric orientation. The worldview profile is further confounded by the fact that individuals who are biracial by heritage and who choose not to identify with a single racial group may have a worldview that is qualitatively different than that of individuals who are not biracial. Their lineages are different, society's reaction toward them is different, and their interactional experiences with the world are different. Although important, it is beyond the scope of this article to address adequately this particular topic among bicultural and multicultural individuals. Root (1996), however, provided a comprehensive discussion of this issue as well as the multiracial experiences of bicultural individuals.

Given its importance, it is necessary, therefore, for the clinician or diagnostician to have information on the client's level of acculturation and worldview prior to the onset of any assessment or intervention procedure. Such information is imperative because not all clients who appear to belong to a particular cultural group in terms of appearance and surname will share the same worldviews, values, and perceptions. To avoid stereotyping, the service provider should gather information on the client's cultural orientation from the interview, or assessment measures, prior to formulating a treatment conceptualization or diagnostic considerations. According to Dana (1992), the information should reflect the relative contributions from the dominant and nondominant cultures in the client's cultural orientation. Such information can assist the clinician or diagnostician in the determination of appropriate assessment measures, clinical formulations, and intervention strategies. As service providers, clinicians and diagnosticians should be ever vigilant of their own values and worldviews. They should also be willing to examine the potential impact of their values on African American clients. Their understanding of this group's cultural values and idiosyncrasies will be greatly enhanced if they resist making value judgments before adequate sociocultural information has been collected, challenge stereotypes and assumptions, and avoid imposing their own worldviews onto clients.

Treatment Issues

Because of past and current experiences with racism and prejudices, many African American clients are distrustful of European American therapists (E. J. Smith, 1981). Ridley (1984) contended that "cultural paranoia" feeds distrust and is, in fact, a major variable that influences disclosure in African American clients. According to several researchers (Ho, 1992; Ridley, 1984; E. J. Smith, 1991), this particular response pattern is a healthy reaction to institutional racism. It allows African Americans to understand racism without personalizing its ill effects. It affords African Americans the time and ability to process various interactional patterns with European Americans so that the most

Table 1 Summary of Eurocentric and Africentric Characteristics

Characteristic	*Eurocentrism*	*Africentricism*
Values	Emphasis on individual rights	Emphasis on group and relationships
	Authoritative orientation	Democratic orientation
	Nuclear family structure	Extended family structure
	Emphasis on youthfulness	Emphasis on maturity
	Independence oriented	Interdependence oriented
	Assertive and competitive	Compliant and cooperative
	Thrive under conflict	Thrive under harmony
	Freedom oriented	Security oriented
	Written tradition	Verbal tradition
Guiding principles of action	Fulfillment of individual needs	Achievement of collective or cultural goals
	Individual responsibility	Group or cultural responsibility
Behavior orientation	Self-actualization	Collective actualization
	Projection of feelings	Expression of feelings
Time orientation	Future oriented	Here-and-now oriented
	Time determined	Event determined
Ethical orientation	Morality anchored in people	Morality anchored in relationships
Language usage	Standard English	Standard and nonstandard English
Client—therapist communication	Ambiguous approach	Concrete, tangible approach
	Cause-effect orientation	Environmentally influenced
	Physical and mental health distinction	Combined physical and mental health
	Long-term goals	Immediate and short-range goals
Communication style	Speak fast to control listener	Speak with affect
	More eye contact when listening	Direct or prolonged eye contact when speaking; less when listening
	Nonverbal markers (head nods)	Interrupt when can (turn taking)
	Quick responding	Quicker responding
	Objective, task oriented	Affective, emotional, interpersonally oriented
History	Based on immigrants' experience	Based on slavery experience
	Romanticize war	Avoidance of conflict
Status and power	Measured by economic possessions	Measured by noneconomic possessions
	Credentials, titles, and positions	Status in the community
	Believe better than other systems	Believe as good as other systems
Aesthetics	Music and art based on European cultures	Music and art based on multiple cultures, primarily African American
	Women: blonde, thin, young	Women: multiple personal roles
	Men: athletic ability, power, status	Men: multiple personality qualities
Religion	No tolerance for deviation (monodeity)	Tolerant of others' interpretations of God

appropriate response can be emitted. It provides a tool of discernment for African Americans to better understand the deep and surface messages of European Americans. Thus, cultural paranoia has served as a survival tool for many African Americans. To expect these individuals to give up this particular adaptive skill during the initial phase of therapy is unreasonable and, probably, ill-advised. Understanding cultural paranoia, however, is a critical step to comprehending the African American client within his or her cultural context.

Getting clients to self-disclose is half of the therapy or assessment battle. Being able to receive the communication from clients and to react in an objective and a culturally respectful manner is the other half of the battle. Despite an increase in literature that describes the changing social, educational, and economic status of African Americans, many clinicians and diagnosticians continue to base their perceptions on stereotypes and unchallenged assumptions (Pedersen, 1987). Greene (1985), Paniagua (1994), and D. W. Sue and Sue (1990) have identified several phenomena that might adversely affect the counseling or assessment process. None of these experiences are productive. Most of them, in fact, are counterproductive with African American clients. Following is a brief explanation of each area.

1. *Communication difficulty:* Effective communication is the key to effective therapy. Without it, there is no constructive therapeutic outcome. When clinicians and diagnosticians are working with African American clients, communication becomes even more significant. Culturally, African Americans are expressive and communicative people. If they feel comfortable in the relationship or the situation, they become interactive and expressive. Multiple examples of this behavioral style are seen in church services, interactions between friends and family members, and moments of expressiveness. If uncomfortable, African Americans frequently become guarded, distrustful, and nonverbal. For many of these individuals, history has shown that to do otherwise is detrimental to their emotional, economic, or physical viability. Because of experiences many African Americans have had within mental health and social service systems, they have learned that cultural paranoia is the most adaptive personality style and that discernment is the most effective way to communicate with individuals who do not share the same cultural background (Carter, 1991; Ridley, 1984). Without an effort by therapists to overcome this barrier, their diagnoses, conceptualizations, and interpretations will be, at best, suspect.

2. *Race-based countertransference:* As a phenomenon, countertransference involves the projection of feelings and thoughts by the therapist onto the client. At times, the countertransference can be constructive; at other times, it can be counterproductive. Nevertheless, it manifests itself in many ways: being overprotective with clients, rejecting or disrespecting clients, requiring constant reinforcement and approval, seeing oneself in clients, or compulsively giving advice. The therapist's own emotional needs or unresolved conflicts become entangled in the therapeutic relationship and, thereby, obstruct or destroy his or her sense of objectivity. Unsupervised, countertransference can be therapeutically unproductive and potentially unethical. Supervised, countertransference can provide the therapist with valuable information that could be used for therapeutic gain. The insidiousness of race and racial thoughts, however, makes race-based countertransference extremely difficult to monitor. Without forethought, the therapist or diagnostician could react to perceived stereotypical or racially isolated experiences in a negative way. Without insight, the therapist or diagnostician could then project his or her reaction onto the client without assuming any responsibility for his or her part of the interaction. When the client fails to return for continued treatment or assessment, or if therapy fails to progress as

planned, the client is then labeled as being resistant to treatment

3. *Racism and race-based prejudice:* Although disallowed by the code of ethics (American Psychological Association, 1992), subtle and overt forms of race-based prejudices exist within the field of psychology. It is inevitable and unrealistic to think otherwise in a race-conscious society. They are manifested in research arenas and academia when a Eurocentric-only perspective is presented. They are exhibited in clinical settings when a Eurocentric worldview is the overarching theoretical orientation of the practice. They are exhibited within diagnostic settings where culturally biased measures are used to assess ethnic minority clients. When the Eurocentric worldview, normative standard, and clinical conceptualizations are used uncritically with African American clients, the therapist or diagnostician is acting in an ethnocentric manner. He or she is indicating by his or her therapy and assessment choices that the Eurocentric standard is appropriate and unbiased. Despite repeated empirical studies that have discussed the cultural biases of various theoretical orientations, cognitive ability instruments, and psychological measures, numerous psychologists practice exclusively in accordance with a Eurocentric standard and act as if the refuting data do not exist. Thus, cultural differences may be viewed negatively and interpreted as an indication of pathology.

4. *Color blindness:* As a perception, color blindness may be humanistically egalitarian. As an approach in therapy, however, color blindness may be potentially insulting. To believe that racial color is not important and that all clients are the same is commendable in a non-race-based hierarchical society. Unfortunately, in the United States, such is not the case. Race may not necessarily be an important factor for the therapist, evaluator, or diagnostician; however, to assume that it is not important to the African American client is presumptuous and culturally insensitive. The implied message to the client is that one's race is important as long as it is not used as a mitigating factor or explanation for a difficult situation or affective experience. Hall (1997) referred to this marginalization of the client's race as *cultural malpractice.* In her article, she pointedly discussed the adverse impact of this particular perceptual myopia on client-therapist relationships, graduate education and training programs, and the future of psychology. On the basis of her description, if the field of psychology does not change or adapt its current theoretical thoughts and practices to more effectively meet the needs of a multicultural society, the prognosis for cross-cultural fertilization within each of these domains is bleak.

5. *Limited definition of familial roles and boundaries:* Within the traditional European American culture, the nuclear family consists of two parents and biological children—dogs are optional. Within the African American culture, the nuclear family can consist of biological children, stepchildren, nonbiological relatives, and a parent or parents—dogs are not included. Within the former group, roles and functions are culturally defined (i.e., based on traditional definitions). Within the latter group, roles and functions are situationally defined (i.e., based on emotional necessity). Within social services and mental health settings, the former group is the prototype of a defined family. Conversely, within these same settings, the latter group is the prototype of a cultural anomaly. Besides being ethnocentric, the implied message of this limited definition is that the Eurocentric definition of family is ideal whereas the African American definition is disorganized and dysfunctional. From an Africentric perspective, families are not limited by geographic location, blood ties, or marital status. Family consists of anyone, regardless of family of origin, who is invested in maintaining the viability of the family group or structure.

6. *Limited definition of normalcy:* Because of the contextual nature of normalcy, all behaviors

that the client exhibits must be evaluated within their cultural context. As a mitigating factor, an individual's culture can influence etiological determinations, clinical conceptualizations, and the definition of normalcy. If African American clients' behaviors are defined by European American standards and definitions of normalcy, then the clinician and diagnostician are at risk of clinical misdiagnoses and mistreatment.

7. *Inappropriate racial labels:* Although most non-European American cultural groups have had their cultural identity defined over the years by European American demographers and sociologists, African Americans are one of the few cultural groups whose racial identity has been defined and redefined on a continual basis (Baldwin, 1976; Carter, 1995; Cross, 1971; Helms, 1984; Parham, 1989; T. W. Smith, 1992). As a cultural group, they have gone from being Niggers, to Nigras, to Negroes, to Colored, to Blacks, to Afro-Americans, to African Americans. For some cultural researchers, the label is more than a semantic difference (Akbar, 1984; Carter, 1991; Dana, 1998; Helms, 1984; Parham & Helms, 1981). For African Americans, it represents a worldview, ethnic identity, and cultural affiliation. For many non-African Americans, it represents a nominal demarcation. To ignore the importance of the racial label with an African American client implies cultural insensitivity, cultural ignorance, or both. Conversely, to acknowledge its significance suggests respect, sensitivity, and sincerity. For therapeutic gain or diagnostic information, the latter mind-set would be more productive when working with African American clients.

Treatment Recommendations

From an Africentric perspective, treatment should include three phases. The first phase, pretreatment, involves equipping oneself to work with African American clients. Although not all African Americans are alike, there are some sociocultural commonalities that transcend geographic and economic differences. There is a common history within this country, there are common experiences with discrimination and institutional racism, and there is a sense of cultural connectedness that has endured over time and geographical distance. If the clinician or diagnostician is unfamiliar with the current and historical details of these commonalities and the impact they have on the personality development of African Americans, then he or she needs to become a "student" of the culture. Such an endeavor could occur at a practical as well as a theoretical level. From a practical perspective, the clinician should (a) explore the autobiographical literature of African Americans who have described their experiences as cultural beings within this country, (b) attend culturally specific conferences that address issues pertaining to African Americans (i.e., those of the Association of Black Psychology and National Association of Black Social Workers), (c) participate in various workshops that explore cross-cultural dynamics and experiences, and (d) confer with African American colleagues and consultants regarding possible transference and countertransference issues within cross-cultural dyadic relationships. From a theoretical perspective, the clinician should read, process, and discuss with colleagues the writings of various African American researchers and academicians who have focused their scholarly activities on the experiences of African Americans. As a starting point, Akbar (1984), Baldwin (1979, 1980, 1985), and Nobles (1976) have provided further information on the Africentric perspective and Africentric psychology. Similarly, R. Jones (1996) provided a comprehensive summary of various diagnostic measures that are sensitive to the unique emotional and behavioral patterns of African Americans. Finally, Carter (1995), Helms (1984, 1990), Helms and Carter

(1991), Parham (1989), Parham and Helms (1981), and Ridley (1984) have provided various clinical conceptualizations that are unique to the identity structure and clinical experiences of African Americans.

There is, indeed, an abundance of literature on African Americans and their culture. The aforementioned articles are only a minuscule sample of the wealth of material that exists within the professional literature. Because of the multitude of clinical and empirical thoughts regarding African Americans, it would be an unyielding, if not impossible, endeavor to attain a comprehensive knowledge base of their cultural experiences. Despite the numerous cross-cultural opportunities for dialogue within professional organizations, the abundance of cross-cultural literature within professional journals, and the encouragement by various clinicians and academicians for further cross-cultural development within psychology, most European American clinicians fail to take the first step of setting aside their cultural ethnocentricity in order to gain the necessary skills and knowledge needed to be culturally competent clinicians with African American clients.

The second phase of treatment, assessment and evaluation, involves understanding the details of the client's issues from a multicultural perspective. This particular task is a twofold process. The first part requires the service provider to assess his or her own cultural identity and to reconcile any unresolved issues prior to working with the culturally different client. If not, the service provider's unresolved issues may interfere with the therapeutic relationship and, thereby, compromise the treatment or evaluation process. The second part of the process involves the assessment of the client's cultural identity. Such an assessment, however, warrants considerable discernment and cultural sensitivity. Cultural identity does not necessarily equal assumed identity. Similarly, the therapist's desire to integrate cultural issues into the therapeutic process may not necessarily have the desired positive result that he or she had hoped for. There are numerous African Americans who have assumed a European American identity and worldview. There are some European Americans who have adopted an Africentric worldview. There are members of both racial groups who have blended the two perspectives in a way that is consistent with their lifestyle. Finally, there are bicultural and multicultural individuals who may choose to identify with one or the other cultural group. To assume an African American client has adopted a particular worldview or cultural identity before asking is, at best, presumptuous and, at worst, potentially insulting. In addition, the initiation of a discussion of the client's cultural affiliation has the potential of either endearing the client to the therapist or endangering the therapeutic relationship. The former reaction may result from the client's believing that the therapist is culturally sensitive; the latter reaction may result from the client's perceiving that the therapist is culturally presumptuous.

Several models are presented in the literature that explore the various stages of racial identity development among African Americans (Cross, 1971; Helms, 1984, 1990; Helms & Carter, 1991; A. C. Jones, 1985; Parham & Helms, 1981). Helms (1984), in particular, articulated the various stages of racial identity development and explored the bidirectionality of the client-therapist relationship. She also provided a clear description of the dynamics of monocultural and cross-cultural therapy dyads and the common affective issues that encapsulate these interactional exchanges. It would not do the model justice for me to present it in the detail that it deserves within the context of this article; her book on racial identity development as well as her articles serve that function. Although not specific to African Americans, Dana (1993, 1997, 1998) has provided a conceptual overlay that complements Helms's racial identity theory. His model is based on two major assumptions: Assessment and treatment strategies must be derived from the client's cultural worldview, and diagnostic specificity from a cross-cultural perspective must be derived from both culture-specific (emic) and culture-general (etic) sources. Combined, these two sources of information provide a contextual understanding of the intrapersonal and interpersonal experiences of African Americans. Without this contextual juxtaposition, the information that is gathered about the African American client's presenting problems becomes incomplete.

Synthesized integration is the third phase of the treatment process. It involves the synthesis of the client's presenting problems, culturally contextual history, racial identity development, and intervention strategies. With clients who share similar cultural experiences with the clinician or diagnostician, this task can be challenging. With clients who do not share similar cultural experiences with the service provider, this task can be an arduous process. Combining the conceptual elements of Dana's (1997) multicultural assessment intervention model and Helms's (1990) racial identity developmental stages allows the elements of the Africentric perspective to be integrated into a culturally consistent and contextually therapeutic framework.

The model that I propose is based on four major premises: (a) African Americans have unique cultural values, behavioral idiosyncrasies, and worldviews that are similar in some ways but radically different in most ways from those of European Americans and other ethnic minority groups; (b) the ongoing experiences and effects of racism and discrimination impact African Americans' personality dynamics and racial identity development; (c) competent assessment, conceptualization, and intervention require a working knowledge of paradigm differences between the Eurocentric and Africentric perspectives; and (d) specific information about the African American culture and the client's worldview can serve to increase the reliability and validity of the assessment process and improve the diagnostic labels and efficacy of subsequent interventions. Table 2 provides the conceptual template for the proposed culturally sensitive assessment and treatment model for African Americans. Next, I provide a description of the model's components with suggested questions for further clarification.

1. *Worldview:* A person's worldview is his or her conceptualization of the world, interactions between people, philosophy of life, and value systems. In fact, as a philosophy and approach to life, it can be independent of race. It is neither dichotomist nor nominal. Rather, a person's worldview can exist along a continuum and remain context specific. Despite its flexibility, most people have a predominant worldview that includes overarching characteristics that permeate most of their thoughts, intrapersonal beliefs, and interpersonal relationships. For this particular domain, the evaluator should assess the client's worldview along the Eurocentric-Africentric continuum. In assessing this particular domain, he or she should explore the following areas: Where along the continuum is the client's predominant worldview? What are the predominant value areas that characterize the client's worldview? If the client's worldview is contextual, what are the factors within the various areas that would make it contextual? What are the personal, environmental, and sociocultural influences that contribute to the client's worldview?

Table 2 Culturally Sensitive Assessment and Treatment Model for African Americans

	Client's Assessed Worldview			
Model Component	*Predominantly Eurocentric*	*Mostly Eurocentric*	*Mostly Africentric*	*Predominantly Africentric*
Racial identity stage*	Preencounter	Encounter	Integrated	Immersion-emersion
Treatment goals	Individual actualization	Balance with more individual goals than cultural goals	Balance with more cultural goals than individual goals	Cultural actualization
Assessment measures (if necessary)	Standard measures	Modified measures with Eurocentric focus	Modified measures with Africentric focus	Culture-specific measures
Conceptual synthesis	Monocultural (Eurocentric)	Cross-cultural with Eurocentric emphasis	Cross-cultural with Africentric emphasis	Monocultural (Africentric)
Intervention strategies	Universal strategies	Combined with Eurocentric emphasis	Combined with Africentric emphasis	Culture-specific strategies
Therapist race preference	European American	Either with European American preference	Either with African American preference	African American
Racial issues	Client initiated	Client-therapist initiated	Therapist-client initiated	Therapist initiated
Diagnoses	Appropriate	Appropriate with clarification	Appropriate with clarification	Inappropriate

*I intentionally switched the order of Helms's (1990) last two stages of racial identity. From a worldview perspective, both the preencounter and the immersion-emersion stages represent the polarities of cultural self-isolation. Conversely, the Eurocentric and integrated stages represent the blending of ideological thoughts and attitudes.

2. *Racial identity stage:* On the basis of Helms's (1990) stages of racial identity, what would be the client's predominant racial identity stage? What personal experiences, family and peer influences, environmental components, and sociocultural factors have influenced the client's racial identity development? Did the client's racial identity development occur in a stepwise manner? If not, what events caused changes in the developmental pattern?

3. *Treatment goals:* What are the primary treatment goals that the client wants to work on while in therapy? Are the goals consistent with the client's worldview (i.e., Eurocentric or Africentric) or a balance of the two perspectives? If the goals are somewhat balanced, is there an individualized or a cultural inclination or drift? What specific precipitants (e.g., personal vs. cultural) are prompting the client to work on certain goals?

4. *Assessment measures:* The choice of assessment measures should be based on the client's worldview. If the client is predominantly Eurocentric, then standard measures can be used to supplement the clinical interview. If the client is mostly Eurocentric or mostly Africentric in his or her orientation, then standard measures are

only appropriate with modifications, disclaimers of the test's cultural limitations, or clarification of cultural differences that may affect the assessment process. If the client is predominantly Africentric, the culture-test mismatch may rule out ethical use of standard measures. With clients who are predominantly or mostly Africentric, the clinician could use various emic (i.e., culture-specific) measures that have been standardized with predominantly African Americans. For a detailed description of the various culture-specific measures, refer to R. Jones (1996).

5. *Conceptual synthesis:* On the basis of collected data (i.e., racial identity stage, treatment goals, assessment measures) from the client as well as collaterals, what is the clinician's synthesized conceptualization of the client's intrapersonal experiences, interpersonal interactions, and sociocultural adjustment? Are the treatment goals congruent with the clinical picture that the client presents in therapy? If not, what is causing the incongruity?

6. *Intervention strategies:* On the basis of the client's worldview, what specific intervention strategies should the clinician recommend? For the most efficacious results, the recommendations should be congruent with the worldview. The more Africentric the worldview, the more active the role of the clinician. He or she may need to serve multiple roles as well as multiple functions with the African American client. Also, the more Africentric the client, the greater the involvement from the African American community and its various components. Conversely, the more Eurocentric the client, the more the clinician can rely on standard intervention strategies based on the therapist's orientation and comfort level.

7. *Therapist race preference:* With this particular domain, was the race of the therapist an important issue in the client's consideration of therapy? If racial preference was an important determinant, what were the factors that made it important to the client? Was the therapist's race an important enough factor to determine the therapy outcome? If so, what impact did it have on the therapy process?

8. *Racial issues:* The client's worldview should determine who initiates the discussion about racial issues. Given its sensitive nature, it would probably be more prudent for the client to initiate it if his or her worldview is predominantly or mostly Eurocentric. Conversely, if the client's worldview is predominantly or mostly Africentric, then he or she probably would not mind if the evaluator initiated discussion on the topic. Regardless of the client's worldview, caution, sensitivity, and respect should be exercised by the evaluator when discussing this issue. If asked by the client, the evaluator should be open, reflective, and honest about his or her feelings and thoughts. Because of ongoing experiences with European Americans, most African Americans can sense the evaluator's level of sincerity and self-disclosure.

9. *Diagnoses:* The appropriateness of the diagnoses should be contingent on the client's worldview. Because the current diagnostic system is Eurocentric in its orientation and emphasis, it would be appropriate, in its present form, only for clients who are predominantly Eurocentric. The more the client drifts from that end of the worldview continuum, the less reliable the diagnosis. Cultural factors, historical issues, race-based experiences, and personality dynamics may become significant variables; the current diagnostic system, therefore, may not represent accurately the complexity of the African American client's personality structure. As general guidelines in working with African American clients, the following are offered to clinicians as suggested intervention strategies:

10. *Be willing to adopt flexible roles.* In traditional mental health settings, professional roles are relatively prescribed: Clinicians provide therapy, social workers provide case management, and psychologists provide evaluation services. Given the utilization pattern of African Americans in mental health settings, the service provider may have only one opportunity to "hook" the person into the program. If that opportunity is to be maximized, then he or she may have to serve a variety of functions. To meet the client's sociocultural and emotional needs, the service provider may need to be a clinician, adviser, advocate, facilitator, consultant, educator, and social intervener. The presenting problem should serve as the determining factor for the roles. When task-oriented and behaviorally specific services are provided, the African American client will feel affirmed, assisted, and assured that mental health services can be of value.

11. *Be sensitive to cultural idiosyncrasies and be willing to discuss racial differences.* Open discussions of racial differences within the therapeutic context affirm the client's cultural orientation and experiences as well as normalize the dynamics of crosscultural relationships. Such discussions also reduce racial tension and anxiety and help the therapist be more comfortable and sensitive to the client's expectations. If the client is unwilling to discuss, or acknowledge, racial differences, the service provider should not press the issue. If pressed, the client may become guarded, resistant, and ambivalent.

12. *Include the church and extended family in the assessment and therapy process.* The strength of the African American community lies in its churches and extended families (Griffith, English, & Mayfield, 1980; Taylor & Chatters, 1986). Within the African American community, the church can serve as a source of spiritual and political strength. Similarly, the extended family can serve as a source of emotional and cultural stability. Unlike the European American definition, *extended family* includes any combination of individuals who live within the same community and who share an emotionally intimate relationship. It can include relatives, nonrelatives, older individuals, and community leaders; it is not limited to biological links. Given the function of these institutions for African Americans, they should be used in as many ways as possible. As a direct form of intervention, the assistance of community members could facilitate the treatment and evaluation processes in ways that might have been previously unavailable to the service provider. As an indirect form of intervention, the community members could serve as consultants in areas that could supplement the primary treatment protocol.

13. *Use a problem-solving approach that focuses on the client's everyday experiences.* Many African American clients prefer and expect a quick solution to problems they identify as essential. Consistent with the history of service utilization, African Americans tend to use services only when it is absolutely unavoidable and only for a very brief period. Consistent with the Africentric orientation, African Americans tend to be here-and-now oriented and problem focused. Thus, intrapsychic development tends to be overshadowed by their everyday struggles in meeting basic needs. As problems are identified and solved with problem-solving techniques, credibility and sense of trust are enhanced. Although interested, most African Americans have neither the financial resources nor the time to become "self-actualized" within a European American sociocultural structure.

14. *Focus not on deficits but on the client's social, emotional, and cultural strengths.* For many African Americans, life is socially and economically difficult. The sources of the difficulty

may include personality style and idiosyncrasies, life circumstances, educational limitations, and financial constraints All cultural groups experience elements of these difficulties. For African Americans, however, the struggle to maintain one's emotional stability is further exacerbated by ongoing discrimination and racism. Focusing on the deficits not only further deteriorates the client's struggling self-worth but also adds another burden that must be reconciled. Focusing on the client's strengths and on what he or she has accomplished, despite sociocultural barriers, provides a sense of affirmation and a culturally contextual reality.

15. *Use the client's cultural context as the foundation for diagnostic clarification and inquiry.* Cultural information can provide additional background data that could clarify diagnostic and clinical inquiries. Without the information, the clinician and diagnostician are at risk of either overdiagnosing or underdiagnosing the African American client's presenting problems. Sickle-cell anemia and high blood pressure, for example, are two such physical disorders that have strong emotional symptomatology and cultural relevance. Focusing on the symptoms without recognizing the disorder could prolong treatment without symptom abatement. It may also be legally and ethically questionable if the clinician or diagnostician follows a course of action when a referral or a more appropriate course of treatment is warranted. Researchers, clinicians, and diagnosticians barely understand the impact of continuous discrimination and racism on the personality structure of African Americans. However, if a parallel is drawn between the experiences of African Americans and those of other ethnic groups who have endured cultural atrocities, then the insidious impact of these experiences on the personality structure and development of African Americans would be equally profound. The diagnoses of behavioral symptoms and the conceptualization of cases must be tied into (the client's cultural context. Recognizing the cultural phenomenon is the first step in providing appropriate treatment. Understanding its etiology and incorporating that information in training programs, literature, and clinical settings become the more challenging next step. Overdiagnosing might result in unnecessary or inappropriate treatment protocols; underdiagnosing might result in inadequate or unrealistic treatment protocols.

Summary

If one accepts the premise that clients are multidimensional, then one must acknowledge the significant effect of personal demographics on their personality structure. Race is only one of these major demographics; gender, age, sexual orientation, and socioeconomic status are other equally influential factors and are significant enough to warrant further investigation. For utility purposes, I chose to focus on only one of these dimensions: race. To be culturally competent diagnosticians with African American clients, clinicians must incorporate conceptual models and worldviews that are not predominantly Eurocentric in origin or focus. To be effective therapists with African American clients, clinicians must be willing to step out of their professional "comfort zone" and seek out experiences and strategies that have proven to be efficacious with cross-cultural clients. Neither of these tasks is easy; both of these tasks require ongoing supervision, literature searches, workshops, and personal growth. Neither of these tasks is professionally overwhelming; both of these tasks contribute to skills, knowledge, and attitudes that are more congruent with being a culturally competent therapist, diagnostician, and evaluator.

References

Akbar, N. (1984). Africentric social sciences for human liberation. *Journal of Black Studies, 14,* 395–414.

Allison, K. W., Crawford, I., Echemendia, R., Robinson, L., & Kemp, D. (1994). Human diversity and professional competence: Training in clinical and counseling psychology revisited. *American Psychologist, 49,* 792–796.

American Psychological Association. (1992). Ethical principles of psychologists and code of conduct. *American Psychologist, 47,* 1597–1611.

Armstrong, H., Ishiki, D., Heiman, J., Mundt, J., & Womack, W. (1984). Service utilization by Black and White clientele in an urban community mental health center: Revised assessment of an old problem. *Community Mental Health Journal, 20,* 269–281.

Baldwin, J. A. (1976). Black psychology and Black personality; Some issues for consideration. *Black Books Bulletin, 4,* 6–11.

Baldwin, J. A. (1979). Theory and research concerning the notion of Black self-hatred: A review and reinterpretation. *Journal of Black Psychology, 5,* 51–77.

Baldwin, J. A. (1980). The psychology of oppression. In M. K. Asante & A. Vandi (Eds.), *Contemporary Black thought* (pp. 95–110). Beverly Hills, CA: Sage.

Baldwin, J. A. (1985). Psychological aspects of European cosmology in American society. *The Western Journal of Black Studies, 9,* 216–223.

Baldwin, J. A., & Hopkins, R. (1990). African American and European American cultural differences as assessed by the worldviews paradigm: An empirical analysis. *The Western Journal of Black Studies, 14,* 38–52.

Bennett, M. J. (1986). Toward ethnorelativism: A developmental model of intercultural sensitivity. In R. M. Paige (Ed.), *Cross cultural orientation: New conceptualizations and applications* (pp. 27–69). Lanham, MD: University Press of America.

Burham, M. A., Hough, R. L., Karno, M., Escobar, I. I., & Telles, C. A. (1987). Acculturation and lifetime prevalence of psychiatric disorders among Mexican Americans in Los Angeles. *Journal of Health and Social Behavior, 28,* 89–102.

Carter, R. T. (1991). Cultural values: A review of empirical research and implications for counseling. *Journal of Counseling and Development, 70,* 164–173.

Carter, R. T. (1995). *The influence of race and racial identity in psychotherapy: Toward a racially inclusive model.* New York: Wiley.

Cross, W. E., Jr. (1971). The Negro-to-Black conversion experience: Towards a psychology of Black liberation. *Black World, 20,* 13–27.

Dana, R. H. (1992). Assessment of cultural orientation. *SPA Exchange, 2*(2), 14–15.

Dana, R. H. (1993). *Multicultural assessment perspectives for professional psychology.* Boston; Allyn & Bacon.

Dana, R. H. (1997). Multicultural assessment and cultural identity: An assessment—intervention modal. *World Psychology, 3,* 121–141.

Dana, R. H. (1998). *Understanding cultural identity in intervention and assessment.* Thousand Oaks, CA: Sage.

Gallo, J. J., Marino, S., Ford, D., & Anthony, J. C. (1995). Filters on the pathway to mental health care: Sociodemographic factors. *Psychological Medicine, 25,* 1149–1160.

Geary, L. E., Brown, D. R., Milburn, N. G., Ahmed, F., & Booth, J. (1989). *Depression in Black American adults: Findings from the Norfolk Area health study.* Washington, DC: Institute of Urban Affairs.

Goodman, A. R., & Siegel, C. (1978). Differences in White/non-White community mental health center service utilization patterns. *Evaluation and Program Planning, 1,* 51–63.

Greene, B. A. (1985). Considerations in the treatment of Black patients by White therapists. *Psychotherapy, 22,* 389–393.

Griffith, E. E. H., English, T., & Mayfield, V. (1980). Possession, prayer, and testimony: Therapeutic aspects of the Wednesday night meeting in a Black church. *Psychiatry, 43,* 120–128.

Hall, C. (1997). Cultural malpractice: The growing obsolescence of psychology with the changing U.S. population. *American Psychologist, 52,* 642–651.

Havassy, B. E., & Hopkin, J. T. (1989). Factors predicting utilization of acute psychiatric inpatient services by frequently hospitalized patients. *Hospital and Community Psychiatry, 40,* 820–823.

Helms, I. E. (1984). Toward a theoretical explanation of the effects of race on counseling: A Black and White model. *The Counseling Psychologist, 12,* 153–165.

Helms, J. E. (1990). *Black and White racial identity: Theory, research, and practice.* New York: Greenwood Press.

Helms, J. E., & Carter, R. T. (1991). Relationships of White and Black racial identity attitudes and demographic similarity to counselor preferences. *Journal of Counseling Psychology, 38,* 446–457.

Ho, M. K. (1992). *Minority children and adolescents in therapy.* Newbury Park, CA: Sage.

Homer, D., & Vanderhuis, K. (1981). Cross cultural counseling. In G. Althen (Ed.), *Learning across cultures* (pp. 30–50). Washington, DC: National Association of Foreign Student Affairs.

Ibrahim, F. A. (1985). Effective cross cultural counseling and psychotherapy. *Counseling Psychologist, 13,* 625–638.

Jones, A. C. (1985). Psychological functioning in Black Americans: A conceptual guide for use in psychotherapy. *Psychotherapy, 22,* 363–369.

Jones, R. (1996). *Handbook of tests and measurements for Black populations* (Vols. 1 and 2). Hampton, VA: Cobb & Henry.

Katz, J. H. (1985). The sociopolitical nature of counseling. *The Counseling Psychologist, 13,* 615–624.

Kearney, M. (1975). Worldview theory and study. In B. J. Siegel (Ed.), *Annual review of psychology* (Vol. 4, pp. 247–270). Palo Alto, CA: Annual Reviews.

Lindsey, K. P., & Paul, G. L. (1989). Involuntary commitments to public mental institutions: Issues involving the overrepresentation of Blacks and assessment of relevant functioning. *Psychological Bulletin, 106,* 171–183.

McIntosh, J. L. (1984). Suicide among Native Americans: Further tribal data and considerations. *Omega: The Journal of Death and Dying, 14,* 215–229.

Moscicki, E. K., Locke, B. Z., Rae, D. S., & Boyd, J. H. (1989). Depressive symptoms among Mexican Americans: The Hispanic Health and Nutrition Examination Survey. *American Journal of Epidemiology, 130,* 348–360.

Neighbors, H. W. (1984). Professional help use among Black Americans: Implications for unmet need. *American Journal of Community Psychology, 12,* 551–566.

Nobles, W. W. (1976). Black people in White insanity: An issue for Black community mental health. *Journal of Afro-American Issues, 4,* 21–27.

Paniagua, F. A. (1994). *Assessing and treating culturally diverse clients: A practical guide.* Thousand Oaks, CA: Sage.

Parharm, T. A. (1989). Cycles of psychological Nigrescence. *The Counseling Psychologist, 17,* 197–226.

Parham, T. A., & Helms, J. E. (1981). The influence of Black students' racial identity attitudes on preference for counselors' race. *Journal of Counseling Psychology, 28,* 250–257.

Pederson, P. B. (1987). *Handbook of cross cultural counseling and therapy.* Westport, CT: Greenwood Press.

Ridley, C. R. (1984). Clinical treatment of the non-disclosing Black client: A therapeutic paradox. *American Psychologist, 39,* 1234–1244.

Root, M. (1996). *The multiracial experience: Racial borders as the new frontier.* Thousand Oaks, CA: Sage.

Rumbaut, R. G. (1989). Portraits, patterns, and predictors of the refugee adaptation process. In D. W. Hatnes (Ed.), *Refugees as immigrants: Cambodians, Laotians, and Vietnamese in America* (pp. 138–182). Totowa, NJ: Rowman & Littlefield.

Scheffler, R., & Miller, A. B. (1989). Demand analysis of mental health service use among ethnic subpopulations. *Inquiry, 26,* 202–215.

Smith, E. J. (1981). Cultural and historical perspectives in counseling Blacks. In D. W. Sue (Ed.), *Counseling the culturally different: Theory and practice.* New York: Wiley.

Smith, E. J. (1991). Ethnic identity development: Toward the development of a theory within the context of majority/minority status. *Journal of Counseling and Development, 70,* 181–188.

Smith, T. W. (1992). Changing racial labels: From "Colored" to "Negro" to "Black" to "African American" *Public Opinion Quarterly, 56,* 496–544.

Snowden, L. R., & Cheung, F. K. (1990). Use of inpatient mental health services by members of ethnic minority groups. *American Psychologist, 45,* 347–355.

Somervell, P. D., Leaf, P. I., Weissman, M. M., Blazer, D. G., & Bruce, M. L. (1989). The prevalence of major depression among Black and White adults in five U.S. communities, *American Journal of Epidemiology, 130,* 725–735.

Sue, D. W. (1978). World views and counseling. *Personnel and Guidance Journal, 56,* 458–462.

Sue, D. W., & Sue, S. (1987). Cultural factors in clinical assessment of Asian Americans. *Journal of Consulting and Clinical Psychology, 55,* 479–487.

Sue, D. W., & Sue, D. (1990). *Counseling the culturally different: Theory and practice.* New York: Wiley.

Sue, S. (1977) Community mental health services to minority groups. *American Psychologist, 22,* 616–624.

Sue, S., & Marishima, J. K. (1982). *The mental health of Asian Americans.* San Francisco: Jossey-Bass.

Sue, S., & Zane, N. (1987). The role of culture and cultural techniques in psychotherapy: A critique and reformulation. *American Psychologist, 42,* 37–45.

Taylor, R, I., & Chatters, L. M. (1986). Church-based informal support among elderly Blacks. *The Gerontologist, 26,* 637–642.

Wells, K. B., Goldin, J., & Hough, R. L. (1989). Acculturation and the probability of use of health services by Mexican-Americans. *Health Services Research, 24,* 237–257.

13

Native Americans

Hilary N. Weaver

Many social workers never expect to encounter a Native American client. Native people are often perceived as relics of a distant past who live on isolated reservations in a few regions of the country. In fact, Native Americans are a growing population that resides across the country in urban, suburban, and rural settings. Social workers who do not expect to see Native clients may fail to recognize that some of their clients are indeed Native Americans.

At the time of the 2000 census, there were 4.1 million Native Americans (including Alaska Natives). This accounts for 1.5% of the U.S. population. Of these, 2.5 million people (.9% of the population) identified as solely Native American, and 1.6 million (.6% of the population) identified as a mixture of Native American and some other group. In 1990, there were 2 million Native Americans, equaling 8% of the population. The 2000 data for those who identify solely as Native American represents a 26% increase over the 1990 figure, and the data on Native Americans of mixed heritage represents a 110% increase over the 1990 figure[1] (Ogunwole, 2002).

Forty-three percent of Native Americans live in the West, 31% in the South, 17% in the Midwest, and 9% in the Northeast United States. More than half of the Native population lives in 10 states, with the largest populations being in California (627,562) and Oklahoma (391,949). The cities with the largest Native populations are New York City (87,241) and Los Angeles (53,092). The largest Native Nations or tribes are the Cherokee (729,533), Navajo (298,197), Sioux (261,632), Chippewa (255,576), Latin American Indian (180,940), and Choctaw (142,123).[2] The largest group of Alaska Natives is the Eskimo (54,761) (Ogunwole, 2002).

There are many different definitions of a Native American. Each Native Nation (also known as a tribe) has its own criteria for membership. These criteria are often based on the amount of Native ancestry someone has (blood quantum). There is extensive intermarriage between Native Americans and non-Natives or among Native Americans from different nations, thus raising the question of the identity of their offspring. Some Native Nations are matrilineal and only consider someone to be a tribal member if that person's mother is a member of that nation. Others are patrilineal and trace descent only through the father. Still others accept members with Native heritage through either their mother or father. When a Native person is formally considered a member or citizen of a Native Nation, that person is listed on the tribal rolls and is considered enrolled. Being enrolled allows access to a variety of tribal entitlements such as payments based on treaties or social services offered under tribal auspices. Enrollment confers other rights such as the ability to vote in tribal elections and the right to own land on a particular reservation.

Although Native Nations set criteria for enrollment, competing definitions also exist of who is a Native American. The federal government has its own definitions that are typically based on blood quantum. Different federal programs use different definitions for Native Americans in their eligibility requirements. The U.S. census uses the terms *American Indian* and *Alaska Native,* defined as "a person having origins in any of the original peoples of North and South America (including Central America), and who maintain tribal affiliation or community attachment" (U.S. Census Bureau, 2001). This definition is based primarily on social roles and does not consider blood quantum.

Many different terms are used to refer to the original inhabitants of the Americas including *Native American, American Indian, indigenous, First Nations People, Native,* and *Indian.* There is no consensus about which term is most appropriate, although many people have strong preferences. These terms are often used interchangeably, but *American Indian* and *Indian* have somewhat narrow meanings and exclude many but not all of the indigenous people of Alaska. The term *Native American* is broader and includes Alaska Natives as well as indigenous people found in the continental United States. The term *Native American* may also include indigenous people from other parts of the United States and its territories, such as Native Hawaiians, Samoans, and Guamanians. The terms *indigenous* and *Native,* though sometimes used in a narrow sense, can be used for original inhabitants of any area. For instance, these terms may refer to the original inhabitants of New Zealand (Maori) or the original inhabitants of Scandinavia (Sami). *First Nations People,* a common term for the original inhabitants of Canada, has gained some popularity among Native people in the United States. This term is often linked to a strong sense of sovereignty and political awareness. Although seen by many younger people as a positive term, it is not widely used by elders and may be unfamiliar to many non-Native people. Given the lack of precision in these terms, it is often best to use the most specific term possible. For instance, when referring to someone from the Hopi Nation, it may be most appropriate to use the term *Hopi* rather than any of the broader terms. Many indigenous people identify primarily with their nation (e.g., Seneca) or clan (e.g., Beaver, a network of extended families within the Seneca) rather than with an umbrella label like Native American or American Indian. The terms *Native, Native American, First Nations,* and *indigenous* are used interchangeably here when use of more specific terms is not possible.

This chapter gives an overview of social work with First Nations people. The significant diversity within and among Native Nations sets the context for discussion. The chapter also presents information on knowledge, skills, and values/attitudes necessary for cultural competence, and presents issues for cultural competence on micro and macro levels.

Knowledge for Cultural Competence

A qualitative study designed to operationalize the elements of cultural competence with Native

Americans found that helping professionals need to be knowledgeable in four areas: diversity, history, culture, and contemporary realities (Weaver, 1999b). Diversity is an overarching concept. The history, culture, and contemporary realities of indigenous people vary, both within and among nations.

Diversity

More than 500 distinct Native Nations exist within the boundaries of what is now the United States. Some of these nations straddle the borders with Canada and Mexico. Indigenous nations never shared a single social structure, value system, religion, or language. Although there are some commonalities among indigenous groups within a particular region, there is considerable diversity among and within Native Nations. Understanding this diversity is key to culturally competent social work practice with First Nations people.

The diversity among Native peoples makes it difficult to gather accurate, generalizable information (McNeil, Porter, Zvolensky, Chaney, & Kee, 2000). Generalizations often lead to stereotypes. When working with Native clients, it is important to know which Native Nations they are affiliated with because information about one group (e.g., Chickasaw) may not be applicable to another (e.g., Blackfeet). The diversity across indigenous groups presents challenges to researchers. It is often difficult to recruit adequate numbers of different groups of Native people for meaningful intertribal comparisons. Thus, the usefulness of research as a guideline for practice is limited.

Likewise, the diversity among Native Nations presents challenges for practitioners. For example, variables tentatively associated with violence, such as male restrictiveness, male authority, and socioeconomic stress, vary widely across Native groups. Whether an indigenous client is from a matrilineal or patrilineal nation has far-reaching implications for the community context of domestic violence (Hamby, 2000).

There are also intertribal differences in help-seeking behavior. For example, military veterans from the Northern Plains and the Southwest differ significantly in their use of Western-based services and traditional healing options for mental and emotional problems (Manson, 2000). Likewise, helping professionals developing alcohol prevention programs must consider the heterogeneity of First Nations people. Comprehensive, community-based approaches must be shaped by local culture (Moran & May, 1995).

Some Native Americans live on reservations but others do not. Researchers have long been interested in exploring differences between reservation dwellers and their urban counterparts. A study commissioned by the Administration on Aging found most elders only have a grade school education although urban elders were more likely than their reservation counterparts to have a high school degree (29% compared with 17% of reservation dwellers). Elders on reservations appear to have a higher risk of social isolation, even though extended family members are more available in reservation environments. Generally, urban elders have better mental and physical health. Needs are high and service utilization is low for both groups, but urban elders are more likely to seek help from agencies (John, 1991).

Native Americans differ in many variables including income and education. Native people also differ in their level of knowledge and adherence to cultural traditions. Even among elders on reservations, there is a wide range of values and behaviors. Some are very knowledgeable and grounded in traditional ways but others are not (Kavanaugh, Absalom, Beil, & Schliessmann, 1999).

History

Many social problems result from centuries of forced change (Fleming, 1992). Administrators and service providers must be knowledgeable of the history of various Native American groups to develop effective services in indigenous communities (Swinomish Tribal Mental Health Project, 1991).

It is important to understand and to validate a Native client's sense of history. Often, helping professionals do not know the history of indigenous groups and are surprised to learn that what they have been taught about history and even pre-history is quite different from the perspective of many First Nations people. For example, non-Native people have often been taught that Native Americans are not actually indigenous but were early migrants across the Bering Strait from Asia. There is substantial conflict between the Bering Strait theory of immigration and creation stories of First Nations people that tell of migrations across physical and spiritual dimensions (Fleming, 1992).

Loss of Children. One of the most painful aspects in the history of Native Nations is the loss of their children, first to government-sponsored or government-sanctioned boarding schools, and subsequently to fostercare and adoption. After the U.S. Civil War, it became federal policy to remove children, often forcibly, from their families and communities. They were placed in boarding schools, often far from their homes, where they were taught Christianity and vocational skills to assimilate and "civilize" them. In these schools, children were forbidden to speak their languages and practice their spiritual traditions. Physical, emotional, and sexual abuse were common.

The impact of forced acculturation in boarding schools has left a lasting legacy (Fleming, 1992). Boarding schools led to loss of indigenous languages as well as to high rates of depression, illness, and death. Many children taken to boarding schools became ashamed of their cultural heritage and disowned the values and lifestyles of their families. Others assumed dysfunctional behaviors and exhibited symptoms such as rebelliousness, distrust, withdrawal, and depression. If former boarding school residents returned to their tribal communities, they often had difficulty fitting into a way of life they no longer completely understood. Lack of indigenous role models during childhood severely stunted their social and emotional development as Native American people. In adulthood, many of these children developed severe problems such as alcoholism, depression, or violent behavior (Swinomish Tribal Mental Health Project, 1991).

The boarding school era was a time of child removal and assimilationist social policies. The subsequent era of Native American adoptions continued in the same vein (George, 1997). Many First Nations children were taken from their families, ostensibly on charges of neglect and the belief they would be better off with White families than living in poverty on reservations under the influence of their "savage" parents. For example, the Boys and Girls Aid Society of Oregon, the largest adoption agency in that state, found many adoptive homes for Native children with White families. Between 1944 and 1977, 94 percent of Native children in this agency were adopted by non-Native families (Collmeyer, 1995). Loss of children was equated with loss of a future. If children were raised outside Native, cultural traditions, there could be no cultural continuity and, thus, Native people would cease to exist as distinct cultural entities. "Adoption represented a spiritual death and rupture in the social fabric of the tribe that could never be repaired" (George, 1997, p. 171).

Alienation of indigenous children from their families and communities through boarding schools, fostercare, and adoption has led to significant cultural loss. As a result of these experiences, many Native people have lost their ability to speak their indigenous languages. Native people who cannot speak their languages often feel a deep sense of loss, shame, guilt, sadness, and anger (Swinomish Tribal Mental Health Project, 1991). Loss of language and cultural traditions often caused a rift between those who retained cultural knowledge and those who did not. Many children who returned from the schools or who were raised in White families were unable to communicate with their grandparents and older community members who continued to speak only their traditional languages.

The removal of Native children also disrupted the transmission of parenting skills across generations. Children raised in an institutional setting were without positive role models when they became parents themselves. The extensive physical, emotional, and sexual abuse common in the boarding schools left this new generation of parents with dysfunctional and often brutal ways of interacting with their children (Morrisette, 1994; Weaver & White, 1999).

Suppression of Spirituality. The history of indigenous people in the United States is filled with examples of spiritual oppression and denial of religious freedom. Misunderstandings and ethnocentric assumptions led to active persecution of indigenous spiritual practices. In the late 1800s, many indigenous religions and ceremonies such as the Sun Dance and the Potlatch were outlawed, despite the fact that this is in direct opposition to freedom of religion promised in the U.S. Constitution. The suppression of indigenous spirituality, in turn, led to practices going underground and the loss of some traditional knowledge (Swinomish Tribal Mental Health Project, 1991).

Alcohol and Disease as Tools of Cultural Destruction. Alcohol played a significant role in the history of indigenous and non-indigenous interactions. Most Native Nations had no contact with alcohol until Europeans introduced it as a trade item. Only a few nations in the Southwest developed forms of wine and beer. When alcohol was used before White contact, it involved controlled, supervised use in ritualized occasions, and did not involve excessive drunkenness (Abbott, 1996).

European colonizers used alcohol as a tool of conquest and cultural destruction (Maracle, 1993; Swinomish Tribal Mental Health Project, 1991). Fur traders and frontiersmen paid for Native goods using alcohol. Native people were encouraged to drink heavily and become intoxicated. Alcohol has been implicated as being used to swindle Native people and take their land.

Disease has also been implicated as a tool of conquest. Historically, population loss from disease decimated Native populations far more than did overt acts of war. Native people had no immunities to diseases common in Europe and thus died in large numbers when exposed to illnesses such as smallpox. As this lack of immunity became apparent to European and later American military commanders, they began to deliberately spread disease among indigenous people as a way of weakening their foes, thus clearing the land for European settlement (Stiffarm & Lane, 1992).

Growing European and European-American Domination. During the early history of interactions between European nations and Native Nations, treaties were made to govern how these groups would interact. Treaties designated rights and lands to be retained by First Nations people and those to be given up in exchange for various types of payments. Treaties were subsequently made between the U.S. federal government and Native Nations. According to the U.S. Constitution, treaties are the supreme law of the land.

At the time of original contact between European colonists and First Nations people, the Native Nations held more power. That changed as European immigrants became more numerous. As the balance of power shifted, the new Americans were able to violate treaties with minimal fear of repercussions. They forced one-sided treaty agreements on Native Nations with diminishing power. Even though the federal government has violated all treaties, they continue to govern many modern day interactions between First Nations people and the United States (Clinton, Newton, & Price, 1991).

At times, the United States used military force to remove Native people from land set aside for them. History contains many examples of these forced removals. The most famous were the Trail of Tears, in which the Cherokee were forced to leave their traditional lands in the Southeastern United States and walk 1,500 miles to Oklahoma, and the Longest Walk., in which 9,000 Navajo were forced to walk 300 miles to be imprisoned at Bosque Redondo (Stiffarm & Lane, 1992). Forced marches and subsequent confinement often led to the death of large segments of indigenous populations.

Culture

First Nations people come from many different cultures. Some Native people follow traditional indigenous beliefs and values whereas others do not. It is important to keep in mind the cultural diversity among First Nations people, yet some common cultural elements are found in many Native traditions. These include a fluid sense of time, spirituality, emphasis on the group over the individual, and respect.

Time. Most Native cultures have a fluid sense of time. Many Native people view being "ruled by the clock" as unnatural and unhealthy. Rigidly following the dictates of a clock diminishes natural life rhythms and destroys the quality of human interactions and relationships (Swinomish Tribal Mental Health Project, 1991). When viewed from a deficit perspective, this fluid sense of time is interpreted as chronic lateness, laziness, lack of caring, and disrespect. The indigenous concept of time, however, is much more person-centered than is the Western concept. Native people are likely to take time to interact with others rather than stating they have no time for them and rushing off to appointments. It can be challenging for social workers to accommodate this fluid sense of time within a restrictive agency context. If possible, being available for a block of time (drop-in hours) may be more effective than scheduling specific appointment times.

Spirituality. Spirituality plays an important role in maintaining and restoring health in Native cultures. Disease is perceived as lack of balance or harmony with the Creator and nature, thus requiring both material and spiritual remedies. A study of Native elders found that faith and frequency of prayer were strongly correlated with mental health and other aspects of social functioning (Meisenhelder & Chandler, 2000).

In contrast to dominant society views, indigenous people view spiritual, mental, physical, and social aspects of their lives as connected and continuously interacting. Indigenous spirituality goes beyond a belief system to incorporate guidelines for behavior. It is a spiritual necessity to live a balanced life in harmony with all other beings. To be out of balance or to deny the interconnectedness of all creation risks the well-being of individuals, families, and communities. For traditional Native Americans, spirituality is a part of every aspect of life including worldview, relationships, health and illness, healing, and ways of grieving (Swinomish Tribal Mental Health Project, 1991).

Many First Nations people experience the eagerness of non-indigenous people to discuss and participate in Native spiritual practices as intrusive and rude. Non-Native helping professionals need to respect the private nature of many indigenous spiritual beliefs and practices

(Swinomish Tribal Mental Health Project, 1991). Past exploitation, distortion, and laws that have prohibited indigenous spiritual traditions have left Native people protective of their spiritual practices and reluctant to share information with outsiders.

Social workers can learn basic information on cultural and spiritual practices outside the context of the social work relationship. In this way, they can avoid exploiting the client. Reading and viewing videos can provide this background information without overstepping boundaries. In particular, a recent PBS video, *In the Light of Reverence,* can be useful for understanding the importance of sacred traditions and the reluctance of many Native people to share this information.

Primacy of the Group. A sense of identity is rooted in group membership. Native people often refer to themselves as members of the Native community, regardless of their geographic location. Many Native Americans identify first with their nation or tribe and second with a clan or society to which they belong. Some express fear that knowledge of, or identification with, non-Native culture is equivalent to loss of indigenous culture (Fleming, 1992).

Social cooperation is often valued over independent decision making. The wishes and plans of individuals must be balanced along with the needs of family and community members (Swinomish Tribal Mental Health Project, 1991). This emphasis on the group leads to strong mutual support networks. The well-being of the group is paramount.

Social control is often maintained through indirect mechanisms such as gossip, shaming, withdrawal of approval, humor, and teasing (Swinomish Tribal Mental Health Services, 1991). These methods are often used to teach children what behaviors are expected of them and reinforce the behavioral expectations of all community members. Likewise, adults who behave outside community norms are likely to experience teasing, shaming, and gossip.

Respect. Respect is emphasized in all social interactions. There are appropriate ways to communicate respectfully with others, including limiting eye contact and not interrupting someone who is speaking. People are accorded respect for the different roles they fulfill within a community. Elders are respected for their knowledge and wisdom, children are respected as the future of Native Nations, and leaders are respected for their willingness to sacrifice their own needs on behalf of First Nations communities.

Respect is a key value in all interactions, yet displays of respect often conflict with dominant society values. For example, at home Native American children learn to listen respectfully without asking questions. In school, they are confronted with a very different set of expectations and requirements for success, thus leaving them confused and unable to succeed in one or both environments (Swinomish Tribal Mental Health Project, 1991).

Contemporary Realities

Many Americans think of Native people primarily within a historical context and fail to recognize that Native cultures are still vital, even though many ways of life have changed. Romantic notions of Native Americans wearing beads and feathers perpetuate the idea of indigenous cultures as monolithic and static. Because few people have in-depth contact with Native Americans, these romantic notions go unchallenged (Fleming, 1992).

Understanding the contemporary realities of Native people involves understanding the context of federal policies that significantly affect Native people, the dynamics of tribal governments that continue to function with some sovereignty while subsumed under federal authority, social problems and their relationship to a legacy of colonialism, and the strengths and vitality that have withstood centuries of oppression.

The Context of Federal Policies. Because of their unique relationship with the federal government, Native people are subject to intrusion by many federal bureaucracies. Native people have federal policies and regulations that apply solely to them. The federal government still treats Native people as its wards, and, as such, it often holds and manages money for both Native Nations and individual Native people. In this role as guardian, the federal government also has the power to sue entities such as states on behalf of Native people when they are treated unjustly (e.g., illegal seizing of land).

One of the most important areas of involvement in the lives of Native people, especially relevant to social workers, is the Indian Child Welfare Act (ICWA). ICWA is a federal law and thus does not apply to indigenous people from Native Nations that are not federally recognized or are located outside the United States (e.g., the. Shinnecock of New York State that only have state recognition). Thus, some states have passed similar legislation to extend comparable protection to indigenous people within their borders that are not covered under ICWA. Washington state has a tribal-state agreement that goes beyond ICWA to extend services to Canadian Natives and members of non-federally recognized tribes in Washington state (Bending, 1997). New York State has a similar law (Weaver & White, 1999).

The Indian Child Welfare Act was passed in response to the large numbers of Native American children being raised by non-Native families, either through fostercare or adoption. Under ICWA, Native Nations have the right to assume jurisdiction over fostercare and adoption proceedings involving their children. A social agency involved in fostercare or adoption proceedings for a Native American child must notify the child's nation. That nation has the right to handle the case itself if it chooses. Another critical provision of ICWA states that cultural continuity is in the best interest of the child. When Native American children are placed in fostercare or for adoption, the following order must be followed: (1) placement with the extended family, (2) placement with a family from the same Native Nation, (3) placement with any Native American family, then (4) placement with any qualified family (Barsh, 1996). A social worker who has a case covered by ICWA must contact the child's nation immediately. The nation has the right to handle the case itself, work with a non-Native social service department on the case, or relinquish the case entirely to a non-Native social service department. The provisions of ICWA are not diminished by subsequent legislation. For example, the Multiethnic Placement Act, designed to remove barriers to transracial placements, and the Adoption and Safe Families Act, designed to reduce the time children spend in fostercare, specifically state they do not apply to cases covered by ICWA.

Contemporary Tribal Governments. Native Nations have retained sovereignty that allows them to continue to operate their own governments. Although Native Nations are subject to federal laws and oversight, they are not subject to state laws unless this right is specifically granted by the federal government or Native Nations themselves. Today most Native Nations have an elected government, often led by a tribal president and tribal council. Many have law enforcement and social service systems in place that serve their members. As a result of the Indian Reorganization Act of 1934, many Native Nations have constitutions modeled on those of states; however, a few nations continue to function with traditional leaders such as chiefs and clan mothers. Still others have an official, elected government but retain vestiges of traditional forms of governance.

Today, many tribal governments are striving for culturally appropriate economic development and self-sufficiency after generations of federal domination and imposed dependency. Because Native Nations retain vestiges of sovereignty, each has a right to determine which types of economic development best meet its needs. Tribal revitalization is a way to overcome the legacy of historical tragedies and keep identity and language alive. This means cultural renaissance in contemporary terms, not returning to a way of life of past centuries, often referred to as going back to the blanket (Fleming, 1992). Often, however, members of Native Nations are divided over economic development opportunities such as casinos, tourism, and exploitation of natural resources. What some Native people see as positive sources of income, others view as devastating compromises to cultural and spiritual integrity.

Social and Health Problems. Native Americans experience a variety of health and social problems, many as a direct result of colonization and dependency created by the federal government. For example, the cycle of neglect and subsequent removal of children and disruption of families is a lasting consequence of the boarding schools (Swinomish Tribal Mental Health Project, 1991). The social science literature on Native people suggests that they suffer disproportionately from a variety of problems including diabetes (Gilliland, Mahler, Hunt, & Davis, 1999; Kavanaugh et al., 1999), tuberculosis, suicide, alcohol-related problems (Kavanaugh et al., 1999), mental health problems (Narduzzi, 1994), and rapidly increasing incidence of, and mortality from, cardiovascular disease, cancer, and other chronic diseases (Gilliland et al., 1999). Native Americans are overrepresented in the homeless veteran population (by at least 19%), and they exhibit more severe alcohol problems (40% more than Whites) but fewer psychiatric problems than other homeless veterans (Kasprow & Rosenheck, 1998).

Probably the most widely known and stereotyped social problem of Native communities is that of alcohol dependence. Alcohol takes a disproportionate toll in Native American communities, resulting in a higher rate of alcohol-related deaths than in the general population (Moran & May, 1995). There is significant diversity in alcohol use among First Nations groups and within groups based on age and gender. For example, although stereotypes lead many to believe that all Native people are heavy drinkers, the Navajo abstain at twice the rate of the U.S. population. Among Native people in general, abstinence is particularly common among those middle-aged and older. The disparity between Native Americans and the general population of the United States is greatest among younger groups. Native American youth use alcohol earlier, with more frequency, in greater amounts, and with more negative consequences than do non-Natives. Alcohol has negative consequences for both males and females but is frequently a bigger problem for males (Moran & May, 1995). A study of Native American adolescents in the Northwest found that Native males attribute their drinking to heredity and fate. Native females were more likely to attribute their drinking to environmental events like problems at home (Sage & Burns, 1993).

Native people experience high rates of violence and trauma. Injury morbidity and mortality far exceed other groups. A study conducted at a trauma center in Seattle, Washington, found high injury rates, including a high proportion of intentional injuries (e.g., suicide, homicide), and a significant proportion of injuries among the homeless. Alcohol plays a major role in injuries among Native Americans (more than three-fourths of those injured were legally intoxicated). Risk for injury is increased by poverty, unemployment, and inadequate education that lead to homelessness and substance abuse (Sugarman & Grossman, 1996).

Interpreting the Research. Statistics on Native people must be interpreted cautiously. Misclassification of Native Americans in studies is a major problem that limits data quality (Weaver, 1999c). For example, some data in the Northwest underestimates the number of Native people by one-third (Sugarman & Grossman, 1996).

Some research now disputes the high rates of social and health problems alleged among First Nations people. For instance, although empirical evidence is limited, scholars often suggest that higher rates of psychopathology exist among Native people than their non-Native peers (McNeil et al., 2000); yet a study of depression and conduct disorder in Native and non-Native children found no difference in parent and child self-ratings of conduct disorders. Non-Native teachers, however, rated the Native children higher on conduct disorders, possibly because of negative bias resulting from cultural distance. All children rated themselves higher on depression than did the adults rating them (Dion, Gotowiec, & Beiser, 1998).

Cultural Loss. Even though some First Nations people have successfully retained their traditions, cultural loss is perceived to be a major threat in many Native communities. "Historical theft of Indian lands, outlawing of Indian spiritual practices, the massive removal of Indian children from their families, and the introduction of alcohol have all contributed to cultural loss, and have made it difficult for young people to develop a healthy cultural identity. Many native languages have been lost. The imposition of non-Indian values has weakened traditional Indian culture and thereby jeopardized individual psychological health" (Swinomish Tribal Mental Health Project, 1991, p. 43).

Loss of cultural identity and negative self-images contribute to mental health problems and are problems in and of themselves. Psychological well-being cannot be maintained without a sense of cultural vitality. Lack of a strong, positive cultural identity puts people at risk for depression, alcohol abuse, and destructive behaviors (Swinomish Tribal Mental Health Project, 1991).

Continuity and Strengths. Native communities continue to exist as distinct cultural entities with many strengths. Even when federal policies interrupted values transmission, wisdom, beliefs, and practices are strengths that have survived (Long & Curry, 1998). Communities are striving to revitalize traditions through programs that teach language and culture. Many youth now participate in kindergarten or grade school immersion programs that teach language. The importance of the group reinforces socially acceptable behaviors and emphasizes the value of learning traditions (Swinomish Tribal Mental Health Project, 1991).

First Nations people of all ages are seeking and reclaiming cultural knowledge and traditions. A study of Native women (predominantly Oneida) revealed they handle multiple roles through integration and balance of traditional and contemporary feminine strengths in a positive, culturally consistent manner. Healing the spirit is done through returning to traditions to reclaim the self (Napholz, 2000).

Native communities, especially on tribal lands, are becoming more assertive in their resistance to exploitation. For example, many Native communities have begun to restrict researchers' access because of past problems. Currently, there is heightened suspicion of researchers, particularly from the dominant society. Access to Native communities may be restricted or denied by tribal governments (Beauvais & Trimble, 1992; McNeil et al., 2000). Informal gatekeepers may restrict access for various projects and research for the protection of the community (Beauvais & Trimble, 1992).

Skills for Cultural Competence

A survey of Native American helping professionals identified that both general skills and containment skills are important in delivering culturally competent services to Native Americans (Weaver, 1999b). Although the skills themselves can be generic, the guiding frameworks within which the skills are applied (i.e., theories that guide interventions in particular situations or with certain types of clients) are far from neutral. Social work theories and practices often have a Eurocentric bias and are ineffective with Native American people (Bending, 1997).

Engaging

Social workers should try to recognize and set aside the stereotypes they hold about Native Americans. Most research has overemphasized and given credibility to selected negative beliefs about Native Americans. The continued focus on alarming rates of self-destructive behavior promotes an image of the drunken, suicidal Native American. It is important to have balanced treatment that explores strengths, resilience, and contributions (Fleming, 1992). Social workers must strive to overcome stereotypes so they see their clients as individuals and can engage them as such.

Engaging Native American clients may be a lengthy process. Establishing trust may be difficult and involve testing the social worker's commitment. There is a connection between engaging individual clients and establishing trust in the Native American community. For example, some social agencies in rural Alaska ask staff to participate in events in the Native community. As Native community members see helping professionals at these events, they begin to understand that these professionals have an ongoing commitment to serving the Native community and are not detached individuals who only interact with Native people in a hierarchical relationship during a 9–5 job. Helping professionals who establish a presence in Native communities encourage Native people to feel comfortable seeking services. Helping professionals may feel awkward about learning about Native cultures and not wish to intrude or be voyeuristic. Events that are likely to be open to the public such as festivals and pow wows are good opportunities to learn through observation and listening. Social agencies like the American Indian Community House in New York City regularly publish newsletters with announcements of events and protocols for visitors. Events such as ceremonies are generally closed to the public and would not be publicly announced.

Assessing

Assessments of Native American clients must consider indigenous cultural norms. Examination of the cultural context allows the helping professional to judge how a client's behaviors fit within a range of what is typical. Helping professionals need to take the time to explore the client's perception of the problem or situation.

Indigenous concepts of health and illness differ considerably from non-Native diagnostic categories such as those in the *Diagnostic and Statistical Manual (DSM).* Constructs such as depression, as operationalized through Western psychiatric conceptualizations, are not necessarily meaningful in an indigenous context. The lack of equivalence between indigenous expressions of illness and Western psychiatric disorders makes culturally appropriate assessments challenging (Allen, 1998; Swinomish Tribal Mental Health Project, 1991). Recent changes in the *DSM* have taken an important step in acknowledging culture's role in shaping symptom expression and the course of mental illnesses (Manson, 2000); however, additional changes are needed to adequately address cultural identity and cultural elements in the therapeutic relationship for Native American youth (Novins et al., 1997).

Using Western criteria in assessing First Nations clients is inappropriate and can be a form of institutional racism. Indeed, applying the diagnostic criteria that fit members of one culture to assess members of another culture is cultural imperialism (Swinomish Tribal Mental Health Project, 1991). Forcing the problems of Native clients into Western categories can distort their true nature.

Although many standardized assessment tools have been developed to explore issues such as depression, self-esteem, suicidality, and alcohol dependence, most of these tools have not been developed or modified for use with Native Americans. The universal applicability of standardized tools is questionable (Allen, 1998); therefore, social workers who use such tools should do so with caution. Where Native American assessment tools exist, those designed for specific tribal groups are usually non-existent or do not have established validity or conceptual equivalence (Allen, 1998). One exception to this is the tribally specific and carefully tested Zuni Life Skills Development Curriculum (LaFromboise & Howard-Pitney, 1995).

Many assessment tools, developed specifically for use with Native Americans, attempt to measure cultural identity. See, for example, the work of Young, Lujan, and Dixon (1998); Garrett and Pichette (2000); and Zimmermann, Ramirez-Valles, Washienko, Walter, and Dyer (1996). Many of these cultural assessment instruments, however, conceptualize culture along a linear continuum, thus failing to account for the complexities of cultural identity. The Orthogonal Model of Cultural Identity and its measurement scale, though not developed exclusively for Native American youth, has been used extensively and successfully with this population. This tool assesses identification with one culture independently from others, thus allowing for identification with more than one culture (Oetting & Beauvais, 1991; Weaver, 1996).

Another tool that measures cultural identity, the Urban American Indian Identity model and scale, expands on earlier models of identity. This model contains four stages (internalization, marginalization, externalization, and actualization) that tap into the identity development process from internalized oppression and group deprecation to positive integrated self and group identity. This model considers identity as formed within the context of self, group, environment, and a historical relationship with the dominant society. The model predicts depression, self-esteem, and other psychological wellness (Walters, 1997).

Other assessment tools have been developed or modified to measure Native American clients on a variety of variables. For example, the. Native American Cultural Involvement and Detachment Anxiety Questionnaire was developed with tribal college students to measure anxiety about social involvement with Native Americans, cultural knowledge, economic issues, and social involvement with the majority culture (McNeil et al., 2000). Another assessment instrument, the Center for Epidemiological Studies Depression Scale, appears to be capable of identifying depression in some populations of Native elders, as long as a higher cutoff point is used to avoid mislabeling people as depressed (Curyto, Chapleski, Lichtenberg, Hodges, Kaczynski, & Sobeck, 1998). Likewise, an instrument has been developed to measure knowledge, attitudes, and behaviors regarding physical activity and diet for Native youth in grades 3 through 5 (Stevens et al., 1999).

Intervening

Culturally competent service delivery begins with a strong grounding in general helping skills such as listening and problem solving. Listening in a cross-cultural context can be challenging since the helping professional may have expectations about what the client is likely to say, based on his or her own cultural context.

Containment skills are a particular set of skills useful with many types of clients and particularly important when working with Native American clients because of cultural communication norms. Containment skills are those in which the social worker refrains from speaking too quickly or too much, thus promoting productive silence (Shulman, 1999). By displaying patience and allowing the session to proceed at a comfortable pace, significant material will often emerge.

One helping professional describes the importance of listening in her work with Native Americans of the Great Plains region:

> As a nurse I am used to listening, to gathering a history to make an assessment and coming to a diagnosis. But in truly listening to Lakota people, one is usually led—often in a round-about way—to a deeper, more significant issue. If we fail to listen until they finish speaking, we never really get to hear the real thoughts or concerns. While we are used to being fast and as efficient as possible, Lakota see this as a lack of interest in them and as an insincere attempt to help them. I must spend time, settle into a chair, and be very present to be trusted. (Kavanaugh et al., 1999, p. 20)

Non-Natives often misinterpret periods of silence that can be common among First Nations people. For many Native people, "the non-verbal aspects of conversation are often regarded as more important than the words exchanged. Often, much is left unsaid. Many Indian people are highly skilled at 'reading between the lines': they pick up on nuances of tone, gesture and glance. Often Indian people can exchange a great deal of information in a very few words" (Swinomish Tribal Mental Health Project, 1991, p. 189).

Resisting the temptation to be verbally assertive in conducting the social work interview is often the most productive approach with Native American clients. Likewise, it can be helpful for social workers to consciously monitor their non-verbal behavior to ensure they are not being physically assertive in ways that may inhibit the interview. Avoiding eye contact can be a way of respecting privacy. The firmness typical of American handshakes may be misconstrued for aggressiveness and lead to negative impressions. First Nations people often express negative feelings subtly. Feelings may be shut down because of prior experiences of trauma and deprivation (Swinomish Tribal Mental Health Project, 1991).

Social work skills must be integrated into interventions in culturally appropriate ways. One of the few empirically validated approaches to working effectively with Native Americans involves culturally grounded behavioral approaches to preventing poor dietary practices, tobacco, and other substance misuse (Schinke, 1996). Culturally grounded approaches include using elders to teach about traditional foods and tobacco use as a ceremonial rather than recreational practice. This culturally based information is used to encourage behavior change.

Another important area for work with Native Americans is in acknowledging and addressing issues of grief and loss, both related to historical trauma and to contemporary social problems. Many Native people have experienced significant losses and trauma that need to be grieved and mourned. Traditions provide ways for dealing with grief and loss that are important in maintaining mental health (Swinomish Tribal Mental Health Project, 1991). Social workers such as Yellow Horse Brave Heart are leading the way in developing culturally appropriate clinical interventions to address these critical needs. (See, for example, Brave Heart-Jordan & DeBruyn, 1995; Weaver & Yellow Horse Brave Heart, 1999).

Networking with indigenous helpers such as medicine men and women is important for helping professionals. Social workers can form cooperative relationships with indigenous healers that include mutual referrals and collaboration in helping some clients. Forging links with traditional healers can be critical in providing mental health services (Swinomish Tribal Mental Health Project, 1991).

Conducting culturally appropriate interventions is challenging in and of itself and has become even more complicated by outside constraints such as managed care. The length of time needed to truly establish trust as a foundation for a sound working relationship may no longer be possible in some settings. The helping relationship is likely to be significantly impaired when a culture that values time in social conversation and establishing relationships is faced with managed care and similar time-limited ways of helping (Abe-Kim & Takeuchi, 1996; Kavanaugh et al., 1999).

Helping professionals need to be aware of indigenous communication norms. Disclosure in the therapeutic context may be difficult. Individuals who refrain from talking may be seen as resistant or unwilling to work. Native clients may use indirect communication to share intimate information. This may be misunderstood if it appears the client is discussing someone else or a hypothetical situation. Stating "I" messages directly conflicts with the value of humility and may be a barrier to treatment for some First Nations clients (Wing, Crow, & Thompson, 1995).

The factors that predict mental health difficulties in the general population of elders do not always predict difficulties for Native elders. In fact, income, education, and social support are not good predictors of mental health status for Native elders, and physical health and coping are predictors for both Natives and non-Natives. Significant differences between men and women, and urban and reservation populations, influence the strength of predictors of mental health in Native American elders (Narduzzi, 1994).

Conflicts between traditional beliefs and practices and Western models of care result in barriers to service. Focus groups of Native elders and young women in Oregon explored traditional beliefs and their relationship to prenatal care. The study found a breakdown in transmission of traditional health beliefs because of federal assimilation policies and the death of elders. Traditional care was often not available and Western care was perceived as culturally inappropriate and hostile, thus leaving many without services (Long & Curry, 1998).

Many Native people still seek traditional forms of healing for social and health problems. Western and traditional care may be complementary, with different types of care sought for different maladies. A study of Native military veterans in the Southwest and Northern Plains found that 16 percent reported using traditional healing. The Southwestern sample used traditional healing more often, possibly because this was more available to them than was Western medical care (Gurley et al., 2001).

Culturally competent interventions with Native American clients should incorporate the use of containment skills such as listening, patience, and silence. The needs of clients should guide the work rather than the social worker's preference for particular models or methods. Respect for culturally based beliefs, values, and behaviors must also be an integral part of choosing and implementing interventions.

Values/Attitudes for Cultural Competence

A survey of Native American helping professionals identified four major values or attitudes associated with culturally competent services for Native Americans: (1) helper wellness and self-awareness, (2) humility and willingness to learn, (3) respect, open-mindedness, and a non-judgmental attitude, and (4) social justice (Weaver, 1999b). Although in part, these values are already present in helping professionals and are often what led them to these professions in the first place, these values and attitudes can also be cultivated and enhanced.

The work of social workers and other helping professionals can be very stressful. Helping professionals are often confronted with difficult situations such as removing a child from an abusive family, reaching out to mentally ill people living on the streets, and helping a client heal after the death of a loved one. In particular, the multiproblem situations experienced by many Native American clients can seem overwhelming. To effectively assist clients, helping professionals must be aware of their own feelings and reactions.

Social workers who fail to recognize and take care of their own needs are likely to experience compassion fatigue, become less effective in their work, and may ultimately suffer physical and emotional symptoms themselves. The self-awareness component, critical in the helping professions, can help professionals recognize their own needs, biases, and reactions to certain types of clients. Supervision is an important venue to assist helping professionals to deal with stress that accumulates in day-to-day work. Helping professionals can look to other sources to replenish their energy and emotions. Such sources may include physical exercise, spending time in a peaceful, secluded mountain setting, getting a massage, or participating in spiritual activities or prayer. To be effective helpers, it is important that helping professionals have balance in their own lives.

In a quest for balance and wholeness, some new age religions have turned to Native American spirituality. Native Americans often experience this as exploitation. Helping professionals who experience their own spiritual hunger have sometimes hoped to meet these needs through Native American clients by asking them about spiritual practices and indigenous belief systems. Clearly, the social work relationship exists to meet the needs of clients, not the needs of professionals. Although it is important for helping professionals to meet their own needs, this must be done outside of the social work relationship. To place these expectations on clients is unethical.

It is important to be open to learning from clients. Professionals who think they must know it all hold themselves to an impossible standard. This attitude reinforces the hierarchical status difference between clients and helping professionals. Approaching the helping relationship with humility and recognizing there are many things the professional does not know leaves the door open for learning.

Humility can be reinforced by deliberately entering cross-cultural situations to learn to empathize with cultural minority groups. Cross-cultural encounters in minority communities allow people from the dominant society to experience what it is like to not understand the cultural context, including expected behavior. As cultural outsiders, they may not understand all the jokes and may be regarded with uncertainty or suspicion (Hamby, 2000). Helping professionals can identify cross-cultural learning situations like pow wows or Native American community events through indigenous publications and Web sites.

Social workers will often find that clients have different beliefs, values, and behaviors than they do. How the social worker responds to these differences is crucial. A century ago, early social workers saw themselves as role models and encouraged clients to conform to their standards. This is no longer done consciously, but helping professionals who do not reflect on value differences and approach them with respect may still replicate these value-laden practices.

Most helping professionals today would agree it is important to show respect for clients and their beliefs, but keeping an open mind and being non-judgmental can be difficult tasks. Helping professions need to move beyond simply agreeing to be respectful to actually demonstrating respect for differences in their practice. Respect can be demonstrated through actively listening to clients' concerns and values and choosing interventions accordingly.

Oppression and discrimination faced by many Native Americans are much more than just artifacts of a distant past. Many contemporary problems faced by First Nations people originate in society or in the relationship between indigenous people and the federal government. Counseling, concrete services, and other direct practice approaches can be important in alleviating the symptoms of many social ills, but the exclusive use of such approaches is like putting a bandage on a problem that requires surgery.

Advocacy and activism have been part of the social work repertoire since its beginning. Social workers have long recognized the importance of going from "case to cause." In other words, the problems of one client are often experienced by many and may require macro-level solutions. If a Native American family approaches an agency in need of food, it is important to provide food, but this is often not a solution to the problem. In fact, poverty is a major problem in many Native communities, with reservations consistently constituting some of the poorest areas of the country. It is important to look at the root causes of hunger and poverty in First Nations communities, such as few job opportunities, lack of transportation in isolated areas, and centuries of federal policies that systematically destroyed traditional Native economies and created ongoing dependency on federal programs.

Case Example

Lorena and George White are an elderly Shoshone couple living in Boise, Idaho. They were referred to the Goodman Family Services Agency by their minister for assistance in processing paperwork for the Home Energy Assistance Program (HEAP). Bruno Smith, their assigned caseworker, met with them in his office. He assisted them with the paperwork and inquired about other concrete service needs such as meal preparation and housekeeping services. He allowed plenty of time in his appointment with them and didn't rush them when they were slow responding to his questions. After the initial appointment, he called them to make sure their service needs were being met through the referrals he initiated. Bruno scheduled a home visit after two weeks to assess their living situation and see if they had additional needs before closing the case. During this meeting, they mentioned their son recently had his leg amputated because of diabetes and he was having difficulty adjusting to this loss. They asked if Bruno might be able to help.

In this case, knowledge, skills, and values/attitudes helped facilitate the work in several areas:

- Knowledge of the mistrust that Native Americans often feel for service providers led Bruno to take extra time in establishing a relationship.
- Knowledge about culturally based communication norms helped Bruno to allow silence during the interview and maximize his use of containment skills.

- By not rushing Lorena and George in the interviews, Bruno helped them feel comfortable and relaxed. This led to their concerns emerging naturally.
- Bruno took time to reflect on his feelings and beliefs about Native American clients in general and Native elders in particular. He had heard that Native people had an earth-centered spirituality and was surprised that this couple was referred by an Episcopal minister. Bruno vowed to keep an open mind and try to monitor his own stereotypes so they would not influence the work.
- Native American clients often feel more comfortable trusting helping professionals with minor or concrete issues before raising more emotional or difficult problems. Bruno's competent handling of Lorena and George's need for concrete services, along with his thorough follow-up and cultivation of the relationship, led to a preliminary trust that resulted in the identification of other needs. If Bruno continues to address this family's needs in a culturally competent manner, he and his agency are likely to develop a good reputation that will lead to other Native clients seeking services.

Cultural Competence in Social Policies

The unique relationship between the federal government and Native Americans has led to significant policy regulation in virtually all aspects of Native American life. For example, the allotment policy, also known as the Dawes Act, destroyed the collective ownership of Native lands and declared unallotted land surplus, leading to the loss of more than 100 million acres or two-thirds of all reservation land between 1887 and 1934 (Churchill & Morris, 1992). Likewise, policies have threatened the economic base of Native Nations. For example, the federal government interfered with traditional Diné subsistence when it issued an edict that the Diné's sheep were to be taken away for fear of overgrazing. Relocation policies of the 1950s shaped where Native people should live by promising jobs in urban areas. Termination policies, also originating in the 1950s, legislated away the very existence of whole Native Nations. The current policies of federal recognition still dictate who the federal government acknowledges to be a Native American. Policies also affect Native Americans by governing what services and funding are available for social and health programs.

Little quality research is available, thus leaving policy makers and program planners with no empirical information to use (Narduzzi, 1994). The majority of federal policies have been unilateral with little meaningful input from Native people. One exception to this rule is the Indian Child Welfare Act of 1978. The law was crafted with significant input from Native people, including indigenous helping professionals. Although implementation of this policy has been hindered by inadequate funding and training (Bending, 1997), it is a significant piece of legislation that differs from all other social welfare legislation, it applies only to First Nations people, and it clearly identifies cultural continuity as in the best interest of the child.

Policy makers need to be knowledgeable about First Nations cultures so they can develop and implement culturally congruent policies. Input from First Nations people can help ensure that policies are appropriate and effective. In the past, federal policies have had a predominantly destructive impact on indigenous cultures. Culturally competent policy makers have the potential to develop meaningful programs and regulations that encourage First Nations' self-sufficiency and eliminate federal paternalism.

Cultural Competence in Social Agencies

Indigenous values do not easily blend with mainstream mental health expectations and requirements. This is particularly a problem in record keeping, staff roles, and diagnosis. Funding authorities must recognize the need for flexibility and innovation, or bureaucratic requirements may inadvertently stifle culturally appropriate programs (Swinomish Tribal Mental Health Project, 1991).

Social service programs run by Native Nations often have more fluid program structures, less defined and more flexible boundaries, and more complex client-provider role relationships than do their non-Native counterparts (Swinomish Tribal Mental Health Project, 1991). Although outsiders may view these programs as unprofessional, they serve an important function in meeting the needs of First Nations people.

Just like individual practitioners, agencies need to reflect on their work and how their services invite or inhibit Native American clients. Agency administrators and boards of directors need to ask themselves critical questions about how they incorporate the principles of cultural competence in every aspect of service delivery and agency governance. Self-awareness must lead to behavior change in the struggle for cultural competence.

Community Interventions

Many social problems have their roots in the relationship between Native Americans and the larger society, and thus require macro-level analysis and change. Social workers can use advocacy and community organizing skills to begin to address these large scale needs.

Helping professionals can use their skills to assist Native communities to conduct needs assessments to plan meaningful services (Weaver, 1999a). Through such assessments, service providers can begin to recognize gaps in, and duplication of, services. A community-based needs assessment can also serve as a catalyst for coalition building.

Indigenous social workers have become adept at using macro-level social work skills to bring about important change in, and on behalf of, First Nations communities. For example, Wilma Mankiller, a Cherokee BSW, used her skills to bring plumbing and sanitation services to the people of the Cherokee Nation before going on to become her nation's first female Principal Chief. Likewise, Ada Deer, a Menominee MSW, used her advocacy skills to help overturn the federal termination of her nation before being appointed Director of the Bureau of Indian Affairs, Assistant Secretary of the Interior. These notable women have set excellent examples of how helping professionals can use macro-level skills to bring about important change.

The voices of Native people need to be respected and incorporated in research and program planning. Researchers often adhere to scientific ethics but disregard local ethics (Piquemal, 2001). Many Native people believe this leads to misappropriated knowledge: knowledge that has been acquired under the pretense of helping the Native community but that ultimately does not provide any benefits. Informed consent has different meanings in cross-cultural situations. Consent must be an ongoing process of renegotiation. Data must come back to the Native community.

Images of Native Americans continue to promote stereotypes and influence Native youth to see themselves in negative ways as bloodthirsty savages, pitiful drunks, or mystics lost in a modern world they can't understand. Use of Native American names and images in mascots and advertising, such as the Washington Redskins football team or Crazy Horse malt liquor, is a form of discrimination. Many Native people condemn the use of these types of images as demeaning and hurtful. Using the names of other cultural groups would not be tolerated. These images assault self-esteem. Self-image is clearly linked to other social problems such as violence and substance abuse (Hatfield, 2000).

Conclusion

Native Americans are a diverse population with a long history of government regulation and subsequent mistrust of helping professionals. Mistrust is a natural outcome of a legacy of racism, cultural imperialism, and cultural incompetence. Cultural competence begins with understanding the impact of historical and contemporary losses and how these coexist with strengths and resilience that facilitate survival in a context of colonization.

Helping professionals must strive for cultural competence at all levels of practice including direct services, program planning, and policy development. Only through culturally competent work at all levels of helping can we begin to truly alleviate the extensive social and health problems affecting First Nations people.

Exercises

Exercise #1: Examining local service provision to Native Americans.

Identify the major Native American groups in your area including their approximate numbers and location. Contact three major social service agencies that serve these areas. Find out how many Native clients they serve each year and what types of services they provide to this population. Based on these inquiries, make some tentative conclusions about how well the needs of the Native American community are being met by these agencies. Discuss your tentative findings and begin to make hypotheses about what these agencies are doing that may make them hospitable or inhospitable to local Native Americans. Make recommendations for improvement.

Exercise #2: Applying the Indian Child Welfare Act.

Reflect on the following case example: Janie Singer from Santa Clara Pueblo has recently been reported for child abuse of her three young children. The charges have been verified, and you need to make foster care arrangements for the children. Does the Indian Child Welfare Act apply in this case? If so, what steps do you need to take?

Exercise #3: Experiential learning activities in Native American communities.

Attend a pow wow, social, or other Native American gathering or festival that is open to the public. What can you learn about communication norms and social etiquette from this experience? How can you apply what you have learned in a social work setting?

Additional Resources

Bachman, R. (1992). *Death and Violence on the Reservation.* New York: Auburn House.

This book gives an excellent overview of the extent of violence in Native American communities. The author uses statistics on arrests, imprisonment, and mortality to present a side of Native American life that is unfamiliar to most non-Native people. Helping professionals can use this information to become better informed about the social environment of many Native people, then go beyond these statistics to apply a strengths perspective in their work.

In the White Man's Image. (1992). American Experience Series. Public Broadcasting Service.

This video recounts the historical development of the boarding school system with a particular focus on Carlisle, one of the first and most famous Native American boarding schools. First person accounts and commentary by historians are presented. The video includes "before and after" pictures taken of Native American children when they first arrived at the school and after their traditional clothes were taken away and their hair was cut and styled to illustrate how they were remade "in the white man's image."

Jaimes, M. A. (1992). *The State of Native America: Genocide, Colonization, and Resistance.* Boston: South End Press.

This edited book provides key information on laws, policies, and historical developments that have influenced contemporary Native Americans. Topics covered include the political nature of early indigenous population estimates, issues of sovereignty in a colonial context, and rights to natural resources. This information provides important contextual information for helping professionals and identifies numerous issues in need of advocacy.

Maracle, B. (1993). *Crazywater: Native Voices on Addiction and Recovery.* Toronto: Penguin Books.

This book provides numerous personal stories of indigenous people and their encounters with alcohol. These narratives clearly depict a diversity of experiences including a variety of therapeutic solutions. While these narratives are taken from the Canadian context, the book provides useful insights into indigenous struggles with addiction for helping professionals in both the United States and Canada.

Ogunwole, S. U. (2002). *The American Indian and Alaska Native Population: 2000.* U.S. Bureau of the Census.

This brief narrative provides an accessible overview of U.S. census material on Native Americans. The material includes information on residential patterns, age, education, and other demographic information. The size of various Native populations and changing demographic patterns are identified.

Notes

1. In 1990, the census did not allow people to designate more than one racial or ethnic group. Therefore, precise comparisons between 1990 and 2000 census figures are not possible, making it difficult to determine how much the Native American population has grown.

2. The categories used by the census do not necessarily coincide with the labels used by many indigenous people. For example, the term Sioux, considered outdated and even offensive by some indigenous people, is used by the census to represent a combined grouping of Lakota, Dakota, and Nakota people, and the census term Latin American Indian is a conglomerate of tribal groupings.

References

Abbott, P. J. (1996). American Indian and Alaska Native aboriginal use of alcohol in the United States. *American Indian and Alaska Native Mental Health Research, 7*(2), 1–13.

Abe-Kim, J. S., & Takeuchi, D. T. (1996). Cultural competence and quality of care: Issues for mental health service delivery in managed care. *Clinical Psychology: Science and Practice, 3*(4), 273–295.

Allen, J. (1998). Personality assessment with American Indians and Alaska Natives: Instrument considerations and service delivery style. *Journal of Personality Assessment, 70*(1), 17–42.

Barsh, R. L. (1996). The Indian Child Welfare Act of 1978: A critical analysis. In J. R. Wunder, *Recent Legal Issues for American Indians, 1968 to the Present.* New York: Garland, 219–268.

Beauvais, F., & Trimble, J. E. (1992). The role of the researcher in evaluating American Indian alcohol and other drug abuse prevention programs. In M. A. Orlandi, R. Weston, & L. G. Epstein (Eds.) *Cultural Competence for Evaluators: A Guide for Alcohol and other Drug Abuse Prevention Practitioners Working with Ethnic and Racial Communities.* Rockville, MD: Office of Substance Abuse Prevention, U.S. Department of Health and Human Services. 147–171.

Bending, R. L. (1997). Training child welfare workers to meet the requirements of the Indian Child Welfare Act. *Journal of Multicultural Social Work, 5*(3/4), 151–164.

Brave Heart-Jordan, M., & DeBruyn, L. (1995). So she may walk in balance: Integrating the impact of historical trauma in the treatment of American Indian women. In J. Adelman & G. Enguidanos (Eds.), *Racism in the lives of Women: Testimony, Theory, and Guides to Antiracist Practice.* New York: Haworth Press, 345–368.

Churchill, W., & Morris, G. T. (1992). Key Indian laws and cases. In M. A. Jairnes (Ed.), *The State of Native America: Genocide, Colonization, and Resistance.* Boston: South End Press, 13–21.

Clinton, R. N., Newton, N. J., & Price, M. E. (1991). *American Indian Law. Cases and Materials.* Charlottesville, VA: Michie Company.

Collmeyer, P. M. (1995). From "Operation Brown Baby" to "Opportunity": The placement of children of color at the Boys and Girls Aid Society of Oregon. *Child Welfare, 74*(1), 242–263.

Curyto, K. J., Chapleski, E. E., Lichtenberg, P. A., Hodges, E., Kaczynski, R., & Sobeck, J. (1998). Prevalence and prediction of depression in American Indian elderly. *Clinical Gerontologist, 18*(3), 19–37.

Dion, R., Gotowiec, A., & Beiser, M. (1998). Depression and conduct disorder in Native and non-Native children. *Journal of the American Academy of Child and Adolescent Psychiatry, 37*(7), 736–742.

Fleming, C. M. (1992). American Indians and Alaska Natives: Changing societies past and present. In M. A. Orlandi, R. Weston, & L. G. Epstein (Eds.), *Cultural Competence for Evaluators: A Guide for Alcohol and other Drug Abuse Prevention Practitioners Working with Ethnic/Racial Communities.* Rockville, MD: Office of Substance Abuse Prevention, U.S. Department of Health and Human Services, 147–171.

Garrett, M. T., & Pichette, E. F. (2000). Red as an apple: Native American acculturation and counseling with or without reservation. *Journal of Counseling and Development, 78,* 3–13.

George, L. J. (1997). Why the need for the Indian Child Welfare Act? *Journal of Multicultural Social Work, 5*(3/4), 165–175.

Gilliland, F. D., Mahler, R., Hunt, W. C., & Davis, S. M. (1999). Preventive health care among rural American Indians in New Mexico. *Preventive Medicine, 25*(2), 194–202.

Gurley, D., Novins, D. K., Jones, M. C., Beats, J., Shore, J. H., & Manson, S. M. (2001). Comparative use of biomedical services and traditional healing options by American Indian veterans. *Psychiatric Services, 52*(1), 68–74.

Hamby, S. L. (2000). The importance of community in a feminist analysis of domestic violence among American Indians. *American Journal of Community Psychology, 28*(5), 649–672.

Hatfield, D. L. (2000). The stereotyping of Native Americans. *The Humanist, 60*(5), 43–45.

John, R. (1991). *Defining and Meeting the Needs of Native American Elders: Applied Research on their Current Status, Social Service Needs, and Support Network Operation.* Lawrence: University of Kansas.

Kavanaugh, K., Absalom, K., Beil, W., & Schliessmann, L. (1999). Connecting and becoming culturally competent: A Lakota example. *Advances in Nursing Science, 27*(3), 9–31.

Kasprow, W. J., & Rosenheck, R. (1998). Substance use and psychiatric problems of homeless Native American veterans. *Psychiatric Services, 49*(3), 345–350.

LaFromboise, T., & Howard-Pitney, B. (1995). Zuni Life Skills Development Curriculum:

Description and evaluation of a suicide prevention program. *Journal of Counseling Psychology, 42*(4), 479–486.

Long, C. R., & Curry, M. A. (1998). Living in two worlds: Native American women and prenatal care. *Health Care for Women International, 19*(3), *205–215.*

Manson, S. M. (2000). Mental health services for American Indians and Alaska Natives: Need, use, and barriers to effective care. *Canadian Journal of Psychiatry, 45*(7), 617–626.

Maracle, B. (1993). *Crazy Water: Native Voices on Addiction and Recovery.* Toronto: Penguin Books.

McNeil, D. W., Porter, C. A., Zvolensky, M. J., Chaney, J. M., & Kee, M. (2000). Assessment of culturally related anxiety in American Indians and Alaska Natives. *Behavior Therapy, 31*(2), 301–325.

Meisenhelder, J. B., & Chandler, E. N. (2000). Faith, prayer, and health outcomes in elderly Native Americans. *Clinical Nursing Research, 9*(2), 191–203.

Moran, J. R., & May, P. A. (1995). American Indians. In J. Philleo &. F. L. Brisbane (Eds.), *Cultural Competence for Social Workers: A Guide for Alcohol and other Drug Abuse Prevention Professionals Working with Ethnic/Racial Communities.* Center for Substance Abuse Prevention, 3–39.

Morrisette, P. J. (1.994). The holocaust of First Nations people. *Contemporary Family Therapy, 16*(5), 381–392.

Napholz, L. (2000). Balancing multiple roles among a group of urban midlife American Indian working women. *Health Care for Women International, 27*(4), 255–266.

Narduzzi, J. L. (1994). *Mental Health among Elderly Native Americans.* New York: Garland.

Novins, D. K., Bechtold, D. W., Sack, W. H., Thompson, J., Carter, D. R., & Manson, S. M. (1997). The *DSM-IV* outline for cultural formulations: A critical demonstration with American Indian children. *Journal of the American Academy of Child and Adolescent Psychiatry, 36*(9), 1244–1252.

Oetting, E. R., & Beauvais, F. (1991). Orthogonal cultural identification theory. The cultural identification of minority adolescents. *International Journal of the Addictions, 25*(5A & 6A), 655–685.

Ogunwole, S. U. (2002). *The American Indian and Alaska Native Population: 2000.* U.S. Bureau of the Census. http://www.census.gov/population/www/cen2000/briefs.html

Piquemal, N. (2001). Free and informed consent in research involving Native American communities. *American Indian Culture and Research Journal, 25*(1), 65–79.

Sage, G. P., & Burns, G. L. (1993). Attributional antecedents of alcohol use in American Indian and Euroamerican adolescents. *American Indian and Alaska Native Mental Health Research, 5*(2), 46–53.

Schinke, S. (1996). Behavioral approaches to illness prevention for Native Americans. In P. M. Kato & T. Mann (Eds.), *Handbook of Diversity Issues in Health Psychology,* New York: Plenum Press, 367–387.

Shulman, L. (1999). *The Skills of Helping Individuals Families, Groups, and Communities.* Irasca, IL: F. E. Peacock.

Stevens, J., Cornell, C. E., Story, M., French, S. A., Levin, S., Becenti, A., Gittelsohn, J., Going, S. B., & Reid, R. (1999). Development of a questionnaire to assess knowledge, attitudes, and behaviors in American Indian children. *American Journal of Clinical Nutrition, 69*(4), 773s–781s.

Stiffarm, L. A., & Lane, P., Jr. (1992). The demography of Native North America: A Question of American Indian survival. In M. A. Jaimes (Ed.), *The State of Native America: Genocide, Colonization, and Resistance.* Boston: South End Press, 23–53.

Sugarman, J. R., & Grossman, D. C. (1996). Trauma among American Indians in an urban county. *Public Health Reports, 111*(4), 321–327.

Swinomish Tribal Mental Health Project. (1991). *A Gathering of Wisdoms, Tribal Mental Health: A Cultural Perspective.* LaConner, WA: Swinomish Tribal Community.

U.S. Census Bureau. (2001). Current Population Survey. http://www.census.gov

Walters, K. L. (1997). Urban lesbian and gay American Indian identity: Implications for mental health service delivery. In L. B. Brown, *Two Spirit People: American Indian Lesbian Women and Gay Men*. Binghamton, NY: Haworth Press, 43–65.

Weaver, H. N. (1996). Social work with American Indian youth using the orthogonal model of cultural identification. *Families in Society: The Journal of Contemporary Human Services, 77*(2), 98–107.

Weaver, H. N. (1999a). Assessing the needs of Native American communities: A Northeastern example. *Evaluation and Program Planning: An International Journal, 22*(2), 155–161.

Weaver, H. N. (1999b). Indigenous people and the social work profession: Defining culturally competent services. *Social Work, 44*(3), 217–225.

Weaver, H. N. (1999c). Through indigenous eyes: A Native American perspective on the HIV epidemic. *Health and Social Work, 24*(1), 27–34.

Weaver, H. N., & Yellow Horse Brave Heart, M. (1999). Examining two facets of American Indian identity: Exposure to other cultures and the influence of historical trauma. *Journal of Human Behavior in the Social Environment, 2*(1/2), 19–33.

Weaver, H. N., & White, B. J. (1999). Protecting the future of indigenous children and nations: An examination of the Indian Child Welfare Act. *Journal of Health and Social Policy, 10*(4), 35–50.

Wing, D. M., Grow, S. S., & Thompson, T. (1995). An ethnonursing study of Muscogee (Creek) Indians and effective health care practices for treating alcohol abuse. *Family Community Health, 18*(2), 52–64.

Young, Y. K., Lujan, P., & Dixon, L. D. (1998). I can walk both ways. *Human Communication Research, 25*(2), 252–275.

Zimmermann, M. A., Ramirez-Valles, J., Washienko, K. M., Waiter, B., & Dyer, S. (1996). The development of a measure of enculturation for Native American youth. *American Journal of Community Psychology, 24*(2), 295–310.

14

Counseling and Psychotherapy With Asian American Clients

Nolan Zane
Teru Morton
June Chu
Nancy Lin

In working with Asian American populations, it is important to appreciate and account for the social and psychological diversity that exists among members of this ethnic minority group. Generalizing about any group is perilous, particularly when considering peoples with roots in Asia, which comprises 30 percent of the Earth's total land mass and is home to over three-fifths of this planet's population, with the inhabitants ranging from preliterate hunter-gatherers to cosmopolitan multilingual urbanites (Columbia Encyclopedia, 2001). It is therefore best to consider the specific background of an Asian American client and to be cautious in the tendency to generalize information across distinct ethnic groups.

Moreover, to make counseling or treatment recommendations for such a diverse group becomes even more challenging in view of the limited amount of empirically based information available on cultural influences in treatment. The bulk of the research reviewed in this chapter involves primarily group or population-focused studies in which research has examined ethnic or cultural group influences on therapy process and outcomes. Although this parameter-based research has provided important information about the mental health treatment experiences of ethnic minorities, the focus on group differences often has obscured important variations among members of a particular minority group. More significantly, the descriptive nature of this research has precluded exact determination of how culture affects the treatment experience and eventual outcomes. Recently, greater emphasis has been placed on variable-focused studies that examine how specific psychological elements associated with ethnic or cultural group differences affect treatment or moderate treatment effectiveness. This shift to study culturally based variables such as cultural value orientation, cultural identity, control orientation, shame and stigma, etc., allows us to better explain and understand the specific effects of cultural influences.

Given these limitations, we proceed as judiciously as we can, outlining the demographics and sociopolitical history of Asian American subgroups, reviewing key cultural tendencies, issues, and conflicts likely to be encountered in counseling and psychotherapy, drawing out some implications for working with this population and offering several illustrative case studies. We recognize that culture is only one relevant factor in establishing an explanatory model for mental illness, and that, depending on the circumstances, other aspects may be more influential. The literature reviewed represents trends that have been observed and should be considered as general guidelines for working with Asian American clients. However, when possible (as addressed by the research), we will also discuss individual differences in psychological dimensions, as well as inter-ethnic and intra-ethnic group differences.

Demographics and Sociopolitical History

Asians began immigrating to North America in the 1840s, up to six generations ago. More recently, new waves of immigrants have once again substantially augmented the Asian population. The 2000 United States Census showed Asian Americans increasing from 7.27 million in 1990 to 10.24 million in 2000, a 46 percent growth rate (U.S. Census Bureau, 1990; U.S. Census Bureau, 2000). They are presently the fastest growing ethnic group in North America. The percent of foreign-born people in this country is higher than it has been in more than half a century, and more of these foreign-born individuals (28 percent) come from Asia than any other continent. The largest subgroups among the overall Asian American community are Chinese Americans (2.4 million), Filipino Americans (1.9 million), Asian Indians (1.7 million), Vietnamese Americans (1.1 million), Korean Americans (1.1 million), and Japanese Americans (0.8 million). Smaller subgroups together represent 1.3 million additional Asian Americans.

Asian Americans are a very heterogeneous group, not only because of clearly distinct countries of origin but also because of unique sociopolitical histories concerning their arrival in North America. The first Asian immigrants were men from southern China, who began arriving in 1848 for the Gold Rush in California and western states. Soon after, Americans' fears of losing jobs to Chinese workers led to the 1882 Chinese Exclusion Act, banning further immigration. This ban was repealed in 1943 when the United States recognized China as an ally in World War II and relaxed its immigration laws somewhat. With the 1882 ban on Chinese immigration, Japanese immigrants began to arrive to work Hawaii's sugar plantations, but anti-Japanese sentiments grew there as well. A 1907 Executive Order prohibited Japanese migration to the U.S. mainland from Hawaii and Mexico, the 1908 Gentlemen's Agreement restricted immigration from Japan to wives of Japanese already in the United States, and the 1924 Immigration Bill ended further immigration from Japan altogether. Relations with Japan deteriorated just prior to World War II, a conflict characterized by markedly anti-Japanese sentiments. In 1942, Executive Order 9066 permitted forcible removal of Japanese Americans from the west coast to internment camps. This political history is unique to Japanese Americans, but other aspects of anti-Asian discrimination and racism have targeted all of the Asian American groups.

Laborers from Korea began arriving in Hawaii to work the sugar plantations in 1903. The 1907 Executive Order banned them, along with the Japanese, from migrating to the mainland United States, and the 1924 Oriental Exclusion act prevented almost all Korean migration to this country. Korean migration resumed after World War II ended, with the arrival of the Korean wives and children of United States military servicemen. U.S. support during and after the Korean War was influential in later waves of immigration.

When Spain ceded the Philippines to the United States in 1892, Filipinos became United States nationals, and unrestricted immigration was permitted so that they could work the cane fields and pineapple plantations of Hawaii, orchards of California, and fisheries and canneries of Washington, Oregon, and Alaska. More Filipino immigrants arrived in response to the 1946–1965 recruitment drives of the U.S. Armed Forces during the Cold War of the 1950s. Immigration was severely reduced when the Philippines later achieved commonwealth status. However, the Immigration Act of 1965 resulted in substantial increases in Asian immigration when the national origins system was replaced with the fixed quota system of 20,000 people from each foreign country.

Large numbers of Vietnamese war refugees came to the United States in the 1970s after the fall of Saigon. The United States resettlement policy often distributed refugees across diverse areas of the United States to sponsoring individuals and groups responsible for helping them find employment, education, and other services (Tran, 1991). Recently, diplomatic ties between the United States and Vietnam have been reestablished, prompting a second wave of Vietnamese immigrants (Banerjee, 2001).

Profiles of other recent immigrants differ widely. Many Southeast Asians, Laotians, Hmong, Cambodians, and Vietnamese were refugees who fled retaliatory persecution for supporting the United States. Many of these refugees have often experienced economic and psychosocial adjustment challenges upon their arrival in the United States. By contrast, the Asian Indian population tends to have a higher mean income and level of education than all other Asian American groups, and it has grown the fastest in the last decade (106 percent), growth which is attributed in part to the creation of H-1B visas that encourage high-tech industry immigrants from Asia (KTVU/Fox 2, 2001).

As a whole, Asian Americans reside predominantly in urban settings (96 percent live in metropolitan areas). About half of all Asian Americans live in the western United States, with 20 percent in the Northeast, 19 percent in the South, and 12 percent in the Midwest. Their rate of growth from 1990 to 2000 was significant across many states: e.g., 10 percent in Arkansas, 110 percent in South Dakota, 94 percent in New Jersey, 83 percent in Pennsylvania (Armas, 2001), 78 percent in Florida (Word, 2001), 71 percent in Michigan (Warikoo, 2001), and 61 percent in California (KTVU/Fox 2, 2001).

Family Dynamics and Issues

Although substantial inter-group heterogeneity exists among Asian Americans, these groups share certain commonalities of family structure and functioning. A number of factors mitigate these tendencies, the most notable being the effects of acculturation on Asian American families and their members (cf. Lee, 1989). However, certain family tendencies in child rearing practices, communication patterns, role relations and expectations, as well as potential sources of interpersonal conflict persist among Asian Americans despite societal pressures to acculturate in social, political, financial, and educational domains (Ching, McDermott, Fukunaga, Yanagida, Mann, & Waldron, 1995).

Child Rearing Practices

Confucius laid the general template for Asian families centuries ago—a vertical structure with father at its head, mother deferential and supportive of him, and children obedient to and respectful toward both authority figures. To reinforce core family values such as work ethic and academic achievement, parents may use shame, guilt, or an appeal to duty and responsibility to help children understand that they must not embarrass, shame, or dishonor their families (Isomura, Fine, & Lin, 1987). Even across many generations residing in North America, Asian Americans continue to see families as responsible for their individual members' behavior (Lin, Miller, Poland, Nuccio, & Yamaguchi, 1991). Asian Americans value family lineage, considering that the behavior of any individual reflects upon and impacts both preceding and future generations of the family. Thus, it is vital that counselors and therapists understand an individual's identity and place within the family context whenever conducting therapy with Asian Americans (Sodowsky, 1991). Traditional Asian emphases on paternal hierarchy, authoritative parenting, filial piety, interdependence, conformity, and saving face can contrast with the Western preference for more child independence and egalitarian parenting, an approach in which children are taught about individuality, the need for autonomous functioning, self-reliance, and the uniqueness of their personal qualities.

There are, of course, variations in how Asian groups socialize these traditional Asian values (Uba, 1994). For example, Chinese Americans tend to closely supervise children, emphasize achievement, and view child rearing as a mother's responsibility. Filipino Americans tend to lull, carry, and play with their infants, but Korean Americans may view playing with children as undermining the children's respect for adults. Southeast Asian parents tend to become more restrictive as children grow older, gradually increasing their emphasis on such things as disobedience, failure to fulfill responsibilities, and aggression toward siblings. Taken as a whole, however, many Asian American parents still differ appreciably from mainstream American parents. For example, in contrast to Asian parents, White American parents tend to see play with children as an integral part of the learning process, and they often treat their children as equals or at least as participants in the decision making process. Asian American mothers often anticipate the needs of their children, while White American mothers are inclined to want their children to verbalize their needs. Attachment and interaction patterns between mother and child reflect cultural values, and differences in these practices across cultures often result in unique socioemotional, identity development, and individuation processes (cf. Takahashi, 1986).

Communication Patterns and Norms

Traditional Asian families emphasize collectivist values of interdependence, conformity, and harmony; communication is indirect, implicit, nonverbal, and intuitive. Direct confrontations are avoided (Hsu, 1983). Japanese consider emotional expression to be "bad form," and Japanese language has restrictive words for affect expression (McDermott, Char, Robillard, Hsu, Tseng, & Ashton, 1983; Takeuchi, Imahori, & Matsumoto, 2001). Filipino women demonstrate the use of *delicadeza* for nonconfrontational communication (Araneta, 1993), and Koreans use *noonchi,* a "measuring with eyes," or intuitive perception of others (Kim, 1993). Love and affection are not expressed verbally as much as shown through the mutual fulfillment of obligations and consideration of tending to physical needs. A language of emotions is characteristic of Western cultures, and traditional Asian cultures tend to view emotions as a sign of weakness and disgrace. For example, as Chinese Americans report becoming more "American," their reports of affective behavior show increased variation (Tsai & Levenson, 1997), reflecting the Westernized tendency for more open and verbal affective expression.

Because so much of communication in Asian cultures is through indirect means, intra-familial conflict and misunderstandings often occur. Older generation parents who have grown accustomed to certain styles of interacting may not be able to fully express themselves directly, but their more Americanized children may not be fully able to "read" these meaningful cues. The more acculturated children may also be more vocal, and this further upsets the family hierarchy, as the younger generation family members may unwittingly overstep certain cultural norms and expectations such as the appropriate display of deference and respect to elders.

Attitudes Toward Marriage and Relationships

With the more traditional, less acculturated families, marriage is not seen as an individual decision based upon love but as a union between families, emphasizing the appropriate match in economic and social status of the families rather than the romantic inclinations of the spousal relationship. Whereas Westerners raise children to become autonomous individuals who are able to lead their own lives separate from their parents, Asians raise their children with a respect for the familial role in their present and future lives. Asian Americans who are raised by parents holding one worldview of family and marriage, yet grow up in a society where love and affective emotion are bases for relationships, may find themselves in conflict when they choose to marry an individual for love. The difficulties that individuals may encounter when marrying someone from another culture must also be kept in mind. Some Asians look down on Asian women who marry non-Asians: they see these women as "business girls" whose only goal is economic advancement (Ratliff, Moon, & Bonacci, 1978). And the strong in-group and out-group inclinations of Asian American groups (Tanaka, Ebrero, Linn, & Morera, 1998) may cause interracial marriage to be considered a betrayal of the family heritage. Factors that increase the rates of out-group marriage include acculturation and assimilation to North American society (Kitano, Fujino, & Sato, 1998) and dissatisfaction among Asian women with the gender hierarchy of traditional Asian cultures (Kitano et al., 1998).

Worldviews Relative to the Family and Extended Relationships

The collectivistic values characteristic of many Asian Americans also have a large impact on identity and sense of the self, which differ markedly from typical Western self-perceptions (Landrine, 1992; Markus & Kitayama, 1991). The Western view of "self" assumes that people are completely independent and separate from others, whereas the Asian view of "self" emphasizes social influences, with each person defined in relation to others. Sense of self, particularly in first generation immigrants, is strongly tied to family and ethnic groups (Sodowsky, Kwan, & Pannu, 1995). With so much of psychotherapy predicated on the Western perspective of self, it is not surprising that therapy dropout rates are so high for Asian American clients. Enmeshment, codependence, lack of individuation, social anxiety, and other psychopathological labels are frequently given erroneously to this group by practitioners who impose the Western conceptualization of self onto the behavior of Asian Americans.

Holistic cognitive orientations, which emphasize interrelationships and interconnectedness, also clearly influence the perceptions of many Asian Americans. Compared to other groups, Asians are highly context-sensitive, attending to the whole environment rather than to its focal features (Ji, Peng, & Nisbett, 2000; Tsai, 1999). Additionally, they are more inclined toward dialectical thinking, the "cognitive tendency toward acceptance of contradiction" (Peng & Nisbett, 2000, p. 742). They are able to deal with contradictions by compromising and finding truth in two contradictory ideas, rather than insisting upon only one correct premise. For example, Morris and Peng (1994) found that Chinese individuals process behavior using situational factors, preserving contextual information in their mental representations and simulating counterfactual situations in addressing problem situations, which results emphasize to the salience of context, audience, and dialectic thinking. The Asian worldview, whereby attention is directed toward the environment rather than inward to the self, has important implications for cognitively oriented practitioners, in that highly context-specific problem formulations and dialectic thinking that encourage compromises in conflict resolution can be used by the therapist in treatment.

Similarly, the holistic thinking of Asian philosophies is counter to the mind-body dualism of Western thinking. Asian languages typically blend descriptors of psychological experiences with physical body sensations. Moreover, excessive emotions are believed to endanger both relationships with others and one's own physical well-being (Hsu, 1983). Asians may therefore voice mental illness in somatic terms, and their children may monitor physical symptoms and communicate with somatic representations, which poses problems for Western practitioners, who are unaccustomed to working with somatic complaints as indicators of mental distress. This tendency also creates difficulty in Asian American families, where older generations call for help indirectly or somatically, but their more Westernized children require more verbal and explicit descriptions of mental health problems than elders are able to provide.

In sum, East-West cultural differences involve collectivism/interdependence versus individualism/autonomy, hierarchical versus egalitarian structures, indirectness versus emotional expressiveness, holistic integration versus separation of mind, body, and spirit, an interconnected versus separated sense of self, and a sense of belonging to a small nuclear family versus an extended clan, including a web of past ancestors and yet-to-be-born progeny. For Asian Americans, these cultural conflicts and tensions take place as much in the family as they do within the individual, and they continue to present in various forms across generations as accultarative forces that vary in their effects on different family members.

Age and Cohort Issues

Adolescents and Young Adults

Asian American adolescents and young adults face cultural challenges in the developmental issues of establishing their identity, establishing a career of some kind, and choosing a partner. In identity development, they must navigate the powerful cross pressures to adhere to more traditional family and cultural traditions and to become "more American." The question "Who am I?" is often quite a different issue to Asian American youth than it was for their parents. Table 1 shows the dominant frameworks for conceptualizing the development of Asian American ethnic identity. All three frameworks listed assume that an identity acknowledging and integrating both ethnic and majority cultures results in optimal psychological well-being and functioning (Phinney, Cantu, & Kurtz, 1997). In some ways, the ambivalence and, at times, hostility often observed among Asian American youth toward their ethnicity and culture may be considered "rational" and normal in view of the bicultural pressures and demands usually experienced by these youth.

It is important that mental health professionals help them work through filial piety/individuation and other differential acculturation-accelerated conflicts (e.g., overt expression of emotions and caring vs. emotional self-restraint, asserting one's opinion and needs vs. deference and respect for elders, promoting oneself vs. modesty and self-effacement), enabling them to leave treatment with a better integrated answer to their "Who am I?" question, irrespective of the presenting problem.

Another stressor commonly experienced by Asian American youth is the enormous pressure they feel to excel academically. The Chinese, like many other Asian groups, have a long tradition of academic aspirations for their children, dating back to the centuries-old Mandarin system (Lam, Chan, & Leff, 1995). This parental emphasis on work ethic and academic achievement is reinforced by the reality that many Asian American youth are excluded or discouraged from pursuing other avenues of achievement (Sue & Okazaki, 1990). In addition, the "American Model Minority" myth can often marginalize this group as docile, hard working, and upwardly mobile—respected but disliked (Lin & Fiske, unpublished manuscript). Given these circumstances, many Asian American youth feel that they have little choice but to excel in academics, and they see scholastic failure as unacceptable personally and as a major disappointment to the family.

Table 1 Models of Ethnic Identity and/or Ethnic Identity Development

Racial/Cultural Identity Development Model (R/CID) (Sue & Sue, 1990)	
Stage 1	Conformity—individual rejects ethnic identity in favor of host culture
Stage 2	Dissonance—individual begins to question their initial rejection of their ethnic group
Stage 3	Resistance & Immersion—individual completely identifies with Asian American culture, actively rejecting the host culture
Stage 4	Introspection—individual questions their complete immersion in their ethnic culture, and begins search for self-identity
Stage 5	Integrative Awareness—individual is secure in ethnic identity and appreciates other racial/ethnic groups
Tse's (1999) Stage Model of Ethnic Identity Development	
Stage 1	Ethnic unawareness—individual is unaware of minority status
Stage 2	Ethnic ambivalence/evasion—individual actively distances self from ethnic group; adopts the host group culture
Stage 3	Ethnic emergence—individual realizes that joining the ethnic group is not possible, and begins to seek other affiliations
Stage 4	Ethnic identity incorporation—individual joins their ethnic minority group
Phinney's (1989) Model of Ethnic Identity Development	
Stage 1	Diffusion/Foreclosure—individual does little exploration of ethnic identity
Stage 2	Moratorium—individual engages in active ethnic identity search, increased awareness about the importance of ethnicity
Stage 3	Identity achieved—individual has come to terms with their ethnic identity and emerges identified with their ethnic group

Elderly

Elderly Asian Americans face very different problems from the youth. They experience developmentally related losses of their parental, work, marital, and other roles (Merton, 1957). Moreover, aging in a culturally incongruent society exacerbates these losses. Traditionally the elderly are revered and respected in Asian countries; traditions of filial piety dictate that elderly parents' children fulfill their needs, care for them, treat them with reverence, and obey their wishes and plans (Hines, Garcia-Preto, McGoldrick, Almeida, & Weltman, 1992). If Americanized adult children do not fulfill these obligations and expectations, the personal and cultural incongruencies that elderly Asian Americans feel can lead to increasing tension, conflict, and dysphoria (Kim, Hurh, & Kim, 1993). Among people age 75 and older in San Francisco during 1987–1996, 20 percent of suicides were committed by Asian Americans, a rate disproportionately higher than that of other ethnic groups (Shiang, 1998).

Refugees and Recent Immigrants

There is a clear contrast in the circumstances of refugees versus immigrants (Matsuoka, 1990). While immigrants voluntarily left their native lands to pursue better opportunities or reunite with loved ones in North America, refugees were forced to abandon their homes and seek safety elsewhere. Asian refugees, particularly those from Southeast Asia, have typically experienced significant and protracted trauma involving persecution or genocidal campaigns, torture or containment as prisoners of war, abrupt severance from ancestral homelands, rupture of extended kinship networks, loss of family members, often through traumatic events, and protracted family separation or long stays in crowded refugee camps en route to this country (Matsuoka, 1990; Nicholson & Kay, 1999). As a group, refugees are typically burdened with more mental health problems and have fewer resources than other Asian immigrants for coping with the continuing stresses of adjusting to their new environment.

Recent or new immigrants from Asia vary widely in education, income, and country of origin, but all experience some degree of acculturative stress as they struggle to adjust to their new environment, find employment, enter schools, and learn English. Western education, employment, urbanization, and settlement patterns, along with changes in socialization practices and pressures to conform to the Western culture, are just a few of the many new stressors that may be encountered when adapting to American culture (Sodowsky, Lai, & Plake, 1991). Settling in a densely Asian community can provide supports for traditional structures and values but can correspondingly diminish the speed of adaptive acculturation. In any case, new immigrant families often must work long hours, isolating themselves from local culture and practices (Lam et al., 1995). The immigrant wife who works outside the home may help relieve financial stress on the family but augment other difficulties by inadvertently undermining the patriarchal family structure. Commonly, immigrant children become English-fluent faster than their parents, thereby becoming the primary interpreters and culture brokers, further destabilizing the traditional family system.

Experience as an Ethnic Minority

Asian Americans are oftentimes the targets of racism in its various forms. This country's long history of anti-Asian legislation (exclusionary acts, the internment of the Japanese Americans during World War II, anti-miscegenation laws, etc.) reflects the fact that Asian Americans have not been seen as Americans, but as foreigners. Ying, Lee, and Tsai (2000) found that racial discrimination decreases subjective competence ratings for both foreign-born and U.S.-born Chinese Americans, with this effect being stronger for the latter. These researchers hypothesize that immigrants, retaining psychological attachment to their native culture, may be more able to distance or buffer themselves from discrimination than are persons of Asian descent who are born in the United States. American-born Asian Americans, though in their home country, must repeatedly confront the question "*Where are you from?*" which implies foreign status. For Asian Americans, being accepted as American is considered "achieved and provisional, rather than taken-for-granted and stable" (Kibria, 2000). Research indicates that racial discrimination produces the same psychological and physical stress effects that other psychosocial stressors do (Williams, Spencer, & Jackson, 1999), and mental health practitioners should anticipate the additional issues that Asian clients may bring to therapy concerning their place in this society that often involve their experiences of marginalization, alienation, and discrimination.

Gender Issues

Traditionally, Asian societies have well-defined social roles, especially in the context of family (Marsella, 1993; Uba, 1994; Sue, 1999). Social roles across genders are no exception. Although there is a trend toward increasing gender equality, Asian cultures tend to encourage men and women to hold different responsibilities and to abide by rules of conduct that emphasize social stability over individual rights. For East Asian societies such as those found in China, Korea and Japan, Confucian teachings have strictly differentiated proper behavior for each sex (Hong et al., 1993).

"The most beautiful and gifted girl is not so desirable as a deformed boy" (Hong, Yamamoto, Chang, & Lee, 1993) reflects the traditional preeminence and perceived desirability of boys, who are needed to carry on the family name and perform necessary family rituals. With a legacy of male favoritism, it is not surprising that even today implicit expectations for boys and girls can be very unequal. Among Asian Americans, eldest sons (as well as individuals with no siblings) may feel special pressure to carry on the family line (L. Nguyen. & Peterson, 1992; N. A. Nguyen & Williams, 1989), succeed economically (Espiritu, 1999), and become caretakers of aging parents (Sue, 2001). This dutiful familial role is at odds with the freewheeling, independent, "own-man" image of American masculinity and career success (Sue, 1999). Therefore, Asian American men may present with conflicts over family responsibility and obligations versus the emphasis on autonomy, overt masculinity, and self-reliance that characterizes male behavior in American society. Historically, Asian daughters have been devalued, expected to be obedient and modest, and perceived as belonging to their future husband's household (Morrow, 1989; Lee & Cynn, 1991). Strict adherence to these values is now rare among modern Asian American households, but the tendency to be more liberal with sons than with daughters often persists. Less acculturated parents typically grant less social freedom to daughters than they would to sons. If women marry, they are usually expected to subordinate their personal agendas and careers to those of their spouses and to share the husband's family responsibilities, including taking care of the parents-in-law in their old age. If husbands spend most of their time away from home, care of elderly in-laws can become solely the daughter-in-law's responsibility. Many Asian American women feel caught in competing cross-pressures to defer to their husbands and take care of in-laws, while being assertive and independent achievers in the context of American society.

Homosexual and transgender Asians and Asian Americans may experience emotional distress compounded by a cultural heritage emphasizing family (Baytan, 2000). Research aimed at describing the experiences of these individuals is needed. Because many Asian cultures are family-based and do not have acceptable models for different lifestyles, lesbian and gay individuals may understandably feel the need to hide their sexuality from their families in order to avoid both personal rejection and family shame. In addition, most Asian cultures do not openly discuss issues of sexuality. Therefore, the idea of "coming out" is not likely to be a familiar concept. Consequently, there may be few social supports for individuals experiencing the double jeopardy of being both an ethnic and sexual minority.

Spiritual Beliefs, Values, and Practices

Hundreds, if not thousands, of religions are practiced in Asia (Central Intelligence Agency, 2001). For more than 2,000 years, the elements of Confucianism, Buddhism, Taoism, Hinduism, animism, and shamanism have blended to yield some main principles as well as a host of alternative belief systems and attendant alternative therapies. Even though some Asian immigrants bring a tradition of Christianity with them from their country of origin or convert to Christianity after arriving in North America, the underlying beliefs, values, and philosophies of their earlier religious traditions continue to exert powerful and inchoate influences on them (Tan & Dong, 2000).

Unlike the Confucian doctrine of righteous action and moral codes of conduct, Buddhism prescribes a program of passive acceptance, detachment from desire, and meditation. A Buddhist believes that only by extinguishing one's personal desires and attachments can suffering be overcome and the spiritual self liberated and fully awakened. The Buddhist practice of meditation to elicit "evenly hovering attention" is compatible with the here-and-now "mindfulness" of some humanistic treatments, such as gestalt approaches, and with certain cognitive-behavioral approaches (Finn & Rubin, 2000).

Taoism emphasizes the inseparability of the body, psyche, and spirit, as well as a connection with nature through quiet reflection, balanced diet, breathing techniques, and disciplined living to promote health and longevity. It is the basis of traditional Chinese medicine, which provides a variety of cures to ailments attributed to an imbalance of the social or physical world (Unschuld, 1985). *Feng shui,* a form of geomancy addressing physical environmental factors, and *tai chi chuan,* a martial art form combining physical exercise and mental discipline, are two of the derivatives. The worldviews of many Asian Americans incorporate the complementary forces of *yin* and *yang,* and of *chi,* one's life energy. Many Taoist concepts are making their way into a variety of new Asian-influenced alternative approaches to restoring and maintaining well-being that are beginning to coalesce in North America.

Hinduism, originating in the Indian subcontinent, posits numerous gods and goddesses, is reflected in numerous rituals, prescribes yoga as a spiritual path, and explains the development of a soul through karma and reincarnation. Karma is inherently a belief in one's personal responsibility—"as a man sows, so shall he reap," if not in this lifetime then in the next—and in the essential fairness of life (Sharma, 2000).

Animism, the oldest spiritual tradition worldwide, deifies nature in spirit forms that can then be worshipped and interacted with symbolically. Illnesses can result from malevolent or displeased spirits, sometimes sent by other people casting a curse or spell (Unschuld, 1985). Rituals to appease or distract the spirits are prescribed, often involving the actual or symbolic sacrifice of an animal or object in exchange for the nature spirit's release of the sick person's spirit. Shamanism is closely related to animism. The human and spirit worlds are held to be linked, such that disturbance in one creates disturbance in the other, and problem solving in one brings peace in the other (Vitebsky, 1995). Shamans, chosen by the spirits (Howard, 1998), may manifest their spiritual calling through hearing voices, speaking in tongues, having a physical or mental anomaly, or possessing an unusual ability to communicate with animals or read the signs of nature. They are both celebrated and marginalized in their own society. Shamanism is widespread in Asia, particularly among people marginalized from the official power structure: individuals from rural areas, women, and ethnic minorities (K. Howard, personal communication, March 18, 1999).

Together, the strains of Confucianism, Buddhism, Taoism, Hinduism, animism, and shamanism have woven an almost countless number of specific cults across the vast continent of Asia, most of which identify afflictions along with their etiologies and remedies. Asian spiritual beliefs emphasize the centrality of family and clan, the place of individuals in a larger cosmos, the spiritual connection with deceased ancestors as a link to the spirit world, and a holistic view of body, mind, and spirit. Beyond this, the therapist must tactfully probe for spiritual and culture-specific explanations of the manifest symptoms and attendant culture-prescribed remedies.

Culture-bound syndromes, symptom clusters that are identified and mediated in particular cultural contexts, may sometimes be observed in Asian clients, particularly if they are immigrants from rural areas. Table 2 shows some of the better-documented Asian culture-bound syndromes, although there are many others not yet commonly seen in the West. These syndromes can only be understood by viewing their etiologies and symptom manifestations from a spiritual and culturally relativistic perspective.

View of Mental Health Professions

By tradition, Asian Americans see mental health problems as shameful—reflecting moral weakness in the individual and family, disgracing ancestors and future generations, and resulting from the past sins by family members. Families often shield mentally ill members from the public to save face and to avoid shame and stigma. Many only seek outside help as a last resort in acute stages (Zane & Sue, 1996). Moreover, many Asian Americans conceptualize mental illness very differently from views of mental health professionals. Many Western forms of psychotherapy require (a) a separation of mental from physical problems in symptoms, causes, and cures, which can be at odds with Asian holistic approaches; (b) a level of self-disclosure that offends notions of privacy

Table 2 Asian Culture-Bound Syndromes

Name in English	*Asian Names*	*Endemic Area*	*Cultural Explanation*	*Symptoms*
Divine Illness	Shin-byung	Korea	Invasion by angry ancestral spirits onto descendants with weak constitutions, caused by improper observance of ritual.	Sense of double-facedness (*ijung-inkyukja*), persistent and sometimes acute physical pain, sleeplessness, fatigue, anxiety, sudden outbursts of anger and distress.
Penis Retraction Syndrome	Koro Suo yang Siok iong, or Shuk yang Rok-joo Jinjinia bemar	Malaysia China, Hong Kong, & Taiwan Thailand Assam	Spirit invasion, excessive masturbation.	Sudden intense fear and sensation of the penis retracting into the abdomen resulting in death; a female correlate, in which the vulva and nipples recede into the body, also exists.
Qi-gong Psychotic Reaction or Cultivation Insanity	Zho hwo ru mwo	China	Practicing *qi gong* with an unrighteous mind, resulting in spirit or animal possession and has various mentalities such as pursuing a *qi gong* state to show off.	Time-limited psychotic episode of dissociative, paranoid, or other psychotic and non-psychotic symptoms after participating in qigong (a folk health-enhancing body movement/meditative exercise).
Neurasthenia	Shenjing shuairuo Shinkei shitsu	China, Japan	Imbalance of the body, environmental stress, weak bodily constitution.	Physical and mental fatigue, dizziness, headaches, and other pains, difficulty concentrating, memory loss, sleep disturbance.
Spirit Possession	Hsieh-ping Shin-byung	Taiwan, Korea	Possession by an ancestral spirit who is trying to communicate with family members.	Tremor, delirium, visual or auditory hallucinations, disorientation; trancelike state.
Fear of Wind/Fear of Cold	Pa-feng/ Pa-leng	China	Fear of excessive *yin* energy from wind and cold.	Phobic fear of wind and cold, respectively; bundling up in warm clothes, eating "hot" foods.
No translation found	Taijin kyofusho	Japan	Over-nurturance by maternal figure.	Intense fear of offending or embarrassing others with one's body, body parts, or bodily functions; hypersensitivity of one's appearance, odor, facial expressions, and movements.

Name in English	*Asian Names*	*Endemic Area*	*Cultural Explanation*	*Symptoms*
Soul Loss	Imu Latah Amurakh, Irkunii, Ikota, Olan, Myriachit, and Menkeiti Bah-tschi, Bah-tsi, & Baah-ji Mali-mali & Silok	Japan (Ainu & Sakhalin), Malaysia, Siberia, Thailand, Philippines	Soul loss or detachment due to a sudden shocking event.	Hypersensitivity to sudden fright, dissociative or trancelike behavior, command obedience, echolalia, or echopraxia.
Anger Syndrome	Hwa-byung or wool-hwa-byung	Korea	Suppression of deep anger.	Insomnia, fatigue, panic, fear of impending death, dysphoric affect, indigestion, anorexia, dyspnea, palpitations, generalized aches and pains, and a feeling of a mass in the epigastrium.
** No translation found **	Amok	Malaysia Philippines	Being irreparably wronged.	Brooding, followed by sudden violent frenzy, ending with amnesia.
Semen-loss Syndrome	Dhat & Jiryan Sukra prameha Shen kui & Shen k'ui	India, Sri Lanka China	Loss of life energy from too much sexual intercourse, nighttime emission or masturbation; yang energy deficiency.	Dizziness, backache, headaches, mental and physical fatigue, insomnia, frequent dreams, complaints of sexual dysfunction (i.e., impotence, premature ejaculation)

and propriety in a face-conscious culture; (c) a focus on interpersonal conflict and direct confrontation, which is difficult for harmony-oriented individuals; (d) a language of emotion not always consonant with cultural cognitive and communication forms; and (e) an emphasis on individuation and pursuit of personal wants and needs in contrast to collectivistic norms and obligations emphasized by the Asian cultures. In view of these cultural incongruities between psychological treatment and Asian values and worldviews, it is not surprising that Asian Americans are relatively skeptical about the Western mental health profession, relatively unlikely to present for treatment, and relatively likely to drop out prematurely (from the therapist's point of view). Liu, Pope-Davis, Nevitt, and Toporek (1999) therefore strongly suggest that therapists consider clients' acculturation level and perceptions of mental health. Atkinson and Girn (1989) found that attitudes toward professional psychological help are directly related to acculturation, suggesting that psychological services need to be modified if immigrants are to view such help as legitimate and credible.

In addition to this wariness or skepticism, many Asian American individuals and families simply lack awareness about mental health services and their usefulness. Providers wishing to better serve Asian Americans, particularly the newer immigrants and refugees, may want to focus on alternative means of outreach—innovative arrangements with ESL programs, employers, churches, schools, medical clinics, and civic associations salient to this group, as well as outreach efforts to community elders and indigenous healers. These approaches can help establish culture-consonant and community-endorsed approaches to prevention, early detection and treatment, and community empowerment. Language-appropriate written materials, translators, and support groups are often needed.

Strategies for Counseling and Psychotherapy

The preceding discussion has addressed some of the major East-West differences the mental health practitioner should be aware of in preparing to work with Asian Americans, and it pointed to the enormous heterogeneity in this group. Next we list a number of suggestions for approaching an Asian American client or family. These strategies are tendered in the spirit of working hypotheses that can guide counseling and treatment but should not be considered as specific prescriptive courses of action. Rather, it is suggested the practitioner amend and adapt these strategies as an accurate reading of the clients and their issues may suggest alternative or even opposing approaches.

Establish Credibility and Initial Formality

Most Asian Americans have traditions of scholarship and respect for authority. The practitioner can establish initial credibility by comfortably accepting the "doctor" or "*sensei*" (esteemed teacher for Japanese) expert authority role. Demonstrating capacity for cross-cultural effectiveness and inspiring confidence in one's ability to help are of paramount importance in the critical first encounter. Use of formal names (e.g., Mrs. Huong, Dr. Lee) with correct pronunciations is suggested. It is also advisable to show distinct respect to elders and to acknowledge traditional structures by addressing husband before wife and adults before children initially. If the client bows slightly at the time of handshake or other salutation, it is courteous to reciprocate the gesture. If a business card is offered, it should be treated with the same respect that would be shown the person. If a modest gift is given, the counselor or therapist should accept it humbly to the degree possible (Yang, 1994). Particularly in the first session, decorum, dignity, and respect will be valued. Honoring the client is never inappropriate, regardless of ethnic background, but it becomes exceedingly important with face-conscious Asian American clients. It is easier to become less formal, but much harder to become more so after the initial meeting.

Permit Indirect Contextual Communication and Low Emotional Expressiveness

If clients present with a nonlinear contextual interactional style, the practitioner is advised to respect this form of communication, permit it, and indeed join in it, at least initially. This may appear as initial conversational "small talk" or even "beating around the bush" as both parties search for cues to contextualize the other (e.g., their background, acquaintances in common, familiarity with the client's culture, capacity to help). The counselor or therapist should listen for information and store it for later use, in turn using this style of communication to subtly inform the client of his or her knowledge, experience, and capacity to provide meaningful help. In this initial interaction, one should avoid unnecessarily intrusive questions and demands for high emotional expressiveness and confrontations until it appears appropriate to venture in those directions; it is good to permit silences in conversational turn taking, however difficult this may be. This is all part of high context communication. Contrary to the inscrutable stereotypes, Asian American clients typically communicate a rich amount through metaphors, subtle nonverbal language, choice of words said and not said, and the use of silence, so the counselor's challenge is to slow down, watch for issues of face and dialectic, and for holistic modes of thinking, and learn the codes of communication. This indirect, high context communication and low emotional expressiveness is most likely to be seen with more traditional and less acculturated Asian Americans, at the beginning of sessions and when focusing on particularly difficult issues.

Assess Acculturation and Ethnic Identity

Accurate assessment of acculturation level on different dimensions and of ethnic identity requires that a counselor generate hypotheses from intake information; this should be a dominant activity in the first session. Moreover, this assessment may continue on refined points and issues throughout a treatment episode. Incorrect assessment can lead to grievous albeit unwitting offenses to the client and to inappropriate, ineffective diagnosis, treatment plans, and intervention modalities. The less acculturated the Asian American client, the more salient the following guidelines will be. The more "Americanized" the client, the more the counseling can resemble that of mainstream clients, although cultural issues are still paramount even for very acculturated individuals. Lethal *faux pas* can occur if a practitioner treats an Asian American as less acculturated than the client feels he or she is (invoking "foreignness" challenges) or as more acculturated (e.g., requiring intimate disclosures, display of intense emotions, or use of confrontational strategies or lapsing into informality too early). The practitioner should remember, in assessing acculturation, that (a) it is uneven, and a client may be very American in some areas of functioning and very Asian in others; (b) it continues for at least several generations, and family members may be at different acculturative levels and issues; and (c) people cannot always report accurately on their level of acculturation, so responses to direct queries may not always be accurate and/or may reflect socially desirable biases.

In contrast to acculturation, ethnic identity refers to how individuals think of and present themselves. Referencing oneself as Chinese American, or Asian American, or Chinese, or just American indicates which group the client identifies with and may inform the therapist about the sociopolitical aspects of the client's worldview. In assessing ethnic identity, the provider will want to assess degree of "Chineseness," "Hmongness," and so on, as well as degree of "Americanness." Many highly acculturated individuals view themselves as strongly bicultural, with high proficiency in both cultures. Careful assessment of acculturation and ethnic identity is even more important when clients are racially and ethnoculturally blended individuals and families. The practitioner who is successful in these assessments will be rewarded with clients exploring with them, in time, the dilemmas and conflicts around acculturative or identity issues with which they may be involved.

Use of Interpreters

When the client cannot speak English with sufficient proficiency and an interpreter is needed, trust issues and miscommunication problems can arise. Bilingual interpreters and service providers should have training in working with service providers and vice versa. The interpreter typically sits next to the client (and sometimes just slightly behind), so the client and provider can face one another and address each other directly. This underscores the primary relationship between therapist and client, maximizes nonverbal communication between them, and minimizes the diffusion and distortion in communication and relationship-building inherent in adding a third party. When speaking, the counselor or therapist should address the client: "When did these problems begin, Mr. Lee?" is preferable to "Ask him when these problems began." Interpreters should translate literally, resisting the temptation to impose lay or personal understandings onto the material they translate, thereby introducing an unknown personal bias into the discussion. For example, "I drank lemon grass tea and tried Chi Gung again for a while, but the pains kept getting worse and my son insisted I come here" is more informative than "He hasn't had any psychological treatment before." Accurate interpretation can at least double the time for assessment or a treatment session. Although it is clearly resource intensive, utilizing a professional interpreter is preferred to using a bilingual family member, because of the likely distortions and other dynamics related to family shame and face saving.

Honor Face and Face Saving

Maintenance of face and avoiding loss of face can be an important dynamic in effective relationships between Asian American clients and their practitioners. Face issues are implicated in many different aspects of treatment for Asian Americans. For example, studies have shown that loss of face is negatively related to self-disclosure in treatment situations, especially when the client discloses about his or her most intimate relationships. Moreover, differences in a person's preference for different treatment approaches (i.e., directive vs. nondirective approach) can be better explained by loss of face than by a competing model based on differential treatment expectations between Asians and Whites (Zane & Mak, 2003). Dignifying the client, normalizing rather than pathologizing, positively framing and reframing, emphasizing strengths and skill building rather than deficits, etc., are all useful with face-conscious clients. In addition, in keeping with the social sense of self of many Asian Americans, face presentation and maintenance concerns are common in issues brought to therapy.

How can the newly unemployed immigrant father save face in his community when he is now financially dependent on his daughter? How can the family accept the unorthodox career or marriage choice or sexual orientation of their firstborn son without losing face in their church or neighborhood? In the contextual Asian worldview, actions are judged within a specific situation and as seen from the perspective of salient others. For example, if a couple with marital difficulties presents with a list of the ways in which they cope, this list can be elaborated and commended, using positive frames, postponing the direct focus on undisclosed dysfunctions until the couple becomes more trusting and familiar with the therapist. Perceived denial, minimization, internal inconsistencies, poor role performances, and conflicts within the family can indeed be addressed, but the practitioner is advised to use tact and diplomacy, capitalizing on Asian capacities with metaphors, dialectical thinking, and high context communication where possible, to ensure that face remains honored.

Emphasize Structured, Directive, and Goal-Directed Problem Solving

Many Asian Americans may respond well to directive, structured, problem-focused approaches, especially at the beginning of treatment (Root, 1985; Tan & Dong, 2000). Worldviews and styles of communication, thinking, and perceiving that are potentially disparate, along with face-related concerns, create an unfamiliar situation for the client who is in therapy in which the stimulus field is potentially too open, with too much room for misunderstanding and miscommunication regarding what is expected and what is acceptable. Firm, goal-directed structure and leadership from the practitioner can reduce the ambiguity and face threat in this situation. For example, Kim (1993) advocates a directive approach emphasizing the practitioner's authority, expertise, and knowledge when working with Korean clients. In addition, for the many Asian American clients who often present with major somatic discomfort (e.g., chest pain, headache, breathing difficulty) rather than more psychological symptoms, framing the therapeutic interaction in a formal medical model and treating somatic complaints directly before addressing the associated situational, emotional, and social problems is recommended (Kinzie & Leung, 1993). While certainly some relatively Westernized Asian Americans will seek out reflective, nondirective, open-ended process-oriented therapies, this will not be the preferred mode of intervention for most of this clientele. Indeed, if psychoanalysis is attempted in a language in which the client is not fully proficient, the analyst should expect significant transference associated with whether the immigrant is idealizing or retreating from the new country, its language, and its providers (Litjmaer, 1999). Practitioners are advised to be explicit, by the end of the first session where possible, in describing the treatment plan—the specific goal and time frame, along with what will be required of the client, what procedures will be like, and what research supports those procedures. Structure, directiveness, and problem-focused approaches enhance the practitioner's credibility and the client's hope and comfort, increasing the chances of return visits.

Emphasize the Family Context

Family treatment should be very carefully implemented when working with Asian American clients. In family-based treatment, it is important to acknowledge traditional authority lines in ways that are sensitive to participating members. When an intergenerational conflict between individualist and collectivist values presents, it is advisable to couch it first from the collectivist stance as a way of recognizing the family as a whole. The more "Westernized" younger clients will likely recognize and respond positively to approaches that assume caring, wisdom, and authority from the older cohort. Reassured elders will then be more comfortable supporting their children's pursuits.

The power of Asian American families when they mobilize to support changes in individual or family functioning cannot be overstated. The practitioner should cast a wide net in determining the family system, since some recently immigrated families have key members still back in the home country, whose presence is still felt in a very immediate sense. Other families may keep a shrine in the home for deceased family members, on which they regularly place offerings—again reflecting the very real referred presence of another's influence on the current family dynamics. Even when the family therapy modality is not used, familial relationships and issues of collective face are still likely to surface in the counseling or treatment transactions.

Employ Spiritual Resources

Cultural consonance and efforts to work within the client's spiritual worldview enhance the credibility, attractiveness, and effectiveness of the treatment plan. For example, a colleague who uses biofeedback successfully for Asian Americans with anxiety disorders sometimes engages them first in a discussion of "chi" enhancement and alignment. Christian Asian American clients prefer Christian practitioners (Misumi, 1993; Tan & Dong, 2000), and will likely respond favorably to referencing Christian values and beliefs. American-born contemplative Buddhists may find cognitive behavioral and humanistic approaches which focus on "mindfulness" quite attractive and consonant with their meditation practices; they may actually be disproportionately involved in these forms of therapy (Finn & Rubin, 2000).

Exploration of the religious and spiritual aspects of the Asian American client often yields important material for therapy. Is the Japanese American's "it can't be helped" (*"shi kata ga nai"*) attitude using the passive acceptance of Buddhist teachings in a positive or negative way? Is the Asian Indian American using the concept of karma to accept or to avoid personal accountability and responsibility? Does the Chinese American's Taoist perspective suggest treatment goals that are couched in terms of balance, or seem compatible with incorporation of meditation or use of a *tai chi* or *chi gung* group as an adjunct to treatment? Are the behaviors of the recent immigrant from a rural outer island in the Philippines in fact a culture-bound syndrome, not psychiatric but spiritual in etiology and remedy? Many American-born contemplative Buddhists are articulate about their beliefs and choice of spiritual leader (Finn & Rubin, 2000), and it is appropriate to explore these significant resources for growth or problem resolution efforts.

Therapists working with Asian American clients will want to be able to identify and access as needed the rich assortment of monks, priests, ministers, shamans, healers, and spiritual teachers their clients look to—sometimes as consultants, sometimes as referral sources or referrals, sometimes for adjunctive roles in treatment. Therapists will also want to remain alert to the potentially beneficial practices of their Asian American clients' spiritual systems (e.g., meditation, yoga, martial arts, and other mental-physical practices) and be able to work alongside these practices synergistically, from a holistic perspective where possible.

Enhance Own Cultural Understandings and Cultural Connections

There is a large and growing body of knowledge available about the many facets of Asian American subpopulations and their experiences and worldviews. Mental health practitioners can increase their understanding of these various subgroups by mastering not only the professional literature but also the growing body of autobiographies, nonfiction accounts, and fictional novels and stories by Asian American authors or about Asian American subjects. Films, plays, and other lively arts also can enhance cultural understandings for the interested learner. Participating in activities of the local Asian American community and joining community groups that attract Asian Americans are other useful and productive ways of gaining greater insights into (and comfort with) cultural practices, forms of communication, and worldviews. This kind of learning by cultural immersion appears to enhance cultural understandings in qualitatively different ways. Bicultural individuals in a mainstream setting behave in accord with the mainstream norms, but behave quite differently in settings where they are the majority, so immersion in those ethnic community settings usually affords rich new perspectives and enhanced multicultural competencies. Community connections also provide the treatment adjuncts, referral sources, cultural materials, and cultural consultants so important for those who serve the culturally diverse.

Enhance Both Asian and American Connections of Client

Asian Americans experience the mixed blessing of biculturalism, each in his or her own way at any given time. Rarely do they seek treatment for bicultural or ethnic identity issues per se, but rather for managing their problems at work, their relationships and health, and the other problems of living. However, because issues of biculturalism, acculturative dynamics, and ethnic identity evolution seem forever part of the substrate, the practitioner might consider setting ancillary goals regarding improved identity alignment and enhanced empowerment in connections with both the mainstream American culture and organizations and the ethnic Asian ones. Outcomes may be measured as improved self-efficacy, greater comfort in declaring one's identity, greater ease in navigating across cultures, stronger connections with both mainstream and ethnic community organizations and values, or comfort in taking more leadership as a bridge person of sorts. It is our experience that when counseling or psychotherapy with Asian Americans is successful, this is an unsought but nonetheless significant benefit. The following case examples illustrate some of the strategies that have been discussed.

Case Examples

Roles, Obligations, Face, and Grief

David Uyemoto is the hospital liaison to the four grown children of Mrs. Watanabe, a 95-year-old Japanese American who came to the United States as a picture bride, was long ago widowed, and has recently declined rapidly from Alzheimer's disease. Uyemoto's job is to help the children attend their mother's last days and make necessary decisions. These children are well-educated professionals with a 30-year age spread, acculturated in varying degrees. Only the two eldest speak Japanese; the women have out-married; and the youngest has divorced. Now they are arriving from all corners of the country.

At the family's request, Uyemoto holds several family counseling sessions around issues of who will pay for what expense, when to stop applying unusual life-saving means, and what kind of funeral *"Okasan"* would want. In these sessions, the traditional duty of the eldest son clashes with pragmatics—some younger daughters are better informed and more skilled in performing the executive and case managerial duties that are his by tradition. Power issues surface: Should sons, particularly the eldest one, have greater decision-making power, or should the family function as a simple democracy? Japanese family dynamics of guilt and obligation become apparent. The siblings quarrel softly and obtusely about issues of filial piety: Who has done what to support *Okasan* and be there for her, along the way and at the end? The discussion about the funeral centers on what "a good Japanese" funeral would be like, but disagreements of what "Japaneseness" means reflect the acculturative heterogeneity within the sibling group. Mrs. Watanabe was Buddhist for most of her life, but had begun attending services and social events at the nearby Japanese Methodist church, where Japanese was spoken.

Dr. Uyemoto presides over the Watanabe children's decision-making sessions, staying task-focused and directing the group's discussion, while probing the different perspectives of the children. The reunited siblings interact intensely outside of their sessions with Uyemoto, grateful for the privacy to work through, outside of his presence, the intimate family matters of mourning, filial piety, and sibling rivalry, and to define what being "Japanese" and "American" mean to them as they confront the loss of *Okasan*, the most Japanese of them.

For the third anniversary of Mrs. Watanabe's death, the time of ascent to Buddhist heaven, the siblings contract Dr. Uyemoto to preside over their reunion, although none of them is a practicing Buddhist. Here the discussion covers their evolved sense of what being Japanese American means, their mourning and recovery, and their appreciation to Uyemoto for managing their journey together in such a fruitful and healing way.

Cultural Adaptations in Crisis and Mourning

The local Refugee Resettlement program calls Ann Lorenzo to attend a crisis. An eight-year-old Hmong boy has hung himself. Lorenzo drives to the public housing project where the family lives and sits on the floor of the cramped living room with a translator, the parents, and some younger children. The conversation does not much resemble a typical psychotherapy session with mainstream clients. Family members seem transfixed with fear, unable to keep from glancing to the corner where the boy has hung himself with an electric cord. They talk about "ghosts" (per the translator), and want more than anything to change dwellings, to switch to a different unit in the project. The young translator is clearly embarrassed, calls them superstitious, and notes what his supervisor has told him—that this is not possible, given the housing rules.

In this difficult situation, Lorenzo develops the family's trust in three ways. She attends the boy's funeral in the town's Paupers Field. She successfully intervenes with the public housing authority to have the family moved to a different unit. She finds shamans in the local Hmong community and elicits the family's agreement that they be put in touch with each other. Later she learns that several sessions of shamanistic rituals have occurred to banish destructive spirits, and the family is at peace that their young child is safely home in their ancestral spirit world.

Lorenzo later meets with the family three more times. In these sessions, working with the same translator, she helps connect the father with a maintenance job, compliments the younger children for their growing grasp of English and exhorts them to help and obey their parents, and focuses extensively on the mother, who is deteriorating, complaining of incapacitating headaches, refusing to learn English, and remaining very disconnected from the extant Hmong community. Lorenzo recruits a kind and solicitous Hmong woman in the ESL program to serve as a volunteer sponsor, and this volunteer befriends the disconsolate mother, bringing her herbal headache remedies and inducting her to the ESL program. The client becomes a regular member of the Hmong ESL program, developing friendship supports in the community while learning English. Over time her headaches cease.

The typical issues of mourning the boy's death were never part of the therapy directly presided upon by Lorenzo, but instead were addressed by Lorenzo's attendance at the funeral, the introduction of the community shamans, and the recruitment of the outreach volunteers from the Hmong community. This resulted in strengthening the family and enhancing its adaptation to this new country, and it improved relations between the Hmong community and the mental health establishment.

References

Araneta, E. G. (1993). Psychiatric care of Filipino Americans. In A. C. Gaw (Ed.), *Culture, ethnicity, and mental illness* (pp. 377–411). Washington, DC: American Psychiatric Press, Inc.

Armas, G. C. (2001). Asian population jumps across country [Electronic version]. *The Detroit News,* Retrieved August 8, 2001, from http://detnews.com/2001/census/0103/09/197658.htm

Atkinson, D. R., & Gim, R. H. (1989). Asian-American cultural identity and attitudes toward mental health services. *Journal of Counseling Psychology, 36*(2), 209–212.

Banerjee, N. (2001, May 17–23). Census releases data on Asian subgroups. *Asian Week,* p. 8.

Baytan, R. (2000). Sexuality, ethnicity and language: Exploring Chinese Filipino male homosexual identity. *Culture, Health and Sexuality, 2*(4), 391–404.

Central Intelligence Agency. (2001). *World factbook.* Retrieved August 10, 2001, from http://www.cia.gov/cia/publications/factbook/index.html

Ching, J. W. J., McDermott, J. F., Fukunaga, C., Yanagida, E., Mann, E., & Waldron. J. A. (1995). Perceptions of family values and roles among Japanese Americans: Clinical considerations. *American Journal of Orthopsychiatry, 65*(2), 216–224.

Columbia Encyclopedia, Sixth Edition. (2001). Asia. *Bartleby.com,* Retrieved February 25, 2002, from http://www.bartleby.com/65/as/Asia.html

Espiritu, Y. L. (1999). Gender and labor in Asian immigrant families. *American Behavioral Scientist, 42,* 628–634.

Finn. M., & Rubin, J. B. (2000). Psychotherapy with Buddhists. In P. C. Richards & A. E. Bergin (Eds.), *Handbook of psychotherapy and religious diversity* (pp. 317–340). Washington, DC: American Psychological Association.

Hines, P. M., Garcia-Preto, N., McGoldrick, M., Almeida, R., & Weltman, S. (1992). Intergenerational relationships across cultures. *Families in Society, 73*(6), 323–338.

Hong, W., Yamamoto, J., Chang, D. S., & Lee, F. (1993). Sex in a Confucian society. *Journal of the American Academy of Psychoanalysis, 21,* 405–419.

Howard, K. (1998). *Korean shamanism: revivals, survivals, and change.* Seoul, Korea: Royal Asiatic Society, Korea Branch, Seoul Press.

Hsu, J. (1983). Asian family interaction patterns and their therapeutic implications. *International Journal of Family Psychiatry, 4,* 307–320.

Isomura, T., Fine., S., & Lin, T. (1987). Two Japanese families: A cultural perspective. *Canadian Journal of Psychiatry, 32,* 282–286.

Ji, L. J., Peng, K., & Nisbett, R. E. (2000). Culture, control, and perception of relationships in the environment. *Journal of Personality & Social Psychology, 78,* 943–955.

Kibria, N. (2000). Race, ethnic options, and ethnic binds: Identity negations of second-generation Chinese and Korean Americans. *Sociological Perspectives, 43*(1), 77–95.

Kim, K. C., Hurh, W. M., & Kim, S. (1993). Generation differences in Korean immigrants' life conditions in the United States. *Sociological Perspectives, 36*(3), 257–270.

Kim, L. I. C. (1993). Psychiatric care of Korean Americans. In A. C. Gaw (Ed.), *Culture, ethnicity, and mental illness* (pp. 347–375). Washington, DC: American Psychiatric Press, Inc.

Kinzie, J. D., & Leung, P. K. (1993). Psychiatric care of Indochinese Americans. In A. C. Gaw (Ed.), *Culture, ethnicity, and mental illness* (pp. 281–304). Washington DC: American Psychiatric Press.

Kitano, H. H. L., Fujino, D. C., & Sato, J. T. (1998). Interracial marriages: Where are the Asian Americans and where are they going? In L. C. Lee & N. W. S. Zane (Eds.), *Handbook of Asian American psychology* (pp. 233–260). Thousand Oaks, CA: Sage Publications.

KTVU/Fox 2 and Associated Press. (2001). CA's population soars [Electronic version]. *Baysinsider.com.* Retrieved July 26, 2001, from http://www.bayinsider. com/news/2001/05/24/census.html

Lam, D. H., Chan, N., & Leff, J. (1995). Family work for schizophrenia: Some issues for Chinese immigrant families. *Journal of Family Therapy, 17*(3), 281–297.

Landrine, H. (1992). Clinical implications of cultural differences: The referential versus the indexical self. *Clinical Psychology Review, 12*(4), 401–415.

Lee, E. (1989). Assessment and treatment of Chinese-American immigrant families. *Journal of Psychotherapy and the Family, 6*(1–2), 99–122.

Lee, J., & Cynn, V. (1991). Issues in counseling 1.5 generation Korean Americans. In C. Lee & B. Richardson (Eds.), *Multicultural issues in counseling: New approaches to diversity* (pp. 127–140). Alexandria, VA: American Association for Counseling and Development.

Lin, K. M., Miller, M. H., Poland, R. E., Nuccio, L., & Yamaguchi. (1991). Ethnicity and family involvement in the treatment of schizophrenic patients. *Journal of Nervous & Mental Disease, 179*(10), 631–633.

Lin, M. H., & Fiske, S. T. (in press). Attitudes toward Asian Americans: Developing a prejudice scale.

Litjmaer, R. M. (1999). Language shift and bilinguals: Transference and counter-transference implications. *Journal of the American Academy of Psychoanalysis, 27,* 611.

Liu, W. M., Pope-Davis, D. B., Nevitt, J., & Toporek, R. L. (1999). Understanding the function of acculturation and prejudicial attitudes among Asian Americans. *Cultural Diversity and Ethnic Minority Psychology, 5*(4), 317–328.

Markus, H. R., & Kitayama, S. (1991). Culture and self: Implications for cognition, emotion, and motivation. *Psychological Review, 98*(2), 224–253.

Marsella, A. J. (1993). Counseling and psychotherapy with Japanese Americans: cross-cultural considerations. *American Journal of Orthopsychiatry, 63*(2), 200–208.

Matsuoka, J. K. (1990). Differential acculturation among Vietnamese refugees. *Social Work, 35*(4), 341–345.

McDermott, J. R, Char, W. R, Robillard, A. B., Hsu, J., Tseng, W.-S., & Ashton, G. C. (1983). Cultural variations in family attitudes and their implications for therapy. *Journal of the American Academy of Child Psychiatry, 22*(5), 454–458.

Merton, R. K. (1957). *Social theory and social structure.* New York, NY: The Free Press.

Misumi, D. (1993). Asian-American Christian attitudes towards counseling. *Journal of Psychology and Christianity, 12,* 214–224.

Morris, M. W., & Peng, K. (1994). Culture and cause: American and Chinese attributions for social and physical events. *Journal of Personality & Social Psychology, 67* (6), 949–971.

Morrow, R. D. (1989). Southeast Asian child rearing practices: Implications for child and youth care workers. *Child & Youth Care Quarterly, 18* (4), 273–287.

Nguyen, N. A., & Williams, H. L. (1989). Transition from East to West: Vietnamese adolescents and their parents. *Journal of the American Academy of Child and Adolescent Psychiatry, 28,* 505–515.

Nguyen, L., & Peterson, C. (1992). Depressive symptoms among Vietnamese-American college students. *Journal of Social Psychology, 133,* 65–71.

Nicholson, B. L., & Kay, D. M. (1999). Group treatment of traumatized Cambodian women: A culture-specific approach. *Social Work, 44*(5), 470–479.

Peng, K., & Nisbett, R. E. (2000). Dialectical responses to questions about dialectical thinking. *American Psychologist, 55*(9), 1067–1068.

Phinney, J. S. (1989). Stages of ethnic identity development in minority group adolescents. *Journal of Early Adolescence, 9*(1–2), 34–49.

Phinney, J. S., Cantu, C., & Kurtz, D. (1997). Ethnic and American identity as predictors of self-esteem among African American, Latino, and White adolescents. *Journal of Youth and Adolescence, 26,* 165–185.

Ratliff, B. W., Moon, H. F., & Bonacci, G. A. (1978). Intercultural marriage: The Korean-American experience. *Social Casework, 59,* 221–226.

Root, M. P. P. (1985). Guidelines for facilitating therapy with Asian American clients. *Psychotherapy, 22,* 349–356.

Sharma, A. R. (2000). Psychotherapy with Hindus. In P. S. Richards & A. E. Bergin (Eds.), *Handbook of religious diversity* (pp. 341–365). Washington, DC: American Psychological Association.

Shiang, J. (1998). Does culture make a difference? Racial/ethnic patterns of completed suicide in San Francisco, CA 1987–1996 and clinical applications. *Suicide and Life-Threatening Behavior, 28*(4), 338–354.

Sodowsky, G. R. (1991). Effects of culturally consistent counseling tasks on American and international student observers' perception of counselor credibility: A preliminary investigation. *Journal of Counseling and Development, 69,* 253–256.

Sodowsky, G. R., Kwan, K.-L. K., & Pannu, R. (1995). Ethnic identity of Asians in the United States. In J. G. Ponterotto & J. Casas (Eds.), *Handbook of multicultural counseling* (pp. 123–154). Thousand Oaks, CA: Sage Publications.

Sodowsky, G. R., Lai, E. W. M., & Plake, B. S. (1991). Moderating effects of sociocultural variables on acculturation attitudes of Hispanics and Asian Americans. *Journal of Counseling and Development, 70,* 194–204.

Sue, D. (1999). Asian American masculinity and therapy: The concept of masculinity in Asian American males. In G. R. Brooks & G. E. Good (Eds.). *The new handbook of psychotherapy and counseling with men* (pp. 780–795). San Francisco, CA: Jossey-Bass.

Sue, D. W., & Sue, D. (1990). *Counseling the culturally different: Theory and practice* (2nd ed.). New York, NY: John Wiley & Sons.

Sue, S. (2001). Mental health: Culture, race, and ethnicity. *A supplement to Mental Health: A Report of the Surgeon General.* United States Department of Health and Human Services.

Sue, S., & Okazaki, S. (1990). Asian-American educational achievement: A phenomenon in search of an explanation. *American Psychologist, 45,* 913–920.

Takahashi, K. (1986). Examining the strange-situation procedure with Japanese mothers and 12-month-old infants. *Developmental Psychology,* 22(2), 265–270.

Takeuchi, S., Imahori, T. T., & Matsumoto, D. (2001). Adjustment of criticism styles in Japanese returnees to Japan. *International Journal of Intercultural Relations, 25*(3), 315–327.

Tan, S., & Dong, N. J. (2000). Psychotherapy with members of Asian American churches and spiritual traditions. In P. S. Richards & A. E. Bergin (Eds.), *Handbook of psychotherapy and religious diversity* (pp. 421–444). Washington, DC: American Psychological Association.

Tanaka, J. S., Ebrero, A., Linn, N., & Morera, O. F. (1998). Research methods: The construct validity of self identity and its psychosocial implications. In N. Zane & L. C. Lee (Eds.), *Handbook of Asian American Psychology* (pp. 21–79). Thousand Oaks, CA: Sage.

Tran, T. V. (1991). Family living arrangement and social adjustment among three ethnic groups of elderly Indochinese refugees. *International Journal of Aging & Human Development, 32*(2), 91–102.

Tsai, J. L. (1999). Culture. In D. Levinson, J. J. Ponzetti, & P. F. Jorgensen (Eds.), *Encyclopedia of human emotions, Vols. 1 & 2* (pp. 159–166). New York, NY: Macmillan Reference.

Tsai, J. L., & Levenson, R. W. (1997). Cultural influences on emotional responding: Chinese American and European American dating couples during interpersonal conflict. *Journal of Cross Cultural Psychology, 28,* 600–625.

Tse, L. (1999). Finding a place to be: Ethnic identity exploration of Asian Americans. *Adolescence, 34*(133), 121–138.

Uba, L. (1994). *Asian Americans: Personality patterns, identity, and mental health.* New York, NY: The Guilford Press.

U.S. Census Bureau. (2000). *Profile of General Demographic Statistics: 2000.* Washington, DC: U.S. Government Printing Office.

U.S. Census Bureau. (1990). *Summary of General Characteristics of Asian or Pacific Islander Persons and Households: 1990.* Washington, DC: U.S. Government Printing Office.

Unschuld, P. (1985). *Medicine in China: A history of ideas.* Berkeley: University of California Press.

Vitebsky, P. (1995). *The shaman.* 1st American ed. Boston: Little. Brown.

Warikoo, N. (2001). Asian populations leaps 71%: Metro area shops, eateries, churches attest to the influx [Electronic version]. *Detroit Free Press,* Retrieved August 8, 2001, from www.freep.com/ news/census/ casia29_20010329.htm

Williams, A., Ota, H., Giles, H., Pierson. H. D., Gallois, C., Ng, S. H., Lim, T.-S., Ryan, E. B., Somera, L., Maher, J., Cai, D., & Harwood, J. (1997). Young people's beliefs about intergenerational communication. *Communication Research, 24*(4), 370–393.

Williams, D. R., Spencer, M. S., & Jackson, J. S. (1999). Race, stress, and physical health. In R. J. Contrada and R. D. Ashmore (Eds.), *Self, social identity, and physical health* (pp. 71–100). NewYork: Oxford University Press.

Word, R. (2001). Florida's Asian population increases dramatic 77.7%. *Tcpalm.com,* Retrieved July 26, 2001, from www.tcpalm .com/news/florida/23sasian.shtml

Yang, M. M. (1994). *Gifts, favors, and banquets: The art of social relationships in China.* Ithaca, NY: Cornell University Press.

Ying, Y. W., Lee, P. A., & Tsai, J. L. (2000). Cultural orientation and racial discrimination: Predictors of coherence in Chinese American young adults. *Journal of Community Psychology, 28*(4), 427–442.

Zane, N., & Mak, W. (2003). Major approaches to the measurement of acculturation among ethnic minority populations: A content analysis and an alternative empirical strategy. In G. Marin, P. Balls Organista, & K. M. Chun (Eds.), *Acculturation: Advances in theory, measurement, and applied research* (pp. 39–60). Washington, DC: American Psychological Association.

Zane, N., & Sue, S. (1996). Health issues of Asian Pacific American adolescents. In M. Kagawa-Singer & P. A. Katz (Eds.), *Health issues for minority adolescents* (pp. 142–167). Lincoln, NE: University of Nebraska Press.

PART III

Sensitivity and Responsiveness to Consumers

Part III of the Reader focuses on the centrality of providers' sensitivity and responsiveness to consumer expectations regarding the therapeutic recovery and healing process. A sensitive and responsive mental health practitioner may need to adopt a variety of roles to meet expectations of consumers suffering from the effects of poverty, oppression, racism, and stigma. The six articles in Part III provide an entry point for providers in their journey to become more attentive to the quality of their interactions with consumers.

The first manuscript of Part III, by Neuliep (2006), provides an authoritative overview of the relationship between language and culture—paradoxically, a topic often ignored in the multicultural mental health literature. Neuliep focuses our attention on four types of verbal communication styles (direct-indirect, elaborate-succinct, personal-contextual, and instrumental-affective), an understanding of which is crucial to providing sensitive and culturally competent mental health services.

The second article by Sue et al. (2007) provides a taxonomy of racial microaggressions (i.e., slights, insults, and derogatory remarks) aimed at people of color. Intentional or unintentional negative discourse of this type will clearly impair the development of a therapeutic alliance between the client and mental health provider.

The third article by Anthony (2000) offers a set of recovery-based standards that county adult and child systems of care can use as they move from deficit-based to recovery-oriented mental health systems. A recovery orientation views consumers as capable of recovering from their mental illness. Also implied within this orientation is mental health system change that includes treatment, crisis intervention, case management, rehabilitation, enrichment, rights protection, basic support, self-help, and wellness promotion.

The fourth manuscript by Arredondo (2002) focuses our attention on the challenges of providing mental health services to historically marginalized, disenfranchised, and underserved individuals. Arredondo reminds us of the diversity of opinions and worldviews of historically marginalized people. Counseling competencies are offered to begin to address interpersonal and organizational barriers to effective mental health services with members of these groups.

The fifth manuscript by Ponterotto, Utsey, and Pedersen (2006) provides a brief and readable overview of empirical measuring instruments used to assess prejudice, cultural competence, racism-related stress, racial and ethnic identity, and multicultural personality correlates. Routinely incorporating information embodied in these measures could positively affect mental health service delivery.

The last article in Part III is by the California Network of Mental Health Clients (2000). The goal of the article is to help mental health providers become more sensitive and responsive to the culture of being a mental health client or consumer. Client issues of pervasive discrimination, stereotyping, and stigma predominate for many community mental health clients and must be countered with client empowerment and social justice advocacy.

15

The Verbal Code

Human Language

James W. Neuliep

The language faculty is a system, a subsystem of the brain . . . its major elements don't appear to exist in other similar organisms . . . to a large extent it appears to be determined by our biological endowment and is essentially invariant across the species.

—Noam Chomsky[1]

The capacity of the human brain to acquire language may be the distinguishing feature that separates humans from the rest of the living beings on the planet. Our ability to put thoughts into a code in order to communicate with someone else empowers us beyond imagination. Other living beings are larger, stronger, faster, and smaller, but no other living being has the capacity for language. Language has put humans on top of the evolutionary ladder. Because of their capacity for language, humans have become the most powerful living beings on earth. The purpose of this chapter is to explore the idea of language and how it varies across cultures. This chapter will outline the relationship between language and culture by first exploring the Sapir-Whorf hypothesis. The second part of this chapter will outline the fundamental structure of language, including a discussion of the concept of a universal grammar that applies to all languages. The third part of this chapter will look at universals of language that are shared across cultures. The fourth part of the chapter focuses on how the use of language differs across cultures, including a look at elaborate and restricted codes and cross-cultural comparisons of language style.

The Relationship Between Language and Culture

Linguist and cultural anthropologist Zdenek Salzmann points out that, historically, anthropologists and linguists often grouped language, culture, and race together as though any one of them automatically implied the other two. Contemporary linguistic anthropologists generally agree, however, that culture, race, and language are historically distinct. In other words, a person's race does not determine what language he or she will speak. However, the language of a particular culture and the thought processes of its people are closely related.[2]

Sapir-Whorf Hypothesis

In 1928, anthropologist and linguist Edward Sapir published a paper in the journal *Language* that changed the face of the study of language and culture. Sapir's thesis was that the language of a particular culture directly influences how people think. In the paper, he wrote,

> The network of cultural patterns of a civilization is indexed in the language which expresses that civilization. . . . Language is a guide to "social reality." . . . Human beings do not live in the objective world alone . . . but are very much at the mercy of the particular language which has become the medium of expression for their society.[3]

Sapir continued to argue that the ways in which people perceive the world around them, including their natural and social environments, are essentially dictated by their language. In fact, Sapir argued that the speakers of different languages see different worlds. Strongly influenced by Sapir was one of his students, Benjamin Whorf.[4] Whorf was persuaded by Sapir's writings and further developed this line of thought. In 1940, Whorf wrote,

> The background linguistic system (in other words the grammar) of each language is not merely a reproducing instrument for voicing ideas but rather is itself the shaper of ideas. . . . We dissect nature along lines laid down by our native languages.[5]

Like Sapir, Whorf believed the people who speak different languages are directed to different types of observations; therefore, they are not equivalent as observers and must arrive at somewhat different views of the world.[6] Sapir and Whorf's ideas received a great deal of attention and have become well-known as the Sapir-Whorf hypothesis. Salzmann contends that the Sapir-Whorf hypothesis delineates two principles. One is the principle of linguistic determinism, which says that the way one thinks is determined by the language one speaks. The second is the principle of linguistic relativity, which says that the differences among languages must therefore be reflected in the differences in the worldviews of their speakers. These principles raise some important issues for cross-cultural communication. If how we think is a reflection of the language we speak, then the speakers of two very different languages must think very differently. This could render effective and successful intercultural communication extremely difficult, if not insurmountable.

Salzmann and other contemporary linguists and anthropologists maintain that the Sapir-Whorf hypothesis may be a bit exaggerated. Today, most linguists believe that the vocabulary and grammar of a particular language parallel the "nonverbal" culture. In other words, the geographic, climatic, kinesic, spatial, and proxemic aspects of a culture are emphasized and accented in a culture's language. Salzmann notes, for example, that in Pintupi (one of the aboriginal languages of Australia) there are at least ten words designating various kinds of holes. Mutara is a special hole in a spear, Pulpa refers to a rabbit burrow, Makarnpa is the burrow of a monitor lizard, and Katarta is the hole left by a monitor lizard after it has broken the surface after hibernation. Moreover, linguists believe that the syntactic features of a language influence how speakers of that language categorize and mentally organize their worlds. For example, speakers of English use the personal pronoun "you" whether they are addressing one or several children, adults, old persons, subordinates, or individuals much superior in rank than themselves. Other languages operate differently. When addressing someone, speakers of Dutch, French, German, Italian, Russian, and Spanish must choose between the "familiar" personal pronoun and the "polite" personal pronoun and/or the corresponding verb form. In English, the word *teacher* refers to a person who teaches, whether it is a man or a woman. In German, *lehrer* is the masculine form of teacher and *leherin* is the feminine form. In this way, speakers of Dutch, French, German, and Italian may be more conscious of the status differences between them and another person because their language requires them to use words designating the power differential.[7]

Therefore, most linguists now believe that the users of a particular language may overlook or ignore objects or events that speakers of another language may emphasize. John B. Carroll modifies the Sapir-Whorf hypothesis by arguing that to the extent that languages differ, language users organize their experiences differently based on the vocabularies and grammars provided by their respective languages. Carroll notes that these cognitions will affect behavior.[8]

The Structure of Human Language

All languages are a systematic set of sounds, combined with a set of rules, for the sole purpose of creating meaning and communicating.[9] Any human language is made up of a set of sounds. These sounds are represented symbolically in the language's alphabet. In English, for example, there are approximately 40 sounds represented in an alphabet of 26 letters. The Korean script, called Hangul, consists of 16 consonants, of which there are five basic forms, and 10 vowels. According to Kenneth Katzman, the Hebrew alphabet of 22 letters (five of which have a different form when they appear at the end of a word) consists entirely of consonants. The language is written from right to left without vowels. Thus, the word *kelev* (i.e., dog) appears as the Hebrew equivalents of, from right to left, k, l, and v. If you are not familiar with Hebrew it is impossible to know how to pronounce a word from the way it is written. During the eigth century, a system was developed for indicating vowels through the use of small dots and dashes placed above and below the consonants. These signs are still in use today, but they are confined to schoolbooks, prayer books, and textbooks for foreigners, and are not to be seen in newspapers, magazines, or books for general use.[10] The written form of Japanese consists of three major alphabets. A fourth alphabet, called romaji, is a Romanization using English letters. All four alphabets are used simultaneously in any given piece of writing. The first alphabet, called kanji, consists of more than 5,000 borrowed characters from Chinese. The word kanji means "Chinese character." Kanji are the Chinese characters used in written Japanese. Each kanji character represents an idea or concept, rather than a simple sound. The meaning of the character changes when the combination of characters varies. For an example, see Figure 1.

To be able to read a Japanese newspaper, you would need to know and understand at least 2,000 basic characters. Moreover, you would have to learn the different readings or compounds of two or more kanji. There are more than 4000 kanji compounds. The Japanese also have two phonetic alphabets, called *hiragani* and *katakana*. Hiragani consists of 46 characters.

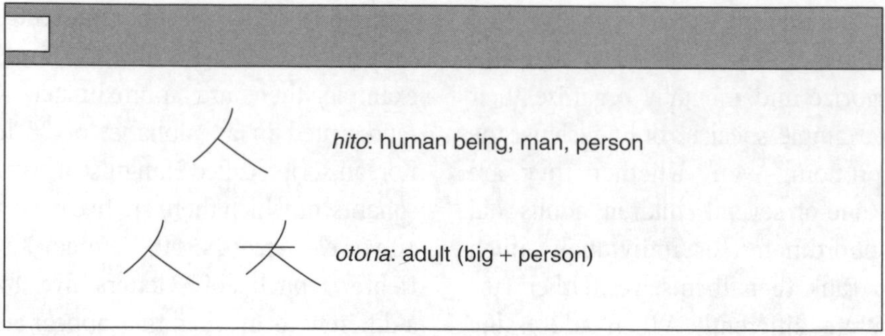

Figure 1 Kanji Examples

These are phonetic sounds that make up the kanji and are used to change verb tenses. The katakana also consists of 46 sounds. The katakana sounds coincide with the hiragana but the characters are different. Katakana is used for all foreign words coming from outside of Japan.[11]

Sounds and Symbols

The letters of a language's alphabet are symbols representing sounds. These small units of sound are called phonemes. In English the letter *c* represents the sound "see" or "ka," the letter *a* represents the sound "ah," and the letter *t* represents the sound "tee." In combination, phonemes become words; that is, morphemes, the smallest meaningful unit of sound. When coarticulated, the sounds "ka," "ah," and "tee" create the word/morpheme "cat."

There is no natural or inherent relationship between the sounds and their accompanying alphabet. That is, there is no intrinsic or immanent relationship between the symbol *c* and the "see" sound, the *a* and the "ah" sound, or the letter *t* and the "tee" sound. That *c* represents the "see" sound is completely random and arbitrary. Likewise, there is also no natural relationship between any word and its referent. In other words, there is no natural or necessary relationship between the word *cat* and that fuzzy little animal walking across the room. In Spanish, which uses a similar but different sound system, the fuzzy little animal walking across the floor is called *gato,* in Japan it is *neiko,* and in French it is *chat.* Each of the different languages uses a different set of sounds to refer to the same referent.

Although the letters and the sound systems of any two languages may be different, the function of an alphabet is the same across languages—to symbolize sound. A symbol is an arbitrarily selected and learned stimulus representing something else. The ability to represent sounds with symbols seems to be limited to humans. To be sure, animals can learn to associate sounds with behaviors, but they can do so only at a very rudimentary level. Jo Liska has developed a hierarchy of symbolic abstraction that allows us to see where humans and animals are distinct in terms of language and symbol use.[12] The hierarchy is, from bottom to top, symptoms, ritual semblances, iconic semblances, proper symbols, conceptual symbols, and syntactic symbols.

According to Liska, *symptoms* constitute the foundation for all animal communication. These are biologically "hard-wired" in the central nervous system. The employment of symptoms is unconscious and stimulated by events in the physiological conditions of the animal. Examples of symptoms are pupil dilation, blushing, piloerection, estrous, and vocalizations. A dog's growl at the sign of another dog is symptomatic. Liska maintains that these behaviors are fixed and immune to short-term environmental changes. Symptoms are automatic, involuntary, and primary. Liska labels *ritual semblances* as exaggerated symptoms that are relatively conscious. Examples include posed facial expressions, gestures of pantomime, begging, and signs of submission. Dogs and cats often exaggerate their begging routines in order to receive table scraps. *Iconic semblances* are related to ritual semblances in that these are signs that represent their referents. A map, blueprint, and photograph of a dog are iconic semblances that are isomorphic to their referents. Liska suggests that iconic semblances are probably restricted to humans. Early cave drawings by our ancestors might be considered iconic semblances. Moving up Liska's ladder of symbolic abstraction are *proper symbols.* These refer to a specific stimulus that labels some aspect of reality. Proper symbols provide the means for naming others, objects, or events. The word "cat" is a proper symbol for the fuzzy little animal. Proper symbols are acquired through stimulus-response learning. Over time, we learn to associate the fuzzy little animal with the word "cat." On the other hand, *conceptual* symbols create symbolic reality and refer to concepts that exist only in the minds of the users such as "liberty," "democracy," and "freedom." Unlike proper symbols, conceptual symbols have no physical referent. The stimulus response pattern for acquiring proper symbols cannot account for the acquisition of conceptual symbols because there is no external stimulus (e.g., such as a cat) for which to associate the symbol. Finally, at the top of the symbolic hierarchy are syntactic symbols. These symbols express grammatical relationships between other symbols such as possession, function, and tense. Syntactic symbols are the means by which language is patterned, organized, and structured.[13]

According to Liska, many mammals and birds communicate using ritual semblances, and some species of primates seem to be able to acquire and use proper symbols. When well-trained and monitored, apes seem to acquire language presented to them visually. Yet their natural communication repertoire appears to be based on symptoms and ritual semblances. Apes seem to have the capacity for language, but as humans use it, language has not yet emerged among wild-living apes. Liska contends that all animals "communicate," but we humans have made it our single most distinguishing characteristic. To be sure, argues Liska, other animal species may possess "advanced" communication systems. Apes engage in a whole host of symptomatic and emblematic signs. Whales sing intricate songs that vary over time. Killer whales (i.e., orcas) use calls that seem to vary from group to group. Wolves use a complicated set of postures for coordination of the pack. But unlike animals, we seem compelled to create and invent symbols. As Liska avows, humans seem to communicate because we *need* to.[14]

Syntax and Universal Grammar

Along with a system of sounds, all languages have a set of rules for combining the sounds to create meaning. The set of rules, or grammar, is called syntax. Through syntax, sentences are generated. Through syntax, sound and meaning are connected. Noam Chomsky is perhaps the most recognized linguist in the world. For the past 50 years, Chomsky has developed a fascinating theory about syntax.[15] Chomsky contends that although the 5,000 or so languages that are spoken in the world today appear to be very different, they are, in fact, remarkably similar. Moreover, Chomsky asserts that the obvious differences among languages are actually quite trivial. Chomsky maintains that the languages spoken on the planet today are all dialects of one common language—human language.[16]

Chomsky argues that all human languages share a *universal grammar* that is innate in the human species and culturally invariant. Chomsky and other linguists claim that every normal child is genetically programmed for human language. Just as humans are programmed to walk upright, so are humans programmed with universal grammar. Chomsky says that language is as much a part of the human brain as the thumb is a part of the human hand. Lila Gleitman, a linguist at the University of Pennsylvania, maintains that human language is not innate in the same way as bee language or horse language may be innate, or in the sense that human visual sensation is innate. Humans do not "learn" how to see. Humans do, however, learn a specific language. The acquisition of a particular language (e.g., English, Japanese) is influenced by the specific cultural environment in which a child is born.[17] In other words, no individual language is universal to human beings. Children learn their specific language by being exposed to it in their cultural environment. Children born and raised in China learn to speak Chinese, whereas children born and raised in Norway learn to speak Norwegian, not because of their race or ethnicity, but because of their cultural environment. The commonalities between the different languages (e.g., Chinese and Norwegian) are so striking that Chomsky and other linguists are convinced that the fundamental syntax for all languages is universal and that the particular languages of a particular culture are simply dialects of the universal grammar. For example, there are two fundamental syntactical structures to all human languages. The first is that all languages, the world over, rely on either word order or inflections to convey meaning. Most languages rely on both to a greater or lesser extent. English, for example, relies heavily on word order. The phrase "The man is in the car" means something very different from "The car is in the man." English also uses inflection to carry meaning. Inflections are changes to words to indicate grammatical relationships such as number, case, gender, tense, and so on. For example, to indicate the plural of something in English, we add the letter "s" to the end of words. A single fuzzy little animal is called a "cat," and two fuzzy little animals are called "cats." The language of the Warlpiri people of Australia relies almost exclusively on inflection rather than word order. Latin also relies heavily on inflection. The point is that word order and inflection are a part of all languages. As linguist Dan Slobin asserts,

> In a way [language] it's like the human face. A human face is very simple, two eyes, a nose, and a mouth. You can draw a simple sketch of it. But look at the incredible diversity. Each one of us has a uniquely different face. Yet each face is obviously a human face. Languages are the same. Each one is obviously a different language but they're clearly examples of the same kind of system.[18]

Lila Gleitman forwards two additional arguments in favor of the universality of language.[19] The first is that language learning proceeds uniformly among children within and across cultures. Chinese children and Norwegian children learn language at the same time in their development. All normal children begin to use language at about the same time, across cultures. Linguist Steven Pinker of the Massachusetts Institute of Technology has observed that sometime around their first birthday, babies start to understand and use words. At about eighteen months, the children's vocabulary, across all cultures, increases at a rate of one word every two hours and continues to grow through adolescence. At this time, two-word strings appear. These two-word combinations are highly similar across cultures. Children announce when objects appear, disappear, and move about. According to Pinker, by the age of three years, a child's vocabulary grows dramatically and he or she can produce fluent grammatical conversation. Such sentences,

> though quite short, illustrate the child's knowledge and competence of the basic structure of language (e.g., appropriate word order, and so on). For example, even though he or she has never had a lesson on English grammar, an English-speaking child might say "I want cookie," but would never say, "Want I cookie." By the age of five or so, children in normal learning settings begin to use complex sentences.[20]

Gleitman argues that even in cases where the learning environment changes, children learn language at essentially the same rate. For example, studies indicate that a child's language learning rate is basically unaffected by differences in mothers' speech. Furthermore, deaf and blind children learn language at the same time and rate as children with normal hearing and sight. Gleitman points out that the vocabulary and syntax of sign languages are essentially the same as in spoken languages. At about the age of two, deaf children start to put gestures together into elementary two- and three-gesture sentences. By five years of age they are constructing complex, multigesture sentences. In addition, blind children have little trouble acquiring terms that describe visual experiences. Gleitman suggests that because blind children are unable to see, phrases referring to sight (e.g., "Look at that!") might be absent from their speech. Yet such terms are some of the first to appear in the blind children's vocabulary. For example, in response to the command "look up," blind children raise their hands instead of their heads. When they are told that they can "look but not touch," blind children very slowly stretch out their hands and cautiously touch the object. When told "go ahead and look," they handle the object with enthusiasm.[21]

The second point supporting the universality of language argument is that children across cultures acquire many linguistic generalizations that experience alone could not have taught them. Children of all cultures say things that no one could have taught them. Chomsky argues that in advance of experience, children of all cultures are already equipped with an understanding of the basic structure of any human language. Like walking, or growing hair, language is encoded into the genetic makeup of normal functioning human beings. By the age of three, for example, there are any number of things children cannot do, such as tie their own shoes, perform mathematical computations, or spell most words. By the age of three, however, children can construct meaningful sentences in ways that no one has ever taught them.[22] Moreover, as Pinker notes, the sentences they create are grammatically correct. Indeed, asserts Pinker, children never make some mistakes. For example, a child might ask "What did you eat your eggs with?" but the child would never say "What did you eat your eggs and?" which seems to be a straightforward extension of the statement "I ate ham and eggs." The interesting point here is that no one has ever taught the child not to end sentences with the word *and.* Pinker and Chomsky argue that children never make such errors because to do so would violate some principle of universal grammar. Below is another example provided by Pinker. In this example, a language learner who hears the (a) and (b) sentences could quite sensibly extract a general rule that, when applied to the (c) sentence, would yield sentence (d). But the resulting sentence (d) is something no one would say.

(a) We expect the bird to fly.
(b) We expect the bird will fly.
(c) The bird is expected to fly.
(d) The bird is expected will fly.[23]

The proposition that all languages share a universal grammar that is innate to humans is widely accepted among contemporary linguists. But these linguists also recognize that all human languages are somewhat different. For example, although virtually all languages rely on some form of word order to construct sentences, the word order may vary across languages. For example, the word order for a sentence in most European languages is subject-verb-object, as in the sentence "I watch television." In Japanese, however, the order is subject-object-verb, as in the sentence "I television watch." In addition, Japanese, like other Asian languages, does not contain a grammatical equivalent to plurality, as can be found in English.[24] The Swahili alphabet lacks the letters *c, q,* and *x,* but contains a number of its own. The letter *dh* is pronounced like the *th* of "this," and *gh* like the German *ch.* Whereas English grammatical inflections occur at the end of a word, in Swahili everything is done at the beginning. *Kitabu* is the Swahili word for "book," but the word for "books" is *vitabu.* This word falls into the so-called Ki Mi class, one of eight in the Swahili language. Others are the M Mi class (e.g., *mkono* = hand, *mikono* = hands; *mji* = town, *miji* = towns); and the M Wa class, used mainly to refer to people (e.g., *mtu* = man, *watu* = men; *mjinga* = fool, *wajinga* = fools). Thus, "one big book" in Swahili is *kitabu kikubwa kimoja,* which translates as "book-big-one," but "two big books" is *vitabi vikubwa viwili.*

Many languages are read from left to right, as in English. Most languages of the Middle East, however, including Arabic, Hebrew, and Persian, are read from right to left. Korean writing differs considerably from most other languages, in that the letters of each syllable are grouped together into clusters, as if the English word "seldom" were written:

S D		S E L
E O	or	D O M
L M		

The point here is that although human languages across the globe have much in common, each is unique in some way.[25]

All human languages have a set of rules that are used to combine the language's sounds into meaningful units. Complex languages exist even in remote parts of the world, where people have yet to be exposed to modern technology and media. Papua New Guinea, for example, is where some of the most isolated people on earth live, and yet it is probably the most linguistically diverse country. Among the population of 3 million people, there are more than 750 languages spoken; about one-fifth of the total number of languages on Earth. Some of the languages are spoken by fewer than 1,000 people. In his longitudinal work with the Menya people of Papua New Guinea, Carl Whitehead has found that the Menya use a language that is as complex as any other language. He argues that one of the most remarkable features of the Menya language is its verb system. Some Menya verbs, according to Whitehead, can have as many as 2,000 to 3,000 different forms as compared to English, where a verb can have up to five forms. Languages such as Menya are as highly rule governed as any other language. In this sense, there is no such thing as a primitive language.[26]

Universals of Language

Another reason why so many linguists believe that all languages evolved from a universal grammar is their numerous commonalities. All languages are remarkably similar. For example, all languages have some way of labeling objects, places, or things (like the English noun). All languages have a way of naming action (like the English verb). All human languages have some way of stating the negative (e.g., it is *not* raining out), a way to construct interrogatives, and a way of differentiating between singular and plural.[27]

According to Salzmann, the uniquely human way of communicating via speech shares several other universal features, regardless of culture, race, and particular lexicon. First, Salzmann notes that all human speech is transmitted via a vocal-auditory channel. Conversely, some sounds produced by animals are not vocal or are not received auditorily (e.g., bees have no ears). An important advantage of the vocal-auditory channel for humans is that the rest of the body is left free to carry on other activities. Second, speech sounds are emitted from their source of origin in all directions, making it possible to determine the location of the source. Functionally this is important because the sender and the receiver do not have see each other to communicate. This is also important because it enables speakers to communicate without necessarily being face to face—for example, from around corners, or in the dark. Third, speech sounds are heard within a very limited range and only during production. Soon after, they are lost. In this sense speech is transitory. Fourth, speech is also interchangeable. We are capable of repeating what others say. This is not true of many animal species. Fifth, human speakers are equipped with complete intrapersonal feedback. As speakers, we can hear ourselves and are capable of monitoring our own messages. Sixth, speech is specialized. Human speech has only a single function; that is, to communicate. Seventh, speech can be displaced from time and space. We can talk about something that happened 1,000 years ago, or project what we think will happen 1,000 years from now. Eighth, what a person may say can be completely false. Ninth, speech is reflexive. We use language to talk about language. Finally, tenth, the speakers of any language can learn a second language or even several languages in addition to their native tongue.[28]

Generative Grammar

One of the most remarkable features of any language's rule structure is that it allows the speakers to generate sentences that have never before been spoken. Chomsky refers to this aspect of language as its *generative grammar.* From a finite set of sounds and a finite set of rules, speakers of any language can create an infinite number of sentences, many of which have never before been uttered yet are easily comprehended by other speakers of the same language.[29]

Most of the sentences you have produced today have never before been spoken by anyone on the planet, and yet everyone understood them. Linguist George A. Miller contends that any sentence more than 20 words in length has probably never before been spoken. Miller demonstrates this through example. According to Miller, suppose it is possible for someone to choose the next word that he or she is going to say from a list of 10 possible words. Continuing on, assume that the second word someone is going to speak is also one of 10 possible words. At this point the total number of possible combinations of two-word sentences is 10 times 10, or 100 possible two-word sentences. Now assume that the person is to select a third word out of a possible 10 words. The number of possible three-word sentences is 10 to the third power, or 1,000 possible sentences (see Figure 2).

Moving on to a fourth possible word, out of a list of 10 possible words, the number of potential four-word sentences is 10 to the fourth power, or 10,000 possible sentences. The number of possible messages is increasing very rapidly as the length of the message increases. Following this example, the number of possible 20-word sentences is 10 to the 20th power, or 100,000,000,000,000,000,000 possible sentences. Based on this example, Miller alleges that the number of possible sentences in any language is essentially infinite.[30]

Elaborated and Restricted Codes

Although the world's 5,000 or so languages have much in common, the style or fashion in which they are used by the people who speak them differs from culture to culture. In fact, speakers of the same language often use it differently. Some of these differences may be explained by Hall's concept of high- and low-context cultures. Persons in high-context cultures generally rely more on their nonverbal code than on their verbal code to communicate, whereas members of low-context cultures rely extensively on the verbal code during communication.

Basil Bernstein argues that the use of linguistic codes is closely related to the social structure of a particular culture. First, Bernstein differentiates between language and speech. As it is described above, Bernstein

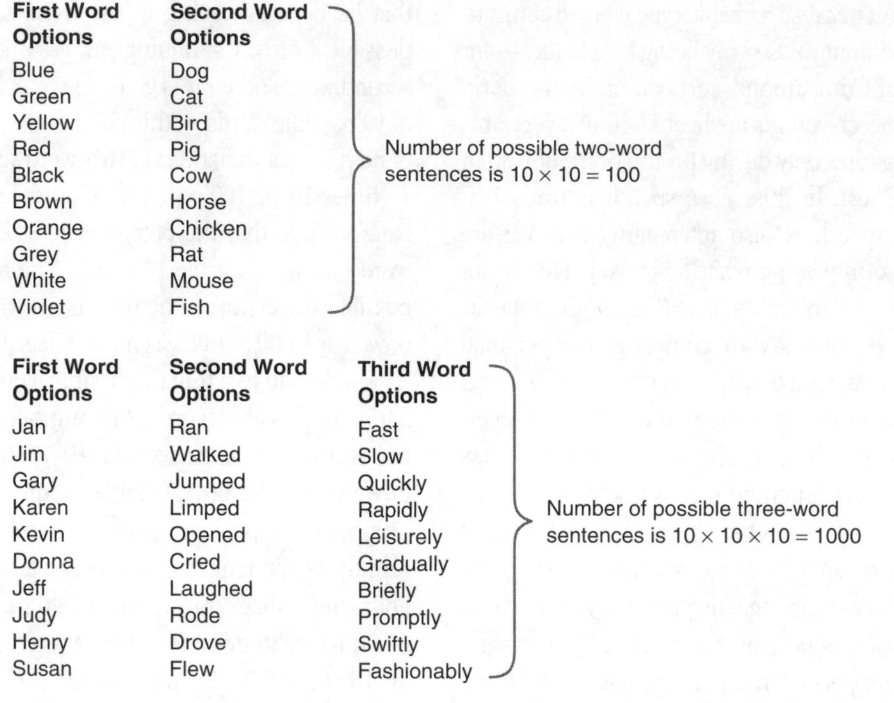

Figure 2

agrees that language is a system of sounds and syntax that allows speakers to represent their reality and generate an infinite number of sentences. In fact, he argues that all languages are equal in terms of their ability to represent reality. Speech, on the other hand, is at the mercy of the social circumstances wherein it is employed. Bernstein maintains that whereas language symbolizes what is *possible* to do, speech symbolizes what is actually occurring. The social context of communication sets up the boundaries for the type of speech that is preferred, obligated, or prohibited. As the social context varies, the speakers of the language will generate different kinds of speech, even if they speak the same language. The social system delimits the speaker's options in terms of language use. The speech codes, then, are not defined in terms of lexicon or syntax, but by the social structure of the culture.[31]

Broadly speaking, Bernstein identifies two types of linguistic/speech codes: elaborated and restricted. A restricted code is one wherein the options (not necessarily the vocabulary) are limited as to what the speaker can say or do verbally. A restricted code is considered a status-oriented speech system. The code reinforces the social system by restricting or limiting its speakers to a limited number of linguistic options during communication. Restricted codes are most often seen in high-context cultures wherein the status of the interactants dictates who says what to whom and how it is said. When interactants of a high-context, collectivistic culture communicate, their words and phrases are strictly prescribed, leaving them little choice about what to say or how to say it. In this way, their code is "restricted" and is highly predictable. Bernstein points out that the Chinese, for example, operate with a restricted code, yet have one of the most complex languages on earth. Chinese people need to learn several thousand characters in order to read and write, but they speak with a restricted code because the social system (highly status and group oriented) dictates what can be said to whom in a given social circumstance. Restricted codes also emerge in individualistic cultures as interactants develop close relationships. Restricted codes can be found in what Bernstein calls "closed" communities, such as prison camps and criminal subgroups, but can develop within any social structure where the individuals share social identifications (e.g., spouses, co-workers, and so on). In this way, restricted codes show up in both high- and low-context cultures, although they tend to be more salient across the entire culture in a high- rather than low-context culture.[32]

With an elaborated code, speakers can choose from among a variety of linguistic options to communicate. Bernstein argues that speakers using an elaborated code are able, via the social system, to put their thoughts, intents, and goals into an explicit verbal message. Bernstein argues that elaborated codes develop in circumstances where the speakers' intents are unknown or vary widely, as in individualistic cultures. Because the individual speaker's intent is unclear, the speaker has a variety of linguistic options available from which to choose. The speaker must expand and elaborate so that his or her intentions are clearly communicated. Any language will allow the speaker to do that, but the social system regulates it. The social structure of an elaborated code user is such that considerable flexibility exists in one's role prescription. To communicate one's intent, the speaker must be given much linguistic latitude. In this way, it is very difficult to predict the vocabulary and syntax of a speaker using an elaborated code. Students in the United States, for example, may have no idea what kinds of things a new professor will say on the first day of class. Students in China, on the other hand, can probably predict quite accurately the kinds of messages their professor will send. In the United States, the culture generally uses an elaborated code, whereas in China, it is restricted.[33]

Cross-Cultural Communication Styles

Although the capacity for language is universal, the language of a particular culture must be learned by its members. Moreover, cultures seem to have a predominant manner, fashion, or style in which they use their language. Communication theorists William Gudykunst and Stella Ting-Toomey argue that at different language acquisition stages, children learn not only the structure and lexicon of their culture's language, but also the various styles of language interaction unique to their culture. Such language style reflects the affective, moral, and aesthetic patterns of a culture. Gudykunst and Ting-Toomey describe a culture's verbal style as its tonal coloring of a message that is communicated through shades of tonal qualities. Gudykunst and Ting-Toomey describe four verbal communication styles that have been identified by intercultural theorists. The styles are direct-indirect, elaborate-succinct, personal-contextual, and instrumental-affective. Variations of these styles may exist in any culture, but typically one style tends to dominate within a culture.[34]

Direct-Indirect

According to Gudykunst and Ting-Toomey, cultures differ in the degree to which speakers disclose their intentions through precise and candid verbal communication. Persons using a direct style employ overt expressions of intention. In using a direct style, interactants assert self-face needs. Such messages clearly articulate the speaker's desires and needs. Direct styles are often used in low-context, individualistic cultures. Conversely, an indirect style, which is often seen in high-context and collectivistic cultures, is one where the speaker's intentions are hidden or only hinted at during interaction. The use of ambiguity and vagueness is characteristic of an indirect style. In high-context cultures, there is no need to articulate every message. True understanding is implicit, coming not from words but from actions in the environment. Moreover, indirect communication prevents potentially embarrassing moments that might threaten the face of either speaker.[35]

The direct style is preferred in cultures such as the United States, England, Australia, Germany, and Israel, among others. In the United States we frequently use such phrases as "for sure," "no question," "without a doubt." We value verbal precision and self-expression. Americans are encouraged to "speak their mind." We are so direct and candid that we will even announce to an entire room when we are going to use the bathroom, as in "I'll be right back, I have to use the restroom." Gudykunst and Ting-Toomey allege that Israel is also considered a direct culture, perhaps even more so than the United States. Fedarko points out that many Israelis use the direct style of *dugri* (straight talk) that is quintessentially Israeli. Israelis value communication that is simple, direct, and honest. A speaker displaying dugri places substance before style and makes no attempt at pretense or deception. Some have referred to Israel as an "in your face" culture when it comes to interacting.[36] Germans, too, value frankness and directness in their interaction with others and are especially fond of the use of examples. Along with their direct style is an absence of small talk. Hall and Hall maintain that in their quest for direct and candid talk, Germans despise social chit-chat. Sometimes, Germans are perceived by their European counterparts as brutally frank.[37]

The use of an indirect style of language is seen in many Asian cultures. Indirectness is valued in these cultures because saving face and harmony in social relationships are highly valued. Directness threatens both of these goals. According to Gudykunst and Ting-Toomey, Japanese speakers, for example, limit themselves to implicit and even ambiguous use of words such as "maybe" and "perhaps." Children in Japan are taught not to be self-centered, and those who take the initiative are generally not rewarded. Japanese mothers typically use rhetorical questions and tone of voice and context to express disapproval. Sumiko Iwao argues that there is an unspoken belief among Japanese that verbalizing deep feelings spoils their value. To the Japanese, being understood without words is far more cherished than precise articulation. Iwao asserts that in Japan, interpersonal communication is based on a great deal of guessing and reading between the lines. Directness is disagreeable and repugnant. The ability to correctly grasp what a person thinks and feels without verbal expression is considered a sign of closeness between two persons. In marital relationships verbal communication is thought to be unnecessary. Iwao calls Japan "a culture of no words." She alleges that this may be due to the high value placed on masculinity. According to Japanese ideals, the most masculine of men is a man of few words who does not disclose personal weakness by complaints or expose his innermost thoughts and feelings, especially to his wife.[38] To a certain degree, the French are indirect. Hall and Hall argue that the French often indulge in small talk and prefer some mystery in their interaction with others. They maintain that the French will often talk around the point they wish to make.[39]

An Intercultural Conversation: Direct and Indirect Speaking

To some extent direct and indirect modes of communication are universal. Indirect modes, for example, are often used out of simple politeness. But direct modes of communication are seen most often in cultures like the United States, whereas indirect modes are seen in many Asian cultures, such as Japan, Korea, and China. The following dialogue takes place between a young couple who have been dating for a short time. The man is a U.S. student, and the woman is from an Asian culture. Note the misunderstanding that results as a consequence of the use of direct and indirect modes of communication.[40]

Jim: Ya know, Michiko, I really enjoy the time we spend together. I really like you. I've been so happy since we met.

Michiko: Hmmm, thank you.

Jim: I mean, I feel like I've learned so much about you and your culture.

Michiko: Yeah, it's very interesting.

Jim: I'm so glad you came to the United States. Do you like it here? What is your favorite thing about us?

Michiko: Well, it's pretty big. It's very nice here.

Jim: What do you think about Americans?

Michiko: I don't know. Maybe I haven't been here long enough to know.

Jim: You must think something!

Michiko: Well, I'd probably have to think about it.

Jim: I mean, do you like us?

Michiko: Well, I don't really know that many Americans yet.

In all likelihood, Jim is not going to get much of an answer from Michiko. She continues throughout the dialogue using rather general answers to Jim's very specific and direct questions about her feelings toward the United States. Michiko might believe that Jim is being far too direct and invading her privacy. Besides, the fact that she has traveled halfway around the world should be indicative of her desire to be here, right? There must be something about the United States that attracted her. Michiko cannot possibly say something critical about the United States because she would lose face, as would Jim, as a native. She relies on imprecise and indefinite answers.

Elaborate, Exacting, and Succinct Styles

According to Gudykunst and Ting-Toomey, the elaborate, exacting, or succinct communication style deals with the quantity and/or volume of talk that is preferred across cultural groups. There are three levels—an elaborate style, which emphasizes flashy and embellished language; an exacting style, where persons say no more or less than is needed; and a succinct style characterized by the use of concise statements, understatements, and even silence.[41] An elaborate style of communication can be seen in many Arab, Middle Eastern, and Afro-American cultures. Many Middle Easterners tend to use metaphors, similes, and adjectives in everyday conversation. African Americans, too, prefer personalized, often exaggerated, spontaneous styles of interaction. Kochman writes,

> Stylistic self-expression within Black culture is characterized by dramatic self-conscious flair. . . . Black stylistic self-expression is also characterized by inventive (humorously ironic) exaggeration as in the self-promotion of demonstrably capable aspects of self ("If you've got it, flaunt it") or even by less demonstrably positive capabilities ("If you don't have it, flaunt it anyway"), which is all part of Afro-American boasting: the "making of one's noise." As Hollywood Henderson said, "I put a lot of pressure on myself to see if I can play up to my mouth." But exaggeration also serves to characterize (and neutralize the impact of) negative situations, such as poverty ("The soles on my shoes are so thin, I can step on a dime and tell you whether it's heads or tails").[42]

Americans tend to prefer an exacting style of interaction consistent with a "Just the facts" mentality popularized by the *Dragnet* television series of the 1960s. A succinct style can be found in Japan, China, and some Native American (e.g., Apache, Navajo) cultures. These cultures value the use of concise talk and silence. To the Chinese, silence is a means to maintain social control in a situation. Stowell points out that the Chinese, in general, do not value verbal skills. In fact, speaking skills in general are considered immoral. The skilled speaker may be labeled as "having a flattering mouth," "an oil-mouth," or a "honey-mouth." Chinese children are taught to be cautious about the use of words. The Chinese say "One should use the eyes and ears, not the mouth," and "Disaster emanates from careless talk." The Chinese consider the wisest and most trustworthy person as the one who talks the least but the one who listens, watches, and restricts his or her verbal communication.[43]

The American Indian tribes of the Navajo and Apache also value the use of silence as a way to deal with ambiguity. Steven Pratt, an actively participating member of the Osage tribe, and Lawrence Weider, a professor of communication, argue,

> To the real Indian, it appears that White Americans who are strangers to each other may freely engage in conversation in such places as the supermarket check-out line. Commercial airlines provide an even more intense opportunity for easy conversation between strangers. Seatmates often disclose their life histories to each other. In the culture of real Indians, these are extraordinary and improper ways to behave, especially when both parties are real Indians. When real Indians who are strangers to one another pass each other in a public space, wait in line, occupy adjoining seats, and so forth, they take it that it is proper to remain silent and to not initiate conversation. Being silent at this point is a constituent part of the real Indian's mode of communicating with others, especially other Indians.[44]

The use of an elaborated, exacting, or succinct style is closely related to Hall's high- and low-context communication and Bernstein's classification of restricted and elaborated codes. Gudykunst and Kim contend that restricted codes resemble jargon or shorthand speech in which speakers are almost telegraphic. This seems to correlate with a succinct style. Conversely, Bernstein asserts that elaborated codes rely heavily on verbal amplification for message transmission with much less emphasis on the nonverbal code or environmental cues. This seems to correspond with the elaborate style.[45]

Personal and Contextual Style

Gudykunst and Ting-Toomey define the personal communication style as one that amplifies the individual identity of the speaker. Such a style stresses and underscores "personhood." This style is often seen in individualistic cultures. A personal style relies on the use of first-person pronouns in sentence construction. Person-oriented language stresses informality and symmetrical power relationships. For example, English has only one form for the second person, that is, *you*. Regardless of whether they are speaking to someone of higher, equal, or lower status, English speakers use the same form for the second person. For example, if we were to meet the President of the United States, we might say, "It's nice to meet you." If we were to meet a new colleague or neighbor, we could say, "It's nice to meet you." If we meet our new colleague's first-grade daughter, we might say, "It's nice to meet you." The personal nature of our language does not distinguish status or rank via pronoun usage.

Moreover, in the United States, we tend to treat each other with informality and forgo the use of formal titles and strict manners. These cultural attitudes are reflected in our personal verbal style. As Condon notes, two of the most frequently used words in English are "I" and "you." He points out that for many Americans, it is difficult to talk for any length of time without using pronouns. In Japan, however, there are at least ten words that might be equivalent to the English "I."[46] In addition, Storti notes that the Thai language has twelve forms of the pronoun "you."[47]

On the other hand, assert Gudykunst and Ting-Toomey, a contextual style accentuates and highlights one's role identity and status. In cultures that employ a contextual style, the social context dictates word choice, especially personal pronouns. For example, when using Thai language, one must look carefully at the situation, including the status and intimacy level among the interactants, in order to decide what form of pronoun to use. Unlike a personal style, where pronoun usage is consistent across situations, contextual-style language varies across situations. The correct form of pronoun is contingent on the context. Storti notes that German and French, for example, have familiar and formal forms of the pronoun *you.* The decision to use one form over another is based on the context of the interactants.[48] To use the familiar form with an unfamiliar interactant would be inappropriate. Germans are well known for their formality and strict use of titles, even among friends. German neighbors who have known each other for years still use the title "Herr" when addressing each other. June Ock Yum maintains that a fundamental function of many East Asian languages is to recognize the social status, degree of intimacy, age, and sex of the interactants. These types of demographics will influence the degree of formality and the use of honorifics in the language code. Many Asian languages highlight status differences and asymmetrical power relationships. According to Samuel Martin, Korean and Japanese have what he calls two "axes of distinction"—the axis of address and the axis of reference. In the axis of address, the speaker carefully chooses language based on the status role of the speakers. With the axis of reference, the speaker chooses language based on the speaker's attitude about the subject of communication. Yum provides the example of the phrase "to eat." In English, "to eat" is "to eat" regardless of with whom one is eating (e.g., a friend, a parent, or the President of the United States). In Korean, however, there are at least three different ways to say "to eat" depending on the role of the speakers: *muka-da* (plain), *du-shin-da* (polite), and *chap-soo-shin-da* (honorific).[49]

The Japanese use a contextual style, and their language includes an elaborate system of honorifics. Honorifics are linguistic forms that communicate respect according to one's rank and the rank of those to whom one is speaking. Honorifics take the form of suffixes to nouns, adjectives, and verbs. For example, the informal form of the verb "to go," *iku,* is used when speaking with someone to whom one is intimate. If the person with whom one is interacting is a stranger or is older, then the politeness marker, *-masu,* appears, as in *iki-masu.* If the person with whom one is interacting is socially superior, then the honorific form of the verb "to go," *irassyaru,* is used.[50] Hooker notes that one cannot learn to speak Japanese without learning the honorific language forms, including syntax and grammar, for defining one's social status. According to Hooker, through most of Japanese history, learning the language meant experiencing and reinforcing the social differences that ordered society. He points out that there was a time in Japanese history when one literally could not construct a sentence without defining one's own social class and the social class to whom one was speaking. In addition, Hooker notes, Japanese honorifics are a gendered system. Women's speech tends to be filled with honorifics and a sense of deference (i.e., honor, regard) to males.[51]

An Intercultural Conversation: Personal and Contextual Styles

In the following interaction, Jim is a student at a local university. He was born and raised in the United States. Akira is an exchange student from Japan. Jim and Akira are eating dinner together in a local restaurant. They have known each other for only a short time. Not only is

Jim's style of communication overtly personal, but he's also quite direct.

Jim: Hey buddy, what do you think of this American restaurant? I really like it.

Akira: Yes, Mr. Jim. This is very nice.

Jim: I always prefer restaurants like this, kinda casual but good food. I come here a lot. Do you go out to eat much in Japan?

Akira: Japanese restaurants are nice, too.

Jim: Yeah, but do you go out to eat much?

Akira: Sure, Japanese people like restaurants.

Jim: Whenever I come here I usually order the same thing. It's kinda funny, but since I like it, I figure I may as well eat it. I have a lot of friends that do that.

Akira: Sure.

Jim: Yeah, I was thinking the other day that since the dorm food sucks so bad, I should go out to eat more often.

Akira: Yes, that's a good idea.

Jim is trying to involve Akira in the conversation by relating to him his personal experiences and preferences. Jim uses the first person "I" no fewer than 11 times and even refers to Akira as "Buddy." Akira never refers to himself in the first person. Akira generally defers to Jim and says little, even addressing Jim as "Mr. Jim." As a foreigner, Akira probably sees Jim as socially superior and uses a formal title. Moreover, rather than talking about his personal preferences, Akira mentions that Japanese people enjoy restaurants.

Instrumental and Affective Style

Gudykunst and Ting-Toomey define an instrumental verbal style as sender-based and goal-outcome based. The instrumental speaker uses communication to achieve some goal or outcome. Instrumental messages often are constructed to persuade and influence others and to maintain one's face. Yum says that instrumental-style users believe that communication should end after some goal has been attained and outcomes can be assessed, such as friends gained, opponent defeated, or some form of self-fulfillment has been reached.[52] Julia Wood reports that men in the United States engage in an instrumental style more often than U.S. women. U.S. women, on the other hand, use collaborative and cooperative talk.[53] An affective communication style is receiver and process oriented. The affective speaker is concerned not so much with the outcome of the communication, but with the process. In cultures where an instrumental style predominates, the burden of understanding often rests with the speaker. The speaker carefully chooses and organizes his or her messages in order to be understood by the audience. In cultures where an affective style is used, the responsibility of understanding rests with both parties; that is, the speaker and the listener. Affective speakers carefully watch for the reactions of their listener. Verbal expressions are insinuated and quite subtle. Affective speakers often operate on an intuitive sense and are nonverbally expressive. Hall and Hall assert that before getting down to business, the French prefer to establish a mood or a feeling, and a certain amount of intuition is required on the part of the listener in order to discover the meaning.[54] Condon argues that where Americans like to talk about themselves, Japanese talk about each other. The Japanese are very conscious of the other person with whom they are interacting; it is an interdependent concern unlike the American concern for independence. Condon notes,

> The difference in orientations is apparent when friends who have not seen each other for a while happen to meet. Americans are likely to ask about each other and tell each other about where they have been or what they have been doing.

> Who speaks first does not seem to matter very much. When Japanese friends meet, one is likely to begin by thanking the other for some previous favor or gift or letter that was sent. Most often, a reference to the last time they were together is part of this greeting. Thus, they re-establish a particular continuing relationship.[55]

Samuel Martin contends that the Japanese language has a complex array of polite formulas, or stock phrases, that have a leveling effect in just about any social situation. Martin argues that foreigners traveling in Japan can increase their effectiveness if they memorize these 20 or 30 polite formulas. Martin states that, to some extent, Japanese conversation is all formula and no content.[56] Perhaps the affective style of the Japanese is best reflected in Haiku poetry. Haiku is a very short form of poetry popular in Japan. Haiku poems always deal with some aspect of the season. Japanese Haiku poets are required to communicate a vivid impression using only 17 Japanese characters. The Haiku poem is concise while simultaneously communicating a deep spiritual understanding. From the reader of Haiku, much effort is required. One of the most popular Haiku poets was Basho, who lived some 300 years ago, but whose poetry is still used as the definitive model for contemporary Haiku poets.

> Waterjar cracks:
> I lie awake
> This icy night.
> Lightning:
> Heron's cry
> Stabs the darkness.
> Sick on a journey:
> Over parched fields
> Dreams wander on.[57]

Chinese communication is also said to be more affective than instrumental. Becker argues that Chinese people reject debate and argumentation during the process of communication.[58] June Ock Yum believes that Confucianism has a large impact on Chinese communication and asserts that the Chinese emphasize a process and receiver orientation. According to Confucian philosophy, the primary function of communication is to initiate, develop, and maintain social relationships. Yum states that in China, it is important to engage in small talk before initiating business and to communicate personalized information. The Chinese view communication as a never-ending interpretive process. During a conversation, Chinese do not calculate what they give or receive. To do so, states Yum, would be to think about immediate personal profits, which conflicts with the Confucian notion of mutual faithfulness. The Chinese are disgusted by purely business-like transactions that are carefully planned and orchestrated.[59] Echoing Yum's seminal work, Stowell contends that Chinese is a listener-responsible language, rather than a speaker-responsible language, as is English. In a listener-responsible language, the listener is required to construct the meaning based on his or her relationship with the speaker. The Chinese view communication as an interdependent process whereby both speaker and listener are active participants who, together, create meaning.[60]

An Intercultural Conversation: Instrumental and Affective Speaking

In the following dialogue, Mr. Benton has traveled to China to introduce Mr. Yeh-Ching to a new operating system. Mr. Benton is coming from a culture that values an instrumental style of speaking, so he wants to get right down to business. Mr. Yeh-Ching, on the other hand, wants to establish a relationship before discussing any business possibilities. Mr. Benton and Mr. Yeh-Ching are meeting at a local restaurant in Beijing.[61]

Mr. Benton: Ah, Mr. Yeh-Ching. I've been waiting awhile. Had you forgotten about our meeting?

Mr. Yeh-Ching: Good morning, Jerry, it is so nice to see you.

Mr. Benton: Well . . . I'm glad you're finally here. I have all the material you need to see about the new computers we're installing. Here's our plan . . .

Mr. Yeh-Ching: Jerry, have you seen much of our city?

Mr. Benton: Well . . . I really don't have much time for sightseeing. This isn't a vacation, ya know. Business, business, business. My boss expects me to close this deal today and be back in New York by the weekend. So, here's my idea for installation.

Mr. Yeh-Ching: Our city is so beautiful and full of history. Please allow me to arrange a tour for you. We can go together.

Mr. Benton: I'd love to, but ya know . . . business is business.

Mr. Yeh-Ching: Can I arrange a tour for you? My staff would be delighted to get to meet you.

Mr. Benton: No thanks, but I'd like to show you something. Look at these new configurations for the computers we're installing. Now . . . notice that—

Mr. Yeh-Ching: Here is a menu. This restaurant has some very interesting Chinese dishes that I would like for you to try.

Mr. Benton: Oh, I grabbed a bite to eat at the Hilton. Go ahead and eat, though. I can show you the production schedule.

Chances are pretty good that Mr. Yeh-Ching will not buy Mr. Benton's new computer system. To an affective speaker like Mr. Yeh-Ching, Mr. Benton is too concerned about his business and not concerned enough about the personal side of business; that is, relationships. Affective speakers are sometimes suspicious of people who refuse to get to know each other before striking a deal.

Cross-Cultural Conflict Styles

As in any relationship, whenever two people from different cultures come together and exchange verbal and nonverbal messages, conflict can emerge. Conflict often surfaces as a result of incompatible goals, limited or inadequate resources, differing opinions on important topics, and so on. Intercultural conflict involves emotional frustrations or a clash of expectations based on cultural differences. Communication professor Stella Ting-Toomey has spent much of her professional career studying conflict and communication conflict styles across cultures. Ting-Toomey has observed that how people manage communication during conflict differs considerably across cultures. She notes that people from different cultures often use different communication styles during conflict.[62] According to Ting-Toomey, conflict style refers to a person's overall orientation toward initiating and managing conflict. Ting-Toomey maintains that a person's conflict style is based on two communication dimensions. The first dimension is the degree to which a person asserts a *self-face need;* that is, seeks to satisfy his or her own interests during conflict. The second is the degree to which a person is cooperative (i.e., *other-face need)* and seeks to incorporate the interests of the other.[63] The combination of assertiveness, or self-face need, and cooperativeness, or other-face need, defines five styles of managing conflict.

The degree to which a person asserts a high self-face need while simultaneously discounting the other-face need defines the *dominating* communication style. On the other hand, the person who assumes a high self-face need while also attending to the needs of the other-face takes on an *integrating* style. The person who tries to balance both self-face and other-face needs takes on a *compromising* style. The person using an *avoiding* style ignores both self-face need and other-face need. The person who puts the other-face need ahead of self-face need assumes an *obliging* style (see Figure 3).

Some research has shown that a culture's individualism-collectivism orientation affects the preference of conflict management style. Although the research is not conclusive, many studies have shown that persons from Asian cultures, many of which are collectivistic, generally prefer avoiding and obliging styles, especially when compared to the United States (an individualistic culture), where we see a preference for dominating and integrating styles. Related research has shown that Middle Eastern managers prefer integrating styles of conflict management over dominating and compromsing.[64]

Language and Ethnic Identity

A fundamental way in which groups distinguish themselves from other groups, and thereby maintain their group identity, is through the language they speak. Within groups, status and hierarchy are recognized primarily through the use of language. Often, immigrant groups maintain their cultural heritage and identity by using their native language in their host culture and by teaching it to their children. Other immigrant groups may discourage the use of their native tongue so as to establish themselves as legitimate members of their new culture. McNamara argues that immigrants entering a new culture may have to redefine their former social identity. In a study of Hebrew-speaking Israeli immigrants in Australia, McNamara found that as the Israeli immigrants changed their social identities, there was a corresponding change in their attitudes favoring English over Hebrew. The subjects in McNamara's study were considered *yordin*, a term with negative connotations referring to Israelis living abroad. Among other things, language identified the *yordin* as an outgroup in Australia. As with most migrant

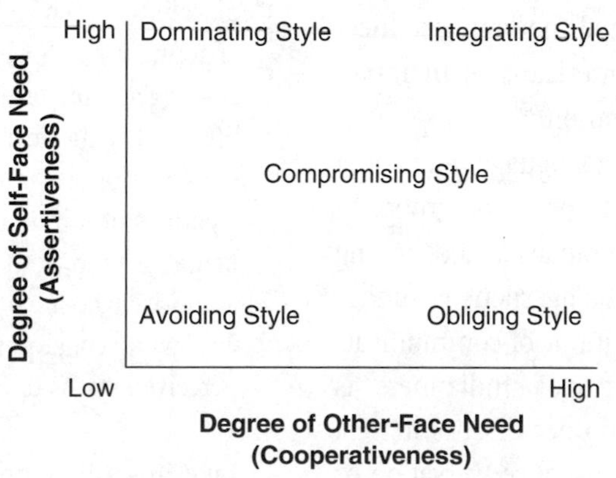

Figure 3

languages used in Australia, Hebrew had low status. By learning and speaking English and teaching it to their children, the yordin were able, to some extent, to manage their negative social identities in their new host culture.[65]

Patricia SanAntonio conducted research on the language practices of an American computer company based in Japan. This particular company required its employees to speak English. Because they wanted to hire native Japanese persons with business expertise and English skills, however, they had trouble attracting high-quality candidates. In order to compete with other Japanese companies, they hired new college graduates who lacked proficient English skills. The result was that they had a workforce with a great deal of English-speaking variety; that is, some were quite competent, whereas others struggled considerably. Because English was so important to the company, the ability to speak English and to interact with American managers became a real source of power within the company. SanAntonio argued that within the Japanese context, language and identity are inextricably linked, and that the ability and willingness for Japanese employees to use English identified them and their desire to become integrated into the organization. SanAntonio concluded that the English-only policy created a boundary between the Japanese and Americans such that Japanese input was reduced. The policy essentially circumvented the Japanese hierarchy and allowed the Americans to maintain control within the organization.[66]

Intraculturally, the use of language can mark a person as a member of a particular group. In their analysis, Weider and Pratt argue that among some Native Americans, being silent is fundamental in the real Indian's mode of communicating. Moreover, the topic of one's "Indianness" is forbidden; "real" Indians do not discuss it. Real Indians do not engage in casual conversation or idle chit-chat with other Indians. Weider and Pratt note that individuals who initiate small talk or openly discuss their Indianness are disqualified from the group of "real" Indians.[67] In Gerry Philipsen's seminal research on speaking "Like a Man in Teamsterville," he argued that to present oneself as a man requires an implicit understanding of the communication rules of the particular speech community of real men. "Real" men in Teamsterville engage in a variety of communicative strategies that signal their membership in the group. Real men do not rely on speech as their primary mode of self-expression. Only in situations where the interactants are equal (e.g., two "Men") is speaking allowed. Here, speaking serves as a means for solidarity. Speaking is restricted when the communicants are unequal, as in cases where a man is interacting with someone of higher status, such as a boss, or of lower status, such as a wife/girlfriend or children. Moreover, speaking is discouraged when a man must assert his power or influence over others, as in cases where he is responding to an insult to himself or his wife/girlfriend, in cases of disciplining children, and in asserting himself in political or economic discussions. In these types of contexts nonverbal communication is preferred. In some cases, men may be silent, but in others they may react physically, as in the case of responding to an insult. As Philipsen argues,

> In critical symbolic ways, as protector and as master of a house the Teamsterville man disvalues speech as a resource for male role enactment. . . . Speech is not an integral part of earning a living or other aspects of economic life. . . . For the Teamsterville man, minimal emphasis of talk in work settings is one part of a pattern of minimal talk with outsiders to the neighborhood, with persons in positions of authority who are not long-time associates, and with white collar persons, with whom there is a perceived status difference.[68]

Like any other group in the United States, African Americans are identified by their use of language, specifically Ebonics. Moreover, Blacks clearly identify themselves in terms of their use of Ebonics. Smitherman estimates that 80 to 90 percent of all African Americans use some form of Ebonics in some situations. Weber asserts that Ebonics is critical in fostering Black identity in the United States for at least three reasons. First, Weber maintains that because Blacks experience life differently from other groups, they need a language to express their unique experience. Second, Black language bridges the economic, educational, and social gap among Blacks. Weber states that Ebonics "is the language that binds, that creates community for blacks, so that the brother in the three-piece Brooks Brothers suit can go to the local corner where folks 'hang out' and say, 'hey blood, what it is?' and be one with them." Finally, Ebonics expresses a political statement that Blacks have not relinquished a vital part of themselves—that is, language—and that they can maintain control over at least one part of their lives.[69]

The controversy over Ebonics is both political and linguistic. Linguists disagree about whether Ebonics is a dialect (of English) or a language by itself. If a language is defined as a set of sounds, combined with a set of rules, for the purpose of communicating, then Ebonics should be considered a language. A dialect is typically thought of as a regional variety, or subset, of a language. Dialects are distinguished by their variations in vocabulary, grammar, and pronunciation from other regional varieties. As Smitherman notes, the labels "language" and "dialect" are equally respectable among linguists. The term *dialect* has, however, taken on negative connotations among the public.[70] Politically, the debate centers on the appropriateness of Ebonics in various social settings, such as schools. Politically, some factions argue that Ebonics is appropriate and should be taught in schools. For example, in December 1996, the Oakland, California, School Board wrote,

> BE IT RESOLVED that the Board of Education officially recognizes the existence, and the cultural and historic bases of West and NigerCongo African Language Systems, and each language as the predominantly primary language of African-American students . . . BE IT FURTHER RESOLVED that the Superintendent in conjunction with her staff shall immediately devise and implement the best possible academic program for imparting instruction to African American students in their primary language for the combined purposes of maintaining the legitimacy and richness of . . . "Ebonics" . . . and to facilitate their acquisition and mastery of English language skills.[71]

The resolution prompted an anti-Ebonics movement spearheaded by Peter King (New York), member of the U.S. House of Representatives. On January 9, 1997, King introduced House Resolution 28, which read, in part, that no federal funds should be used to pay for or support any program that is based on the premise that Ebonics is a legitimate language.[72] Linguistic and political arguments notwithstanding, Ebonics is clearly a medium of expression for many African Americans. Ebonics not only serves as a vehicle for communication, but also fosters a sense of identity and community among those who speak it.

Do You Speak American?

In 2004, celebrated award-winning author and journalist Robert MacNeil traveled across the United States exploring how the English language is used throughout the various regions of the country. MacNeil wanted to answer the question, What does it mean to "speak American"? Throughout his travels, MacNeil discovered that the English used in the United States differs considerably from region to region, among ethnic and social groups, and by age and gender. In addition, MacNeil found that many people shift from one version of English to another depending on the person with whom they are speaking.[73]

Linguists often argue over the term *Standard English;* that is, the variety of English spoken in the United States that is considered correct. Some linguists argue that there is a right and a wrong way to speak English and that certain correct forms should always be used. But most linguists also recognize that different varieties of English exist in different geographical areas. As we move from region to region across the country, we can hear differences in pronunciation, grammatical structures, vocabulary, and pitch. Most people think of such differences as *accents;* hence, the phrase "Southern accent" is used to describe the speech of people who live in the southern United States. Another term often used by sociolinguists (scholars who study language as it is used in various social contexts) is *dialect;* that is, a language variety associated with a particular region or social group. An accent or dialect should not be confused with *slang* or *jargon.* Slang refers to words or expressions typically used in informal communication. Slang words often do not last long, and other slang replaces them. Jargon refers to the specialized or technical vocabulary used by persons in the same group, such as doctors, lawyers, computer specialists, and so on. Many sociolinguists now use the term *language variety* to refer to the way a particular group of people uses language.[74]

Throughout the United States a debate rages over whether English should be the *official* language. An official language is one that has been specifically designated in the constitution of a country or territory. More than half the countries in the world have official languages, including Egypt, Saudi Arabia, Syria, Lebanon, Kuwait, Jordan, Palestine, and Libya, all of whom designate Arabic as their official language. The federal government of the United States does not recognize an official language, but 30 states have established English as the official state language.[75]

Speakers of a particular dialect often believe that their language variety is the best, correct, and standard way to speak. They may even believe that their language variety is so standard that it is not even considered a dialect. Noted sociolinguist Walt Wolfram argues that everyone speaks some form of dialect. Wolfram maintains that it is not possible to speak a language without speaking a dialect of that language. Moreover, he dispels the myth that dialects result from unsuccessful attempts of people to speak the correct form of a language. Instead, Wolfram contends that speakers acquire their dialect by adopting the speech features of those around them, not by failing in their attempts to adopt

States With English as the Official Language

Alabama	Indiana	New Mexico (with Spanish)
Alaska	Iowa	North Carolina
Arkansas	Kentucky	North Dakota
California	Louisiana (with French)	Puerto Rico (with Spanish)
Colorado	Massachusetts	U.S. Virgin Islands
Florida	Mississippi	Utah
Georgia	Missouri	Virginia
Hawaii (with Hawaiian language)	Montana	Wyoming
	Nebraska	
Illinois	New Hampshire	

standard language features. Dialects, like all language systems, are systematic and regular, and they function as any standard language variety.[76]

Estimating the number of dialects in the United States is difficult. Some linguists argue that there may be as few as only three, whereas others contend that there are as many as 25 dialects in the United States (which would include Ebonics, Spanglish, and Chicano English). Still others maintain that it is impossible to count the possible language varieties in the United States. A few U.S. dialects are discussed below.

Appalachian English (AE). Appalachian English (AE) is spoken by people in the Appalachian mountains from eastern Pennsylvania to North Carolina. Perhaps the most distinctive feature of AE is *a-prefixing;* that is, putting an *a-* sound before words that end in *-ing,* as in, "I was a-slippin' and a-slidin' on the ice," or "What are you a-doin' here so early?" The a-prefix can only occur with verb complements, with -ing participles that function as nouns. Thus, the sentence "The man went a-sailin' " is appropriate, but the sentence "The man likes a-sailin' is not." [77]

Cajun English. Cajun English, sometimes called Linguistic Gumbo, is the term that describes the variety of French spoken in south Louisiana. It originates in the language spoken by the French and Acadian people who settled in Louisiana in the 17th century. Five features distinguish Cajun English, including vowel pronunciation, stress changes, the lack of the /th/ phonemes, nonaspiration of /p/, /t/, and /k/, and lexical differences. Cajuns talk extremely fast, their vowels are clipped, and French terms abound in their speech.[78]

R-Less or R-Dropping Dialects. Regional differences in how the *r* sound is pronounced distinguish one dialect from another. The *r* sound before a vowel (e.g., red, bread) is pronounced much the same way across the United States. But in many dialects of the East Coast (e.g., Boston, New York), the *r* sound before a consonant is dropped and speakers of such dialects lengthen the preceding vowel sound, as in "paahk the caah."[79]

California English. In recent years much attention has focused on the "Valley Girl" dialect phenomenon (e.g., "Gag me with a spoon!"). But California is very diverse ethnically, with substantial Black and Hispanic populations. Thus, the stereotypic "Valley Girl" dialect is spoken mostly by the White population. In such speech, the vowels of *hock* and *hawk, cot* and *caught,* are pronounced the same—so *awesome* rhymes with *possum.* Also, the vowels in *boot* and *boat* (called back vowels because they are pronounced in the back of the mouth) all have a tendency to move forward in the mouth, so that the vowel in *dude* or *spoon* (as in "gag me with a . . .") sounds a little like the word *you,* or the vowel in *pure* or *cute.* Also, *boat* and *loan* often sound like *bewt* and *lewn*—or *eeeeuuw.*[80]

Language has an immense impact on how individuals see themselves and others within any cultural milieu. Language is perhaps the major marker that people use to categorize and group others.

Summary

All human languages are made up of a system of sounds, syntax, and semantics. The sole purpose of language is to communicate. Historically, linguists once believed that language was tied to race and culture. Contemporary linguists have discounted that notion in favor of the idea that languages are essentially human and are not unique to any particular race or culture. As humans, regardless of culture, we are born with a universal grammar that allows us to learn the particular language of our culture. Any individual language is simply a subset of the universal grammar that is embedded in our brains. Considerable evidence shows that children (even deaf and blind children) acquire language in the same way at about the same time. Moreover, children are able to construct grammatically correct sentences without ever having been formally taught.

Language is a guide to social reality, helping people to observe events around them and to organize their thoughts. Moreover, language is so powerful that speakers can generate an infinite number of never-before-spoken sentences that are completely comprehensible by speakers of the same language. Although the universal grammar of all languages is similar, persons from different cultures use different styles of language, ranging from direct to indirect, personal to contextual, instrumental to affective, and elaborate to succinct. Direct-indirect style refers to how speakers reveal their intentions. The personal-contextual style refers to the degree to which speakers focus on themselves during communication or on their partner. Instrumental styles are goal oriented, whereas affective styles are process oriented. Elaborate and succinct styles refer to the actual quantity or volume of talk that is preferred. These different styles probably reflect cultural values and beliefs.

References

1. Searchinger, G. (Director & Producer). (1996). *The human language series: Part I: Colorless green ideas* [Film]. (Available from Ways of Knowing, Inc. 200 West 72nd Street, New York, NY 10023).

2. Salzmann, Z. (1993). *Language, culture, & society.* Boulder, CO: Westview.

3. Sapir, E. (1929). The status of linguistics as a science. *Language, 5,* 207–214.

4. Salzmann, *Language, culture, & society.*

5. Whorf, B. (1940). Science and linguistics. *Technology Review, 42,* 229–231, 247–248.

6. Whorf, B. (1940). Linguistics as an exact science. *Technology Review, 43,* 61–63, 80–83.

7. Salzmann, *Language, culture, & society.*

8. Carroll, J. B. (1963). Linguistic relativity, contrastive linguistics, and language learning. *International Review of Applied Linguistics in Language Teaching, 1,* 1–20.

9. Chomsky, N. (1965). *Aspects of the theory of syntax.* Cambridge: MIT Press; Goss, B., & O'Hair, D. (1988). *Communicating in interpersonal relationships.* New York: Macmillan.

10. Katzner, K. (1975). *Languages of the world.* New York: Funk & Wagnalls.

11. Tohsaku, C. K. (1997). *Japanese "Kanji"* [Online]. Available: http://edweb.sdsu.edu/courses/edtec670/cardboard/card/k/kanji.html

12. Liska, J. (1993). Bee dances, birdsongs, monkey calls, and cetacean sonar: Is speech unique? *Western Journal of Speech Communication, 57,* 1–26.

13. Ibid.

14. Liska, Bee dances, birdsongs, monkey calls, and cetacean sonar.

15. Chomsky, N. (1957). *Syntactic structures.* The Hague: Mouton & Company.

16. Much of this discussion of language is based on interviews with Chomsky and other linguists in Searchinger, *The human language series.*

17. Gleitman, L. P. O. (1993). A human universal: The capacity to learn language. *Modern Philology, 90,* s13–s33.

18. Searchinger, *The human language series.*

19. Gleitman, A human universal.

20. Pinker, S. (1995). Language acquisition. In L. R. Gleitman & M. Liberman (Eds.), *An invitation to cognitive science: Vol. 1: Language* (2nd ed.). Cambridge: MIT Press.

21. Gleitman, A human universal.

22. Searchinger, *The human language series.*

23. Pinker, S., Language acquisition. Some of these examples are from an interview with Pinker in Searchinger, *The human language series.*

24. Heath, J. (1997). *Super-quick overview of characteristics of the Japanese language* [Online]. Available: http://stripe.colorado.edu/-jheath/faq4.html

25. Katzner, *Languages of the world.*

26. Searchinger, *The human language series;* Kulick, D. (1992). *Language shift and cultural reproduction, socialization, self, and syncretism in a Papua New Guinean village.* Cambridge, UK: Cambridge University Press.

27. Ibid.

28. Salzmann, *Language, culture, & society.*

29. Searchinger, *The human language series.*

30. Ibid.

31. Bernstein, B. (1966). Elaborated and restricted codes: Their social origins and some consequences. In A. G. Smith (Ed.), *Communication and culture* (pp. 427–441). New York: Holt, Rinehart and Winston.

32. Ibid.

33. Ibid.

34. Gudykunst, W. B., & Ting-Toomey, S. (1988). Verbal communication styles. In W. B. Gudykunst, & S. Ting-Toomey (Eds.), *Culture and interpersonal communication* (pp. 99–115). Newbury Park, CA: Sage.

35. Gudykunst & Ting-Toomey, Verbal communication styles.

36. Fedarko, K. (1995). Man of Israel: Rabin's stirring life story marks out the mile-posts in the history of his nation. *Time, 146*(20), 68–72.

37. Hall, E. T., & Hall, M. R. (1990). *Understanding cultural differences: Germans, French, and Americans.* Yarmouth, ME: Intercultural Press.

38. Iwao, S. (1993). *The Japanese woman: Traditional image & changing reality.* Cambridge, MA: Harvard University Press.

39. Hall & Hall, *Understanding cultural differences.*

40. This dialogue is very loosely adapted from Storti, C. (1994). *Cross-cultural dialogues: 74 brief encounters with cultural difference.* Yarmouth, ME: Intercultural Press.

41. Gudykunst & Ting-Toomey, Verbal communication styles.

42. Kochman, T. (1990). Cultural pluralism: Black and White styles. In D. Carbaugh (Ed.), *Cultural communication and intercultural contact* (pp. 219–224). Hillsdale, NJ: Erlbaum.

43. Stowell, J. (1996). *The changing face of Chinese communication: A synthesis of interpersonal communication concepts.* Paper presented at the annual convention of the Speech Communication Association, San Diego, CA.

44. Weider, D. L., & Pratt, S. (1990). On being a recognizable Indian among Indians. In D. Carbaugh, (Ed.), *Cultural communication and intercultural contact,* (pp. 45–64). Hillsdale, NJ: Erlbaum.

45. Bernstein, Elaborated and restricted codes: Their social origins and some consequences; Gudykunst, W. B., & Kim, Y. Y. (1997). *Communicating with strangers: An approach to intercultural communication.* New York: McGraw-Hill.

46. Condon, J. C. (1984). *With respect to the Japanese: A guide for Americans.* Yarmouth, ME: Intercultural Press; Gudykunst & Ting-Toomey, *Culture and interpersonal communication.*

47. Storti, C. *Cross-cultural dialogues: 74 brief encounters with cultural differences.*

48. Ibid.

49. Yum, J. O. (1997). The impact of Confucianism on interpersonal relationships and communication patterns in East Asia. In L. A. Samovar, & R. E. Porter (Eds.), *Intercultural communication: A reader* (pp. 78–88), Belmont, CA: Wadsworth; Martin, S. E. (1964). Speech levels in Japan and Korea. In D. Hymes, (Ed.), *Language in culture and society* (pp. 407–415). New York: Harper and Row.

50. Miyagawa, S. *The Japanese language.* (www.-japan.mit.edu/articles/JapaneseLanguage.html). Massachusetts Institute of Technology, 1995.

51. Hooker, R. *The Japanese language* (www.wsu.edu:8080/~dee/ANCJAPAN/language.htm), 1999.

52. Gudykunst & Ting-Toomey, Verbal communication styles; Yum, The impact of Confucianism on interpersonal relationships and communication patterns in East Asia.

53. Wood, J. T. (1997). *Gendered lives: Communication, gender, and culture.* Belmont, CA: Wadsworth.

54. Hall & Hall, *Understanding cultural differences.*

55. Condon, *With respect to the Japanese* (p. 50).

56. Martin, Speech levels in Japan and Korea.

57. *A haiku homepage* [Online]. Available: http://www.dmu.ac.uk/-pkal/haiku.html; *The shiki internet salon* [Online]. Available: http://mikan.cc.matsuyama.u.acjp/-shiki/

58. Becker, C. B. (1986). Reasons for the lack of argumentation and debate in the Far East. *International Journal of Intercultural Relations, 10,* 75–92.

59. Yum, The impact of Confucianism on interpersonal relationships and communication patterns in East Asia.

60. Stowell, *The changing face of Chinese communication;* Lustig, M. W., & Koester, J. (1996). *Intercultural competence: Interpersonal communication across cultures.* New York: HarperCollins.

61. This dialogue is adapted from Copeland, L. (Producer). (1983). *Managing the overseas assignment* [videorecording]. San Francisco: Copeland Griggs Productions.

62. Ting-Toomey, S., & Oetzel, J. G. (2003). Cross-cultural face concerns and conflict styles. In W. B. Gudykunst (Ed.), *Cross-cultural and intercultural communication* (pp. 127–147). Thousand Oaks, CA: Sage.

63. The concepts of assertiveness and cooperativeness are found in a number of sources, including Thomas, K. W., & Kilmann, R. H. (1974). *Thomas-Kilmann conflict MODE instrument.* New York: XICOM, Tuxedo; Rahim, M. A. (1983). A measure of styles of handling interpersonal conflict. *Academy of Management Journal, 26,* 368–376; Ting-Toomey, S., (1988). Intercultural conflict styles: A face-negotiation theory. In Y. Y. Kim & W. B. Gudykunst (Eds.), *Theories of intercultural communication* (pp. 213–235). Newbury Park, CA: Sage.

64. Ting-Toomey & Oetzel, Cross-cultural face concerns and conflict styles.

65. McNamara, T. F. (1988). Language and social identity: Israelis abroad. In W. B. Gudykunst (Ed.), *Language and ethnic identity* (pp. 59–72). Clevedon, UK: Multilingual Matters, Ltd.

66. SanAntonio, P. M. (1988). Social mobility and language use in an American company in Japan. In W. B. Gudykunst (Ed.), *Language and ethnic identity* (pp. 35–44). Clevedon, UK: Multilingual Matters, Ltd.

67. Weider & Pratt, On being a recognizable Indian among Indians.

68. Philipsen, G. (1990). Speaking "like a man" in Teamsterville: Culture patterns of role enactment in an urban neighborhood. In D. Carbaugh (Ed.), *Cultural communication and intercultural contact* (pp. 11–20). Hillsdale, NJ: Erlbaum.

69. Smitherman, G. (2000). *Talkin that talk: Language, culture and education in African America.* New York: Routledge; Weber, S. (1994). The need to be: The socio-cultural significance of black language. In L. A. Samovar & R. E. Porter (Eds.), *Intercultural communication: A reader* (pp. 221–226). Belmont, CA: Wadsworth.

70. Smitherman, G. *Talkin that talk.*

71. Excerpt taken from Smitherman, *Talkin that talk* (p. xi).

72. Richardson, E. (1998). The anti-Ebonics movement: "Standard" English only, *Journal of English Linguistics, 26,* 156–170.

73. MacNeil, R., & Cran, W. (2005). *Do you speak American?* New York: Random House; *Do you speak American?* Online source: www.pbs.org/speak

74. MacNeil & Cran, *Do you speak American?* Online source: www.pbs.org/speak; Wolfram, W., & Schilling-Estes, N. (1998). *American English: Dialects and variation.* Oxford, UK: Basil Blackwell.

75. *List of official languages.* (2005). Wikipedia: The Free Encyclopedia. Online source: http://en.wikipedia.org/wiki/List_of_official_languages

76. Wolfram & Schilling-Estes, *American English.*

77. A-prefixing in Appalachian English: Archaism or innovation? *Do you speak American?* Online source: www.pbs.org/speak/seatosea/americanvarieties/a-prefixing/background

78. Stirring the linguistic gumbo. *Do you speak American?* Online source: www.pbs.org/speak/seatosea/americanvarieties/cajun/

79. Fought, J. (2004). *Starting with the coast* [Online]. Available: http://www.pbs.org/speak/seatosea/americanvarieties/southern/

80. Eckert, P., & Mendoza-Denton, N. (2002). Getting real in the Golden State. *Language Magazine, 1*(7), 29–30, 33–34.

16

Racial Microaggressions in Everyday Life

Implications for Clinical Practice

Derald Wing Sue

Christina M. Capodilupo

Gina C. Torino

Jennifer M. Bucceri

Aisha M. B. Holder

Kevin L. Nadal

Marta Esquilin

Although the civil rights movement had a significant effect on changing racial interactions in this society, racism continues to plague the United States (Thompson & Neville, 1999). President Clinton's Race Advisory Board concluded that (a) racism is one of the most divisive forces in our society, (b) racial legacies of the past continue to haunt current policies and practices that create unfair disparities between minority and majority groups, (c) racial inequities are so deeply ingrained in American society that they are nearly invisible, and (d) most White Americans are unaware of the advantages they enjoy in this

Editor's note: Lillian Comas-Diaz served as the action editor for this article before Derald Wing Sue joined the *American Psychologist* Editorial Board as an associate editor on January 1, 2007.

Authors' note: Derald Wing Sue, Christina M. Capodilupo, Gina C. Torino, Jennifer M. Bucceri, Aisha M. B. Holder, Kevin L. Nadal, and Marta Esquilin, Department of Counseling and Clinical Psychology, Teachers College, Columbia University. Aisha M. B. Holder is now at Fordham University.

society and of how their attitudes and actions unintentionally discriminate against persons of color (Advisory Board to the President's Initiative on Race, 1998). This last conclusion is especially problematic in the mental health professions because most graduates continue to be White and trained primarily in Western European models of service delivery (D. W. Sue & Sue, 2003). For that reason, this article focuses primarily on White therapist–client of color interactions.

Because White therapists are members of the larger society and not immune from inheriting the racial biases of their forebears (Burkard & Knox, 2004; D. W. Sue, 2005), they may become victims of a cultural conditioning process that imbues within them biases and prejudices (Abelson, Dasgupta, Park, & Banaji, 1998; Banaji, Hardin, & Rothman, 1993) that discriminate against clients of color. Over the past 20 years, calls for cultural competence in the helping professions (American Psychological Association, 2003; D. W. Sue, Arredondo, & McDavis, 1992) have stressed the importance of two therapist characteristics associated with effective service delivery to racial/ethnic minority clients: (a) awareness of oneself as a racial/cultural being and of the biases, stereotypes, and assumptions that influence worldviews and (b) awareness of the worldviews of culturally diverse clients. Achieving these two goals is blocked, however, when White clinicians fail to understand how issues of race influence the therapy process and how racism potentially infects the delivery of services to clients of color (Richardson & Molinaro, 1996). Therapists who are unaware of their biases and prejudices may unintentionally create impasses for clients of color, which may partially explain well-documented patterns of therapy underutilization and premature termination of therapy among such clients (Burkard & Knox, 2004; Kearney, Draper, & Baron, 2005). In this article, we describe and analyze how racism in the form of racial microaggressions is particularly problematic for therapists to identify; propose a taxonomy of racial microaggressions with potential implications for practice, education and training, and research; and use the counseling/therapy process to illustrate how racial microaggressions can impair the therapeutic alliance. To date, no conceptual or theoretical model of racial microaggressions has been proposed to explain their impact on the therapeutic process.

The Changing Face of Racism

In recent history, racism in North America has undergone a transformation, especially after the post–civil rights era when the conscious democratic belief in equality for groups of color directly clashed with the long history of racism in the society (Jones, 1997; Thompson & Neville, 1999). The more subtle forms of racism have been labeled *modern racism* (McConahay, 1986), *symbolic racism* (Sears, 1988), and *aversive racism* (Dovidio, Gaertner, Kawakami, & Hodson, 2002). All three explanations of contemporary racism share commonalities. They emphasize that racism (a) is more likely than ever to be disguised and covert and (b) has evolved, from the "old fashioned" form, in which overt racial hatred and bigotry is consciously and publicly displayed, to a more ambiguous and nebulous form that is more difficult to identify and acknowledge.

It appears that modern and symbolic racism are most closely associated with political conservatives, who disclaim personal bigotry by strong and rigid adherence to traditional American values (individualism, self-reliance, hard work, etc.), whereas aversive racism is more characteristic of White liberals (Dovidio & Gaertner, 1996, 2000). Aversive racists, according to these researchers, are strongly motivated by egalitarian values as well as antiminority feelings. Their egalitarian values operate on a conscious level, while their antiminority feelings are less conscious and generally covert (DeVos & Banaji, 2005). In some respects, these three forms of racism can be ordered along a continuum; aversive racists are the least consciously negative, followed by modern and symbolic racists, who are somewhat more prejudiced, and finally by old-fashioned biological racists (Nelson, 2006).

Although much has been written about contemporary forms of racism, many studies in health care (Smedley & Smedley, 2005), education (Gordon & Johnson, 2003), employment (Hinton, 2004), mental health (Burkard & Knox, 2004), and other social settings (Sellers & Shelton, 2003) indicate the difficulty of describing and defining racial discrimination that occurs via "aversive racism" or "implicit bias"; these types of racism are difficult to identify, quantify, and rectify because of their subtle, nebulous, and unnamed nature. Without an adequate classification or understanding of the dynamics of subtle racism, it will remain invisible and potentially harmful to the well-being, self-esteem, and standard of living of people of color (U.S. Department of Health and Human Services, 2001). Ironically, it has been proposed that the daily common experiences of racial aggression that characterize aversive racism may have significantly more influence on racial anger, frustration, and self-esteem than traditional overt forms of racism (Solórzano, Ceja, & Yosso, 2000). Furthermore, the invisible nature of acts of aversive racism prevents perpetrators from realizing and confronting (a) their own complicity in creating psychological dilemmas for minorities and (b) their role in creating disparities in employment, health care, and education.

The Manifestation of Racial Microaggressions

In reviewing the literature on subtle and contemporary forms of racism, we have found the term *racial microaggressions* to best describe the phenomenon in its everyday occurrence. First coined by Pierce in 1970, the term refers to "subtle, stunning, often automatic, and nonverbal exchanges which are 'put downs'" (Pierce, Carew, Pierce-Gonzalez, & Willis, 1978, p. 66). Racial microaggressions have also been described as "subtle insults (verbal, nonverbal, and/or visual) directed toward people of color, often automatically or unconsciously" (Solórzano et al., 2000). Simply stated, microaggressions are brief, everyday exchanges that send denigrating messages to people of color because they belong to a racial minority group. In the world of business, the term *microinequities* is used to describe the pattern of being overlooked, underrespected, and devalued because of one's race or gender. Microaggressions are often unconsciously delivered in the form of subtle snubs or dismissive looks, gestures, and tones. These exchanges are so pervasive and automatic in daily conversations and interactions that they are often dismissed and glossed over as being innocent and innocuous. Yet, as indicated previously, microaggressions are detrimental to persons of color because they impair performance in a multitude of settings by sapping the psychic and spiritual energy of recipients and by creating inequities (Franklin, 2004; D. W. Sue, 2004).

There is an urgent need to bring greater awareness and understanding of how microaggressions operate, their numerous manifestations in society, the type of impact they have on people of color, the dynamic interaction between perpetrator and target, and the educational strategies needed to eliminate them.

Our attempt to define and propose a taxonomy of microaggressions is grounded in several lines of empirical and experiential evidence in the professional literature and in personal narratives.

First, the work by psychologists on aversive racism (Dovidio & Gaertner, 1996; Dovidio et al., 2002), studies suggesting the widespread existence of dissociation between implicit and explicit social stereotyping (Abelson et al., 1998; Banaji et al., 1993; DeVos & Banaji, 2005), the attributional ambiguity of everyday racial discrimination (Crocker & Major, 1989), the daily manifestations of racism in many arenas of life (Plant & Peruche, 2005; Sellers & Shelton, 2003; Vanman, Saltz, Nathan, & Warren, 2004), and multiple similarities between microaggressive incidents and items that comprise measures of race-related stress/perceived discrimination toward Black Americans (Brondolo et al., 2005; Klonoff & Landrine, 1999; Utsey & Ponterotto, 1996) and Asian Americans (Liang, Li, & Kim, 2004) all seem to lend empirical support to the concept of racial microaggressions. Second, numerous personal narratives and brief life stories on race written by White psychologists and psychologists of color provide experiential evidence for the existence of racial microaggressions in everyday life (American Counseling Association, 1999; Conyne & Bemak, 2005; Ponterotto, Casas, Suzuki, & Alexander, 2001). Our analysis of the life experiences of these individuals and the research literature in social and counseling psychology led us to several conclusions: (a) The personal narratives were rich with examples and incidents of racial microaggressions, (b) the formulation of microaggressions was consistent with the research literature, and (c) racial microaggressions seemed to manifest themselves in three distinct forms.

Forms of Racial Microaggressions

Racial microaggressions are brief and commonplace daily verbal, behavioral, and environmental indignities, whether intentional or unintentional, that communicate hostile, derogatory, or negative racial slights and insults to the target person or group. They are not limited to human encounters alone but may also be environmental in nature, as when a person of color is exposed to an office setting that unintentionally assails his or her racial identity (Gordon & Johnson, 2003; D. W. Sue, 2003). For example, one's racial identity can be minimized or made insignificant through the sheer exclusion of decorations or literature that represents various racial groups. Three forms of microaggressions can be identified: microassault, microinsult, and microinvalidation.

Microassault

A microassult is an explicit racial derogation characterized primarily by a verbal or nonverbal attack meant to hurt the intended victim through name-calling, avoidant behavior, or purposeful discriminatory actions. Referring to someone as "colored" or "Oriental," using racial epithets, discouraging interracial interactions, deliberately serving a White patron before someone of color, and displaying a swastika are examples. Microassaults are most similar to what has been called "old fashioned" racism conducted on an individual level. They are most likely to be conscious and deliberate, although they are generally expressed in limited "private" situations (micro) that allow the perpetrator some degree of anonymity. In other words, people are likely to hold notions of minority inferiority privately and will only display them publicly when they

(a) lose control or (b) feel relatively safe to engage in a microassault. Because we have chosen to analyze the unintentional and unconscious manifestations of microaggressions, microassaults are not the focus of our article. It is important to note, however, that individuals can also vary in the degree of conscious awareness they show in the use of the following two forms of microaggressions.

Microinsult

A microinsult is characterized by communications that convey rudeness and insensitivity and demean a person's racial heritage or identity. Microinsults represent subtle snubs, frequently unknown to the perpetrator, but clearly convey a hidden insulting message to the recipient of color. When a White employer tells a prospective candidate of color "I believe the most qualified person should get the job, regardless of race" or when an employee of color is asked "How did you get your job?" the underlying message from the perspective of the recipient may be twofold: (a) People of color are not qualified, and (b) as a minority group member, you must have obtained the position through some affirmative action or quota program and not because of ability. Such statements are not necessarily aggressions, but context is important. Hearing these statements frequently when used against affirmative action makes the recipient likely to experience them as aggressions. Microinsults can also occur nonverbally, as when a White teacher fails to acknowledge students of color in the classroom or when a White supervisor seems distracted during a conversation with a Black employee by avoiding eye contact or turning away (Hinton, 2004). In this case, the message conveyed to persons of color is that their contributions are unimportant.

Microinvalidation

Microinvalidations are characterized by communications that exclude, negate, or nullify the psychological thoughts, feelings, or experiential reality of a person of color. When Asian Americans (born and raised in the United States) are complimented for speaking good English or are repeatedly asked where they were born, the effect is to negate their U.S. American heritage and to convey that they are perpetual foreigners. When Blacks are told that "I don't see color" or "We are all human beings," the effect is to negate their experiences as racial/cultural beings (Helms, 1992). When a Latino couple is given poor service at a restaurant and shares their experience with White friends, only to be told "Don't be so oversensitive" or "Don't be so petty," the racial experience of the couple is being nullified and its importance is being diminished.

We have been able to identify nine categories of microaggressions with distinct themes: alien in one's own land, ascription of intelligence, color blindness, criminality/assumption of criminal status, denial of individual racism, myth of meritocracy, pathologizing cultural values/communication styles, second-class status, and environmental invalidation. Table 1 provides samples of comments or situations that may potentially be classified as racial microaggressions and their accompanying hidden assumptions and messages. Figure 1 visually presents the three large classes of microaggressions, the classification of the themes under each category, and their relationship to one another.

The experience of a racial microaggression has major implications for both the perpetrator and the target person. It creates psychological dilemmas that unless adequately resolved lead to increased levels of racial anger, mistrust, and loss of self-esteem for persons of color; prevent White people from perceiving a different racial reality; and create impediments to harmonious race relations (Spanierman & Heppner, 2004; Thompson & Neville, 1999).

The Invisibility and Dynamics of Racial Microaggressions

The following real-life incident illustrates the issues of invisibility and the disguised problematic dynamics of racial microaggressions.

I [Derald Wing Sue, the senior author, an Asian American] recently traveled with an African American colleague on a plane flying from New York to Boston. The plane was a small "hopper" with a single row of seats on one side and double seats on the other. As the plane was only sparsely populated, we were told by the flight attendant (White) that we could sit anywhere, so we sat at the front, across the aisle from one another. This made it easy for us to converse and provided a larger comfortable space on a small plane for both of us. As the attendant was about to close the hatch, three White men in suits entered the plane, were informed they could sit anywhere, and promptly seated themselves in front of us. Just before take-off, the attendant proceeded to close all overhead compartments and seemed to scan the plane with her eyes. At that point she approached us, leaned over, interrupted our conversation, and asked if we would mind moving to the back of the plane. She indicated that she needed to distribute weight on the plane evenly.

Both of us (passengers of color) had similar negative reactions. First, balancing the weight on the plane seemed reasonable, but why were we being singled out? After all, we had boarded first and the three White men were the last passengers to arrive. Why were they not being asked to move? Were we being singled out because of our race? Was this just a random event with no racial overtones? Were we being oversensitive and petty?

Although we complied by moving to the back of the plane, both of us felt resentment, irritation, and anger. In light of our everyday racial experiences, we both came to the same conclusion: The flight attendant had treated us like second-class citizens because of our race. But this incident did not end there. While I kept telling myself to drop the matter, I could feel my blood pressure rising, heart beating faster, and face flush with anger. When the attendant walked back to make sure our seat belts were fastened, I could not contain my anger any longer. Struggling to control myself, I said to her in a forced calm voice: "Did you know that you asked two passengers of color to step to the rear of the 'bus'?" For a few seconds she said nothing but looked at me with a horrified expression. Then she said in a righteously indignant tone, "Well, I have never been accused of that! How dare you? I don't see color! I only asked you to move to balance the plane. Anyway, I was only trying to give you more space and greater privacy."

Attempts to explain my perceptions and feelings only generated greater defensiveness from her. For every allegation I made, she seemed to have a rational reason for her actions. Finally, she broke off the conversation and refused to talk about the incident any longer. Were it not for my colleague who validated my experiential reality, I would have left that encounter wondering whether I was correct or incorrect in my perceptions. Nevertheless, for the rest of the flight, I stewed over the incident and it left a sour taste in my mouth.

The power of racial microaggressions lies in their invisibility to the perpetrator and, oftentimes, the recipient (D. W. Sue, 2005). Most White Americans experience themselves as good, moral, and decent human beings who believe in equality and democracy. Thus, they find it difficult to believe that they possess biased racial attitudes and may engage in behaviors that are discriminatory (D. W. Sue, 2004). Microaggressive acts can usually be explained away by seemingly nonbiased and valid reasons. For the recipient of a microaggression, however, there is always the nagging question of whether it really happened (Crocker & Major, 1989). It is difficult to identify a microaggression, especially when other explanations seem plausible. Many people of color describe a vague feeling that they have been attacked, that they have been disrespected, or that something is not right (Franklin, 2004; Reid & Radhakrishnan, 2003). In some respects, people of color may find an overt and obvious racist act easier to handle than microaggressions that seem vague or disguised (Solórzano et al., 2000). The above incident reveals how microaggressions operate to create psychological dilemmas for both the White perpetrator and the person of color. Four such dilemmas are particularly noteworthy for everyone to understand.

Dilemma 1: Clash of Racial Realities

The question we pose is this: Did the flight attendant engage in a microaggression or did the senior author and his colleague simply misinterpret the action? Studies indicate that the racial perceptions of people of color differ markedly from those of Whites (Jones, 1997; Harris Poll commissioned by the National Conference of Christians and Jews, 1992). In most cases, White Americans tend to believe that minorities are doing better in life, that discrimination is on the decline, that racism is no longer a significant factor in the lives of people of color, and that equality has been achieved. More important, the majority of Whites do not view themselves as racist or capable of racist behavior.

Minorities, on the other hand, perceive Whites as (a) racially insensitive, (b) unwilling to share their position and wealth, (c) believing they are superior, (d) needing to control everything, and (e) treating them poorly because of their race. People of color believe these attributes are reenacted everyday in their interpersonal interactions with Whites, oftentimes in the form of microaggressions (Solórzano et al., 2000). For example, it was found that 96% of African Americans reported experiencing racial discrimination in a one-year period (Klonoff & Landrine, 1999), and many incidents involved being mistaken for a service worker, being ignored, given poor service, treated rudely, or experiencing strangers acting fearful or intimidated when around them (Sellers & Shelton, 2003).

Dilemma 2: The Invisibility of Unintentional Expressions of Bias

The interaction between the senior author and the flight attendant convinced him that she was sincere in her belief that she had acted in good faith without racial bias. Her actions and their meaning were invisible to her. It was clear that she was stunned that anyone would accuse her of such despicable actions. After all, in her mind, she acted with only the best of intentions: to distribute the weight evenly on the plane for safety reasons and to give two passengers greater privacy and space. She felt betrayed that her good intentions were being questioned. Yet considerable empirical evidence exists showing that racial microaggressions become automatic because of cultural conditioning and that they may become connected neurologically with the processing of emotions that surround prejudice (Abelson et al., 1998). Several investigators have found, for example, that law enforcement officers in laboratory experiments will fire their guns more often at Black criminal suspects than White ones (Plant & Peruche, 2005), and

Table 1 Examples of Racial Microaggressions

Theme	*Microaggression*	*Message*
Alien in own land When Asian Americans and Latino Americans are assumed to be foreign-born	"Where are you from?" "Where were you born?" "You speak good English."	You are not American.
	A person asking an Asian American to teach them words in their native language	You are a foreigner.
Ascription of intelligence Assigning intelligence to a person of color on the basis of their race	"You are a credit to your race."	People of color are generally not as intelligent as Whites.
	"You are so articulate."	It is unusual for someone of your race to be intelligent.
	Asking an Asian person to help with a math or science problem.	All Asians are intelligent and good in math/sciences.
Color blindness Statements that indicate that a White person does not want to acknowledge race	"When I look at you, I don't see color."	Denying a person of color's racial/ethnic experiences.
	"America is a melting pot."	Assimilate/acculturate to the dominant culture.
	"There is only one race, the human race."	Denying the individual as a racial/cultural being.
Criminality/assumption of criminal status A person of color is presumed to be dangerous, criminal, or deviant on the basis of their race	A White man or woman clutching their purse or checking their wallet as a Black or Latino approaches or passes	You are a criminal.
	A store owner following a customer of color around the store	You are going to steal/You are poor/You do not belong.
	A White person waits to ride the next elevator when a person of color is on it	You are dangerous.
Denial of individual racism A statement made when Whites deny their racial biases	"I'm not racist. I have several Black friends."	I am immune to racism because I have friends of color.
	"As a woman, I know what you go through as a racial minority."	Your racial oppression is no different than my gender oppression. I can't be a racist. I'm like you.
Myth of meritocracy Statements which assert that race does not play a role in life successes	"I believe the most qualified person should get the job."	People of color are given extra unfair benefits because of their race.
	"Everyone can succeed in this society, if they work hard enough."	People of color are lazy and/or incompetent and need to work harder.

Theme	*Microaggression*	*Message*
Pathologizing cultural values/communication styles The notion that the values and communication styles of the dominant/White culture are ideal	Asking a Black person: "Why do you have to be so loud/animated? Just calm down."	Assimilate to dominant culture.
	To an Asian or Latino person: "Why are you so quiet? We want to know what you think. Be more verbal." "Speak up more."	
	Dismissing an individual who brings up race/culture in work/school setting	Leave your cultural baggage outside.
Second-class citizen Occurs when a White person is given preferential treatment as a consumer over a person of color	Person of color mistaken for a service worker	People of color *are* servants to Whites. They couldn't possibly occupy high-status positions.
	Having a taxi cab pass a person of color and pick up a White passenger	You are likely to cause trouble and/or travel to a dangerous neighborhood.
	Being ignored at a store counter as attention is given to the White customer behind you	Whites are more valued customers than people of color.
	"You people . . ."	You don't belong. You are a lesser being.
Environmental microaggressions Macro-level microaggressions, which are more apparent on systemic and environmental levels	A college or university with buildings that are all named after White heterosexual upper class males	You don't belong/You won't succeed here/There is only so far you can go.
	Television shows and movies that feature predominantly White people, without representation of people of color	You are an outsider/You don't exist.
	Overcrowding of public schools in communities of color	People of color don't/shouldn't value education.
	Overabundance of liquor stores in communities of color	People of color are deviant.

that Afrocentric features tend to result in longer prison terms (Blair, Judd, & Chapleau, 2004). In all cases, these law enforcement officials had no conscious awareness that they responded differently on the basis of race.

Herein lies a major dilemma. How does one prove that a microaggression has occurred? What makes our belief that the flight attendant acted in a biased manner any more plausible than her conscious belief that it was generated for another reason? If she did act out of hidden and unconscious bias, how do we make her aware of it? Social psychological research tends to confirm the existence of unconscious racial biases in well-intentioned Whites, that nearly everyone born and raised in the United States inherits the racial biases of the society, and that the most accurate assessment about whether racist acts have occurred in a particular situation is most likely to be made by those most disempowered rather than by those who enjoy the privileges of power (Jones, 1997; Keltner & Robinson, 1996). According to these findings, microaggressions (a) tend to be subtle, indirect, and unintentional, (b) are most likely to emerge, not when a behavior would look prejudicial, but when other rationales can be offered for prejudicial behavior, and (c) occur when Whites pretend not to notice differences, thereby justifying that "color" was not involved in the actions taken. Color blindness is a major form of microinvalidation because it denies the racial and experiential reality of people of color and provides an excuse to White people to claim that they are not prejudiced (Helms, 1992; Neville, Lilly, Duran, Lee, & Browne, 2000). The flight attendant, for example, did not realize that her "not seeing color" invalidated both passengers' racial identity and experiential reality.

Dilemma 3: Perceived Minimal Harm of Racial Microaggressions

In most cases, when individuals are confronted with their microaggressive acts (as in the case of the flight attendant), the perpetrator usually believes that the victim has overreacted and is being overly sensitive and/or petty. After all, even if it was an innocent racial blunder, microaggressions are believed to have minimal negative impact. People of color are told not to overreact and to simply "let it go." Usually, Whites consider microaggressive incidents to be minor, and people of color are encouraged (oftentimes by people of color as well) to not waste time or effort on them.

It is clear that old-fashioned racism unfairly disadvantages people of color and that it contributes to stress, depression, shame, and anger in its victims (Jones, 1997). But evidence also supports the detrimental impact of more subtle forms of racism (Chakraborty & McKenzie, 2002; Clark, Anderson, Clark, & Williams, 1999). For example, in a survey of studies examining racism and mental health, researchers found a positive association between happiness and life satisfaction, self-esteem, mastery of control, hypertension, and discrimination (Williams, Neighbors, & Jackson, 2003). Many of the types of everyday racism identified by Williams and colleagues (Williams & Collins, 1995; Williams, Lavizzo-Mourey, & Warren, 1994) provide strong support for the idea that racial microaggressions are not minimally harmful. One study specifically examined microaggressions in the experiences of African Americans and found that the cumulative effects can be quite devastating (Solórzano et al., 2000). The researchers reported that experience with microaggressions resulted in a negative racial climate and emotions of self-doubt, frustration, and isolation on the part of victims. As indicated in the incident above, the senior author experienced considerable emotional turmoil that lasted for the entire flight. When one considers that people of color are exposed continually to microaggressions and that their effects are cumulative, it becomes easier to understand the psychological toll they may take on recipients' well-being.

We submit that covert racism in the form of microaggressions also has a dramatic and detrimental impact on people of color. Although microaggressions may be seemingly innocuous and insignificant, their effects can be quite dramatic (Steele, Spencer, & Aronson, 2002). D. W. Sue believes that "this contemporary form of racism is many times over more problematic, damaging, and injurious to persons of color than overt racist acts" (D. W. Sue, 2003, p. 48).

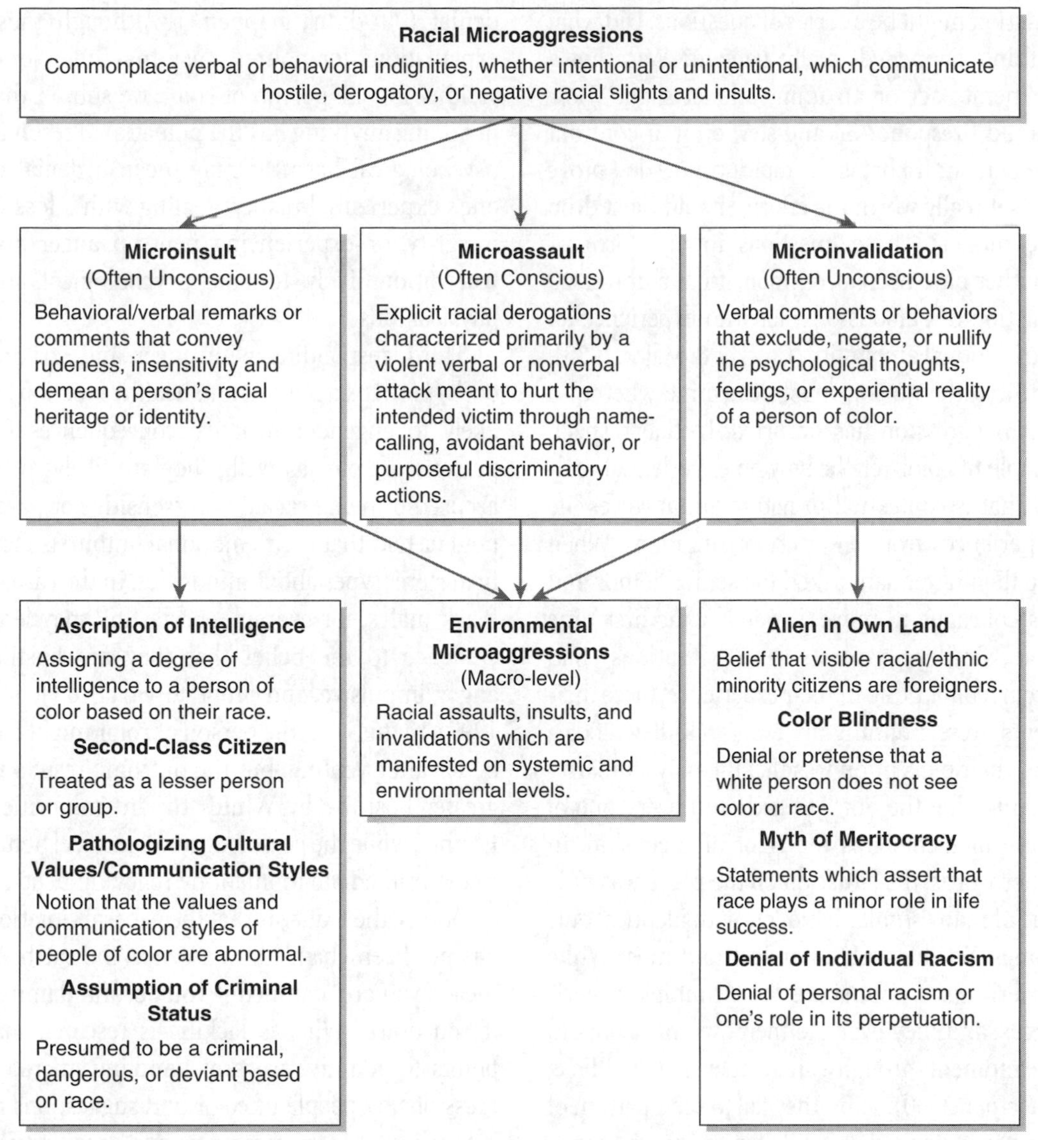

Figure 1 Categories of and Relationships Among Racial Microaggressions

It has been noted that the cumulative effects of racial microaggressions may theoretically result in "diminished mortality, augmented morbidity and flattened confidence" (Pierce, 1995, p. 281). It is important to study and acknowledge this form of racism in society because without documentation and analysis to better understand microaggressions, the threats that they pose and the assaults that they justify can be easily ignored or downplayed (Solórzano et al., 2000). D. W. Sue (2005) has referred to this phenomenon as "a conspiracy of silence."

Dilemma 4: The Catch-22 of Responding to Microaggressions

When a microaggression occurs, the victim is usually placed in a catch-22. The immediate reaction might be a series of questions: Did what I think happened, really happen? Was this a deliberate act or an unintentional slight? How should I respond? Sit and stew on it or confront the person? If I bring the topic up, how do I prove it? Is it really worth the effort? Should I just drop the matter? These questions in one form or another have been a common, if not a universal, reaction of persons of color who experience an attributional ambiguity (Crocker & Major, 1989).

First, the person must determine whether a microaggression has occurred. In that respect, people of color rely heavily on experiential reality that is contextual in nature and involves life experiences from a variety of situations. When the flight attendant asked the senior author and his colleague to move, it was not the first time that similar requests and situations had occurred for both. In their experience, these incidents were nonrandom events (Ridley, 2005), and their perception was that the only similarity "connecting the dots" to each and every one of these incidents was the color of their skin. In other words, the situation on the plane was only one of many similar incidents with identical outcomes. Yet the flight attendant and most White Americans do not share these multiple experiences, and they evaluate their own behaviors in the moment through a singular event (Dovidio & Gaertner, 2000). Thus, they fail to see a pattern of bias, are defended by a belief in their own morality, and can in good conscience deny that they discriminated (D. W. Sue, 2005).

Second, how one reacts to a microaggression may have differential effects, not only on the perpetrator but on the person of color as well. Deciding to do nothing by sitting on one's anger is one response that occurs frequently in people of color. This response occurs because persons of color may be (a) unable to determine whether a microaggression has occurred, (b) at a loss for how to respond, (c) fearful of the consequences, (d) rationalizing that "it won't do any good anyway," or (e) engaging in self-deception through denial ("It didn't happen."). Although these explanations for nonresponse may hold some validity for the person of color, we submit that not doing anything has the potential to result in psychological harm. It may mean a denial of one's experiential reality, dealing with a loss of integrity, or experiencing pent-up anger and frustration likely to take psychological and physical tolls.

Third, responding with anger and striking back (perhaps a normal and healthy reaction) is likely to engender negative consequences for persons of color as well. They are likely to be accused of being racially oversensitive or paranoid or told that their emotional outbursts confirm stereotypes about minorities. In the case of Black males, for example, protesting may lend credence to the belief that they are hostile, angry, impulsive, and prone to violence (Jones, 1997). In this case, the person of color might feel better after venting, but the outcome results in greater hostility by Whites toward minorities. Further, while the person of color may feel better in the immediate moment by relieving pent-up emotions, the reality is that the general situation has not been changed. In essence, the catch-22 means you are "damned if you do, and damned if you don't." What is lacking is research that points to adaptive ways of handling microaggressions by people of color and suggestions of how to increase the awareness and sensitivity of Whites to microaggressions so that they accept responsibility for their behaviors and for changing them (Solórzano et al., 2000).

Racial Microaggressions as a Barrier to Clinical Practice

In a broad sense, counseling and psychotherapy can be characterized as the formation of a deeply personal relationship between a helping professional and a client that involves appropriate and accurate interpersonal interactions and communications. For effective therapy to occur, some form of positive coalition must develop between the parties involved (D. W. Sue & Sue, 2003). Many have referred to this as the "working relationship," the "therapeutic alliance," or the "establishment of rapport" (D. W. Sue & Sue, 2003). A strong therapeutic relationship is often enhanced when clients perceive therapists as credible (trustworthy and expert) and themselves as understood and positively regarded by their therapists (Strong & Schmidt, 1970). Helping professionals are trained to listen, to show empathic concern, to be objective, to value the client's integrity, to communicate understanding, and to use their professional knowledge and skills to aid clients to solve problems (Grencavage & Norcross, 1990).

As a therapeutic team, therapist and client are better prepared to venture into problematic areas that the client might hesitate to face alone. Research suggests that the therapeutic alliance is one of the major common factors of any helping relationship and is correlated with successful outcome (Lui & Pope-Davis, 2005; Martin, Garske, & Davis, 2000). More important, however, are findings that a client's perception of an accepting and positive relationship is a better predictor of successful outcome than is a similar perception by the counselor (Horvath & Symonds, 1991). Thus, when clients do not perceive their therapists as trustworthy and when they feel misunderstood and undervalued, therapeutic success is less likely to occur. Oftentimes, the telltale signs of a failed therapeutic relationship may result in clients being less likely to self-disclose, terminating prematurely, or failing to return for scheduled visits (Burkard & Knox, 2004; Kearney, Draper, & Baron, 2005).

Although the task of establishing an effective therapeutic relationship applies to the entire helping spectrum, working with clients who differ from the therapist in race, ethnicity, culture, and sexual orientation poses special challenges. White therapists who are products of their cultural conditioning may be prone to engage in racial microaggressions (Locke & Kiselica, 1999). Thus, the therapeutic alliance is likely to be weakened or terminated when clients of color perceive White therapists as biased, prejudiced, or unlikely to understand them as racial/cultural beings. That racism can potentially infect the therapeutic process when working with clients of color has been a common concern voiced by the President's Commission on Mental Health (1978) and the Surgeon General's Report on *Mental Health: Culture, Race and Ethnicity* (U.S. Department of Health and Human Services, 2001). It has been postulated that therapist bias might partially account for the low utilization of mental health services and premature termination of therapy sessions by African American, Native American, Asian American, and Latino/Hispanic American clients (U.S. Department of Health and Human Services, 2001).

Yet research also reveals that most people in our nation believe in democracy, fairness, and strong humanistic values that condemn racism and the inequities that it engenders (Dovidio et al., 2002). Such a statement is arguably truer for mental health professionals, whose goals are to help rather than hinder or hurt clients of color. Both the American Psychological Association and the American Counseling Association have attempted to confront the biases of the profession by passing multicultural guidelines or standards that denounce prejudice and discrimination in the delivery of mental health services to clients of color (American Psychological Association, 2003; D. W. Sue et al., 1992). Like most people in society, counselors and therapists experience themselves as fair and decent individuals who would never consciously and deliberately engage in racist acts toward clients of color. Sadly, it is often pointed out that when clinician and client differ from one another along racial lines, however, the relationship may serve as a microcosm for the troubled race relations in the United States. While many would like to believe that racism is no longer a major problem and that the good intentions of the helping profession have built safeguards against prejudice and discrimination, the reality is that they continue to be manifested through the therapeutic process (Utsey, Gernat, & Hammar, 2005). This is not to suggest, however, that positive changes in race relations have not occurred. Yet, as in many other interactions, microaggressions are equally likely to occur in therapeutic transactions (Ridley, 2005).

The Manifestation of Racial Microaggressions in Counseling/Therapy

Microaggressions become meaningful in the context of clinical practice, as relational dynamics and the human condition are central aspects of this field. The often unintentional and unconscious nature of microaggressions (Dilemma 2: Invisibility) poses the biggest challenge to the majority of White mental health professionals, who believe that they are just, unbiased, and nonracist. Further, mental health professionals are in a position of power, which renders them less likely to accurately assess (Dilemma 1: Conflict of Racial Realities) whether racist acts have occurred in their sessions. Thus, the harm they perpetrate against their clients of color is either unknown or minimized (Dilemma 3: Minimal Harm). Microaggressions not only oppress and harm, but they place clients of color in the unenviable position of a catch-22 (Dilemma 4).

In clinical practice, microaggressions are likely to go unrecognized by White clinicians who are unintentionally and unconsciously expressing bias. As a result, therapists must make a concerted effort to identify and monitor microaggressions within the therapeutic context. This process is reminiscent of the importance of becoming aware of potential transference and countertransference issues between therapist and client and how they may unintentionally interfere with effective therapy (Woodhouse, Schlosser, Crook, Ligiero, & Gelso, 2003). The inherent power dynamic in the therapeutic relationship further complicates this issue, as therapists are in a position of power to make diagnoses and influence the course of treatment. The power dynamic between therapist and client also affects the catch-22 of responding to microaggressions because clients may be less likely to confront their therapists and more likely to question their own perceptions in the event of a microaggression.

Table 2 provides a few examples of microaggressions in counseling practice under each of the nine categories identified earlier. Under Color Blindness, for example, a client of color stresses the importance of racial experiences only to have the therapist reply, "We are all unique. We are all individuals" or "We are all human beings or the same under the skin." These colorblind statements, which were intended to be supportive, to be sympathetic, and to convey an ability to understand, may leave the client feeling misunderstood, negated, invalidated, and unimportant (especially if racial identity is important to the client). Moreover these statements presume that the therapist is capable of not seeing race and impose a definition of racial reality on the client (Neville et al., 2000).

Under Denial of Individual Racism, a common response by Whites to people of color is that they can understand and relate to experiences of racism. In Table 2, under this category,

Table 2 Examples of Racial Microaggressions in Therapeutic Practice

Theme	*Microaggression*	*Message*
Alien in own land When Asian Americans and Latino Americans are assumed to be foreign-born	A White client does not want to work with an Asian American therapist because "she will not understand my problem."	You are not American
	A White therapist tells an American-born Latino client that he/she should seek a Spanish-speaking therapist.	
Ascription of intelligence Assigning a degree of intelligence to a person of color on the basis of their race	A school counselor reacts with surprise when an Asian American student had trouble on the math portion of a standardized test.	All Asians are smart and good at math.
	A career counselor asking a Black or Latino student, "Do you think you're ready for college?"	It is unusual for people of color to succeed.
Color blindness Statements which indicate that a White person does not want to acknowledge race	A therapist says, "I think you are being too paranoid. We should emphasize similarities, not people's differences" when a client of color attempts to discuss her feelings about being the only person of color at her job and feeling alienated and dismissed by her co-workers.	Race and culture are not important variables that affect people's lives.
	A client of color expresses concern in discussing racial issues with her therapist. Her therapist replies with, "When I see you, I don't see color."	Your racial experiences are not valid.
Criminality/assumption of criminal status A person of color is presumed to be dangerous, criminal, or deviant on the basis of their race	When a Black client shares that she was accused of stealing from work, the therapist encourages the client to explore how she might have contributed to her employer's mistrust of her.	You are a criminal.
	A therapist takes great care to ask all substance abuse questions in an intake with a Native American client, and is suspicious of the client's nonexistent history with substances.	You are deviant.
Denial of individual racism A statement made when Whites renounce their racial biases	A client of color asks his or her therapist about how race affects their working relationship. The therapist replies, "Race does not affect the way I treat you."	Your racial/ethnic experience is not important.
	A client of color expresses hesitancy in discussing racial issues with his White female therapist. She replies "I understand. As a woman, I face discrimination also."	Your racial oppression is no different than my gender oppression.

(Continued)

Table 2 (Continued)

Theme	*Microaggression*	*Message*
Myth of meritocracy Statements which assert that race does not play a role in succeeding in career advancement or education	A school counselor tells a Black student that "if you work hard, you can succeed like everyone else." A career counselor is working with a client of color who is concerned about not being promoted at work despite being qualified. The counselor suggests, "Maybe if you work harder you can succeed like your peers."	People of color are lazy and/or incompetent and need to work harder. If you don't succeed, you have only yourself to blame (blaming the victim).
Pathologizing cultural values/communication styles The notion that the values and communication styles of the dominant/White culture are ideal	A Black client is loud, emotional, and confrontational in a counseling session. The therapist diagnoses her with borderline personality disorder. A client of Asian or Native American descent has trouble maintaining eye contact with his therapist. The therapist diagnoses him with a social anxiety disorder.	Assimilate to dominant culture.
	Advising a client, "Do you really think your problem stems from racism?"	Leave your cultural baggage outside.
Second-class citizen Occurs when a White person is given preferential treatment as a consumer over a person of color	A counselor limits the amount of long-term therapy to provide at a college counseling center; she chooses all White clients over clients of color.	Whites are more valued than people of color.
	Clients of color are not welcomed or acknowledged by receptionists.	White clients are more valued than clients of color.
Environmental microaggressions Macro-level microaggressions, which are more apparent on a systemic level	A waiting room office has pictures of American presidents.	You don't belong/Only white people can succeed.
	Every counselor at a mental health clinic is White.	You are an outsider/You don't exist.

we provide the following anecdote: A client of color expresses hesitancy in discussing racial issues with his White female therapist. She replies, "I understand. As a woman, I face discrimination too." The message is that the therapist believes her gender oppression is no different from the client's experiences of racial/ethnic oppression. This response is problematic because such attempts by the therapist to explain how he or she can understand a person of color's experience with racism may be perceived by the client as an attempt to minimize the importance of his or her racial identity, to avoid acknowledging the therapist's racial biases, or to communicate a discomfort with discussing racial issues. Furthermore, the therapist excuses himself or herself from any blame or fault in perpetuating racism and the power of racism. This failure to acknowledge the significance of racism within and outside of the therapy session contributes to the breakdown of the alliance between therapist and client. A therapist's willingness to discuss racial matters is of central importance in creating a therapeutic alliance with clients of color (Cardemil & Battle, 2003).

Under the category Alien in Own Land, many Asian Americans and Latino/Hispanic Americans report that they are commonly seen as perpetual foreigners. For example, a female Asian American client arrives for her first therapy session. Her therapist asks her where she is from, and when told "Philadelphia," the therapist further probes by asking where she was born. In this case, the therapist has assumed that the Asian American client is not from the United States and has imposed through the use of the second question the idea that she must be a foreigner. Immediately, a barrier is created in the helping relationship because the client feels invalidated by the therapist (she is perceived as a foreigner, not a U.S. citizen). Unfortunately, the Asian American client is unlikely to question her therapist or point out the bias because of the power dynamic, which causes her to harbor resentment and ill feelings toward the therapist.

We contend that clients of color are at increased risk of not continuing in the counseling/therapy session when such microaggressions occur. Worse yet, they will not receive the help they need and may leave the session feeling worse than when they first sought counseling. Because it is unlikely that clinicians intentionally create hostile and unwelcoming environments for their ethnic minority clients, it can be assumed that these biases are being expressed through microaggressions. Therapists can convey their bias to their ethnic minority clients in myriad ways, such as by minimizing symptoms for Asian Americans on the basis of a false belief in the "model" minority (D. W. Sue & Sue, 2003) or by placing greater emphasis on symptoms such as paranoid delusions and substance abuse in Native Americans and Africans Americans, who are believed to suffer from these afflictions (U.S. Department of Health and Human Services, 2001).

Last, White counselors and therapists can impose and value their own cultural worldview while devaluing and pathologizing the cultural values of their ethnic minority clients. Previous research has shown that pathologizing clients' cultural values has been a major determinant of clients of color discontinuing psychotherapy (S. Sue, Fujino, Hu, & Takeuchi, 1991). Many clients of color may feel misunderstood by their therapists because of a lack of cultural understanding. Asian American or Latino American clients who enter therapy to discuss family issues such as feeling obligated, stressed, or overwhelmed with excess family responsibilities may be encouraged by therapists to speak out against their families or to make decisions regardless of family support or expectations. Therapists may be unaware that they may be directly invalidating cultural respect for authority and imposing an individualistic view over a collectivist one.

Future Directions in the Understanding of Racial Microaggressions

With respect to racism, D. W. Sue (2004, p. 762) has stated that the greatest challenge society and the mental health professions face is "making the 'invisible' visible." That can only be accomplished when people are willing to openly and honestly engage in a dialogue about race and racism. In that respect, the education and training of mental health professionals must incorporate issues of race and culture. One would ordinarily expect that mental health professionals would be more willing than most to dialogue on this topic, but studies suggest that White clinicians receive minimal or no practicum or supervision experiences that address race and are uncomfortable broaching the topic (Knox, Burkard, Johnson, Suzuki, & Ponterotto, 2003). Many White trainees in therapy dyads experience anxiety in the form of poor articulation, faltering and/or trembling voices, and mispronunciation of words when directly engaged in discussions about race (Utsey et al., 2005). It is interesting that such nonverbal behaviors also serve as a form of racial microaggression. When helping professionals have difficulty addressing race issues, they cut off an avenue for clients of color to explore matters of bias, discrimination, and prejudice.

Education and Training and Racial Microaggressions

It is clear that mental health training programs must support trainees in overcoming their fears and their resistance to talking about race by fostering safe and productive learning environments (Sanchez-Hucles & Jones, 2005). It is important that training programs be structured and facilitated in a manner that promotes inquiry and allows trainees to experience discomfort and vulnerability (Young & Davis-Russell, 2002). Trainees need to be challenged to explore their own racial identities and their feelings about other racial groups. The prerequisite for cultural competence has always been racial self-awareness. This is equally true for understanding how microaggressions, especially those of the therapist, influence the therapeutic process. This level of self-awareness brings to the surface possible prejudices and biases that inform racial microaggressions. A first step for therapists who want to integrate an understanding of racism's mental health effects into the conceptualization of psychological functioning is to undergo a process of learning and critical self-examination of racism and its impact on one's life and the lives of others (Thompson & Neville, 1999). For White clinicians, it means addressing the question "What does it mean to be White?" and being fully cognizant of their own White racial identity development and how it may intrude on people of color (Helms, 1992, 1995). In addition, it has been suggested that articulating a personal theory of reality and of therapeutic change in the context of an environment of racism is one way to begin integrating knowledge of racism with the practice of psychotherapy (Thompson & Neville, 1999). Education and training must aid White clinicians to achieve the following: (a) increase their ability to identify racial microaggressions in general and in themselves in particular, (b) understand how racial microaggressions, including their own, detrimentally impact clients of color, and (c) accept responsibility for taking corrective actions to overcome racial biases.

Research on Racial Microaggressions

A major obstacle to understanding racial microaggressions is that research is in a nascent state. Researchers continue to omit subtle racism and microaggressions from their research agendas, and this absence conveys the notion that covert forms of racism are not as valid or as important as racist events that can be quantified and "proven." In fact, omitting microaggressions from studies on racism on the basis of a belief that they are less harmful encourages the profession to "look the other way." Moreover, the fact that psychological research has continued to inadequately address race and ethnicity (Delgado-Romero, Rowland, & Galvin, 2005) is in itself a microaggression. Pursuing a line of research examining how cross-racial dyadic compositions impact the process and outcome of counselor/client interactions would be a tremendous contribution to the field of counseling and clinical psychology. Helms and Cook (1999) noted that racial consciousness is a critical consideration in determining White therapists' ability to operate effectively in cross-racial dyads.

For mental health purposes, it would be useful to explore the coping mechanisms used by people of color to stave off the negative effects of microaggressions. The fact that people of color have had to face daily microaggressions and have continued to maintain their dignity in the face of such hostility is a testament to their resiliency (D. W. Sue, 2003). What coping strategies have been found to serve them well? A greater understanding of responses to microaggressions, both in the long term and the short term, and of the coping strategies employed would be beneficial in arming children of color for the life they will face. Such research is necessary because without documentation and analysis to help better understand microaggressions, the threats that they pose and the assaults that they justify can be easily ignored or downplayed (Solórzano et al., 2000). Studying the long-term impact that microaggressions have on mental health functioning, self-esteem, self-concept, and racial identity development appears crucial to documenting the harm microaggressions inflict on people of color. The taxonomy of microaggressions proposed here may make it easier to explore other social psychological questions as well.

First, it is highly probable that microaggressions vary in their severity and impact. As indicated, a microassault does not evoke a guessing game because the intent of the perpetrator is clear. However, the racist intent of microinsults and microinvalidations is less clear and presents different dilemmas for people of color. Some questions to ponder include the following: (a) Are the three forms of racial microaggressions equal in impact? Are some themes and their hidden messages more problematic than others? Although all expressions may take a psychological toll, some are obviously experienced as more harmful and severe than others. (b) Is there a relationship between forms of racial microaggressions and racial identity development? Recent research and formulations on White racial identity development and the psychosocial costs of racism to Whites (Helms, 1995; Spanierman, Armstrong, Poteat, & Beer, 2006) imply that forms of racial microaggressions may be associated with certain statuses or trait clusters. (c) Finally, is it possible that different racial/ethnic groups are more likely to encounter certain forms of racial microaggressions than others? A preliminary study suggests that Asian Americans are prone to be victims of microinvalidations with themes that revolve around "alien in one's own land" (D. W. Sue, Bucceri, Lin, Nadal, & Torino, 2007) rather than microinsults with themes of "criminality." Is it possible that Blacks are more likely to be subjected to the latter than to the former? What about Latinos and American Indians?

Second, the challenge in conducting research aimed at understanding microaggressions involves measurement. Adequate assessment tools need to be created to effectively explore the new and burgeoning field of microaggression research. Although there are several promising race-related stress and discrimination measures, such as the Perceived Ethnic Discrimination Questionnaire (PEDQ; Brondolo et al., 2005), the Color-Blind Racial Attitude Scale (COBRAS; Neville et al., 2000), the Index of Race Related Stress (ERRS; Utsey & Ponterotto, 1996), and the Schedule of Racist Events (SRE; Klonoff & Landrine, 1999), none of them is directly aimed at distinguishing between categories of racial microaggressions or their intentional or unintentional nature. The PEDQ uses four subscales that broadly measure stigmatization, harassment, workplace discrimination, and social exclusion; the COBRAS is specific to a person's minimization of race and racism; the IRRS uses Jones's (1997) framework to measure individual, institutional, and societal racism; and the SRE is aimed at measuring frequency of racist incidents. All contain examples of racial microaggressions that support our taxonomy, but none makes conceptual distinctions that allow for categorical measurements of this phenomenon. It seems imperative that specific instruments be developed to aid in understanding the causes, consequences, manifestations, and elimination of racial microaggressions.

Conclusion

Nearly all interracial encounters are prone to the manifestation of racial microaggressions. We have chosen mainly to address the therapeutic relationship, but racial microaggressions are potentially present whenever human interactions involve participants who differ in race and culture (teaching, supervising, training, administering, evaluating, etc.). We have purposely chosen to concentrate on racial microaggressions, but it is important to acknowledge other types of microaggressions as well. Gender, sexual orientation, and disability microaggressions may have equally powerful and potentially detrimental effects on women, gay, lesbian, bisexual, and transgender individuals, and disability groups. Further, racial microaggressions are not limited to White–Black, White–Latino, or White–Person of Color interactions. Interethnic racial microaggressions occur between people of color as well. In the area of counseling and therapy, for example, research may also prove beneficial in understanding cross-racial dyads in which the therapist is a person of color and the client is White or in which both therapist and client are persons of color. Investigating these combinations of cross-racial dyads would be useful, because it is clear that no racial/ethnic group is immune from inheriting the racial biases of the society (D. W. Sue, 2003). We encourage future research in these two areas because all forms of microaggressions have detrimental consequences.

References

Abelson, R. P., Dasgupta, N., Park, J., & Banaji, M. R. (1998). Perceptions of the collective other. *Personality and Social Psychology Review, 2,* 243–250.

Advisory Board to the President's Initiative on Race. (1998). *One America in the 21st century: Forging a new future.* Washington, DC: U.S. Government Printing Office.

American Counseling Association. (1999). *Racism: Healing its effects.* Alexandria, VA: Author.

American Psychological Association. (2003). Guidelines on multicultural education, training, research, practice, and organizational change for psychologists. *American Psychologist, 58,* 377–402.

Banaji, M. R., Hardin, C., & Rothman, A. J. (1993). Implicit stereotyping in person judgment. *Journal of Personality and Social Psychology, 65,* 272–281.

Blair, I. V., Judd, C. M., & Chapleau, K. M. (2004). The influence of afrocentric facial features in criminal sentencing. *Psychological Science, 15,* 674–679.

Brondolo, E., Kelly, K. P., Coakley, V., Gordon, T., Thompson, S., & Levy, E. (2005). The Perceived Ethnic Discrimination Questionnaire: Development and preliminary validation of a community version. *Journal of Applied Social Psychology, 35,* 335–365.

Burkard, A. W., & Knox, S. (2004). Effect of therapist color-blindness on empathy and attributions in cross-cultural counseling. *Journal of Counseling Psychology, 51,* 387–397.

Cardemil, E. V., & Battle, C. L. (2003). Guess who's coming to therapy? Getting comfortable with conversations about race and ethnicity in psychotherapy. *Professional Psychology: Research and Practice, 34,* 278–286.

Chakraborty, A., & McKenzie, K. (2002). Does racial discrimination cause mental illness? *British Journal of Psychiatry, 180,* 475–477.

Clark, R., Anderson, N. B., Clark, V. R., & Williams, D. R. (1999). Racism as a stressor for African Americans. *American Psychologist, 54,* 805–816.

Conyne, R. K., & Bemak, F. (2005). *Journeys to professional excellence: Lessons from leading counselor educators and practitioners.* Alexandria, VA: American Counseling Association.

Crocker, J., & Major, B., (1989). Social stigma and self-esteem: The self-protective properties of stigma. *Psychological Review, 96,* 608–630.

Delgado-Romero, E. A., Rowland, M., & Galvan, N. (2005). The continuing and evolving challenge of race and ethnicity in empirical counseling and counseling psychology research: A reply. *Counseling Psychologist, 33,* 559–564.

DeVos, T., & Banaji, M. R. (2005). American = White? *Journal of Personality and Social Psychology, 88,* 447–466.

Dovidio, J. F., & Gaertner, S. L. (1996). Affirmative action, unintentional racial biases, and intergroup relations. *Journal of Social Issues, 52,* 51–75.

Dovidio, J. F., & Gaertner, S. L. (2000). Aversive racism and selective decisions: 1989–1999. *Psychological Science, 11,* 315–319.

Dovidio, J. F., Gaertner, S. L., Kawakami, K., & Hodson, G. (2002). Why can't we all just get along? Interpersonal biases and interracial distrust. *Cultural Diversity and Ethnic Minority Psychology, 8,* 88–102.

Franklin, A. J. (2004). *From brotherhood to manhood: How Black men rescue their relationships and dreams from the invisibility syndrome.* Hoboken, NJ: Wiley.

Gordon, J., & Johnson, M. (2003). Race, speech, and hostile educational environment: What color is free speech? *Journal of Social Philosophy, 34,* 414–436.

Grencavage, L. M., & Norcross, J. C. (1990). Where are the commonalities among the therapeutic common factors? *Professional Psychology: Research and Practice, 21,* 372–378.

Helms, J. E. (1992). *A race is a nice thing to have: A guide to being a white person or understanding the white persons in your life.* Topeka, KS: Content Communications.

Helms, J. E. (1995). An update of Helms's White and people of color racial identity models. In J. G. Ponterotto, J. M. Casas, L. A. Suzuki, & C. M. Alexander (Eds.), *Handbook of multicultural counseling* (pp. 181–191). Thousand Oaks, CA: Sage.

Helms, J. E., & Cook, D. (1999). *Using race and culture in counseling and psychotherapy: Theory and process.* Needham Heights, MA: Allyn & Bacon.

Hinton, E. L. (2004, March/April). Microinequities: When small slights lead to huge problems in the workplace. *DiversityInc.* (Available at http://www.magazine.org/content/files/Microinequities.pdf)

Horvath, A. O., & Symonds, B. D. (1991). Relationship between working alliance and outcome in psychotherapy: A meta-analysis. *Journal of Counseling Psychology, 38,* 139–149.

Jones, J. M. (1997). *Prejudice and racism* (2nd ed.). Washington, DC: McGraw-Hill.

Kearney, L. K., Draper, M., & Baron, A. (2005). Counseling utilization by ethnic minority college students. *Cultural Diversity and Ethnic Minority Psychology, 11,* 272–285.

Keltner, D., & Robinson, R. J. (1996). Extremism, power, and imagined basis of social conflict. *Current Directions in Psychological Science, 5,* 101–105.

Klonoff, E. A., & Landrine, H. (1999). Cross-validation of the Schedule of Racist Events. *Journal of Black Psychology, 25,* 231–254.

Knox, S., Burkard, A. W., Johnson, A. J., Suzuki, L. A., & Ponterotto, J. G. (2003). African American and European American therapists' experiences of addressing race in cross-racial psychotherapy dyads. *Journal of Counseling Psychology, 50,* 466–481.

Liang, C. T. H., Li, L. C., & Kim, B. S. K. (2004). The Asian American Racism-Related Stress Inventory: Development, factor analysis, reliability, and validity. *Journal of Counseling Psychology, 51,* 103–114.

Locke, D. C., & Kiselica, M. S. (1999). Pedagogy of possibilities: Teaching about racism in multicultural counseling courses. *Journal of Counseling and Development, 77,* 80–86.

Lui, W. M., & Pope-Davis, D. B. (2005). The working alliance, therapy ruptures and impasses, and counseling competence: Implications for counselor training and education. In R. T. Carter (Ed.), *Handbook of racial-cultural psychology and counseling* (pp. 148–167). Hoboken, NJ: Wiley.

Martin, D. J., Garske, J. P., & Davis, M. K. (2000). Relations of the therapeutic alliance with outcome and other variables: A meta-analytic review. *Journal of Counseling and Clinical Psychology, 66,* 832–837.

McConahay, J. B. (1986). Modem racism, ambivalence, and the Modern Racism Scale. In J. F. Dovidio & S. L. Gaertner (Eds.), *Prejudice, discrimination and racism* (pp. 91–126). Orlando, FL: Academic Press.

National Conference of Christians and Jews. (1992). *Taking America's pulse: A summary report of the National Conference Survey on Inter-Group Relations.* New York: Author. (Available at http://eric.ed.gov/ERICDocs/data/ericdocs2/content_storage_01/0000000b/80/23/84/59.pdf)

Nelson, T. D. (2006). *The psychology of prejudice.* Boston: Pearson.

Neville, H. A., Lilly, R. L., Duran, G., Lee, R., & Browne, L. (2000). Construction and initial validation of the Color Blind Racial Attitudes Scale (COBRAS). *Journal of Counseling Psychology, 47,* 59–70.

Pierce, C. (1995). Stress analogs of racism and sexism: Terrorism, torture, and disaster. In C. Willie, P. Rieker, B. Kramer, & B. Brown (Eds.), *Menial health, racism, and sexism* (pp. 277–293). Pittsburgh, PA: University of Pittsburgh Press.

Pierce, C., Carew, J., Pierce-Gonzalez, D., & Willis, D. (1978). An experiment in racism: TV commercials. In C. Pierce (Ed.), *Television and education* (pp. 62–88). Beverly Hills, CA: Sage.

Plant, E. A., & Peruche, B. M. (2005). The consequences of race for police officers' responses to criminal suspects. *Psychological Science, 16,* 180–183.

Ponterotto, J. G., Casas, J. M., Suzuki, L. A., & Alexander, C. M. (2001). *Handbook of multicultural counseling.* Thousand Oaks, CA: Sage.

President's Commission on Mental Health. (1978). *Report of the President's Commission on Mental Health.* Washington, DC: U.S. Government Printing Office.

Reid, L. D., & Radhakrishnan, P. (2003). Race matters: The relations between race and general campus climate. *Cultural Diversity and Ethnic Minority Psychology, 9,* 263–275.

Richardson, T. Q., & Molinaro, K. L. (1996). White counselor self-awareness: A prerequisite for multicultural competence. *Journal of Counseling and Development, 74,* 238–242.

Ridley, C. R. (2005). *Overcoming unintentional racism in counseling and therapy* (2nd ed.). Thousand, Oaks, CA: Sage.

Sanchez-Hucles, J., & Jones, N. (2005). Breaking the silence around race in training, practice, and research. *Counseling Psychologist, 33,* 547–558.

Sean, D. O. (1988). Symbolic racism. In P. A. Katz & D. A. Taylor (Eds.), *Eliminating racism: Profiles in controversy* (pp. 53–84). New York: Plenum.

Sellers, R. M., & Shelton, J. N. (2003). The role of racial identity in perceived racial discrimination. *Journal of Personality and Social Psychology, 84,* 1070–1092.

Smedley, A., & Smedley, B. D. (2005). Race as biology is fiction, racism as a social problem is real. *American Psychologist, 60,* 16–26.

Solórzano, D., Ceja, M., & Yosso, T. (2000, Winter). Critical race theory, racial microaggressions, and campus racial climate: The experiences of African American college students. *Journal of Negro Education, 69,* 60–73.

Spanierman, L. B., Armstrong, P. L., Poteat, V. P., & Beer, A. M. (2006). Psychosocial costs of racism to Whites: Exploring patterns through cluster analysis. *Journal of Counseling Psychology, 53,* 434–441.

Spanierman, L. B., & Heppner, M. J. (2004). Psychosocial Costs of Racism to Whites Scale (PCRW): Construction and initial validation. *Journal of Counseling Psychology, 51,* 249–262.

Steele, C. M., Spencer, S. J., & Aronson, J. (2002). Contending with group image: The psychology of stereotype and social identity threat.

In M. Zanna (Ed.), *Advances in experimental social psychology* (Vol. 23, pp. 379–440). New York: Academic Press.

Strong, S. R., & Schmidt, L. D. (1970). Expertness and influence in counseling. *Journal of Counseling Psychology, 17,* 81–87.

Sue, D. W. (2003). *Overcoming our racism: The journey to liberation.* San Francisco: Jossey-Bass.

Sue, D. W. (2004). Whiteness and ethnocentric monoculturalism: Making the "invisible" visible. *American Psychologist, 59,* 759–769.

Sue, D. W. (2005). Racism and the conspiracy of silence. *Counseling Psychologist, 33,* 100–114.

Sue, D. W., Arredondo, P., & McDavis, R. J. (1992). Multicultural competencies/standards: A call to the profession. *Journal of Counseling and Development, 70,* 477–486.

Sue, D. W., Bucceri, J., Lin, A. I., Nadal, K. L., & Torino, G. C. (2007). Racial microaggressions and the Asian American experience. *Cultural Diversity and Ethnic Minority Psychology, 13,* 72–81.

Sue, D. W., & Sue, D. (2003). *Counseling the culturally diverse: Theory and practice* (4th ed.). New York: Wiley.

Sue, S., Fujino, D. C., Hu, L., & Takeuchi, D. (1991). Community mental health services for ethnic minority groups: A test of the cultural responsiveness hypothesis. *Journal of Consulting and Clinical Psychology, 59,* 533–540.

Thompson, C. E., & Neville, H. A. (1999). Racism, mental health, and mental health practice. *Counseling Psychologist, 27,* 155–223.

U.S. Department of Health and Human Services. (2001). *Mental health: Culture, race, and ethnicity—A supplement to Mental Health: A Report of the Surgeon General.* Rockville, MD: U.S. Department of Health and Human Services, Substance Abuse and Mental Health Services Administration, Center for Mental Health Services.

Utsey, S. O., Gernat, C. A., & Hammar, L. (2005). Examining White counselor trainees' reactions to racial issues in counseling and supervision dyads. *Counseling Psychologist, 33,* 449–478.

Utsey, S. O., & Ponterotto, J. G. (1996). Development and validation of the Index of Race-Related Stress (IRRS). *Journal of Counseling Psychology, 43,* 490–502.

Vanman, E. J., Saltz, J. L., Nathan, L. R., & Warren, J. A. (2004). Racial discrimination by low-prejudiced Whites. *Psychological Science, 15,* 711–719.

Williams, D. R., & Collins, C. (1995). US socioeconomic and racial differences in health: Patterns and explanations. *Annual Review of Sociology, 21,* 349–386.

Williams, D. R., Lavizzo-Mourey, R., & Warren, R. C. (1994). The concept of race and health status in America. *Public Health Reports, 109,* 26–41.

Williams, D. R., Neighbors, H. W., & Jackson, J. S. (2003). Racial/ethnic discrimination and health: Findings from community studies. *American Journal of Public Health, 93,* 200–208.

Woodhouse, S. S., Schlosser, L. Z., Crook, R. E., Ligiero, D. P., & Gelso, C. J. (2003). Client attachment to therapist: Relations to transference and client recollections of parental caregiving. *Journal of Counseling Psychology, 50,* 395–408.

Young, G., & Davis-Russell, E. (2002). The vicissitudes of cultural competence: Dealing with difficult classroom dialogue. In E. Davis-Russell (Ed.), *The California School of Professional Psychology handbook of multicultural education, research, intervention, and training* (pp. 37–53). San Francisco: Jossey-Bass.

17

A Recovery Oriented Service System

Setting Some System Level Standards

William A. Anthony

In the 1990s a number of state mental health systems, behavioral managed care entities, and county systems of care declared that their service delivery systems were based on the vision of recovery. A recovery vision of service is grounded in the idea that people can recover from mental illness, and that the service delivery system must be constructed based on this knowledge. In the past, mental health systems were based on the belief that people with severe mental illness did not recover, and that the course of their illness was essentially a deteriorative course, or at best a maintenance course. As systems strive to create new initiatives consistent with this new vision of recovery, new system standards are needed to guide the development of recovery oriented mental health systems. Based on research on previous system initiatives and current consensus around accepted recovery practices and principles, a set of system standards that are recovery focused are suggested to guide future system developments.

The 1990s has been called the "decade of recovery" (Anthony, 1991). Two seminal events of the preceding decade paved the way for the concept of recovery from mental illness to take hold in the 1990s. One factor was the writing of consumers (e.g., Anonymous, 1989; Deegan, 1988; Houghton, 1982; Leete, 1989; McDermott, 1990; Unzicker, 1989). For the preceding decades, and culminating in the decade of the 1980s, consumers had been writing about their own and their colleagues' recovery. The consumer literature suggests that recovery is a deeply personal, unique process of changing one's attitudes, values, feelings, goals, skills, and/or roles. It is a way of living a satisfying, hopeful, and contributing life. Recovery involves the development of new meaning and purpose in one's life as one grows beyond the catastrophic effects of psychiatric disability (Anthony, 1993). Conceptual and empirical studies on the recovery process have begun to appear (Spaniol, Gagne, & Koehler, 1999; in press). Based on the writings of consumers,

Table 1 identifies several assumptions about the recovery process that can be used to guide service system development.

In addition to the conceptual work of consumers, the other major factor precipitating the acceptance of the recovery-vision was the empirical work of Harding and her associates, whose research and analytic work initially impacted the field in the 1980s. Over the years Harding (1994) and her colleagues have reviewed a number of long term research studies including their own (Harding, Brooks, Ashekaga, Strauss, & Brerer, 1987a, 1987b) that suggested that a deteriorating course for severe mental illness is not the norm. The possible causes of chronicity may be viewed as having less to do with the disorder and more to do with a myriad of environmental and other social factors interacting with the person and the illness (Harding, Zubin, & Strauss, 1987, p. 483). It was the ongoing analysis of long term outcome studies by Harding and associates that provided the empirical basis for the recovery vision.

In contrast to Harding's research and the emerging consumer literature throughout most of the 1980s and officially until the appearance of *DSM-III-R,* the belief was that severe mental illness, particularly schizophrenia, was a deteriorative disease (American Psychiatric Association, 1980). This seemingly definitive diagnostic conclusion turned out to be ill conceived and inhibited acceptance of the recovery vision. Antithetical to the concept of gradual deterioration due to mental illness over time is the concept of recovering over time from mental illness. Harding's later work (Desisto, Harding,

Table 1 Assumptions About Recovery

Factors/Items	*Reasons*
1. Recovery can occur without professional intervention.	Professionals do not hold the key to recovery, consumers do. The task of professionals is to facilitate recovery; the task of consumers is to recover. Recovery may be facilitated by the consumer's natural support system.
2. A common denominator of recovery is the presence of people who believe in and stand by the person in need of recovery.	Seemingly universal in the recovery concept is the notion that critical to one's recovery is a person or persons in whom one can trust to "be there" in times of need.
3. A recovery vision is not a function of one's theory about the causes of mental illness.	Recovery may occur whether one views the illness as biological or not. The key element is understanding that there is hope for the future rather than understanding the cause in the past.
4. Recovery can occur even though symptoms reoccur.	The episodic nature of severe mental illness does not prevent recovery. As one recovers, symptoms interface with functioning less often and for briefer periods of time. More of one's life is lived symptom free.
5. Recovery is a unique process.	There is no path to recovery, not one outcome. It is a highly personal process.
6. Recovery demands that a person has choices.	The notion that one has options from which to choose is often more important than the particular option one initially selects.
7. Recovery from the consequences of the illness is sometimes more difficult than recovering from the illness itself.	These consequences include discrimination, poverty, segregation, stigma, and iatrogenic effects of treatment.

Source: Adapted from Anthony (1993).

McCormick, Ashikaga, & Brooks, 1995a, 1995b) involved a comparison of the long term outcome of people with psychiatric disabilities in two different states. This masterfully designed three-decade-long follow up examined what might account for system-wide differences in consumers' recovery and once again confirmed as consumers had been saying, that recovery from mental illness was happening.

System Planning and the Recovery Vision

During the 1990s increasing numbers of states and counties adopted a recovery vision as the overriding vision for their system planning. The Community Support System (CSS) perspective as to the critical services needed to be helpful to people with psychiatric disabilities became a part of the thinking of many system planners and administrators. Most comprehensive mental health system initiatives in the 1980s and 1990s can be traced to the CSS conceptualization of basic services (National Institute of Mental Health, 1987). Anthony (1993) used the CSS model as a basis for describing the essential services of a recovery oriented system. Based on the CSS framework, the Center for Psychiatric Rehabilitation has identified the quintessential outcome of each service intervention and the description of the process each service uses to achieve that outcome (Anthony, Cohen, Farkas, & Gagne (in press). (See Table 2.)

The Boston University Center for Psychiatric Rehabilitation, along with its organizational consultation affiliate, BCPR, is directly aware of recovery initiatives in selected states in which they have been consulting, including such states as California, Iowa, New York, Ohio, and Washington. The Center is currently collaborating with the National Association of State Mental Health Directors (NASMHPD), the National Association of Consumer/Survivor Mental Health Administrators (NAC/SMHA), and the Consumer Organization Networking and Technical Assistance Center (CONTAC) to describe and evaluate the extent to which state

Table 2 Essential Services in a Recovery Oriented System

Service Category	*Description*	*Consumer Outcome*
Treatment	Alleviating symptoms and distress	Symptom relief
Crisis intervention	Controlling and resolving critical or dangerous problems	Personal safety assured
Case management	Obtaining the services client needs and wants	Services accessed
Rehabilitation	Developing clients' skills and supports related to clients' goals	Rule functioning
Enrichment	Engaging clients in fulfilling and satisfying activities	Self-development
Rights protection	Advocating to upload one's rights	Equal opportunity
Basic support	Providing the people, place, and things clients need to serve (e.g., shelter, meals, health care)	Personal survival assured
Self-help	Exercising a voice and a choice in one's life	Empowerment
Wellness	Promoting healthy lifestyles	Health status improved

Source: In Anthony, Cohen, Forces, & Gagne. (in press). Adapted from Cohen, M., Nemee, P., Farkas, M., & Forbess, R. (1988). *Training technology: Case management.* Boston: Center for Psychiatric Rehabilitation.

mental health systems have implemented policies and practices that promote recovery.

Jacobsen and Curtis (2000) have already examined several states' recovery based planning, focusing on how states are using specific strategies to work toward a recovery vision. These strategies include: developing recovery vision statements; educating personnel about recovery; increasing the involvement of consumers and family in planning and service delivery; and implementing "user-controlled" services.

Relevant Systems Level Research

Perhaps the most straightforward definition of a system—and a definition most relevant to today's mental health service system in particular—is that a service system is a combination of services organized to meet the needs of a particular population (Sauber, 1983). A difficulty in creating a mental health service system stems from the varied, multiple needs of the client population. Since deinstitutionalization, many different service systems have been designated as responsible for meeting one or more of the individual needs of persons with long-term psychiatric disabilities (e.g., mental health, health, substance abuse, vocational rehabilitation, social security). The diverse needs of persons with severe psychiatric disabilities for housing, health care, economic, educational, vocational, and social supports dictates coordination between multiple service providers. The mental health service system has become the primary system responsible for preventing individuals who need services from being ignored or falling through the cracks. The challenge to the mental health field has been to develop a mental health service system that could consistently meet the diverse needs of all clients (Reinke & Greenley, 1986). In essence, not only must effective and relevant services be available, but they must also be well-coordinated so that they are easily accessible and efficient, without controlling the consumer to the point of simply replicating the state mental hospital in the community. No doubt the most pressing, obvious national example of service system fragmentation is the system of services for people who have been labeled dually diagnosed, i.e., people with psychiatric disabilities and substance abuse problems (Drake, McLaughlin, Pepper, & Minkoff, 1991; Ridgely, Goldman, & Willenbring, 1990; Ridgely & Dixon, 1995).

Although many studies have noted that multiple, fragmented service systems can interfere with effective service delivery to persons with psychiatric disabilities, until the 1980s little systems-level research was undertaken (Anthony & Blanch, 1989). In 1977, Armstrong reported that 135 federal programs in 11 major departments and agencies had direct impact on people with mental illness. He reported that many of the failures of deinstitutionalization could be attributed to funding disincentives and lack of coordination among these programs (Armstrong, 1977). Other early evidence of the need for system development and integration included the interrelationship of health and mental health as demonstrated by the frequent conflict between services rendered by primary care physicians and mental health professionals (Burns, Burke, & Kessler, 1981). Currently, the integration of behavioral managed care and physical health care is a major concern of those planning managed care systems. Also making system development difficult is the fact that existing funding streams have conflicting regulations and eligibility criteria (Dickey & Goldman, 1986).

Moreover, the lack of coordination directly affects clients. Tessler (1987) found that when clients do not connect with resources after discharge from inpatient care, their overall community adjustment is poorer and there are more complaints about them. On the other hand, poor coordination is sometimes blamed for failures actually due to insufficient resources or inappropriate services (Solomon, Gordon, & Davis, 1983). At some point, the sheer quantity of services (or lack thereof) does affect quality. Research has not yet clarified the relationship between the numbers, types, or coordination of services and client outcome.

Anthony and Blanch (1989) categorized various attempts at ensuring the integration of services into four types, according to whether they emphasized (a) legislated relationships and program models, (b) financing mechanisms, (c) strategies for improving interagency linkages, and/or (d) assignment of responsibility. Many initiatives have, of course, incorporated several of these elements.

Within the last several decades, data collection on systems level interventions has occurred sporadically. One example is the previously mentioned work of Harding (Desisto, et al., 1995a, 1995b) that involved comparing the long-term outcome of people with psychiatric disabilities served by two different systems in two separate states. This study concluded that differences in recovery outcome were probably due to system-wide differences in psychiatric rehabilitation programming. Another example is the ongoing research investigating various CSS services. In the 1990s the National Institute of Mental Health and later the Center for Mental Health Services (CMHS) initiated nation-wide a number of research demonstrations of essential CSS service components, including vocational rehabilitation, case management, crisis response services, and other supportive services (Jacobs, 1998). An analysis of the results of 29 projects found that the majority of the studies reported positive findings on one or more of the following outcomes: symptomatology, consumer outcomes (e.g., competitive employment), satisfaction with services, and service utilization. More recently, ongoing CMHS demonstrations should inform system planners and policy makers into the next decade.

Another CMHS sponsored research initiative examined the impact of service integration on housing outcomes for persons who were homeless and mentally ill using data from the Access to Community Care and Effective Services and Supports (ACCESS) program (Cocozza, Steadman, & Dennis, 1997; Rosenheck et al., 1998). Results showed a significant relationship between measures of service system integration and independent housing outcomes.

A final example of systems level research is the effort launched by the Robert Wood Johnson (RWJ) foundation in the late 1980s. The RWJ initiative was based on the fundamental assumption that a central authority would enhance continuity of care, and that such improvements would lead to improved client outcomes. Nine cities were selected on a competitive basis to develop community-wide systems of care (Shore & Cohen, 1990). Within the five-year demonstration period each city was expected to create a local mental health authority that would assume central responsibility for developing and coordinating public sector services. For the most part the RWJ system initiative did not attempt to improve practitioner competencies and program standards; rather, RWJ focused almost exclusively on organization and financing. Little significant consumer impact was found (Lehman, Postrado, Roth, McNary, & Goldman, 1994; Shern et al., 1994).

Origin of the Recovery Oriented System Standards

Unlike the development of standards for particular program models, there are no standards for recovery oriented systems. Typically, standards have been most often considered in the development of model programs, such as Assertive Community Treatment (ACT), (Teague, Drake, & Ackerson, 1995), IPS (Becker & Drake, 1993; Drake, 1998), Clubhouse (Beard, Propst, & Malamud, 1982) and Choose-Get Keep (Anthony, Howell, & Danley, 1984; Anthony, Cohen, Farkas, & Gagne [in press]). A comparable set of standards has not been advanced for a recovery oriented mental health system. Furthermore, there is no model of a recovery oriented mental health system currently operating, although as pointed out previously, a number of systems are declaring the development of a recovery oriented system to be their intent. Direction and guidelines are needed to stimulate and reinforce the development of a recovery oriented system. The system that existed for most of the last century was based on the notion that people with severe mental illness do not recover, and that maintenance and care of people with severe mental illness should be the goal.

Lacking a currently functioning model system for guidance, it becomes necessary to suggest the system level standards that might be helpful for system designers. The recovery oriented system standards outlined in Table 3 are meant to serve as a starting point of reference and as a guide for system development. Furthermore, the identification of system standards on which each system is based allow for system level research to be more meaningful. In addition, technical assistance for system development can use the standards as a jumping off point.

The particular standards identified in Table 3 are derived from several sources. First, they are consistent with the systems level research that has so far occurred. Secondly, they are compatible with the aforementioned recovery principles. Lastly, the system level consultants of the Boston University Center for Psychiatric Rehabilitation and its affiliate BCPR reviewed each standard and made changes to the standards based on their consultative experience. Standards were not included unless there was consensus. Over the last 17 years consultants from these organizations have on average provided technical assistance and training in about 17 states and three countries per year.

Recovery System Standard Dimensions

The standards have been grouped according to the system level dimension which best describes the focus of the standard. However, this categorization of standards is done for ease of presentation and not as part of a deliberate attempt to characterize how system standards must be organized. As the standards are used, modified, and refined, new ways to organize and name the system dimensions will no doubt occur.

Design

The mission and outcomes of the system incorporate the language of recovery. Consumers and their families are integrally important in the design process. The identified mission and consumer outcomes include such dimensions as improvements in role functioning, empowerment, consumer satisfaction, and quality of life. The mission is achieved through a set of identified services (see Table 2) which, when combined together, contribute to the achievement of the recovery outcomes (Anthony, 1993). A specific *service* (e.g., crisis intervention services, case management services) is defined by its unique process and outcomes. A *setting* is defined by its location (e.g., inpatient, community mental health center). A *program* is defined by certain administrative, staffing, and service standards (e.g., intensive case management program, clubhouse program). The system is designed around the CSS configuration of

Table 3 Characteristics of a Recovery Oriented System

System Dimension	*Recovery System Standard*	*Example of Current Nonrecovery Standard*
Design	Mission includes recovery vision as driving the system	Mission includes description of service principles (e.g., community of care)
	Mission implies recovery measure as overall outcome for system (e. g., empowerment, role functioning)	Mission implies no measures of recovery outcome (e.g., comprehensive range of services)
	Care of needed services are identified for system (e.g., treatment rehabilitation)	Case set of programs or settings are identified for system (e.g., day treatment programs and inpatient settings)
Evaluation	Primary consumer outcomes identified for each service are measurable and observable (e.g., number of cases, percentage of people employed)	Outcomes for each service are process measures or program quality measures only (e.g., number of people seen in service time before first appointment)
	Consumer and family measures of satisfaction included in system evaluation	Consumer and family perspective are not actively sought for system evaluation
Leadership	Leadership constantly reinforces recovery session and recovery system standards	Leadership vision focused on developing specific programs of settings
Management	Policies insure that a core set of processes (e.g., protocols) are described for area identified service	Policies do not insure that service protocols guide service delivery
	Policies expect programs within each service have policies and procedures directly related to implementing the service process	Policies and procedures are about staffing, physical setting, and so forth, and not about service process
	Policies insure that MIS system collects information on service process and outcomes	Policies focus MIS on collecting information on types of clients served and costs but not on service processes and outcomes
	Policies insure that supervisors provide feedback to supervisors on service process protocols as well as on progress toward consumer goals	Policies on supervision do not focus on supervision, providing feedback on protocols and consumer goals primarily on symptomatology and medication
	Policies encourage service programs to be recovery friendly (i.e., procedures are compatible with recovery values)	Policies encourage service programs in value compliance and professional authority
	Policies encourage the assignment of service staff to greatest effect possible, based on competencies and preferences	Policies direct service staff to be assigned primarily by credentials
Integration	Function of case management is expected to be performed for each consumer who wants or needs it	Case management function is not expected to be provided to all who want or need it
	Standardized planning process across services that is guided by consumer outcomes	Planning process varies between services and is not guided by consumer outcomes

(Continued)

Table 3 (Continued)

System Dimension	*Recovery System Standard*	*Example of Current Nonrecovery Standard*
Integration	Policies encourage the development and implementation of system integration strategies to achieve specific consumer outcomes	Policies on system integration strategies do not address development, implementation, and evaluation of such strategies
	Referrals between services include consumer outcomes expected of service provider	Service referring includes consumer descriptions rather than consumer outcomes
Comprehensiveness	Consumer goals include functioning in living, learning, working and/or social environments	Consumer goals do not include functioning in living, learning, working, and social environments (typically only residential environments)
	Consumer goals include functioning in nonmental health environments, not controlled by the mental health setting (e.g., YMCA, religious organizations)	Consumer goals emphasize adjustment in mental health environments
	Consumer goals include outcomes from any of the identified services	Consumer goals include outcomes for only a few identified services
	Policies insure that programs provide an array of setting and a variety of levels of supports within a setting	Policies allow programs to provide a limited array of setting and support within settings
Consumer Involvement	Consumer are activity sought for employment at all levels of organization	Consumers are not actively sought for employment at all levels of employment
	User controlled self-help services are available in all geographic areas	User-controlled, self-help services are not available or available in only a few geographic areas
	Consumers and families integrally involved in system design and evaluation	Consumers and families are involved in a token way in system design and evaluation—if at all
Cultural Relevance	Policies insure that assessments, planning and service interventions of personnel enable them to provide competent manner	Policies with respect to assessments, planning, and services intervention do not take cultural diversity into consideration
	Policies insure that the knowledge, skills, and attitude of personnel enable them to provide effective care for the culturally diverse populations that might wish to use the system	Policies related to personnel do not attend to issues of cultural diversity
	Policies insure that setting and programs and the access to them reflect the culture of their current and potential consumers	Policies only insure that setting programs are compatible with the predominant culture
Advocacy	Advocates for a holistic understanding of people served	Advocates primarily for particular programs setting or disciplines
	Advocates for consumers to have the opportunity to participate in community rules	Advocates for consumers to have the opportunity to participate in mental health programs

System Dimension	*Recovery System Standard*	*Example of Current Nonrecovery Standard*
Advocacy	Advocates for an understanding of recovery potential of people served	Advocates for understanding of recovery potential of people served is lacking
Training	Policies insure that all levels of staff understand recovery vision and its implications within service categories	Policies make no mention of recovery vision nor its implications for services
	Policies encourage selection and training methods designed to improve knowledge, attitudes, and skills reserved to conduct particular service that staff is implementing	Policies on selection and training based on interests of staff or training coordinator
Funding	Dollars across services are expended based on consumer expressed needs	Dollars across services are expended based on information other than consumer needs
	Dollars across services are expended based on expected process and outcome of services	Dollars across services are expended based on historical traditional funding
Access	Access to service environments is by consumer preference rather than professional preference	Access to service environments is based primarily on professional decisions
	Access to service environments is not contingent upon using a particular mental health service	Access to service environments is based primarily on participation in certain mental health services
	Access to living, learning, working, and social environments outside mental health system is expected	Access to living, learning, working, and social environments outside mental health system is not encouraged

services and is not designed around a specific set of programs or settings; rather programs and settings must indicate which of the services they provide and on what consumer outcomes they will be held accountable; For example, a PACT program may indicate that they provide treatment, rehabilitation, crisis intervention, and case management services, and that they are accountable for implementing the process associated with each of those services.

Evaluation

Each program providing services in the system must identify the unique consumer outcomes they will achieve. For example, in rehabilitation services, no matter what the rehabilitation program is called (e.g., IPS, Clubhouse) and no matter what the setting (e. g., psychosocial rehabilitation center, mental health center), the service must achieve improvements in the consumers' role functioning (see Table 2). Treatment services must achieve symptom alleviation, and so on. Outcomes assessments must always include the perspectives of consumers and family members.

Leadership

The vision of recovery must be present in most all of the leadership's written and public statements. Recovery is such a paradigm shifting notion (Anthony, 1991), that its fundamental assumptions and principles must constantly be reinforced. Recovery is a vision incompatible with the mission of the mental health system of the past century. The leadership must demonstrate through their words and actions that they and everyone else in the system need to "buy in" to this dramatically new direction.

Management

System management, through system level policies and procedures, must ensure that each individual service define itself by the unique process they use. Service protocols are developed and implemented so that the basic service processes are possible to monitor (Anthony, 1998). An MIS system exists for each service. For example, the basic protocol for case management might include process components such as setting a service goal, planning, linking, and negotiating for service access. The protocol for rehabilitation might include setting the overall rehabilitation goal, functional assessment, resource assessment, planning, skill development, and resource development. Supervisory sessions revolve around effective ways to implement the protocol. System management looks for "recovery oriented" values in the programs they fund, and staff assignment to programs is based, to the greatest extent possible, on competencies and preferences, rather than credentials.

Integration

The system polices include the provision of case management for all who need and want it. Each service, within the array of services offered by the system, has a standardized planning process that shares some common process elements across services, that is, each service contains the major process elements that are standard across services. Common process elements might be: an *assessment* of the consumer's goal(s), a *plan* to reach the goal(s), and specific *interventions* to achieve the goal(s). For example, enrichment services might perform an assessment to determine which enrichment activities the consumer prefers, *plan* how to access that activity, and *intervene* by providing or arranging the preferred recreational, social, and so forth activity according to the plan. Case management services might *assess* the person's service goal, *plan* for accessing those services, and *intervene* through linking and/or negotiating for those services. In addition, when referrals occur between different service programs, the referral includes a specific description of the consumer outcomes the receiving service is expected to achieve.

Comprehensiveness

All the possible residential, work, educational, and social environments in which a consumer might potentially function are included as a consumer goal(s) and measurable consumer outcome(s). Functioning in nonmental health environments (e.g., schools, social clubs) are included as goals. It is the policy of the system that consumer supports that facilitate a consumer's functioning are provided in a wide variety of environments. A particular support exists in more than one environment. For example, intensive residential support may be provided in group residences, but also in an individual's own apartment.

Consumer Involvement

Selection and recruitment materials for staff throughout the system target consumers and family members for employment, as well as voluntary service on boards. User-controlled services are available in all the designated catchment areas served by the system.

Cultural Relevance

The *system* promulgates policies designed to increase the possibility that the system reflects the culture of the consumers served. Specifically, policies on cultural competence address the training and experience of practitioners, the assessment, planning, and intervention process, and culturally relevant programs and procedures to access them.

Advocacy

System advocacy occurs for the recovery vision, for a holistic understanding of the persons served, and for consumers to have the opportunity to participate fully in community roles.

Training

System level policies on training are designed so that delivery of specific services is improved; training is grounded in the vision of recovery, and not just in the interest of certain staff.

Funding

Funding from the system is based on the consumers' recovery goals. Funding directly supports the processes and outcomes that the system is designed to achieve.

Access

Policies encourage access to services based on the consumers' goals rather than professional preference. Access is not contingent upon the consumer attending certain mental health services. For example, access to housing is not contingent on taking medication. Access to nonmental health environments is expected.

Conclusions

As system planners use all or some of these standards they will undoubtedly modify, refine, and/or add to these standards. This first attempt at providing recovery oriented system standards should prove useful in a number of ways. First of all, it can provide direction to system planners as they develop proposals for their system. It can provide a basis for consumer and family advocacy and monitoring at the system level. The standards can be used in system level research and evaluation of recovery oriented systems, and as a framework to make comparisons across systems. Lastly, as these standards outlined in Table 3 are put into use, it will further encourage the operationalization of these standards.

These recovery oriented system standards are a first step in moving a system with no recovery vision to a system that believes that consumers can develop meaningful and purposeful lives, despite having experienced the catastrophe of severe mental illness. A mental health system guided by a recovery vision must have policies and procedures in place to increase the possibility of recovery occurring—for the system itself as well as for those it serves.

References

American Psychiatric Association. (1980). *Diagnostic and statistical manual of mental disorders* (3rd ed.). Washington, DC: Author.

Anonymous. (1989). How I've managed chronic mental illness. *Schizophrenia Bulletin, 15,* 635–640.

Anthony, W. A. (1991). Researching the unresearchable! *Psychosocial Rehabilitation Journal, 140,* 1.

Anthony, W. A. (1993). Recovery from mental illness: The guiding vision of the mental health service system in the 1990s.

Psychosocial Rehabilitation Journal 16(4), 11–23.

Anthony, W. A. (1998). Psychiatric rehabilitation technology: Operationalizing "black box" of the psychiatric rehabilitation process. *New Directions for Mental Health Services, 79,* 79–87.

Anthony, W. A., & Blanch, A. K. (1989). Research on community support services: What have we learned? *Psychosocial Rehabilitation Journal, 12*(3), 55–81.

Anthony, W. A., Cohen, M. R., Farkas, M., & Gagne, G. (in press). *Psychiatric rehabilitation* (2nd ed.). Boston: Boston University, Center for Psychiatric Rehabilitation.

Anthony, W. A., Howell, & Danley, K. S. (1984). Vocational rehabilitation of the psychiatrically disabled. In M. Mirabi (Ed.), *The chronically mentally ill: Research and services* (pp. 215–237). Jamaica, NY: Spectrum Publications.

Armstrong, B. (1977). A federal study of deinstitutionalization: How the government impedes its goal. *Hospital and Community Psychiatry, 28,* 417, 425.

Beard, J. H., Propst, R. N., & Malamud, T. J. (1982). The Fountain House model of psychiatric rehabilitation. *Psychosocial Rehabilitation Journal, 5*(1), 47–53.

Becker, D. R., & Drake, R. E. (1993). *A working life: The individual placement and support (IPS) program.* Concord, NH: Dartmouth Psychiatric Research Center.

Burns, B. J., Burke. J. D., & Kessler, L. G. (1981). Promoting health-mental health coordination: Federal efforts. In A. Broskowski, E. Marks, & S. H. Budman (Eds.), *Linking health and mental health.* Beverly Hills, CA: Sage Publications.

Coccozza, J. J., Steadman., H. J., & Dennis, D. (1997). *Implementing system integration strategies: lessons from the ACCESS program.* New York: Policy Research Associates.

Cohen, M. R., Nemec, P. B., Farkas, M. D., & Forbess, R. (1988). *Psychiatric rehabilitation training technology: Case management* (Trainer package). Boston: Boston University, Center for Psychiatric Rehabilitation.

Deegan, P. F. (1988). Recovery: The lived experience of rehabilitation. *Psychosocial Rehabilitation Journal 11*(1) 11–19.

DeSisto, M. J., Harding, C. M., McCormick, R.V, Ashikaga, T., & Brooks, G. W. (1995a). The Maine and Vermont three-decade studies of serious mental illness: 1. Matched comparison of cross-sectional outcome. *British Journal of Psychiatry, 167,* 331–338.

DeSisto, M. J., Harding, C. M., McCormick, R. V., Ashikaga, T., & Brooks, G. W. (1995b). The Maine and Vermont three decade studies of serious mental illness: II. Longitudinal course comparisons. *British Journal of Psychiatry, 167,* 338–341.

Dickey, B., & Goldman, H. H. (1986). Public health care for the chronically mentally ill: Financing operation costs: Issues and options for local leadership. *Administration in Mental Health, 14,* 63–77.

Drake, R. E. (1998). A brief history of the individual placement and support model. *Psychiatric Rehabilitation Journal, 22*(1), 3–7.

Drake, R., McLaughlin, E., Pepper, B., & Minkoff, K. (1991). Dual diagnosis of major mental illness and substance disorder. In K. Minkoff (Ed.), *New Directions for Mental Health Services, No. 50* (pp. 3–12) San Francisco: Jossey Bass, Inc.

Harding, C. M. (1994). An examination of the complexities in the measurement of recovery in severe psychiatric disorders. In R. J. Ancill, S. Holliday, & G. W. MacEwan (Eds.), *Schizophrenia: Exploring the spectrum of psychosis* (pp. 153–169). Chichester: J. Wiley & Sons.

Harding, C. M., Brooks, G. W. Ashikaga, T., Strauss, J. S., & Breier, A. (1987a). The Vermont longitudinal study of persons with severe mental illness, I. Methodology, study sample, and overall status 32 years later. *American Journal of Psychiatry, 144,* 718–726.

Harding, C. M., Brooks, G. W., Ashikaga, T., Strauss, T. S., & Breier, A. (1987b). The Vermont longitudinal study of persons with severe mental illness: II. Long-term outcome of subjects who retrospectively met DSM-III criteria for schizophrenia. *American Journal of Psychiatry, 144,* 727–735.

Harding, C. M., Zubin, J., & Strauss, J. S. (1987). Chronicity in schizophrenia: Fact, partial fact, or artifact? *Hospital and Community Psychiatry, 38,* 477–486.

Houghton, J. F. (1982). Maintaining mental health in a turbulent world. *Schizophrenia Bulletin, 8,* 548–552.

Jacobs, J. (Ed.) (1998). *Community support research demonstration grants, 1989–1996: Major findings and lessons learned.* Rockville. MD: Center for Menial Health Services.

Jacobson, N., & Curtis, L. (2000). Recovery as policy in mental health services: Strategies emerging from the states. *Psychiatric Rehabilitation Journal, 23*(4), 333–341.

Leete, E. (1989). How I perceive and manage my illness. *Schizophrenia Bulletin, 15,* 197–200.

Lehman, A., Postrado, L., Roth, D., McNary, S., & Goldman., H. (1994). Continuing of care and client outcomes in the Robert Wood Johnson Foundation Program on chronic mental illness. *Milbank Quarterly, 72*(1), 105–122.

McDermott, B. (1990). Transforming depression. *The Journal, 1*(4), 13–14.

National Institute of Mental Health. (1987). *Toward a model plan for a comprehensive, community-based mental health system.* Rockville, MD: Division of Education and Service Systems Liaison.

Reinke, B., & Greenley, J. R. (1986). Organizational analysis of three community support program models. *Hospital and Community Psychiatry, 37,* 624–629.

Ridgely, M., & Dixon, L. (1995). Policy and financing issues in the care of people with chronic mental illness and substance abuse disorders. In A. F. Lehman & L. B. Dixon (Eds.), *Double jeopardy: Chronic mental illness and substance abuse.* (pp. 277–295). New York: Harwood Academic Publishers.

Ridgely, M., Goldman, H., & Willenbring, M. (1990). Barriers to the care of persons with dual diagnoses: Organizational and financial issues. *Schizophrenia Bulletin, 16,* 123–132.

Rosenheck, R., Morrissey. J., Lam, J., Calloway, M., Johnson, M., Goldman, H., Randolph, F., Blasinsky, M., Fontana, A., Calysn, R., & Teague, G. (1998). Service system integration, access to services, and housing outcomes in a program for homeless persons with severe mental illness. *American Journal of Public Health, 88*(11), 1610–1615.

Sauber, S. R. (1983). *The human services delivery system.* New York: Columbia University Press.

Shern, D., Wilson, N., Coen, A. S., Patrick, D., Foster, M., Bartsch, D., & Demmler, J. (1994). Client outcomes II: Longitudinal client data from the Colorado treatment outcome study. *Milbank Quarterly, 72*(1), 123–148.

Shore, M., & Cohen, M. D. (1990). The Robert Wood Johnson Foundation program on chronic mental illness: An overview. *Hospital and Community Psychiatry, 41*(11), 1212–1216.

Solomon, P., Gordon, B., & Davis, J. M. (1983). An assessment of aftercare services within a community mental health system. *Psychosocial Rehabilitation Journal, 7*(2), 33–39.

Spaniol, L., Gagne, C., & Koehler, M. (1999). Recovery from serious mental illness: What it is and how to support people in their recovery. In R. E. Marinelli, & A. E. Dell Orto (Eds.), *The psychological and social impact of disability* (4th ed.). New York: Springer.

Spaniol, L., Gagne, C., & Koehler, M. (in press). The recovery framework in rehabilitation: Concepts and practices from the field of serious mental illness. In J. R. Finch & D. P. Moxley (Eds.), *Sourcebook of rehabilitation and mental health services.* New York: Plenum.

Teague, G. B. Drake, R. E., & Ackerson, T. H. (1995). Evaluating use of continuous treatment teams for persons with mental illness and substance abuse. *Psychiatric Services, 46*(7), 689–695.

Tessler, R. C. (1987). Continuity of care and client outcome. *Psychosocial Rehabilitation Journal, 1*(1), 39–53.

Unzicker, R. (1989) On my own: A personal journey through madness and reemergence. *Psychosocial Rehabilitation Journal, 13*(1), 71–77.

18

Counseling Individuals From Marginalized and Underserved Groups

Patricia Arredondo

Background and Context

The Civil Rights Act of 1964 was a historical milestone for U.S. history as a whole but in particular for individuals and groups who, based on circumstances of birth or other unplanned life experiences, were victims of prejudice, discrimination, and segregation. Title VII of the act prevented discrimination in employment, education, and housing based on national origin, religion, or ethnic and racial background. At the time, the presumed beneficiaries of this legislation were persons of color, particularly African Americans living in the racially segregated South. With the creation of the Equal Employment Opportunity Commission, there was an expectation that there would be a change in exclusionary practices with respect to education, employment, housing, and so forth. The assumption was that the law would prevail, put the fear of God into employers and others in decision-making roles, and "level the playing field" for those typically disenfranchised based on their color, religion, and cultural background.

Another consequence of the civil rights movement led by individuals such as the Reverend Martin Luther King, Jr., was the creation of other movements that led to new federal and state laws and organizational policies about the rights of marginalized groups and individuals. These included the Chicano civil rights movement in the late 1960s and early 1970s, part of which was the struggle for farmworkers' rights led by Cesar Chavez; the renewed women's movement of the late 1960s and the 1970s; the declassification of gay and lesbian identity as a "diagnosable" category in the third edition of the *Diagnostic and Statistical Manual of Mental Disorders* (American Psychiatric Association, 1980); the Gray Panthers organization, founded by senior citizens with a social justice agenda; and children's rights groups that emerged as a result of heightened awareness of child abuse, an increase in the numbers of single-parent homes, and other conditions that adversely affected the health and emotional development of children. Although the Civil Rights Act established sanctions against discrimination in certain life areas, there is still a limit to how widely the law is applied and enforced. Unfortunately, the act does not provide protection for many who are in marginalized groups, and it seems that on a fairly regular basis, a new group takes on marginalized status.

How do marginalized groups come into being? Marginalized groups have always existed in the United States, but it was with the 1964 Civil Rights Act that Americans began to legislate protection and rights for certain groups based on race, religion, national origin, and gender. Nevertheless, sociopolitical and economic conditions as well as nationalistic premises have always provided a context for defining "in" and "out" groups. Examples begin with the Declaration of Independence and the determination made by its signers concerning who would and would not be considered a "free man." The fights for legislation to grant voting rights to women and non-Whites are also indicative of the historical marginal status of women and people of color in the United States.

Other contextual factors include what L. Robert Kohls (1988) has described as "the values Americans live by." These include self-reliance, individualism, competition, self-help, and futurism. The value that many Americans place on the "survival of the fittest" and "pulling oneself up by one's own bootstraps" suggests that if individuals cannot demonstrate self-sufficiency, there must be something deficient about them. Based on historical marginalization and contemporary situations that are out of their control, the members of certain groups are ascribed this identity and are pushed outside of the mainstream, where they are recipients of social welfare and are considered worthy of derision and rejection.

In the preceding discussion, I have attempted to describe the interdisciplinary focus of this chapter. In order to discuss counseling plans and strategies with clients from different marginalized groups, counselors require ecological, economic, sociopolitical, and historical knowledge about those groups. Furthermore, counseling educators and practitioners need to be informed about sources they can turn to so that they can assure that they will be ethical, culturally competent, and relevant in the delivery of caring and respectful services.

Marginalization and Identity-Related Models and Contexts

Who becomes a member of a disenfranchised or marginalized group or one with a specialty status designation? In many respects, the bulk of this volume, and of other books such as Blank and Slipp's *Voices of Diversity* (1994) and Atkinson and Hackett's *Counseling Diverse Populations* (1995), is concerned with groups that have been rendered different based on sociopolitical designations, unchangeable dimensions of their personal identities, or as a result of life circumstances that cause them to "assume" a new status. Whether an individual is an immigrant or refugee, a person of color, or elderly, there is an automatic ascription and assumption of group identity.

One could argue that each individual in the world holds various group membership identities or affiliations, with varying benefits and liabilities based on those identities. However, in the United States many individuals are automatically labeled, based on certain identity factors, some of which are inherent, as members of particular marginalized groups. This tendency to apply such labels or descriptors to others might be called "labelese." Although it is generally an unconscious practice, people have a greater tendency to label based on negative perceptions or opinions of others for whom they hold low regard (Arredondo, McCarthy, & D'Andrea, 2000).

In spite of how individuals become reduced to a "marginalized" group identity, such as "gays" or "physically disabled," practitioners in counseling, community psychology, social work, public health, and other helping professions usually attempt to understand individuals more holistically. Most counselors and psychologists would agree that all persons hold multiple identities; this is what makes us the unique individuals we are. In the personal dimensions of identity (PDI) model (Arredondo & Glauner, 1992), the A, B, C framework provides some broad classifications. The A dimension classifications are assumed at birth and are often the least changeable. These include gender, ethnicity, culture, and sexual orientation. The dimension of physical disability (e.g., hearing impairment, multiple sclerosis) is seen as the result of either birth or a life experience that has long-term consequences.

The A dimensions in the PDI model are often discussed in terms of "isms," which tends to become a means of identifying groups that have become the target of adverse, difficult, and otherwise exclusionary and marginalizing life experiences. For example, sexism is generally directed toward women, racism toward people of color, and classism toward persons of lower socioeconomic status. "Linguicism" is linguistically related racism (Chen-Hayes, Chen, & Athar, 1998); this form of discrimination is based upon speakers' accents and is generally aimed at immigrants. Because these classifications put figurative identity stamps on individuals associated with these groups, they have become groups in need of special attention in the context of counseling and mental health practices. At the same time, they are individuals and groups that the helping professions have not historically addressed in a proactive way. These are not the YAVIS (young, attractive, verbal, intelligent, and social) clients that counseling students generally see in practicums or internships.

Classification also affects expectations and assumptions about members of these groups as well as the ways in which they are perceived and treated. Professionals following the medical, pathology-oriented model in counseling and psychotherapy have generally described the women in marginalized groups as passive and predisposed to certain psychological diagnoses, such as hysteria and depression. One consequence of this, far too often, has been treatment with medication. Viewed by therapists through such stereotypical lenses, these women are often rendered helpless and dependent. Certain treatments follow, and these women are reduced to one single stereotyped dimension—their gender—viewed from a deficit perspective.

The C dimension of the PDI also helps to explain how marginalization or special categorization may develop. This dimension refers to historical eras and events that are not always within individuals' control; contextual or ecological factors, such as sociopolitical factors and geographic and regional conditions; and legacies that individuals have inherited from their families, their nations, or other circumstances that have preceded or occurred during their lifetimes. An example comes from the continuing devastation in sub-Saharan Africa due to the AIDS epidemic. In a January 2000 *Newsweek* article headlined "10 Million Orphans," the authors describe an emerging marginalized group—the children who have become orphans because their parents died of AIDS. They report projections that by the end of 2000, "10.4 million children under 15 will have lost their mothers or fathers or both parents to

AIDS" (Masland & Nordland, 2000, p. 42). The effects of becoming an orphan introduce another set of conditions into the lives of these children as well: poverty, malnutrition, dropping out of school, becoming exploited through drug use and prostitution, and, for many, eventually becoming victims of AIDS themselves.

In the United States, American Indians were not only the target of exploitation and marginalization; as Gaw (1993) puts it, their culture experienced a holocaust. As a result of government policies and refusal to honor treaties, American Indians nearly became extinct. The population of today's 556 tribes equals only 1.2 million persons. According to Gaw, five-sixths of the Native American population died as the result of epidemics, forced relocations, and direct armed attacks on entire communities by the U.S. Cavalry. Over the years, Native children were taken by force from their homes and sent to government boarding schools, where they were coerced into "unlearning" their Indian ways; some never returned to their tribes. In the minds of Indian people, being Indian was a matter of survival. History indicates that reality. Writers of American Indian history underscore the "nonperson" status that affects many Indians' self-perception, suggesting that self-segregation or otherwise marginalizing oneself may be a direct consequence of negative self-image and low self-regard.

The B dimension of the PDI model offers another set of group and individual identities that are described as more fluid, by choice or through developmental opportunities (see Figure 1). Some of these identities include educational and military experience, health care practices, and social/recreational outlets. When we think of groups such as the rural poor, the chronically mentally ill, or children orphaned as a result of AIDS, the notion of access to desirable health care, education, and "good" employment seems unlikely. In fact, we presume that marginalized individuals have few options and choices in life. Even today, American Indians must show proof of tribal membership in order to receive certain services. It is well-known that persons who live in poverty are uninsured and therefore more at risk with respect to emotional and physical well-being.

On a global basis, Chiu (1996) observes that mental health professionals need to be "more aware of cross cultural differences in psychiatric patients" (p. 129). He contends that worldwide migration across national boundaries has increased as a result of the fall of the Soviet Union, growth in international businesses, and increased access to international travel. Recent immigrants have multiple stressors to deal with at once, and many must try to cope while living in countries that are culturally, linguistically, and religiously different from their countries of origin. Without adequate support networks and culturally competent mental health services, such individuals may manifest severe psychiatric disturbances.

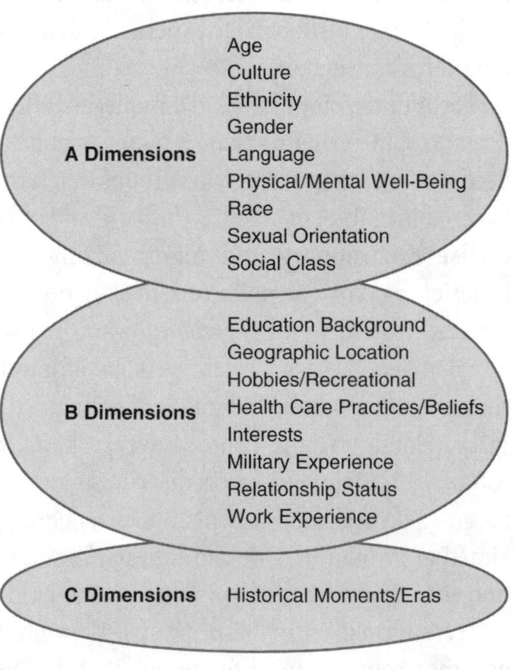

Figure 1 Dimensions of Personal Identity

Sociologist Harold Isaacs (1975) has examined the phenomenon of groups' becoming marginalized in relation to basic group identity. Although Isaacs focuses on ethnic groups, his work can help to inform our understanding of who takes on marginal status. One thing we know is that marginal status is not based on a group's numbers alone; other criteria and conditions operate to contribute to group marginalization. Isaacs indicates that basic group identity embodies a "ready-made set of endowments and identifications which every individual shares with others from the moment of birth by the chance of the family into which he/she is born at that given time in that given place" (p. 31). Although there is an emphasis on the biological, Isaacs states that there are also "common holdings of the group . . . the social features, the 'shared sameness' that enter in all their complex ways into the making of the individual ego identity" (p. 32).

Referring again to the A and C dimensions of the PDI model, shared biological and social features emerge as two characteristics that contribute to a group classification, such as gender, although they do not necessarily indicate shared group identity. For example, African American women and White women have gender in common, but this does not necessarily mean that members of these groups share other forms of sameness. The heterogeneity of marginalized groups is often overlooked; that is, outsiders may view all individuals of a particular group identity as the same and indistinguishable. Those who resort to labelese might assert, "If you've seen one, you've seen them all."

Isaacs (1975) also considers the criteria of individuals' sense of belongingness and the quality of individuals' self-esteem. Eric Erikson and Kurt Lewin have written about negative identity and the "uncertainty of belongingness," respectively. In a discussion of adolescent gang behavior, Erikson (1968) notes that for a gang member, having a negative identity is better than having no sense of identity at all. Lewin (1935) theorizes that the status of not belonging affects an individual's dealings with others, be they more or less powerful. In essence, a person can see him- or herself as more powerful and thereby special based on group affiliation and the group's perceived status.

Indeed, persons in specialized or marginalized groups typically are portrayed or perceived as being powerless, victims of circumstances, or victimizers. Often they are seen as being responsible for their own plight in life; we call this "blaming the victim." An orphan who feels responsible for the fact that his mother had AIDS and died, leaving the child destitute and ill, is blaming the victim—in this case, himself. Often, people with disabilities seem to be blamed for their own lack of full ability. For example, individuals who are hearing impaired often find that the burden of accommodation to their disability lies with them—they have to make themselves understood.

Another way of understanding the phenomena associated with marginalized identity and group status is through examination of the effects of social standing, ordinant groups, and prestige and power factors (Fouad & Brown, 2000). Similar to the PDI model's A dimension of social class (Arredondo & Glauner, 1992), social standings are legacies transmitted across generations; these are also associated with some of the PDI's B dimensions, including educational attainment, occupational status, and the consequential or inherited economic resources. In fact, the cycles of poverty and privilege offer interesting parallels in their perpetuation, although the realities are quite different.

Individuals who are descendants of those who arrived in the New World on the *Mayflower* often claim high social standing, and it is well-known, particularly in the New England area, that certain family names connote privilege and social rank. Interestingly, religion, gender, and race also interact with social standing, resulting in terms such as *WASP* (White Anglo-Saxon Protestant), *blueblood,* and *Brahmin.* Individuals in marginalized groups would not be perceived as holding these identities.

Members of "ordinant groups" are given higher social standing based on self-perception and the perceptions of others (Fouad & Brown, 2000). This goes back to the premise mentioned earlier, that not all persons are accorded equity or seen as naturally worthy of respect. For example, it is well-known that African American women are paid less than White women, and that White women with lesser education and economic resources are not viewed with the same regard as their more educated and economically advantaged sisters. It has often been stated that "perceptions become reality," and when it comes to determining who belongs to a marginalized group, a combination of particular A and B dimensions of identity alone may predispose certain individuals to this status.

Prestige and power are also factors that distinguish those with high social standing from those with marginalized identities. According to Fouad and Brown (2000), prestige criteria include "occupational prestige, subjective status, consumptive behavior, group participation (including types of persons comprising the groups and the type of activities engaged in by the groups), and evaluations of racial, religious, and ethnic groups" (p. 384). Additionally, "normative" color and cultural behavior are criteria that receive "relative value, acceptance, and appreciation by the larger societal group" (p. 384). For example, members of the Muslim faith are seen as non-Christian, and their religious practices and attire are often deemed foreign and are not valued or appreciated. With respect to "normative" color, East Asians from Pakistan and Egyptians who may be more visibly "white" are likely to be viewed more positively by members of the majority culture than are some of their darker-skinned peers.

The power factor plays a key role in the definition of marginal group status and, of course, in the control of an individual's destiny. The determination of who is eligible for the Welfare to Work Program, Head Start, farm subsidies, AIDS treatment, family assistance, subsidized housing, and subsidies for prescription medications, among other life-sustaining, basic benefits, is often in the hands of legislators who are far removed from the situations of marginalized groups and who base their decisions on social status, ordinant group standing, and prestige.

Additionally, it is rare that an individual with marginalized group status crosses into a category with higher social standing. With the passage of the Civil Rights Act, more women and persons of color became candidates for public office, making them eligible to gain a part of the power factor. However, in the past 5 years fewer women have sought public office, and persons of color who have become elected officials have often found their professional and personal practices, both prior to and during their tenure in office, subject to heightened scrutiny. That such a small percentage of elected officials has been subjected to a disproportionate amount of scrutiny is noteworthy; it suggests that the White political majority still yields the power and influence to determine credibility and acceptability.

Minority Identity

To this discussion must be added the minority identity development (MID) model (Atkinson, Morten, & Sue, 1992). The self and other attitudinal categories of this stage model amplify the preceding discussion of social standing, personal identity, and the PDI model. The four attitudinal categories of the MID model are attitudes toward self, attitudes toward others of the same minority group, attitudes toward other minority groups, and attitudes toward the dominant group. The basic premises of the model are (a) that members of minority groups grow up in a culture of oppression and discrimination and (b) that they are then presumed to be deficient. Consequently, the deck is stacked against members of ethnic and racial minority groups, and minority group members are thus the subordinates in an automatic dominant-subordinate relationship with members of the dominant group. Thus, in the first MID stage, conformity, individuals accept their second-class status and are often self-deprecating; idealize the dominant White, able-bodied, heterosexual group; devalue others of the same minority group status; and view other minority groups as unacceptable and to be avoided.

This model can be readily applied to marginalized groups. In fact, some women, gays and lesbians, and persons with disabilities have remarked about the relevance of this model for their individual experiences. If the hearing impaired, for example, are perceived as inadequate as a group, all individuals who are hearing impaired assume that status, and although they may accept their impairment, they still have to contend with external perceptions and expectations about them. Returning again to individuals suffering from AIDS or HIV, it is conceivable that such persons may believe that they must accept unkind treatment from members of the dominant group—persons who do not have AIDS or who are not HIV-positive—and also discriminate against others with AIDS/HIV in order to fit in and be accepted.

For mental health practitioners, the minority identity development model, the personal dimensions of identity model, and the concepts of basic group identity, negative identity, sense of belonging or unbelonging, and social standing offer very valuable frameworks for working with members of marginalized groups. Therapists must recognize the complexity of forces that impinge on individuals in such groups and the situational and historical contexts that may predetermine their marginalized status; they must also be aware of the prevailing forces and laws that may be available to assist these individuals, but that are often manipulated by those with power and control.

It is fairly easy to have intellectual discourse and to hypothesize about marginalized groups, but it is another experience entirely to be identified as a member of such a group. In the next section, I identify some of the groups that are "accorded" marginalized status in the United States.

Who Belongs to Marginalized Groups?

Within the United States, marginalized groups have historically included the four major ethnic and racial minority groups: African Americans/Blacks, American Indians, Asians, and Latinos, or those of Hispanic heritage. Also marginalized are the disabled, women, gays and lesbians, and the poor. The obvious ways in which these groups differ from the mainstream are in color, gender, physical health, sexual orientation, and economic resources. Over the years, social status for some individuals associated with these groups has shifted, particularly for White women of educational accomplishment and economic means. At the same time, with increasing diversity of cultural identities, rapid changes in technology, increasing emphasis on financial wealth, and changes in family patterns, constellations, and values, the seeds have been sown for the creation of new marginalized groups.

In a recent publication titled *Advocacy in Counseling*, edited by Lewis and Bradley (2000), the majority of the 16 chapters suggest the need for advocacy in counseling with members of historically marginalized groups and others who are emerging with this identity. Among the groups addressed by the contributors to the volume are African American clients; Native American Indian and Alaska Native clients; Latinos/as; multiracial families; youth; older adults; lesbian, bisexual, gay, and transgendered persons; people with HIV/AIDS; and women in the criminal justice and addiction treatment systems. The issues discussed include gender-based equity, nonviolence, addictions, linguicism, and domestic violence. In other literature on marginalized groups, authors have included those who belong to nonmainstream religious groups, victims of child abuse, Black women prisoners, and families living under extreme environmental conditions (e.g., in urban areas and in the unhealthy, unsanitary conditions found in parts of Appalachia; Atkinson & Hackett, 1995).

In these discussions, authors have a tendency to refer to the group identity phenomenon in a monolithic way, obfuscating differences and the heterogeneity within groups that are attributed marginalized status. For example, rural White youth may have some commonalities with rural youth of color, but not across all dimensions of personal identity. Color certainly makes for a different life experience, as well as how an individual is valued by those outside of his or her group. Additionally, one must keep in mind that all youth, whether rural or urban, are part of family and community systems that add further definition. Poor rural families may constitute a marginalized group, and separating the youth from the family would not necessarily facilitate developmental processes or the "success" of particular counseling interventions.

However, it is important to note that the poor rural teenagers and adults who form these marginalized families do have particular types of issues and stressors that are different from those of other kinds of families. One good example comes from Brown's (1998) study of adolescent girls in rural Maine. By virtue of their physical environment, their limited economic and educational opportunities, and the historical repetition of cultural practices in their local environment, these girls reported that they knew what was in store for them. The kinds of dreams for adulthood that many teenagers from other environments might hold were not even a consideration for them. Their worldview was already formed, and they expected to follow the same life script as had their parents and grandparents. They were aware of the prevailing "groupthink" and how it meant their remaining in this colonized situation (I discuss colonization in more detail in the next section).

As we return to the questions of who is a member of a marginalized group and what distinguishes a marginalized group, a set of factors emerge. These include the phenomenon of colonization, the definition of marginalization by those in power, the need for legislation to protect marginalized individuals and groups, economic disempowerment, environmental and living conditions of hardship, (more often than not) group members' being of color or of multiracial background, and lack of access to advocacy, power, or other means of changing the conditions that maintain a group's marginal status. All of these conditions place severe limitations on individuals and bring about negative consequences, many of which cannot be controlled, such as poor access to health care and basic survival resources.

The phenomenon of colonization is a contextual factor that is relevant to this discussion. In her review of anticolonial Chicana feminism, Teresa Córdova (1999) notes: "Colonialism has imbedded its memory in our spirits. After stripping us of our institutions, our resources, and our history, the colonizer asserts his superiority and declares us deficient and deserving of our fate" (p. 11). In Córdova's review, several terms corresponding to the concept of colonialism emerge, such as *subjugation, occupation, patriarchy, racism, struggle, loss of identity, sexism, racism, classism,* and *dehumanization.* Many marginalized groups have experienced various forms of colonization as defined through this language, and many are maintained in that group status by the perpetuation of these same practices by those in power.

In a discussion of the mestizo worldview, Ramirez (1998) brings forth the deficit perspective about indigenous peoples. Ramirez cites Mannoni, a French psychoanalyst who wrote in the early 1960s, who asserted that the Native peoples of the Americas wanted to be colonized and dependent. According to Mannoni (1960), the arrival of the conquerors from Spain was "unconsciously expected—even desired—by the future subject peoples" (p. 644; quoted in Ramirez, 1998, p. 6).

The reality of "colonization" leads us back to the historical and sociopolitical context and to the observations that in the United States freedom has not rung true for every person, and that the determination of deficiency and social value by the privileged continues to maintain the status quo for marginalized groups and to engender new ones.

Effects of Being in a Marginalized Group

The discussion thus far suggests that individuals in groups with marginalized status generally do not benefit from that status. In fact, far more often, they have adverse experiences because of the assumptions made about them by others. Stereotyping is often used to exclude individuals or to control them; those who label assume a position of power over those whom they stereotype. Fiske (1993) notes that "stereotypes are intrinsically controlling of other people" (p. 621) and that "stereotyping operates in the service of control" (p. 623). She observes that the use of power, stereotyping, and control leads to the development of asymmetries between two individuals or two groups.

If we take the example of persons with physical disabilities, we can see that assumptions and perceptions about people in marginalized groups—in this case individuals' physical limitations and even their intelligence—often result in the application of stereotypes. One consequence of such stereotypes is that the disabled, as a group, are among the most underemployed in the United States. The stereotypes applied to people with disabilities control perceptions of their ability to work, and those in power (e.g., employers or hiring managers) make choices and exert their power based on these stereotypes.

International examples can also be invoked. Through apartheid, the colonizers of South Africa marginalized and ruled the majority population of Africans. Those years of segregation and dominance left millions disempowered in their homeland. Similar examples can be pointed to in South America, where indigenous groups have managed to preserve themselves in spite of linguicism, racism, and deliberate genocide.

Another example can be found in the growing numbers of elderly in the United States. Because the American culture values youthfulness and fitness and does not respect or have high regard for older individuals, many are rendered invisible. This manifests in the struggles many elderly face in securing access to adequate and affordable housing, health care, and the means to meet other daily life needs. One effect of the marginal status of older Americans is the tendency of many to infantilize them. The perception may be that seniors have to be treated like children because they are physically weaker, more often have hearing impairments, cannot help themselves, and cannot advocate on their own behalf. Such stereotypical thinking on the part of mental health professionals will naturally lead to interventions that are not necessarily respectful of individual seniors. When counseling interventions are built on premises of client deficiency and helplessness, the dignity of the client is undercut. In mental health settings, clinicians and administrators have the power to set the climate and standards of care for elderly clients. If they base these on stereotypes rather than on respect for the client and concern for the client's dignity, they are not paying proper attention to their professional duty. As Fiske (1993) notes, stereotyping is often linked to such a lack: "We are a society where people in power stereotype in part because they do not have to pay attention" (p. 621).

Some effects of being part of a marginalized group may be less easily discerned than others but are still powerful because they are psychological in nature. These include low self-esteem, poor self-concept, learned helplessness, and self-marginalization. As self-fulfilling prophecy sets in, individuals in marginalized groups believe they "deserve" to be marginalized.

Córdova's (1999) discussion of the colonial mentality and identity is again relevant here; she describes the concept of *identity to power* (p. 32). In examining the marginalized individual's or group's position in relation to the colonizer or group in power, Córdova suggests that there are three possible identities a colonized individual can assume: overseer, imposter, or wimp (p. 33). Presumably, a person who takes on the role of overseer works to ensure that others in his or her group stay in place and do not resist their assigned role. Overseers and imposters are individuals who identify with their aggressors and take on dehumanizing behavior toward others in their group or in similarly disenfranchised groups.

These roles often become evident when tension develops between ethnic and racial minority groups. The theory is that these groups, in their attempts to obtain power, sometimes turn on each other or develop a pecking order and demonstrate the characteristics of oppressors, overseers, and imposters. Among the homeless, conflicts sometimes result in homicide when one member of a group is perceived to be weak or is seen as not playing by the local rules. Colonization is an insidious condition that historically has been imposed by members of the dominant White male group upon those they see as weaker, expendable, and less valuable as people.

Atkinson and Hackett (1995) discuss some forms of discrimination, from negative stereotypes to physical violence, that affect persons with disabilities, elders, women, and gays and lesbians. They also identify social, economic, and environmental discrimination against members of these groups. They report that children with disabilities are "overrepresented among those physically abused" (p. 77). They note also that the elderly experience victimization both from actual crimes and through their fear of being victims of crime. Atkinson and Hackett also describe other forms of discrimination that affect women and have led to women's marginalization as a group. These include social inequality, economic disadvantage, lack of maternity and child support, occupational segregation and comparable work, wage discrimination, gender role stereotyping, and victimization. Like other groups described above, women in general are the victims of the use and abuse of power by those in control.

In addition, women of color are further victimized as a result of their color. For example, studies of sexual harassment in the workplace indicate that women of color, particularly African American women, are more often the victims of such harassment. It has been hypothesized that this is so because women of color are perceived as more vulnerable and less powerful than White women, with few resources of support or advocacy within the organizations where the harassment occurs.

Another effect for counseling of the classifying of whole groups is that clinical approaches and theoretical positions are developed based on assumptions about group members that may not be true. For example, in an article on sexual orientation, Klein, Sepekoff, and Wolf (1990) note that research on sexual orientation has been restricted because of "rigidly demarcated orientations and derived norms from clinical populations that often have been biased" (p. 65). Such an approach minimizes the complexity of sexual orientation and its multifaceted, dynamic process. In clinical practice, such limitations can prove detrimental; for instance, a clinician may impose issues on a client because of the client's gay or lesbian identity. Similarly, some have asserted that a person's "culture" is the explanation for his or her psychological or life issues. The challenge for the clinician is to go beyond the marginalized status or visible identity of the client, without ignoring it, and allow the individual to define the problem or issue, rather than make presumptions about reasons for the client's marginalized status.

Invisibility is still another effect of membership in a marginalized group. Gays and lesbians as well as those who are hearing and visually impaired have reported this type of experience. Have you ever noticed how people respond to a visually impaired person as he or she attempts to cross the street? Some bystanders act as though they cannot "see" the person. With the hearing impaired, people often focus on trying to be "heard," and so speak loudly when addressing such individuals. In work environments, gays and lesbians tend to be invisible in many organizations because of the penalties associated with their being open about their sexual identity. There are many emotional costs to invisibility; marginalized individuals may hear themselves or other members of their groups joked about or ridiculed, and many experience isolation, a sense of "unbelonging," and stress as a result of being different. Being marginalized or classified in some way as a member of a special population introduces many psychological and daily life stressors.

Shared Worldview of Marginalized Individuals and Groups

When an individual self-defines as a member of a marginalized group or has that status attributed to him or her, this suggests that he or she holds a worldview that clinicians need to recognize and understand. A person's worldview comprises his or her belief system and values, and thus dictates the individual's norms of behavior, such as how he or she communicates.

Worldview has been described as encompassing an individual's perceptions of the relationship between locus of control and attribution of responsibility. Sue (1978) presents a model that involves the four elements of internal locus of control, internal attribution of responsibility, external locus of control, and external attribution of responsibility; an individual's worldview may manifest a combination of these categories. It is inconceivable that persons in a marginalized group would see themselves as having internal control and internal responsibility. In fact, most circumstances are out of their control, because of oppression and their inherent lack of power.

The worldviews that seem most closely aligned with the plight of marginalized individuals are those that combine external locus of control and internal attribution of responsibility or external locus of control and external attribution of responsibility. Individuals such as immigrants and refugees may recognize that their status and access to educational and health care services is dictated by government policies, but they may still believe they have responsibility for ministering to their own needs and life objectives. Persons with an "external-external" worldview have probably assumed a position of learned helplessness for a number of reasons. They may have concluded over time that no matter how hard they try, they are not going to be taken seriously because of their marginal status, that there is no one who will advocate for them, and that they can only be passive participants in the life circumstances that surround them. In others words, they have given up on helping themselves.

Life experiences also contribute to individuals' worldviews. Life experiences drive a person's beliefs about his or her self-efficacy, power or lack thereof, and sense of self-respect. When one speaks with homeless persons, mothers on public assistance, or elderly persons in assisted living, for example, one quickly notices that they are well aware of how others see them. I once found myself consulting to some mental health providers in several state hospitals. Theirs was a challenging job, and they were well credentialed to work with different ranges of the mentally ill, but these professionals often communicated their low expectations and perceptions of these patients. They made numerous disrespectful comments in the presence of the patients, including a comment about one patient's inability to do little more than "vegetate." They appeared to be unwilling to advocate for their patients, and their attitude of subjugation was open and accepted. Clearly, not all providers are like these, but such attitudes seem to prevail in particular institutions, making one wonder about the continued victimization of the mentally ill.

Empowerment and disempowerment are two processes often talked about in counseling. Empowerment is often presumed to be an individual process, driven by a person's desire to change things for him- or herself. If an individual has inherited the legacy of several generations of marginalization owing to his or her group membership, it is highly unlikely that he or she will be able to self-empower. In fact, given the historic worldview of disempowerment, the pattern will likely continue. An example comes from the high incidence of pregnancy among Latina and African American teenagers. One of my counseling students shared her dismay when an 18-year-old client of hers gleefully informed her that she was to have her third child. As class members processed the case in terms of the counselor's potential biases and judgments in working with the client, they also explored explanations for the teenager's joy. One of the conclusions reached was that many of these young women feel powerless, and having a child gives them something to be proud of and even raises their status in their home communities.

In counseling situations, empowerment is often seen as a desirable process. However, it is equally important for counselors to consider the context or situation in relation to the promotion of individual empowerment. Is it possible, for example, for a homeless family to seek health care services if they are uninsured? Can an individual with limited English proficiency be successful in securing a Head Start spot for her child? Unless therapists have walked in the shoes of marginalized persons, they may find it hard to appreciate the sense of profound disempowerment and lack of hope held by many. Because the factors of access and equity are barriers to individuals in marginalized groups, counselors may in fact have only an abstract understanding of marginalized individuals' life situations. This limits counselors' engagement and inhibits their firsthand learning.

Competencies for Working More Effectively With Individuals From Marginalized Groups

The multicultural counseling competencies laid out by the Association for Multicultural Counseling and Development (AMCD) specify that counselors must be aware of their own worldviews and of their perceptions of different identity factors as these relate to themselves and to the clients they serve (Arredondo et al., 1996; Sue, Arredondo, & McDavis, 1992). Not surprisingly, many counselors have had limited experiences with members of marginalized groups; they may even consciously avoid contact with such groups. Because of the factors of access and equity that often prevent individuals in marginalized groups from seeking mental health services, counselors may never have had opportunities to work with and thereby learn from this broad, complex, and in-need clientele. To try to reduce some of the barriers, the AMCD has proposed a number of multicultural counseling competencies (Arredondo et al., 1996), which appear in adapted form below. (Changes added to the competencies in 1996 appear in italics.)

Counselor Awareness of Own Cultural Values and Biases

1. Culturally skilled counselors can articulate the beliefs of their own cultural and religious groups as these relate to sexual orientation, able-bodiedness (versus physical disabilities), and so forth, and the impact of these beliefs in a counseling relationship.
2. Culturally skilled counselors are able to recognize the sources of their own comfort/discomfort with respect to differences in terms of race, ethnicity, and culture, *as well as different disabilities, the elderly, different sex and sexual orientations, lower socioeconomic means and status, homelessness, and so forth.*
3. Culturally skilled counselors are able to identify differences (as described in the PDI model; Arredondo & Glauner, 1992) and are nonjudgmental *and willing to learn* about those differences.
4. Culturally skilled counselors possess knowledge and understanding about how oppression, racism, discrimination, and stereotyping affect them personally and in their work *and how these dynamics affect the lives of individuals in marginalized groups.*
5. Culturally skilled counselors can specifically identify, name, and discuss privileges that they personally receive in society due to their race, socioeconomic background, gender, physical abilities, sexual orientation, and so on.
6. Culturally skilled counselors possess knowledge about their social impact on others. They are knowledgeable about communication differences, how their style may clash with or foster the counseling process with others different from themselves based on the A, B, and C dimensions of the PDI model, and how to anticipate the impact they may have on others.
7. Culturally skilled counselors can give three to five concrete examples of situations in which they modified their communication style to complement that of a culturally different person *in terms of physical disability, age, poverty status, prisoner, and so forth,* how they decided on the modification, and the result of that modification.
8. Culturally skilled counselors can identify specific attitudes, beliefs, and values from their own heritage and cultural learning that support behaviors that demonstrate respect for and valuing of differences and those that impede or hinder respect for and valuing of differences *based on homelessness, different religious practices, HIV/AIDS condition, physical disabilities, and so forth.*

Counselor Awareness of Client's Worldview

1. Culturally skilled counselors are aware of their negative and positive emotional reactions toward members of other racial and ethnic groups, individuals from marginalized groups such as persons from Appalachia, war refugees, gays, lesbians,

and transgendered individuals, those who are members of non-Christian religious groups, and so forth that may prove detrimental to the counseling relationship.

2. Culturally skilled counselors identify their common emotional reactions about individuals and marginalized groups and observe their own reactions in encounters. For example, do they feel fear when a homeless person approaches them, or anxiousness when they drive through a neighborhood considered to be one populated by families of lower socioeconomic status?
3. Culturally skilled counselors are aware of stereotypes and preconceived notions that they may hold toward other racial and ethnic minority groups as well as those with marginalized group status, such as children and families in poverty or religious minorities.
4. Culturally skilled counselors possess specific knowledge about the groups with which they are working. They are aware of the life experiences, cultural heritages, and historical backgrounds of their culturally different clients and clients from marginalized groups in that community. This particular competency is linked to the minority identity development models available in the literature.
5. Culturally skilled counselors understand how being a member of a marginalized group can affect personality formation, vocational choices, manifestation of psychological disorders, help-seeking behavior, and the appropriateness or inappropriateness of counseling approaches.
6. Culturally skilled counselors understand and have knowledge about sociopolitical influences that impinge on the lives of individuals from marginalized groups by limiting access and further dehumanizing of individuals.
7. Culturally skilled counselors can identify the implications of such concepts as internalized oppression, institutional racism, privilege, and the historical and current political climate regarding immigration, poverty, and public assistance.
8. Culturally skilled counselors are aware of legal and legislation issues that affect various communities and individuals who are members of marginalized groups.
9. Culturally skilled counselors can discuss and define the concept of cultural invasion or oppression as described in Paulo Freire's (1993) theoretical framework on oppression.
10. Culturally skilled counselors can discuss concepts such as social standing, ordinant groups, and power and prestige factors as they apply to understanding barriers for members of marginalized groups.
11. Culturally skilled counselors can discuss factors and experiences that may contribute to the worldviews of members of marginalized groups.
12. Culturally skilled counselors can provide explanations for the perpetuation of marginalized groups.
13. Culturally skilled counselors have knowledge of the family structures, hierarchies, values, and beliefs of different marginalized groups.

Culturally Appropriate Intervention Strategies

1. Culturally skilled counselors seek out educational, consultative, and training experiences to improve their understanding of and effectiveness in working with culturally different populations *and individuals who are members of marginalized groups.*
2. Culturally skilled counselors maintain active referral lists and continuously seek

new referrals that are relevant to the different needs of clients along A and B dimensions of the PDI model *and those from marginalized groups.*

3. Culturally skilled counselors familiarize themselves with relevant research and the latest findings regarding mental health and mental disorders that affect *individuals from marginalized groups.*
4. Culturally skilled counselors can discuss recent research regarding such topics as mental health, career decision making, education and learning, and *employment options as they relate to individuals from marginalized groups.*
5. Culturally skilled counselors can discuss how the generic characteristics of counseling and therapy may clash with the values and *worldviews of individuals from marginalized groups.*
6. Culturally skilled counselors *can advocate on behalf of individuals from marginalized groups when they recognize the barriers to access and service based on institutional oppression.*
7. Culturally skilled counselors can identify and communicate possible alternatives that would reduce or eliminate existing barriers within their own institutions and within local, state, and national decision-making bodies.
8. Culturally skilled counselors use assessment instruments appropriately with clients from marginalized populations.
9. Culturally skilled counselors recognize possible historical and current sociopolitical biases in the *Diagnostic and Statistical Manual of Mental Disorders (DSM)* system of diagnosis as these *relate to different marginalized groups.*
10. Culturally skilled counselors can discuss traditional ways of helping, *such as prayer, 12-step programs, and networks of support, that have been deemed effective with individuals from different marginalized groups.*
11. Culturally skilled counselors take responsibility for educating their clients regarding the processes of psychological intervention, such as goals, expectations, legal rights, and the counselor's orientation *in counseling.*
12. *Culturally skilled counselors develop far-reaching programs or interventions to identify and serve members of marginalized groups, such as school dropouts; gay, lesbian, and bisexual youth; and seniors in assisted living.*

Summary

Marginalized groups will always exist, putting pressure on professionals in the mental health field to become proactive in their approach to members of these groups. A few years ago, California voters passed Proposition 209, which eliminated public services, including mental health counseling, for undocumented immigrants. Many California counselors have since struggled with a dilemma: Do I break the law or help someone in need?

The field of mental health has been politicized by insurers and legislators, and this has had negative consequences for the profession and its constituents. Counselors must become more politically active within their own professional associations, more aware of federal and state legislation that can affect their work and their clients' well-being, and more engaged in advocacy behavior to create more equity in provision of and access to mental health services. The challenges for mental health professionals are many because of social changes taking place worldwide. Counselors, psychologists, and other mental health practitioners must acquire a better understanding of the phenomena of multiculturalism, migration, and immigration, and the accompanying stressors and coping mechanisms used by different individuals and groups. By assuming new roles as change agents, mental health professionals will ensure the mental health well-being of future generations. To activate these roles, they must have a commitment to working with marginalized and underserved individuals, a willingness to enhance their skills to meet the counseling competencies proposed, and a belief that the profession can make a difference in the lives of marginalized persons.

Topics for Further Discussion

1. From a historical perspective, how did some groups come to be marginalized in the United States? What have been some of the contributing factors/events?
2. Discuss the legislation that began the move to grant rights to disenfranchised groups in the United States. How was it operationalized when it was passed? How is it operationalized today?
3. Who did the signers of the Declaration of Independence consider to be a "free man"? Who was not a "free man," and why?
4. Describe some of the forces and factors today, nationally and globally, that are contributing to the establishment of new marginalized groups?
5. What can be done to prevent marginalization of individuals and groups through societal action?
6. How might an individualist worldview contribute to the maintenance of groups with power?
7. Discuss the roles that stereotyping, power differentials, and White privilege play in maintaining the status quo for those in power.
8. Discuss "labelese" and how it functions.
9. Explain the phenomenon of colonization and how it applies to individuals and groups who are and are not marginalized.
10. Discuss the personal dimensions of identity model as it relates to one or more marginalized groups. Be sure to look at within-group differences.
11. Describe the attitudinal categories in the minority identity development model and apply them to one or more visibly marginalized groups.
12. Describe some of the effects of being marginalized on individuals and groups.
13. Identify the combination of locus of control and attribution of responsibility that describes the worldview that may be most widely held by marginalized individuals and groups.
14. Discuss the characteristics of ordinant groups and how they function within groups perceived to be heterogeneous and not marginalized.
15. Discuss national and global conditions that are contributing to the evolution of new marginalized groups.
16. How does racism affect or interact with marginalization?
17. What are some institutional practices that may perpetuate the marginalization of different groups?
18. Specify four or five competencies required for counselors to work ethically and effectively with marginalized individuals and families.
19. Name two or three counseling courses in which discussion of marginalized groups can readily occur. What competencies can be specified?
20. Describe institutional competencies for better serving marginalized individuals and groups.

References

American Psychiatric Association. (1980). *Diagnostic and statistical manual of mental disorders* (3rd ed.). Washington, DC: Author.

Arredondo, P., & Glauner, T. (1992). *Personal dimensions of identity model.* Boston: Empowerment Workshops.

Arredondo, P., McCarthy, J., & D'Andrea, M. (2000, June). "Label-ese" as a form of control. *Counseling Today,* pp. 21, 31–32.

Arredondo, P., Toporek, R., Brown, S. P., Jones, J., Locke, D. C., Sanchez, J., & Stadler, H. (1996). Operationalization of the multicultural counseling competencies. *Journal of Multicultural Counseling and Development, 24,* 42–78.

Atkinson, D. R., Morten, G., & Sue, D. W. (1992). *Counseling American minorities: A cross-cultural perspective* (4th ed.). Dubuque, IA: William C. Brown.

Atkinson, D. R., & Hackett, G. (1995). *Counseling diverse populations.* Dubuque, IA: Brown & Benchmark.

Blank, R., & Slipp, S. (1994). *Voices of diversity: Real people talk about problems and solutions in a workplace where everyone is not alike.* New York: AMACOM.

Brown, L. (1998). *Raising their voices.* Cambridge, MA: Harvard University Press.

Chen-Hayes, S., Chen, M., & Athar, N. (1998, November). Challenging linguicism: Action strategies for counselor and client-colleagues. *Counseling Today,* pp. 28, 30.

Chiu, T. L. (1996). Problems caused for mental health professionals worldwide by increasing multicultural populations and proposed solutions. *Journal of Multicultural Counseling and Development, 24,* 129–140.

Córdova, T. (1999). Anti-colonial Chicana feminism. In R. D. Torres & G. Katsiaficas (Eds.), *Latino social movements: Historical and theoretical perspectives* (pp. 11–41). New York: Routledge.

Erikson, E. (1968). *Identity: Youth and crisis.* New York: W. W. Norton.

Fiske, S. T. (1993). Controlling other people. *American Psychologist, 48,* 621–628.

Fouad, N. A., & Brown, M. T. (2000). Role of race and social class in development: Implications for counseling psychology. In S. D. Brown & R. W. Lent (Eds.), *Handbook of counseling psychology* (3rd ed., pp. 379–402). New York: John Wiley.

Freire, P. (1993). *Pedagogy of the oppressed* (Rev. 20th anniversary ed., R. R. Barr, Trans.). Albany: State University of New York Press.

Gaw, A. C. (1993). *Culture, ethnicity, and mental health.* Washington, DC: American Psychiatric Press.

Isaacs, H. R. (1975). *Idols of the tribe: Group identity and political change.* New York: Harper & Row.

Klein, F., Sepekoff, B., & Wolf, T. (1990). Sexual orientation: A multi-variable dynamic process. In T. Geller (Ed.), *Bisexuality: A reader and source book* (pp. 64–81). Ojai, CA: Times Change.

Kohls, L. R. (1988). *The values Americans live by.* Yarmouth, ME: Intercultural Press.

Lewin, K. (1935). *A dynamic theory of personality.* New York: McGraw-Hill.

Lewis, J., & Bradley, L. (Eds.). (2000). *Advocacy in counseling: Counselors, clients, and community.* Greensboro, NC: ERIC-CASS.

Mannoni, O. (1960). Appel de la federation de France du FLN. *El Moudjahid, 59,* 644–645.

Masland, T., & Nordland, R. (2000, January 17). 10 million orphans. *Newsweek,* pp. 42–45.

Ramirez, M. (1998). *Multicultural/multiracial psychology.* Northvale, NJ: Jason Aronson.

Sue, D. W. (1978). Eliminating cultural oppression in counseling: Toward a general theory. *Journal of Counseling Psychology, 16,* 419–428.

Sue, D. W., Arredondo, P., & McDavis, R. J. (1992). Multicultural counseling competencies and standards: A call to the profession. *Journal of Counseling and Development, 70,* 644–688.

19

Assessments of Prejudice, Cultural Competence, Stressful Effects of Racism, Racial and Ethnic Identity, and the Multicultural Personality

Joseph G. Ponterotto

Shawn O. Utsey

Paul B. Pedersen

Terrorists create terror; terror creates fear and anger; fear and anger create aggression; and aggression against citizens of different ethnicity or religion creates racism and, in turn, new forms of terrorism.

—P. G. Zimbardo, past president of the American Psychological Association (2001, p. 50)

In Chapter 1 of *Preventing Prejudice: A Guide for Counselors, Educators, and Parents* (Ponterotto, Utsey, & Pederson, 2006), we pointed out how easily prejudice can develop and how pervasive it is in the United States. This is particularly the case for subtle, modern racism in White Americans. How can we determine or measure how racist we are—how racist or prejudiced our children, students, or colleagues may be? In the last half century, researchers, particularly in social and counseling psychology, have developed countless measures, assessments, and tests to quantify prejudicial thinking and attitudes. In this chapter, we list some of the more popular and well-researched measures, and we provide references for readers who may be interested in gathering more information on a particular assessment.

In this chapter, we also review empirical measures of racial identity development, multicultural personality, and multicultural competence, because these constructs are correlated with prejudice and multicultural awareness. More specifically, individuals with higher levels of racial identity, multicultural personality, and multicultural competence tend to be less prejudiced and more comfortable and competent when interacting in culturally diverse situations. Furthermore, as noted in Part II of this book, individuals who score higher on the constructs also appear to have higher psychological health and quality of life in general.

Finally, this chapter briefly reviews instruments that measure the stressful effects of racism for select racial and ethnic minority groups.

Measures of Racism, Prejudice, and Homophobia

Table 1 summarizes popular and more recently developed measures or assessments of racism, prejudice, and homophobia. The first column of the table specifies the instrument name and the original citations that describe the development and initial validity and reliability of the measure. Column 2 defines the construct that the instrument purports to measure. Column 3 specifies the dimensionality of the instrument. Dimensionality determines, from a psychometric point of view, whether the instrument yields one total score (unidimensional) or multiple, somewhat distinct subscales (or factors), in which case it can be classified as a multidimensional instrument. We also note the number of items per subscale or factor, as well as the total number of items in the instruments.

Columns 4 and 5 note our assessment of the instruments' pattern of score reliability and validity. Instead of getting statistically complex in our assessment here, we use an accessible summative index of the instruments' psychometric strength. Each instrument's score reliability and validity strength is evaluated as *limited, adequate,* or *strong,* based on the following criteria.

Limited

This classification is applied to instruments that may have been used in only a few studies, that have a limited sampling base (in terms of geography, age, and so forth), and that do not have consistently satisfactory indexes of internal score reliability (that we define as coefficient alpha = .70) across diverse samples. These instruments also may not have indexes of stability (test-retest reliability) over time. Furthermore, the measures in this category may not have adequate construct validity as measured by both exploratory and confirmatory factor analyses. Readers should remember that reliability and validity are not stable characteristics of instruments or measures themselves, but are instead characteristics of scores on a measure or assessment administered to a particular sample in a particular place and at a particular time under certain testing conditions (see Constantine & Ponterotto, 2005; Thompson, 2002). For this reason, it is important that score reliability and validity be calculated for each administration of the measure.

Adequate

We characterize an instrument as generally having adequate score reliability and validity if the measure has been used in multiple studies (usually 5 to 10), has evidenced consistently satisfactory internal consistency score reliability (mean or median coefficient alpha at .70 and higher across studies), and presents some evidence of test-retest reliability (stability) as well. Furthermore, adequate measures also have undergone large-sample exploratory factor analysis (an assessment of construct validity) documenting the proposed factor structure (that

Table 1 Measures of Racism, Prejudice, and Homophobia

Measure (and Developers)	*Construct (and Audience)*	*Factors (and Item Number)*	*Reliability*	*Validity*	*Psychometric Critiques*
Quick Discrimination Index (Ponterotto, Burkard et al., 1995, 2001; Utsey & Ponterotto, 1999)	Subtle racial and gender prejudice (adolescents and adults)	Racial attitudes (9) Racial comfort (7) Gender attitudes (7) Total items = 30	Adequate to strong	Adequate to strong	Burkard et al. (2001), Biernat & Crandall (1999), Ponterotto et al. (2002)
Modern Racism Scale (McConahay, 1986)	Whites' racial attitudes toward Blacks (adolescents and adults)	Unidimensional, 6- and 7-item versions	Adequate	Adequate	Sabnani & Ponterotto (1992)
Institutional Racism Scale (Barbarin & Gilbert, 1981)	Institutional racism (adolescents and adults)	Indices of racism (8) Strategies to reduce racism (11) Extent of strategy use (7) Agency climate (6) Administrative efforts (20) Personal efforts (20) Total items = 72	Adequate	Adequate	
Situational Attitude Scale (Sedlacek & Brooks, 1970)	Initially Whites' attitudes toward Blacks; modified to assess attitudes toward women, male sex roles, persons with disabilities, and children (adolescents and adults)	10 interpersonal scenarios with 10 items each Total items = 100	Adequate	Adequate	
Motivation to Control Prejudice Reactions (Dunton & Fazio, 1997)	Motivation to control expressions of prejudice (adolescents and adults)	Concern with acting prejudiced (11) Restraint to avoid dispute (6) Total items = 17	Adequate	Adequate	Burkard et al. (2001)

(*Continued*)

Table 1 (Continued)

Measure (and Developers)	*Construct (and Audience)*	*Factors (and Item Number)*	*Reliability*	*Validity*	*Psychometric Critiques*
Modern Homophobia Scale (Raja & Stokes, 1998)	Heterosexual attitudes toward lesbian women and gay men (adolescents and adults)	Attitudes toward lesbians (24) Attitudes toward gay men (22) Total items = 46	Adequate	Adequate	Burkard et al. (2001)
Lesbian, Gay, and Bisexual Knowledge and Attitudes Scale for Heterosexuals (Worthington et al., 2005)	Heterosexual knowledge and attitudes toward lesbian, gay, and bisexual individuals (heterosexual late adolescents and adults)	Hate (6) Knowledge (5) Civil rights (5) Religious conflict (7) Affirmativeness (5) Total items = 28	Adequate	Adequate	
Racial Bias Preparation Scale (Fisher, Wallace, & Fenton, 2000)	Adolescent perceptions of multicultural preparation messages received from primary caregivers (all adolescents)	Reactive (10) Proactive (10) Total items = 20	Limited	Limited	

is, whether the measure is unidimensional or multidimensional). Finally, adequate measures have also evidenced convergent and criterion-related validity through theoretically predicted significant correlations with related constructs.

Strong

We generally reserve this evaluation for those measures that have been used in many studies (10 or more) across diverse geographic regions and samples and that have evidenced consistently satisfactory levels of score reliability (internal consistency [coefficient alpha] and test-retest stability) across samples. Strong measures most often have construct (factor structure) evidence supported by both large-sample exploratory and confirmatory factor analyses, and they have evidence of score-convergent and criterion-related validity. These measures may also have been used internationally and give evidence of generalizable psychometric support.

Finally, column 6 of Table 1 lists references for extensive critical reviews and evaluations of the psychometric strengths and limitations of scores emanating from the specific measures. There are a good number of measures presented that have not yet received such a rigorous evaluation, often by a third party. Some of the measures are too new, with too little use, to warrant an integrative evaluation at this time. For students and professionals or whoever may be interested in using one of the instruments for his or her own research, we highly suggest reading all of the development studies listed in column 1, as well as the critical reviews of the instruments cited in column 6.

Featured Instrument: Quick Discrimination Index

From Table 1, we feature the Quick Discrimination Index (QDI; Ponterotto, Burkard, et al., 1995; Utsey & Ponterotto, 1999). The QDI is one of the more frequently used measures of more subtle racial and gender bias. It includes three subscales or factors: Cognitive Racial Attitudes (9 items), Affective Racial Attitudes (7 items), and Cognitive Gender Attitudes (7 items). Critical reviews of the QDI (see column 6 of Table 1) have found scores from the QDI across many samples to have consistently satisfactory indexes of internal consistency reliability, with the median coefficient alpha for the Cognitive Racial Attitude factor .85; for the Affective Racial Attitude factor, .77; and for the Cognitive Gender Attitude factor, .71. Indexes of test-retest reliability, construct validity, criterion-related validity, and confirmatory factor structure have also been adequate (see Ponterotto, Potere, et al., 2002, for the latest critical review).

The QDI has also been used internationally, with wording adaptations for samples in the United Kingdom and South Africa and a full translation in Chinese.

Measures of Multicultural Counseling Competence

Table 2 summarizes 10 measures of professional counselors' (and other mental health professionals) perceived competence to work with culturally diverse clientele. Seven of the measures focus on competence to work with racially and ethnically diverse clients; two focus on competence in counseling lesbian, gay, and bisexual clients. The 10th measure listed in Table 2 tests the multicultural training environment for training programs in counseling. Each measure is evaluated along the same criteria described in detail earlier.

Table 2 Measures of Multicultural Counseling Competence

Measure (and Developers)	*Construct (and Audience)*	*Factors (and Item Number)*	*Reliability*	*Validity*	*Psychometric Critiques*
Multicultural Counseling Knowledge and Awareness Scale (Ponterotto et al., 1996; Ponterotto, Gretchen, et al., 2002)	Self-reported perceptions of multicultural counseling competence (counselors and other mental health professionals)	Knowledge (20) Awareness (12) Total items = 32	Adequate to strong	Adequate to strong	Constantine & Ladany (2001); Ponterotto & Potere (2003); Kocarek et al. (2001); Constantine, Gloria, & Ladany (2002)
Multicultural Counseling Inventory (Sodowsky et al., 1994)	Same as above	Awareness (10) Knowledge (11) Skills (11) Relationship (8) Total items = 40	Adequate to strong	Adequate to strong	Constantine & Ladany (2001), Pope-Davis & Nielsen (1996), Ponterotto & Alexander (1996), Kocarek et al. (2001)
Multicultural Awareness-Knowledge-and-Skills Survey (D'Andrea et al., 1991; Kim et al., 2003)	Same as above	Awareness (20) Knowledge (20) Skills (20) Total items = 60	Adequate to strong	Adequate to strong	Constantine & Ladany (2001), Ponterotto & Alexander (1996), Kocarek et al. (2001)
California Brief Multicultural Competency Scale (Gamst et al., 2004)	Same as above	Nonethnic ability (7) Knowledge (5) Awareness (6) Sensitivity (3) Total items = 21	Adequate to strong	Adequate to strong	
Cross-Cultural Inventory–Revised (LaFromboise et al., 1991)	Observer report assessment of counselor multicultural competency (counseling supervisors)	Unidimensional Total items = 20	Adequate	Adequate	Ponterotto & Alexander (1996)

Measure (and Developers)	*Construct (and Audience)*	*Factors (and Item Number)*	*Reliability*	*Validity*	*Psychometric Critiques*
Multicultural Competence in Student Affairs–Preliminary 2 (Pope & Mueller, 2000)	Self-perceived multicultural competence in student affairs professionals	Unidimensional Total items = 34	Adequate	Adequate	Pope, Reynolds, & Mueller (2004)
Multicultural Counseling Competence and Training Survey–Revised (Holcomb-McCoy & Day-Vines, 2004)	Self-perceived multicultural competence in school counselors	Terminology (4) Knowledge (19) Awareness (9) Total items = 32	Adequate	Adequate	
Lesbian, Gay, and Bisexual Affirmative Counseling Self-Efficacy Inventory (Dillon & Worthington, 2003)	Perceived self-efficacy in working with lesbian, gay, and bisexual clients in an affirmative framework (mental health practitioners and students)	Apply knowledge (13) Advocacy skills (7) Self-awareness (5) Assessment (4) Relationship (3) Total items = 32	Adequate	Adequate	
Sexual Orientation Counselor Competency Scale (Bidell, 2005)	Self-perceived competence in counseling gay, lesbian, and bisexual clients	Skills (11) Attitudes (10) Knowledge (8) Total items = 29	Adequate	Adequate	
Multicultural Environmental Inventory–Revised (Pope-Davis et al., 2000; Toporek et al., 2003)	Multicultural integration within counseling graduate programs	Curriculum and supervision (11) Climate and comfort (11) Honesty in recruitment (3) Multicultural research (2) Total items (27)	Adequate	Adequate	

We found all 10 measures to possess generally adequate to strong psychometric properties (score reliability and validity) across samples. The Multicultural Knowledge and Awareness Scale (Ponterotto et al., 1996; Ponterotto, Gretchen, et al., 2002), the Multicultural Counseling Inventory (Sodowsky, Taffe, Gutkin, & Wise, 1994), and the Multicultural Awareness-Knowledge-and-Skills Survey (D'Andrea, Daniels, & Heck, 1991) are the most frequently used self-report measures. The Cross-Cultural Counseling Inventory– Revised (LaFromboise, Coleman, & Hernandez, 1991) is the most frequently used observer or supervisor evaluation form of a trainee's multicultural competence.

Five newer measures that we believe hold strong research promise include Dillon and Worthington's (2003) Lesbian, Gay, and Bisexual Affirmative Counseling Inventory, Bidell's (2005) Sexual Orientation Counselor Competency Scale, Pope and Mueller's (2000) Multicultural Competence in Student Affairs–Preliminary 2 Scale, Holcomb-McCoy and Day-Vines' (2004) Multicultural Counseling Competence and Training Survey–Revised, and Gamst et al.'s (2004) California Brief Multicultural Competency Scale. These measures are quite new and have not undergone extensive independent use and critique; nonetheless, the development studies introducing these new measures were very strong, and we see the instruments as potential major contributions to the competency research.

Featured Instrument: Multicultural Counseling Knowledge and Awareness Scale

The MCKAS is a careful revision of the original Multicultural Counseling Awareness Scale (MCAS; Ponterotto et al., 1996). It includes two factor-analytically derived subscales: Knowledge (20 items) and Awareness (12 items). MCKAS factor scores have witnessed satisfactory internal consistency reliability, with the mean coefficient alpha across 22 geographically dispersed samples falling at .90 (median was .91) for the Knowledge scale, and .78 (median was also .78) for the Awareness scale. The MCKAS subscales also have satisfactory test-retest reliability and criterion-related validity, and the factor structure has been supported using both exploratory and confirmatory factor analyses (see Ponterotto & Potere, 2003, for the latest in-depth critical review).

Measures of Teachers' Multicultural Competence

Table 3 summarizes six measures of teachers' multicultural competence. The majority of these measures focus on teachers at the elementary, middle, and high school level. As a group, these measures have undergone less use and less psychometric scrutiny than the measures in the other tables in this chapter. As a result, all of these instruments are rated as only *limited* to *adequate* in regard to psychometric strength. The newest measure in the group is the Multicultural Awareness-Knowledge-and-Skills Survey for Teachers, by D'Andrea et al. (2003). This measure is an adaptation of their popular counselor competency measure of the same name (refer back to Table 2). We believe this measure holds good promise, but as of yet there is not enough research on the measure to rate its psychometric strength above the *limited* category.

Featured Instrument: Teacher Multicultural Attitude Scale

The Teacher Multicultural Attitude Scale (TMAS; Ponterotto et al., 1998) is a 20-item

Table 3 Measures of Teachers' Multicultural Competence

Measure (and Developers)	*Construct (and Audience)*	*Factors (and Item Number)*	*Reliability*	*Validity*	*Psychometric Critiques*
Teacher Multicultural Attitude Survey (Ponterotto et al., 1998)	Multicultural awareness and sensitivity (K–12 teachers)	Unidimensional Total items = 20	Limited to adequate	Limited to adequate	Ponterotto et al. (2003)
Multicultural Awareness-Knowledge-Skills Survey for Teachers (D'Andrea, Daniels, & Noonan, 2003)	Perceived self-reported multicultural competence (K–12 teachers and teacher education students)	Awareness (8) Knowledge (13) Skills (20) Total items = 41	Limited	Limited	
Cultural Diversity Awareness Inventory (Henry, 1986)	Multicultural sensitivity (adult educators)	Unidimensional Total items = 28	Limited	Limited	Ponterotto et al. (2003)
Multiethnic Climate Inventory (P. E. Johnson & R. E. Johnson, 1996)	Cultural attitudes and biases (K–12 teachers)	Cultural encapsulation (5) Cultural hostility (5) Majority dominance (5) Minority suppression (5) Total items = 20	Limited	Limited	Ponterotto et al. (2003)
Multicultural Teaching Concerns Survey (Marshall, 1996)	Concerns regarding working with culturally diverse students (K–12 teachers)	Competence (11) Strategies and techniques (11) Bureaucracy (4) Family and group knowledge (5) Total items = 31	Limited	Limited	Ponterotto et al. (2003)
Racial Ethical Sensitivity Test (Brabeck et al., 2000)	Ethical sensitivity to racial, ethnic, and gender intolerance (K–16 teachers and educators)	Stimulus.vignettes of ethical violations, unidimensional, with 37 ethical violations assessed	Limited	Limited	Ponterotto et al. (2003)

unidimensional (yields one total score) measure of K–12 teachers' multicultural awareness and sensitivity. More specifically, teachers making high scores on the TMAS are "aware of multicultural issues in education; are open, receptive, and embracing of cultural diversity; and believe cultural diversity and multicultural education enhance the learning environment for all students" (Ponterotto, Mendelsohn, et al., 2003, p. 196). The TMAS has witnessed satisfactory score internal reliability (coefficient alpha = .86) and test-retest stability (.80 at 3-week interval), as well as promising factor-analytic and criterion-related validity support.

Measures of the Stressful Effects of Racism

Table 4 summarizes six assessments that attempt to measure and quantify, on some level, the impact of racism on the lives of U.S. minority group members. Four of the six measures focus on racism experienced by African Americans, one focuses on the impact of racism on Asian Americans, and one is more general and can apply to the impacts of racism on minority group members in general. As noted in Table 4, we perceive a wide variety of psychometric strength in the selected sample of instruments: Some have only limited psychometric support, and others have adequate to strong support. The newest measure in the group is Liang, Li, and Kim's (2004) Asian American Racism-Related Stress Inventory. Although it is relatively new, we already rate this instrument as having *limited* to *adequate* reliability and validity support because of three systematic development studies reported by its authors.

In the study of racism generally, more attention has been paid to measuring racial and prejudicial attitudes rather than on the detrimental impact these attitudes have on both perpetrators and victims. As such, research that measures the impact of racism is critical to researchers' understanding so that prevention and intervention efforts and programs can be better and more holistically informed.

Featured Instrument: Index of Race-Related Stress–Brief Version

The Index of Race-Related Stress–Brief Version (IRRS-B; Utsey, 1999) is a 22-item factor-analytically reduced version extracted from the longer IRRS (Utsey & Ponterotto, 1996). The IRRS-B includes three factors (or subscales): Cultural Racism, with 10 items; Institutional Racism, with six items; and Individual Racism, also with six items. Coefficient alphas for the three factors were, respectively, .78, .69, and .78. Evidence of score construct and criterion-related validity was demonstrated through confirmatory factor analysis and through theoretically predicted significant correlations with other racism measures.

Measures of Racial and Ethnic Identity Development

Table 5 summarizes basic information on racial and ethnic identity development measures. By far the most extensively used measures in this category are racial identity measures developed by Janet E. Helms and her colleagues, as well as the general ethnic identity measure developed by Jean S. Phinney. Newer measures holding extensive promise in this category are the Cross Racial Identity Scale and the Oklahoma Racial Attitude Scale. Both of these instruments, despite being relatively new, have already received a psychometric rating of *adequate* from us because of careful, systematic development and testing of instrument items (see Table 5).

Table 4 Measuring the Stressful Effects of Racism

Measure (and Developers)	*Construct (and Audience)*	*Factors (and Item Number)*	*Reliability*	*Validity*	*Psychometric Critiques*
Index of Race-Related Stress (Utsey & Ponterotto, 1996)	Everyday stress experienced by African Americans (late adolescent and adult African Americans)	Cultural racism (16) Institutional racism (11) Individual racism (11) Collective racism (8) Global racism (46) Total items = 46	Adequate to strong	Adequate to strong	Utsey (1998a)
Index of Race-Related Stress–Brief Version (Utsey, 1999)	Same as above	Cultural racism (10) Institutional racism (6) Individual racism (6) Global racism (22) Total items = 22	Adequate to strong	Adequate to strong	Utsey (1998a)
Perceived Racism Scale (McNeilly et al., 1996)	Perceptions of White racism experienced over a lifetime as well as within the past year (late adolescent and adult African Americans)	Employment Academic Public realm Racist statements (Subscale items unclear) Total items = 51	Limited	Limited	Utsey (1998a)

(Continued)

Table 4 (Continued)

Measure (and Developers)	*Construct (and Audience)*	*Factors (and Item Number)*	*Reliability*	*Validity*	*Psychometric Critiques*
Racism and Life Experience Scale–Brief Version (Harrell, 1994)	Impact of racism (minority group members)	Racism-self (20) Racism-group (12) Total items = 32	Limited	Limited	Utsey (1998a)
Schedule of Racist Events (Landrine & Klonoff, 1996)	Frequency of racial discrimination in past year or over entire lifetime (African American late adolescents and adults)	Recent racist events (6) Lifetime racist events (6) Appraisal of racist events (6) Total items = 18	Limited	Limited	Utsey (1998a)
Adolescent Discrimination Distress Index (Fisher et al., 2000)	Adolescence distress from institutional, educational, and peer contexts (all adolescents)	Institutional (6) Educational (4) Peer (5) Total items = 15	Limited	Limited	
Asian American Racism-Related Stress Inventory (Liang et al., 2004)	Perceptions of race-related stress (Asian American late adolescents and adults)	Sociohistorical (14) General (8) Perpetual foreigner (7) Total items = 29	Limited to adequate	Limited to adequate	

Table 5 Measuring Racial and Ethnic Identity

Measure (and Developers)	*Construct (and Audience)*	*Factors (and Item Number)*	*Reliability*	*Validity*	*Psychometric Critiques*
Black Racial Identity					
Black Racial Identity Attitude Scale (Helms & Parham, 1996)	Cross's (1971) model of psychological nigrescence (African Americans)	Pre-encounter (14) Encounter (4) Immersion-emersion (9) Internalization (12) 11 filler items Total items = 50 (Short form = 30)	Adequate	Adequate	Fischer & Moradi (2001)
Multidimensional Inventory of Black Identity (Sellers et al., 1997; Shelton & Sellers, 2000)	Dimensions of African American Identity (African Americans)	Nationalist (9) Oppressed (9) Assimilationist (9) Humanist (9) Centrality (8) Private regard (7) Total items = 51	Limited	Limited	Fischer & Moradi (2001)
African Self-Consciousness Scale (Baldwin & Bell, 1985)	Baldwin's (1981) Africentric theory (African Americans)	Total items = 42	Adequate	Limited	Fischer & Moradi (2001)
Cross's Racial Identity Scale (Vandiver et al., 2001, 2002)	Cross's (Cross & Vandiver, 2001) revised model of psychological nigrescence (African Americans)	Assimilation (5) Miseducation (5) Self-hatred (5) Anti-White (5) Afrocentricity (5) Multiculturalism (5) Total items = 40	Adequate	Adequate	

(Continued)

Table 5 (Continued)

Measure (and Developers)	*Construct (and Audience)*	*Factors (and Item Number)*	*Reliability*	*Validity*	*Psychometric Critiques*
White Racial Identity					
White Racial Identity Attitude Scale (Helms & Carter, 1990)	Helms's (1984) theory of White identity (White Americans)	Contact (10) Disintegration (10) Reintegration (10) Pseudoindependence (10) Autonomy (10) Total items = 50	Limited to adequate	Adequate	Helms (2005); Fischer & Moradi (2001)
White Racial Consciousness Development Scale (Claney & Parker, 1989; Parker, Moore, & Neimeyer, 1998)	Helms's (1984) theory of White identity (White Americans)	Contact (3) Autonomy (3) Disintegration (2) Pseudoindependence (2) Reintegration (2) Behavioral autonomy (3) Total items = 15	Limited	Limited	Choney & Rowe (1994)
Oklahoma Racial Attitude Scale (Choney & Behrens, 1996; LaFleur et al., 2002)	Rowe et al.'s (1994) racial consciousness model (White Americans)	Dissonant (4) Avoidant (3) Reactive (8) Dependent (3) Conflictive (8) Integrative or dominant (8) Total items = 34	Adequate	Adequate	Fischer & Moradi (2001)
Multigroup Ethnic Identity Measure (Phinney, 1992)	Social and developmental identity paradigms (all groups)	Ethnic identity (14) Other group orientation (6) Total items = 20	Adequate	Adequate	Fischer & Moradi (2001); Ponterotto, Gretchen, et al. (2003)

Measures of the Multicultural Personality

The theory of the multicultural personality posits that Americans with more of a multicultural worldview and orientation toward life will not only be more comfortable in an increasingly culturally diverse society but will also evidence higher levels of psychological health and quality of life in general. We believe that the multicultural personality is a promising area for future research.

Table 6 lists measures that assess components of the multicultural personality. It is important to remember that instruments reviewed in Tables 1 through 5 also tap components of the multicultural personality through related constructs. The Multicultural Personality Questionnaire (MPQ) profiled in Table 6 is the broadest and most comprehensive measure of the multicultural personality currently available. The MPQ consists of five factors (or subscales): Cultural Empathy, Open-Mindedness, Social Initiative, Emotional Stability, and Flexibility. The MPQ was developed in the Netherlands by Professors Karen van der Zee and Pieter van Oudenhoven (2000), and these researchers, along with their colleagues, have conducted a series of studies highlighting the validity and utility of the MPQ in predicting psychological adjustment and quality of life for English-speaking expatriates living in various countries. Ponterotto et al. (2005) have adapted the MPQ slightly for research with North American samples.

The Miville-Guzman Universality-Diversity Scale measures a narrower construct relating to comfort with diversity and the valuing of both similarities and differences among people. This instrument has witnessed adequate score reliability and validity across multiple samples. The Psychological Costs of Racism to Whites Scale and the Racial Justice Action Scale are new measures that we believe have good promise as components of the multicultural personality construct.

Guidelines for Selecting Multicultural Instruments

This chapter has reviewed a number of multicultural-focused instruments across the areas of prejudice, racism, homophobia, multicultural competence, the stressful effects of racism, racial and ethnic identity development, and the multicultural personality. Paper-and-pencil instruments are one type of tool that counselors, educators, and administrators can use to assist their own professional development and to supplement their work with clients and students. These instruments are not panaceas, and they cannot substitute for meaningful personal and professional experience or seasoned clinical judgment.

Any instrument used by counselors, teachers, administrators, supervisors, or managers should be selected with caution. One general rule is not to administer to clients, students, or parents any instrument that you yourself have not completed. Here are four additional guidelines that we use when selecting instruments for practice, research, program evaluation, and supervision.

1. Does the instrument have face validity to you? Despite the psychometric properties specified for the instrument, are you comfortable with the scale? Are you satisfied with the wording, format, layout, and length of the instrument? Do you believe the instrument items accurately measure the construct of interest? Is the wording (e.g., reading level needed for reliable comprehension) appropriate for your target sample? Are there bilingual or translation issues that need to be addressed? Are you

Table 6 Component Measures of the Multicultural Personality

Measure (and Developers)	*Construct (and Audience)*	*Factors (and Item Number)*	*Reliability*	*Validity*	*Psychometric Critiques*
Multicultural Personality Questionnaire (van der Zee & van Oudenhoven, 2000, 2001)	Multicultural effectiveness in expatriates (organizational and personnel psychology) (all groups)	Cultural empathy (18) Open-mindedness (18) Social initiative (17) Emotional stability (20) Flexibility (18) Total items = 91	Adequate	Adequate	
Miville-Guzman Universality-Diversity Scale (Miville et al., 1999)	Awareness and acceptance of both similarities and differences among people	Unidimensional Total items = 45	Adequate	Adequate	Burkard et al. (2001)
Miville-Guzman Universality-Diversity Scale–Short Form (Fuertes et al., 2000)	Awareness and acceptance of both similarities and differences among people	Unidimensional Total items = 15	Adequate	Adequate	
Psychosocial Costs of Racism to Whites Scale (Spanierman & Heppner, 2004)	Psychosocial costs of racism for Whites	White empathy (6) White guilt (5) White fear (5) Total items = 16	Adequate	Adequate	
Racial Justice Action Scale (Kingsbury, Schiffner, Qin, & Cheng, 2005)	McClintock's continuum of social action against oppression	Proactive stance (5) Awareness and support (10) Working against equality (5) Total items = 20	Limited	Limited	

confident that the items will not be offensive to your selected participants?

2. Has the instrument generated scores over multiple samples that could be considered reliable and valid? Have previous research studies using the instrument clearly described the sample, procedures, and indexes of reliability and validity? If the instrument claims to be multidimensional, is there empirical and rational support for scoring and interpreting subscales separately?

3. Remember that when requesting an instrument from an author or publisher it is equally important to request up-to-date research reports assessing score reliability and validity on the instrument. Simply having a copy of the instrument itself with scoring directions will not suffice. You are ethically bound, before using an instrument, to assess its psychometric strengths and limitations.

4. When you use an instrument, it is important to follow the author's or publisher's scoring directions very carefully. For many instruments, certain items need to be reverse-scored before a total score can be tallied; other instruments require complex score transformations. If you have questions about how an instrument is to be used or scored, contact the author or publisher directly. When you write up the results of your study, be sure to include score means, standard deviation, and coefficient alphas for all subscales scored. *Remember, score reliability is a function of instrument scores with a particular sample in a particular place under particular testing conditions; therefore it is essential to report score coefficient alphas for every sample tested.* Furthermore, it is general ethical testing policy to save your actual data for 5 years and make that data available to interested researchers.

References

Constantine, M. G., & Ponterotto, J. G. (2005). Evaluating and selecting psychological measures for research purposes. In F. T. L. Leong & J. T. Austin (Eds.), *The psychology research handbook: A guide for graduate students and research assistants* (2nd ed., pp. 104–113). Thousand Oaks, CA: Sage.

Thompson, B. (Ed.). (2002). *Score reliability: Contemporary thinking on reliability issues.* Thousand Oaks, CA: Sage.

D'Andrea, M., Daniels, J., & Heck, R. (1991). Evaluating the impact of multicultural counseling training. *Journal of Counseling and Development, 70,* 143–150.

D'Andrea, M., Daniels, J., & Noonan, M. J. (2003). New developments in the assessment of multicultural competence: The Multicultural Awareness-Knowledge-Skills-Survey-Teacher Form. In D. B. Pope-Davis, H. L. K. Coleman, W. M. Liu, & R. Toprek (Eds.), *Handbook of multicultural competencies* (pp. 154–167). Thousand Oaks, CA: Sage.

Dillon, F., & Worthington, R. L. (2003). The Lesbian, Gay and Bisexual Affirmative Counseling Self-Efficacy Inventory (LGB-CSI): Development, validation, and training implications. *Journal of Counseling and Development, 50,* 235–251.

Bidell, M. P. (2005). The Sexual Orientation Counselor Competency Scale: Assessing attitudes, skills, and knowledge of counselors working with lesbian, gay, and bisexual clients. *Counselor Education and Supervision, 44,* 267–279.

Gamst, G., Dana, R. H., Der-Karabetian, A., Aragon, M., Arellano, L., Morrow, G., & Martenson, L. (2004). Cultural competency revised: The California Brief Multicultural Competence Scale. *Measurement and Evaluation in Counseling and Development, 37,* 163–183.

Holcomb-McCoy, C. C., & Day-Vines, N. (2004). Exploring school counselor multicultural competence: A multidimensional concept. *Measurement and Evaluation in Counseling and Development, 37,* 154–162.

LaFromboise, T. D., Coleman, H. L. K., & Hernandez, A. (1991). Development and factor structure of the Cross-Cultural Counseling Inventory–Revised. *Professional Psychology: Research and Practice, 22,* 380–388.

Ponterotto, J. G., Baluch, S., Greig, T., & Rivera, L. (1998). Development and initial score validation of the Teacher Multicultural Attitude Survey. *Educational and Psychological Measurement, 58,* 1002–1016.

Ponterotto, J. G., Burkard, A. W., Rieger, B. P., Grieger, I., D'Onofrio, A., Dubuisson, A., et al. (1995). Development and initial validation of the Quick Discrimination Index (QDI). *Educational and Psychological Measurement, 55,* 1026–1031.

Ponterotto, J. G., Costa, C. I., Brobst, K., Kowalewska, D., Mendelsohn, J., Scheinholtz, J., et al. (2005). *Multicultural personality dispositions and psychological well-being.* Unpublished manuscript, Division of Psychological and Educational Services, Fordham University, New York.

Ponterotto, J. G., Gretchen, D., Utsey, S. O., Rieger, B. P., & Austin, R. (2002). A revision of the Multicultural Counseling Awareness Scale. *Journal of Multicultural Counseling and Development, 30,* 153–180.

Ponterotto, J. G., Potere, J. C., & Johansen, S. A. (2002). The Quick Discrimination Index: Normative data and user guidelines for counseling researchers. *Journal of Multicultural Counseling and Development, 30,* 192–207.

Ponterotto, J. G., Rieger, B. P., Barrett, A., Harris, G., Sparks, R., Sanchez, C., et al. (1996). Development and initial validation of the Multicultural Counseling Awareness Scale. In G. R. Sodowsky & J. C. Impara (Eds.), *Multicultural assessment in counseling and clinical psychology* (pp. 247–282). Lincoln, NE: Buros Institute of Mental Measurements.

Pope, R. L., & Mueller, J. A. (2000). Development and initial validation of the Multicultural Competence in Student Affairs–Version 2 (MCSA–2) Scale. *Journal of College Student Development, 41,* 599–608.

Utsey, S. O. (1999). Development and validation of a short form of the Index of Race-Related Stress (IRRS–Brief Version). *Measurement and Evaluation in Counseling and Development, 32,* 149–167.

Utsey, S. O., & Ponterotto, J. G. (1996). Development and validation of the Index of Race Related Stress (IRRS). *Journal of Counseling Psychology, 43,* 490–501.

Utsey, S. O., & Ponterotto, J. G. (1999). Further factorial validity assessment of scores on the Quick Discrimination Index (QDI). *Educational and Psychological Measurement, 59,* 325–335.

van Der Zee, K. I., & van Oudenhoven, J. P. (2000). The Multicultural Personality Questionnaire: A multidimensional instrument of multicultural effectiveness. *European Journal of Personality, 14,* 291–309.

20

Client Culture Trainings/ Focus Groups Project Report

The California Network of Mental Health Clients

Acknowledgements

Planning Group: Cultural Competency Committee/CNMHC, Madelaine Bacon, Pearl Johnson, Ben Jones, Maria Maceira, Chandra Ogden, Delores Percy, Jose Rangel, Vickie Reis, Alice Washington

Presenters	
Central Valley:	Maria Maceira Ben Jones Sally Zinman Connie Moreno
Far North:	Vickie Reis Madelaine Bacon Rachel Querrero
Bay Area:	Alice Washington Maria Mar Maria Fuentes
South:	Marietta Logan-Curry Delores Percy Cora Fullmore
Far South:	Chandra Ogden Irma Kendricks Walter Philips

Report prepared by: Sally Zinman; Administrative support: Kathy Trevino

Executive Summary

Background

In order to further the knowledge base about client culture, the California Network of Mental Health Clients (CNMHC) held 5 trainings/ focus groups, one in each of the five geographic and governmental regions of the CNMHC, to explore what client culture means to clients. In *The Plan for Culturally Competent Specialty Mental Health Services, Addendum, Required Components for Implementation Plan, Consolidation of Specialty Mental Health Services (Phase 11)*, there is cursory mention of "consumer culture." The goal of the Trainings/Focus Groups was to engage the client community and, ultimately, the mental health community, in exploring and expanding the concept of client culture and its usefulness.

Format

A Training/Focus Group was held in each of Regions. The format (Appendix A) consisted of presentations from mental health professionals on the current knowledge about cultural competency and the mental health system including the managed care cultural competency plan requirements and clients on client culture as a distinct culture. (See summary of these presentations in Appendixes C, D, and E.) These presentations were followed by a focus group. The Focus Questions which framed the group discussion were:

> How do you define client culture? What are its major characteristics?
>
> What are the similarities between client culture and ethnic cultures, both positive and negative?
>
> How does a competent mental health system provide services that are sensitive to client culture?
>
> Is defining client culture and identifying it as a separate culture useful?

A Questionnaire consisting of these Focus Questions was available to participants in case they preferred writing their responses instead of or in addition to verbal participation. Twenty-two written Questionnaires were returned to the CNMHC. See Appendix B.

Trainings/Focus Groups were held in:

Modesto (Central Valley Region) on May 23, 1998; Redding (Far North Region) on May 30, 1998; San Jose (Bay Region) on June 13, 1998; Los Angeles (South Region) on June 20, 1998; and Carlsbad (Far South Region) on June 29, 1998.

A composite of 135 clients participated in the Focus Groups, with some Regions having ample and others scant participation: Central Valley: 12 participants; Far North: 35 participants; Bay Area: 47 participants; South: 30 participants; Far South: 11 participants.

Responses in the group discussion were recorded on flip charts and notes and audio tapes from three of the regions were available for this report.

Data Compilation Method

Each unique response from all of the Focus Groups was entered from the flip charts and notes and individual Questionnaires. (Obviously, in the group discussions, when a response was voiced it usually was not repeated since it become a group comment, while individual written responses were repeated.) When a similar response was repeated, this was indicated. Phrases capturing the nuances of the similar responses were noted. In some cases, like categories were joined. (For example, alternative treatments were joined with client-run alternatives, or the organizing and support aspects of the client movement were joined.) The cumulative responses of any one unique response were calculated and responses with the highest number viewed as client choice for the purpose of this study.

Summary

Question 1: How do you define Client Culture? What are its characteristics?

The experience of discrimination was the most repeated characteristic of client culture, with 12 responses, described as "treated poorly"; "stereotyped"; "second class citizens"; and "disparaged." This was followed by describing the mental health client movement and its support and organizing activities as constituting client culture, with 8 responses, described as "coming together and sharing, speaking with one voice, our movement"; "helping each other, nurturing each other, supporting each other"; "like a family, supporting each other"; "community of self-empowerment—at all levels"; and "unity is a culture—the new culture." Equally important as a characteristic of client culture was being marginalized, 8 responses, described as "isolated"; "feel different"; and "being an outcast." Poverty was an important characteristic of client culture, 7 responses, described as "economics a culture"; "unemployment"; "low level jobs"; and "isolated by poverty."

Both the experience of forced treatment and bad treatment, and oppression, had 6 responses. Low self-esteem had 5 responses, described as "internalize low images of us."

Question 2: What are the similarities between client culture and ethnic cultures, both positive and negative?

Discrimination and stigma were seen as the most shared characteristics between client culture and ethnic cultures, with 17 responses, described as "bottom of barrel"; "scapegoated for society's problems"; "looked at as a group, not as a person" and "negative stereotypes, socially and personally." Second in number of responses was that client culture and ethnic cultures consist of movements for change, 7 responses, described as "civil rights, empowerment movements"; "collective action, peer support, self-help groups, common resources"; "another civil rights movement." Poverty and class issues had 5 responses, described as "substandard housing, lower paying jobs"; "economic status—difficulty getting housing"; and "environments unsafe—bad neighborhoods." Both client cultures' and ethnic cultures' concentration on social justice issues had 5 responses and their shared experience of oppression had 4 responses. (See Data Section for a complete list of responses.)

Question 3: How does a competent mental health system provide services that are sensitive to client culture?

There are a cluster of ideas within the same range of number of responses to this question. Dealing with quality of life issues such as housing and employment had the highest responses, 12, described as "address real needs of clients, housing, employment"; "real needs of the whole person"; and "build community. supports." Second in importance toward developing a competent mental health system was mental health professionals "dropping the stereotypes and recognizing that we are all equals," 10 responses, described also as "whole system would have to change so as to see providers/clients as equals"; "respect clients as a coach rather than a psycho-therapist" and "empathy instead of sympathy." Next in number of responses was listening to consumers and groups, 9 responses, and developing client-run alternatives/alternative treatment modalities, 9 responses. These were described as "listen to perspective of client, don't tell us what we should think," "ask clients what they want," and "self-help programs, recovery centers," client-run agency providers; and "alternative treatment approaches." Consumer involvement in policy-making had 8 responses, described as "poll consumers as to programs they like when making cutbacks;

and include consumers in "all levels of decision-making." (See Data Section for a complete list of responses.)

Question 4: Is defining client culture and identifying it as a separate culture useful?

The overwhelming response to this question was yes, 18 responses, not including the positive comments in which agreement was indicated by the comment. There was some caution, however. There was concern that defining client culture might institutionalize negative stereotypes (2 responses). One participant exclaimed that many, particularly the negative, characteristics of client culture were circumstances, not culture. Primary concerns about identifying client culture as a separate culture were the danger of ghettoizing ourselves, becoming myopic and refusing to venture outside of our chosen culture, the concern of further sub-dividing cultures among ourselves, and of perpetuating the polarization of them and us.

The most repeated positive response to this question, 14 responses, was that defining client culture and identifying it as a separate culture were useful as a mechanism to organize for social change and to support each other, described as "gives us strength, we are not alone"; "yes, if it helps us to de-stigmatize ourselves"; social identity necessary to take action"; "can enhance and empower those that come behind us"; and "useful in fighting for our rights and supporting each other." Another reason why defining client culture was believed to be important was as a mechanism to promote a more client sensitive and thus more competent mental health system, described as, "train mental health system in how we live everyday, help them to understand us better and thus provide better services"; "help fit services to needs of the individual"; "without knowing our culture, denying proper services"; and "in order to treat the whole patient, work within parameters of said 'client world.' " Participants also expressed that defining client culture was useful as a mechanism to "know who you are, your own environment," 5 responses, described as "know yourself first, a transitional strategy"; "define ourselves—create our own culture"; and "we as a group of people should be acknowledged, teach people, who we are."

(See Data Section for a complete list of responses.)

Preliminary Observations

1. Clients self-identify as being victims of discrimination and stereotyping more than any other client culture characteristic. Discrimination and stereotyping pervades the first three Questions. They are the most repeated responses when defining client culture and its similarities to ethnic cultures. Moreover, the second most significant characteristic of a competent mental health system is one in which mental health professionals unlearn stereotypical thinking and "recognize that we are all equal."

2. Almost as frequent as references to discrimination and stereotyping is the awareness and importance of the mental health client movement, which is viewed as giving us a united voice for change and a vehicle for mutual support. The client movement is described as both a major characteristic of client culture and the prime use for defining client culture as a separate culture. The client movement is second in responses in Questions 1 and 2 and first in importance in Question 4. Its relation to our identity as victims of discrimination and stereotyping is clear. As a participant said in answering if defining client culture was useful, "Yes, if it helps us to de-stigmatize ourselves."

3. A client competent mental health system is viewed as one that deals with quality of life issues, such as housing, employment, and community supports. "Seeing the whole person" had the most responses in Question 3 and was

repeated in Question 4, when clients described how defining client culture could result in a more competent mental health system.

4. A clear consensus that emerged from the focus groups was that defining client culture was useful as a mechanism for change of the mental health system and societal attitudes and practices toward clients.

Data Collected[1]

Question 1: How do you define client culture? What are its characteristics?

Poverty (7)

Unemployment

Poor jobs

Isolated by poverty

Economics a culture

Low self-esteem (5)

Internalized low images of us

Confusion

Self-doubt based on conflicting information

Go to same center, organization, health place

To get something done for us (2)

Involved with County

Discrimination (12)

Treated poorly

Laugh, gossip, and intimidate

Discriminated with regard to cost of the professional services we request

Lack of health care parity

Treated as second class citizens

Stereotyped

Disparaged

Being an outcast

High intelligence (2)

Very smart

High resilience (2)

Survivors

School interrupted (1)

Humor (1)

Forced treatment (6)

Incarceration

Drugged

Drugged without consent

Only other group of people allowed to be incarcerated—other group criminal

Justice

Demeaning treatment

Oppressed (6)

Same medical diagnosis (4)

Common problem—illness

Same problem

Marginalized (8)

Isolated

Feel different

Being an outcast

We are different

Share the same language (1)

Activities of movement, support and political (8)

Independent—free of system

Alternative methods of healing

Support groups of equals

Coming together and sharing, speaking with one voice, our movement

A group that shares beliefs, needs, values, traditions, weaknesses—work together to meet the needs, strengthen their weakness; build on their strengths, and achieve their goals

Compassion, understanding and sympathies based on similar histories and backgrounds

Helping each other/nurturing each other/supporting each other

Like a family supporting each other

Diverse (3)

A culture inclusive of everyone—gay, lesbian, ethnic backgrounds

Diversity should not be feared should be embraced

Don't put clients in one basket—see us as the richness of the community

Aggressively independent (2)

Dependency (2)

Silence/fear (2)

System wore us out, taught us to be frightened

Anger

Question 2: What are the similarities between client culture and ethnic cultures, both positive and negative?

Oppression (4)

Being enslaved by "mental illness"

Victimized

Rights issues—even to having access (5)

Facing social justice issues

Confronting social justice issues

Fighting for rights

Another civil rights movement

Discrimination/stigma—(15)

Bottom of barrel

Scapegoat for society's problems

Mislabeling—based on misunderstanding

Discrediting clients—culture's knowledge

Looked at as a group, not a person

See people as a group—not as an individual, understanding the diversity

Negative stereotypes—socially and personally

Labeling

Stereotyped like ethnic culture

Treated like tokens

Anger and defiance (2)

Fiercely independent (2)

Built in distrust of authority

Don't trust authority

Separatists (2)

Sense of clanhood

Poverty, class issues (5)

Negative—grouped with ethnic groups in terms of discrimination

Sub-standard housing, low paying jobs

Quality of life

Economic status—difficulty getting housing

Environment unsafe—bad neighborhoods

Economic pressures

Organized for change, movements for change (7)

Civil rights, empowerment movements

Collective action, peer support, self-help groups

Fighting for the rights—housing, jobs, living conditions

Celebrating ourselves—rejoice in ourselves

Suppressed—won't be suppressed anymore

Another civil rights movement

Positive support from others with same background (2)

Suicide rate high in ethnic cultures (1)

Drug use (1)

Both have special needs (1)

Client culture—need medication and therapy in order to function

Ethnic—need connection to their heritage in order to preserve their self-identity

Diversity of talent, ideas, opinions, assumptions (3)

Co-optation—like ethnic movement/culture (1)

Internal conflict in both (2)

Turn on each other, conflict within our own ranks

Other disabilities not judged (2)

Not a value judgment on other disabilities

Ability to survive (2)

Knowing where and how to reach out to find proper agencies

Ethnic cultures teach you—learn to develop coping skills

Ethnic culture—parents share culture with children

Psychiatric disability—not given same kind of guidance from family (1)

Perception that client movement is racist (2)

Ethnic culture—physical similarities, not same with client culture (1)

Both have closet members (2)

Self denigration—self-fulfilling prophesy creates chronic mental illness

Internalize what people say about you

Question 3: How does a competent mental health system provide services that are sensitive to client culture?

Drop stereotypes/training on client culture, history of client movement, find out what their (clients) life is like (10)

Professional should have to try psychotropics

Recognition that we are all equal

Whole system would have to change, see providers/clients as equals

Challenging idea of providers and clients—should be equal, points on a continuum

Respect clients as a coach rather than a psychotherapist

Empathy not sympathy

Identify me as a citizen, with all the patient's rights

Not treating us like tokens

Close financial gap between mental health professionals and clients

Listening to consumers and groups (9)

Listen to perspectives of client—don't tell us what we should think

Ask clients what they want

Listening to clients

Being informed of backgrounds and culture

Make me a part of my treatment/planning team

Staff go with norms, not the individual needs

Deal with quality of life issues—housing, employment (12)

Address real needs of clients housing, employment

Build community support

Value needs of the whole person

Spirituality—god as part of recovery

See the whole person

Client culture part of a holistic approach to client care

Adapt their services to fit our culture—i.e. be aware of transportation

Advocacy (2)

Advocacy—external from and internal to system

Consumer employment in mental health delivery system (4)

Peer counseling

Consumer involvement in policy making (8)

Include consumers in negotiation for contracts

Poll consumers as to programs they like when making cutbacks

Evaluation of services that target consumers

All levels of decision making

Client alternatives—client agency providers (9)

Consumer run conservators

Alternative treatment approaches

Alternative medicine

Supporting a healthy lifestyle—exercise each night, etc.

By allowing sports—musical—humorist satire, activities to the maximum

Client owned and run recovery villages

Peer support

Self-help programs/recovery centers

Can't be competent without us—use client run pilot projects as models

Training for client volunteers (2)

Self-advocacy training so effective on Boards

A voluntary system (4)

Stop forced treatment

Limiting forced treatment

Validate client cultural preferences taken into account

Recognize choice to be homeless, gay, lesbian, etc.

Change Social Security methods of calculation (1)

By having proper education relating to profession (2)

Learn more about interrelationship about medication and other things

Have more celebrations (2)

More social activities for clients

Go into community where people live (1)

Maintain confidentiality (2)

Lack of information from doctors (2)

Be more honest in answering clients questioning, instead of patronizing

Putting high functioning mentally ill people with low functioning not a good idea (2)

Finding services for clients that are of various intellect

Hiring staff who have sensitivity to the culture (4)

Recruit and train people from different cultures

Cultural events with different costumes

Professionals of different cultural backgrounds to provide services to clients of different ethnic cultures

Collaboration efforts with other groups—any kind of groups (1)

Serve physically and mentally disabled together, not separately (2)

Educate staff around physical and mental health—training them for both

Question 4: Is defining client culture and identifying it as a separate culture useful?

Yes—(18)

Train mental health system in how we live everyday, help them to understand us better and thus provide better services (11)

To be culturally competent to us

To empathize with us

In order to treat the whole patient, work within parameters of said "client world"

Be sensitive to client's individual needs

Without knowing client culture—denying proper services

Help fit (services) to needs of the individual

Clients being treated in better ways—more human—better housing

To provide services in relation to client culture

To be able to assess (access) client needs in relation to societal pressure

Yes, if it helps us to de-stigmatize ourselves (organize for change)

Sensitivity to client culture; will cause mental health system to be competent

Adopt other services to fit our culture, transportation

Shows other consumers we have a common voice, similar experiences, a united voice (14)

Gives us strength—we are not alone—peer support/leads to recovering and organizing

Peers best friends you can have

Organized action

We are a resource for each other

Transitional strategy

Acceptance, understanding, compassion, empathy for fellow "sufferers"

Ability to share common experiences

Also can be beneficial if it brings persons of like nature or with similar problems together and these people work together to overcome the oppression and discrimination that exists

A human rights community amidst opposing social realities

Yes, for it gives us a purpose to exist

To be pro-active in our daily lives, fight back

Useful in sense of community, how we work together

Speak with a common voice

Social identity necessary to take action

Strengthen self-empowerment

Best ways to get rid of stigma, etc.

Can enhance and empower those who come behind us

Strengthening and self-empowerment

Useful in fighting for our rights

Supporting each other

In our best interest, any other culture banded together have gotten things done

Speak out regarding our shared values

We should make change through the value of ourselves

Help us to focus on issues (5)

Know yourself first, a necessary transitional strategy

Define ourselves—create our own culture

I define myself

Important to know who you are; your own environment

We are a group of people who should be acknowledged, teach people who we are. As smart as they are, but just different.

Shows society its negative creation (1)

Concerns

May maintain negative stereotypes

Is not a culture, is circumstances

Client culture not to label and isolate clients

Negative aspect—when one becomes myopic and won't go outside culture of chosen identification

No, if we make distinctions among ourselves, sub-divide more (2)

Perpetuates them and us

Fear mental illness will be only identification, don't ghettoize ourselves

Separates us out, however, many of us are in closet anyway

No—gender is the real issue or—have to address gender first

Note

1. The heading of each category was the first response in that category.

APPENDIX A

Training/Focus Group Agenda

Professional Trainer

Current knowledge about cultural competency; Cultural competency in the mental health plan.

Client Trainer(s)

A discussion about client culture as a separate culture.

Focus Group following the presentations

Questions:

How do you define client culture? What are its major characteristics? What are the similarities between client culture and ethnic cultures, both positive and negative? How does a competent mental health system provide services that are sensitive to client culture? Is defining client culture and identifying it as a separate culture useful?

APPENDIX B

Training/Focus Group Questionnaire

How do you define client culture? What are its major characteristics?

____

____

____

____

____

____

What are the similarities between client culture and ethnic cultures, both positive and negative?

______

______

______

______

______

______

How does a competent mental health system provide services that are sensitive to client culture?

______

______

______

______

______

______

Is defining client culture and identifying it as a separate culture useful?

______

______

______

______

______

______

APPENDIX C

Client Culture

Introduction:

I. Defining Culture
   A. Definition of culture from *Intercultural Communications* by Maurice Rappaport

II. Personal Experiences
   A. Impact of oppressive mechanisms on quality of life; cultural shock
   B. Personal empowerment
   C. Steps to success

III. Client Culture: Oppressive Mechanisms
   A. Diagnosis/labeling
   B. Medication
   C. Hospitalization
   D. Societal/familial stigma
   E. Economic impact
   F. Housing
   G. Feeling different
   H. Culturally incompetent services
   I. Forced treatment

IV. Client Culture: Empowerment
   A. Self-help
   B. Peer advocacy and support
   C. Education
   D. Alternative mental health services
   E. Political Activism

V. History of the Client Movement
   A. The beginning, how it came about
   B. Present day
   C. Hopes for the future

APPENDIX D

A Discussion About Client Culture as a Separate Culture

A culture does exist among mental health clients. We are calling it client culture.

Culture, as defined in the Addendum for the Consolidation of Specialty Mental Health Services (Phase II), is "the integrated pattern of human behavior that includes thought, communication, actions, customs, beliefs, values and institutions of a racial, ethnic, religious or social group . . . A particular individual' s cultural identity may involve the following parameters among others: ethnicity, race, language, age, country of origin, acculturation, gender. socioeconomic class, religious/ spiritual beliefs and sexual orientation."

How have I been impacted by what I define as client culture? Well, I have been affected by both oppressive mechanisms and empowering mechanisms of client culture. The oppressive mechanisms include:

A. Diagnosis/labeling—I am no longer known as Alice, a black lady, or a very tall girl. I am now a consumer, a schizophrenic, or am mentally ill. In reality, I am a person.

B. Hospitalization/forced treatment—I was locked up. No freedom. Controlled by the clicking of keys going into a lock on the door to my freedom, my life. Treated differently because of being a mental health client.

C. Economic impact—I was suddenly poor when I became a client. I couldn't go everywhere or buy anything. I had to wear clothing that I couldn't get into because my medications had made me so fat. Poor.

D. Housing—I live in a house known as a place where crazy people live. We are known because the cops and ambulances have been there so many times.

E. Feeling different—I am different enough, but being a client really negatively reflects upon anything else about me I may feel makes me different.

F. Culturally incompetent services—I had to fight for my dignity while in therapy. Services are not respectful and do not celebrate us as clients.

Everyone is unique and beautiful, and this *is* how we should celebrate each other. When I achieved this type of attitude and helped the people I dealt with in the system learn this attitude also, I had encountered some empowering mechanisms of client culture. I became empowered with peer support, educating myself about my mental health and getting involved in self-help. I learned how to advocate for myself and became involved in system reform.

I am still empowered today because now I know how to stay free.

APPENDIX E

A Discussion About Client Culture as a Separate Sub-Culture

What Is the Definition of This Client Culture? (Major Characteristics)

Mental health consumers have a variety of similar life experiences. Experiences such as symptoms and medication responses, and shared difficulties with family, housing, employment, and institutionalization unify us. It is easier to identify with someone whose experiences we share. To identify with and be part of a group creates cultural ties which gives strength because we then know we are not alone. It is a shortcut to closeness.

This cultural tie has helped many of us to move forward in our recovery. Finding peers in a world full of stigma helped me significantly in many ways. It helped with my self-esteem. My peers validated my experience by sharing theirs with me. Every time I reassured someone that this mental health issue was not their fault, I was also giving myself the same message.

With regard to my recovery and maintaining a level of health that allows me to accomplish things I want to do, my mental-health peers, who are a part of my community and sub-culture, are a big factor supporting my health. As an example, they are there when I call at 6:00 in the morning in an accelerated state, they make helpful, loving, non-judgmental suggestions. When they are temporarily experiencing heightened symptoms, I want to be there for them. Both sides of this equation are good for my spirit: to know that I have friends in a sub-culture that can understand and assist me and to be able to offer support to someone else and experience the thanks and generosity of others. This sub-culture gives us a context to learn good things about ourselves and to accept without recrimination the challenges that we live with.

Advocacy and support are healthy byproducts of the consumer self-help movement. When we reach a saturation point with irritations such as stigma, discrimination, and shoddy treatment by some professionals and institutions we may experience hopelessness, depression, and anger. Sometimes this will motivate us to make change for the improvement of our lives and for those in our consumer/survivor sub-culture, our peers.

Nothing in the consumer movement has been accomplished in a vacuum. Our cultural experience is one in which we have built upon this leadership of others. We will continue to do so. Consider how our consumer issues were first championed by people in California like: Howie the Harp, Salty Zinnman, Jay Mahler, Roy Crewe, Ron Schraiber, Corinne Camp, and countless others. Our consumer sub-culture should continue to be valued and nurtured because as a whole, working together, we can accomplish much more than anyone alone on the Internet, in Washington D.C. or as the only powerful leader in a particular geographic area.

The California Network of Mental Health Clients is a grand cultural network with a powerful role in learning about our needs, goals, and direction. It can also be a powerful representative advocacy vehicle. Our numbers are our strength. Our Consumer/Survivor culture spans across many ethnicities and economic cultures.

Although one in five families experiences mental health problems, we continue to be stigmatized, under-funded in the area of medical advancement/research, housing and even discriminated with regard to access to the professional services we require. Although most of us consider the Health

Parity Legislation to be of great importance, somehow, it has not passed. Meanwhile, insured medical benefits for mental health services in the private sector have been decreased by 54%; one in ten families receives education they need to understand and help their loved ones with mental illness.

A good example of powerful advocacy is what the community supporting the developmentally delayed have been able to accomplish. They have created more funding, opportunity, and services for their people. As an example, my sister-in-law has a developmental disability, mental retardation. I am happy for her that she is pleased with her environment and proud of herself when she brings home her check of $10 a month. She has a large support staff that allows her to have a work place and to bring home her own money. This brings her so much joy. I know mental health consumers who could use similar services. There is a tremendous loss of potential to society and to individuals, when we are not encouraged and assisted to develop to the best of our abilities, whatever that may be. This is an example of lack of parity between systems, created by society, serving people with similar needs.

As a Mexican-American (first generation born in America), coming from a poor fruit-picking family, I learned about discrimination at an early age, long before I started having mental health symptoms. You can only "turn the other cheek" for so long before you get angry. I made a decision to channel my energy into starting self-help groups.

I couldn't understand or accept shoddy treatment by temperamental staff members while in psychiatric hospitals. I remember a few, very painful instances of isolation in psychiatric hospitals that seemed to last for torturous days which were anything but therapeutic. Now I'm at a point where I feel the necessity to work with our local Junior College Psychiatric Technician Program and I am on their advisory committee. My goal is to make changes. Anger can motivate an individual to do positive things if it is harnessed and correctly directed.

More than anything the consumer cultural experience has prevented me from turning that anger inward. Instead it has helped me to channel my anger into a positive force for change to better the situation for my cultural peers and myself.

I would like to share this simple message: if some issue bothers you enough to make you angry or worse, depressed, about yourself, work at changing it. Try to find people to help you. They don't have to be someone of your same sub-culture but they must believe in what you want to accomplish and of course unite the group that is your sub-culture. Work with the California Network of Mental Health Clients and ask for their suggestions and support. *Part of being a sub-culture is that we are a resource for each other.*

What Are the Negative Similarities Between Client and Ethnic Cultures?

A negative aspect of any culture it when one becomes myopic and wants nothing to do with groups outside of the culture of chosen Identity. People cheat themselves when they do not feel strong enough to venture outside of their safe sub-culture. We can choose to live in a cocoon with small range of diversity. Isn't that the kind of discriminate we don't want practiced against us?

A Mental Health System Provides Services That Are Sensitive to Client Culture When It:

- Nurtures self-reliance and systems that allow people to identify with their consumer culture.
- Assists consumers who are interested to become support staff for their peers and hires them to do a variety of meaningful work in the mental health service system where they can also serve as role-models.

- Includes consumers in design and implementation of new projects, which foster more independence and less dependence.
- Includes consumers in the negotiations when contractors must be chosen from outside of the public mental health system.
- Polls consumers as to which services they prefer when making decisions about starting new programs or cutting back existing services.
- Learns how consumers benefit from the services they currently receive.

Addendum: 2003–2004 Legislation and Public Policy

The following issues are listed by legislative number and the position adopted by the CNMHC Board of Directors Executive Committee in April 2003:

AB 111 Corbett Child abuse: mental suffering Monitor

Establishes mental suffering as unlawful abuse and tries to describe it. Can be used in custody cases. Encourages law enforcement agencies to collaborate with mental health professionals to address the needs of children and families exposed to violence. Includes pairing law enforcement officers with mental health personnel so that the mental health personnel may help offer immediate assistance to the children at the time of the emergency call, as well as making referrals to the appropriate agencies.

While the PEPP and the Executive Committee members support the dialogue that establishes a link between child abuse and mental suffering and appreciated the attempt to have law enforcement work in conjunction with mental health staff, the concerns included: the types of documentation kept on the children involved; the possible labeling of assisted children; what authority/agency would determine the referrals and services offered to the designated children; the potential of having a label/diagnosis used against parents in a custody dispute.

Staff was directed to express these concerns with Assemblymember Corbett's office for clarification.

AB 348 Chu Mental health: involuntary confinement: psychologists Support as written

Allows the attending practitioner to have authority over all aspects of the treatment plan, including lifting a commitment. Increases psychologists' ability to make the same determinations as psychiatrists, specifically release authority.

This legislative piece was initially introduced last year and failed to pass through the legislative process by the close of session. AB 348 could be amended during the session and the committee members wished to review the CNMHC position as these changes were incorporated.

AB 376 Chu CA Mental Health Planning Council: composition Monitor

Adds representatives of labor organizations of both private and public employees who work in mental health settings to the CA Mental Health Planning Council as full members.

There were many questions expressed and the majority of committee members felt that more information was needed prior to adopting a position.

AB 939 Yee Telemedicine: psychiatric inpatient hospital services: reimbursements Monitor

Provides reimbursement from Medi-Cal to psychiatrists for telemedicine services. CNMHC Board members were concerned about the lack of findings of need. While this practice has been accepted in other sectors of health services, this proposed legislation did not state that it was drafted in response to an essential and immediate necessity.

AB 1042 Parra Inmates: use of pepper spray in State Department of Mental Health facilities Oppose

Requires Department of Corrections to issue pepper spray to Department of Corrections medical technical assistants while on duty and assigned to State Department of Mental Health facilities.

AB 1102 Yee Peace officers: training relating to the mentally ill Support if amended

Increases training of peace officers by four 10-hour days (40 hours) specifically for subject of "handling" of persons with mental illness. This proposed additional training would use mental health consumers for one day of the training in training.

It was determined that CNMHC should request direct participation of clients in the design, development, and presentation of any training that is given to persons who have "first response" responsibility.

AB 1370 Yee Mental health: community treatment facilities: program Oppose

Reduces oversight of the use of seclusion and restraints in community treatment facilities that treat youth with mental disabilities. Prohibits the DMH from imposing the higher standards for S & R that are required in other psychiatric facilities. Prohibits the DMH from requiring 24-hour onsite nursing staff and reduces the required bi-monthly on-site visits to once every six months.

This legislation was introduced during the last legislative session and failed to become law.

AB 1371 Yee Human research subjects Support

Requires that any investigator involved in human subjects research disclose his/her financial interest in the project to potential participants. Increases maximum liability and fines for violation. Also requires a participant's primary physician to determine the participant's capacity to meaningful consent.

AB 1424 Mountjoy Minors: psychotropic drugs Support

States that denying psychotropic drugs to a child does not constitute a finding of neglect. Provides that a parent or guardian's refusal to allow a child to be given medical treatment does not, by itself, make the child eligible to become a dependent of the juvenile court. This legislation was introduced last legislative session and failed passage by closure of year.

AB 1475 Steinberg Housing: homeless Support

Revises criteria and sets new priorities for Housing and Emergency Shelter Trust Fund Act of 2002 to include projects for homelessness.

This proposed legislation could utilize the Trust Fund Act as an adjunct to the AB 34/2034 programs, to provide housing for the people in these programs. Housing has been the biggest (and most expensive) obstacle in the implementation of the AB 34/2034 programs.

SB 130 Chesbro Seclusion & restraints spot bill Support in principle

Legislative language not yet available. Sen. Chesbro has held hearings on this subject and has included client testimony in the background research. The CNMHC committee members support the continuation of client involvement throughout the development of this proposed legislation. In response to the directive by the CNMHC membership, the CNMHC committees support any and all reduction of involuntary seclusion and restraints that would eventually lead to complete elimination.

SB 372 Margett Involuntary detention: grave disability Oppose

Relates to the criteria of gravely disabled for a condition in which a person has been found mentally incompetent and a pending indictment or information charging the person with a felony involving death or serious bodily harm or serious threat to someone's well being and the person is unable to assist counsel in his/her defense (summary). This kind of conservatorship is called a Murphy Conservatorship, which allows for indefinite involuntary commitment. This bill would expand the criteria of Murphy Conservatorships to include a pending complaint of a serious violent offense. In current law a person to have a Murphy Conservatorship has to have had a preliminary hearing or grand jury hearing on the complaint/charge. The expanded criteria would allow a Murphy Conservatorship—indefinite involuntary commitment—based on a complaint without the independent review of the facts that a preliminary hearing or grand jury hearing permits.

SB 372 was heard before the Senate Health and Human Services Committee and, after testimony by CNMHC and other mental health advocates, was sent back to the author with possible reconsideration.

SSI/SSP—possible benefit reductions Oppose

The Governor's budget proposal for 2003–04 includes the suspension of COLA and a $49 monthly reduction in SSI benefits for the aged, blind, and disabled. This proposal is before the Legislature and will be considered as part of the final budget bill to be determined by July 1, 2003. At this time the Legislature has taken no position on the benefit cut and the outcome is uncertain. It is felt by groups that advocate for disability rights that this proposal has had very little discussion on the policy level and has been given even less media exposure. CNMHC stands with these disability advocacy groups in their opposition to this cruel proposal. Any reduction of the SSI/SSP benefit award would result in deprivation for the recipient, and place stable housing in jeopardy. The lack of COLA increases in both 2003 and 2004, as proposed, will place SSI/SSP recipients in deepening poverty. The proposed reductions asking those Californians, already vulnerable to our failing economy, to help pay for the State budget deficit is unconscionable and unacceptable.

MediCal Optional Benefits Oppose

The Governor's budget proposal also includes the elimination of MediCal optional benefits: adult dental services, medical supplies, podiatry, acupuncture, chiropractic services, psychology, independent rehabilitation centers, occupational therapy, non-emergency medical transportation, optician/optical lab services, hospice, durable medical equipment, optometry, hearing aids, prosthetics, speech/audiology services, orthotics. and physical therapy—all for a grand total of only $362 million in general fund savings.

These services are not only medically necessary but support quality of living for people with disabilities. This proposal is also opposed by CNMHC and all other disability rights advocates.

Source: California Department of Mental Health, 2000.

PART IV

Sociocultural Diversities

Part IV provides, through nine articles and chapters, a selective introduction to the literature on mental health service delivery to members of groups in which race or ethnicity may not be the most salient focus of professional concern. This broader focus includes women, men, lesbians, gays, poor persons, older adults, and individuals with disabilities.

The first article by Hill, Thorn, and Packard (2000) provides a thorough overview of the intrapersonal (i.e., cognitive loss, stamina, health problems) and interpersonal (i.e., caregiving, friendships, retirement, death of spouse) issues facing older adults. Due to better nutrition and medical interventions, this population is living longer and increasing as a proportion of the total population. The authors offer two theoretical models of development to organize prevention and intervention strategies for this population.

The second article by Cox (2005) continues the discussion on ethnicity and aging by focusing on ethnicity and chronic disease among subgroups of ethnic elderly. Culturally competent health care for older adults of color requires that providers be knowledgeable about the values, beliefs, and traditions of this growing population segment.

The third article of Part IV by Hinrichsen (2006) extends the previous discussion by linking the American Psychological Association's multicultural guidelines to older adults. Diversity issues facing older adults are critically reviewed with an emphasis on changing teaching, supervision, and clinical practice.

The fourth manuscript by Hansen, Gama, and Harkins (2002) provides a rationale for the continued incorporation of gender and cultural factors in multicultural counseling. Helpful strategies for bridging the coverage gap between gender and the multicultural literature are provided.

In the fifth manuscript by Fukuyama and Ferguson (2000), the focus shifts to people of color who happen to identify as lesbian, gay, or bisexual. The oppression (i.e., racism, sexism, heterosexism) that these individuals may experience is reviewed and critiqued, and recommendations for effective counselor advocacy and intervention are offered.

In the sixth article, Greene (2005) reminds us that oppressive ideologies in the mental health field negatively influence clinical practice by facilitating social injustice and creating barriers to culturally competent interventions. Greene argues for greater sensitivity for clients who manifest multiple identities/diversities (e.g., race/ethnicity, sexual orientation, gender, disability, social class, and age) and hence may also experience multiple oppressions as a result of these identities.

The seventh article by Smith (2005) examines the relationship between mental health service delivery and poor clients. Smith reviews over four decades of psychological literature that indicates a consistent "class-bias" toward the treatment of working-class and poor people. A discussion on how therapists can avoid "class-related attitudinal barriers" is provided.

Hopps and Liu (2006), in the eighth manuscript of Part IV, examine the role of social class in psychology from a social justice perspective. Hopps and Liu note that the field of psychology continues to grapple with the construct of social class. The authors offer a definition of social class based in part on a person's self-perceived social standing. A discussion and literature review of social class as it pertains to the delivery of health care is provided.

The last article by Sotnik and Jezewski (2005) examines the relationship between culture and disability services to foreign-born persons. Issues of culture, worldview, diversity, acculturation, and cultural competence are related to people with disabilities and the greater disability service delivery system.

21

Counseling Older Adults

Theoretical and Empirical Issues in Prevention and Intervention

Robert D. Hill

Brian L. Thorn

Ted Packard

It has been widely documented that the nature of the U.S. population has changed dramatically in the past 50 years. Trends most prominent in this changing demography include large increases in the number of individuals living into old and very old age. The number of adults 65 and older has increased dramatically since 1980, and will continue to increase at a rate faster than the general population for years to come (U.S. Bureau of the Census, 1996).

These issues were not unanticipated by counseling psychologists. In 1980, a major contribution in *The Counseling Psychologist,* which focused on identifying the most important issues in 2000 A.D., highlighted the psychological and social problems associated with the aging of the U.S. population. Of the many scholars in counseling psychology who contributed to this issue, John Whitely (1980) noted that "general and substantial increase in life expectancy" (p. 4) would be apparent by 2000 A.D. and that "[a]s human life expectancy is extended by advances in nutrition and medicine, counseling psychologists can help individuals master the challenges associated with aging" (p. 6).

This prediction has become a reality. The Census Bureau has documented that in 1990 the average life expectancy in the United States (from birth to death) was 75.4 years (National Center for Health Statistics, 1995), and it is projected to approach 80 years by the year 2000 (Takamura, 1998; U.S. Bureau of the Census, 1996). A major question concerns the extent to which increasing life expectancy will influence social issues and public policy. What follows is a brief summary of several important issues associated with increased aging of the population that likely will be relevant to counseling psychology.

First, and most obvious, is the fact that because people are living longer there will be a greater representation of older adults in our population. The percentage of individuals 65 years of age and older now makes up approximately 8% of the U.S. population. If current trends continue, this will increase to 15% by the year 2010, meaning that approximately 40 million U.S. citizens will be dealing with the physiological and psychological realities of old age. In addition, increasing life expectancy also means that the number of individuals living into very old age will increase. In contrast to the 16% increase in those between the ages of 65 and 74 years between 1990 and 2010, the number of persons who are 75 years of age and older is expected to increase by 50%, and the number of those 85 years and older will double (U.S. Bureau of the Census, 1992, 1996). Issues facing the very old include dealing with progressive increases in disability, changes in family structure, bereavement, and death and dying. Although there is some research examining quality of life and psychological functioning in very old adults (e.g., centenarians), we know relatively little about assessing and ameliorating the challenges facing these individuals (see Bäckman, Small, Wahlin, & Larsson, in press; Kropf & Pugh, 1995; Pooh, Sweaney, Clayton, & Merriam, 1992).

What can be anticipated, however, is that addressing the needs of the very old will require counseling pyschologists and other mental health specialists to provide services in a variety of contexts that have not been in their traditional domain of professional practice. These contexts likely will include adult day care, nursing home, and transitional residential care, as well as a range of assisted living contexts. Several articles by counseling psychologists have highlighted this issue as an important future trend for our specialty (see Crose & Kixmiller, 1994; Lopez, 1980; Myers & Salmon, 1984; Nagel, Cimbolic, & Newlin, 1988).

Second, the heterogeneity of the older population will be great in terms of individual and cultural diversity. It is well known, for example, that females currently make up the majority of the older adult population because they have a longer life expectancy than men (Atchley, 1997; Nathanson, 1990; U.S. Bureau of the Census, 1996). What is less well known, and may have even greater long-term social consequences, are the very rapid increases in older ethnic minority populations, including African Americans, Hispanics, and Asian Americans (Atchley, 1997; Schneider & Grueling, 1990). In their national survey of older adults, The American Association of Retired Persons (AARP) reported that in 1994 ethnic minority groups totaled 14% of all older adults residing in the United States (8% were African American, 4% were Hispanic/Latino/a, 2% were Asian or Pacific Islander, and 1% were Native American/Alaska Native). By 2030, AARP estimates that the total minority representation could become as high as 25% (AARP, 1998). In her overview of aging issues for the 21st century, Takamura (1998) noted that by 2020 "the number of elderly Hispanic Americans is expected to increase by 300% . . . the number of elderly African Americans is expected to increase by 102% . . . [and among] Asian and Pacific Islander[s] a 358% increase is anticipated" (p. 411).

Although there is a growing literature in counseling psychology examining the special issues facing individuals from ethnic minority groups, very few studies have examined the impact of aging on ethnic minorities. This oversight contrasts with the growing literature in other professional disciplines (e.g., social work, nursing, gerontology) examining the range of psychological issues facing older ethnic minority adults (for example, see Gelfand, 1994; Markides & Black, 1996; Sakauye, 1996; Thurmond, 1996).

Finally, the scientific literature clearly documents that as individuals age, the prevalence of chronic disease and age-related disability increases. Even though the quality of life in older adults has improved, the prevalence of age-related disability in this population remains high, especially as individuals progress into very old age. Nearly 25% of individuals 85 years and older report needing assistance to live independently, and 20% report needing assistance with daily self-care (Atchley, 1997). In this regard, some degenerative conditions, such as Alzheimer's disease, that have a differential diagnosis based on age are becoming more commonplace in contemporary society (e.g., with late onset after 65 years and early onset 65 years or less by DSM-IV diagnostic standards; American Psychiatric Association, 1994). The cost of age-related degenerative disease states is enormous, both in terms of economic impact and psychological demands (Alloul et al., 1998; Raskind & Peskind, 1992). The potential for counseling psychologists to serve the needs of older adults with disabling conditions is enormous but relatively unaddressed.

In sum, with individuals in our society living longer, it has become critical to understand the nature of aging and how counseling psychologists can play a role in helping old and very old adults negotiate the physical, social, and psychological challenges associated with the aging process. This chapter (1) examines the theoretical and empirical literature both within and outside counseling psychology, with the goal of elucidating a meaningful conceptualization of old age that is consistent with the framework of normative adaptation and change that has been associated historically with counseling psychology; (2) explores concerns that are consistent with the range of issues and problems that older individuals face as a result of the aging process; (3) highlights counseling strategies and treatment recommendations for addressing older adult issues that are grounded in theory and research; and (4) recommends essential competencies that will enable counseling psychologists to work effectively with older adult clients.

Because counseling psychology interventions have been defined typically within a normative as opposed to a pathological framework (see Gelso & Fretz, 1992), this chapter highlights issues in normal aging. Issues in pathological aging such as Alzheimer's disease and related dementias (Edwards, 1993; Hill, Bäckman, & Stigsdotter-Neeley, in press; Nordhus, VandenBos, Berg, & Fromholt, 1998); late-life chronic psychiatric illness (Birren, Sloane, & Cohen, 1992; Carstensen, Dornbrand, & Edelstein, 1996; Hersen & Van Hasselt, 1998; Woods, 1996); and chronic disability and issues in long-term care associated with pathological aging (Gatz, 1996; Gatz & Smyer, 1992) are addressed elsewhere in the literature. The goal of this chapter is to provide theoretically and empirically grounded information that can be applied to professional practice specifically geared to counseling psychologists. To achieve this goal, we use three case vignettes as examples of typical (or normative) problems older adults may face as part of the aging process. By revisiting these case examples at different points in the chapter, we hope to demonstrate how counseling psychologists can provide meaningful psychological services to older individuals.

Case Vignettes

Cognitive Loss

Jim is a 76-year-old European American man who is concerned about his failing memory. He had a long career as an insurance salesman whose territory covered a large rural area of a western U.S. state. He prided himself on his ability to recognize and remember the names of seldom seen clients and acquaintances; consequently, he perceives himself as "very good with names and faces." Jim reports that he enjoyed his career. On retirement at age 65, he devoted time to volunteer work and church-related activities. Jim noted that in recent years he has had greater difficulty remembering peoples' names when he has encountered them in unexpected places. He says he has come to counseling because he is distressed over his memory problems that appear to have worsened significantly over the past few years. Recently, Jim could not remember the name of a familiar person in his church congregation until prompted. His wife, who attended the session with Jim, noted that in the past year she has not been able to rely on him for remembering phone numbers and important dates (e.g., grandchildren's birthdays) as she did in the past. His family physician, who works in the same multidisciplinary group practice where Jim sought counseling, suggested that Jim seek advice from the psychologist on staff. Jim says, "My family doctor told me you might be able to help me find some answers. She said something about medication and testing. I have this terrible fear that these memory losses may be the first sign of Alzheimer's disease."

Caregiving

Juanita is an 83-year-old Hispanic woman who has been caring for her 84-year-old husband, Antonio, for several years. Antonio was diagnosed with Alzheimer's disease five years ago. Juanita was referred for counseling by a social worker from a local community action agency which does in-home visits with very frail older adults as well as home-bound disabled people. Juanita says that she is very discouraged. She reports a happy marriage of 60 years with Antonio and that they have 4 children, 12 grandchildren, and 7 great grandchildren. She has two sisters and one brother who live nearby. Juanita states that her family is very supportive, especially her oldest unmarried daughter who offered recently to move in with them as a way to help. However, as Antonio's condition has worsened, some of Juanita's other children have suggested that he be permanently placed in a nursing home. Taking their advice, Juanita met with the administrator of a local nursing home, but decided against pursuing this option because, according to Juanita, "when we were married by Father Santiago in the Holy Trinity Church, he said that our marriage was for better or worse and until death do us part, and that's how it has always been. I could never live with myself if I placed Antonio in there. And even though he is not able to talk with me right now, we've been through tough times before, and I think we can get through this one as well. It's just that I am very lonely and believe that Antonio is never going to be what he was once. I wish my old age with Antonio could be comfortable instead of all hard work and sadness. Maybe I should just give up and ask my daughter, Carlita, to move in and help me take care of Antonio, but she has her own life to live too."

Career Issues

John is a 54-year-old European American man who has worked for a manufacturing company for 27 years. He was referred for counseling by the employee-relations department. One month prior to John's first counseling session the company merged with another firm, and he was laid off in the process. John was unable to exercise the company's early retirement option because the minimum retirement age was 55 years. Further, John reported that he was "not ready to retire" and was anxious about the prospect of not being able to continue working to support his family. John met a few times with a benefits counselor who gave him several career inventories and said that his profile was a close match to "farmer." He reported that this score probably reflected his long-standing hobby of gardening. He reported that a lot of emphasis in his "exit" counseling was placed on getting his resume updated, working hard to develop a job information network, and developing strategies for using the newspaper and the Internet to identify prospective jobs quickly. John has become discouraged with prospects for finding a new job and angry that all of his years of service (e.g., employee of the year awards) were rewarded with an abrupt and unanticipated dismissal. He states, "I'm really discouraged because who is going to hire an old man when there are 10 younger and more up-to-date people looking for the same positions? I was counting on this job getting me to retirement."

These vignettes represent distinctly different issues that individuals may encounter in older age, with the likelihood of facing such problems increasing as the aging process progresses into very late life. It is noteworthy that such issues are not confined to certain persons or specifiable classes of people. Thus, in many respects the challenges highlighted in this chapter occur as part of the normal aging process. Models of aging that fully capture problems in everyday living, therefore, must focus on what happens to normal individuals as they age. The two models that are presented next elucidate underlying physical and psychological processes in normal aging.

Developmental Models of Aging

The process of aging in late life has been discussed by a number of authors and from a variety of conceptual and theoretical perspectives. These efforts have included focusing on theoretical conceptualizations, such as activity level, disengagement, abandonment, role involvement, and socioenvironmental influences (see Fry, 1992, for a general summary of these and other social theories of aging). These theoretical propositions differ with respect to their empirical support and direct use for counseling psychologists working with older adults. However, given that aging is a universal process, a theoretical model for professional practice with the aged should be flexible enough to allow for cultural variations, while at the same time provide a framework for understanding biological, social, and intrapersonal changes that are a predictable part of the aging experience. In addition, such a model should be practical enough to guide the development of remedial, preventive, and educative interventions that are distinguishing features of counseling psychology (see Gelso & Fretz, 1992).

In this section, two models of normal aging are presented that have direct bearing on the development of an approach to professional practice that is grounded in principles associated with counseling psychology. These are Paul Baltes's Selective Optimization with Compensation Theory (Baltes, 1987, 1993, 1997; Baltes, Dittrnann-Kohli, & Dixon, 1984; Baltes, Staudinger, & Lindenberger, 1999) and Robert Atchley's Continuity Theory (Atchley, 1989, 1992, 1997). Both of these conceptual models address real-world issues facing older adults and have been supported by empirical research.

Selection, Optimization, and Compensation

Selection, optimization, and compensation (SOC) is a general theoretical framework for human development, described as a metatheory by P. B. Baltes (1997). It borrows heavily from concepts in human abilities research that have elucidated a two-process model of intellectual function: crystallized and fluid intelligence (Horn, 1968, 1978, 1982; Horn & Cattell, 1966). Crystallized intelligence is reflected in mental abilities that depend on sociocultural influences such as formal schooling or learning due to informal exposure to one's culture (e.g., reading, interacting with people). Components of crystallized intelligence are exemplified by vocabulary ability and language usage, as well as the retrieval, integration, and synthesis of factual knowledge. On the other hand, fluid intelligence reflects processes that are inherent within the individual and that are postulated to operate independently of acculturation. Fluid intelligence is commonly quantified through novel tasks designed to measure processing speed, reaction time, working memory, and pattern recognition, as well as perception of simple and complex relationships. The predominance of developmental research that has examined these two forms of intelligence in adulthood has consistently found that they are differentially affected by aging. Much of the early research reported that crystallized intelligence was relatively stable in adulthood and old age, whereas fluid intelligence tended to decline progressively with advancing age (Horn & Donaldson, 1976; Rabbitt, 1993; Salthouse, 1991). More recent research assessing very old cohorts has documented that even crystallized intelligence may show measurable age-related declines as early as 65 years of age (Giambra et al., 1995).

Baltes's reconceptualization of these constructs reflects two fundamental expansions of the fluid/crystallized dichotomy of human abilities across the life span: the two-process model extends beyond intellectual functioning to encompass the broader domain of adaptation, and these two processes may interact with one another, inasmuch as stability in crystallized processes may compensate for age-related losses in fluid processes.

To set his theory apart from the human abilities literature, P. B. Baltes (1997) relabeled the components of his two-process categorization scheme as *crystallized pragmatics* and *fluid mechanics.* Baltes describes these processes as follows:

> Using a computer metaphor, one can conceptualize the fluid mechanics as reflecting the neurophysiological "hardware" or cognitive primitives of the human brain as it was shaped by biocultural evolution . . . crystallized cognitive pragmatics can be understood as the culture-based "software" of the mind. They reflect the bodies of knowledge and information that cultures provide in the form of factual and procedural knowledge about the world, human affairs, socialization, and human agency. (p. 373)

A central feature of Baltes's model is that although there is inevitable decline across the life course, learning continues to occur throughout adulthood and even into very old age. This life span learning capacity is labeled as "plasticity" or the unused "reserve" capacity that is engaged when a person is confronted with a novel learning situation. The ability to change cognitive capability through plasticity intervention has been documented in a series of studies where older adults have improved their memory performance in response to systematic and intensive, mnemonic strategy training (Kliegl, Smith, & Baltes, 1989, 1990). Even in these instances, however, older adults still perform substantially less well than skilled younger adults, with distributions of scores of younger and older subjects on standard memory training tasks often showing little or no performance overlap (P. B. Baltes & Kliegl, 1992). In other words, as long as there is some reserve capacity in fluid mechanics, there may be selective improvement in old age on some abilities. Pathological conditions, such as dementia, often are characterized by severe restrictions in plasticity, and it may be that variations across individuals on this latent variable could distinguish between normative and pathological processes in age-related decline (M. M. Bakes, Kuhl, Gutzmann, & Sowarka, 1995).

P. B. Baltes (1997) has noted that the decomposition of the "life span architecture" is not limited to physical function, but includes psychological and cultural processes as well.

Although his conceptualization of inevitable decline is a relatively pessimistic view of aging, it is indeed a well-established fact that the ultimate end of the aging process is death, a normative process of complete decomposition (McCue, 1995). Although there is great variability among individuals in this process, the overall balance of developmental gains and losses inevitably shifts toward the loss side of the ledger in very late life.

A somewhat different picture has emerged, however, from an innovative series of studies by Baltes and his colleagues at the Max Planck Institute on the impact of crystallized culture-based pragmatics on intellectual functioning in old age (P. B. Baltes, 1993; P. B. Baltes, Lindenberger, & Staudinger, 1995; P. B. Baltes & Staudinger, 1993). In these studies, operational definitions of "wisdom" were developed, a construct related to factual and procedural knowledge that flows from sociocultural experience. In contrast to working memory and processing speed, performance curves of subject responses to wisdom tasks did not decline precipitously with advancing age but remained relatively level into the 70- and 80-year-old age range. An important generalization from this research is that, to a degree as yet unknown, crystallized culture-based pragmatics can offset, partially, the inevitable declines associated with biologically based fluid mechanics. As Baltes succinctly stated, "Better software can lead to higher performance even if the hardware is of lesser quality" (P. B. Baltes, 1993, p. 582). More information will be presented about the importance of "wisdom" as an acquired, meaning-based adaptive skill in older age in a later section of the chapter.

P. B. Baltes (1997) has identified three adaptive processes, *selection, optimization,* and *compensation,* that are applicable across the life span and that older adults engage in to deal with the pervasive effects of age-related decline. These processes contribute to the high degree of individual variability in old age, particularly with regard to psychological and cognitive functioning. *Selection* refers to the processes by which individuals become more discriminatory in their choice of activities on which to expend time and energy. For example, it is well documented that in advanced age older adults tend to alter their overall social network and focus on relationships that are perceived to have higher potential satisfaction and value, such as with family and close relatives (Lansford, Sherman, & Antonucci, 1998; van Tilburg, 1998). Freund and Baltes (1998) have further decomposed the concept of selection into *elective selection* or *loss-based selection.* Elective selection involves life span regulative processes that are involved in selecting from a pool of alternative developmental pathways to maximize adaptation. In contrast, loss-based selection involves responses that are designed specifically to address the decline (or loss) of previously available capabilities. The goal of selection in this regard is to maximize adaptation by minimizing the complexity of options associated with a specific life task (e.g., simplifying one's finances to make them more manageable).

Optimization refers to processes by which individuals, including older persons, develop increased functional efficacy via learning, practice, and experience. A considerable body of research has focused on developmental processes of optimization through models of education and learning that are specific to older adults (Jenkins, 1979; Willis, 1985). Finally, compensation is the conscious effort employed to mitigate limitations and losses in functional ability associated with the aging process. Lifelong learning and cultural support facilitate the individual's strategic use of these three strategies, and it is noteworthy that the underlying processes are influenced by individual difference factors, such as educational level, intellectual capacity, and culture (Hill, Wahlin, Winblad, & Bäckman, 1995).

P. B. Baltes et al. (1999) provide an excellent example of how adaptation in normal aging involves the interaction of these processes. This example may also help to elucidate further the relative role of each component process within this larger synergistic phenomenon.

> When the concert pianist Arthur Rubinstein, as an 80-year-old, was asked in a television interview how he managed to maintain such a high level of expert piano playing, he hinted . . . First; he played fewer pieces *(selection);* he practiced these pieces more often *(optimization);* and to counteract his loss in mechanical speed he now used a kind of impression management, such as playing more slowly before fast segments to make the latter appear faster *(compensation).* (pp. 483–484)

This example highlights the superordinate premise that the components of SOC generally focus on facilitating personal agency and helping individuals to maintain or regain control over important aspects of their lives that may be compromised due to age-related declines. This premise is critical in the development of interventions in normal aging (and some aspects of pathological aging) because research has documented a positive relationship between a sense of personal control and quality of life in community as well as institutional contexts (Langer & Rodin, 1976; J. Rodin, 1986; J. Rodin & McAvay, 1992). SOC may represent a concrete articulation of specific mechanisms by which personal control is preserved across the adult life span and especially in old age where absolute functional capacity is diminished.

Throughout this chapter, SOC will be used as guiding principles underlying intervention approaches tailored to issues in normal aging. It is important to note that these constructs are consistent with the remedial, educative, and preventive roles that Gelso and Fretz (1992) recommend for counseling psychologists who intervene with adult developmental issues across the life span.

Continuity Theory

Continuity theory is a generic social-psychological theory of aging based on the premise that the sense of identity in older individuals is influenced substantially by how they perceive themselves in changing contexts and the extent to which altered circumstances influence their view of themselves. Continuity theory views enduring individual characteristics and external events or contexts as modifiers of personal change. Atchley (1989) summarized the theory as follows:

> Continuity Theory holds that, in making adaptive choices, middle-aged and older adults attempt to preserve and maintain existing internal and external structures, and they prefer to accomplish this objective by using strategies tied to their past experiences of themselves and their social world. Change is linked to the person's perceived past, producing continuity in inner psychological characteristics as well as in social behavior and in social circumstances. Continuity is thus a grand adaptive strategy that is promoted by both individual preference and social approval. . . . In middle and later life, adults are drawn by the weight of past experience to use continuity as a primary adaptive strategy for dealing with changes associated with normal aging. (p. 183)

Atchley distinguished between internal and external continuity. *Internal continuity* involves the extent to which the inner structures and processes of the person guide adaptation. In this regard, such characteristics as temperament, emotional ability, and personal energy tend to dictate adaptation or predict the degree of change that a person is able to make in a new context. Atchley (1989) noted that "[i]nternal continuity is a healthy capacity to see inner change as connected to the individual's past and to see the individual's past as sustaining and supporting and justifying the new self" (p. 184). *External continuity*, on the other hand, represents the extent to which the societal structures (e.g, one's social circle, cultural group, family, coworkers) influence the self by interacting with one's internal identity. Atchley explained, "Continuity of activities, skills, and environments [external continuity] is a logical result of . . . optimum satisfaction from life" (p. 184).

Both these sources of continuity work to stabilize one's sense of self and limit the extent to which change is possible. Thus, in the latter half of the adult life span internal and external continuity will be powerful moderating factors in determining how older adults approach new tasks in a familiar context (e.g., managing the household following the death of a spouse), adapt to a changing context (e.g., moving to a retirement community), or deal with personal challenges to the self that are part of the aging process (e.g., age-related disability).

This theory has strong use for counseling interventions in that it is based on the premise that individuals are not different fundamentally in old age from earlier points in the life cycle, and each person can be understood using developmental themes that are stable or invariant within the individual across the life span. This premise is supported by research that has documented the stability of individual characteristics, including personality style (Costa & McCrae, 1980, 1992), cognitive stylistics (Shapiro, 1965), and vocational and personal interests (Hansen, 1984). Counseling strategies that have been effective in helping to maintain well-being in old age, such as life review (Gatz et al., 1998), are based on principles of internal continuity, or maintaining a consistent sense of self in the face of age-related change.

Fundamental Concepts to Consider

Several fundamental concepts emerge that are important for building an approach to counseling tailored to fit problems and issues prominent in normal and even in pathological aging. We believe these concepts can be generalized across age cohort, sex, ethnic, and socioeconomic groups.

1. Aging involves normative developmental processes that are inherently destructive, but despite its inevitability, decline can be buffered by cultural factors.
2. Individuals cope with a wide variety of issues in older age. Coping is influenced by lifelong adaptive or maladaptive styles that involve intra- and interpersonal factors.
3. Change is critical in optimal adaptation to age-related problems and issues, and the nature of adaptation is influenced by characteristics of the individual and their social context.
4. Aging is associated with a set of acquired characteristics (e.g., wisdom, spirituality) that exert a stabilizing influence in the presence of age-related decline, and "successful aging" is associated with the cultivation of these qualities.

The Role of Age-Related Decline

Most issues facing older adults are associated with age-related decline. Noteworthy in the three vignettes presented earlier are issues of loss, including cognitive decline, deterioration of a meaningful relationship, and termination of a long-time job. In Table 1 these losses are included as part of a larger constellation of late-life issues classified according to whether they are normative or nonnormative and intra- or interpersonal. This list of issues is not exhaustive, but represents examples of common challenges facing older adults. For a more complete treatment of problems and issues of loss facing older adults, readers may consult Birren and Schaie (1996), Nordhus et al. (1998), and Carstensen et al. (1996).

Division of such issues into a 2 × 2 taxonomy may seem to oversimplify the wide array

Table 1 Issues Facing Older Adults

Intrapersonal	Cognitive loss Diminished stamina and dexterity Diminished sensory functioning	Alzheimer's disease Cardiovascular disease Arthritis Osteoporosis Stroke
Interpersonal	Caregiving of a parent Maintaining friendships Retirement from work Death of a spouse (if female)	Divorce Death of a child Death of a younger sibling

of problems and concerns that are part of the aging experience. However, this kind of schema can focus attention clearly on critical aspects of the aging experience that have great likelihood of enhancing quality of life. In the first vignette, with regard to Jim's concern that he might be in the early stages of Alzheimer's disease, the overriding issue is not the symptoms per se, but what they may mean in predicting Jim's future functioning. Helping Jim assess the qualitative nature of his experienced loss (e.g., distinguishing between what is normal memory loss in older age versus what is nonnormative loss due to disease) is an important first step in any effective intervention strategy (American Psychological Association, 1998).

Addressing initial issues of loss is paramount for building working relationships with older clients. Although it may seem unduly pessimistic to point out to an older client that cognitive loss in later life is a normal and expected process, knowing one's "baseline" capability, adjusted for age, helps to challenge the faulty assumption that any cognitive loss is due to disease processes. In fact, Alzheimer's disease, resulting in nonnormative cognitive loss, affects only 4% to 8% of the overall population of individuals aged 65 years and older (American Psychiatric Association, 1994; American Psychological Association, 1998; Raskind & Peskin, 1992).

Counseling psychologists working with older adults need to understand the kind of developmental loss that would be considered "normative" in old and very old age, as well as an estimated time interval when an individual might face such issues. A client, for example, who has concerns about caring for parents may benefit from knowing that decrements in memory are encountered frequently by older adults sometime between the ages of 50 and 70 years (Ostrosky-Solis, Jaime, & Ardila, 1998). Expecting such events to occur can help individuals develop anticipatory strategies to minimize negative impacts on them and their families.

The concept of age-related decline is seen most clearly in the experience of dying, which was described earlier as a normative process (McCue, 1995). Although physical death in old age often results from disease, the actual event is best viewed as a normal end state of very late life (Hill, Packard, & Lund, 1996; Ingebretsen & Solem, 1998).

Conceptualizing issues as intra- or interpersonal in nature raises the question of how much individual control one can have over problems associated with aging. In the first vignette, loss of cognitive function is primarily an individual issue, but it may also affect others. This is also the case in the third vignette where a long-term job is lost either through planned or unplanned processes. Such experiences most directly affect the aging individual, but there also may be indirect effects on the family system (e.g., loss of income may change the family's socioeconomic status).

Conversely, issues that are primarily interpersonal, such as Juanita's caring for a cognitively impaired spouse in the second vignette, may have interpersonal effects on the identified caregiver. In this regard, the caregiver's capacity to cope with the problem may be influenced by multiple intrapersonal factors such as the care receiver's mental or physical condition, or the premorbid relationship that the caregiver had with the care receiver (Cavanaugh, 1998). Identifying such factors for the caregiver, and in some instances the care receiver, will help to normalize some of the personal burdens that the caregiver will inevitably experience (Query & Flint, 1996; Robinson & Thurnher, 1979).

An important factor in conceptualizing and intervening in age-related issues or problems is the role of culture. The second vignette portrays a Hispanic woman who is caring for her elderly husband, and as noted in the vignette, church and family play large roles in guiding the caregiver's decisions about her future and the future of her spouse. It is critical that the counselor work to incorporate the unique characteristics of the older individual in relation to the issue of concern, as well as demonstrating sensitivity to the individual's cultural context. For example, to address Juanita's concerns adequately, the counselor may need to seek out additional information about the culture and traditions of this family system. It is likely that Juanita's dilemma can be addressed more effectively through culturally appropriate means, including, for example, collaborative meetings between local church leaders and the family. In this example, relevant literature sources, such as Atkinson and Hackett (1997), Daley, Applewhite, and Jorquez (1989), and Torres-Gil (1987), may aid the counselor in understanding the various cultural issues associated with caregiving.

The Role of Continuity

In this section, specific aspects of Atchley's (1989) continuity theory are highlighted that are central to the model we are suggesting for counseling older adults. The basic assumptions of this model include (1) adult identity as relatively consistent and stable across the life span, (2) older adults acting in ways that are consistent and reaffirming of their identity, and (3) older adults, more than other age groups, using past experiences to address current issues and problems.

Although there have been numerous studies documenting the stability of adult personality characteristics over time (McCrae & Costa, 1990, 1991, 1994), Atchley's theoretical proposition of continuity in adult life span development provides a heuristic vehicle for translating these concepts into intervention strategies for working with older adults. In response to a major contribution in *The Counseling Psychologist* by Fry (1992), Atchley noted:

> What promotes life satisfaction [in older age]? There is substantial support for the idea that life satisfaction is enhanced if aging people can continue the expression of lifelong values in familiar relationships and environments. Thus continuity theory offers a framework that can be used to discover how each person has historically produced life satisfaction for her/himself. It also provides clues to what sorts of changes might threaten the life satisfaction of a person. (p. 339)

This statement suggests that individual coping with the wide array of issues of old age is the product of the person's long-term adaptive style and involves both intra- and interpersonal factors. This highlights the role of long-standing characteristics and traits that are an integrated part of the individual, and the interaction of such individual traits with the immediate and extended family system. In other words, coping in old age generally involves accessing intra- or interpersonal resources that already exist as part of the earlier adult coping repertoire.

For counseling psychologists who work with older adults, developing treatment plans that focus on helping older clients actualize their existing coping repertoires to address specific problems likely will be more helpful than approaches that require the older adult to establish new mind-sets or use new approaches to problem solving (Brammer & Abrego, 1981; Smyer, 1984). This is not to say that older clients will not benefit from new ideas or treatment recommendations. However, maximizing the probability that counseling interventions will be perceived as useful requires a thorough understanding of the older client's developmental history and sensitivity as to whether the strategies will be perceived as consistent with the client's identity.

In the third vignette. John views himself as career-obsolete because of his age. However, he likely has acquired characteristics from his life experiences, including a stable sense of self (e.g., likes, dislikes, needs, preferences, personal strengths, and mastery of life tasks) that may be used in helping him access coping strategies for dealing with his job loss. For example; one task of the counselor may be to help John reframe the search for work as an opportunity to find employment that better fits his enduring sense of self. Such a model of counseling has been described in detail by Brammer and Abrego (1981) for developing skills to cope with normative transitions in middle adulthood. Their model has direct application for working with older adults facing career transition issues, such as job loss or retirement.

The Role of Change

As discussed, a sense of consistency is critical in helping older adults manage issues related to changing internal and external contexts. However, the notion of change is essential in balancing stability with needs for adaptation, personal growth, and self-improvement (Mahoney, 1991). This does not mean that older persons are not capable of making large changes with respect to their lifestyle behaviors and patterns; however, there are several aspects of the change process that may differentiate older from younger adults. For example, there is empirical support for the assumption in continuity theory that stable internal structures are more difficult to alter in old age (Atchley, 1989). Further, controlled interventions have documented the role of age-related processes in diminishing plasticity or learning potential in old age (P. B. Baltes, Dittmann-Kohli, & Kliegl, 1986; Lindenberger, Mayr, & Kliegel, 1993).

The counseling and clinical literature also has documented that adaptive attitudes and behaviors may no longer suffice, but previously useful behaviors practiced over longer time intervals are more resistant to change (see Schlossberg, 1981; Smyer, 1984). This is also documented amply by aversive health-related lifestyle behaviors, such as cigarette smoking and alcohol abuse, that have been shown to be highly resistant to change in older age (Ganzini & Atkinson, 1996; Hill, Campbell, Thomas, & Soo-Tho, 1998). In addition, as behavioral routines are rehearsed repeatedly over long periods of time, they become connected to a larger set of values and beliefs that form the underlying identity of the individual (Castro, Newcomb, McCreary, & Baezconde-Garbanati, 1989). This is demonstrated by instances in which adaptive behavior that was maintained in one context continues in a new context, even though its use may no longer exist.

Consistent across all age groups is the psychological reality that stable change usually occurs in small steps. Mahoney (1991) noted that "significant psychological change is rarely easy or rapid" (p. 283). With regard to older adults, the magnitude of change, in absolute terms, may be constrained substantially by the individual's relational and intrapersonal context. The qualitative nature of change may also be different for older adults, thus highlighting the development of a rationale for change, as well as the practice of involving the older individual's mature system of values and beliefs, especially those that have been supported throughout the life span (i.e., one's sense of internal continuity). Stated practically, the reason for change must be compelling enough to the older client that the client is willing to risk changing long-standing beliefs and values that have been a source of security and well-being in the past.

Change associated with inevitable decline is an integral part of aging. Although biological change is an undisputed reality in late adulthood, it is insufficient in and of itself to portray accurately the individual's experience of growing old. Smyer (1984) has noted that aging is multidimensional and can be conceptualized best by considering interactions among biological, personal/psychological, physical/environmental, and social/cultural processes that underlie individual differences in the aging individual. He noted that "while it is assumed that development continues throughout the life span, the pace of development varies across individuals, and within the same individual, different biological and psychological systems or functions age at different rates" (p. 25). Even though the aging process is biologically destructive, it is overly simplistic to stereotype aging as homogeneous decline. What is critical is the wide variations in individual differences in biological aging. For example, it is well known that individuals tend to live longer if they come from higher socioeconomic strata, are better educated, and have easier access to medical care (Takamura, 1998; Worldwatch Institute, 1994). Some research suggests that education may have a preventive effect on the emergence and course of degenerative disease states such as dementia (Mortimer & Graves, 1993). These sociocultural factors are just a few of the many variables that play a prominent role in the nature and the course of aging in any given individual.

Rowe and Kahn (1987) coined the term "successful aging" to highlight that some individual differences in the aging process may be associated with nonloss or gains when compared with the average or "usual" individual. For example, through exercise some may show gains in physical endurance in comparison to the typical loss experienced by the average adult in the same age cohort who does not exercise (Stones & Kozma, 1996). What this concept implies is that older adults not only differ with regard to aging, but are able to influence the aging process themselves. Such potential is an example of the concept of plasticity that was discussed in an earlier section of the chapter (P. B. Baltes, 1993; P. B. Baltes & Baltes, 1980) and, as implied by Mahoney (1991), the flexibility to alter the negative progression of aging through cultural, social, and economic factors adds to our uniqueness as human beings.

Meaning-Based Characteristics of Successful Aging

In their well-known MacArthur Foundation studies of aging, Rowe and Kahn (1998) drew several important thematic conclusions about the defining characteristics of successful aging: "If successful aging is to be more than the imitation of youth, however, we must also ask whether there are valued human attributes that increase with age, or that might do so under appropriate conditions of opportunity and encouragement" (p. 139).

This passage suggests that successful aging is associated with a set of acquired personal characteristics that exert a stabilizing influence on individuals in the presence of age-related decline. These characteristics are a highly personalized part of the fully developed self and are commonly identified by such terms as wisdom (Sternberg, 1990), self-actualization (Maslow, 1968), and spirituality (Worthington, 1989). It is important to note that although such attributes are personal in nature, they also are associated with the ability to integrate experiences across the life span into a comprehensive understanding about how to function effectively and meaningfully in the world. Because much of the empirical literature examining characteristics of successful aging has focused on wisdom, this section elaborates this construct and explores relationships between wisdom and successful adaptation to age-related change.

Despite the fact that researchers have developed elaborate definitions of what wisdom entails (see P. B. Baltes, 1993; P. B. Baltes & Smith, 1990; Clayton & Birren, 1980; Holliday & Chandler, 1986; Orwoll & Perlmutter, 1992; Sternberg, 1990) or is not (Meacham, 1992), it remains an elusive and difficult construct to define. Most existing knowledge about wisdom comes from examining implicit conceptualizations of what it means to be "wise." For example, Holliday and Chandler asked a wide range of people of all ages to nominate individuals who they considered wise and to generate descriptors of their nominees. The descriptions then were compared with terms extracted from the literature to yield a set of distinctive characteristics of wisdom, including (1) exceptional understanding (e.g., seeing things within a larger context); (2) superior judgment (e.g., thinking carefully before deciding); (3) general competence (e.g., curious, intelligent); (4) interpersonal skills (e.g., fair, reliable, mature); and (5) social unobtrusiveness (e.g., discreet, nonjudgmental). A noteworthy characteristic of individuals nominated as wise was that, for the most part, they were older than the nominators themselves, a finding that supported the researchers' postulated relationship between positive aging and wisdom.

In a related vein, P. B. Baltes, Staudinger, Maercker, and Smith (1995) defined wisdom as a set of complex skills for dealing with problems in everyday living and as "expert-levels of performance in the fundamental pragmatics of life" (P. B. Baltes, Staudinger, et al., 1995, p. 155). An implicit assumption of this conceptualization is that wisdom is manifested most fully in old age and can be acquired through actively developing skills in the planning, conduct, and interpretation of life. To test their assumption, the researchers identified "wise" individuals through a nomination procedure and asked them to respond to two standardized vignettes designed to test for wisdom-related skills (Staudinger, Smith, & Baltes, 1994). One vignette portrayed a life-planning issue (a woman attempting to reconcile conflict between her desire to begin a late-life career and her family responsibilities) and an existential life crisis (the threat of suicide by a friend who was despondent over the meaninglessness of life). P. B. Baltes, Staudinger, et al. also attempted to control for the relative effects of age by recruiting a young and old control group of individuals of similar socioeconomic status. They also controlled for wisdom-related knowledge by recruiting an older group of clinical psychologists who, as a professional group, were predicted to perform very highly on these two tasks. Individuals nominated for their wisdom outperformed the young and old control groups on both tasks. Their performance also was equal to the older clinical psychologists. Thus, P. B. Baltes, Staudinger, et al. concluded that (1) unlike physiological processes and cognitive functions that deteriorate with age, wisdom does not appear to decline but may be enhanced in some individuals as a consequence of the aging process; (2) there are specific life span conditions that facilitate the development of wisdom; and (3) it may be possible to identify specific skills that are markers of wisdom and amenable to training.

From this and related studies (Sternberg, 1990), several identifying characteristics of wisdom have been noted consistently. Specifically, wisdom can be defined as exceptional understanding and judgment, combined with superior ability to use such processes in competent ways and to communicate to others the hypotheses and conclusions reached. With regard to late-life adaptation, Labouvie-Vief (1992) noted that wisdom is the ability to integrate life experiences with rational thought in ways that facilitate an approach to life that may have adaptive advantages in coping with age-related change.

Thus, unlike the pessimistic view of age-related decline previously discussed, what is suggested here is the possibility that for some individuals aging may facilitate the acquisition of attributes that can increase the individual's capacity to cope in old and very old age. P. B. Baltes et al. (1995) noted that wisdom is a core construct that provides "insights into the quintessential aspects of the human condition and human life, including its biological finititude, cultural conditioning, and interindividual variations. At the center of this body of knowledge and its application are questions concerning the conduct, interpretation, and meaning of life" (p. 155).

Most research suggests that wisdom is more prevalent in older than in younger adults, even though there is much variability across individuals (P. B. Baltes & Staudinger, 1993). Although the ability to be wise is related to a number of factors, including intelligence and creativity (Sternberg, 1985), wisdom is a broad construct that is activated in situations requiring the management of existential issues of meaning, suffering, life, and death. Although research has not conceptualized wisdom as a member of a broader collection of maturationally based constructs, such as spirituality and self-actualization, for the purposes of this chapter these concepts are viewed as having a number of common features. They tend to develop as a part of the aging process, and include specific abilities that enhance coping with many negative aspects of aging. They can also be used to process problems of everyday living across the life span.

A body of research has identified spirituality as another important life span maturational construct that can be a core feature of internal continuity (Atchley, 1997). Although the elucidation of a spirituality construct that can be validated and used to assess quality of life or coping has been problematic (see Ellison, 1994; Weiland, 1995; Worthington, 1989), spirituality has been found to be a dynamic life span phenomenon. Intrinsic aspects of religiosity, such as one's personal convictions and internal belief structures, have been found to be positively associated with optimal mental health (Bergin, 1983; Bergin, Masters, & Richards, 1987). Within counseling psychology, Worthington has perhaps best articulated a life span view of the development and maintenance of religious values and beliefs. A central feature of his conceptualization is the integral role that religiosity plays in both normative and idiosyncratic life transitions. Using this conceptualization, Worthington highlighted a number of life span issues that might benefit from spirituality-based counseling, including dealing with death, sexuality, alcohol and drug abuse, career issues, interpersonal relationships, and parenting. Recent research has focused on examining the efficacy of counseling strategies that involve salient aspects of religiosity, such as hope and forgiveness, to address life span developmental issues (McCullough, Worthington, & Rachal, 1997; Worthington et al., 1997).

Thus, when working with older adults, it may be useful to identify such maturational characteristics to understand more fully how an individual may cope with the realities of aging. In the third vignette, John is unexpectedly released from his long-term job. His initial response to this loss is to focus narrowly on the job itself and his altered sense of meaning as a former employee. In John's words, "I'm discouraged because who is going to hire an old man when there are 10 younger and more up-to-date people looking for the same jobs? I was counting on this job to get me to retirement." The benefits counselor provided several suggestions that all were focused on helping John secure new employment as soon as possible. Although these suggestions may have some value, accessing larger meaning-based processes may encourage John to reinterpret his job loss in a way facilitative of more optimal long-term adjustment. For example, allowing John to explore more deeply his conceptualization of retirement may help him reframe his job loss as a transition to activities potentially more fulfilling given his relative stage in life.

This kind of approach to career counseling has been highlighted in a series of studies examining the importance of stable intraindividual constructs (e.g., personality factors, lifelong goals, relational structures, religiosity) in predicting optimal adjustment to late-life career transitions such as retirement (see Payne, Robbins, & Dougherty, 1991; Robbins, Lee, & Wan, 1994). From such research, it could be postulated that simply engaging in a job search without a life span oriented self-evaluation process may exacerbate disillusionment about the relationship between work and other activities that John may value as he progresses into old and very old age (e.g., family, other meaningful personal relationships, self-enhancement activities).

A General Framework

The fundamental principles presented are critical in understanding the aging process and in developing meaningful counseling interventions tailored to older adults. Atchley (1992) noted that although continuity theory can explain the processes of normative psychosocial adaptation in late life, it also can be useful for designing counseling strategies for maintaining a sense of cohesiveness in the face of change due to unexpected discontinuities, such as disease or unanticipated economic change (e.g., job loss). Baltes's selective optimization with compensation theory provides a framework not only for understanding adult cognitive functioning during later years, but also the management of a range of developmental events in late life (Freund & Baltes, 1998). Integrating these theories with the defining principles of counseling psychology can produce a general framework for counseling psychologists' conceptualization of late life issues, as well as a practical guide for intervening with older adults.

Major Themes

A first step in developing a framework tailored to issues of older adulthood, and grounded in principles of counseling psychology, is to review the distinguishing features of counseling psychology described by Gelso and Fretz (1992). These features are both philosophical and practice oriented and, for the most part, are consistent with the developmental theories presented earlier.

Gelso and Fretz's first major theme states that counseling psychology approaches personal change from a normative, nonpathological perspective. Smyer (1984) highlighted this concept as follows: "Often, the counselor's initial task is to assist the older client in differentiating the normal aging process from pathological or abnormal processes" (p. 25). This concept also was elaborated earlier as a central feature of the theory of selective optimization with compensation as it relates to older age. Tailoring this nonpathological theme to older adults requires redefining normative processes in terms of the extent to which optimization is possible. Stated in more practical terms, a 60-year-old marathon runner cannot maintain the same objective race times she achieved when 25 years of age; however, it still may be possible to have the fastest marathon time among her peers in a 60-year-old age cohort.

A second major theme highlighted by Gelso and Fretz (1992) is the idea that counseling psychologists focus on strengths and personal assets. With respect to older adults, this means using previously developed positive coping skills to address predictable, and even unpredictable, issues that arise as part of the aging process. This "strength" theme is a central feature of continuity theory as Atchley (1992) noted:

> The main difference between older clients and younger ones is that the older clients often come with a stronger sense of what coping strategy has worked well for them in the past, and if that approach is no longer working, then the counselor may want to deal first with why strict continuity is not adaptive in the current situation. (pp. 339–340)

Inherent in this theme is the notion that it may be possible to access meaning-based maturational characteristics (e.g., wisdom, spirituality) as an integral part of coping. This may be as simple as providing a context for the individual to explore a problematic issue within the framework of these processes as suggested by Worthington (1989). It also may be as proactive as identifying characteristics that may be brought to bear on new issues (e.g., the capacity to forgive others) and encouraging older clients to use their strengths in addressing problems (e.g., reconciling negative memories of a recently deceased spouse).

A third theme from Gelso and Fretz (1992) is the perspective that emphasizes person-environment interactions rather than an exclusive focus on either the person or the environment. Individuals are intertwined inextricably with their sociocultural environment and must be understood in this context. This concept is a fundamental premise of SOC theory, and for this reason can be important in developing a framework for counseling older adults. Smyer (1984) proposed a counseling model for older adults that involves examining stressors in later life related to changes in physical functioning and in the sociocultural context as well. He presented a range of age-related problems that often are viewed from a single perspective (e.g., sleep disturbance in old age) and recommended ways to address these issues more completely by using a broader, multidimensional paradigm of adaptation and coping consistent with the themes noted earlier.

Conceptualizing older adults from holistic perspectives and avoiding stereotypic notions (e.g., "to be old is to be physically sick"; Rowe & Kahn, 1998) has the potential of being viewed by older adults as more relevant and meaningful. In their review of outcome research with older adults, Wellman and McCormack (1984) noted the importance of using a multidisciplinary team counseling approach. This notion is consistent with viewing older adult issues from a person-environment perspective.

Interventions that focus on helping older adults increase their sense of personal control through either altering external conditions that limit personal control or maximizing their sense of control through use of SOC principles have great potential for enhancing quality of life in old age. A powerful example of such an intervention was demonstrated in an early study conducted by Langer and Rodin (1976), who altered a floor of a nursing home to maximize the extent to which individual residents on the floor could take responsibility for their care. Residents in this "increased responsibility" group reported that they felt happier and were more active than those in the comparison control floor at posttesting and after 3 weeks. In a follow-up study, R. Rodin and Langer (1977) noted that this enhanced sense of well-being among the residents on the "increased responsibility" floor remained after 18 months. Given the benefits of such an intervention in nursing home residents for enhancing the quality of life, it is our contention that the role of personal control for facilitating well-being in normal aging may be enormous.

The Role of the Counseling Psychologist

The themes described in this chapter may be applied broadly to the remedial, preventive, and educative or developmental professional roles of counseling psychologists enumerated by Gelso and Fretz (1992). The next section describes how counseling psychologists can use these roles in intervening with older adults.

The Remedial Counseling Role

This role involves assisting older individuals or groups with the resolution of problems that have resulted from impaired functioning. With the knowledge that decline is part of normal aging but can be moderated to some extent through compensation and optimization, the concept of remediation takes on relativistic meaning. For example, research indicates that cognitive functioning, particularly episodic memory performance, declines in old age (Kausler, 1994; Salthouse, 1991). For the individual who is experiencing age-associated memory impairment, encoding and recall strategies that were employed as a younger person (e.g., rapid repetition of information) may not be an effective compensation strategy. Thus, it becomes critical to search for solutions that can optimize performance in a declining system. For example, writing information down (e.g., making a shopping list, recording appointments in a day planner) may compensate for the heavy burden of encoding and retrieving large amounts of data that are accessed only infrequently (see Intons-Peterson & Newsome, 1992). However, for information that cannot be accessed from written material such as names and faces and personal identification numbers, older adults may benefit from learning mnemonic strategies that facilitate encoding and retrieval (Intons-Peterson & Newsome, 1992; Plude & Schwartz, 1996; Yesavage, Lapp, & Sheikh, 1989).

The Preventive Counseling Role

This role involves anticipating potential problems and intervening to eliminate or minimize their occurrence in the future. Preventive interventions may involve imparting information in advance of an issue (e.g., preparing a living will) that helps to guide choices before the issue of concern arises. An excellent example of a preventive intervention is helping very old adults create safer living spaces to deal with predictable future mobility impairments (Sterns & Camp, 1998). This is highlighted by research examining the wide range of technologies, such as handheld environmental control units (e.g., light dimmers or remote VCR and television controls), in aiding performance and minimizing accidents associated with everyday tasks in the home. This research also suggests that technologies can help to extend functional independence into very advanced age (Czaja, 1997). For example, memory for prescription taking in older adults has been improved by converting text-based medication regimens (commonly found on pill bottles) to pictorial or iconic images (Morrell, Park, & Poon, 1989). This strategy has been shown to improve adherence to medication regimens in older adults by capitalizing on spatial memory processes that are more resistant to age-related decline than is verbal memory (Park, Puglisi, & Smith, 1986).

Preventive interventions involve (1) helping older clients identify conditions or situations that hinder the successful negotiation of important everyday tasks (e.g., moving around the house); (2) collaborating with clients in developing realistic strategies to deal with identified conditions or situations (e.g., the reorganization of furniture); and (3) dealing with psychological barriers that impede effective functioning (e.g., "Moving my furniture around so I won't fall is a sign that I am becoming more dependent."). Psychological barriers often arise around complex tasks, such as driving an automobile, that are connected to an individual's internal sense of continuity (e.g., independence), where the action itself has become dangerous because of sensory, motor, or cognitive deficits associated with advanced aging (Persson, 1993; Sterns & Camp, 1998).

The Educative and Developmental Counseling Role

This role includes interventions that are meant to provide skills that build resistance to maladaptive functioning. As noted by Gelso and Fretz (1992, p. 6), "the distinction between the developmental and preventive roles is often subtle—a matter of degree rather than kind." With regard to age-related education, it is important for counseling psychologists to provide relevant information to help older adults understand issues that arise as a consequence of the aging experience. As highlighted in the first vignette, John is concerned that his memory loss is due to Alzheimer's disease. In assessing John's cognitive performance, the counselor can explain the etiology and progressive nature of Alzheimer's disease. This may help to reassure John that his condition likely is not due to a degenerative disease, while at the same time educating him about more valid warning signs of Alzheimer's disease. Therefore, in addition to reducing current anxiety that his memory loss is a symptom of disease, education about the nature of Alzheimer's disease may also decrease the possibility that John will erroneously interpret normal memory lapses in the future.

The three basic counseling roles noted above are not mutually exclusive when working with older adults. In fact, it may be that counseling psychologists regularly assume all three roles while addressing issues or problems. As a way to demonstrate how this might occur, consider the case of a retired high school teacher who is referred to a counselor by a geriatric physician for psychological problems secondary to progressive vision impairment due to macular degeneration. This disease of the eye, more commonly experienced by older adults, involves degeneration of the central part of the retina (Schieber, 1992). Consequences include a progressive loss in the ability to distinguish fine visual details, which can significantly limit adaptation to one's living environment (Research to Prevent Blindness, 1994). In this example, the visual disability may be accompanied by affective symptoms such as those found in depression or anxiety.

To address this issue, the counselor can begin with a thoughtful assessment to clarify the range of the client's difficulties and their relationship to her symptoms of distress. Such an assessment will probably involve contacting and collaborating with the physician who diagnosed the client's visual impairment. The counselor assesses directly the extent to which the client's impairment is influencing her sense of well-being and provides the client with accurate information about the extent and nature of her disease *(educative role)*. Counseling may be employed to treat the client's experience of distress by encouraging greater acceptance of diminished visual capability, while at the same time helping her to learn ways to remain functionally independent in the presence of the impairment *(remedial* or *rehabilitative role)*. The counselor also may help the client to develop strategies to prevent additional problems due to her progressive vision impairment. For example, a retired high school teacher, who presumably is comfortable in a classroom setting, might be encouraged to enroll in a community program that provides adaptive living assistance for visually impaired adults *(preventive role)*. Such an intervention not only would serve an educative function, but also might assist the client in developing a support group sensitive to her needs and facilitative of her efforts to adapt to declining visual capability.

In this example, the depressed mood and anxious affect are not viewed as psychopathological symptoms but instead as normative psychological manifestations predictably experienced by an individual facing a progressive disability. Interventions would focus on helping the client to compensate for declining function by selectively emphasizing other assets from the client's own familiar repertoire of skills, activities, and contexts *(optimization).* Such an approach would maximize external continuity and bolster a sense of internal continuity (e.g., "How have you learned to solve problems before?").

The reality of physical and cognitive decline in older age generally means that adjustments are needed when considering such questions as "What level of adaptive functioning is reasonable to expect from this person?" and "How does one build on strengths when formerly cherished abilities have deteriorated with age?" Such questions highlight the importance of having a comprehensive theoretical framework for understanding the developmental processes and critical issues of late life in contrast to earlier stages of adulthood.

Applying the General Framework to Issues of Older Adults

In this section, the three vignettes presented previously are used to illustrate how the framework we have described can be applied to the common problems in everyday living that face individuals advanced in age. Note that the organization of these vignettes focuses on (1) defining the problem, (2) assessing the situation, and (3) intervening for change. Potential roles and functions of counseling psychologists within these three broad categories will be illustrated.

Cognitive Loss

Defining the Problem

Jim is expressing fear of the future more than concern about current problems. He wants to know if his "trouble remembering things" (names and faces of acquaintances) is indicative of the onset of Alzheimer's disease. A basic issue is whether his forgetfulness is normative for a 76-year-old man. Jim and his wife are aware that he used to be able to retrieve information more readily from long-term memory. Extra concentration no longer results automatically in recalling the desired information. Jim realizes that this represents a decrement in his cognitive abilities and knows that forgetfulness is one of the signs of Alzheimer's disease. Baltes's theory, discussed previously, describes this type of cognitive loss as a decrease in plasticity, or reduced efficiency in fluid mechanics, and posits that it is normal for a man in his mid-70s to experience diminished cognitive plasticity to some degree.

Another important dimension of Jim's presenting concern is fear of losing his identity and his connection to important relationships. Many older people experience fear of Alzheimer's disease to such an extent that it undermines their health and well-being (Centofanti, 1998). Here again is the underlying question of whether Jim's forgetfulness is normative. To understand the nature of Jim's fear, Atchley's (1989) continuity theory provides a useful heuristic. Losing one's identity, as is experienced in advanced Alzheimer's disease, represents a major disruption of internal continuity. Connections between one's internal and external world are lost. Family and friends experience disruptions in the continuity of their external worlds when familiar relational dynamics with the disabled loved one gradually shift to unpredictable and sometimes incomprehensible interactions. The intensity of people's fear of losing their identity in this way is evidence of the importance of maintaining continuity in our world.

In sum, although Jim's forgetfulness is problematic, he is experiencing intense fear that his difficulty retrieving names is symptomatic of a disease process that could ultimately rob him of his cognitive capabilities and disconnect him from the relationships that mean the most to him.

Assessing the Situation

An informed counselor likely will begin the assessment process with an understanding that epidemiological studies have found the prevalence of dementia of the Alzheimer's type in the adult population to be only 4% to 8% in individuals 65 years of age and over (*DSM-IV*, American Psychiatric Association, 1994; American Psychological Association, 1998). Assessment procedures selected for this client should be comprehensive yet balanced with a focus on methods that are relevant to the client's presenting concerns. To address the issue of whether the memory problem is normative, one of the first questions is whether the forgetfulness is encountered when Jim is extending his reserve cognitive capacity (plasticity). In other words, is remembering names a routine process given ample memory cues?

Desirable appraisal techniques with Jim will include a clinical interview and a mental status exam to assess his overall cognitive functioning, as well as the nature of his memory complaint (American Psychological Association, 1998). With regard to overall cognitive functioning, the counselor might use the Dementia Rating Scale (DRS; Mattis, 1988), a brief screening instrument for dementia. This instrument is easy to administer and has well-developed norms for distinguishing cognitive performance that may or may not be indicative of dementia. Performance on such an instrument can be used to address whether the memory problems Jim is experiencing are due to disease processes (i.e., nonnormative) or normative changes associated with aging. It may be that Jim previously functioned well above normal in the area of name and face recollection but now has moved into the average range of functioning. This sort of change may be alarming to him but does not necessarily indicate the onset of dementia.

At a more specific level, the counselor also might administer the Memory Assessment Scales (MAS; Williams, 1991) which provide a comprehensive measure of memory functioning. This instrument is particularly appropriate for Jim because it includes measures that assess both immediate and delayed recall for names and faces. Jim states that his problems with recall have been primarily with infrequently encountered people and only recently with the name of a more familiar church associate. Therefore, the assessment inquiry can be directed toward the determination of whether this represents cognitive loss that is beyond what would be expected for someone of Jim's age and capability. The MAS also measures reserve capacity by comparing Jim's functioning with comprehensive age-based norms for individuals in his age range. Finally, the assessment process should include an inquiry into the typical strategies used by Jim for remembering names. Knowing how Jim approaches this task may be important in the design of remedial interventions.

Intervening for Change

If the results from the DRS were indicative of dementia, the counselor should refer Jim for a comprehensive neuropsychological assessment by a qualified neuropsychologist who has specialty skills for diagnosing dementia. If Jim's condition is diagnosed as dementia, the counseling psychologist could work cooperatively with Jim, his family, the diagnosing specialist, and other professionals in the community to develop a treatment plan to deal with the predictable cognitive loss and changes in everyday functioning that are associated with this disease state.

In the more likely event that Jim's memory problems are determined to be within the normal range, the counselor can intervene in several ways. First, Jim and his wife can be educated about normative memory changes and what it means to suffer typical cognitive losses associated with older age *(educative role).* For many older individuals, the knowledge that problems are normative is an effective reliever of distress. As part of educating Jim about his name-face memory difficulties, it also might be important to acknowledge the relative difficulty of remembering names or faces. This task involves retrieving precise information with minimal verbal cues (i.e., you don't get credit for recalling only part of a first name). Thus, it likely will be important to convey that name recall is a difficult issue for people across the life span.

Second, counseling may be employed to help resolve persistent affective, spiritual, or existential issues, such as grief or fear associated with impending death or declining health. When Jim understands and accepts the normal functional declines he is experiencing, he is likely to reexamine his choices of daily activities in an effort to focus his energy and time on those endeavors which capitalize on his remaining strengths and maximize his sense of well-being. Doing so will help Jim to maintain internal continuity in the face of external change and discontinuity *(remedial role).*

Finally, preventative interventions may be employed to help Jim learn to compensate for memory deficits by using other retained abilities. The counselor working with Jim may prescribe cognitive exercises that help to optimize or maintain as much as possible, his extant memory skills. For example, a simple memory aid such as a cue card, and some additional focused concentration, may help Jim retrieve more easily the names of new people he meets at church or in his volunteer activities. Another possibly helpful strategy may be to use written lists and notes, something Jim has not needed to do in the past. Part of this training should help Jim better understand the nature of memory (e.g., effective encoding facilitates retrieval) so that he can use this new knowledge in developing compensatory strategies to offset his emerging deficits *(preventive role).*

Caregiving

Defining the Problem

Juanita's presenting problem originates not from concerns about her own cognitive and adaptive functioning, but from the increasingly difficult task of caring for her husband who has had a diagnosis of Alzheimer's disease for several years. In terms of the theoretical models outlined previously, she is experiencing a serious disruption in external continuity. The husband who has been an important part of her life for at least 60 years is no longer able to reciprocate in the intimate interactions of their shared relationship. Juanita may be experiencing the loss of her husband even though he remains alive and physically present. Because external continuity helps us to maintain a sense of internal continuity, she likely is feeling a loss of identity and an impaired sense of self. Considering that Juanita is 83, it also is likely that she is experiencing some degree of physical decline that hinders her ability to provide 24-hour care for her husband.

The question of whether Juanita's experience is normative is also relevant here but in a somewhat different way. In this case, the question takes the form of "Is it a normative experience for an 83-year-old woman to be struggling with the difficulties of providing care to a husband with a severe cognitive disability?" Further, it is important to address Juanita's expressed concern regarding the future consequences of continuing the caregiving role into very late life.

Assessing the Situation

A competent assessment in this case is one that is both culturally sensitive and prescriptive with regard to potential intervention strategies. Juanita is not presenting with concerns about her own cognitive functioning, so the primary means of assessment would involve soliciting her help in developing a thorough and developmentally appropriate psychological and social history. Juanita's issues are likely best understood within the context of her cultural, familial, and economic situation. As part of this assessment, questions should explore Juanita's beliefs about aging, beliefs about her role as a spouse, the nature of her relationship with her children and other family members, and her understanding and level of use of available support resources (e.g., the role of her church).

Clarifying the extent and nature of her husband's functional deficits also will be important. This might be accomplished by obtaining measures of her husband's adaptive functioning or ability to care for himself. This activities of daily living assessment procedure will involve determining the extent to which her husband requires help in negotiating self-care behaviors (e.g., bathing, toileting, transferring, eating, dressing; Katz, 1983). It also may be useful to assess Juanita for depression by using an age-appropriate measure of her affective state (e.g., the Geriatric Depression Scale; Yesavage, 1986), keeping in mind that many older people will use words like "lonely" and "sad" in ways that essentially downplay a significant level of depression (Weiner, 1992).

Intervening for Change

Juanita clings to the hope that she and her husband will "get through this," implying that she may not have a comprehensive understanding of her husband's demented condition. This may be especially problematic if her husband is not able to engage in self-care behaviors, which would mean that Juanita carries an extra-heavy caregiving burden. The counselor, therefore, may want to help Juanita understand that Alzheimer's is a degenerative disease and that her husband's condition predictably will worsen. Such information may help Juanita to feel less conflict about outside help, especially as the caregiver role becomes more difficult with her husband's continuing decline *(educative role)*. The counselor may intervene by helping Juanita deal with grief issues associated with the loss of her husband as a coequal companion. The counselor also can help Juanita explore culturally appropriate ways that she can be "comfortable" in old age even in the presence of her caregiving role *(remedial role)*. For example, an intervention involving her family could help Juanita find ways to meet her own needs by refocusing on alternative assets, such as relationships with other family members, to help rebuild her sense of external continuity. This could also involve exploring the potential benefits and costs associated with her daughter's plan to move in and share some of the caregiving responsibilities with Juanita for a period of time *(preventive role)*.

Career Issues

Defining the Problem

Using the conceptual models discussed earlier, the counselor might view John's issue as an unexpected turn regarding a major life event. Retirement from work often is a normative event; however, at age 54 John's job loss can be considered nonnormative because of his age and the unexpected and sudden change in his life. For these reasons, John's concern about maintaining a sense of well-being and financial stability are adaptive psychological responses.

Referring again to Atchley's (1989) notion of continuity, we can describe John's concerns in terms of a major disruption in external continuity, while internal continuity (John's sense of himself) hopefully will remain intact.

John's reported anxiety and discouragement indicate that his sense of intrapersonal cohesiveness is threatened. Because he has worked with the same company for 27 years and planned to stay there until retirement, vocational stability has played an important role in maintaining John's sense of inner well-being by providing continuous external reinforcement for his self-concept as the breadwinner of the family.

John's concerns include doubt about his value as a potential employee in a job market where he is competing for jobs with younger and possibly less expensive candidates. In this context, John places a high value on youth. His concerns imply that he feels less able to learn new skills, and, from a practical standpoint, he may be correct. From the theories presented earlier, we predict that as people age they tend to focus selectively on activities and environments that are compatible with their inner cognitive structures and needs in an effort to optimize daily functioning. In addition, as people grow older they lose some of their ability to focus concurrently on multiple activities. Although this decline usually happens slowly during the middle adult years, it may be that at age 54 John has a subjective awareness of a somewhat decreased aptitude for retraining. John is faced with an unanticipated change in his external environment at a time when he likely feels less able to adapt to that change.

Assessing the Situation

An assessment of John's concerns might follow a twofold process: (1) determine what elements have served to maintain his internal and external continuity over the years with regard to career and (2) ascertain to what extent his identity and sense of self have been affected by his job loss.

The benefits counselor approached John's situation from a perspective more appropriate for someone in early adulthood. Results from the career inventories may provide a useful starting place for exploration and clarification of John's skills, interests, and values, but he probably already has a relatively clear understanding of what he does well, what he likes, and what he dislikes in a career (i.e., internal and external continuity).

It may also be important to understand how much of John's identity is centered around his career. To some degree, the weight given to the importance of one's career in maintaining personal identity is related to gender ideology and cultural factors. Men from some cultural and age-cohort groups place great emphasis on the importance of one's career in defining who and what they represent (Atchley, 1997). If family, friends, religion, and other activities outside of work are emphasized to an equal or greater extent, then John's sense of self likely will remain largely intact and his identified concerns may be confined to providing financial support for his family and saving for retirement. Conversely, if John's career is the primary foundation of his identity, then he may be vulnerable to prolonged anxiety or depression until he is able to reenter the workforce in a career that can maintain his sense of identity as an employed and "useful" individual.

Intervening for Change

Several intervention approaches may be helpful for John. First, he can be reminded about the value of his past experience and repertoire of functional skills that can be applied to a variety of work activities. His discouragement about his future employability may, in part, result from thinking too narrowly about career options. Such pessimism may have been reinforced by

the benefits counselor. Thus, John may benefit from information about a wide range of work options available to him, given his accumulated talents and skills *(educative role)*. This type of counseling can encourage John to consider creatively many possibilities for future employment, including making use of his established network of friends, colleagues, and acquaintances. If, for example, John has been involved over the years with community clubs or civic activities, he may find that his best and most attractive employment leads come from contacts in those areas of his life.

Clarification of John's assets and skills may help him to evaluate better his strengths, abilities, and interests as the foundation for building a new career. Counseling may also help John to resolve issues of lower self-worth that may have emerged in the aftermath of his job loss. Therapy in this context may best be perceived as a variation on the theme of grief counseling. By grieving his lost job and lost youth, and then moving on, John may feel freer to refocus his energy and attention on a new area that is consistent with his values and self. Through this process, he may be more likely to look back on this point in his life as a painful yet important time for him in restructuring his values and priorities *(remedial role)*.

Successful counseling may include the provision of information, in a sensitive and supportive way, about the wisdom that can be gained through finding meaning in his loss. In spite of the economic uncertainty that comes with being unemployed, if John is able to turn his loss into an opportunity for personal growth, then he will likely look back and perceive this unexpected turn of life events as a positive milestone. For example, John's initial job loss could become the turning point which leads to an interesting new career that is more flexible with regard to his family interests and brings him increased life satisfaction during his later working years *(preventive role)*.

Intervention Competencies

Our vignettes have illustrated that counseling psychologists already possess many skills necessary for intervening with older adults. A goal of this chapter not only has been to build a conceptual foundation descriptive of the adult aging experience but also to help in developing counseling interventions. However, adequate preparation for addressing the many mental health issues that are part of the aging experience necessitates counseling psychologists having (1) comprehensive knowledge of the aging process, (2) expertise in assessment of older adults, and (3) skill in developing counseling strategies in a variety of older adult contexts.

Knowledge of the Aging Process

Modest amounts of relevant information about the aging process and professional practice with older adults have been published in counseling psychology specialty journals and texts. A quarter of a century ago, this fact was apparent to Sidney Pressey (Pressey, 1973; Pressey & Pressey, 1972), one of the founders of the specialty of counseling psychology, who, as an 83-year-old resident in a nursing home, recommended ways for counseling psychologists to address issues of the old and very old. Pressey also expressed concern over the dearth of gerontological research in the counseling psychology literature and the general lack of awareness in the discipline about the kinds of psychological issues that are prevalent in old age. Pressey and Pressey noted that

> an old-age counselor, especially if so functioning in an institution [nursing home] . . . has research opportunities now almost unrecognized. . . . Indeed, in the notable favorable environment of the best institutions it should be possible to investigate potentials regarding longevity, maintained ability, and personality as nowhere else. (p. 366)

Since these early writings, two major contributions have appeared in *The Counseling Psychologist* that have highlighted counseling strategies for older adults (Smyer, 1984) and contemporary theories of aging (Fry, 1992). However, as noted throughout this chapter, adequately addressing issues of old and very old clients requires integration of comprehensive developmental theories of aging and specialized counseling strategies and interventions.

Gerontological knowledge has expanded dramatically, especially in the past 10 years. Numerous journals now exist dedicated solely to issues of the old and very old (e.g., *Journal of Gerontology, Journal of Mental Health and Aging, Clinical Gerontologist, Educational Gerontology, Psychology and Aging, Journal of the American Geriatrics Society).* Active professional organizations have developed, such as the Gerontological Society of America, a multidisciplinary organization that addresses the broad spectrum of physical, psychological, and social issues of adult development and aging. Within the National Institutes of Health, the National Institute of Aging annually funds single and multidisciplinary research which examines diverse issues facing the old and very old. Developing a gerontological knowledge base from these various sources is an essential activity for counseling psychologists who desire to develop proficiency skills for working with older adults.

Within the American Psychological Association, members of Division 20 (Adult Development and Aging), working in concert with psychologists from Division 12 (Clinical Psychology), recently drafted a report enumerating qualifications for practice in clinical and applied geropsychology (APA Interdivisional Task Force on Clinical and Applied Geropsychology, 1998). From these guidelines, three levels of training in geropsychology were proposed. Level 1 (generic training in aging and adult development) is encouraged for all licensed psychologists, because it is likely that most will encounter older adult clients in their professional practice as the general population ages. Level 2 (specific training in the provision of psychological services to older adults) is recommended for psychologists who wish to include an older adult clientele as part of their professional practice. In addition to obtaining information about the aging process, Level 2 training involves developing proficiency in identifying and treating some of the more common psychological issues facing older adults. Level 3 (specialized training, including comprehensive supervised experience in the provision of psychological services to older adults) is for psychologists wishing to become specialists in the psychological treatment of older adults. Level 3 requires demonstrated competence in working with older or very old clientele. At all three levels of training, psychologists are expected to develop awareness of assessment instruments and procedures (Segal, Coolidge, & Hersen, 1998) and intervention strategies (Gatz et al., 1998; Myers, 1990) that are specific to older adults. The next two sections highlight each of these areas of gerontological practice.

Issues in Assessing Older Adults

Given that older adults experience normative and nonnormative problems and issues that are common in individuals across the life span (e.g., depression, anxiety) and unique to old age (e.g., Alzheimer's disease), it is critical to assess the extent to which psychological issues or problems can influence everyday functioning in older age. Even for those psychological issues common in younger cohorts, the presenting symptoms can differ significantly between younger and older adults, as is found in the role of impaired cognitive function as a symptom of depression (Poon, 1992; Woods, 1996). Counseling psychologists who desire to work with older adults need to develop competency in

assessing cognitive, affective, and physical aspects of functioning in old and very old age. Thus, it is critical to have access to assessment instruments and procedures that have been standardized, validated, and normed on older populations. Fortunately, there are a number of useful references to guide the practitioner in this regard (American Psychological Association, 1998; Davies, 1996; Poon, 1986; Segal et al., 1998).

An assessment issue that is critical in geropsychology is the identification and gauging of age-related dementias, of which Alzheimer's disease is the most prominent subtype. The most widely used definition of dementia can be found in the *DSM-IV* (American Psychiatric Association, 1994). Briefly, dementia is characterized by profound and global impairment in one or more areas, including speech and writing, fine and gross motor coordination, encoding and/or retrieving of familiar and unfamiliar objects and people, and the ability to plan, execute, and monitor purposeful behavior. In dementia, complex reasoning ability is severely impaired, as well as the ability to function independently in everyday contexts.

It is beyond the scope of this chapter to provide a comprehensive overview of dementia and its assessment; however, this disorder can have a dramatic impact on an individual's sense of personal control and the ability to use compensatory mechanisms (SOC) to deal with late-life issues. Atchley (1989) has noted that, with regard to continuity theory, deteriorative disease states such as dementia represent one of the more profound disruptions to a person's sense of internal continuity. Counseling psychologists who desire to work with older adults should be familiar with a range of screening examinations that have been normed on older populations and can identify individuals who have cognitive deficits sufficient to warrant more in-depth assessment for dementia-related disorders. These screening examinations should include methods for assessing mental status (e.g., Blessed Dementia Index; Blessed, Tomlinson, & Roth, 1968; Mini-Mental Status Exam; Folstein, Folstein, & McHugh, 1975; Dementia Rating Scale; Mattis, 1988), as well as measures of self-care and adaptive function (Activities of Daily Living; Katz, 1983). Several excellent resources are available that provide an introduction and guide to screening for dementia (Hill et al., in press; Nordhus et al., 1998; Poon et al., 1992; Woods, 1996).

In addition to identifying specific instruments for assessing particular issues facing older adults (e.g., memory function, functional independence), it is important to consider qualitative aspects of the testing context. To obtain useful performance measures from older clients, administration procedures must be adapted to the specific age-related characteristics of the client (e.g., hearing deficits, psychomotor slowing). Segal et al. (1998) provided a useful set of guidelines for assessing older adults:

1. Ensure that the testing environment maximizes sensory cues for the older client.
2. Relax time constraints to optimize performance in the presence of predictable behavioral slowing that occurs in old and very old age.
3. Ensure that the purpose and procedure of the assessment is presented clearly to older clients.
4. Show respect and understanding for older clients by openly discussing issues of concern (e.g., age differences between client and therapist).
5. Make use of ancillary sources of information that can help in understanding and interpreting the performance of older clients (e.g., involving family members in the assessment process, especially if the family is caring for the older client).
6. Maintain a therapeutic approach when evaluating older clients, such as showing

concern for the client's well-being during the assessment.

7. Consider the client's related medical conditions or medication use as a source of variation that may influence the outcome of the assessment.

Thus, it is important to consider qualitative issues in the testing environment, as well as specific instruments for obtaining representative indicators of cognitive, affective, or physical functioning. Finally, because aging can interact with other individual difference variables (e.g., gender, ethnic background, socioeconomic status), the relevance of these sources of individual and cultural diversity should also be considered (e.g., assessing an individual for dementia who has very little formal education).

Tailoring Counseling Interventions to Older Adult Contexts

As described earlier, consideration of person-environment fit is important when intervening with older clients. This is particularly important because of the wide range of contexts in which older adults may reside, apart from traditional home environments. Such contexts include but are not limited to retirement communities, assisted living centers, and skilled nursing facilities. There are even specialized skilled nursing homes for older adults diagnosed with dementia that provide focused care tailored to the psychological and behavioral problems associated with this disorder (Alzheimer's disease care units; Ohta & Ohta, 1988). Although counseling psychologists can provide useful services to older adults in these settings, models of intervention within the field of counseling psychology, for the most part, have not been developed for many of these contexts.

In a cross-sectional survey of 124 nursing home administrators, Crose and Kixmiller (1994) reported that management of psychological issues facing their older residents was the most frequently cited concern. Problems related to depression, loneliness, anxiety, and withdrawal were identified repeatedly. A relatively low percentage of administrators reported employing psychologists or other mental health professionals to assist with these issues. Like Pressey (1973), the authors contended that nursing homes can be particularly fertile environments for counseling psychologists to address the needs of older adults, particularly as members of multidisciplinary teams. Because a primary goal of nursing homes is to enhance resident well-being, nonmedical approaches that focus on person-environment interactions likely will result in intervention efforts that are more responsive to the physical and psychological needs of nursing home residents (see Langer & Rodin, 1976; R. Rodin & Langer, 1977).

Impaired mobility is a significant barrier to obtaining health care services (Melcher, 1988). Other disciplines, such as social work, nursing, and medicine, have developed elaborate in-home procedures for treating the very old. Like these related disciplines, counseling psychologists must develop proactive models of assessment and intervention for older citizens limited in their ability to use traditional community mental health services.

Counseling psychologists have yet to develop models of care that address specifically issues facing older adults. Like others across the life span, older adults deal with transitions associated with the aging process, and there is a substantial knowledge base that has emerged from counseling psychology for negotiating transitional experiences in adulthood (Brammer & Abrego, 1981; Schlossberg, 1981). Hopefully, the unique life-transition issues that characterize older and very old adults will begin to be addressed systematically and comprehensively by counseling psychologists in the near future. With our traditional emphases on normative development, assets and strengths, and person-environment interactions, we are well positioned to make substantive contributions in this increasingly critical arena.

Directions for Future Research and Theory

As the number of older adults in our society increases relative to younger-aged groups, the focus of science and public policy will place a greater emphasis on the range of psychological issues facing older adults. It is within this context that counseling psychologists may play an important role. This chapter has highlighted strategies for prevention and intervention for normative issues of adjustment and transition in old age. It also may be important for counseling psychology to focus on the generation of conceptual and empirical knowledge about the aging process. Several areas are highlighted below that are consistent with traditional research emphases in counseling psychology and relevant to the aging experience in our contemporary society.

1. There is a need to develop models of career development that better elaborate the nature of career transition in later adulthood. Although research from counseling psychology cited earlier in this chapter has examined factors that predict adjustment to retirement in old age (Payne et al., 1991; Robbins et al., 1994), traditional conceptualizations of retirement as the end of career are not reflective of contemporary vocational trends across the adult life span (Canaff, 1997). In addition, developing and validating counseling approaches that are consistent with the older adult career transition experience seem warranted.

2. As highlighted by Gelso and Fretz (1992), models of counseling have historically emphasized normative developmental issues, and the literature that has conceptualized the aging phenomenon within the field has focused predominantly on normal aging (see Fry, 1992; Schlossberg, 1981; Smyer, 1984). Models of aging that impact research and training should be more inclusive of nonnormative issues, such as chronic disease and disability (American Psychological Association, 1998; Gatz, 1996), dementias (Centofanti, 1998; Edwards, 1993), and issues of long-term care (Nagel et al., 1988; Ohta & Ohta, 1988). The need for counseling psychologists not only to possess appropriate skills, but to have expanded knowledge about nonnormative chronic conditions that are prominent among the old and very old is also necessary if counseling psychologists are to be perceived as relevant service providers to older consumers (Crose & Kixmiller, 1994).

3. As noted earlier in this chapter, the fastest growing segment of older adults are those who are 85 years of age and older (Backman et al., in press), and there is a growing body of research examining the special issues facing this very old group (Ritchie, 1998; Smith & Baltes, 1997). One example that highlights this phenomenon are issues related to death and dying, which have been relatively unaddressed in counseling psychology. The extent to which counseling psychologists are able to address the needs of the very old will depend, in part, on development of a knowledge base that incorporates issues of death and dying within models of transition and change that are integral to counseling psychology.

4. The chapter highlighted preventive, remedial, and educative roles that counseling psychologists can adopt addressing normative issues in late life. Several examples were provided describing how these roles might be applied to specific late-life issues. Outcome research is needed that provides empirical support for the effectiveness of these interventions in addressing various age-specific issues.

To date, outcome research examining counseling psychology interventions with older adults lags far behind what is available in other mental health specialties, including clinical psychology and social work (American Psychological Association, 1998; Carstensen et al., 1996; Gatz, 1996; Gatz & Smyer, 1992; Nordhus et al., 1998).

5. As noted early in the chapter, the changing demographics of the aging population indicate that a substantial number of older adults will be from ethnic minority groups. Some of the issues facing older ethnic minority adults include dealing with the economic challenges of poverty in old age, transmission of culture to younger generations, and the impact of ethnicity on access to social services (Harris, 1998). Although models of counseling exist that are specific to ethnic minority populations, many of these do not address the interaction of age and ethnicity (Atkinson & Hackett, 1997; Sue, Zane, & Young, 1994). Future research is needed to elucidate counseling approaches that consider special issues facing older adults from ethnic minority groups.

Summary

This chapter has highlighted two theoretical models well adapted to the development of prevention and intervention strategies for issues facing adults in later life. These models of aging are comprehensive, deal with the qualitative aspects of the aging experience, and are consistent with the defining characteristics of counseling psychology (cf. Gelso & Fretz, 1992). P. B. Baltes's (1997) selective optimization and compensation theory addresses the pervasive experience of loss related to growing older. Atchley's (1989) continuity theory provides explanatory mechanisms for maintaining consistency and a stable sense of self in old and very old age. Several fundamental principles were presented from these models that illuminate the aging experience, including physical and psychological decline, age-related change, continuity, and the role of maturationally acquired characteristics as resources for meaning and coping. We noted that although there is great variability in how individuals negotiate the aging experience, death is the end result of aging and the ultimate equalizer of humankind. Finally, we examined how counseling psychology as a professional specialty is well positioned to address many of the normative issues associated with the aging experience, as well as to assist older adults in negotiating many of the nonnormative events that occur in old age, such as loneliness and depression. We maintain that, if counseling psychology is to remain a strong and relevant professional specialty into the 21st century, addressing the psychological issues of the old and very old must be an integral part of its professional mission.

References

Alloul, K., Sauriol, L., Kennedy, W., Laurier, C., Tessier, G., Novosel, S., & Contandriopoulos, A. (1998). Alzheimer's disease: A review of the disease, its epidemiology and economic impact. *Archives of Gerontology and Geriatrics, 27,* 189–221.

American Association of Retired Persons. (1998). *Profile of older Americans.* Washington, DC: Author.

American Psychiatric Association. (1994). *Diagnostic and statistical manual for mental disorders* (4th ed.). Washington, DC: Author.

American Psychological Association. (1998). *Interdivisional task force on clinical and applied geropsychology.* Washington, DC: Author.

Atchley, R. C. (1989). A continuity theory of normal aging. *Gerontologist, 29,* 183–190.

Atchley, R. C. (1992). What do social theories of aging offer counselors? *The Counseling Psychologist, 20,* 336–340.

Atchley, R. C. (1997). *Social forces in aging* (8th ed.). Belmont, CA: Wadsworth.

Atkinson, D. R., & Hackett, G. (1997). *Counseling diverse populations* (2nd ed.). Boston: McGraw-Hill.

Bäckman, L., Small, B. J., Wahlin, A., & Larsson, M. (in press). Cognitive functioning in the very old. In F. I. M. Craik & T. A. Salthouse (Eds.), *Handbook of aging and cognition* (2nd ed.). Mahwah, NJ: Erlbaum.

Baltes, M. M., Kuhl, K-P., Gutzmann, H., & Sowarka, D. (1995). Potential of plasticity as a diagnostic instrument: A cross validation and extension. *Psychology and Aging, 10,* 167–172.

Baltes, P. B. (1987). Theoretical propositions of life-span developmental psychology: On the dynamics between growth and decline. *Developmental Psychology, 23,* 611–626.

Baltes, P. B. (1993). The aging mind: Potential and limits. *Gerontologist, 33,* 580–594.

Baltes, P. B. (1997). On the incomplete architecture of human ontogeny: Selection, optimization, and compensation as foundation of developmental theory. *American Psychologist, 52,* 366–380.

Baltes, P. B., & Baltes, M. M. (1980). Plasticity and variability in psychological aging: Methodological and theoretical issues. In G. E. Gurski (Ed.), *Determining the effects of aging on the central nervous system* (pp. 41–66). Berlin, Germany: Schering.

Baltes, P. B., Dittmann-Kohli, F., & Dixon, R. A. (1984). New perspectives on the development of intelligence in adulthood: Toward a dual-process conception and a model of selective optimization with compensation. In P. B. Baltes & O. G. Brim, Jr. (Eds.), *Life-span development and behavior* (Vol. 6, pp. 33–76). San Diego, CA: Academic Press.

Baltes, P. B., Dittmann-Kohli, F., & Kliegl, R. K. (1986). Reserve capacity of the elderly in age-sensitive tests of fluid intelligence: Replication and extension. *Psychology and Aging, 1,* 172–177.

Baltes, P. B., & Kliegl, R. K. (1992). Further testing of limits of cognitive plasticity: Negative age differences in a mnemonic skill are robust. *Developmental Psychology, 20,* 121–125.

Baltes, P. B., Lindenberger, U., & Staudinger, U. M. (1995). Die zwei gesichter der intelligenz in alter [The two faces of intelligence in old age]. *Spektrum der Wissenschaft, 10,* 52–61.

Baltes, P. B., & Smith, J. (1990). The psychology of wisdom and its ontogenesis. In R. J. Sternberg (Ed.), *Wisdom: Its nature, origins, and development* (pp. 87–120). Cambridge, England: Cambridge University Press.

Baltes, P. B., & Staudinger, U. M. (1993). The search for psychology of wisdom. *Current Directions in Psychological Science, 2,* 75–80.

Baltes, P. B., Staudinger, U. M., & Lindenberger, U. (1999). Lifespan psychology: Theory and application to intellectual functioning. *Annual Review of Psychology, 50,* 471–507.

Baltes, P. B., Staudinger, U. M., Maercker, A., & Smith, J. (1995). People nominated as wise: A comparative study of wisdom-related knowledge. *Psychology and Aging, 10,* 155–166.

Bergin, A. E. (1983). Religiosity and mental health: A critical reevaluation and meta-analysis. *Professional Psychology: Research and Practice, 14,* 170–184.

Bergin, A. E., Masters, K. S., & Richards, P. S. (1987). Religiousness and mental health reconsidered: A study of an intrinsically religious sample. *Journal of Counseling Psychology, 34,* 197–204.

Birren, J. E., & Schaie, K. W. (Eds.). (1996). *Handbook of the psychology of aging* (4th ed.). San Diego, CA: Academic Press.

Birren, J. E., Sloane, R. B., & Cohen, G. D. (1992). *Handbook of mental health and aging* (2nd ed.). New York: Academic Press.

Blessed, G., Tomlinson, B., & Roth, M. (1968). The association between quantitative measures of dementia and of senile changes in the cerebral grey matter of elderly subjects. *British Journal of Psychiatry, 114,* 797–811.

Brammer, L. W., & Abrego, P. J. (1981). Intervention strategies for coping with transitions. *The Counseling Psychologist, 9,* 19–36.

Canaff, A. L. (1997). Later life career planning: A new challenge for career counselors. *Journal of Employment Counseling, 34,* 85–93.

Carstensen, L. L., Dornbrand, L., & Edelstein, B. A. (Eds.). (1996). *The practical handbook of clinical gerontology.* Thousand Oaks, CA: Sage.

Castro, J. G., Newcomb, M. D., McCreary, C., & Baezconde-Garbanati, L. (1989). Cigarette smokers do more than just smoke cigarettes. *Health Psychology, 8,* 107–129.

Cavanaugh, J. C. (1998). Caregiving to adults: A life event challenge. In E. H. Nordhus, G. R. VandenBos, S. Berg, & P. Fromholt (Eds.), *Clinical geropsychology* (pp. 131–135). Washington, DC: American Psychological Association.

Centofanti, M. (1998). Fear of Alzheimer's undermines health of elderly patients. *APA Monitor, 29,* 6. Washington, DC: American Psychological Association.

Clayton, V. P., & Birren, J. E. (1980). The development of wisdom across the life span: A reexamination of an ancient topic. In P. B. Baltes & O. G. Brim, Jr. (Eds.), *Life-span development and behavior* (Vol. 3, pp. 103–135). San Diego, CA: Academic Press.

Costa, P. T., Jr., & McCrae, R. R. (1980). Still stable after all these years: Personality as a key to some issues in adulthood and old age. In P. B. Baltes & O. G. Brim, Jr. (Eds.), *Life-span development and behavior* (Vol. 3, pp. 65–102). New York: Academic Press.

Costa, P. T., Jr., & McCrae, R. R. (1992). Trait psychology comes of age. In T. Sonderegger (Ed.), *Nebraska Symposium on Motivation, 1991* (pp. 169–204). Lincoln: University of Nebraska Press.

Crose, R., & Kixmiller, J. S. (1994). Counseling psychologists as nursing home consultants: What do administrators want? *The Counseling Psychologist, 22,* 104–114.

Czaja, S. J. (1997). Using technologies to aid the performance of home tasks. In A. D. Fisk & W. A. Rogers (Eds.), *Handbook of human factors and the older adult.* San Diego, CA: Academic Press.

Daley, J. M., Applewhite, S. R., & Jorquiez, J. (1989). Community participation of the elderly Chicano: A model. *International Journal of Aging and Human Development, 29,* 135–150.

Davies, S. (1996). Neuropsychological assessment of the older person. In R.T. Woods (Ed.), *The handbook of the clinical psychology of ageing* (pp. 441–474). New York: Wiley.

Edwards, A. J. (1993). *Dementia.* New York: Plenum Press.

Ellison, C. G. (1994). Religion, the life stress paradigm and the study of depression. In J. S. Levin (Ed.), *Religion in aging and health* (pp. 78–121). Thousand Oaks, CA: Sage.

Folstein, M. F., Folstein, S. E., & McHugh, P. R. (1975). Mini mental state: A practical method for grading the cognitive state of patients for the clinician. *Journal of Psychiatric Research, 12,* 189–198.

Freund, A. M., & Baltes, P. B. (1998). Selection, optimization, and compensation as strategies of life management: Correlations with subjective indicators of successful aging. *Psychology and Aging, 13,* 531–543.

Fry, P. S. (1992). Major social theories of aging and their implications for counseling concepts and practice: A critical review. *Counseling Psychologist, 20,* 246–329.

Ganzini, L., & Atkinson, R. M. (1996). Substance abuse. In J. Sadavoy, L. W. Lazarus, L. F. Jarvik, & G. T. Grossberg (Eds.), *Comprehensive review of geriatric psychiatry II* (2nd ed., pp. 659–692). Washington, DC: American Psychiatric Press.

Gatz, M. (1996). Aging and mental disorders. In J. E. Birren & K. W. Schaie (Eds.), *Handbook of the psychology of aging* (4th ed., pp. 365–382). San Diego, CA: Academic Press.

Gatz, M., Fiske, A., Fox, L. S., Kaskie, B., Kasl-Godley, J. E., McCallum, T. J., & Loebach, J. (1998). Empirically validated psychological treatments for older adults. *Journal of Mental Health and Aging, 4,* 9–46.

Gatz, M., & Smyer, M. (1992). The mental health system and older adults in the 1990s. *American Psychologist, 47,* 741–751.

Gelfand, D. (1994). *Aging and ethnicity: Knowledge and services.* New York: Springer.

Gelso, C. J., & Fretz, B. R. (1992). *Counseling psychology.* New York: Harcourt Brace.

Giambra, L. M., Arenberg, D., Zonderman, A. B., Kawas, C., & Costa, P. T. (1995). Adult life span changes in immediate visual memory and verbal intelligence, *Psychology and Aging, 10,* 123–139.

Hansen, J. C. (1984). The measurement of vocational interests: Issues and future directions. In S. D. Brown & R. Lent (Eds.), *Handbook of counseling psychology* (pp. 99–136). New York: Wiley.

Harris, H. L. (1998). Ethnic minority elders: Issues and interventions. *Educational Gerontology, 24,* 309–323.

Hensen, M., & Van Hasselt, V. (1998). *Handbook of clinical geropsychology.* New York: Plenum Press.

Hill, R. D., Bäckman, L., & Stigsdotter-Neeley, N. (in press). *Cognitive rehabilitation in old age.* New York: Oxford University Press.

Hill, R. D., Campbell, B. W., Thomas, L. A., & Soo-Tho, K. M. (1998). Perceptions of well-being in older smokers. *Journal of Mental Health and Aging, 4,* 271–280.

Hill, R. D., Packard, T., & Lund, D. (1996). Bereavement. In J. A. Sheikh (Ed.), *Treating the elderly* (pp. 45–74). San Francisco: Jossey-Bass.

Hill, R. D., Wahlin, A., Winblad, B., & Bäckman, L. (1995). The role of demographic and life style variables in utilizing cognitive support for episodic remembering among very old adults. *Journal of Gerontology: Psychological Sciences, 50,* 219–227.

Holliday, S. G., & Chandler, M. J. (1986). Wisdom: Explorations in adult competence. In J. A. Meachum (Ed.), *Contributions to human development* (Vol. 17, pp. 1–96). Basel, Switzerland: Karger.

Horn. J. L. (1968). Organization of abilities and the development of intelligence. *Psychological Review, 75,* 242–259.

Horn, J. L. (1978). Human ability systems. In P. B. Baltes (Ed.), *Life-span developmental psychology* (Vol. 1). New York: Academic Press.

Horn, J. L. (1982). The theory of fluid and crystallized intelligence in relation to concepts of cognitive psychology and aging in adulthood. In F. I. M. Craik & S. Trehub (Eds.), *Aging and cognitive processes* (Vol. 8, pp. 237–278). New York: Plenum Press.

Horn, J. L., & Catell, R. B. (1966). Refinement and test of the theory of fluid and crystallized intelligence. *Journal of Educational Psychology, 57,* 253–270.

Horn, J. L., & Donaldson, G. (1976). On the myth of intellectual decline in adulthood. *American Psychologist, 31,* 701–719.

Ingebretsen, R., & Solem, P. E. (1998). Death, dying, and bereavement. In I. H. Nordhus, G. R. VandenBos, S. Berg, & P. Fromholt (Eds.), *Clinical geropsychology* (pp. 177–181). Washington, DC: American Psychological Association.

Intons-Peterson, M. J., & Newsome, G. L., III. (1992). External memory aids: Effects and effectiveness. In D. J. Herrmann, H. Weingartner, A. Searleman, & C. McEvoy (Eds.), *Memory improvement: Implications for memory theory* (pp. 101–122). New York: Springer-Verlag.

Jenkins, J. J. (1979). Four points to remember: A tetrahedral model of memory experiments. In L. S. Cermak & F. I. M. Craik (Eds.), *Levels of processing in human memory* (pp. 426–446). Hillsdale, NJ: Erlbaum.

Katz, S. (1983). Assessing self-maintenance: Activities of daily living, mobility, and instrumental activities of daily living. *Journal of the American Geriatrics Society, 31,* 721–727.

Kausler, D. H. (1994). *Learning and memory in normal aging.* San Diego, CA: Academic Press.

Kliegl, R. K., Smith, J., & Baltes, P. B. (1989). Testing-the-limits and the study of adult age differences in cognitive plasticity of a mnemonic skill. *Developmental Psychology, 25,* 247–256.

Kliegl, R. K., Smith, J., & Baltes, P. B. (1990). On the locus and process of magnification of age differences during mnemonic training. *Developmental Psychology, 26,* 894–904.

Kropf, N. P., & Pugh, K. L. (1995). Beyond life expectancy: Social work with centenarians. *Journal of Gerontological Social Work, 23,* 121–137.

Labouvie-Vief, G. (1992). Wisdom as integrated thought: Historical and developmental perspectives. In R. J. Sternberg (Ed.), *Wisdom: Its nature, origins, and development* (pp. 52–83). Cambridge, England: Cambridge University Press.

Langer, E. J., & Rodin, J. (1976). The effects of choice and enhanced personal responsibility for the aged: A field experiment in an institutional setting. *Journal of Personality and Social Psychology, 34,* 191–198.

Lansford, J. E., Sherman, A. M., & Antonucci, T. C. (1998). Satisfaction with social networks: An examination of socioemotional selectivity across cohorts. *Psychology and Aging, 13,* 544–552.

Lindenberger, U., Mayr, U., & Kliegl. R. K. (1993). Speed and intelligence in old age. *Psychology and Aging, 8,* 207–220.

Lopez, M. A. (1980). Social-skills training with institutionalized elderly: Effects of a precounseling structuring and overlearning on skill acquisition and transfer. *Journal of Counseling Psychology, 27,* 286–293.

Mahoney, R. (1991). *Human change processes: The scientific foundations of psychotherapy.* Chicago: Basic Books.

Markides, K. S., & Black, S. A. (1996). Race, ethnicity, and aging: The impact of inequality. In R. H. Binstock & L. K. George (Eds.), *Handbook of aging and the social sciences* (4th ed., pp. 153–170). San Diego, CA: Academic Press.

Maslow, A. (1968). *Toward a psychology of being.* Princeton, NJ: Van Nostrand-Reinhold.

Mattis, S. (1988). *Dementia rating scale.* Odessa, FL: Psychological Assessment Resources.

McCrae, R. R., & Costa, P. T., Jr. (1990). *Personality in adulthood.* New York: Guilford Press.

McCrae, R. R., & Costa, P. T., Jr. (1991). Adding Licbe and Arbeit: The full five-factor model and well-being. *Personality and Social Psychology Bulletin, 17,* 227–232.

McCrae, R. R., & Costa, P. T., Jr. (1994). The stability of personality: Observations and evaluations. *Current Directions in Psychological Science, 3,* 173–175.

McCue, J. D. (1995). The naturalness of dying. *Journal of the American Medical Association, 273,* 1039–1043.

McCullough, M. E., Worthington, E. L., Jr., & Rachal, K. C. (1997). Interpersonal forgiving in close relationships. *Journal of Personality and Social Psychology, 73,* 321–336.

Meacham, J. A. (1992). The loss of wisdom. In R. J. Sternberg (Ed.), *Wisdom: Its nature, origins, and development* (pp. 181–211). Cambridge, England: Cambridge University Press.

Melcher, J. (1988). Keeping our elderly out of institutions by putting them back in their homes. *American Psychologist, 43,* 543–647.

Morrell, R. W., Park, D. C., & Poon, L. W. (1989). Quality of instruction on prescription drug labels: Effects on memory and comprehension in young and old adults. *Gerontologist, 29,* 345–345.

Mortimer, J. A., & Graves, A. B. (1993). Education and other socioeconomic determinants of dementia and Alzheimer's disease. *Neurology, 43,* 39–44.

Myers, J. E. (Ed.). (1990). Techniques for counseling older persons [Special issue]. *Journal of Mental Health Counseling, 12*(3).

Myers, J. E., & Salmon, H. E. (1984). Counseling for older persons: Status, shortcomings and potentialities. *Counseling Psychologist, 12,* 39–53.

Nagel, J., Cimbolic, P., & Newlin, M. (1988). Efficacy of elderly and adolescent volunteer counselors in a nursing home setting. *Journal of Counseling Psychology, 35,* 81–86.

Nathanson, C. A. (1990). The gender-mortality differential in developed countries: Demographic and sociocultural dimensions. In M. G. Ory & H. R. Warner (Eds.), *Gender, health, and longevity: Multidisciplinary perspectives* (pp. 3–23). New York: Springer.

National Center for Health Statistics. (1995). *Vital Statistics of the United States, 1990, 2* (Pt. A). Washington, DC: U.S. Government Printing Office.

Nordhus, E. H., VandenBos, G. R., Berg, S., & Fromholt, P. (1998). *Clinical geropsychology.* Washington, DC: American Psychological Association.

Ohta, R. J., & Ohta, B. M. (1988). Special units for Alzheimer's disease patients: A critical look. *Gerontologist, 28,* 803–808.

Orwoll, L., & Perlmutter, M. (1992). The study of wise persons: Integrating a personality perspective. In R. J. Sternberg (Ed.), *Wisdom: Its nature, origins, and development* (pp. 160–177). Cambridge, England: Cambridge University Press.

Ostrosky-Solis, F., Jaime, R. M., & Ardila, A. (1998). Memory abilities during normal aging. *International Journal of Neuroscience, 93,* 151–162.

Park, D. C., Puglisi, J. T., & Smith, A. D. (1986). Memory for pictures: Does an age-related decline exist? *Journal of Psychology and Aging, 1,* 11–17.

Payne, E. C., Robbins, S., & Dougherty, L. M. (1991). Goal directedness and older adult adjustment. *Journal of Counseling Psychology, 38,* 302–308.

Persson, D. (1993). The elderly driver deciding when to stop. *Gerontologist, 33,* 88–91.

Plude, D. J., & Schwartz, L. K. (1996). Compact disc-interactive memory training with the elderly. *Educational Gerontology, 22,* 507–521.

Poon, L. W. (1986). *Clinical memory assessment.* Washington, DC: American Psychological Association.

Poon, L. W. (1992). Toward an understanding of cognitive functioning in geriatric depression. *International Psychogeriatrics, 4,* 241–266.

Poon, L. W., Sweaney, A. C., Clayton, G. M., & Merriam, S. B. (1992). The Georgia centenarian study. *International Journal of Aging and Human Development, 34,* 1–17.

Pressey, S. L. (1973). Old age counseling: Crises, services, potentials. *Journal of Counseling Psychology, 20,* 356–360.

Pressey, S. L., & Pressey, A. (1972). Major neglected need opportunity: Old-age counseling. *Journal of Counseling Psychology, 19,* 362–366.

Query, J. L., Jr., & Flint, L. J. (1996). The caregiving relationship. In N. Vanzetti & S. Duck (Eds.), *A lifetime of relationships* (pp. 455–483). Pacific Grove, CA: Brooks/Cole.

Rabbitt, P. (1993). Does it all go together when it goes? *Quarterly Journal of Experimental Psychology: Human Experimental Psychology, 46,* 385–434.

Raskind, M. A., & Peskind, E. R. (1992). Alzheimer's disease and other dementing disorders. In J. E. Birren, R. B. Sloane, & G. D. Cohen (Eds.), *Handbook of mental health and aging* (2nd ed., pp. 457–482). New York: Academic Press.

Research to Prevent Blindness. (1994). *Progress report.* New York: Author.

Ritchie, K. (1998). Mental health of the oldest old: The relevance of centenarian studies to psychogeriatric research. *International Psychogeriatrics, 10,* 7–9.

Robbins, S. B., Lee, R. H., & Wan, T. T. H. (1994). Goal continuity as a mediator of early retirement adjustment: Testing a multidimensional model. *Journal of Counseling Psychology, 41,* 18–26.

Robinson, B., & Thurnher, M. (1979). Taking care of aged parents: A family cycle transition. *Gerontologist, 19,* 586–593.

Rodin, J. (1986). Aging and health: Effects of the sense of control. *Science, 233,* 1271–1276.

Rodin, J. (1990). Control by any other name: Definitions, concepts, and processes. In J. Rodin, C. Schooler, & K. W. Schaie (Eds.), *Self-directedness cause and effects throughout the life course* (pp. 1–17). Hillsdale, NJ: Erlbaum.

Rodin, J., & Langer, E. J. (1977). Long-term effects of a control relevant intervention with the institutionalized aged. *Journal of Personality and Social Psychology, 35,* 897–902.

Rodin. J., & McAvay, G. (1992). Determinants of change in perceived health in a longitudinal study of older adults. *Journal of Gerontology, 47,* 373–384.

Rowe, J. W., & Kahn, R. L. (1987). Human aging: Usual and successful. *Science, 237,* 143–149.

Rowe, J. W., & Kahn, R. L. (1998). *Successful aging.* New York: Pantheon Books.

Sakauye, K. (1996). Ethnocultural aspects. In J. Sadavoy, L. W. Lazarus, L. F. Jarvik, & G. T. Grossberg (Eds.), *Comprehensive review of geriatric psychiatry* (2nd ed., pp. 197–221). Washington, DC: American Psychiatric Press.

Salthouse, T. A. (1991). *Theoretical perspectives on cognitive aging.* Hillsdale, NJ: Erlbaum.

Schieber, F. (1992). Aging and the senses. In J. E. Birren, R. B. Sloane, & G. D. Cohen (Eds.), *Handbook of mental health and aging* (2nd ed., pp. 252–306). San Diego, CA: Academic Press.

Schlossberg, N. K. (1981). A model for analyzing human adaptation to transition. *The Counseling Psychologist, 9,* 2–18.

Schneider, E. L., & Grueling, J. M. (1990). The aging of America: Impact on health care costs. *Journal of the American Medical Association, 263,* 2335–2340.

Segal, D. L., Coolidge, F. L., & Hersen, M. (1998). Psychological testing of older people. In I. H. Nordhus, G. R. VandenBos, S. Berg, & P. Fromholt (Eds.), *Clinical geropsychology* (pp. 231–257). Washington, DC: American Psychological Association.

Shapiro, D. (1965). *Neurotic Styles.* New York: Basic Books.

Smith, J., & Baltes, P. B. (1997). Profiles of psychological functioning in the old and oldest old. *Psychology and Aging, 12,* 458–472.

Smyer, M. A. (1984). Life transitions and aging: Implications for counseling older adults. *The Counseling Psychologist, 12,* 17–37.

Staudinger, U. M., Smith, J., & Baltes, P. B. (1994). *Manual for the assessment of wisdom-related knowledge [Materially NR. 46 Des Max-Plank-lnstituts for Bildungsforschung].* Berlin, Germany: Max Planck Insitute for Human Development and Education.

Sternberg, R. J. (1985). Implicit theories of intelligence, creativity, and wisdom. *Journal of Personality and Social Psychology, 49,* 607–627.

Sternberg, R. J. (Ed.). (1990). *Wisdom; Its nature, origins, and development.* Cambridge, England: Cambridge University Press.

Sterns, H. L., & Camp, C. J. (1998). Applied gerontology. *Applied Psychology: An International Review, 47,* 175–198

Stones, J. J., & Kozma, A. (1996). Activity, exercise, and behavior. In J. E. Birren & K. W. Schaie (Eds.), *Handbook of the psychology of aging* (4th ed., pp. 338–364). San Diego, CA: Academic Press.

Sue, S., Zane, N., & Young, K. (1994). Research on psychotherapy with culturally diverse populations. In A. E. Bergin & S. L. Garfield (Eds.), *Handbook of psychotherapy and behavior change* (4th ed., pp. 783–820). New York: Wiley.

Takamura, J. C. (1998). An aging agenda for the 21st century: The opportunities and challenges of population longevity. *Professional Psychology: Research and Practice, 29,* 411–412.

Thurmond, D. P. (1996). *Choosing to meet the need: A guide to improve targeting of title III services to low-income minority elderly.* Washington, DC: National Association of Area Agencies on Aging.

Torres-Gil. F. (1987). Hispanics: A special challenge. In A. Pifer & L. Bronte (Eds.), *Our aging society: Paradox and promise* (pp. 219–242). New York: Norton.

United States Bureau of the Census. (1992, July). Growth of America's oldest old population. *Profiles of America's elderly, No. 2.* Washington DC: U.S. Government Printing Office.

United States Bureau of the Census. (1996). *Current population reports, special studies, 65+ in the United States* (pp. 23–190). Washington, DC: U.S. Government Printing Office.

van Tilburg, T. (1998). Losing and gaining in old age: Changes in personal network size and social support in a four-year longitudinal study. *Journals of Gerontology: Psychological Sciences and Social Sciences, 53,* 313–323.

Weiland, S. (1995). Interpretive social science and spirituality. In M. A. Kimble et al. (Eds.). *Aging, spirituality and religion: A handbook* (pp. 589–611). Minneapolis, MN: Fortress Press.

Weiner, M. B. (1992). Treating the older adult: A diverse population: Psychoanalysis of the midlife and older patient [Special issue]. *Psychoanalysis and Psychotherapy, 10,* 66–76.

Wellman, R. E., & McCormack, J. M. (1984). Counseling with older persons: A review of outcome research. *The Counseling Psychologist, 12,* 81–95.

Whitely, J. (1980). Counseling psychology in the year 2000 A.D. *The Counseling Psychologist, 8,* 2–8.

Williams, M. J. (1991). *Memory assessment scales.* Camberwell, Australia: Psychological Assessment Resources.

Willis, S. L. (1985). Towards an educational psychology of the older adult learner: Intellectual and cognitive bases. In J. E. Birren & K. W. Schaie (Eds.), *Handbook of the psychology of aging* (2nd ed., pp. 818–847). New York: Van Nostrand-Reinhold.

Woods, R. T. (1996). Mental health problems in late life. In R. T. Woods (Ed.), *Handbook of the clinical psychology of aging*. New York: Wiley.

Worldwatch Institute. (1994). *Vital signs*. New York: Norton.

Worthington, E. L. (1989). Religious faith across the life span: Implications for counseling and research. *The Counseling Psychologist, 17,* 555–612.

Worthington, E. L., Jr., Hight, T. L., Ripley, J. S., Perrone, K. M., Kurusu, T. A., & Jones, D. R. (1997). Strategic hope-focused relationship-enrichment counseling with individual couples. *Journal of Counseling Psychology, 44,* 381–389.

Yesavage, J. A. (1986). The use of self-rating scales in the elderly. In L. W. Poon (Ed.). *Clinical memory assessment of older adults.* Washington, DC: American Psychological Association.

Yesavage, J. A., Lapp, D., & Sheikh, J. I. (1989). Mnemonics as modified for use by the elderly. In L. W. Poon, D. C. Rubin, & B. A. Wilson (Eds.). *Everyday cognition in adulthood and late life* (pp. 598–611). Cambridge, England: Cambridge University Press.

22

Ethnicity and Care

C. Cox

Deciding when care is needed, who should provide it, and how it should be offered is a multifaceted decision. The response is determined not only by the older person's impairment or disability level, but also by the values, traditions, and culture of the group to which the senior belongs. Among the critical factors that can influence the perception and development of frailty is ethnicity. In fact, ethnicity, because it relates to the individual's role in society and interactions with others, provides the context in which factors such as gender, family, and the use of services are organized.

It is critical to remember that culture itself is not a constant and that adherence to ethnic values and traditions varies with many other factors. Ethnicity remains a very complex phenomenon that can be affected by birthplace, years after immigration, and assimilation. Viewing each particular group, subgroup, and even family in terms of its own unique background and experiences is essential in understanding responses to impairments and to needs for care.

Ethnicity encompasses a distinct way of viewing and reacting to the world. Race, religion, or national origin are markers of ethnicity, with individual members classified according to the degree to which they identify with a specific group as well as the extent to which others consider them to be "ethnic" (Shibutani & Kwan, 1965).

Ethnic groups commonly hold distinct cultural beliefs, values, and norms. These can influence the aging process, determining the ways in which individuals are expected to age, their status, and their relationships, including the ways in which persons should care for and be involved with those who become impaired. As important as ethnicity may be as a critical influence on the care of older persons, it is not a constant force. Age, acculturation, and socioeconomic status contribute to the saliency of ethnicity as a force in a person's life (Markides, Liang, & Jackson, 1990).

Given the fact that ethnic culture and attitudes can affect care, it is imperative to recognize that ethnic disparities also exist within the caregiving network. Studies continue to show that professionals and systems maintain biases and discriminatory attitudes that affect services received by minority elders (White-Means, 2000, Johnson & Smith, 2002). According to the Institute of Medicine (2002), racial and ethnic minorities in the United States receive lower quality care than non-minority Whites. Among the factors contributing to this disparity are clinical uncertainty, stereotypical behavior, and conscious bias that can extend to prejudice.

Impairment and Ethnicity

The prevalence of chronic diseases varies by race and ethnicity. Black and Hispanic elderly have higher levels of diabetes than White non-Hispanics, with Black elderly also having much higher rates of hypertension (National Center for Health Statistics, 1999). The same data also show Black elderly as reporting more limitations in their activities and being more likely to have difficulties performing activities of daily living than White elderly. Other national data (Carrasquillo, Lantigua, & Shea, 2000) show Hispanic elders as having similar levels of ADL and IADL dependencies as White non-Hispanics, with Blacks again having the highest level of impairments and requiring the use of assistive devices. Data on differences in cognitive impairment indicate greater rates of impairment among Hispanic elders than among other groups (Gurland et al., 1997; Tang et al., 1998; Carasquillo et al., 2000). Studies also indicate that compared with White non-Hispanic elderly, Hispanics have lower rates of Alzheimer's disease but higher rates of vascular dementia (Fritz, Ortiz, & Ponton, 2001). Puerto Ricans have been found to be more disabled than Blacks or Whites with the disability beginning early in life and continuing into old age. In addition, variations among subgroups of ethnic populations are also apparent. In comparison with Mexican Americans and Cuban Americans, Puerto Rican elderly have greater levels of disability (Burnette & Mui, 1995).

Responses to Impairment

As ethnicity influences one's view of the world, it may also influence the perception of impairment. Disabilities or impairments that limit an older person's functioning may be perceived as an expected part of the normal course of aging. Within this perspective, an impairment may be accepted as a natural occurrence and not perceived as a symbol of decline or dependency. Older persons will not perceive themselves as dependent if they are able to provide some type of support or assistance to other family members.

This type of exchange or mutual assistance, whether financial, emotional, hands-on, or even symbolic, promotes the older person's sense of self-esteem and connectedness while permitting him or her to continue to play a role within the family (Becker, Beyee, Newsorn, & Mayern, 2003). The importance of social roles in responses to impairment is further underscored by research showing that maintaining roles and some personal control assists older persons adapt to declines in health, and actually reduces disability (Seeman, Baker, Richardson, & Tinetti, 1996). For example, if older persons are depended upon for child care or other assistance, they are less likely to identify themselves as disabled or impaired.

However, though these attitudes and behaviors may assist in adaptation, they may also affect the decision to seek care. In some instances, as the person feels responsible for some aspect of the family's well-being, he or she may deny his/her own need for care. The result is that care is sought only when the illness or impairment has become significantly disabling. In addition, older persons who feel responsible for assisting the family may deny their own impairments in order to continue in their traditional roles.

Responses of ethnic groups to cognitive impairments in the elderly warrant specific attention. Frequently, dementia is not recognized by families that regard cognitive deficits and behavioral problems as a normal part of aging. Ethnic groups assign meaning to dementia according to their own values, norms, and beliefs, which further influence their own caregiving activities as well as their use of services. Thus, to the extent that families are accepting of cognitive impairments in their older relatives, they are less likely to seek medical care and treatment for symptoms. Therefore, many remain at risk of not receiving medications that can slow the course of illness or help reduce symptoms.

At the same time, it is critical that any attempt to understand a group's responses to impairments considers the social milieu and environment in which the persons live. Thus, histories of poor access to care, inadequate services, and culturally insensitive providers can affect the older person's responses to symptoms and impairments, particularly his or her proclivity to seek formal assistance. In addition, little knowledge or education regarding the nature of impairments or appropriate treatments can further affect the ways persons respond.

African Americans

As discussed earlier, African American elderly, compared with other groups, are more likely to have functional impairments and difficulties with the activities of daily living. The population rates their health as more poor than either White or Hispanic elderly (Benson & Marano, 1998). As well as being more likely to have life-threatening illnesses such as heart disease and hypertension, they also have high rates of arthritis, which can severely restrict mobility. In addition, African American elderly are more likely to report being ill and to be disabled at an earlier age than their White peers.

At the same time, older Black persons are less likely to receive appropriate health care services than White elderly. Often they lack access to such care as screenings, physical and occupational therapies that may be available to other groups due to a lack of knowledge about techniques, limited income, and limited insurance. Given the low income status of many Black elderly, a reliance on Medicaid and Medicare, and their concentrations in urban centers, they often lack access to physicians who can assist them in receiving such services and thus race becomes a key factor in explaining the use of community health care (White-Means, 2000). In addition, when they do receive medical care, they receive lower-cost procedures and services, even under Medicare (Lee, Gehlbach, Hosmer, Red, & Baker, 1997).

Studies on the use of home care services by older African Americans have found varying results. Whereas some studies indicate the group uses less home care than older non-Hispanic Whites (Mui & Burnette, 1994; Wallace, Levy-Storms, Kingston, & Andersen, 1998), others find that race does not affect use and that any differences that do occur are dependent on income and Medicaid status (Miller et al., 1996).

Hispanics

Data from the 1999 Medical Expenditures Panel Survey is used to describe the health of Hispanics aged 50 years and older (Center for an Aging Society, 2003). The data reveal that the proportion of older Hispanics having at least one chronic condition is similar to that of non-Hispanic Whites. However, Hispanics are less likely than other groups to see a physician or to use other health care providers such as optometrists, psychologists, chiropractors, physical therapists, occupational therapists, or social workers.

Less than one third of older Hispanics with chronic conditions had insurance coverage for prescription drugs compared with 39% of non-Hispanic Blacks and 52% of non-Hispanic Whites. Hispanics are also more likely to be either uninsured (27%) or dependent on Medicaid (24%) than the other groups. For those over the age of 65, more than one third are dependent solely on public programs (i.e., Medicaid and Medicare) for their health care.

Only 20% of Hispanics, compared to 81% of non-Hispanic Blacks and 60% of non-Hispanic Whites, have Medicare and private insurance.

The disparities in health care for Hispanics with chronic disease are also noted in the use of preventive and maintenance services. In comparison to other groups with diabetes, hypertension, or heart disease, older Hispanics are less likely than either non-Hispanic Whites or Blacks to have their conditions regularly monitored. The group also reports more difficulty in making appointments with their health care providers and not surprisingly, tends to be less satisfied with their care. Disparities in health care seriously affect the functioning of older Hispanics. For instance, data indicate that this group is much less likely to have hip replacements, even under Medicare, than non-Hispanic Whites suffering from the same arthritic condition (Escalante et al., 2002). Accordingly, these persons continue to be in pain, and their impaired functioning leads to greater dependency. The lack of surgery reflects a lack of familiarity with the procedure and difficulties in communicating with the physician.

Asian Pacific Islanders

Asian Pacific Islander elderly are the second-fastest growing older population in the United States. Projections of future growth indicate that by 2050 Asian Americans will compose 6.3% of the older population, in comparison with 9.3% Blacks and 17.5% Hispanics (U.S. Bureau of the Census, 2000). This population includes several ethnic groups, Japanese, Koreans, Filipinos, Vietnamese, and the largest group, Chinese. Each group maintains its own customs and traditions, and within each population these are likely to be more strongly adhered to by the first generation to immigrate.

Data on the health status of these populations are difficult to obtain due to the absence of any large national database and the lumping together of all of the populations into one group. Data from the American Heart Association show a high prevalence of diabetes, hypertension, and obesity among the older population, with heart disease and stroke the leading causes of death (American Heart Association, 2003). However, data on the overall functional status or limitations of these populations are lacking. Findings that are available tend to be on specific groups in one geographic area.

A study of Filipino, Indian, Japanese, Korean, and Vietnamese adults over age 65 in New York City found that on measures of general physical functioning, mental health, and social functioning, the group rated themselves lower than the general older population (Ryan, 2003). In addition, more than 40% reported depressive symptoms, making depression more prevalent than in the general elderly population. Poor menial health was most likely experienced when they felt a greater cultural gap between themselves and their children and were unable to read English. These limitations as well as their impairments in ADLs are associated with poorer social functioning.

Native Americans

The American Indian elderly are, according to many indices, the most impaired and potentially frail of any ethnic groups. The extent of this impairment is reflected by the fact that at age 45, American Indians experience limitations in their ADLs comparable to those experienced by other groups at age 65 (Cook, 1989). Older American Indians have a higher percentage than Whites of disabilities preventing them from using public transportation, with 71% having limitations in their ability to perform ADLs (Manson & Callaway, 1990).

Rates of chronic diseases such as heart disease, diabetes, and cancer are 600% higher for Native

Americans than for the rest of the population (Office of Minority Health, 2002). Poor health education and health behaviors, poor facilities, and limited services are major causes of this ill health. As an example, one study found that hypertension was frequently not diagnosed or monitored, suggesting that improved measures of detection and management were essential (Rhoades & Buchwald, 2003). Other research found that diabetes among the elderly contributed to poor role performance, health perception, and quality of life (McFall, Solomon, Teshia, & Smith, 2000). Education about the care of diabetes for both patients and their caregivers is needed in order to improve the management of the illness.

Data on the physical functioning of American Indian elders indicate that almost 25% rate themselves as disabled, with approximately 8% reporting more than one disability. In comparison to national data on limitations among the older population, Native Americans report increased limitations and needs for assistance at as young as age 55. At age 55, 30% need assistance with walking in comparison to 11% of the general population age 65 and above (NRCNAA, 1998). It as also important to note that same data indicate that only 65% of elders receive personal assistance to help with their limitations.

Families and Caregiving

It is generally believed that family support networks among ethnic groups are strong and that they provide all the assistance a functionally impaired older relative may require. The fact that minority elderly are underrepresented in nursing homes is understood as evidence of a lack of need for such care and that families are providing for these persons in the community. Just as demographic changes are occurring with the majority population, however, parallel changes are occurring within the ethnic and minority populations.

Younger cohorts move from ethnic areas in inner cities, often leaving the older relatives to cope on their own or providing only minimal amounts of assistance. This lack of involvement can also increase feelings of stress and depression among older persons as they feel neglected and isolated by children who no longer respect them or adhere to traditional values and norms. If expectations not shared by adult children remain strong among the elderly, dissatisfaction can ensue regardless of the efforts that the children make.

Expectations for assistance are strongest among first generation immigrants and those not born in the United States. As younger cohorts become acculturated traditional norms regarding caregiving may change along with the new norms and demands of society. Moreover, among many ethnic minority groups, the low economic status of adult children and other family members, as well as their own health problems, can make it extremely difficult to provide care to an impaired older person. At the same time, little is known about the extent to which family caregiving actually meets the needs of dependent seniors.

References for Informal Care

The degree to which a preference for informal care reflects traditional values and obligations or previous negative experiences with the formal system continues to be debated. Histories of discrimination, poor services, long waits, and culturally insensitive staffs encourage a preference for and a dependence on the family as a source of care. Moreover, in a period when immigrants are falling under increased security regarding their legal status, as well as their eligibility for some programs, the preference may indeed be for informal assistance rather than involvement with formal services.

A study of African American, Puerto Rican, and non-Hispanic Whites in an urban area found culture a more important factor than socioeconomic status in determining the amount of informal care. The two minority groups, regardless of income or disability level, received more informal care than older White persons (Tennstedt & Chang, 1998) Although these findings suggest a cultural preference for informal care, it is difficult to discern whether this preference reflects values and traditions or negative attitudes and experiences with the formal system.

Evidence for the salient role of ethnicity in the caregiving relationship is found in a study of first and second generation Japanese Americans living in Chicago. Filial piety, or support of the older generation, was a strong sentiment among both parents and their adult children (Osako & Liu, 1986). Adult children with more personal resources than their parents continued to accept the norms of filial responsibility, incorporating them into the pattern of American values that emphasize individual choice and independence; the tradition actually assisted in the older individual's transition from an independent to a dependent status.

Even among this population, though, the propensity for familial care may be waning. A study of Japanese American families in Washington State found that they were as interested in nursing home care as others in the population (McCormick et al., 1996) At the same time, a survey of supportive community services use by family caregivers in all groups of Asian Americans found only 15% using them, in comparison with approximately 30% of other caregivers (National Alliance for Caregiving, 1997). This lack of use may partially be explained by the finding that a larger proportion of Asian caregivers did not know what kind of help or information would be useful. Ensuring that educational materials and outreach tailored to specific ethnic groups are developed could foster the use of needed services.

The complexity of unraveling cultural factors from other determinants in the preference for informal care is vividly depicted in findings on Korean elderly. Two levels of service awareness and utilization of community long-term care services in comparison with non-Hispanic Whites were viewed as results of a lack of outreach and information (Moon, Lubben, & Villa, 1998). In addition, this underutilization may also indicate that services themselves are culturally inappropriate and persons are making conscious decisions not to use them (Cho, 1998).

Informal Supports of African American Seniors

Much research has been done on the informal support systems of African American elderly, including the extent to which these systems are available to them. Older African Americans have been found to draw on a varied pool of informal helpers not restricted to immediate family, and in which there is some degree of substitution "When children are unavailable to assist the elderly, other relatives, particularly siblings, will provide care" (Taylor, 1985).

This extended system increases the possibility of others to provide support. But kin and non-kin appear to play varying roles in meeting the needs of the elderly. Kin are found to provide long-term, instrumental assistance based on an obligatory relationship, while non-kin are more likely to provide socioemotional support and care for short-term needs (Taylor & Chatters, 1988). In comparison to White functionally unimpaired older persons, African Americans are more likely to have informal supports that are not members of the immediate family (Burton et al., 1995).

The type, amount, and frequency of help is on a sliding scale in these arrangements.

Increases in disability contribute to increases in the number of available helpers and increased contacts, depending on the proximity of the family. However, the extent to which informal help to African American elderly is available should not be overestimated. The African American elderly are less likely to have spouses and adult children available to provide help and financial assistance.

In a study of the support systems of inner-city African Americans, Johnson and Baher (1990) found that adult children, even when close to the elderly, did not tend to offer instrumental support because of strains and distractions in their own lives. Moreover, older persons resisted being dependent on their children, preferring instead to use formal services such as home help and chore workers. Many with the most serious impairments had no weekly contact with either relatives and friends. Thus, those most in need of support may be the most at risk of being isolated due to their inability to maintain social networks.

The church has been viewed as a source of support for older African Americans, supplementing the social support offered by families (Tayor & Chatters, 1988; Walls & Zarit, 1991). However, research suggests that such assumptions may not be consistently valid. A study of frail urban African Americans found that they did not receive any more assistance than the non-frail from the church or from their families (Bowles et al., 2000). Contrary to assumptions regarding supports, the frail were less likely than others to feel close to their families and did not have greater contact with them. The group used more community services than others and did not report greater support from the church, indicating that the church was not involved in meeting their care needs. These findings reinforce the need to be cautious when assuming that needs of these older persons are being met without formal community help.

The Stress of Caregiving

Ethnicity docs not provide immunity from the stress of caregiving although study results vary on how it relates to caregiver well-being. In a study of burden among Hispanic caregivers, Cox and Monk (1996) found that cultural values and norms continued to govern familial relationships and the care of the elderly. However, strong adherence to these values could have negative consequences on caregiver well-being. It may affect both their response to the use of services as well as the strains they experience. Among Hispanic caregivers, the use of formal services, although alleviating some of the demands placed on the caregiver's time, was associated with greater depression. This finding suggests they felt troubled in not adhering to cultural expectations regarding caregiving (Cox & Monk, 1996).

Other studies on depression among Hispanic caregivers have looked at specific population subgroups. In one study, Mexican American women reported significantly higher rates of depression than either Anglo or African American caregivers (Adams, Aranda, Kemp, & Takagi, 2002). Other research indicates Cuban caregivers are more depressed than non-Hispanic caregivers, with primary risk factors being female and caring for a relative with poor cognitive status (Harwood et al., 2000).

The impact of caregiving on the informal supports of African American elderly is noted in their care of relatives with Alzheimer's disease. A study of African American and White caregivers who had contacted Alzheimer's associations for assistance showed African American caregivers were not immune to the depression and strains experienced by their non-minority peers (Cox, 1999). However, their well-being was more strongly affected by the support they received from others than by the actual status of the patient. Those caregivers maintained very strong expectations for assistance from other family members and when these expectations were not met, they became vulnerable to depression.

These findings imply that care must be taken when attributing particular caregiver responses to specific groups. There may be as much diversity within groups as among individuals. Income, place of residence, relationship, employment, and degree of acculturation, as well as the degree of discrimination or racism experienced, can have distinct influences on a caregiver's use of and response to formal services.

Service Use

With the rates of disability and chronic illness among African American and Hispanic elderly higher than those of non-Hispanic Whites, and their use of institutional care lower, there is an implied need for community care and services. However, many factors can influence such use, including those associated with the individual and with the service itself. Understanding the influence of potential barriers impinging on the decision to use services is fundamental to assuring that specific needs are met.

Individual barriers are those associated with low income, a lack of insurance, inability to speak English or limited English, and immigration status. Persons who are insecure about their residency status and who are unable to understand program guidelines or criteria are particularly vulnerable to these barriers. In addition, individual barriers may refer to adherence to norms regarding the use of services. Thus, a person may be to reluctant to use a support group for fear of stigma associated with sharing problems outside of the family. A family may choose not to use formal home care if the home attendants are from the same ethnic group and may judge them negatively for not providing all of the care themselves.

Services themselves can present barriers by not having ethnically diverse staff, lacking flexibility in their programs, and having little understanding of the groups they intend to serve. Without staff that can easily communicate with persons in their own language, interpreters, or materials that can be understood, programs risk being underutilized by ethnic populations. Users must also be assured the providers they see are as competent and qualified as those seen by other groups (Brach & Fraser, 2000). Locating services in ethnic neighborhoods and close to public transportation further contributes to utilization.

Models of Service Utilization

The Andersen model of health services utilization (Andersen & Newman, 1973) is frequently used to provide a framework for examining the utilization of services by diverse groups. The model depicts utilization as resulting from three sets of factors: predisposing, enabling, and need. Predisposing factors are demographics and socioeconomic characteristics including race and ethnic background. Enabling factors can include economic resources, insurance, living environment, social resources, transportation, and personal resources. Needs encompass physical health, mental health, functional status, and one's own perception that services can help.

The model is often used to compare the use of in-home and community-based services by specific populations. However, in applying the model, it is important to recognize that need itself, often a primary factor in determining service use, may be interpreted differently and thus is not necessarily a prerequisite for service use.

Cox (1999) applied the model to African American and White caregivers of Alzheimer's relatives. Both groups were comparable with regard to the needs of both patient and caregiver, and needs were motivating factors toward service use. Given this similarity, however, the groups differed in their interests in specific services. White caregivers were most interested in obtaining information on the illness and support groups, while the African American caregivers were more interested in day care, home health, referrals, and respite.

In a study applying the model to focus groups of White non-Hispanic and African American seniors, need played a less significant role than other factors in attitudes toward long-term care (Bradley et al., 2002). Predisposing and enabling factors such as attitudes and knowledge, social norms, and perceived control were most important in influencing service-use intention. Accessibility of information about long-term care, feelings toward the norms concerning caregiving, and concerns of privacy and self-determination were most important in predicting whether or not persons would use long-term care services.

Another model of service utilization (Wallace, 1990) views use as affected by structural factors associated with the availability, accessibility, and acceptability of services. Ethnic older adults and their families are at risk of finding barriers in each of these areas. Availability refers to the existence and provision of services. Accessibility involves eligibility criteria, insurance, and income as well as knowledge and awareness of services. Acceptability refers to the staff and the ways in which services are offered. If programs are made congruent with cultural values, recognizing attitudes toward the use of formal assistance and concerns like fear of dependency by older persons, acceptability is increased.

The importance of acceptability of services is reflected in the use of services by Japanese Americans in Seattle (Young, McCormick, & Vitaliano, 2002). The Japanese community was involved in identifying the service needs of Japanese elders and in developing appropriate services such as a nursing home, assisted living, adult day care, and meal services. Accordingly, the services were developed in a way that made them culturally acceptable to both elders and their families. Care was taken to assure that the programs were perceived as an extension of traditional family caregiving. By incorporating attitudes and traditions of the population, the services were viewed positively and were well-utilized.

On Lok

On Lok Senior Health Services in San Francisco is an example of how community care services can be developed to be accessible and acceptable to diverse populations of older adults. On Lok was established in 1971 in response to the health care needs of the frail elderly in San Francisco's Chinatown and surrounding areas. It began as a day care center for the elderly, and then served as a Medicare demonstration model of consolidated services providing all medical and social services.

On Lok has expanded into eight community sites in the San Francisco area. The population served by On Lok is primarily Asian or Pacific Islander (63%), as are the staff (74%) (Kornblatt, Eng, & Hansen, 2003); however, the program also serves large populations of Hispanic and Caucasian elderly. As program participants have become more diverse, a staff training program in cultural diversity has been introduced to increase knowledge about the specific cultures. The program was developed from the responses of staff to a survey that assessed their knowledge and understanding of the cultures of the various groups.

Based upon these responses, the following specific objectives for the training were developed:

1. Increase understanding of how culture determines attitudes, values, and behaviors;
2. Gain an overview of the dimensions of diversity that staff bring to the workplace;
3. Increase inter- and intra-cultural sensitivity toward both On Lok participants and staff;
4. Learn effective communication skills.

The training is seen as having contributed to both staff satisfaction and the quality of care they provide, with staff better able to understand and respond to the concerns and needs of participants.

Reaching Diverse Groups

One of the greatest challenges in meeting the care needs of ethnic elderly in the community is reaching them. For many reasons these persons, particularly those with the most needs, may be the most unconnected or suspicious of the service system. Overcoming the many barriers that can affect their use of services demands both knowledge and commitment by providers.

Working with persons from the community on plans for services development can be fundamental in assuring that programs are congruent with both the values and needs of the intended population. These persons are also important in helping to assure the credibility of the program and in communicating its aims. Including community residents on administrative boards can assist in developing valuable links with the community, crucial to its acceptability.

A key factor in assuring utilization is active outreach. Outreach involves more than having materials in different languages. It involves actively going into the community to develop relationships with groups and to inform them about the services, its intentions, and how it may meet the assistance needs of older persons and their families. Using workers from the same ethnic group as the intended client population can help increase the effectiveness of the outreach effort, as it can be easier for them to communicate and establish rapport. Language barriers affecting understanding of the problems of the older population are also reduced.

Outreach entails going to community fairs, churches, senior centers, physician offices, and other sites that older persons and their relatives may visit. These activities provide an opportunity to describe programs and respond immediately to questions and concerns. They are important in enabling providers to learn about factors affecting service utilization, and thus can help to assure that programs are congruent with the attitudes and expectations of the population.

Staff must be knowledgeable about traditions, norms, and values in order to interact effectively with a population. Through training and education, persons may learn about relevant cultures and become aware of their own biases and perspectives regarding specific groups. Such education can be as important for staff who share the same ethnicity as the clients as for other staff. As an example, if ethnic staff disapprove of a family's use of formal assistance, the attitudes can defer utilization. Thus, ethnic group membership in itself is not sufficient to assure service use.

In designing services, it is essential that programs are presented in a manner sensitive to the cultural nuances of the population. Persons may be deterred from using services if they are confronted with many forms or must be interviewed by many different staff. Such procedures, often common in service agencies, can deter those who are used to more informal and intimate relationships. Collecting information needed for eligibility must be done in ways that are not perceived as intrusive or offending.

The ways programs present themselves can be important determinants in their acceptability.

Many may be deterred from a program that focuses on mental illness or problems, while they would be accepting of one emphasizing growth and change. In the same way, relatives may respond more favorably to support services stressing the ways they can further enable them, rather than those that stress relief from the burdens of caregiving.

Cultural Competency

In recent years a growing recognition of the ethnic plurality of our society has occasioned increased interest in developing culturally competent professionals and services. Cultural competency has been defined as "a set of congruent behaviors, attitudes, and policies that come together in a system or agency or among professionals that permit them to work across cross-cultural situations" (National Association of Social Workers, 1997). Such competency may be viewed as a prerequisite for reaching and serving older ethnically diverse adults and their families.

Cultural competency demands that persons working with ethnic groups be knowledgeable about their values, beliefs, and traditions, and be respectful of them. Practitioners must be able to respond to these persons according to their preferences and their norms for behaviors. Communication is essential for cultural competency, and necessitates some fluency in the language and dialects of the persons being served. In addition, communication also implies understanding nonverbal gestures that persons use in their social interactions with each other and with those outside their ethnic groups. Sensitivity to this communication can be a critical factor in the group's acceptance of the provider and service.

Finally, cultural competency requires that practitioners be accepting of differences (Bhagat & Prien, 1996). Recognizing one's own biases and the ways they affect perceptions and expectations is fundamental to working effectively with culturally diverse older persons. Equally important is the avoidance of stereotyping, or assuming that all members of an ethnic group share the same beliefs and traditions. This is particularly important when working with older persons who may show much stronger adherence to traditional values and norms than their adult children.

Summary

Ethnicity and culture are important influences on the aging process, caregiving, and even the responses of caregivers themselves. Relationships are consistently found between ethnicity and chronic disease as well as seniors' limitations and their responses to them. Such disparities occur even among subgroups of ethnic elderly. At the same time, it remains unclear the extent to which such variations are themselves the results of culture and traditions, or are reflections of continuing disparities resulting from histories of discrimination, poor access, inadequate care, and unresponsive services.

Families continue to play major roles in caring for older ethnic persons in the community and such care is often used to explain their relative lack of use of institutional care. However, many caregivers struggle to meet the demands of their older relatives and are not immune from many of the negative effects of caregiving. Both individual barriers and those presented by services can impact on utilization. Programs must be sensitive and responsive to the needs of cultural groups, their values, and traditions, as well as their previous experiences with formal services. Service utilization depends upon careful planning, the involvement of community persons, well-trained staff, and effective outreach.

Cultural competency refers to the ability of persons to communicate and work effectively with persons from diverse backgrounds. It assumes specific training in cross-cultural work, as well as understanding of personal biases and beliefs that can affect interactions. An important aspect of cultural competency is the ability to accept the validity of differences and another person's values and perspectives.

Finally, it is essential to recognize that ethnicity is not a constant. Its influence on the life of an older person, and the ways he or she perceives impairments, assistance, and care, will vary. Although ethnicity may be an important component in this process, it is not necessarily the only one. Seniors' experiences with formal services and past discrimination can be equally important determinants in the use and choice of care providers.

References

Adams, B., Aranda, M., Kemp, B., & Takagi, K. (2002). Ethnic and gender differences in distress among Anglo American, African American, Japanese American, and Mexican American spousal caregivers of persons with dementia. *Journal of Clinical Geropsychology, 8,* 279–301.

American Heart Association. (2003). *Statistical fact sheet: Populations.* Author.

Andersen, R., & Newman, J. (1973). Societal and individual determinants of medical care utilization in the United States. *Milbank Quarterly, 51,* 95–124.

Becker, G., Beyee, B., Newsom, E., & Mayen, M. (2003). Creating continuity through mutual assistance: Intergenerational reciprocity in four ethnic groups. *Journal of Gerontology: Social Sciences, 58B,* 8151–8159.

Beuson, V., & Marano, M. (1998). Current estimates from the National Health Interview Survey, 1985–1994. In *Vital and Health Statistics* (Vol. 2, p. 110). Hyattsville, MD: National Center for Health Statistics.

Bhagat, R., & Prien, K. (1996). Cross cultural training in organizational contexts. In D. Landis & R. Bhagat (Eds.), *Handbook of intercultural training* (2nd ed.). Thousand Oaks, CA: Sage.

Bowles, J., Brooks, T., Hayes-Reams, P., Butts, T., Myers, H., Allen, W., & Kington, R. (2000). Frailty, family, and church support among urban African American elderly. *Journal of Health Care for the Poor and Underserved, 11,* 87–99.

Brarh, C., & Fraser, I. (2000). Can cultural competency reduce racial and ethnic health disparities? A review and conceptual model. *Medical Care Research and Review, 57,* 181–317.

Bradley, E., McGraw, S., Curry, L., Buckser, A., King, K., Kasl, S., & Andersen, R. (2002). Expanding the Andersen model: The role of psychosocial factors in long-term care use. *Health Services Research, 37,* 1221–1242.

Burnette, D., & Mui, A. (1995). In-home community-based service use by three groups of elderly Hispanics: A national perspective. *Social Work Research, 19(4),* 197–206.

Burton, L., Kasper, J., Shore, A., Cagney, K., LaViest, T., Cubbin, C., & German, P. (1995). The structure of informal care: Are there differences by race? *Gerontologist, 35,* 711–752.

Carrasquillo, O., Lantigua, R., & Shea, S. (2000). Differences in functional status of Hispanic versus non Hispanic white elderly. *Journal of Health and Aging, 12,* 342–361.

Center for an Aging Society, Georgetown University. (2003). *Older Hispanic Americans: Less care for chronic conditions.* Washington, DC: Georgetown University.

Cho, P. (1998). Comment. *Gerontologist, 38,* 317–319.

Cox, C. (1995). Comparing the experiences of black and white caregivers of dementia patients. *Social Work, 40,* 343–349.

Cox, C. (1999). Service needs and use: A further look at the experiences of African American and White caregivers seeking Alzheimer's assistance. *American Journal of Alzheimer's Disease, 14,* 83–101.

Cox, C., & Monk, A. (1996). Strain among caregivers: Comparing the experiences of

African American and Hispanic caregivers of Alzheimer's relatives. *International Journal of Aging and Human Development, 43,* 93–105.

Escalante, A., Barrett, J., del Kincon, I., Connell, J., Phillips, C., & Katz, J. (2002). Disparity in total hip replacement affecting Hispanic Medicare beneficiaries. *Medical Care, 40,* 451–460.

Fritz, L., Ortiz, F., & Ponton, M. (2001). Frequency of Alzheimer's disease and other dementias in a community outreach sample of Hispanics. *Journal of the American Geriatrics Society, 49,* 1301–1308.

Gurland, B., Wilder, D., Lantigua, R., Mayeux, R., Stern, Y., Chen, J., & Killeffer, E. (1997). Differences in rates of dementia between ethnoracial groups. In L. Martin & B. Soldo (Eds.), *Racial and ethnic differences in the health of older Americans* (pp. 233–261). Washington, DC: National Academy Press.

Harwood, D., Barker, Ownby, R., Bravo, M., Aquero, H., & Duaro, R. (2000). Predictors of positive and negative appraisal among Cuban American caregivers of Alzheimer's disease patients. *International Journal of Genuine Psychiatry, 15,* 481–487.

Institute of Medicine. (2002). Unequal treatment: Confronting racial and ethnic disparities in healthcare. Washington, DC: National Academy Press.

Johnson, G., & Baher, B. (1990). Families and networks among older inner city blacks. *Gerontologist, 30,* 726–733.

Johnson, J., & Smith, N. (2002). Health and social issues associated with racial, ethnic, and cultural disparities. *Generations, 26,* 25–32.

Kornblatt, S., Eng., C., & Hansen, J. (2003). Cultural awareness in health and social services. The experience of On Lok. *Generations, 26,* 46–53.

Lee, A., Gehlbach, S., Hosmer, D., Red, M., & Baker, C. (1997). Medicare treatment differences for Blacks and Whites. *Medical Care, 35,* 1173–1190.

Manson, S., & Callaway, D. (1990). Health and aging among American Indians: Issues and challenges for the geriatric sciences. In M. Harper (Ed.), *Minority aging: Essential curricula content for selected health and allied health professions.* Health Resources and Services Administration, DHHS Pub No. HRS (P-DV90-4) Washington, DC: U.S. Government Printing Office.

Markides, K., Liang, J., & Jackson, J. (1990). Race, ethnicity, and aging: Conceptual and methodological issues. In L. George & R. Binstock (Eds.), *Handbook of the social sciences* (3rd ed.). New York: Academic Press.

Miller, B., Campbell, R., Davis, L., Furner, S., Grachelto, A., Prohaska, T., Kaufman, J., Li., M., & Perez, C. (1996). Minority use of community long term care services: A comparative analysis. *Journal of Gerontology: Social Sciences, 51B,* 570–581.

McFall, S., Solomon, T., Teshia, A., & Smith, D. (2000). Health related quality of Native American primary care patients. *Research on Aging 22,* 692–714.

McCormick, W., Ohata, C., Urnoto, J., Young, H., Graves, A., & Kakull, W. (1996). Attitudes towards use of nursing homes and home care in elderly Japanese Americans. *Journal of the American Geriatrics Society, 50,* 1149–1155.

Moon A., Lubben, J., & Villa, V. (1998). Awareness and utilization of community long term care services by elderly Korean and non-Hispanic White Americans. *Gerontologist, 38,* 309–316.

Mui, A., & Burnette, D. (1994). Long term care service use by frail elders: Is ethnicity a factor? Gerontologist, *34,* 190–198.

National Alliance for Caregiving. (1997). *Caregiver data for caregivers to the elderly: 1987 and 1997.* Bethesda, MD: Author.

National Association of Social Workers. (1997). *Code of ethics.* Washington, DC: Author.

National Center for Health Statistics. (1999). *Health and aging chartbook.* Hyattsville, MD: Author.

Office of Minority Health. (2002). *National forum on health disparity issues for American Indians and Alaska Natives.* Denver: Author.

Osako, M., & Liu, W. (1986). Intergenerational relations and the aged among Japanese Americans. *Research on Aging, 8,* 128–155.

Rhoades, D., & Buchwald, D. (2003). Hypertension in older urban Native American primary care patients. *Journal of the American Geriatrics Society, 51,* 774–781.

Ryan, A. (2003). *Asian American elders in New York City: A study of health, social needs, quality of life, and quality of care.* New York: Asian American Federation of New York.

Shibutani, T., & Kwan, K. (1965). *Ethnic stratification.* New York: MacMillan.

Tang, M., Stern, Y., Marder, K., Bell, K., Gurland, B., Lagtigua, R., Andrews, H., Feng, L., Tyeko, B., & Mayeux, R. (1998). The APOE-epsilon 4 allele and the risk of Alzheimer's disease among African Americans, Whites, and Hispanics. *Journal of the American Medical Association, 279,* 751–755.

Taylor, R. (1985). The extended family as a source of support to elderly Blacks. *Gerontologist, 25,* 488–495.

Taylor R., & Chaters, L. M. (1988). Church members as a source of informal social support. *Review of Religious Research, 30,* 193–203.

Tennstedt, S., & Chang, B. (1998). The relative contribution of ethnicity versus socioeconomic status in explaining differences in disability and receipt of informal care. *Journal of Gerontology: Social Sciences, 53B,* 561–570.

U.S. Bureau of the Census. (2000). *National population projections NP-T4.* Washington, DC: U.S. Government Printing Office.

Wallace, S. (1990). The no-care zone: Availability, accessibility, and acceptability in community based long term care. *Gerontologist, 30,* 254–262.

Wallace, S., Levy-Storms, L., Kingston, R., & Andersen, R. (1998). The persistence of race and ethnicity in the use of long term care. *Journal of Gerontology: Social Sciences, 53B,* 5101–5112.

Walls, C. & Zant, S. (1991). Informal support from black churches and the well being of elderly blacks. *Gerontologist, 31,* 490–495.

White-Means, S. (2000). Racial patterns in disabled elderly persons' use of medical services. *Journal of Gerontology: Social Sciences, 55B,* 576–589.

Young, H., McCormick, W., & Vitaliano, P. (2000). Attitudes toward community based services among Japanese American families. *Gerontologist, 12,* 814–825.

23

Why Multicultural Issues Matter for Practitioners Working With Older Adults

Gregory A. Hinrichsen

Some clinicians might wonder whether the American Psychological Association's (APA's) *Guidelines on Multicultural Education, Training, Research, Practice, and Organizational Change for Psychologists* (APA, 2003; henceforth referred to as the *multicultural guidelines*) and *Guidelines for Providers of Psychological Services to Ethnic, Linguistic, and Culturally Diverse Populations* (APA, 1990) have significant real-world relevance to geropsychology. The vast majority of older adults (84%) are White, and an even larger majority of older adults who receive psychological services are White. Most psychologists providing services to older adults are White. Yet race and ethnicity figure into clinical practice with older adults and the lives of older adults in ways that may not be immediately apparent. Considerations of race and ethnicity in the delivery of psychological services to older adults have lagged behind a broader awareness of the importance of these factors for psychologists working with younger adults. In part, this situation reflects the reality that only in recent years has the field of clinical geropsychology professionally defined itself (APA, 2004). In this article, I focus on the relevance of APA's recently adopted multicultural guidelines to clinical practice with older adults. Further, I discuss facts about the lives of minority and ethnic older adults, clinical examples that illustrate how multicultural issues and aging are interwoven, efforts to address multicultural aging, and resources and recommendations on how to incorporate multicultural issues into training and clinical work with older adults.

Those in the field of gerontology have been especially attentive to issues of diversity. Researchers have consistently documented a wide variability among adults with respect to health, finances, political views, social preferences, and other important factors. Mirroring larger societal awareness of the status of

Authors' Note: I thank Merla Arnold, Robert Jerome, and Nanette Kramer for their comments on this article.

minorities, in the 1960s, gerontologists began to focus on issues of older minority group members. Concerns were raised about the situation, dubbed *double jeopardy*, faced by older minorities (Dowd & Bengtson, 1978). As a group, older adults have been the object of widespread stereotypes on the part of the general public as well as health professionals. This phenomenon has been called *ageism* (Butler, 1975). Early studies of ageism, in fact, drew on the theories of racial and ethnic stereotyping of younger adults (Kogan, 1961). Some stereotypes that persist today include the following: Older adults are (a) alike (in fact, they are very diverse); (b) alone and lonely (most are socially integrated); (c) sick, frail, and dependent (most live independently); (d) depressed (they have lower rates of diagnosable depressive disorders than do younger adults); (e) rigid in old age (there is stability of personality into late life); and (f) unable to cope (they are remarkably resilient in the face of late life stresses; APA Working Group on the Older Adult. 1998).

The persistence of misinformation about and stereotyping of older adults by other health professionals has been especially disappointing to geropsychologists. Early in my career, I described the circumstances of a depressed, medically frail older client to a middle-aged psychologist colleague who did not provide services to older people. After hearing of the case, the colleague jokingly remarked. "Well, if I get to that point when I am old, just shoot me." This comment, coming from a person whom I had always considered an astute and sensitive individual, raised concerns in me that are consistent with Guideline 1 of the APA multicultural guidelines (APA, 2003): "Psychologists are encouraged to recognize that, as cultural beings, they may hold attitudes and beliefs that can detrimentally influence their perception of and interactions with individuals who are ethnically and racially different from themselves" (p. 382). Although the comment from the colleague was related to age and not race or ethnicity, it underscored the larger principle articulated in the guideline that negative attitudes toward groups different from one's own may be present even in individuals whose profession is predicated on social justice. At the same time, some gerontologists have raised concerns that not enough attention has been devoted to racial, ethnic, and other dimensions of social diversity in the field of gerontology and that much work remains to be done. For example, one geropsychology colleague working in a geriatric mental health program in an urban area raised the question to staff about how to be more sensitive in the assessment and delivery of services to gay male and lesbian seniors. Some staff found the question amusing as they asserted that gay male and lesbian seniors did not seek mental health services at the facility—an unlikely circumstance given that older gay men and lesbians probably exist in numbers that are comparable to those in younger populations, despite being less visible (Kimmel, 2002).

The Interaction of Age and Race and Ethnicity: Some Facts About Racial and Ethnic Minority Older Adults

In the 20th century, the face of America began to age. In 1900, 5% of Americans were aged (i.e., 65 years of age or older). In 2004, 13% of Americans were aged. By 2030, 20% of the population will be aged. In the 21st century, the face of America will slowly be represented by aged persons of color. Consider these demographic facts about the racial and ethnic makeup of persons 65 years of age and older. In the year

2000, 84% of the aged were White, 8% were Black, 6% were Hispanic, 2% were Asian, and 0.4% were American Indian. It is predicted that in the year 2050, 64% of the aged will be White, 12% will be Black, 16% will be Hispanic, 7% will be Asian, and 0.6% will be American Indian (Federal Interagency Forum on Aging-Related Statistics, 2000). Mirroring larger demographic trends in the United States, increasing numbers of older adults will be minorities. Despite this, a recent issue of the *AARP Bulletin,* a publication of the American Association of Retired Persons, had a cover article titled "Don't Forget Us: How to Save Social Security for the Next Generation," which was accompanied by a photograph of babies, none of whom appeared to be racial or ethnic minorities of the next generation.

Other facts attest to the heterogeneity of older Americans. Educational and economic disparities between White and minority older persons are notable. Seventy-two percent of White older people have a high school diploma, compared with much lower rates for most others (for Black older people, the rate is 44%; for Hispanic older people 29%; and for Asian older people, 65%). The rate of poverty among White older people is 8%, which is a rate much lower than those of others (for Black older people, the rate is 26%; for Hispanic older people, 21%; and for Asian older people, 16%). A sobering fact is that almost half of divorced older Black women live in poverty (Federal Interagency Forum on Aging-Related Statistics, 2000). The median household net worth (i.e., total value of all assets held, including the value of a home) for White older people is $181,000, whereas for Blacks it is $13,000 (Federal Interagency Forum on Aging-Related Statistics, 2000). This disparity in household worth is so large that when I present these figures to students, they routinely assume that I have misstated the figure for Black household net worth ("You mean $130,000, right?"). In one federal report, a footnote confirms that the figure is not a typographic error. Health disparities also exist. Life expectancy from birth for Whites is 77 years, whereas for Blacks it is 71 years. Among White older adults, 74% reported that they are in good health, whereas for Blacks the percentage is 58% and for Hispanics it is 65%. A higher incidence of obesity, diabetes, and hypertension as well as an earlier onset of chronic illness is evident in minority compared with majority older adults.

About 3 million foreign-born persons 65 years of age or older are in the United States. Among them, more than one third were born in Europe, one third in Latin America, and one fourth in Asia. In the future, increasing numbers of foreign-born older adults will likely be from Latin America and Asia. Compared with native-born Americans, older persons who are foreign-born are less educated, more likely to live in poverty, and less likely to obtain health care coverage (He, 2002). Minority older adults underuse mental health services. A wide variety of challenges are faced by minority older adults attempting to access health care. Minority aged delay seeking health care, have less access to specialists, and have greater problems with treatment compliance. Economic and health disparities evident in later life are primarily the legacy of frank racism that was evident in the childhood and adulthood of the current generation of minority older Americans (APA Working Group on the Older Adult, 1998).

Race, Ethnicity, and Diversity in Clinical Practice

Practicing geropsychologists have long discussed the importance of considering several important issues in providing competent psychological services to older adults. These include life span and developmental issues, historical experiences unique to an older cohort, problems common to older people, and the context of older adults' lives (Knight, 2004). Through the framework of transference and countertransference, geropsychologists have also underscored the importance of understanding how age differences (or similarities) might affect client perceptions and behaviors of therapists and vice versa (Genevay & Katz, 1990). Less commonly have ethnic and/or racial differences between therapist and older client been discussed. Regardless of patient age, ethnic or cultural differences between client and therapist are part of the therapeutic dynamic and are usually a fruitful focus of the clinical conversation (Comas-Diaz & Jacobsen, 1991).

"Are You Jewish?"

When I was a 30-year-old psychology intern working in an outpatient geriatric clinic, one of my first older female clients asked, "Are you Jewish?" This simple question from a 78-year-old, depressed, mildly cognitively impaired woman conveyed concerns about perceived differences between client and therapist. This older client and I differed on a variety of statuses, including age, gender, and country of origin. She was older; I was younger. She was female; I was male. She was born in Europe and had immigrated to the United States before World War II; I was born in rural Illinois. Her perception of our differences in ethnicity and religious faith was of most concern. She was raised orthodox Jewish; I was raised Roman Catholic with parents of German and Swedish ancestry. Discussion of the question of whether I was Jewish revealed a number of issues. The client expected that she would have a Jewish service provider because she was seeking services at an institution that had been founded by Jewish philanthropists. In her childhood and young adulthood, educational and economic opportunities were limited for Jews, and she herself had experienced discrimination from non-Jews. At one of the most vulnerable times in her life, could she trust someone who was not Jewish to understand her difficulties and help her? In fact, as an individual raised in a small, culturally homogeneous town in the Midwest, I had much to learn about the larger historical and cultural context of the lives of my older Jewish clients. One source of information was the client herself. Years later, another older Jewish woman born in Europe prefaced a discussion of her early life history by gently asking, "Have you heard of the Holocaust?" This 75-year-old woman was a survivor of a concentration camp and wanted me to understand that this was part of her experience. The Holocaust question shocked me as I realized that she had dealt with people who were unfamiliar with the Holocaust. What was more troubling was that she thought it possible that she might need to educate a health care provider at a Jewish-titled institution about the Holocaust. Nonetheless, she wanted me to understand that she was not seeing a psychotherapist to discuss at length her experience during the Holocaust but rather to better deal with the practical and emotional repercussions of caring for her husband with Alzheimer's disease—which she referred to as "the second Holocaust."

"I Guess You Noticed I'm Black"

How are ethnic or minority service providers perceived by White older clients? An African American psychology intern in her mid-20s whom I supervised began to conduct psychotherapy with a man in his 70s for the treatment of depression triggered by an increasing number of health problems. The intern mentioned that the older client persisted with telling stories about "Negro fellas" in the army during World War II. The emphasis of the stories was usually on how much he liked his Black comrades and the contributions that they made to the army. When asked how she handled this issue, the intern reported she said to the older client, "I guess you noticed I'm Black." This statement led to a productive discussion of a variety of concerns that included worry that he might say something racially related that would offend the intern and concern about whether a Black service provider could understand his experience. At times, during intakes into our geriatric clinic, a prospective client will frankly state, "I'd like a White doctor" or "I want a Jewish doctor." Clinical geropsychologists sometimes have noted that some majority older adults will make disparaging racial or ethnic remarks rarely made by younger adults. In part, open expression of these remarks reflects the reality that the current generation of older adults grew into adulthood during a time when racial and ethnic segregation were government and institution sanctioned and that it was socially acceptable in some circles to publicly and unfavorably caricature racial or ethnic minorities.

"These Are White-Person Questions"

As part of a research study of similarities and differences between Black and White persons caring for a relative with dementia, we asked a series of questions about how individuals chose to cope with the stresses of caregiving (Hinrichsen & Ramirez, 1992). In the course of administering the study instrument, an older Black man remarked to the young Puerto Rican interviewer, "These are White-person questions. I don't choose what I will do. My choices are limited. I just do what I have to do." His remark underscored a number of issues.

1. The interviewer thought that the Black man could speak frankly about "White persons" because she herself was an ethnic minority.
2. Because of a history of discrimination, many minority persons learned in early adulthood that their choices were, in fact, limited. Limited choice in early life is reflected in a diminished sense of control and mastery in later life for minority older people relative to majority older people (Jang, Borenstein-Graves, Haley, Small, & Mortimer, 2003).
3. The questions that we asked study participants were designed by White, well-educated individuals who assumed a shared understanding of language and concepts, including use of Likert-formatted items, to gain information. Convening a focus group of Black older adults prior to undertaking data collection would have been productive. We could have drawn on the focus-group participants to help frame questions and design instruments that made better sense to our older Black study participants. Guideline 4 of APA's multicultural guidelines (APA, 2003) addresses this issue: "Culturally sensitive psychological researchers are encouraged to recognize the importance of conducting culture-centered and ethical psychological research among persons from ethnic, linguistic, and racial minority backgrounds" (p. 388).

Similar assessment issues exist in conducting clinical evaluations of ethnic and minority older adults. One issue arose during the course of a clinical assessment of a 78-year-old woman who had emigrated from India to the United States within the last 5 years. The Indian woman told the interviewer that she looked forward to death. Concerned that the woman may be expressing suicidal ideation, the psychologist invited her middle-aged son to join in the assessment interview. Her son seemed surprised that we thought his mother might be suicidal. When we explained the source of our concern, he said that his mother's thoughts about death reflected her deeply held Hindu beliefs that she had come to the end of her life cycle and that in Indian culture, death was more frankly discussed than it was in Western culture. Her son explained that her welcoming of death also reflected her conviction that she had been a devout Hindu and, as a result, after death she would be reincarnated into a better life.

A clinical assessment issue that my colleagues and I have noted is that some minority older adults perform less well than majority older adults do on cognitive screening instruments such as the Mini-Mental State Exam. At first, these lower screening scores in older minority persons were puzzling, given that subsequent and more thorough evaluations did not reveal the presence of dementia. Research has, in fact, documented that older adults with less education may not perform as well as more educated older adults on such instruments (Crum, Anthony, Bassett, & Folstein, 1993). Some geropsychologists have expressed concern that some widely used neuropsychological instruments do not have norms for older adults much less norms for subgroups of ethnic and minority older adults. Gerontologists have been critical of the assumption that cross-sectional age differences on measures of intellectual functioning are an age effect (Schaie, 1994). On average, older adults' performance on intelligence tests has been found to be lower than that of younger adults. Some concluded this was because the process of aging progressively impaired intellect (i.e., an age effect). In fact, older adults, as a group, have had less access to educational opportunities in early life compared with younger persons and, as a result, in later life perform less well (i.e., a cohort effect).

"Forgive Him, for He Knows Not What He Does"

Several years ago, I was counseling a 68-year-old Jewish woman who was providing care to her 78-year-old husband with advanced Parkinson's disease. Over a period of 10 years, her husband became physically debilitated and cognitively impaired and now required a home health aide. She had recently hired a Caribbean-born Black woman in her early 20s to care for her husband. The aide was a devout Christian woman. Much to my client's consternation, the home health aide made efforts to convert the client from Judaism to Christianity. Things took a turn for the worse when her husband began to call the aide by racial epithets. My client was alarmed by her husband's behavior, cognizant that the aide would be offended by such remarks, and increasingly concerned about leaving her husband alone with the aide. In what I consider a highly skillful way of handling a terribly complicated issue, the client explained to the aide that her husband had dementia and, as a result, would say things that he did not mean. Appealing to the aide's strongly held Christian beliefs, she said, "You know when your Jesus was dying on the cross, he turned his eyes to Heaven and said, 'Forgive them, for they know not what they do.' Would you forgive my husband, for 'he knows not what he does'?" The aide gladly agreed to forgive the husband and made efforts to provide more loving care to him. Shortly thereafter, the husband stopped making disparaging racial remarks.

Race and aging come into play in late life in a way that is not always so evident. Particularly in large urban areas, White older Americans with significant health problems are often cared for by young racially or culturally different home or nursing-home–based health aides. At the most vulnerable time in their lives, some older adults find themselves being cared for in the most direct and intimate way possible by individuals quite different from themselves. Aides are usually poorly paid and may be contending with economic uncertainty and the stresses of living in a new country. Sharp economic differences exist between some older clients and their aides. This potentially volatile mix is rarely addressed openly by institutions or service providers. For older adults, the issue may be manifested in concerns raised about aides. I have heard older clients who receive services at home complain that minority aides "don't understand me," "have children with several men," "don't know how to clean a house," are "irresponsible," "don't really speak English," or are "not real Americans." I have also heard some older clients use racist language. Students new to work with older adults express surprise and dismay that on occasion, their older clients use racial or ethnic caricatures that are rarely publicly uttered by younger persons. One older man said he did not like to watch TV because "there are too many Negroes on those programs." I remind students that older White Americans grew up in a highly racially divided society in which minority groups were viewed unfavorably.

"We Take Care of Elderly in Our Country"

Even majority older adults increasingly find that medical care providers are culturally different from themselves. Growing numbers of foreign medical school graduates have entered the field of psychiatry, and many of them were raised in other countries or cultures. At the Zucker Hillside Hospital, I run a gerontology seminar that, over the years, has included foreign-born psychiatrists who are specializing in geriatric psychiatry. Given widespread misinformation about older adults, one of my chief goals in the seminar is to familiarize all seminar attendees with what is normative about older Americans as well as the great diversity in late life. In discussions about the relationship between older adults and their adult children, remarks from foreign medical school graduates sometimes include "Unlike you, we take care of the elderly in our country." Such remarks are an especially good opportunity to explore cultural differences in relationships between older adults and their adult children. Professionals from other cultures sometimes see older adults living apart from their adult children and the presence of nursing homes in the United States as evidence of lack of concern about older people by their families. Typically, students come to understand that different patterns of relationships between older adults and their families reflect historical, cultural, and economic differences among cultures. Some foreign-born psychiatrists experience being perceived as "the other" by older clients. One foreign-born psychiatrist was annoyed that clients often ask, "Where are you from?" Another expressed frustration that older clients had difficulty understanding what was said because of her accented English. A Pakistani psychiatrist of the Islamic faith sensed that some Jewish clients were uncomfortable with her because of her religion. Some foreign-born mental health care professionals can benefit from efforts to enhance their knowledge and cultural sensitivity to both majority and minority older Americans.

"So I Put on a Suit and Said I Was a Consultant"

I asked an older, retired psychologist friend whether he felt that he was treated differently because of age. He replied in the affirmative. He fell he was treated with less interest and respect by members of his community and also by the medical profession. He found that when he identified himself as a retiree, health care providers were more likely to attribute medical problems to age and not to follow up on the problems with the same vigor as they did before he retired. I asked him what he did about this state of affairs. He responded, "Well, before a medical appointment, I'd put on a suit, bring a briefcase, and tell the doctor I was a consultant." As noted earlier, many older adults experience subtle or not-so-subtle evidence of ageism. Cuddy and Fiske (2002) referred to the "doddering but dear" and "pitied but not respected" nature of ageism. Evidence indicates that in fact, older adults are perceived and treated differently than younger persons are by many groups, including health professionals (Cuddy & Fiske, 2002). As a whole, are older adults a minority group? Pasupathi and Lockenhoff (2002) noted that this issue was addressed by the United States Supreme Court in connection with a case in which the issue under debate was whether older adults deserved protections from discrimination. The Court said they did not in the same way as racial and ethnic minorities did, because most everyone will become old. Nonetheless, it is poignant that majority Americans who live to old age will experience some version of age-based minority group status. To my knowledge, no studies have examined how age prejudice is shaped on the basis of racial or ethnic minority status of the older adult.

What Has Been Done to Address Multicultural Aging?

It is notable that APA's *Guidelines for Providers of Psychological Services to Ethnic, Linguistic, and Culturally Diverse Populations* (APA, 1990) make no mention of aging issues as they bear on race and ethnicity, although other statuses (i.e., gender, sexual orientation) are discussed. This lacuna seems striking given that the majority of older adults are women (of those who reach the age of 85 years, two thirds are women) and that some have characterized aging as a women's issue (Huyck, 1990). In the past, some geropsychologists have privately complained that although APA emphasized the importance of diversity in the delivery of services to children, youth, and younger adults, the old seemed to have been left out of the diversity mosaic. The multicultural guidelines (APA, 2003) incorporate an explicit acknowledgment of age as a factor that may interact with race and ethnicity and therefore is relevant to the delivery of psychological services. By the same token, geropsychologists have been slow to develop research paradigms and models for the delivery of psychological services to racial and ethnic minorities. Noteworthy accomplishments in this area include those of the Gerontological Society of America (GSA). GSA is primarily an organization of research and policy professionals in the field of aging. GSA's Task Force on Minority Issues has made ongoing and substantive efforts to understand, address, and enlarge research studies related to late-life minorities (GSA, Task Force on Minority Issues in Psychology, 1994; Miles, 1999). Published research literature on racial and ethnic minority elders has grown considerably in the last 10 years. The American Society on Aging, a practice-focused professional organization, has done an exemplary job of highlighting issues related to practice with ethnic and minority aging—efforts that are especially evident in its many training workshops. Further, a variety of initiatives have been undertaken to enlarge the number of racial and ethnic minority researchers.

APA's "Guidelines for Psychological Practice With Older Adults" (APA, 2004) address diversity issues in Guideline 5: "Psychologists strive to understand diversity in the aging process, particularly how sociocultural factors such as gender, ethnicity, socioeconomic status, sexual orientation, disability status, and urban/rural residence may influence the experience and expression of health and of psychological problems in later life" (p. 242). A related document was produced by the Veteran's Administration Technical Advisory Group in Geropsychology (TAGG), which developed "Recommendations About the Knowledge and Skills Required of Psychologists Working With Older Adults" (Molinari et al., 2003). TAGG's special ethical issues recommendations encompass the topic of incorporating diversity factors. Recommendations are made for two levels of practice. Level 1 is knowledge and skills for those who see older adults in general clinical practice. Level 2 is for advanced clinical knowledge and experience with older adults. Recommendations for Level 1 psychologists include "The psychologist incorporates cultural, ethnic, and religious factors into his or her geriatric assessments, case conceptualizations, and treatment plans" (Molinari et al., 2003, p. 441). Recommendations for Level 2 psychologists include "The psychologist serves as an expert consultant in considering cultural, ethnic, and religious factors related to geriatric mental health. For example, she or he consults with the local Alzheimer Association on improving the participation of minority caregivers in family support group meetings" (Molinari et al., 2003, p. 441).

A recent and notable effort to explicitly incorporate race and ethnicity into a clinical study is the Resources for Enhancing Alzheimer Caregivers Health (REACH) project. REACH is a multisite clinical research program for family members caring for older adults with Alzheimer's disease. This large study tailored its caregiver support intervention program to be culturally sensitive to issues for African Americans, Cuban Americans, and Mexican Americans (Gallagher-Thompson et al., 2003).

As noted earlier, in urban areas, majority older adults often receive supportive services from minority and foreign-born health aides. The conventional wisdom has been that better care could be provided to older adults residing in nursing homes by educating aides about issues and problems in caring for the aged. In innovative work, Nanette Kramer, Michael Smith, and their colleagues at the Cobble Hill Nursing Home in Brooklyn, New York, looked to the aides as experts in care of frail older people and sought their insights on how optimal care could be provided. Kramer, Smith, Dabney, and Yang-Lewis compiled these perspectives in the publication *Speaking From Experience* (1997), which is accompanied by beautiful photographs of primarily ethnic and minority aides providing care to frail older nursing-home residents. One informal goal of their work was to enhance the dignity and morale in this group of service workers who are often underpaid, underappreciated, and underrecognized for their efforts to care for America's most fragile citizens. A companion training kit, *Working Together: Nursing Assistants Help One Another Manage Stress in Nursing Homes* (n.d.) was also developed. The training kit includes guidance to nursing aides on how to contend with racism and stereotyping on the job.

An especially impressive effort to enhance sensitivity to and education about cultural issues is by the Stanford Geriatric Education Center. The center offers minifellowships in ethnogeriatric education and printed and online educational resources that include a training curriculum in ethnogeriatrics and a compilation of monographs, books, articles, book chapters, research articles, audiovisual materials, journals, newsletters, and Web sites related to ethnogeriatrics. This information may be accessed through http://sgec.stanford.edu/resources.

What Can Be Done to Enhance Multicultural Competence With the Aged?

Learn More

For those who provide psychological services to older adults, it is useful to gain familiarity with multicultural and diversity issues that are relevant to older adults. APA's multicultural guidelines (APA, 2003) are a good starting place for thinking about the general issues that inform clinical practice with all age groups, including the aged. Several excellent textbooks provide an overview of what is known about racial and ethnic diversity among the aged. For those who work with specific racial and ethnic minority aged, it is especially useful to understand the larger historical, cultural, economic, social, and political forces that may have influenced and continue to influence their clients' lives. The Stanford Geriatric Education Center's Web site has well-developed modules on different groups of minority and ethnic aged that will sensitize practitioners to relevant issues. Recommended readings on multicultural issues and aging are listed at the end of this article (see the Appendix).

Teach More

For those who teach or clinically supervise graduate students, discussion of minority and ethnic aging can be interwoven into the existing curricula and supervisory sessions. Because gerontologists historically have been attentive to the heterogeneity of the older population, blending the topics of racial and ethnic diversity into gerontology courses and seminars should be relatively easy. Similarly, clinical geropsychologists who are supervising graduate psychology students often raise transference and countertransference issues that sometimes arise between younger therapists and older clients. As students are often asked to understand that, as a group, older people may have perspectives and values that derive from earlier historical and socialization experiences that differ from younger persons, they can also be asked to grapple with how cohort issues may be mediated by race and ethnicity. If racial and ethnic differences exist between a client and a student therapist, the supervisor can explore whether these differences come into play in the therapeutic relationship. The student can also be encouraged to be attentive to issues of race and ethnicity that may be of concern to the older adult.

Talk More

Topics of race and ethnicity tend to be avoided in daily life and also in professional life. Psychologists can broach a discussion of race, ethnicity, and aging with colleagues who provide services to older adults (Comas-Diaz & Jacobsen, 1991). This discussion can include both perceptions of racial and ethnic minority aged and also majority older adults' perceptions of racial and ethnic minority staff. My experience has been that although staff may initially be hesitant to engage in this discussion, they usually welcome a sensitive and supportive dialogue about race, ethnicity, and aging. When racial and ethnic client–therapist differences are directly raised or hinted at by older adults, pursue them in the clinical conversation. If older adults themselves raise concerns about those racially or ethnically different from themselves, explore those concerns. The psychologist's role is not to challenge or change older adults' racial and ethnic views but rather to try to understand what may underlie them. As noted, some older adults with health problems who need care are uncomfortable with minority health aides because older adults are concerned that aides will not understand their problems; hold values different from their own that may affect care: or will take offense to something they may say, adversely affecting their relationship with the aide.

Appendix

Recommended Readings

American Psychological Association. (2004). Guidelines for psychological practice with older adults. *American Psychologist, 59,* 236–260.

American Psychological Association Working Group on the Older Adult. (1998). What practitioners should know about working with older adults. *Professional Psychology: Research and Practice, 29,* 413–427.

Comas-Diaz, L., & Jacobsen, F. M. (1991). Ethnocultural transference and countertransference in the therapeutic dyad. *American Journal of Orthopsychiatry, 61,* 392–402.

Fried, S., & Mehotra, C. (1998). *Aging and diversity: An active learning experience.* Washington, DC: Taylor & Francis.

Haley, W. E., Han, B., & Henderson, J. N. (1998). Aging and ethnicity: Issues in clinical practice. *Journal of Clinical Psychology in Medical Settings, 5,* 393–409.

He, W. (2002). *The older foreign-born population of the United States: 2000* (U.S. Census Bureau Current Population Reports, Series P. 23–211). Washington, DC: U.S. Government Printing Office.

Wieland, D., Benton, D., Kramer, B., & Dawson, G. (Eds.). (1994). *Cultural diversity and geriatric care: Challenges to the health professions.* New York: Haworth Press.

References

American Psychological Association. (1990). *Guidelines for providers of psychological services to ethnic, linguistic, and culturally diverse populations.* Washington, DC: Author.

American Psychological Association. (2003). *Guidelines on multicultural education, training, research, practice, and organizational change for psychologists.* American Psychologist, *58,* 377–402.

American Psychological Association. (2004). Guidelines for psychological practice with older adults. *American Psychologist, 59,* 236–260.

American Psychological Association Working Group on the Older Adult. (1998). What practitioners should know about working with older adults. *Professional Psychology: Research and Practice, 29,* 413–427.

Author (2005, January). Don't forget us: How to save Social Security for the next generation. *AARP Bulletin, 46,* p. 1.

Butler, R. (1975). *Why survive? Being old in America.* New York: Harper & Row.

Comas-Diaz. L., & Jacobsen, F. M. (1991). Ethnocultural transference and countertransference in the therapeutic dyad. *American Journal of Orthopsychiatry, 61,* 392–402.

Crum, R. M., Anthony, J. C., Bassett, S. S., & Folstein, M. F. (1993, May 12). Population-based norms for the Mini-Mental State Examination by age and educational level. *Journal of the American Medical Association, 269,* 2386–2391.

Cuddy, A. J. C., & Fiske, S. T. (2002). Doddering but dear: Process, content, and function in stereotyping of older persons. In Todd D. Nelson (Ed.), *Ageism: Stereotyping and prejudice against older persons* (pp. 3–26). Cambridge, MA: MIT Press.

Dowd, J. J., & Bengtson, V. L. (1978). Aging in minority populations: An examination of the double jeopardy hypothesis. *Journal of Gerontology, 33,* 427–436.

Federal Interagency Forum on Aging-Related Statistics. (2000). *Older Americans 2000: Key indicators of well-being.* Washington, DC: U.S. Government Printing Office.

Gallagher-Thompson, D., Haley, W., Guy. D., Rupert, M., Arguelles, T., Zeiss, L. M., et al. (2003). Tailoring psychological interventions for ethnically diverse dementia caregivers. *Clinical Psychology: Science and Practice, 10,* 423–438.

Genevay, B., & Katz, R. S. (Eds.). (1990). *Countertransference and older adults.* Newbury Park, CA: Sage.

Gerontological Society of America, Task Force on Minority Issues in Gerontology. (1994). *Minority elders: Five goals toward building a public policy base.* Washington, DC: Author.

He, W. (2002). *The older foreign-born population of the United States: 2000* (U.S. Census Bureau Current Population Reports, Series P23–211). Washington, DC: U.S. Government Printing Office.

Hinrichsen, G. A., & Ramirez, M. (1992). Black and White dementia caregivers: A comparison of their adaptation, adjustment, and service utilization. *Gerontologist, 32,* 375–381.

Huyck, M. H. (1990). Gender differences in aging. In J. E. Birren & K. W. Schaie (Eds.), *Handbook of the psychology of aging* (3rd ed., pp. 124–132). San Diego, CA: Academic Press.

Jang, Y., Borenstein-Graves, A., Haley, W., Small, B. J., & Mortimer, J. A. (2003). Determinants of a sense of mastery in African American and White older adults. *Journals of Gerontology: Series B. Psychological Sciences and Social Sciences, 58B,* 221–224.

Kimmel. D. C. (2002). Aging and sexual orientation. In B. E. Jones & M. J. Hill (Eds.), *Mental health issues in lesbian, gay, bisexual, and transgender communities* (pp. 17–36). Washington DC: American Psychiatric Publishing.

Knight, B. G. (2004). *Psychotherapy with older adults* (3rd ed.). New York: Sage.

Kogan, N. (1961). Attitudes toward old people: The development of a scale and an examination of correlates. *Journal of Abnormal and Social Psychology, 62,* 44–54.

Kramer, N. A., & Smith, M. C. (n.d.). *Working together: Nursing assistants help one another manage stress in the workplace* [Training kit]. Brooklyn, NY: Sephardic Nursing and Rehabilitation Center. Available from http://www.sephardichome.org

Kramer, N., Smith, M., Dabney, J., & Yang-Lewis, T. (1997). *Speaking from experience: Nursing assistants share their knowledge of dementia care.* Brooklyn, NY: Cobble Hill Health Center.

Miles, T. P. (Ed.). (1999), *Full-color aging: Facts, goals, and recommendations for America's diverse elders.* Washington, DC: Gerontological Society of America.

Molinari, V., Karel, M., Jones, S., Zeiss, A., Cooley, S. G., Wray, L., et al. (2003). Recommendations about the knowledge and skills required of psychologists working with older adults. *Professional Psychology: Research and Practice, 34,* 435–443.

Pasupathi M., & Lockenhoff, C. (2002). Ageist behavior. In T. D. Nelson (Ed.). *Ageism: Stereotyping and prejudice against older persons* (pp. 201–246). Cambridge, MA: MIT Press.

Schaie, K. W. (1994). The course of adult intellectual development. *American Psychologist, 49,* 304–313.

24

Revisiting Gender Issues in Multicultural Counseling

L. Sunny Hansen
Elizabeth M. P. Gama
Amy K. Harkins

Although the field of multicultural counseling is more than 25 years old, it is significant that, until the past decade, few researchers or authors had attempted to link gender and counseling across cultures, domestic or international. Gender as a factor often has been neglected or ignored; when acknowledged, it has been commonly treated stereotypically. An extensive body of literature exists on multicultural counseling, cross-cultural counseling, and counseling with women or feminist therapy, but few researchers have integrated culture into feminist therapy or gender into cross-cultural counseling. In much of the counseling literature, culture is generally considered to be synonymous with race or ethnicity. Other possible cultural, contextual, and personal dimensions, such as gender, religion, social class, disability, sexual orientation, and age, although increasingly recognized, often are addressed apart from culture and are all too often ignored even in textbooks specifically addressing multicultural issues.

It is our purpose in this chapter to address the gender dimension in counseling by (a) discussing the interconnectedness of gender and culture, (b) noting the historical and global perspectives on this link, (c) presenting a review of the multicultural and feminist literature, and (d) offering some strategies and suggestions for the areas of counseling, academia, research, and systems interventions. Although we recognize that cross-cultural and multicultural counseling have different origins and research traditions, we use the terms *cross-cultural* and *multicultural* interchangeably. We make a case for a more explicit and integrated link between gender issues in multicultural counseling and cultural issues in feminist therapy.

Constructs That Link Gender and Culture

Whereas some authors argue for a narrow definition of culture (e.g., Locke, 1990), limiting it primarily to race and ethnicity, others support broader, more inclusive definitions that include gender. Fukuyama (1990), for example, suggests a universal or transcultural approach that stresses "the inclusiveness of a wide variety of variables that constitute cultural diversity" (p. 7). Our position is that a broad concept of culture is necessary to explain the present-day reality of most social systems. Within a broad definition of culture, one that conceptualizes culture as "socially shared aspects of experience and knowledge" (Draguns, 1989, p. 3), a dimension such as gender is more than just a demographic variable, as the psychological literature traditionally suggests. Along with race and class, it is one of the salient dimensions of culture.

Gender vs. Sex: Socialization vs. Biology

Ettner (1996) asserts that "gender is the most misunderstood subject of our times" (p. 19). Even though sex differences are biologically determined, children have no gender at birth. Gender is not a natural and inevitable outgrowth of sex. Rather, gender is a social construction; it is "learned and achieved at the interactional level, reified at the cultural level, and institutionally enforced via the family, law, religion, politics, economy, medicine, and the media" (Gagne, Tewksbury, & McGaughey, 1997, p. 479). Social experiences, which are loaded with culturally shaped content regarding what ought to be male and female, give people their genders and associate them with a world of men and a world of women. These worlds have distinctions and similarities. Each is a complex social system with specific norms, traditions, belief systems, and socialization procedures that constitutes a culture of its own, and yet both belong to other cultural dimensions, each of which is unique and all of which overlap.

Gender differences are enculturated in young children through the process of differential socialization. On the basis of minimal biological differences in sex organs and hormones, average size and weight, all national and racial/ethnic cultures have subtle and subliminal ways of imposing their gender role ideologies. Weber (1998) asserts that in Western culture,

> dominant groups define race, gender, and sexuality as ranked dichotomies, where Whites, men, and heterosexuals are deemed superior. Dominant groups justify these hierarchies by claiming that the rankings are a part of the design of nature—not the design of those in power. Subordinate groups resist the binary categories, the rankings associated with them, and the biological rationales used to justify them. (p. 18)

It is precisely because gender is learned that we believe it is possible for people to unlearn, on both individual and societal levels, those dimensions of gender that are limiting, maladaptive, or harmful.

Gender Role Ideology and Stereotyping

Gender role ideology varies somewhat across countries and is patterned after cultural factors. Usually, the residents of developed countries, where comparatively larger numbers of women are employed and in college, have more egalitarian beliefs than do residents of less developed countries, in which women are seen from a more traditional perspective (Williams & Best, 1990). Despite this variation in normative beliefs about what women and men *should* be like, there is an impressive agreement across cultures about what women and men *are* like, leading some authors to suggest that gender stereotyping may be universal (Berry, Poortinga, Segall, & Dasen, 1992).

Despite linguistic, religious, economic, and social differences among the many countries of the world, the process of reproducing the ideology of male superiority from generation to generation and thus perpetuating inequality between the sexes has been remarkably successful. Perhaps the most extensive cross-cultural study concerning gender roles to date is the international investigation conducted by Williams and Best (1982). In their adult study, a total of 2,800 university students (from 28 countries) responded to a 300-item adjective checklist describing psychological characteristics of persons. Each respondent had to judge, for each adjective, whether it was related more to men or to women in his or her country.

Although within-country results showed extensive differentiation in views about gender roles, there was an impressive consensus across countries. Among more than two-thirds of the respondents and at least 20 of the countries, some of the adjectives chosen to describe males were *active, adventurous, aggressive, ambitious, arrogant, assertive, autocratic, clear thinking, courageous, cruel, daring, determined, disorderly, dominant, energetic, enterprising, hardhearted, independent, taking initiative, inventive, logical, rational, realistic, robust, self-confident, strong,* and *wise*. By the same criteria, some of the adjectives used to describe women were *affected, affectionate, attractive, charming, curious, dependent, dreamy, emotional, fearful, gentle, mild, sensitive, sentimental, sexy, softhearted, submissive, superstitious, talkative,* and *weak*. Note that many of the stereotypes associated with women have negative meanings, whereas those associated with men are more positive.

The remarkable similarity across cultures that Williams and Best (1982) found in the university student sample was also shown in a second study (reported in the same book) they conducted with children of two age groups—5–6 years old and 8–9 years old—in 24 countries. The descriptions of male and female were quite similar to the stereotypes evidenced with the adult samples. By age 5 there was already gender stereotyping, and this increased at age 8, when children associated even more of the 32 items with either males or females. Comparisons among countries showed greater similarity in the older age group, leading Williams and Best to conclude that the older children's additional years of experience in their individual cultures had led to greater similarity rather than greater diversity—"a testament to the pancultural similarity in the traits ascribed to women and men" (p. 204).

Williams and Best's (1982) research and the work of Broverman, Broverman, Clarkson, Rosenkrantz, and Vogel (1975) are good examples of series of studies that have found similar results in the stereotypes associated with males and with females. In general, the descriptions can be organized into two dimensions: competency-rationality-assertion and warmth-expressiveness. Men are typically seen as possessing the competency cluster of traits, whereas women personify warmth-expressiveness. Once again, masculine stereotypes are considered more desirable than feminine ones (Broverman, Vogel, Broverman, Clarkson, & Rosenkrantz, 1972).

Despite the fact that no consistent evidence has been found on the presumed differences between males and females in levels of competitiveness, dominance, nurturance, suggestibility, sociability, activity, self-esteem, compliance, analytic ability, anxiety, and achievement motivation (Maccoby & Jacklin, 1974), beliefs about differences between men and women persist in the literature and across cultures. Breakwell (1990) calls such stereotypes "the fulcrum of the social belief system about gender differences" and states that they persist because they serve the valuable purpose of "reify[ing] the gulf between the sexes" (p. 214).

It is important that mental health professionals consider the damaging effects of differential gender role socialization and the subsequent social and cultural pressures for gender conformity as well as sex discrimination. The pressures that individuals may experience in attempting to fulfill particular gender stereotypes, the conflicts that can be generated by the presence of diverse role models or discrepant perceptions concerning what one is and what one should be, can certainly produce psychological distress. It has been suggested that many of the problems women experience stem from their acceptance of a lower-status role stereotype and their conformity to that predetermined image. Similarly, men's problems often result from their lack of success in attaining the high-status, strong, competent, and self-confident male role. With failure, their self-image suffers, and they often deal with the problem in dysfunctional ways (Davenport & Yurich, 1991). Both O'Neil (1981) and Skovholt (1990) point out how men are limited by their socialization. O'Neil describes a masculine mystique in Western cultures that consists of expectations of success and achievement that result in male gender role strain, causing heart disease, emphysema, inability to express emotions, pressures to succeed in a career, and premature death. Skovholt also identifies the restricted emotionality to which boys and men are exposed and describes what he calls "the 180-degree role conflict," in which men are socialized for aggression, violence, and war and then are expected to do a complete reversal and be nurturing and loving husbands and fathers.

Furthermore, the cost of nonconformity to socially deemed gender-appropriate behavior based upon biological sex categories can also be severe. For those whose gender falls somewhere between or outside the gender binary system of maleness/femaleness, the challenge to understand and accept themselves comes with great struggle, and typically they suffer the added trauma of being stigmatized, ostracized, and socially delegitimated or even "erased." The tragedy of Brandon Teena's murder, as depicted in the 1999 Academy Award-winning film *Boys Don't Cry* (directed by Kimberly Peirce), illustrates the high price that may be paid for gender nonconformity.

Instrumentalism and Relationship

With regard to women, feminist writers have criticized traditional psychological theories based on the masculine and individualist model of development. Chodorow (1974) and Gilligan (1982) have both argued that female and male personalities are basically different. On the basis of psychoanalytic theory, Chodorow has proposed a new model of personality development, particularly of gender role acquisition. She argues that male and female differences exist because "women, universally, are largely responsible for early child care and for (at least) later feminine socialization" (p. 43). She further proposes that "in any given society, feminine personality comes to define itself in relation and in connection to other people more than masculine personality does" (p. 44). The female child, being similar to the mother, can develop her gender identity and move into adulthood without rejecting primitive identification with the mother. Because a girl has the opportunity to be around her mother and have a feminine relationship with her, "a girl's gender and gender role identification are mediated by and depend upon real affective relations" (p. 51). A boy's identity formation, on the other hand, involves negation of the relationship with the mother as well as repression and devaluation of all that is feminine so that the boy is able to define himself as different. Consequently, male sex role development implies a stronger pull toward individuation and separation, which males believe is essential for asserting their identity as men.

Gilligan (1982) argues that "the silence of women in the narrative of adult development distorts the conception of its stages and sequence" (p. 156). Her studies, impressive but controversial, attempted to fill in the missing description of women's development, accepted the theory proposed by Chodorow, and investigated the consequences of differential development on the concept of morality among men and women. Her findings show that men's morality and women's morality are based on two different ideologies—an ethic of rights that supports separation and an ethic of care that is associated with attachment. Men's "morality of rights" emphasizes separation, equality, and fairness between claims of others and self, whereas women's "morality of responsibility" emphasizes equity, recognition of differences in need, empathy, and care. In that sense, the psychological logic of relationships and care that underlies women's decisions contrasts with the formal logic of fairness on which the judicial system is based. Gilligan concludes that a woman's sense of self is defined around relationships and care, whereas "power and separation secure the man in an identity achieved through work but leave him at a distance from others" (p. 163).

Some psychologists and social critics have challenged Gilligan's and other feminists' emphasis on sex differences. Hare-Mustin and Marecek (1990), with their social constructivist view of gender, suggest that too much emphasis has been put on sex differences, resulting in an overemphasis on dualistic thinking and dichotomies of masculine and feminine. They argue that although it is true that over time gender roles have been dichotomized in numerous ways, it is time to move beyond the "construction of gender" to deconstruction and then reconstruction of a new way of describing human behavior. Pollitt (1992) makes a similar point when she states that feminists need to move away from what she calls "difference feminism" (emphasizing differences between women and men—e.g., women as caring, men as autonomous) toward "gender feminism," in which both sexes are potentially androgynous. Perpetuating sex difference stereotypes, she argues, ignores the contextual realities of women's lives—including their socioeconomic status—and tends to maintain the status quo. Gilligan has also been criticized for focusing in her work on White middle- and upper-class females and not including girls and women of color (Flansburg, 1993), although her more recent research has been more inclusive.

Heterogeneity and Connectedness

Although it may be the goal of a particular research study to define differences or seek out similarities, it is important to remember that at the individual level, both differences and similarities exist. Comas-Diaz and Greene (1994) point out some of the commonalities and disparities among women of color, White women, and men of color and emphasize both the heterogeneity and connectedness of these groups. Weber (1998) asserts that upon consideration, "most of us occupy both dominant and subordinate positions and experience both advantage and disadvantage in these hierarchies," and concludes that "there are no pure oppressors or oppressed in our society" (p. 24). It is important to remember that if one is to understand another person's experience, one must both appreciate multiplicity and consider how that person's gender, ethnicity, and other social identities interact (Russo, 1998). No one person is either completely like or unlike another person.

Historical and Global Perspectives

Despite the overwhelming similarities across cultures in gender stereotyping, the history of humanity shows variation in issues of inequality and domination across cultures. Eisler (1987) and Lerner (1986) have studied cultures over time and borders. A quick excursion into the field of archaeology, anthropology, history, or women's studies will reveal past times in which women and men were equal partners in the struggles of life, or when women were revered as goddesses. Historian Gerda Lerner (1986), who spent 8 years conducting field research in Mesopotamia, cites the matrilineal and egalitarian nature of early civilizations. She argues that because patriarchy, built on the subordination of women, was a system created later in time, it is also a system that can be changed or eliminated over time.

The myth of male superiority has been perpetuated in religious documents, in textbooks, in the media, in the scientific world, and in daily commonsense psychology. Sigmund Freud described man as the prototype of humanity, described women's development by using a theory based on the development of men, and regarded females as incomplete and as having a weakened superego (Doherty, 1973). Gender role stereotypes have been found to permeate the helping professions, as Broverman et al. (1975) discovered and more recent replications of their work have clearly shown. These revealed a double standard in the definitions of mental health for men and women. Although the concept of the mentally healthy man was no different from the concept of the mentally healthy individual, a significant difference was found between the concept of the mentally healthy adult and the concept of the mentally healthy woman. In other words, a mentally healthy woman was not, by psychological definition, a mentally healthy individual.

Although much more change is needed, the women's movement in the 20th century accomplished much in many countries—from women's right to vote to their right to make choices about their own bodies. Yet there are still cultures in which women are circumcised (U.N. Population Fund, 2000) or forced to marry against their will, and physical and sexual abuse of women and children seems to be common everywhere (Abu-Lughod, 1981). In a discussion of the relationships between women and men in Arab cultures, Abu-Lughod (1981) observes that assumptions that arrangements concerning procreation, child rearing, and division of labor will not change tend to perpetuate the status quo. Male power, she argues, derives from wealth, property, children, and knowledge; when women are no longer considered property, are more free from physical force, have fewer children, and gain knowledge through literacy and education, they will have a greater part in defining their reality, and change will occur. Although the levels of female subordination and abuse vary from culture to culture, gender inequality is still a universal social fact (and a social shame).

In recent years there has been growing recognition of the global nature of women's issues and gender issues across cultures. To underscore the importance of sociocultural context and transnational issues, the U.N. Commission on the Status of Women organized its 1995 conference, held in Beijing, around themes of women's health and violence toward women. In 1993, global outrage over ethnic cleansing and rape of women as part of it helped lead to the acceptance of women's rights as human rights. However, since the fall of the Berlin Wall, the breakup of the former Soviet Union, and other boundary shifting, women in several Eastern European countries have been negatively affected, experiencing higher unemployment rates and less reproductive freedom. More recently, the abusive treatment of women in Afghanistan has brought outrage across cultures and illustrates once again the difficulty of achieving human rights for women. In the 1980s, several nations, including the United States, signed the Convention to Eliminate All Forms of Discrimination Against Women (CEDAW), including violence (United Nations, 1983). By 1999, 162 nations had ratified the agreement, but the United States was not one of them (International Women's Rights Action Watch, 2000).

Organizations such as the Council of Europe, which is based in Brussels, have promoted equality for women and men for many years. In Western Europe in particular, the focus has been on "the equal status of women and men," in Scandinavia called *Likestilling.* A 1992 conference on "equality between women and men in a changing Europe," held in Poland by the Council of Europe in 1992, recognized the many issues resulting from the shifting boundaries, particularly movement from central to free-market economies. One point of agreement among conferees was that equality between women and men is crucial for democracy and the realization of human rights (Hansen, 1997). In addition, the U.N. Population Fund recently released a report titled *The State of the World Population 2000: Lives Together, Worlds Apart: Men and Women in a Time of Change*" (2000). The report examines the impact of gender inequality and systematic discrimination against women and girls on both women and men, and shows an inextricable link between gender inequality and world problems such as poverty, ill health, and overpopulation. The report advocates for partnership between women and men, between governments and civilians, and between rich and poor nations to end gender-based discrimination and violence. This global context is important to the development of women and men of all backgrounds, and transnational networks of men and women are being formed to address issues of human rights, violence, and equality.

As Weber (1998) notes, it is important to remember that

> race, class, gender, and sexuality are contextual. Although they persist throughout history, race, class, gender, and sexuality hierarchies are never static and fixed, but constantly undergo change as part of new economic, political, and ideological processes, trends, and events. Their meanings vary not only across historical time periods, but also across nations and regions during the same period. (p. 16)

Kimmel (2000) makes some very promising predictions for the future of what he calls "the gendered society." He believes that women and men will become not more similar but rather more equal, so that both men and women will be allowed to claim traits that enable them to live the lives they want to live, thereby displaying "a temperamental and psychological flexibility, the ability to adapt to one's environment with a full range of emotions and abilities. . . . Such a transformation does not require that men and women become more like each other, but rather more deeply and fully themselves" (p. 268).

Critique of the Literature

By far the greatest criticism of both feminist and multicultural counseling has been about who is and who is not included in the literature. Much of the literature has ignored or minimized gender or focused on a single dimension, topic, or group (e.g., counseling Latinos, counseling Native American women, Black racial/ethnic identity, psychotherapy with Asian Americans). In so doing, it often has missed the heterogeneity within all cultural groups, including the factors of gender, disability, age, and sexual orientation. Similarly, the literature concerning the counseling of women and feminist therapy has depended heavily on research with White women, as if White women's experience represents a universal norm. Madden and Hyde (1998a) point out that "when women are represented, they tend to be White; when ethnic minorities are represented, they tend to be male," and that "women of color are still invisible in [general] psychology textbooks" (p. 5).

Just as early counseling texts and theories were written mostly by Euro-American men and were assumed to be applicable to women and other groups, current multicultural texts and models, with some notable exceptions, have been written primarily by cultural minority men. (Some of the exceptions are books authored or edited by Pinderhughes, 1989; Helms, 1990; and, more recently, Lee, 1999; and Robinson & Howard-Hamilton, 2000.) Even as women in general and women of color in particular become more visible, it is important to look further into who holds the decision-making power when it comes to grant allocations and acceptance of work for publication. Hall and Greene (1996) encourage us to consider whose values are represented in the psychological literature and to question who may benefit and who may be harmed by them.

Critiques of the Multicultural Literature

Much of the multicultural literature stresses the importance of "worldviews," or how individuals view themselves in their worlds. Many recent models draw from Kluckhohn and Strodtbeck's (1961) grid of different cultural perceptions of human nature, nature, social relationships, time, and activity. Although multiple personal dimensions of identity gain increased recognition in the more recent models, gender is not a central topic in many of them. Some cross-cultural and multicultural researchers, however, do provide fuller and less stereotypical descriptions of gender; for example, Sue and Morishima (1982) observe that there are within-group differences among Asian American women, such as among women of Chinese, Japanese, and Filipino heritage.

Cross (1971), Helms (1984), Atkinson, Morten, and Sue (1989), and Sue and Sue (1999) have introduced the concept of racial identity development—both Black and White—but apart from the dimension of gender. Gender may not be the primary identity for members of cultural groups whose major oppression has been racial/ethnic, but all human beings have gender identities that may add to their subordination in a dominant White society. Because sexism affects both men and women, it is important to recognize the impact of being female or male within a given culture. The multidimensionality and interconnected nature of race, class, gender, and sexual hierarchies are especially visible to those who face oppression along more than one dimension of inequality (Weber, 1998). For example, a poor Latina, a gay African American male, or a disabled Native American female may face double or even triple barriers in a classist, sexist, and racist society. Being an invisible minority—for example, a White gay man or lesbian—carries an additional kind of distress in a homophobic society.

Several authors in the multicultural literature have described gender socialization in patriarchal cultures in which daughters have less freedom and are less valued than sons and women are expected to be submissive to men (Locke, 1992; McGoldrick, Pearce, & Giordano, 1982). Arredondo, Psalti, and Cella (1993) point out that these characteristics may change depending on rates of acculturation and changes in the larger society: For example, among Latinos, greater egalitarianism may occur as families attain middle-class status (Axelson, 1985). Arredondo et al. cite several authors whose works include historical references to women's development, providing a meaningful context for sociocultural understanding (Jordan, 1991; Sage, 1991). They conclude that "there is need to attend to women's individual differences within and across cultural groups; to the interaction of cultural and gender socialization; to forces of sexism, racism, and homophobia and their impact on identity, esteem, and empowerment; and to the portrayals of women in the multicultural counseling literature" (p. 5).

Critiques of the Feminist Literature

Feminist psychology and therapy and gender studies also have been criticized for their lack of attention to women (and men) of color. Reid and Kelly (1994), in their review of research on women of color, charge that psychological research deals with such women as anomalies, and that the search for the "universal woman" (usually meaning White and middle-class or upper-middle-class) has resulted in the omission or invisibility of women of color both as subjects of research and as researchers. Women of color (especially African American women and Latinas) are more likely to be participants in investigations of "atypical or non-mainstream behavior," such as the receipt of welfare, teen pregnancy, homelessness, and criminality. Reid and Kelly also call for reexamination of and new perspectives on how women of color are and should be depicted, describing a transition from a deficit and deviance model to the portrayal of women of color as enactors, enablers, and survivors. On the other hand, they note that in studies of gender and ethnicity, White women should be included, and that the implications of being White and female should not be protected from scrutiny. Among multicultural activists, some movement has occurred in recent years to include Euro-American women (and men) along with the four major ethnic minority groups.

Greene (1994) points out the complexities of issues within given cultural groups and emphasizes the strengths of women in diverse cultures. She confronts the impacts of sexism and racism on women of color and points out the "adaptive" and resourceful strategies these women employ. She notes, for example:

> Each generation of African Americans, usually but not exclusively parenting figures or family members, prepares the next generation for the challenge of being African American in a society that devalues them. African American mothers face a range of unique challenges in socializing their daughters to make psychological sense out of the racist and sexist messages they receive on a routine basis. . . . African American women have made healthy adjustments that are neither deniable nor accidental. Their psychological flexibility is often a reflection of an active socialization process that takes place within their families and communities to prepare its members to confront institutional barriers. (p. 23)

Despite her criticisms of feminist psychology, Espin (1994) asserts that feminist therapy, which acknowledges the impact of social forces on mental health, is uniquely suited to the needs of women of color. By her definition, feminist therapy is more than just "nonsexist therapy"—it involves challenges to authoritarian, patriarchal approaches to psychotherapy and the demonstration of commitment to feminist values. Espin suggests that women of color need growth experiences in addition to therapy; she emphasizes the need for experiences of empowerment, choice, and active social action.

Feminist psychology is also engaged in reconceptualizing gender and culture. The contributions to a 1994 special issue of *Psychology of Women Quarterly* identify six themes and several focal issues that appear to fit the etic or universal approach to transforming theory and research on women (Worell & Etaugh, 1994). Although issues of power, violence, and empowerment of women emerge in the discussion, it is interesting that none of the contributors explicitly addresses culture or women of color except as subpoints. Notice the intersection between the feminist themes addressed in this special issue and some of the themes identified in multicultural counseling:

1. Challenges to the tenets of traditional scientific inquiry
2. A focus on the experience and lives of women
3. A view of power relations as the basis of patriarchal political social arrangements
4. Recognition of gender as an essential category of analysis
5. Attention to the use of language and the power to "name"
6. Promotion of social activism toward the goal of societal change

Landrine (1995) has edited a scholarly indigenous treatise titled *Bringing Cultural Diversity to Feminist Psychology.* A product of a task force created by the Psychology of Women Division of the American Psychological Association (Division 35), the volume was created to integrate the voices of women of color into feminist psychological thinking. The voices are from diverse cultures, including Euro-American cultures, and the contributors convey the important message that culture is also "us," not only "them." Landrine sees "contextual behaviorism" as a useful theoretical framework for linking cultural diversity and feminist psychology.

Integration of Gender and Ethnicity in the Literature

Although both the multicultural and the feminist literatures address "the presence of absence" (absence of gender from the multicultural literature, absence of women of color from the feminist literature), both appear to be moving in the direction of greater multidimensionality and inclusivity in counseling/therapy and in research. Comas-Diaz (1994) and Arredondo et al. (1993) call for an integrative and comprehensive approach to the provision of effective mental health treatment for women of color. They characterize such an approach as one that reconciles psychotherapeutic process with the dual and multiple group memberships of women of color; addresses the effects of minority group membership; acknowledges the confluence of the therapist's and the client's realities; combines traditional psychotherapeutic models with gender, sociocultural, and ethnoracial contexts; and gives critical consideration to experiences of racism, sexism, identity, conflict, oppression, cultural adaptation, and environmental stressors, plus the "internalized colonization" specific to many women of color.

A few recent publications by and about women of color and an expanded view of multiculturalism have begun to integrate gender and ethnicity and other long-overlooked issues into the "mainstream" counseling literature. Wanda Lee (1999), using a broad definition of multicultural counseling in a combined concepts and "groups" approach, includes in her book *An Introduction to Multicultural Counseling* chapters on counseling women, counseling men, and counseling gay men and lesbians. Tracy Robinson and Mary Howard-Hamilton (2000), two African American women, emphasize the convergence of multiple identities, especially race, ethnicity, and gender. Robinson's model on discourses suggests that human characteristics (such as race, sex, sexual orientation, class, and physical disability) operate as status variables in society and that culture-based attitudes about differences evolve within horizontal and hierarchical value systems, resulting in oppressive social consequences (such as racism, sexism, and classism).

Another recent contribution, the second edition of the *Handbook of Multicultural Counseling*, edited by Ponterotto, Casas, Suzuki, and Alexander (2001), is both comprehensive and integrative, to a certain extent. It presents multicultural counseling primarily from a perspective of identities and topics rather than a specific "groups approach." It goes beyond the first edition of the same title by including a section headed "The Intersection of Identities" in which contributors address "sexual orientation in multicultural counseling" and the "interface of feminism and multiculturalism." One of the most innovative parts of this handbook is the introductory section, in which 12 pioneers in multicultural counseling, 6 men and 6 women from diverse racial/ethnic backgrounds, tell their life stories. Most of the women describe the impacts of both culture and gender on their lives. Although the handbook's editors have made an effort to reflect in this second edition a somewhat expanded definition of multiculturalism, they do not include all of the personal dimensions of identity, such as disability and social class. Nonetheless, this volume represents a more inclusive view of multiculturalism and multicultural counseling than did the first edition.

Russo and Dabul (1994), in discussing the dynamic interactions among diversity, feminism, and psychology, make the important point that although feminist psychologists may differ in their definitions of feminism, their explanations of inequalities, and their goals or strategies for prevention and intervention, they have a shared purpose of searching for knowledge that can lead to sociopolitical and personal change and can contribute to the empowerment of women. Russo and Dabul challenge theories that presume essential differences between men and women and assume permanence and resistance to change. They observe that many feminists in the past have not declared questions of power and White patriarchal control primary. Diversity, they assert, must be central to understanding women's lives.

One of the most comprehensive books to address gender and ethnicity is Comas-Diaz and Greene's edited volume *Women of Color: Integrating Ethnic and Gender Identities in Psychotherapy* (1994). Focusing on the interaction of gender and ethnicity in mental health, the contributors to *Women of Color* discuss how cultural relevance and gender sensitivity must be incorporated into therapy with African American, American Indian, Asian and Asian American, Latina, and other populations of women, including professional women of color, lesbians of color, women of color in battering relationships, mixed-race women, and immigrant women.

Arredondo et al. (1993) advocate telling women's stories as presented in the literature about women from specific cultural groups, such as *The Joy Luck Club*, by Amy Tan (1989); *La Chicana*, by Alfredo Mirande and Evangelina Enriquez (1979); and *The Color Purple*, by Alice Walker (1982). They view these narratives as important types of literature that represent unique cultural backgrounds, are written from relatively nonstereotypical contexts, and are truer to women's socialization and development than many other forms of literature.

An emerging and exciting avenue for storytelling has found a creative outlet in narrative therapy. The focus of this form of therapy is on strength and mental health rather than on pathology; the goal is not only to help clients tell their own personal stories but to help them "find strategies for resisting the internalization of negative cultural messages" (Semmler & Williams, 2000, p. 52). By reauthoring negative stories, counselor and client can "deconstruct" cultural narratives that result in feelings of depression, guilt, or anxiety. Semmler and Williams (2000) argue that "piecing together fragments of healing life experiences into new, healing narratives in which clients experience themselves as competent protagonists in their own stories of strength can be empowering indeed" (p. 61). It may be true that "we are as many potential selves as the stories we create" (Lee, 1997, p. 6).

Respect for Cultural Traditions and Moral Dilemmas

We now turn to an issue we believe to be very important to the reconceptualization of gender and multicultural counseling: the generalized idea that all culture-specific behaviors, belief systems, customs, values, and traditions are morally correct and that, therefore, counselors must respect them. The issue of moral relativism is certainly complex. Can people from one culture understand and judge with empathy, fairness, and validity the customs of another culture? Are moral principles universal or culture specific?

With regard to women, we believe that certain practices and their associated values, although traditional or common among certain cultural groups, are morally wrong. For example, we call attention to various forms of abuse to which girls and women are subjected, such as their sale for marriage or prostitution, male domination and consequent wife abuse, polygamy, restriction of liberty, inhuman treatment and torture, and genital mutilation and clitoral circumcision. According to the U.N. Population Fund (2000), approximately 130 million girls and young women worldwide have undergone the painful and dangerous practice of female genital mutilation, and an additional 2 million are at risk each year.

The underlying assumptions that allow such practices to continue are that women are inferior, incompetent to make decisions and run their own lives, and emotionally unstable, and that their sexuality is evil. Obviously, such assumptions can have devastating effects on anyone's perception of self. Whether these assumptions are expressed physically, psychologically, or economically, they prevail in situations in which the dominant group abuses other groups. They represent absence of respect for human freedom and dignity. Furthermore, these are often situations in which the women themselves do not agree with the practices, and in which they are unwilling victims of an unjust social order. Regardless of cultural traditions, such practices indicate prejudice, discrimination, exploitation, and violence, and they need to be condemned. They are practices in which "it is less the case that societies differ morally, and more that some societies (ours included) are involved explicitly in immoral practices" (Kahn, 1993, p. 15). The point is that cultural specificity is no guarantee that certain assumptions, traditions, or behaviors are right when judged in the light of larger human values.

Strategies for Gender-Aware Multicultural Counseling

The following is a summary of selected strategies that we believe might help to bridge the gap between omissions of gender and other dimensions of personal identity in multicultural counseling and omissions of culture in much of traditional counseling and the feminist literature. We include suggestions regarding the counseling of individuals, suggestions for systems interventions, and some ideas for future gender and multicultural research.

Suggestions Concerning Counseling With Individuals

The counseling competencies developed by the Association for Multicultural Counseling and Development have been widely disseminated to the divisions of the American Counseling Association and to professionals involved in counselor training. These competencies include the knowledge, attitudes, and skills that are considered important for counselors who work with diverse populations to possess (Arredondo et al., 1996). Counselors need to include gender as a factor in cross-cultural counseling, and, when addressing gender, they need to do the following: avoid stereotypical treatment; understand that gender role stereotypes are pervasive, that they are reinforced by socialization, and that they erect barriers to the full development of both women and men, especially women and men of color; and be aware of both transference and countertransference in connection with ethnocultural and gender factors (Comas-Diaz & Jacobsen, 1995).

The following knowledge and skills are also required:

- Counselors must be able to help clients of all backgrounds to become more aware of their own racial/ethnic identities (including White racial identity), as well as their gender identities, and the strengths associated with these identities.
- Counselors must be able to help clients of all ethnic backgrounds to assess their multiple identities. (Although members of oppressed populations may cite race/ethnicity as the primary source of their oppression, other identities, such as being female, gay, lesbian, bisexual, disabled, or of a certain religious faith, may be more important at different times in the life cycle.)
- Counselors must become agents of change and try to reduce the barriers of racism, sexism, classism, and other isms that limit the full development of human beings. (They need to be proactive in seeking to reduce violence against women in all its forms—rape, sexual abuse, battering, sexual harassment, emotional abuse, and other forms of power over women—as well as hate crimes against men.)
- Counselors must understand the concept of "White privilege," the unearned privilege that many White people take for granted, as well as other prejudices and biases they might hold toward underserved groups (McIntosh, 1989).
- Counselors must recognize that gender is socially constructed and based on presumed differences between women and men. (They need to be careful about perpetuating stereotypes and maintaining the status quo through overemphasizing gender differences, such as conceptions of women as nurturing and men as autonomous.)
- Counselors need to make use of historical and cultural contexts in attempting to understand diverse cultures, and they need to recognize the heterogeneity of all groups.
- Counselors must be aware of abusive traditions, their underlying ideological assumptions, and their social psychological implications; they must also be aware of the social psychological implications for clients in the event these traditions are challenged. (Even though counselors may understand how morally wrong cultural traditions, values, attitudes, and beliefs are historically constructed, they should neither accept nor recommend that their clients accept and submit to them in the name of cultural differentness or adaptation. However, they must be extremely careful when challenging deeply accepted traditions, so as not to cause breakdowns in communication with clients or jeopardize clients' well-being.)
- Counselors must be able to identify, create, and employ techniques that are appropriate for use with clients from diverse populations. For example, counselors might use strategies of narrative and storytelling to help people of color in particular understand

their heritage and strengths, or they might employ Brown's (1986) gender role analysis technique to obtain more complete pictures of their clients and to help their clients gain more complete pictures of themselves.

- Counselors must become definers of the fields of multicultural and cross-cultural counseling, reframing language and taking care not to label women or men of any culture. (This is especially important for multiethnic and female counselors and researchers.)
- Counselors must recognize that the scientist-practitioner model of training that characterizes most counselor training programs is not sufficient and needs to be expanded to include a third counseling role: that of advocate. Counseling multicultural persons often requires counselors to undertake advocacy (Fassinger, 1998).

Counseling for empowerment should be a goal of all counseling, but especially of counseling with those who have been oppressed and outside of the opportunity structure: gays, lesbians, and bisexuals; people with disabilities; members of racial, ethnic, and religious minority groups; the elderly; low-income persons; and others who have suffered oppression in some way. McWhirter (1994) provides an excellent definition of empowerment in counseling:

> Empowerment is the process by which people, organizations, or groups who are powerless or marginalized a) become aware of the power dynamics at work in their life context, b) develop the skills and capacity for gaining some control over their lives, c) which they exercise, d) without infringing on the rights of others, and e) which coincides with actively supporting the empowerment of others in their community. (p. 12)

Challenges to Academia

In 1998, a special issue of *Psychology of Women Quarterly* featured contributions by feminist authors who addressed the goals and challenges of teaching about gender and ethnicity (Madden & Hyde, 1998b). Although the focus of this issue is undergraduate psychology courses, the information is valuable to all of academia. In an opening editorial in the issue, Russo (1998) notes, "In teaching about diversity, it is important to distinguish between understanding diversity and cataloguing difference" (p. ii). This indeed is a challenge when the subject of diversity is infinite and the teaching term is finite (and only one course in multicultural counseling is available). Madden and Hyde (1998a) suggest two approaches to this problem: (a) Convince the members of the academic psychology community that the issues of gender and ethnicity are so important that they must give up other favorite topics to cover them, or (b) find ways to permeate the discussion of topics within other courses with an understanding of the impacts that gender and ethnicity have on those topics. Each method clearly has advantages and disadvantages.

In an earlier article, Russo and Dabul (1994) offer three ways in which scholars can integrate a feminist perspective into theory and methods of psychology to empower women in all their diversity: (a) Create opportunities for the employment of diverse feminist scholars in academic institutions, where knowledge is created and transmitted; (b) acknowledge women's history in psychology; and (c) resist the use of psychology as a tool "to justify a sexist and racist status quo" (p. 95). Hall and Greene (1996) concur: "The heightened visibility of academic and clinical psychologists, who come from diverse backgrounds themselves, facilitates a growing mandate to dislodge psychology's androcentric, Euro-centric and heterocentric foci from their dominant position" (p. 5). Although this is encouraging, Hall and Greene caution us not to overlook the fact that White males still control much of the decision-making power in the areas of publishing, grant allocations, and other funding.

Suggestions for Research

Although research in multicultural counseling psychology has been very rich in the past few years, in most cases the dimensions of race, ethnicity, gender, social class, and national culture have been analyzed alone. Even research with women often ignores the wide diversity within that sex and disregards other important cultural dimensions, as if women constitute a monolithic group. As Reid and Comas-Diaz (1990a) comment, "Gender research typically fails to include race/ethnic concerns, and . . . studies of ethnic groups often ignore gender issues" (p. 397).

Researchers' neglect in reporting sample characteristics as well as differences and similarities between and among sample populations places serious limitations on the generalizability of their results. It is critical that researchers state clearly how gender, apart from demographic sex categories, is determined in their studies; they must also describe their procedures for inclusion of individuals of any racial or ethnic group, including White participants. And researchers must be specific about their participants. For example, a researcher's statement that the subject of a study is Latina girls may not provide readers with enough information to know whether the results can be generalized to the broad population of Latina girls or whether they are limited to a specific subpopulation of Latina girls. Additionally, participant responses to one forced-choice demographic question regarding sex (asking respondents to choose male or female) on a survey do not provide enough information for anyone to make assumptions about gender—that is, maleness or femaleness. It is time to recognize that we often make an "erroneous assumption that gender will be congruent with sex" (Gagne et al., 1997, p. 503).

Moreover, counseling research must be expanded to consider gender characteristics in combination with other cultural dimensions. The failure to investigate these combined impacts on identity and behavior may create the illusion of homogeneity within each cultural dimension and further contribute to the use of distorted information in theory construction. Two particular efforts that have been made in the direction of such integrative research are worth mentioning. These are a 1990 special issue of *Sex Roles* on gender and ethnicity, edited by Reid and Comas-Diaz (1990b), and a 1993 issue of *Psychology of Women Quarterly* on gender and culture, edited by Unger and Sanchez-Hucles (1993).

The Influence of Positivist Thinking

In psychological research, the pursuit of scientific rigor and universal generalization has been dominated by the positivist/empiricist tradition and has often led investigators to design "tight" and "clean" studies. But the excessive concern with "cleanness" has often produced sterile results that are difficult to generalize, especially in a global and diverse world such as ours. Russo and Dabul (1994) question women's adoption of a scientific method based on reductionism and measures and techniques that are both reductionist and constructed from an androcentric perspective. This approach has had serious implications for psychological research as the pursuit of universal truth and general laws of human behavior often has been conducted at the expense of knowledge concerning race, ethnicity, gender, and social class, and the sociohistorical contingency of action, values, beliefs, attitudes, and motives has been ignored (Gama, 1992).

Positivist principles, such as objectivity, neutrality, replicability, causality, validity, and reliability, are the foundations of quantitative research methods and a dominant model of knowledge construction. Lately, these principles have been subjected to much criticism, and various authors have called for the adoption of alternative research paradigms of greater relevance to the study of men and women (Gama, 1992; Guba & Lincoln, 1994). Both editions of the now-classic *Handbook of Qualitative Research* (Denzin & Lincoln, 1994, 2000) synthesize various qualitative paradigms and strategies for doing such research, and each includes a very informative chapter on feminist approaches. Fortunately, the last decade of the 20th century witnessed in mainstream journals a visible increase in and acceptance of qualitative research, especially with women and multicultural populations. Hall and Greene (1996) point out that the prevailing values of publishers still tend to challenge gender/cultural research. Reports on qualitative research, research that focuses on women of color without comparison to Whites, and research that focuses on sameness rather than difference are not as highly valued as are reports on other kinds of studies.

Even though the quantitative method is rooted in the positivist/empiricist tradition, it does not need to continue under the tyranny of these epistemological assumptions. In research on issues of gender and culture, the most fruitful and enriching approach would be a combination of both qualitative and quantitative methods of observation; this would allow researchers to capture fully the richness of cultural diversity without losing what is universal and common to all individuals.

Suggestions for Systems Interventions

Counselors need to be taught not just skills for changing individuals but strategies for systems interventions and program development aimed at changing institutions as well. This is an important part of the advocacy role and that of the counselor as change agent. As Weber (1998) clearly states, counselors should recognize the "interdependence of knowledge and activism" (p. 13). Counselors need to be involved in the creation of programs designed to address such issues as sexual harassment, school and community safety, violence prevention, and multicultural, gender-fair education (WEEA Equity Resource Center, 2000); programs aimed at reducing stereotyping based on race and gender, such as BORN FREE (Build Options, Reassess Norms, and Free Roles through Educational Equity; Hansen, 1980, 1997); programs for students with disabilities; programs such as the Black, Indian, Hispanic, and Asian Women in Action program (Lindgren, 1991); programs to promote the development of courses on Asian American women and their identity issues (Ibrahim, 1992); programs that address identity development from culture and gender perspectives (Ibrahim, Cameron, & Cheatham, 1992); and programs for boys and adolescent males (Horne & Kiselica, 1999) as well as for girls and young women (Hansen, Walker, & Flom, 1995).

Although racial and gender equity interventions in the United States were diminished in the 1980s, counselors need to be proactive in supporting and implementing policies that enhance all kinds of diversity in their institutions and in the larger society. Institutions need to recognize that in multicultural matters, the personal is political, and they need to be ready to change to meet the needs of increasingly diverse populations.

Multiculturalism, in its broad definition, needs to be incorporated into all parts of counseling psychology programs, including the development and integration of multicultural curricula, the addition of faculty members from diverse groups, and the use of race- and gender-fair texts, instructional materials, and media. Counselors in preparation and counselor education faculty need to become aware of their own multiple identities, biases, and attitudes about difference.

Conclusion

The importance of the incorporation of gender and cultural factors in all of psychology cannot be overstated. The review of the literature presented above indicates that increased attention is being given to gender as a factor in multicultural counseling. Much of this attention is being provided by feminists and women of color, with lesser evidence that men are "owning the problem" or recognizing it to the same degree as are women professionals. Although the incorporation of gender and culture is essential, Weber (1998) encourages us to question whether gender and race determine how people should act out some notion of biological or social imperative. We should consider, too, whether seeing gender and race as immutable facts of people's lives either privileges them or relegates them to certain inferiority. If we keep these issues in mind, we will not overlook the political impacts of social constructions of gender and culture on counseling, academics, research, and social activism.

Although the literature attests that progress has been made in research that addresses issues of gender and culture, counselors and counselors in training, as well as counselor educators, still need to attend to the gender dimension in multicultural counseling.

Topics for Further Discussion

1. How are ways in which issues of gender and culture are addressed in counseling today similar to or different from the ways in which these issues were approached 10–15 years ago?
2. How does a counselor help a client to understand the importance of his or her gender in relation to other aspects of personal identity (e.g., race, ethnicity, disability, sexual orientation, socioeconomic class)?
3. What are the arguments regarding the value of a broad versus a narrow approach to defining culture? Why is this question important?
4. Identify four issues related to gender role socialization and stereotyping. What does research say about these issues across cultures? Why are they important in multicultural counseling?
5. Ask one of your male friends to give you 10 adjectives that he believes best describe what American women are like. Then, ask a female friend to give you 10 adjectives that she believes best describe what American men are like. Compare the two lists. How are they similar? How are they different? To what degree are your friends' descriptions of the opposite sex stereotypical?
6. When we look at gender issues across cultures, what can we say with confidence about the status of women, especially given recent reports from the United Nations, the U.N. Population Fund, and the Council of Europe?
7. Consider Gilligan's (1982) conclusions regarding the morality of men and women. Examine your own standards and patterns. Where do you stand when it comes to making moral judgments? How is your sense of self similar to or different from that described by Gilligan?
8. In what ways are issues of gender and culture seen as "women's issues"? What evidence is there that men in counseling and multiculturalism are beginning to "own the problem" of gender as part of multicultural counseling?
9. There is much discussion, especially in Western cultures, that because patriarchy, which was built on the subordination of women, was created at a time in history, it

can also be eliminated over time. What is your reaction to this point of view? Is patriarchy a characteristic only of Western cultures?

10. How relevant is feminist therapy to women of color? What have been the sources of conflict between women of color and feminists? What has helped counselors and psychologists to recognize the convergence of gender, race, and culture?
11. On what issues do you think you might experience conflict in deciding when it is appropriate to be culturally respectful and when it is important to make judgments about cultural practices based upon your own worldview? What steps might you take to reconcile your conflict?
12. What impacts do a counselor's cultural and gender identities have on his or her counseling relationships? Consider both positive and negative implications.
13. Describe a counseling strategy or question that could be used to assess a client's awareness of his or her cultural identity.
14. What thoughts do you have about gender roles? Are the useful? Are they harmful? Are they based in biology, socialization, or both? How might a counselor's perceptions about gender roles affect his or her counseling relationships?
15. How can a counselor become a client advocate? What might be some barriers to a counselor's empowerment of clients who come from groups that have been traditionally oppressed?
16. Do you accept the argument there are times when gender issues transcend culture? What are some of the universal issues concerning which superordinate values should prevail?
17. Respect for cultural traditions is taught in most counseling and human relations classes. What examples can you give of traditions that many would consider morally wrong? What are the origins of such traditions?
18. Western psychologists and the "men's movement" have pointed out issues facing men and boys today—issues such as the male stereotype that requires men to be strong, lack of emotionality, problems with writing, and problems regarding aggression and intimacy. What additional issues can you identify? Are these just Western issues or do they also apply across cultures?
19. If you were to engage in discussion with some international students in your university, what would you expect to learn about gender roles in their cultures? Why?
20. How can gender and cultural issues be integrated into an academic program?
21. What are some systems intervention programs in your counseling community? Are there any that specifically address gender- or culture-related issues?
22. Imagine a future in which gender and cultural factors do not result in social hierarchies and power inequities. Is such a future possible? What do you see as the future role of research, academic programs, and counseling in relation to gender and culture issues?

References

Abu-Lughod, J. (1981). The relations between men and women: A comparative perspective. *Arab Journal for the Humanities, 1,* 363–378.

Arredondo, P., Psalti, A., & Cella, K. (1993). The woman factor in multicultural counseling. *Counseling and Human Development, 25,* 1–8.

Arredondo, P., Toporek, R., Brown, S., Jones, J., Locke, D. C., Sanchez, J., & Stadler, H. (1996). *Operationalization of the multicultural counseling competencies.* Washington, DC: Association for Multicultural Counseling and Development.

Atkinson, D. R., Morten, G., & Sue, D. W. (1989). A minority identity development model. In D. R. Atkinson, G. Morten, & D. W. Sue (Eds.), *Counseling American minorities: A cross-cultural perspective* (3rd ed., pp. 35–52). Dubuque, IA: William C. Brown.

Axelson, J. A. (1985). *Counseling and development in a multicultural society.* Monterey, CA: Brooks/Cole.

Berry, J. W., Poortinga, Y. H., Segall, M. H., & Dasen, P. R. (1992). *Cross-cultural psychology: Research and applications.* New York: Cambridge University Press.

Breakwell, G. M. (1990). Social beliefs about gender differences. In C. Fraser & G. Gaskell (Eds.), *The social psychological study of widespread beliefs* (pp. 210–225). Oxford: Clarendon.

Broverman, I. K., Broverman, D. M., Clarkson, F. E., Rosenkrantz, P. S., & Vogel, S. (1975). Sex role stereotypes and clinical judgments of mental health. In R. K. Unger & F. L. Denmark (Eds.), *Woman: Dependent or independent variable?* (pp. 164–176). New York: Psychological Dimension.

Broverman, I. K., Vogel, S. R., Broverman, D. M., Clarkson, F. E., & Rosenkrantz, P. S. (1972). Sex-role stereotypes: A current appraisal. *Journal of Social Issues, 28*(2), 59–78.

Brown, L. S. (1986). Gender-role analysis: A neglected component of psychological assessment. *Psychotherapy, 23,* 243–248.

Chodorow, N. (1974). Family structure and feminine personality. In M. Z. Rosaldo & L. Lamphere (Eds.), *Woman, culture and society* (pp. 43–66). Stanford, CA: Stanford University Press.

Comas-Diaz, L. (1994). An integrative approach. In L. Comas-Diaz & B. Greene (Eds.), *Women of color: Integrating ethnic and gender identities in psychotherapy* (pp. 287–318). New York: Guilford.

Comas-Diaz, L., & Greene, B. (1994). Overview: An ethnocultural mosaic. In L. Comas-Diaz & B. Greene (Eds.), *Women of color: Integrating ethnic and gender identities in psychotherapy* (pp. 3–9). New York: Guilford.

Comas-Diaz, L., & Jacobsen, F. M. (1995). Psychopharmacology for women of color: An empowering approach. *Women and Therapy, 16*(1), 85–112.

Cross, W. E., Jr. (1971). The Negro-to-Black conversion experience: Towards a psychology of Black liberation. *Black World, 20,* 13–27.

Davenport, D. S., & Yurich, J. M. (1991). Multicultural gender issues. *Journal of Counseling and Development, 70,* 64–71.

Denzin, N. K., & Lincoln, Y. S. (Eds.). (1994). *Handbook of qualitative research.* Thousand Oaks, CA: Sage.

Denzin, N. K., & Lincoln, Y. S. (Eds.). (2000). *Handbook of qualitative research* (2nd ed.). Thousand Oaks, CA: Sage.

Doherty, M. A. (1973). Sexual bias in personality theory. *Counseling Psychologist, 4,* 67–74.

Draguns, J. G. (1989). Dilemmas and choices in cross-cultural counseling: The universal versus the culturally distinctive. In P. B. Pedersen, J. G. Draguns, W. J. Lonner, & J. E. Trimble (Eds.), *Counseling across cultures* (3rd ed., pp. 3–21). Honolulu: University of Hawaii Press.

Eisler, R. (1987). *The chalice and the blade.* San Francisco: Harper & Row.

Espin, O. (1994). Feminist approaches. In L. Comas-Diaz & B. Greene (Eds.), *Women of color: Integrating ethnic and gender identities in psychotherapy* (pp. 265–286). New York: Guilford.

Ettner, R. (1996). *Confessions of a gender defender.* Evanston, IL: Chicago Spectrum.

Fassinger, R. (1998, August). *Gender as a contextual factor in career services delivery: A modest proposal.* Paper presented at the annual meeting of the American Psychological Association, San Francisco.

Flansburg, S. (1993). *Building self: Adolescent girls and self-esteem.* Newton, MA: Center for Equity and Cultural Diversity, Education Development Center.

Fukuyama, M. A. (1990). Taking a universal approach in multicultural counseling. *Counselor Education and Supervision, 30,* 6–17.

Gagne, P., Tewksbury, R., & McGaughey, D. (1997). Coming out and crossing over: Identity formation and proclamation in a transgender community. *Gender & Society, 11,* 478–508.

Gama, E. M. P. (1992). Toward science-practice integration: Qualitative research in counseling psychology. *Counseling and Human Development, 25,* 1–12.

Gilligan, C. (1982). *In a different voice: Psychological theory and women's development.* Cambridge, MA: Harvard University Press.

Greene, B. (1994). African American women. In L. Comas-Diaz & B. Greene (Eds.), *Women of color: Integrating ethnic and gender identities in psychotherapy* (pp. 10–29). New York: Guilford.

Guba, E. G., & Lincoln, Y. S. (1994). Competing paradigms in qualitative research. In N. K. Denzin & Y. S. Lincoln (Eds.), *Handbook of qualitative research* (pp. 105–117). Thousand Oaks, CA: Sage.

Hall, R. L., & Greene, B. (1996). Sins of omission and commission: Women, psychotherapy, and the psychological literature. *Women and Therapy, 18*(1), 5–31.

Hansen, L. S. (1980). *BORN FREE: Training packets to reduce career-related sex-role stereotyping.* Palo Alto, CA: American Institutes for Research.

Hansen, L. S. (1997). *Integrative life planning: Critical tasks for career development and changing life patterns.* San Francisco: Jossey-Bass.

Hansen, L. S., Walker, J. A., & Flom, B. L. (1995). *Growing smart: What's working for girls in schools.* Washington, DC: American Association of University Women.

Hare-Mustin, R. T., & Marecek, J. (1990). On making a difference. In R. T. Hare-Mustin & J. Marecek (Eds.), *Making a difference: Psychology and the construction of gender* (pp. 1–21). New Haven, CT: Yale University Press.

Helms, J. E. (1984). Toward a theoretical explanation of the effects of race on counseling: A Black and White model. *Counseling Psychologist, 12,* 153–165.

Helms, J. E. (Ed.). (1990). *Black and White racial identity: Theory, research, and practice.* Westport, CT: Greenwood.

Horne, A., & Kiselica, M. (Eds.). (1999). *Handbook of counseling boys and adolescent males.* Thousand Oaks, CA: Sage.

Ibrahim, F. A. (1992). A course on Asian-American women: Identity development issues. *Women's Studies Quarterly, 20*(1–2), 41–58.

Ibrahim, F. A., Cameron, S. C., & Cheatham, H. (1992, March). Identity development from a culture and gender perspective. In F. A. Ibrahim (Chair), *Teaching multicultural counseling.* Symposium conducted at the annual meeting of the American Association for Counseling and Development, Baltimore.

International Women's Rights Action Watch. (2000). *About IWRAW and the convention.* Minneapolis: Author. Retrieved from http://www.igc.org/iwraw/about/overview

Jordan, J. M. (1991). Counseling African American women: "Sister-friends." In C. C. Lee & B. L. Richardson (Eds.), *Multicultural issues in counseling: New approaches to diversity* (pp. 51–64). Alexandria, VA: American Counseling Association.

Kahn, P. H., Jr. (1993, March). *A culturally sensitive analysis of culture in the context of context: When is enough enough?* Paper presented at the biennial meeting of the Society for Research in Child Development, New Orleans.

Kimmel, M. S. (2000). *The gendered society.* New York: Oxford University Press.

Kluckhohn, F. R., & Strodtbeck, F. L. (1961). *Variations in value orientations.* Evanston, IL: Row, Patterson.

Landrine, H. (Ed.). (1995). *Bringing cultural diversity to feminist psychology: Theory, research, and practice.* Washington, DC: American Psychological Association.

Lee, J. (1997). Women re-authoring their lives through feminist narrative therapy. *Women and Therapy, 20*(3), 1–23.

Lee, W. M. L. (1999). *An introduction to multicultural counseling.* Philadelphia: Taylor & Francis.

Lerner, G. (1986). *The creation of patriarchy.* New York: Oxford University Press.

Lindgren, A. (1991, Fall). BIHA serves women of color. *Minnesota Women's Fund News,* pp. 1–3.

Locke, D. C. (1990). A not so provincial view of multicultural counseling. *Counselor Education and Supervision, 30,* 18–25.

Locke, D. C. (1992). *Increasing multicultural understanding: A comprehensive model.* Newbury Park, CA: Sage.

Maccoby, E. E., & Jacklin, C. N. (1974). *The psychology of sex differences.* Stanford, CA: Stanford University Press.

Madden, M. E., & Hyde, J. S. (1998a). Integrating gender and ethnicity into psychology courses. *Psychology of Women Quarterly, 22,* 1–12.

Madden, M. E., & Hyde, J. S. (Eds.). (1998b). Integrating gender and ethnicity into psychology courses [Special issue]. *Psychology of Women Quarterly, 22*(1).

McGoldrick, M., Pearce, J. K., & Giordano, J. (Eds.). (1982). *Ethnicity and family therapy.* New York: Guilford.

McIntosh, P. (1989, July/August). White privilege: Unpacking the invisible knapsack. *Peace and Freedom,* pp. 10–12.

McWhirter, E. H. (1994). *Counseling for empowerment.* Alexandria, VA: American Counseling Association.

Mirande, A., & Enriquez, E. (1979). *La Chicana: The Mexican-American woman.* Chicago: University of Chicago Press.

O'Neil, J. (1981). Male sex role conflicts, sexism and masculinity: Psychological implications for men, women and the counseling psychologist. *Counseling Psychologist, 9,* 61–80.

Pinderhughes, E. (1989). *Understanding race, ethnicity, and power: The key to efficacy in clinical practice.* New York: Free Press.

Pollitt, K. (1992, December 28). Marooned on Gilligan's island: Are women morally superior to men? *The Nation, 255,* 799–807.

Ponterotto, J. G., Casas, J. M., Suzuki, L. A., & Alexander, C. M. (Eds.). (2001). *Handbook of multicultural counseling* (2nd ed.). Thousand Oaks, CA: Sage.

Reid, P. T., & Comas-Diaz, L. (1990a). Gender and ethnicity: Perspectives on dual status. *Sex Roles, 22,* 397–408.

Reid, P. T., & Comas-Diaz, L. (Eds.). (1990b). Gender and ethnicity: Perspectives on dual status [Special issue]. *Sex Roles, 22*(7–8).

Reid, P. T., & Kelly, E. (1994). Research on women of color: From ignorance to awareness. *Psychology of Women Quarterly, 18,* 477–486.

Robinson, T. L., & Howard-Hamilton, M. F. (2000). *The convergence of race, ethnicity, and gender: Multiple identities in counseling.* Upper Saddle River, NJ: Prentice Hall.

Russo, N. F. (1998). Teaching about gender and ethnicity: Goals and challenges. *Psychology of Women Quarterly, 22,* i-iv.

Russo, N. F., & Dabul, A. J. (1994). Feminism and psychology: A dynamic interaction. In E. J. Trickett, R. J. Watts, & D. Birman (Eds.), *Human diversity: Perspectives on people in context* (pp. 81–100). San Francisco: Jossey-Bass.

Sage, G. P. (1991). Counseling American Indian adults. In C. C. Lee & B. L. Richardson (Eds.), *Multicultural issues in counseling: New approaches to diversity* (pp. 23–36). Alexandria, VA: American Counseling Association.

Semmler, P. L., & Williams, C. B. (2000). Narrative therapy: A storied context for multicultural counseling. *Journal of Multicultural Counseling and Development, 28,* 51–62.

Skovholt, T. (1990). Career themes and counseling and psychotherapy with men. In D. Moore & F. Leagren (Eds.), *Problem-solving strategies and interventions for men in conflict* (pp. 39–53). Alexandria, VA: American Counseling Association.

Sue, D. W., & Sue, D. (1999). *Counseling the culturally different: Theory and practice* (3rd ed.). New York: John Wiley.

Sue, S., & Morishima, J. K. (1982). *The mental health of Asian Americans.* San Francisco: Jossey-Bass.

Tan, A. (1989). *The Joy Luck Club.* New York: Ivy.

Unger, K., & Sanchez-Hucles, J. (Eds.). (1993). Gender and culture [Special issue]. *Psychology of Women Quarterly, 17*(4).

United Nations. (1983). Convention on the Elimination of All Forms of Discrimination Against Women (CEDAW). In United Nations (Ed.), *Human rights: A compilation of international instruments* (pp. 43–48). New York: Author.

U.N. Population Fund. (2000). *The state of the world population 2000: Lives together, worlds apart: Men and women in a time of change.* New York: Author. Retrieved October 29, 2000, from http://www.unfpa.org/swp/swpmain.htm

Walker, A. (1982). *The color purple.* New York: Washington Square.

Weber, L. (1998). A conceptual framework for understanding race, class, gender, and sexuality. *Psychology of Women Quarterly, 22,* 13–32.

Williams, J. E., & Best, D. L. (1982). *Measuring sex stereotypes: A thirty-nation study.* Beverly Hills, CA: Sage.

Williams, J. E., & Best, D. L. (1990). *Sex and psyche: Gender and self viewed cross-culturally.* Newbury Park, CA: Sage.

WEEA Equity Resource Center. (2000). *Practical tools and support for gender-fair learning.* (Available from WEAA Equity Resource Center, Education Development Center, 5 Chapel Street, Newton, MA 02458–1060)

Worell, J., & Etaugh, C. (Eds.). (1994). Transforming theory and research with women: Themes and variations [Special issue]. *Psychology of Women Quarterly, 18*(4).

25

Lesbian, Gay, and Bisexual People of Color

Understanding Cultural Complexity and Managing Multiple Oppressions

Mary A. Fukuyama
Angela D. Ferguson

The United States of America is composed of many cultural, ethnic, and national groups. Although this country is considered multicultural by many, the dominant culture is primarily the product of Eurocentric philosophies and values; therefore, the psychological literature, research, theoretical paradigms, and practice are imbued with Eurocentric cultural biases (J. H. Katz, 1985; Sue & Sue, 1990). The inclusion of culturally diverse groups has been conspicuously absent in these domains; when included, they are frequently characterized as deficient, deviant, and inferior (Helms, 1989; Herring, 1989; J. H. Karz, 1985). Consequently, the culturally different have experienced discrimination and prejudice not only in the mainstream American society but also in the field of psychology.

In this chapter the focus is on the intersection of cultural variables (ethnicity, race, gender, class), sexual orientation, and the dynamics of oppression. We intend to challenge the status quo of both mainstream society and Eurocentric psychology as we highlight and examine cultural factors that are salient for lesbian, gay, and bisexual (LGB) people of color. We discuss identity theories (concerned with race, sexual orientation, and gender) and how they affect counseling and therapy with these populations, and we make recommendations for positive interventions. We believe that a theme for LGB people of color in the United States is managing social oppressions that take various forms (e.g., racism, heterosexism, homophobia, biphobia). The chapter is organized into the following sections: assumptions and definitions, critique of identity theories, culture-specific perspectives, and implications for counseling.

Assumptions and Definitions

We have identified three basic assumptions that provide a foundation for this chapter. First, all phenomena have a cultural context. Christensen (1989) defined culture as consisting of "commonalties around which people have developed values, norms, family life-styles, social roles, and behaviors in response to historical, political, economic, and social realities" (p. 275). In the United States, multiple cultures coexist, overlap, and sometimes contradict each other. Studies of acculturation and adaptation indicate that participation in multiple cultures has its unique stressors and implications for mental health. For example, the pressure to assimilate into the dominant culture may result in loss of language, cultural roots, and community ties. For such individuals, the impact is felt in stress, lowered self-esteem, and concurrent social problems such as alcoholism and violence (E. M. J. Smith, 1985). LGB people also feel stress related to "minority status" (DiPlacido, 1998).

Second, we believe that the social structure of American society is based on dominant-subordinate group relations in which the dominant cultural paradigm favors White, heterosexual, male, Christian, and Eurocentric values and marginalizes persons who are different. This structure is at the core of a sociopolitical system that serves to keep the dominant cultural group in economic power and provides these members with privileges not ascribed to those in subordinate roles through various forms of oppression (e.g., sexism, racism). Individuals belonging to or identifying with nondominant cultural groups confront and must cope with one or more forms of oppression on a personal level every day. Oppression itself is a type of "social disease," and it is important not to "blame the victim" for this problem.

Third, the self (identity development, self-esteem, self-concept) is influenced by group memberships. Collective identities (derived from family and ethnic community) may describe more accurately the experiences of people of color than does an individualistic identity. Therefore, psychologists and counselors must examine the dynamics and interactions of multiple cultural identities that are based on group memberships and their accompanying social statuses. Several key definitions follow that clarify further the issues presented in this chapter:

- *Ethnicity:* social groupings based on common ancestry, national origins, foods, music, language, family practices, and political and economic interests. Ethnicity provides an anchor for social identity and historical continuity (McGoldrick, Pearce, & Giordano, 1996).
- *Race:* a determinant of group membership, based largely on geography, national origin, culture, ethnicity, family ties, and economic and political status. Although it was thought to be biologically based, more genetic variability has been found within specified racial groups than between them (King, 1981). Physical characteristics such as skin color have traditionally been used to distinguish group membership, but racial identification is primarily a social construct used to mark social statuses that maintain social divisions and White privilege (Hopps, 1982; Pinderhughes, 1989; Ridley, 1995; Piccard, 1992). In this chapter we prefer to use the phrase "people of color" to describe individuals who belong to visible ethnic or racial minority groups.
- *Racism:* the perpetuation of the myth that Whites are superior to those of other races, which is expressed through social policies

and practices that favor Whites; prejudice in combination with institutional and systemic power (J. H. Katz, 1978; Khowles & Prewitt, 1969). We do not include prejudice or bigotry that may exist among various ethnic groups in this definition because it is not a systemic issue.

- *Sexism:* the belief that men are superior to women and that fulfilling specified gender roles is desirable and morally correct. Sexist policies and practices favor traditional masculine values.

Although it is useful to understand the preceding definitions, it is more important to ask how psychologists explore these constructs with clients. How can one measure an individual's racial identity or understand the extent to which people may hold racist or homophobic ideas and attitudes? The issue of identity development is addressed in the next section.

Critique of Identity Theories

Identity theories have contributed toward an understanding of the relationship between sociocultural factors and the mental health of culturally diverse persons. Various models of identity development have provided a conceptual framework that describes a psychological process by which one moves from nonacceptance to self-acceptance. The relationship of self to one's reference group and to the dominant culture affects this identity development process. Most identity development models are based on a single social identity (e.g., race, gender, or sexual orientation). In this section, we discuss the limitations of single-identity models for understanding LGB individuals' multiple cultural identities. Single-identity theories have overlooked two important dynamics that may exist for LGB people of color: the visibility or invisibility of identity and the saliency of identity. We discuss the negative effects of oppression on members of marginalized groups (Crocker & Major, 1989), and we conclude the section by highlighting some alternative theories applicable to multiple cultural identities.

Identity models have been used to understand an individual's psychological affiliation or connectedness to a particular social identity (Helms, 1990). Several theorists have developed identity models related to race, ethnicity, gender, and sexual orientation (Atkinson, Morten, & Sue, 1989; Banks, 1981; Cass, 1979; Coleman, 1981–1982; Cross, 1991; Downing & Roush, 1985; Helms, 1984, 1986, 1990; McCarn & Fassinger, 1996). Many of the early models of identity explored single social identities and discussed stages or statuses that described the psychological development and experiences of racial identity attitudes (Helms, 1990). Many of these identity models tended to suggest a linear process, although some theorists have discussed the idea that individuals recycle through identity stages in an ongoing process (Parham, 1989).

Identity models also have been developed that describe an individual's perceptions of self related to a particular "ascribed identity" (i.e., that which is attributed to an individual by others; Cross, 1991). These models provide a developmental process for examining the ways in which members of marginalized groups use dominant social groups as reference points for viewing and interpreting themselves and members within their respective reference group. Each stage or ego status represents the extent to which marginalized group members use dominant social groups as reference points. Helms (1990) described this process as the way in which individuals develop their "worldview." She posited that a worldview is a psychological representation of the way in which people view themselves and others relative to their reference group orientation (i.e., group used as reference for self-identity). For example, a young African American woman could identify herself as Black racially but subscribe to White dominant cultural values such as individualism and autonomy.

Many early researchers were interested in understanding the effects of racism and oppression regarding African Americans' racial identity attitudes and reference group orientation. For example, the construct of race represents an individual's "sense of group or collective identity based on one's perception that he or she shares a common racial heritage with a particular racial group" (Helms, 1990, p. 3). The more one perceives a common racial heritage with a particular racial group, the more identification one feels toward that racial group. Identity models provide a conceptual framework for understanding identity attitudes related to reference group orientation, as well as the effects of oppression on both personal and ascribed identity development.

Identity development models also include gender identity and gender role. P. A. Katz's (1979) model described three distinct levels of the way in which boys and girls acquire appropriate gender behavior in terms of sex roles. Other models have examined gender identity relative to female identity. For example, proposed stage models examining female identity have incorporated a feminist developmental perspective (Downing & Roush, 1985; Ossana, Helms, & Leonard, 1992). These models have described the psychological experiences of women's development, particularly in terms of looking at the effects of sexism. However, gender role identity varies within and among cultural groups (Fassinger & Richie, 1997). Many cultures, including the European American culture, value stereotypical gender expectations and ideologies that are associated with patriarchal values (Kimmel & Messner, 1992).

Homophobia (fear of homosexuality) has been used as a means to enforce traditional gender role behavior. For example, boys are coerced into masculine behaviors by threats of being called a "faggot." Girls who act or dress in masculine ways are called "tomboys," although masculinity in girls is not as stigmatizing as femininity in boys. In addition, homophobic comments have been used to dismiss political movements, such as calling feminists "lesbians" as a way to discredit the women's movement (Pharr, 1988).

Until recently, most identity theories and models have been based on single social identities. Theorists have generally discussed and examined a specific social identity as if the group members were homogeneous, monolithic, and lacking multiple identities. Some researchers have attempted to examine multiple layers of identity of culturally diverse individuals in identity formation theories (e.g., Atkinson et al., 1989; Greene, 1986, 1997; Loiacano, 1989; McCarn & Fassinger, 1996; Morales, 1989) and in applications to counseling and psychotherapy (Ferguson, 1995). However, most existing identity theories continue to focus on homogeneous characteristics of group members (Reynolds & Pope, 1991). One of the primary limitations of recognizing only single identities is that individuals who embrace multiple identities are often invisible members within specific social reference groups.

LGB people of color may be coping with feelings of visibility or invisibility in at least two communities in which they live and function: the mainstream LGB community and their respective ethnic communities (Morales, 1989). They are often differentially treated in the White, heterosexual community as well as in their respective heterosexual ethnic communities. Whether visible or not, one's salience of identity, that is, the identity that emerges into one's awareness, often depends on cultural context. An individual's attitudes, feelings, and self-perceptions regarding his or her cultural group memberships are affected by the shifting social, familial, and community contexts the individual moves through on a daily basis. Identities may emerge into awareness as part of group affiliation but also are affected by feelings of difference from the group. For example, an LGB person of color participates in an ethnic community fundraising dinner. She is invisible as a lesbian, and her identity is affected by homophobic comments. Although her ethnic identity may remain salient and steady in its importance, she may have to work actively at reengaging her links as a lesbian in that context (Deaux, 1993).

Psychological identity theories that do not acknowledge concurrent multiple identities obscure the complexity of integrating multiple social identities and coping with multiple forms of oppression. This manner of exploring identity development dismisses the salience of an individual's existing identities. When these theories are applied to counseling interventions, the erroneous belief that an individual has one prominent, superseding identity is perpetuated. Development of a positive sense of self, particularly when the individual is a member of several marginalized groups, is difficult (Greene, 1994; Myers et al., 1991). When an individual is attempting to integrate multiple identities, it is important to examine multiple layers of oppression (e.g., sexism, racism, homophobia). Members of many visible ethnic groups must face the challenging negative societal and internalized oppressions of racism. Many women also must face the challenges of sexism. Many LGB people of color must face the challenges of homophobia or biphobia (fear of bisexuality). Women who are members of visible ethnic minority groups face the challenges of racism and sexism. LGB women of color face at least two or three challenges: racism, sexism, and homophobia. In addition, bisexual people may feel marginalized within the ethnic lesbian or gay community (Rust, 1996). Forms of racism and homophobia differ when directed at women versus men, just as forms of sexism differ when directed at women of color versus White women. Although individuals' experiences and responses to "isms" differ, A. Smith and Stewart (1983) suggest that the commonality "is the internalization of negative self-image, and a negative image of those most like oneself" (p. 3).

The confluence of factors that may affect the development of one's social identities affects the manner in which an individual integrates those identities. The contexts of family, community, cultural norms and expectations, and oppression can inhibit the expression, salience, and acceptance of one or more identities. Using a single identity framework may be ineffectual and perhaps harmful to the individual. One of the indicators of identity development is the "coming out" process; that is, the recognition of sexual identity in self and gradual disclosure of this identity to others. It has been recommended that the models of identity development that emphasize coming out to family and others as a sign of health do not necessarily apply to all LGB people of color (A. Smith, 1997). Counselors and psychologists must be aware of and knowledgeable about the social identities that individuals embrace. They must also assist individuals in understanding those identities relative to their personal and collective group identity development, group memberships, and personal and collective mental health.

Identity models can be used to facilitate understanding of these dynamics by assisting individuals in exploring the impact of oppressions in their lives related to the ways in which they feel more or less accepting of their respective multiple identities. Psychotherapists must also be aware that the identities of LGB people of color are interrelated and that these clients may experience aspects of their multiple identities in uneven ways. Therapists can assist clients in becoming aware of their respective attitudes, feelings, and beliefs related to their multiple cultural identities.

An alternative identity model developed by Oetting and Beauvais (1990–1991) suggested that individuals may identify with more than one cultural group and that these identities may function independently of each other. The authors suggested that one can have a unicultural, bicultural, or multicultural identification. This model may be useful in exploring multiple cultural identities. For example, Mark might feel positive about being Chinese American, neutral about being male, and negative about being gay. Or Cassandra, who is a biracial African American and Jewish, might be proud to be African American, feel distant from her Jewish identity, and be confused about her bisexuality. The therapist should try to understand the interactions and salience of these identities. Biracial or multiracial people may share experiences with bisexual people in that their identities do not fit into unidimensional categories.

Poston (1990) developed a five-stage biracial identity model that may have relevance to the experiences of bisexual persons. Although this model was not formulated based on sexual identity development, there are parallel processes that may describe the coming out processes for bisexuals. The five stages are personal identity, choice of group categorization, enmeshment-denial, appreciation, and integration. The similarities lie in the forced choice of one ethnic identity (like choosing between being gay or straight) when in fact the individual may identify with more than one ethnic group (or, as a bisexual, be attracted to both genders).

Fox (1996) suggested that bisexual identity development is complex and affected by multiple factors, such as gender, social class, age, ethnicity, sexual and emotional attractions, fantasies, and behaviors. He cited other theorists who have focused on bisexual identity as a process of meeting developmental tasks such as resolving homophobia, developing a support system, or dealing with ongoing emotional adjustments concerning issues of labeling, confusion, and uncertainty.

Walters (1997) proposed an urban, gay, American Indian (GAI) identity development model that incorporates a multilevel context inclusive of self-identity and group identity. She also included levels of acculturation, stages of coming out, and group memberships as dimensions of identity development and integration. This multidimensional model appears similar to McCarn and Fassinger's (1996) model, which includes group membership identity development in addition to individual sexual identity development, for lesbians. Developing a sense of group membership with a lesbian and gay community is viewed as a separate but reciprocal process for individual identity development. Group membership identification as being "part of the LGB community" is as important for White LGBs as ethnic community membership is for persons of color. The LGB community provides cultural and social events, support, and political voice, and it substitutes for family for individuals who have been disconnected from their biological families.

These more recent theories that account for multiple cultural identities and cultural complexity have yet to be tested with LGB people of color. We recommend that qualitative research methods be used to elaborate on these experiences. Presently, these models provide a schema for discussing multiple group memberships and identities in interaction with various sources of oppression. We have not addressed other social identities, such as religious identity or the role of parent, but we presume that these roles could be salient and thereby contribute to the complexity of sexual identity development.

Culture-Specific Perspectives

In this section, we discuss some important factors that relate to selected ethnic groups and influence the identity formation process for people of color. However, we have three major reservations to discuss before embarking on this section. First, there is a paucity of research on LGB people of color (Alquijay, 1997; Ferguson, 1995). Soto (1997) reported that in a 10-year review of gay, lesbian, and bisexual publications, less than 5% of the journal articles focused primarily on the area of race or ethnicity. It is a difficult population to study because LGBs are often hidden within their communities. Second, we run the risk of making overgeneralizations about specific ethnic groups because we cannot fully address "within-group" diversity. Third, the concept of sexual orientation is a Western psychological construct not always found in or stigmatized across other cultures. Evidence of bisexual behaviors in diverse cultures around the world is typically found in anthropological literature (Fox, 1996). Ross, Paulsen, and Stalstrom (1988) cited an early cross-cultural study of same-gender sexual behavior in which 64% of the societies included in the study regarded same-gender sexual behavior as normal or socially acceptable for some or all members of the community. The authors suggested that same-gender sexual behaviors can function positively in several ways within a culture: as recreational, as an educational activity (mentoring), as an emotional preference, and as an indication of social status (dominance vs. submission). These authors posited that sexuality is stigmatized when it violates other cultural rules and values. LGB relationships have been stigmatized in Western civilization because they violate a cultural imperative to procreate (a value derived from historic Judeo-Christian values) and depart from gender role expectations. Note that in some cultures, same-gender sexual behavior is not stigmatized, identity is not based on sexuality, and gay liberation is unknown (Herdt, 1990).

We have decided to highlight four broadly defined ethnic groupings: Native Americans, African Americans, Asian Americans, and Latin Americans. This is not meant to diminish the importance of other cultural groups, but it is beyond the scope of this chapter to include all. The racial and ethnic cultural groups discussed in this section have different values, beliefs, customs, and histories in the United States. They do, however, share many commonalities. Under each cultural group heading, the following dimensions are discussed: demographic and historical perspectives, family and community, gender roles, and religion and spirituality. Case examples are discussed in the final section of the chapter.

Native American Perspectives

Demographic and Historical Perspectives

The indigenous population of the United States consists of more than 500 federally recognized and 200 nonfederally recognized tribes (Walters, 1997). Within this culturally diverse population of more than 2 million people, or about 1% of the total population (U.S. Bureau of the Census, 1998), more than 200 languages are spoken, and over 50% live in urban areas. As a collective experience, the history of Native tribes in America is fraught with traumatic relocation (forced movement to reservations), genocide (war and fatal diseases), and overt assimilation pressures (Indian boarding schools, missionary influences). Native peoples continue to be oppressed in the United States as many struggle with poverty, health problems, and cultural discontinuity. In addition to these systemic factors, LGB Native Americans are faced with homophobic stigmatization.

Extended family relations are central in providing support, and tribal social structures determine family role expectations. Because of past genocide, women may feel pressure to or desire to bear children. The degree to which one identifies as Native American or American Indian is influenced by many factors, such as level of assimilation, tribal membership, and residence (reservation vs. urban areas). LGB Native Americans may feel conflicts in allegiances to two oppressed communities. Walters (1997) suggested that American Indian values of kinship, family, cooperation, and collective identity may directly conflict with Eurocentric gay and lesbian values of individuality and coming out openly (which sets one apart from the group). In early Native American history, some native peoples' sexuality (before Christian missionary influences) was described as including procreation, play, and bisexuality (Brown, 1997). Individuals who displayed cross-gender role preferences were described as "two-spirited," that is, possessing both masculine and feminine qualities (Jacobs, Thomas, & Lang, 1997). In some tribes this was valued, but not so in all cases.

Gender Roles

Gender roles and cross-gender behaviors are frequently associated with sexual orientation issues. Gender role behavior (social constructions of masculinity and femininity) is different from sexual orientation, which involves same-gender erotic and affectional attraction and attachment. The phenomenon of cross-gender role behaviors (i.e., males acting like females, females acting like males) is frequently cited in writings about early Native American sexuality. Some precolonial Native American tribes were tolerant of cross-gender role behaviors and regarded individuals who exhibited them as having special powers (Brown, 1997). In some tribes alternative gender roles were seen positively, whereas in others they were regarded negatively (Crow, Wright, & Brown, 1997). Various distinctions in gender roles have been described, including such terms as "not-women, not-men" (Brown, 1997, p. 5) and "hypermasculine males for warriors, ordinary heterosexual males, and homosexual males" (Tafoya, 1997, p. 1). In traditional tribes, gender roles and sexuality were not limited to dualistic categories. Gender alternatives were not seen as particularly threatening in some tribes. Rather, a difference was regarded as something from which to learn. This more accepting attitude can be traced to Native American spirituality.

Religion and Spirituality

Native American religious orientation has been described as inclusive, with all things being sacred (Tafoya, 1997). Sexuality and gender roles were seen on a continuum represented by a circle rather than limited by linear stages or rigid categories. Human growth and development were seen as ever evolving, in contrast to fitting into reductionistic categories.

However, Western values and Christian proselytizing have subjugated most indigenous peoples of today. Hence, many Native Americans have internalized the homophobic or biphobic attitudes found in the mainstream culture. In some Native American traditions, cross-gender roles and bisexuality were regarded positively; such historical roots may aid Native Americans to claim a positive identity based on these precepts. However, regardless of Native traditions, it is important for Whites not to "exoticize" LGB American Indians, not to assume that they have acquired a "two-spirit" valuing of their sexuality (Brown, 1997). Walters (1997) recommended that counselors focus on client resilience and positive coping to deal with the double oppressions of racism and heterosexism.

African American Perspectives

Demographic and Historical Perspectives

African Americans make up about 12% of the total population (more than 34 million people) of the United States (U.S. Bureau of the Census, 1998). They are culturally diverse owing, in large part, to the long history of the slave trade in North America, which brought thousands of culturally different African tribes to the United States. People from the Caribbean islands, which were colonized by Europeans for many years, also immigrated to the United States and have contributed to the cultural diversity in African American communities (Greene, 1997). African American gender roles, cultural values and practices, family systems, and sexuality make up a collection of values and customs from African and European cultures.

Family and Community

The African American community historically has valued family and religion as primary sources of emotional support. Although African Americans' cultural origins are diverse, the community shares common forms of oppression, such as racism, sexism, prejudice, and discrimination. For many African Americans, the family and the community provide support and function "as a refuge and buffer against racism in the dominant culture" (Greene, 1994, p. 395).

LGB African Americans face an additional form of oppression, homophobia, from both the White heterosexual community and the African American heterosexual community. B. Smith (1982) asserted that "heterosexual privilege is the only privilege Blacks have. None of us have racial . . . privilege, almost none of us have class privilege, maintaining 'straightness' is our last resort" (p. 171). She continued by suggesting that although racism and sexism may be experienced by some within the African American community, African American LGB individuals may also be victimized by heterosexual privilege.

This occurrence raises an interesting point relative to an LGB individual's experience of oppressions and the process of coming out within the African American community. Coming out for African Americans may mean the loss of their connection to heterosexual privilege as well as of their refuge against racism. Therefore, when an African American LGB client is reluctant to come out, the psychotherapist should not immediately interpret this hesitation as being the same as ambivalence or confusion about sexual orientation. It may more accurately represent a time when the African American LGB faces the potential of losing a major support system, with less opportunity to develop another community in which to feel safe and affirmed.

For individuals who come out and who are members of visible racial or ethnic groups, the process may be a more complex experience than for White gays and lesbians (Moore, 1997). Loiacano (1989) conducted structured interviews with six African American lesbians and gay men and stated that "choices about coming out to others, becoming involved in primary relationships, and becoming politically active in the [nonheterosexual] community may be complicated by status as a Black American" (p. 22). His results revealed that African Americans may place less value on coming out to others than their White counterparts, for fear that they may "jeopardize needed support as a racial minority" (p. 24). In other words, racial identity had a higher priority than sexual identity.

Gender Roles

Gender role development varies within the African American community; both the White mainstream society and the African American community generate gender role expectations. Gender roles of African American men and women have been greatly influenced by the legacy of slavery in this country. Many African American communities are commonly viewed as matriarchal; it is said that "African American women play critical roles in keeping Black family ties together and in supporting Black men" (B. Smith, 1982, p. 157). These views contradict Eurocentric ideals of masculine and feminine roles. Fassinger and Richie (1997) suggested that gender roles in patriarchal societies such as the United States embrace a stereotypical gender role ideology in which "women should be gentle and expressive while men should be strong and instrumental; women are best suited to homemaking and child rearing while men are suited to paid work outside the home" (p. 86). Both genders may experience conflict in fulfilling respective traditional masculine and feminine expectations owing to racism and discrimination (Shorter-Gooden & Washington, 1996; Wade, 1996).

Perceptions and knowledge regarding sexuality of African American men and women have also been affected by stereotypes and myths, causing conflict and tension in male-female relationships. Throughout the years, perceptions of beauty based on European standards of features such as skin complexion and hair texture have affected greatly the ways in which African Americans see each other as attractive, romantic partners. Historical efforts to control and exploit African Americans' reproduction (B. Smith, 1982) and the existence of extended family systems (Billingsley, 1968) have influenced the manner in which African American men and women perceive themselves in terms of parental roles, parental responsibilities, gender socialization, and expectations.

Religion and Spirituality

Historically the Black church has played important social and political roles in support of African American families and communities (Richardson, 1991). Both spirituality and religion are key factors in the Black community, and both spirituality and faith have been central to the civil rights movement and other social justice issues. Afrocentric spirituality emphasizes harmony among spiritual, physical, and social aspects of life. This orientation may assist African Americans to integrate their sexuality. Although the African American community publicly opposes homosexuality, there may be tacit tolerance of same-gender liaisons on a private level (Monteiro & Fuqua, 1994). Counselors may want to look for commonalities in multiple oppressions to reinforce strategies to resist negative stereotyping and to increase sources for positive self-esteem.

Asian American Perspectives

Demographic and Historical Perspectives

Asian Americans represent a diverse population of persons of Asian descent, recent immigrants, and refugees from the continent of Asia and the Pacific Rim countries, ranging from India and Pakistan to China, Korea, Japan, the Philippines, Southeast Asia, and the Pacific Islands. Approximately 10 million Asian Americans live in the United States, composing nearly 4% of the total population (U.S. Bureau of the Census, 1998), and more than 50% of Asian Americans are foreign born. With such large numbers of immigrants and refugees, one may assume that acculturation and relocation are major influences on identity development (Espin, 1997).

Pacific Islanders often feel excluded from the umbrella term "Asian American." The experiences of Pacific Islanders are more similar to those of indigenous Native Americans owing to American colonialism and missionary influences in the Pacific Rim. Recent events such as the movement to legalize same-gender marriage in Hawaii have brought more attention to the Pacific Island cultures. In addition, there is a movement to reclaim Hawaii's sovereignty and cultural heritage, which includes a more complex view of bisexuality (Hall & Kauanui, 1994).

Family and Community

The family unit is highly valued, and ancestors and intergenerational connections are emphasized. The family is hierarchical in structure, with roles clearly defined by gender, class, and age. Feelings of obligation (filial duty) and shame dictate and control social behaviors.

Chan (1989, 1997) discussed the reasons that LGB Asian Americans are generally invisible. She suggested that the dimensions of "public-self private-self" in East Asian cultures (China, Japan, Korea) dictate the degree of disclosure about intimacy issues. In addition, the self is defined primarily through family and kinship roles, for example, firstborn son. The idea that an individual might come out as a gay man or lesbian is incompatible with the concept of family obligations and duty (Sohng & Ioard, 1996).

Attitudes toward same-gender attraction vary among the different Asian groups (Leong, 1996). Traditional East Asian and South Asian cultures restrict heterosexual contact (i.e., dating is not permitted) but allow intimate friendships and bonding to be expressed in same-gender groupings (e.g., gender-segregated schools). In such settings, same-gender sexual behaviors may be tolerated and not taken seriously.

Acculturation into American culture may also influence the degree of openness about LGB identity. It is possible that coming out is an indicator of acculturation toward the values of individuality and openness of expression. However, coming out may place the Asian American in a conflictual situation. A gay Filipino man, who was politically active in his ethnic community, presented such a dilemma:

> To come out in the Filipino community would be double jeopardy. My first concern was that being openly gay would further jeopardize the serious consideration my political viewpoints would be given in the Filipino community. Secondly, to come out in mainstream society would force me to confront the homophobic attitudes of society at large in addition to the racial discrimination that I was already subjected to as an ethnic minority. (Mangaoang, 1994, p. 39)

Gender Roles

Gender roles have powerful influences that are based on traditions and stereotypes. Traditional gender roles for men and women place men in hierarchical positions of power and women as subservient. Men and women must marry and procreate to continue the family name, and these family roles are more important and salient to identity than sexuality.

Negative stereotypes of Asians exist in the White dominant culture (e.g., they may be viewed as asexual males and exotic females). Such distortions continue to be played out in same-gender relationships. For example, within the gay White male community, the term *rice queen* refers to White men who prefer Asian men (who presumably play out female roles). Other Asian American gay and lesbian themes have been explored in film and theater. The film *The Wedding Banquet* is a humorous approach to parental expectations of a Chinese (gay) son to marry. An Indian film, *Fire,* explores tensions between marital duty and love that develop between two traditional Indian wives who share the same household. Themes of domination were illustrated dramatically in the play *M. Butterfly* by David Henry Hwang (Eng, 1994). The playwright depicted parallels between sexual dominance and political and military dominance by western European powers in Asia.

Religion and Spirituality

A wide variety of religions are represented among Asian Americans, including Hinduism, Islam, Christianity, Buddhism, Confucianism,

Taoism, and indigenous forms of spiritualism. Attitudes toward sexuality vary: There are explicit sacred practices (e.g., tantric traditions), and there is repression (e.g., Catholicism). Most religious traditions regulate heterosexual activity as well as prohibit same-gender activity. Sexuality and spirituality are more closely linked in the Hindu traditions, yet most of the symbolic representations are of the union of the masculine and feminine principles. Psychologists and counselors may need to assess levels of acculturation and familial expectations as central themes in working with Asian American clients.

Latin American Perspectives

Demographic and Historical Perspectives

Latin Americans are a culturally diverse mixture of peoples of indigenous, African, Asian, and European roots. This is the fastest growing ethnic group in the United States, with estimated numbers exceeding 30 million and composing 11% of the total population (U.S. Bureau of the Census, 1998). The largest numbers are Mexican Americans, followed by Puerto Ricans, Cuban Americans, and representatives from Caribbean and Central and South American countries.

Family and Community

Latin Americans are family oriented with values of "family unity, welfare and honor" (Garcia-Preto, 1996, p. 15). The family requires loyalty and fulfillment of obligations, and in turn, it provides protection and care as long as one stays within the family system. Deviations in sexuality may be hidden or overlooked for the sake of family continuity. LGB Latinos feel pressure to marry, if only for appearances (*el que diran,* "what they will say"). Extended family includes both blood relations and those acquired through other commitments such as godparents, in-laws, or children informally adopted. Immigration status also affects family, community relations, and pressures to marry.

Gender Roles

An exploration of gender roles in Latin America provides a foundation for understanding variations in sexual expression. Lara-Cantu (1989) developed a sex role inventory that delineated assertive and aggressive dimensions of masculinity and affective and submissive dimensions of femininity. The ideal of *machismo* (manliness, virility) suggests that men are sexually active, and in some cases, men may be sexually active with other men and not be stigmatized. Zamora-Hernandez and Patterson (1996) noted that there was a higher incidence of bisexuality among Latin American men compared with White men in a study of people with the human immunodeficiency virus (HIV). They also found that men may engage in sex with other men without stigma as long as they assume the active role (vs. the passive, or receptive, role). The homosexual label is reserved for a partner who is "female" in the sex act. However, men who are sexually active with other men do not necessarily conform to these narrow roles.

For Latina women, the ideal of *marianismo* suggests that women are submissive, self-sacrificing, and pure. Just as men are expected to be sexually active, women are expected to be "virgins" until marriage and then to devote themselves to child rearing (Vasquez, 1994). For a Latina woman to be interested in sex, interested in another woman, or sexually active outside of marriage would violate gender role expectations (E. Delgado-Romero, personal communication, May 14, 1998). Latin American women are in a process of discovering their voices about sexuality (Alcaron, Castillo, & Moraga, 1993).

Religion and Spirituality

Religion plays an important role in the life of Latin American families, and Catholicism is the predominant religious influence in Latin American countries. Catholicism frequently merges with indigenous religious customs. Some priests have become social activists with regard to human rights issues, but fighting one type of oppression (economic injustice) does not automatically translate into fighting another (heterosexism). In addition, a recent rise in Protestant fundamentalism could increase homophobic attitudes among Latin Americans. Many religions condemn same-gender sexual behavior, although large extended families may be able to absorb deviations from the heterosexual norm. Cultural factors such as preferred language, acculturation, socioeconomic status, religion, educational level, and family and kinship system need to be accounted for in providing psychotherapy for Latin American clients (Carballo-Dieguez, 1989).

Implications for Counseling

A range of therapeutic issues are raised when working with LGB people of color. In this section we discuss some common themes and make recommendations for practitioners. We again caution the reader about making generalizations but hope that the parameters of this discussion will expand psychologists' abilities to understand the complex dynamics that underlie multiple cultural identities and oppressions. We discuss the impact oppression has on clients' worldviews, the coming out process, and internalized feelings of self-worth. The dynamics of identity saliency and visibility or invisibility are explored. We also make specific recommendations for clinical interventions and discuss selected case examples.

Psychologists are taught to be sensitive to clients' needs and issues but are not taught how to be sensitive to issues of oppression, discrimination, and prejudice. The forces of oppression have shaped the worldviews of clients with multiple identities. As psychologists begin to understand that clients have worldviews that are different from their own, openness to knowing and learning about other cultural groups will increase. Subsequently, psychologists will increase their multicultural counseling competencies (Fassinger & Richie, 1997; Pope & Reynolds, 1997; Sue, Arredondo, & McDavis, 1992; Sue & Sue, 1990).

We recommend that psychologists and counselors examine whether their theoretical orientation allows LGB people of color to feel supported and affirmed in the therapeutic process. Therapists also need to understand clients from a multicultural perspective, which includes exploration of how the individual is affected by various factors such as societal messages, familial messages, group memberships, multiple social identities, oppression, and power. Assessing and understanding the salience of the multiple identities and multiple oppressions of LGB people of color, rather than focusing on only one identity, may assist both the client and the therapist in working through psychological, interpersonal, and emotional issues (Ferguson, 1995).

Coming out is a complex decision-making process for many LGB people of color. There are many places and stages of coming out in one's lifetime; it is a never-ending process. Many LGB people of color have felt diminished and have suffered immeasurably because of oppression. LGB people of color often find refuge in their respective communities and have elected to minimize other aspects of their identities. The decision to disclose sexual orientation—to whom and when—may depend on the intensity of the oppressions. In fact, electing to come out may cause LGB people of color to feel as though they are leaving their place of refuge. Psychologists need to be aware that the decision to come out may bring up feelings of grief and loss. In addition, LGB people of color may have to deal with further oppression in the White gay community. Although LGB people of color may want to affirm their sexual identity, they may not be prepared to leave their cultural environment and enter a hostile social and political climate that may not have sufficient support systems for their psychological well-being. Morales (1989) indicated that LGB people of color balance three identities: "the gay/lesbian community, the ethnic minority community, and the predominantly White mainstream society" (p. 217). For example, by becoming a visible African American LGB, the individual "may run the risk of feeling uprooted as an ethnic person" (Morales, 1989, p. 233).

LGB people of color also may internalize oppression. Feelings of self-hatred and depression and negative attitudes toward the self may be psychological manifestations of internalized oppression. Counselors need to assess the ways in which oppression is experienced from both external and internal sources and how it affects sense of self and perceptions of group memberships. Consider a fictitious case example:

Maria, a 24-year-old Cuban American, feels positive about herself (i.e., positive personal identity). She is in her first relationship with a woman and sees LGB group membership as irrelevant to her own life circumstances (reference group orientation). Maria's mother has mentioned that she is glad that Maria has light features and is seen as White. Currently, Maria does not feel a commitment to any racial group (ascribed identity). However, Maria's presenting problem is that she feels like an "outsider" with her friends. The counselor may want to explore in what ways Maria is affected by oppressions and how they affect her relationship and group affiliations.

Although each identity may be defined separately, there is an interaction between the person's sense of self and his or her group memberships. Psychologists prepared to assess the impact of multiple oppression can assist clients in coping with these effects, in developing more positive attitudes about their identities, and in learning the skills to resist oppression.

Visibility or invisibility of "minority status" influences identity development and group affiliation. When one is a visible target of oppression, one develops skills for coping and resisting both open and covert forms of prejudice. LGB people of color may not have the skills or means for counteracting the additional oppression of homophobia or biphobia. The added weight of this oppression may contribute to anxiety, depression, and isolation. When one is an invisible member of an oppressed group, as is more typical of sexual orientation, one is constantly processing decisions about when and if to self-disclose. This constant self-monitoring and vigilance over safety consume a fair amount of psychological energy. In addition, the unguarded homophobic or biphobic comments from loved ones (who otherwise are supportive) can create inner distress. LGB people of color may decide not to take on yet another form of oppression. For some individuals, the additional pressures may seem like too much, whereas others may feel that they have developed "transferable skills" to fight another oppression (e.g., anti-Semitism, sexism, homophobia, biphobia, and racism).

Some people of color resist labeling by sexual orientation. Gay identity and the gay liberation movement have been associated with the White middle class, wherein individuals are able to break from their families and support themselves autonomously (D'Emilio, 1983). People of color may resist joining the gay liberation movement because it is perceived to be joining with the White oppressor and denying one's family ties. In some ways, a gay identity may be a function of acculturation into American society. As was previously discussed, some men of color engage in same-gender sexual behaviors but do not identify themselves as gay (Tsang, 1994; Zamora-Hernandez & Patterson, 1996). We recommend that clients self-select their identity labels and not be pressured to conform to the customary LGB labels.

We recommend also that counselors and psychologists assist LGB clients to find support systems, which may be groups separate from the White gay community. Such separatist groups may be necessary for cultural immersion and safety. For example, LGB people of color may be able to meet on-line through Internet listservs, bulletin boards, and the World Wide Web (Tsang, 1994). Although virtual communication does not eliminate prejudice, it does allow people of color to find each other for support and socializing. In addition, support groups and social networks exist in large metropolitan areas, such as in San Francisco and Washington, DC. We suggest that LGBs also need heterosexual people of color who are "allies" to counteract the effects of homophobia and heterosexism. For example, how can LGB people of color attend a church where the minister continuously condemns "homosexuality" as a sin? LGBs of color may want to find a more progressive church community but may have to deal with integrating into White churches and adapting to cultural differences in styles of worship.

Hoopes (1979) proposed a cultural learning model for adapting to a pluralistic society that suggests that a multicultural approach uses "selective adoption" of cultural behaviors (p. 18). With LGB people of color, there is a blending of subcultures based on race, ethnicity, gender, and sexual orientation. Members of marginalized groups sometimes have the capacity to bridge groups more easily than persons whose identities are embedded in mainstream culture. Although there are benefits of being biculturally skilled, there are also hidden costs, such as experiencing "cultural strain" when there is intense cross-cultural conflict or dissociating parts of one's self in a cultural context where one part is hostile to another. Consider another fictitious case example:

Dora is a 33-year-old Dakota who has two children, ages 8 and 6. She travels frequently between her tribal home in South Dakota and West Coast urban areas where she has an extended friendship and family network. She has had relationships with both men and women in a "serial monogamous" fashion, and she does not label herself in any particular way regarding her sexual identity. She has formed connections within a lesbian community, and the woman she is currently dating has some concerns about Dora's bisexuality, calling Dora's sexual identity into question. A psychotherapist may want to explore with the client how she negotiates her multiple cultural group connections and identities, as well as explore within the couple relationship the meaning of bisexuality.

Conclusion

Whether intentional or not, the LGB liberation movement challenges heterosexual gender norms for everyone. The mainstream culture benefits from broadened expressions of sexuality and gender roles. LGB persons of color are more likely to cross boundaries of gender, class, race, and ethnic origins and thereby break down the "isms" through multiple group memberships and intergroup relationships. Bisexuals in particular model the concept that human sexuality is expressed on a continuum, not in dichotomous boxes. It is important to resist a pathology model for the sexual identity of LGB people of color. Rather, we encourage psychologists to consider the root causes of oppression to be pathological.

Gloria Anzaldua (1987) wrote about living in the borderlands between Texas and Mexico but extended this geographic experience into the psychological realms through her poetry and trilingual prose. We believe the following quote is a fitting conclusion to this chapter:

> I have been straddling that *tejas*—Mexican border, and others, all my life. It's not a comfortable territory to live in, this place of contradictions. Hatred, anger and exploitation are the prominent features of this landscape. However, there have been compensations for this mestizo, and certain joys. Living on borders and in margins, keeping intact one's shifting and multiple identity and integrity, is like trying to swim in a new element, an "alien" element. There is an exhilaration in being a participant in the further evolution of humankind, in being "worked" on. (Anzaldua, 1987, p. 1)

References

Alcaron, N., Castillo, A., &. Moraga, C. (Eds.). (1993). *The sexuality of Latinos.* Berkeley, CA: Third Women Press.

Alquijay, M. A. (1997). The relationships among self-esteem, acculturation, and lesbian identity formation in Latina lesbians. In B. Greene (Ed.), *Ethnic and cultural diversity among lesbians and gay men* (pp. 249–265). Newbury Park, CA: Sage.

Anzaldua, G. (1987). *Borderlands/La Frontera: The new mestiza.* San Francisco: Spinsters/Aunt Lute Book Company.

Atkinson, D. R., Morten, G., & Sue, D. W. (Eds). (1989). *Counseling American minorities: A cross-cultural perspective* (3rd ed.). Dubuque, IA: William C. Brown.

Banks, J. A. (1981). The stages of ethnicity: Implications for curriculum reform. In J. A. Banks (Ed.), *Multi-ethnic education: Theory and practice* (pp. 129–139). Boston: Allyn & Bacon.

Billingsley, A. (1968). *Black families in White America.* Englewood Cliffs, NJ: Prentice-Hall.

Boykin, K. (1996). *One more river to cross: Black and gay in America.* New York: Doubleday.

Brown, L. B. (1997). Women and men, not-men and not-women, lesbians and gays: American Indian gender style alternatives. In L. B. Brown (Ed.), *Two spirit people: American Indian lesbian women and gay men* (pp. 5–20). New York: Harrington Park Press.

Carballo-Dieguez, A. (1989). Hispanic culture, gay male culture, and AIDS: Counseling implications. *Journal of Counseling and Development, 68,* 26–30.

Cass, V. C. (1979). Homosexual identify formation: A theoretical model. *Journal of Homosexuality, 4*(3), 219–235.

Chan, C. S. (1989). Issues of identity development among Asian-American lesbians and gay men. *Journal of Counseling and Development, 68,* 16–20.

Chan, C. S. (1997). Don't ask, don't tell, don't know. In B. Greene (Ed.), *Ethnic and cultural diversity among lesbians and gay men* (pp. 240–248). Newbury Park, CA: Sage.

Christensen, C. P. (1989). Cross-cultural awareness development: A conceptual model. *Counselor Education and Supervision, 28,* 270–289.

Coleman, E. (1981–1982). Developmental stages of the coming out process. *Journal of Homosexuality,* 7(2–3), 31–43.

Crocker, J., & Major, B. (1989). Social stigma and self-esteem: The self-protective properties of stigma. *Psychological Review, 96,* 608–630.

Cross, W. E. (1991). *Shades of Black.* Philadelphia: Temple University Press.

Crow, L., Wright, J. A., &. Brown, L. B. (1997). Gender selection in two American Indian tribes, in L. B. Brown (Ed.), *Two spirit people: American Indian lesbian women and gay men* (pp. 21–28). New York: Harrington Park Press.

Deaux, K. (1993). Reconstructing social identity. *Society for Personality and Social Psychology, 19,* 4–12.

D'Emilio, J. (1983). Capitalism and gay identity. In A. Snitow, C. Stansell, & S. Thompson (Eds.), *Power of desire: The politics of sexuality* (pp. 100–113). New York: Monthly Review Press.

DiPlacido, J. (1998). Minority stress among lesbians, gay men, and bisexuals: A consequence of heterosexism, homophobia, and stigmatization. In G. M. Herek (Ed.), *Stigma and sexual orientation: Understanding prejudice against lesbians, gay men, and bisexuals* (pp. 138–159). Newbury Park, CA: Sage.

Downing, N. E., & Roush, K. L. (1985). From passive acceptance to active commitment: A model of feminist identity development for women. *The Counseling Psychologist, 13,* 695–709.

Eng, D. L. (1994). In the shadows of a diva: Committing homosexuality in David Henry Hwang's *M. Butterfly. Amerasia Journal, 20,* 93–116.

Espin, O. M. (1997). Crossing borders and boundaries: The life narratives of immigrant lesbians. In B. Greene (Ed.), *Ethnic and cultural diversity among lesbians and gay men* (pp. 191–215). Newbury Park, CA: Sage.

Fassinger, R. E., & Richie, B. S. (1997). Sex matters: Gender and sexual orientation in training for multicultural counseling competency. In D. B. Pope-Davis & H. L. K. Coleman (Eds.), *Multicultural counseling competencies* (pp. 83–110). Newbury Park, CA: Sage.

Ferguson, A. D. (1995). The relationship between African American lesbians' race, gender, and sexual orientation and self-esteem. *Dissertation Abstracts International,* 56(11) A, 4565.

Fox, R. C. (1996). Bisexuality in perspective: A review of theory and research. In B. A. Firestein (Ed.), *Bisexuality: The psychology and politics of an invisible minority* (pp. 3–50). Newbury Park, CA: Sage.

Garcia-Preto, N. (1996). Latino families; An overview. In M. McGoldrick, J. Giordano, & J. K. Pearce (Eds.), *Ethnicity and family therapy* (2nd ed., pp. 141–154). New York: Guilford Press.

Greene, B. A. (1986). When the therapist is White and the patient is Black: Considerations for psychotherapy in the feminist heterosexual and lesbian communities. *Women and Therapy, 5,* 41–65.

Greene, B. (1994). Lesbian women of color: Triple jeopardy in L. Comas-Diaz & B. Greene (Eds.), *Women of color: Integrating ethnic and gender identities in psychotherapy* (pp. 389–427). New York: Guilford Press.

Greene, B. (1997). Ethnic minority lesbians and gay men: Mental health and treatment issues. In B. Greene (Ed.), *Ethnic and cultural diversity among lesbians and gay men* (pp. 216–239). Newbury Park, CA: Sage.

Hall, L. K. C., & Kauanui, J. K. (1994). Same-sex sexuality in Pacific literature. *Amerasia Journal, 20,* 75–81.

Helms, J. E. (1984). Toward a theoretical explanation of the effects of race on counseling: A Black and White model. *The Counseling Psychologist, 12,* 153–365.

Helms, J. E. (1986). Expanding racial identity theory to cover counseling process. *Journal of Counseling Psychology, 33,* 62–64.

Helms, J. E. (1989). Eurocentricism strikes in strange ways and in unusual places. *The Counseling Psychologist, 17,* 643–647.

Helms, J. E. (1990). *Black and White racial identity; Theory, research, and practice.* New York: Greenwood Press.

Herdr, G. (1990). Developmental discontinuities and sexual orientation across cultures. In D. P. McWhitter, S. A. Sandets, & J. M. Reinisch (Eds.), *Homosexuality/heterosexuality: Concepts of sexual orientation* (pp. 208–236). New York: Oxford University Press.

Herring, R. D. (1989). The American Native family: Dissolution by coercion. *Journal of Multicultural Counseling and Development, 17,* 4–15.

Hoopes, D. S. (1979). Intercultural communication concepts and the psychology of intercultural experience. In M. D. Pusch (Ed.), *Multicultural education: A cross-cultural training approach* (pp. 10–38). La Grange Park, IL: Intercultural Network.

Hopps, J. (1982). Oppression based on color [Editorial]. *Social Work, 27,* 3–5.

Jacobs, S. E., Thomas, W., & Lang, S. (1997). *Two-spirit people: Native American gender identity, sexuality, and spirituality.* Chicago: University of Illinois Press.

Katz, J. H. (1978). *White awareness: Handbook for anti-racism training.* Norman, OK: University of Oklahoma Press.

Katz, J. H. (1985). The sociopolitical nature of counseling. *The Counseling Psychologist, 13,* 615–624.

Katz, P. A. (1979). The development of female identity. *Sex Roles, 5,* 155–178.

Kimmel, M. S., &. Messner, M. A. (1992). *Men's lives.* New York: Macmillan.

King, J. C. (I981). *The biology of race.* Berkeley: University of California Press.

Knowles, L., & Prewitt, K. (1969). *Institutional racism in America.* Englewood Cliffs, NJ: Prentice-Hall.

Lara-Cantu, M. A. (1989). A sex role inventory with scales for "machismo" and "self-sacrificing woman." *Journal of Cross-Cultural Psychology, 20,* 386–398.

Leong, R. (1996). *Asian American sexualities: Dimensions of the gay and lesbian experience.* New York: Routledge.

Loiacano, D. K. (1989). Gay identity issues among Black Americans: Racism, homophobia, and the need for validation. *Journal of Counseling and Development, 68,* 21–25.

Mangaoang, G. (1994). From the 1970s to the 1990s: Perspective of a gay Filipino American activist. *Amerasia Journal, 20,* 33–44.

McCam, S. R., & Fassinger, R. E. (1996). Revisioning sexual minority identity development formation: A new model of lesbian identity and its implications for counseling and research. *The Counseling Psychologist, 24,* 508–534.

McGoldrick, M., Pearce, J. K., & Giordano, J. (Eds.). (1996). *Ethnicity and family therapy* (2nd ed.). New York. Guilford Press.

Monteiro, K. P., & Fuqua, V. (1994). Black American gay youth: One form of manhood. *High School Journal, 77*(1–2), 20–36.

Moore, L. C. (1997). *Does your mama know? An anthology of Black lesbian coming out stories.* Decatur, GA; Red Bone Press.

Morales, E. S. (1989). Ethnic minority families and minority gays and lesbians. *Journal of Homosexuality, 17,* 217–239.

Myers, L. J., Speight, S. L., Highlen, P. S., Cox, C. I., Reynolds, A. L., Adams, E. M., & Hanley, P. (1991). Identity development and worldview: Toward an optimal conceptualization. *Journal of Counseling and Development, 70,* 54–63.

Oetting, E. R., & Beauvais, F. (1990–1991). Orthogonal cultural identification theory: The cultural identification of minority adolescents. *International Journal of the Addictions, 25,* 655–685.

Ossana, S. M., Helms, J. E., & Leonard, M. M. (1992). Do "womanist" identity attitudes influence college women's self-esteem and perceptions of environmental bias? *Journal of Counseling and Development, 70,* 402–408.

Parham, T. A. (1989). Cycles of psychological nigrescence. *The Counseling Psychologist, 17,* 187–226.

Pharr, S. (1988). *Homophobia: A weapon of sexism.* Berkeley, CA: Chardon.

Pinderhughes, E. (1989). *Understanding race, ethnicity, and power: The key to efficacy in clinical practice.* New York: Free Press.

Pope, R. L., &. Reynolds, A. L. (1997). Student affairs core competencies: Integrating multicultural awareness, knowledge, and skills. *Journal of College Student Development, 38,* 266–277.

Poston, W. S. C. (1990). The biracial identity development model. *Journal of Counseling and Development, 69,* 152–155.

Reynolds, A. L., & Pope, R. L. (1991). The complexities of diversity: Exploring multiple oppressions. *Journal of Counseling and Development, 70,* 174–180.

Richardson, B. L. (1991). Utilizing the resources of the African American church: Strategies for counseling professionals. In C. C. Lee & B. L. Richardson (Eds.), *Multicultural issues in counseling; New approaches to diversity* (pp. 65–75). Alexandria, VA: American Counseling Association.

Ridley, C. R. (1995). *Overcoming unintentional racism in counseling and therapy: A practitioner's guide to intentional intervention.* Newbury Park, CA: Sage.

Ross, M. W., Paulsen, J. A., & Stalstrom, O. W. (1988). Homosexuality and mental health: A cross-cultural review. *Journal of Homosexuality, 15*(1–2), 131–152.

Rust, P. C. (1996). Managing multiple identities: Diversity among bisexual women and men. In B. A. Firestein (Ed.), *Bisexuality: The psychology and politics of an invisible minority* (pp. 53–83). Newbury Park, CA: Sage.

Shorter-Gooden, K., & Washington, N. C. (1996). Young, Black, and female: The challenge of weaving an identity. *Journal of Adolescence, 19,* 465–475.

Smith, A. (1997). Cultural diversity and the coming out process: Implications for clinical practice. In B. Greene (Ed.), *Ethnic and cultural diversity among lesbians and gay men* (pp. 279–300). Newbury Park, CA: Sage

Smith, A., & Stewart, A. J., (1983). Approaches to studying racism and sexism in Black women's lives. *Journal of Social Issues, 39,* 1–15.

Smith, B. (1982). Racism and women's studies. In G. T. Hull, P. B. Scott, & B. Smith (Eds.), *But some of us are brave* (pp. 157–175). Old Westbury, NY: Feminist Press.

Smith, E. M. J. (1985). Life stress, social support, and mental health issues. The *Counseling Psychologist, 13,* 537–579.

Sohng, S., & Icard, L D. (1996). A Korean gay man in the United States: Toward a cultural context for social service practice. In J. F. Longres (Ed.), *Men of color: A context for service to homosexually active men* (pp. 115–137). New York: Harrington Park Press.

Soto, T. A. (1997). Ethnic minority gay, lesbian, and bisexual publications: A 10-year review. *Division 44 Newsletter, 13,* 13–14.

Spickard, P. R. (1992). The illogic of American racial categories. In M. P. P. Root (Ed.), *Racially mixed people in America* (pp. 12–23). Thousand Oaks, CA: Sage.

Sue, D. W., Arredondo, P., & McDavis, R. J. (1992). Multicultural counseling competencies and standards: A call to the profession. *Journal of Multicultural Counseling and Development, 20,* 644–688.

Sue, D. W., &. Sue, D. (1990). *Counseling the culturally different: Theory and practice* (2nd ed.). New York: Wiley.

Tafoya, T. (1997). Native gay and lesbian issues: The two-spirited. In B. Greene (Ed.), *Ethnic and cultural diversity among lesbians and gay men* (pp. 1–10). Thousand Oaks, CA: Sage.

Tsang, D. C. (1994). Notes on queer n' Asian virtual sex. *Amerasia Journal, 20,* 117–126.

U.S. Bureau of the Census. (1998). Retrieved April 30, 1998 from the World Wide Web: http://www.census.gov.html

Vasquez, M. J. T. (1994). Latinas. In L. Comas-Diaz & B. Greene (Eds.), *Women of color: Integrating ethnic and gender identities in psychotherapy* (pp. 114–138). New York: Guilford Press.

Wade, J. C. (1996). African American men's gender role conflict: The significance of racial identity. *Sex Roles, 34,* 17–33.

Walters, K. L. (1997). Urban lesbian and gay American identity: Implications for mental health service delivery. In L. B. Brown (Ed.), *Two spirit people: American Indian lesbian women and gay men* (pp. 43–65). New York: Harrington Park Press.

Zamora-Hernandez, C. E., & Patterson, D. G. (1996). Homosexually active Latino men: Issues for social work practice. In J. F. Longres (Ed.), *Men of color: A context for service to homosexually active men* (pp. 69–91). New York: Harrington Park Press.

26

Psychology, Diversity, and Social Justice

Beyond Heterosexism and Across the Cultural Divide

Beverly Greene

Introduction

Patricia Williams (1991) tells the following story in her law class on women and notions of property to illustrate what she calls the "semiotics and rhetoric of power relations, of dominance and submission, of assertion and deference, of big and of little . . ." (p. 12). As a psychologist I find this story illustrates the salience of unexamined subjective cultural positioning that is problematic in clinical work.

> Walking down Fifth Avenue in New York I came up behind a couple and their young son. The child, about four or five years old, had evidently been complaining about big dogs. The mother was saying, "But why are you afraid of big dogs?" "Because they're big," he responded . . ." But what's the difference between a big dog and a little dog?" the father persisted. "They're *big*," said the child. "But there's really no difference," said the mother, pointing to a large slathering wolfhound with narrow eyes and the calculated amble of a gangster, and then to a beribboned Pekinese the size of a roller skate . . . flouncing along . . . in that fox-trotty little step that keep Pekinese from ever being taken seriously. "See?" said the father. "If you look really closely you'll see there's no difference at all. They're all just dogs." (Williams, 1991, p. 12)

Williams writes that this position illustrates "the idiocies of High Objectivity" (1991, p. 12) and she uses this story to illustrate a paradigm of thought in which people who are in subordinate social positions are taught to distrust and reject their own perceptions, "not to see what they see." Instead, they are taught to capitulate to the perception of dominant cultural beings who fail to acknowledge their subjective and not objective lens.

This story serves as an appropriate metaphor for the way that socially marginalized people are taught to reject their own perceptions and "not see" their exploitation. It also highlights the ways in which dominant cultural beings can become so immersed into what Williams refers to as the "authoritarianism" of their own world view that they can not only universalize that view but can be oblivious to doing so.

One may ask what the treatment of human problems characterized by the work of mental health professionals with people of diverse identities has to do with social justice. And what does that have to do with subjective sociocultural positioning? As clinicians we are generally concerned with understanding and ameliorating mental health problems. Feminist psychology documents the ways that social inequity has been a significant factor in the mental health problems of women. Feminist psychologists' concerns, however, were initially limited to women, and for that matter to white, well-educated, heterosexual, economically well-off women. Despite their own marginalization as women, early architects of feminist therapies were blind to their own marginalization of other oppressive social practices and their differential effects on women. For example, only middle and upper class women championed the "right to work" as the key to women's liberation. Poor women and women of color always had not only the right but the requirement to work if their families were to survive. However, because women are found in every other social group, evolution of feminist theory by definition had to begin incorporating an analysis of the interactive effects of other forms of social oppression and identities with the oppression of women expressed in sexist and patriarchal ideologies. Interactions between identities is becoming more prominent in our discussions of diversity and multiculturalism, as we move beyond the notion of people having one master identity that is more deserving of attention or more defining of the person than others. Rather, we understand that individuals have multiple identities that interact simultaneously and that any one may be differently salient or meaningful at different developmental junctures and in different contexts.

Identity represents an interaction between the social and internal world. Some of our identities or differences in group membership are private, some are public, some are visible, and some are invisible. However, when the external, social world distorts one's identity and imposes barriers to opportunities based on that identity, the groundwork has been laid for a distorted image of one's self, sense of self-worth and a distorted perception of others. These are fertile conditions for the development of mental health problems. Mental health interventions may assist people who confront this dilemma but if they are not sensitive to social marginalization as a contextual factor it may also harm them.

Among the identities/diversities that attract our concern in mental health are ethno-cultural group membership, sexual orientation, sex, gender identity, disability, social class and age. These are not intrinsic properties of people. They are identities that have a history of being culturally defined, sometimes by law, in ways that make them a locus of social power and/or marginalization. The difference that the aforementioned differences make in people's lives is a function of the meaning ascribed to them and the social power or social disenfranchisement that is associated with them. Oppressive ideologies take human characteristics and predispositions that exist in all people and reduce them to dichotomous categorizations that apply disproportionately or selectively to some people or groups and not others. That characteristic presumably explains their place in the social hierarchy and provides a ready rationale for treatment that is unfair. Oppressive ideologies privilege some identities and devalue others. Individuals are reduced to the category that they belong to and the reality of who they are becomes invisible. The groundwork is then laid to form the rationale describing how we are permitted or even required to regard and treat them.

It is important for us to ask, then, what are the psychological consequences of being socialized to believe that we "belong" to certain groups and treating other people as if they "belong" to certain groups? What is the relationship between systemic oppression and identity? What difference does difference make?

Difference and the Difference That Differences Make

Diversity is a socially constructed concept that simply acknowledges the presence of differences. We must ask, however, why these differences are important? If we are to understand the interpersonal and intergroup tensions that occur when we directly experience or anticipate differences between ourselves and others, we must first ask what difference does that difference make in the person or group's life, why these differences matter, to whom do they matter and who decides which differences make a difference (Greene, 2003)?

My discussion is organized around the human dimensions of race/ethnicity, gender, religion, age, sexual orientation, socioeconomic class and disability. In Western culture these characteristics are considered very important, even to the degree that we have developed conceptualizations of "identities" that are a function of these characteristics. They are also the focus of, as well as the explanation for, tension and distrust between individuals and groups. These characteristics have little meaning beyond the social context in which these dimensions are perceived and defined. We are charged with appreciating the complexity of these issues in the training of human services professionals and in our own practice.

Diversity and multiculturalism are the concepts that we use to describe the study of ethno-racial, gender, sexual orientation, age, disability and other cultural differences between groups and the descriptions of those differences (Greene, 2003). However, analyses in mental health have often avoided raising questions about how these identities or statuses in and of themselves contribute to the client's dilemma, position in the social hierarchy and what the client must do to negotiate the social barriers associated with disadvantaged identity. Overall there has been greater comfort discussing race instead of racism, sex differences as opposed to sexism, minority sexual orientation as opposed to heterosexism, etc. If it were not for racism, sexism, heterosexism, ageism, classism, abilism and other oppressive ideologies, the identities associated with them would not matter as much, nor would discussions of them in the early years of multiculturalism have met with such resistance (Boyd-Franklin, 1993). Given the relational nature of social status it also raises questions about the effects of the theoretician or clinician's position in that hierarchy. How does the theoretician's subjective social and cultural positioning and place in the social hierarchy, their awareness of it or lack of awareness affect the way they conceptualize the psyche and its operation? How does it affect the way they approach and understand the client? Does it enhance that view or obstruct it? Beyond these issues, we must ask what is reenacted in the therapy process itself when the clinician is a member of or strongly identifies with a privileged and dominant group and the patient is/does not. Owens (2000) writes that there is the potential in this scenario for the re-enactment of the normative social power relationship characterized by dominance and subordination. It is incumbent on the therapist to be aware of this potential, to explore it with the client when it occurs and to explore these occurrences in the therapist's own supervision or therapy as well.

Johnson (2001) and Blaine (2000) argue that fear of the unknown is usually given as the reason that people fear and distrust those who are not like them. The implication is that despite our good intentions it is *natural* for us to be uncomfortable with diversity because we are naturally uncomfortable with and afraid of difference (Greene, 2003). However, Johnson (2001) argues that our fears are not based on what we do not know about others, rather, they are a function of all the things that we *think* we know about others based on information that usually involves an accumulated wisdom based on stereotypes and ignorance. When we directly encounter someone who is different, we already harbor assumptions about them despite having never encountered them directly. We are bombarded with information from the media that tells us who and what is considered valuable, productive, trustworthy and warrants protection, as well as who and what is considered disposable, unproductive, dangerous and to be feared and in need of social control. Stereotypes and distortions of groups deemed different from the "norm" often represent the way that it has become convenient or comfortable to perceive them, based on our relationship to them in the social hierarchy rather than on accurate depictions of them. All of these things influence whatever we presume we know about people who are different from us before ever encountering them. Those things that we *think* we know about the unknown or about people who are different are learned ideas. We are not simply born in fear of the unknown or the different, we learn to be afraid (Johnson, 2001). A more detailed discussion of differences, their meaning and their connection to social power may be found in Greene (2003, 2004).

Effects of Social Injustice

Any examination of the effects of social injustice tells us that patterned injustice at the very least leads to less than optimal functioning in any individual, but that is not the whole story. People who belong to marginalized groups are not inevitable psychological cripples. Psychological independence is defined as the ability to mentally remove oneself from malevolent influences of others such that people do not internalize distortions of themselves (Jones, 1997). Its role in maintaining psychological integrity when the environment is ubiquitously hostile is relevant to a more comprehensive understanding of the effects of societal discrimination on its victims and on their development of adaptive coping mechanisms. Jones (1997) argues that people in some disadvantaged groups move within carefully constructed, at times segregated communities, surrounded by the hostility of the dominant culture. However, those communities often facilitate the development of what he calls self-constructed psychological realities. In that context high levels of resilience can be developed. Pinderhughes (1989) observes that individuals who belong to groups associated with power and privilege may be so used to negotiating reality from a position of power that they are ill prepared to cope with adversity or situations where they are not powerful. Hence, resilience is a function of exposure to enough adversity to require the development of strategies to negotiate it but in a context where enough resources are available to do so. It would also seem that while it is important for individuals to be confronted with adversity rather than insulated from it, too much adversity with too little respite and too few resources can overwhelm many individuals, negatively affecting their ability to cope.

West (2002) observes that all Americans experienced, in the aftermath of the 9/11 attacks, the kind of protracted social trauma that socially disadvantaged Americans experience routinely. He explains the latter as a kind of ongoing domestic terrorism that leaves marginalized people unsafe, targets of random violence, hated and unprotected. Understanding the dynamics of how many of these group members have responded in healthy ways may be of use to mental health professionals in assisting people who are coping with other forms of terrorism and the psychological trauma that often results.

Resilience in disadvantaged individuals can enable them to transform adverse circumstances and even thrive despite them. However, Jones (1997) warns that patterned injustice or unwarranted and protracted social or personal hardship, characterized by the experiences of victims of personal or social abuse, leaves people exposed to chronic stressors and challenges that will threaten their "carefully constructed psychological equilibrium" (Jones, 1997, p. 13). Mental health theoreticians and practitioners must understand that tangible psychological and physical energies are required to maintain that equilibrium and that many of our clients pay an emotional and sometimes physical price (expressed in health problems) for survival, even when some group members thrive. Clinicians must resist the temptation of using the existence of survivors as a means of either minimizing the negative effects of the social oppression, resisting the need to blame those who fail to endure those challenges, or suggesting that the social system must be working fairly if some of the disadvantaged group's members manage to overcome some barriers and succeed. To use Williams' (1991) metaphor, we must avoid assuming that even if we can find even one little boy who could wrestle large wolfhounds to the ground, it would not prove that the fear of big dogs held by all of the other little boys was unwarranted.

Social Injustice and Psychological Trauma

It is important to understand the formation of psychological vulnerability and resilience in members of socially disadvantaged groups if we are to use the therapy process competently and if we are to appreciate the sometimes devastating effects of social inequity. How is this connected to subjective cultural positioning and what has this to do with power, privilege and oppressive ideologies? My analysis takes place in the context of the meritocracy myth, the myth of rugged individualism and some of the dynamics that are intrinsic to historical and contemporary social injustice and institutional mental health.

Fine (2002) observes that the myth of rugged individualism, the core of which is the belief that "everyone has choices" and that "opportunity is equally distributed or based on merit," requires the erasure of a history of social oppression and marginalization that is relevant to any analysis of the psychological functioning of socially marginalized persons. In Fine's analysis, maintaining the myth warrants a concomitant idealization of dominant group members that requires keeping secrets about them to maintain the distortion that their idealization represents. It also requires maintaining silence about social pathology or the pathologies of the institutions that we are part of, silence about the incompetence of dominant group members as well as silence about who actually gets but did not deserve. An example of this may be seen in the depiction of poor white people as "trash." We may ask how people who are white and poor are different from other poor people or other white people. The label trash in not so subtle form explains not just who they are, but *why.* The reality of class oppression can be disguised if we assume that something about group members rather than inequity in opportunity explains their condition (Greene, 2000).

Jordan (1997) observes that in the myth of meritocracy, achievements by members of privileged groups are attributed to their individual efforts, and rewards for those efforts are seen as having been earned and deserved. Conversely, people who are vulnerable and disadvantaged are presumed to be getting what they deserve as well, including blame for their condition. In psychotherapy practice, both client and therapist have their own personal stake and role in these beliefs. When psychotherapy paradigms legitimize the social status quo rather than examine it critically, they become instruments of social oppression and control and by definition contribute to social injustice.

Strickland (2000) observes that in the history of institutional mental health we have hospitalized, incarcerated and drugged the psychologically "deviant." Although we give contingencies of reinforcement a polite nod, we continue to place the origins of psychopathology in the individual and not the context. Anxiety, depression, dissociative disorders, anger and rage, accurate perceptions of exploitation and attempts to flee from them represent behaviors that may be desperate and understandable attempts to cope with pathological life conditions or challenges. Those adaptive attempts to cope are themselves pathologized as expressions of defects in the individual. For example, in the mid-1800s a Louisiana surgeon coined the term drapetomania as the diagnosis that described a mental impairment of slaves characterized by their persistent attempts to escape from plantations and bondage (Thomas & Sillen, 1972). Normalizing the abnormality of social pathology driven by oppressive ideologies serves to obscure both the pathology of the dominant group as well as the socially constructed nature of one's placement in the social hierarchy.

When oppressive ideologies are operationalized they represent forms of terrorism and they can create in their survivors not simply a PTSD but what Fine (2002) calls a Post Colonial Stress Disorder. Unlike PTSD, the traumatic process is protracted, inescapable and systemically tied. As such it comes to be perpetuated by people who may not even believe in the oppressive ideologies that are a part of the institution's structure.

Daniel (1995, 2000) cites factors that impede therapists' receptivity to narratives about the role of social marginalization and trauma in clients' lives. She cites the sexual trauma of black women and the disclosure of those experiences that highlight the intersections of race, gender and sexual orientation for group members as an example. In a historical context, who is accusing whom and of what are critical social factors in the ability of therapists to hear social trauma in the patient's narrative. She uses the Anita Hill and Clarence Thomas senate hearings as an example of the continued vulnerability of black women in the workplace and the lack of recognition of that vulnerability even among other black women. Daniel (1995) writes that any analysis about black women's vulnerability is subject to social beliefs about them. What happens if the victim is a black woman who is victimized by a white man? A black man? A white woman? Another black woman? And what happens when class and education are a part of the narrative? I recall many people, many black people, often other women, being furious with Anita Hill, not because they disbelieved her but because they felt that she should be silent about racial dirty laundry, particularly if it was directed at a black man. Many asserted that because she was an educated woman she surely did not have to put up with harassment of any kind. She could simply leave and find another job. The disbelief that class and education do not automatically protect black women from racial and gender vulnerability led to the expectation that Hill should have been silent about her perpetrator. It also fueled the belief that she could not be victimized. Hence not only was her trauma trivialized but she was vilified as a traitor to the race. Such instances can serve to retraumatize the victim. A therapist's ability to hear the potential for traumatizing a client will be a function of the factors Daniel (1995) discusses.

Comas-Diaz (2000) uses the term *cultural allodynia* to describe another form of social trauma characterized by extreme reactions to neutral or ambiguous stimuli caused by insidious ethno-cultural injury. She emphasizes the political nature of diagnosis and treatment and suggests that the failure to acknowledge political process as an ingredient in the failure to see behavioral conditions as a function of cultural reality and power. Hence we must always be alert to acknowledging and analyzing the evolution of strategies designed to move us away from analyses of oppression when such analyses make people uncomfortable. This is particularly important in mental health because therapists' discomfort with these issues will affect their ability to appreciate the client's narrative.

American Legal Scholar Lani Guinier (Guinier & Torres, 2002) uses the miner's canary as a metaphor for political race. Miners often carried a canary into the mines with them as the canary's fragile lungs would cause it to expire from the invisible and odorless toxic gases in the mines long before it would affect the miners. Hence the canary alerted the miners to the poison in the air so that they could get out of the mines before it overpowered them. In mental health paradigms I would extend that analogy to the mental health distress among people who belong to marginalized groups, poor people, people of color, sexual minorities, women, people with disabilities, and old people. Their distress has been viewed historically as an expression of their personal pathology or the group's defect; however they are very much like the miner's canary. Like the canary they are deemed expendable to dominant cultural members and there is a tendency to think that if they are sacrificed, the only harm done is to others like them, who are also expendable. In reality, members of these groups are, like the canary, providing society with a distress signal. If we ignore the problems that disproportionately affect members of marginalized groups, we do so at our own peril because their symptoms are not an expression of their defect; rather they portend a larger, more insidious problem. Their distress is the first sign that there is "poison in the air" in the form of toxic social conditions. If left alone they will affect everyone. Our task then is not to exhaustively study canaries or view them as having defective lungs, devise little air masks to help them better withstand the gas or seek to rehabilitate them. In the miner's analogy, the problem was not the canary, it was the gas in the mines. Many mental health problems are not a function of defective individuals, they are a function of social inequities that become toxic.

The Therapist's Subjective Cultural Positioning and Shame

All psychotherapists are influenced by their own personal cultural identities as well as the culture of whatever theory they embrace. Like any other culture, psychology theory and theorists are embedded in a cultural matrix that is positioned in a cultural context and is not objective. Despite the limitations of theories, Thompson (1989) writes that the failure to explore sociopolitical realities is more attributable to the therapists' countertransference resistance rather than the limitations of specific theories. As therapists we use theoretical paradigms to organize and guide the work;

however, we also allow our experiences with clients to inform what we "know." Theory therefore is a guide, not an absolute determinant of therapeutic interventions. More often, it is the failure of the therapist, often a dominant cultural being or one who is overly identified with dominant cultural paradigms that often include oppressive ideologies, to allow for sufficient self-examination around their own privileged identities, or wish for them, and how it affects their subjectivity that is problematic, not simply the theory per se. Therapists' personal convictions that often interfere with hearing the client are often dominant cultural beliefs that have either accepted and supported or at the very least failed to critique social pathologies that are a function of oppressive ideology. How the therapist is raced, gendered, aged, sexually oriented, etc., affects what they choose to see and what they choose to avoid just as it does in the client. Similarly, theoreticians' understanding of the order of the world, via their subjective cultural lens, informs the theoretical explanations they put forth about human behavior as well as their willingness to examine the nature of constituents of social power and privileged identities in both clients' and therapists' lives.

Social Privilege, Disadvantage and the Therapist's Shame and Guilt

The need to deny the existence and meaning difference in discrepancies of social power differentials between people is often the key to the need to maintain silence around the social inequity associated with differences. When therapists are required to analyze society's realistic power differentials and injustices and their meaning in patient's lives, they must do so in their own lives as well. However, doing so may evoke discomfort with the process and a need to avoid it. To be marginalized may evoke empathy, but to be privileged is to risk evoking anger, resentment and sometimes fear. The reality, however, is that those feelings exist within the therapy process whether therapists choose to talk about them or not. Avoiding them violates the fundamental dictum of therapy, that everything that affects the client is "grist for the mill." Therapy may offer both client and therapist an opportunity to develop connections across differences and the fears about what they make of us and others. Walker (2002) observes that the potential for conflict that is often feared when exploring diversities may be seen as an impasse or as an opportunity to foster and deepen connections across what may seem to be the chasm of difference.

Social privilege and disadvantage are implicated in our understanding of the ego ideal of the therapist. The reality of who we are always falls short of our ideal because by definition the ideal is perfection and therefore unattainable; however, falling short of that ideal often evokes shame and guilt (Holzman, 1995). To avoid experiencing shame and discomfort about privilege we must deny the reality that having a privileged identity means that we may profit at someone else's expense. This denial becomes difficult if we hold a social privilege and we encounter clients who are disadvantaged around that characteristic. The encounter itself can elicit discomfort even if differences and/or their meaning are never overtly discussed. When the reality of privilege materializes, it also challenges therapists' personal beliefs about who they really are. It is unlikely that these issues can be confronted in a client without scrutinizing and challenging one's own sense of self as a mental health service provider. This task can be a painful and difficult but necessary undertaking.

Moncayo (1998) suggests that hierarchical divisions may be found within marginalized groups that are just as tenacious as those between marginalized and dominant/privileged groups. All members of disadvantaged groups are not equally disadvantaged and all do not automatically learn to be any more tolerant of differences than members of the majority. Like members of dominant groups, members of disadvantaged groups with privileged identities may often deny those privileged identities, preferring to focus on their locus of disadvantage. It is usually the majority voices that are most privileged and often deemed to speak for the entire culture. Cultural sisterhood and brotherhood, after all, have all of the complexities and rivalries of sibling relationships.

Conclusion

Psychotherapy can be a powerful tool against social injustice when it validates a client's accurate perception of social as well as personal exploitation as well as the appropriate feelings elicited by unfair treatment. It is helpful when it assists clients in consciously developing adaptive strategies for identifying and addressing ongoing forms of social trauma. Ultimately psychotherapy can be useful in helping clients know the difference between distortions they have been told about themselves, either by family or social pathology, and who they really are.

Every gender is raced, every race is gender coded, and everyone has a sexual orientation and a social class that influences the experience of other aspects of identity. Many people have moved across the boundaries of gender, sexual orientation, and class. People with disabilities constitute a group with permeable boundaries that make it a potential identity for everyone. If they are fortunate enough, people age and grow old. The average American woman is not a size 6, at least not permanently. As we consider a 21st century psychology we are challenged to abandon archaic notions of a master identity and acknowledge that the crucible of identity is really a kaleidoscopic matrix of identities in which we may occupy many different locations at once; that there is a multiplicity of identity in all individuals in which some identities are privileged and some are disadvantaged within the same person; that there is a complex interrelationship of identities that interact in a dynamic manner that transforms and informs one another continually throughout the lifespan. That identity is defined more by context than by the property of a person or persons. Multiple identity paradigms are inherently messy and in the day to day they remind us that we do not *know* what to expect when we begin to explore the complexity of human differences to the degree that we *think* we know.

Mays (2000) offers that psychology must be willing to teach and develop a body of science that is informed by principles of social justice and equity. In this paradigm, research about oppressive ideologies will help to make us more competent when treating clients who are different as well as similar to us. She writes that when social justice informs our perspectives, we become aware that the behaviors that we deem pathological and become a focus of clinical scrutiny are often conditions that are connected to social inequities in health, education and welfare as well as the very paradigms and policies of our own discipline and its practices. Failing to acknowledge and understand the broad and divergent role of societal privilege and disadvantage in clients' lives and their role in our response to and understanding of differences ultimately undermines our attempts to deliver competent clinical services and celebrate the richness of human diversity.

References

Blame, B. (2000). *The psychology of diversity: Perceiving & experiencing social difference.* Mountain View, CA: Mayfield Publishing Co.

Boyd-Franklin, N. (1993). Pulling out the arrows. *Family Therapy Networker, 17*, 54–56.

Comas-Diaz, L. (2000). An ethnopolitical approach to working with people of color. *American Psychologist, 10*, 1319–1325.

Daniel, J. H. (1995). The discourse on Thomas v. Hill: A resource for perspectives on the Black woman and sexual trauma. *Journal of Feminist Family Therapy, 7*, 103–117.

Daniel, J. H. (2000). The courage to hear: African American women's memories of racial trauma. In L. C. Jackson & B. Greene (Eds.), *Psychotherapy with African American women: Innovations in psychodynamic perspectives and practice* (pp. 126–144). New York: Guilford Press.

Fine, M. (2002). The presence of an absence. *Psychology of Women Quarterly, 26*, 9–24.

Greene, B. (2000). Beyond heterosexism and across the cultural divide. Developing an inclusive lesbian, gay and bisexual psychology: A look to the future. In B. Greene & G. L. Croom (Eds.), *Education, research and practice in lesbian, gay, bisexual and transgendered psychology: A resource manual* (pp. 1–45). Thousand Oaks, CA: Sage Publications.

Greene, B. (2003). What difference does a difference make? Societal privilege, disadvantage, and discord in human relationships. In J. Robinson & L. James (Eds.), *Diversity in human interaction: A tapestry of America* (pp. 3–20). New York: Oxford University Press.

Greene, B. (2004). African American lesbians and other culturally diverse people in psychodynamic psychotherapies: Useful paradigms or oxymoron? *Journal of Lesbian Studies, 8*, 57–77.

Guinier, L., & Torres, G. (2002). *The miner's canary: Enlisting race, resisting power, transforming democracy*. Cambridge, MA: Harvard University Press.

Holzman, C. (1995). Rethinking the role of guilt and shame in White women's antiracism work. In J. Adleman & G. Enguidanos (Eds.), *Racism in the lives of women: Testimony, theory and guides to practice* (pp. 325–332). New York: Harrington Park Press.

Johnson, A. G. (2001). *Privilege, power and difference*. Mountain View, CA: Mayfield Publishing Co.

Jones, F. (1997). Eloquent anonymity. [Review of the book Lush life: A biography of Billy Strayhorn.] Readings: *A Journal of Reviews and Commentary in Mental Health, 12*, 10–14.

Jordan, J. (1997). Relational therapy in a nonrelational world. *Work in Progress*, No. 79. Wellesley, MA: Stone Center Working Paper Series.

Mays, V. M. (2000). A social justice agenda. *American Psychologist, 55*, 326–327.

Moncayo, R. (1998). Cultural diversity and the cultural epistemological structure of psychoanalysis: Implications for psychotherapy with Latinos and other minorities. *Psychoanalytic Psychology, 15*, 262–286.

Owens-Patterson, M. (2000). The African American supervisor: Racial transference and counter-transference in interracial psychotherapy supervision. In L. C. Jackson & B. Greene (Eds.), *Psychotherapy with African American women: Innovations in psychodynamic perspectives and practice*. New York: Guilford Press.

Pinderhughes, E. (1989). *Understanding race, ethnicity and power: The key to efficacy in clinical practice*. New York: Free Press/Simon & Schuster.

Strickland, B. R. (2000). Misassumptions, misadventures and the misuse of psychology. *American Psychologist, 55*, 331–338.

Thomas, A., & Sillen, S. (1972). *Racism & psychiatry*. Secaucus, NJ: Citadel Press.

Thompson, C. (1989). Psychoanalytic psychotherapy with inner city patients. *Journal of Contemporary Psychotherapy, 19*, 137–148.

Walker, M. (2002). How therapy helps when the culture hurts. *Work in Progress 1–10.* Wellesley, MA: Wellesley Centers for Women Publications.

Williams, P. (1991). *The alchemy of race and rights.* Cambridge, MA: Harvard University Press.

27

Psychotherapy, Classism, and the Poor

Conspicuous by Their Absence

Laura Smith

Psychotherapy with poor clients has been the subject of an undercurrent of discussion in psychology for the past 40 years. Psychologists have concluded at various points during this period that poor people are neither less interested in nor less able to benefit from the psychotherapeutic process than other demographic groups. Presumptions to the contrary have been linked to therapists' "negative bias" (Lorion, 1974, p. 345) toward them and a lack of educational or supervisory techniques for addressing these biases. Although the intervening years have seen the advent of important multicultural scholarship regarding therapeutic biases around other aspects of difference, classist bias has gone largely unexamined, and psychologists know little more about the therapeutic experiences of poor people today than they did decades ago. Why has psychology fallen short in its service to this segment of society? After first clarifying the use of certain terms and outlining the literature with regard to psychotherapy with poor clients, I suggest that psychotherapists' willingness and ability to work with the poor is compromised by persistent, unexamined classist attitudes, and I present examples of encounters with my own classism in hope of encouraging discussion of these issues.

Definitions

The Poor

Liu et al. (2004) are among the most recent researchers to have documented psychology's

Authors' Note: Portions of this article were included in a presentation to the 112th Annual Convention of the American Psychological Association, Honolulu, Hawaii, July-August 2004. I am deeply appreciative of the guidance that I received in revising an earlier version of this article. I thank Elizabeth Merrick for her careful readings and insightful feedback and Andrew Baer, Carroll Smith, and Sean Kelleher for their support in this article's preparation.

lack of clarity with regard to the use of social class as a construct. Language used to describe populations of interest varies widely; such descriptors include *low income, lower class, low socioeconomic status (SES), poor, economically poor, working poor,* and *disadvantaged.* Calling psychological literature "particularly sloppy," Baker (1996, p. 18) outlined various attempts to operationalize social class, including commonly used divisions based on income or SES that ignore relevant issues such as cultural perspective, social status, and the distinction between mental and physical labor. She also pointed out that class-related constructs are inherently problematic in that they are integral aspects of the stratifications that they purport to describe. A related problem is that the conceptual isolation of class (or any other aspect of social identity, for that matter) is a contrivance that, although helpful for the purpose of discussion, does not accurately represent the complex interactions among class, race, ethnicity, gender, and/or sexual orientation that characterize lived experience. Along these lines, psychologists writing about class have explicated the double jeopardy faced by poor people of color (Boyd-Franklin & Bry, 2000: Espin, 1997), poor immigrants (Azocar, Miranda, & Dwyer, 1996), poor older women (Minkler & Stone, 1985), and poor obese women (Bowen, Tomoyasu, & Cauce, 1999). Given these complexities, it seems unrealistic to think that absolute categorizations and definitions with regard to social class are feasible; psychology's failure to achieve this end is more likely a reflection of the construct itself than of a lack of diligence on the part of psychologists. In this article, people living near or beneath the poverty line will be described as *poor,* a term that should be understood to have the meaning explained by Karon and VandenBos (1977):

> We mean people who have been poor all their lives, whose parents were poor, and who have a high probability of remaining poor. It is thus a social as well as an economic condition. This definition of "poor" does not have sharp boundaries, but includes the unemployed, partially unemployed, and the lower-income members of the working class. (p. 169)

Other terms for this population are used in this article in accordance with the practices of the authors cited.

Classism

Lott (2002) described classism as the result of "class privilege (i.e., unearned advantage and conferred dominance) and power," in words quoted from Moon and Rolison, 1998. Liu et al. (2004) took issue with her definition on the grounds that it captured only one type of classism and excluded, for example, the "classism that lower social class people have against higher social class people" (p. 9). My usage of this term coincides with Lott's. More specifically, the word classism is not used simply to describe prejudiced attitudes that people of one social class might have regarding members of any other social class. Rather, classism, like the other "isms" (e.g., racism, sexism, heterosexism), is a form of oppression. Oppression can be understood as prejudice plus power: It is an interlocking system that involves domination and control of social ideology, institutions, and resources, resulting in a condition of privilege for one group relative to the disenfranchisement of another (Hardiman & Jackson, 1997). Members of both dominant and subordinated groups are capable of prejudice, but only dominant groups have the institutional and cultural power to enforce their prejudices via oppression (Griffin, 1997). Hence, although poor people might certainly harbor prejudices against middle class or wealthy people, these attitudes are not properly referred to as classism according to this definition.

Psychotherapy and Poor Clients

The 1960s

The issue of psychotherapeutic treatment for the poor came into focus with the community mental health center (CMHC) movement of the 1960s. As described by Albee and Gulotta (1997), the Joint Commission on Mental Illness and Health delivered a report to Congress in 1961 that outlined the overwhelming demand being placed on public mental hospitals. Having read the report as a senator, President John F. Kennedy advocated in 1963 for federal funding of research with regard to mental disorders and the construction of 2,000 CMHCs nationwide. During the administration of President Lyndon B. Johnson, limited staffing of CMHCs began.

This proposal, which promised to make psychotherapy available to people of all income levels, appeared against the backdrop of the widely held opinion among psychotherapists of the 1950s and 1960s that most poor people did not have the skills to engage in the therapeutic process, were unlikely to benefit from it, and dropped out prematurely in any event (Graff, Kenig, & Radoff, 1971; Heitler, 1973). Research from that period reviewed by Lorion (1974) indicated that therapists often perceived poor clients as hostile (Hollingshead & Redlich, 1958), crude in language and behavior (Affleck & Garfield, 1961), and a waste of supervisory time (Baum, Felzer, D'Zmura, & Shumaker, 1966). Not surprisingly, researchers found higher class status to be reliably associated with acceptance into psychotherapeutic treatment (Jones, 1974).

The 1970s

As CMHCs opened their doors during the 1970s, a new, more culturally aware interpretation of these treatment difficulties began to emerge: Given that they were faced with middle-class therapists who disliked working with them and held out little hope of a beneficial prognosis, it was no wonder that poor clients failed to show improvement and/or left treatment. Lorion (1973) offered such an assessment, pointing out that no study had established a relation between SES and treatment outcome and suggesting that therapists seemed to be seeking to rationalize their disengagement from the poor. In a review published the following year, Lorion (1974) suggested that therapists' negative attitudes could be important contributors to treatment failures with poor clients, and he lamented the lack of supervisory techniques for addressing these biases. Lorion (1974) also refuted the idea that unrealistic expectations among poor clients rendered them untreatable, for example, that they tended to enter therapy expecting "immediate relief through magical advice" (Jacobs, Charles, Jacobs, Weinstein, & Mann, 1972, p. 667). Lorion (1974) cited research to demonstrate that similar misconceptions are observed at all income levels and suggested that therapists' biases may lead them to overemphasize these misconceptions among poor clients. "Therapist-centered problems," he concluded, "do not justify decisions not to treat. Rather, they should be considered as training-supervisory problems that can be overcome by recognition and discussion" (Lorian, 1974, pp. 351–352).

Similar conclusions were reached in another article published the same year by Jones (1974). Jones outlined the research demonstrating therapists' widespread reluctance to work with poor clients and noted that, "phrased less kindly," this trend could represent "the expression of an ugly class bias" (p. 309). Like Lorion, Jones (1974) posited that "there is no reliable evidence that lower-class clients do not possess the characteristics which clinical wisdom considers necessary for a person to be amenable to psychotherapeutic influence" (p. 317). With regard to the idea that poor people do not understand or want psychotherapy, Jones cited Goin's 1965 investigation of class-related expectations in which 52% of lower-class patients entering a psychiatric clinic indicated that they wished to solve their problems by talking about their feelings and exploring early experiences—in other words, that they expected and hoped to receive insight-oriented therapy.

Siassi and Messer (1976) concurred with the view that "there has been a misplaced emphasis on the role of the patient in attempting to explain negative therapeutic reactions of the lower class patient" (p. 32). They also addressed suggestions from clinicians that psychotherapy be modified or abandoned as a treatment modality for the poor in favor of alternatives such as somatic, symptom-focused, or other "short-cut services" (Siassi & Messer, 1976, p. 32). Acknowledging that poor people may initially approach the therapeutic encounter in despondency, they contended that if therapists have the skills and awareness to "keep low SES patients in treatment beyond the first few interviews, the outcome is at least as good as with higher SES groups" (Siassi & Messer, 1976, p. 33). According to Siassi and Messer (1976), alternative "modalities of care suggested as appropriate for the lower classes may turn out to be inadvertent discrimination in disguise" (p. 32). Smith and Dejoie-Smith (1984) made a similar case with regard to the prescriptive use of behavioral therapy among poor and/or ethnically diverse populations. They demonstrated that claims of its greater effectiveness among such clients lacked empirical validation and cautioned that therapists who made use of such a "cookbook approach" (Smith & Dejoie-Smith, 1984, p. 528) could be perpetuating unsubstantiated generalizations about poor clients.

Other researchers presented evidence of psychotherapeutic treatment offered successfully to poor clients. Pretherapy preparatory experiences were investigated as a method of enhancing rapport between therapists and poor clients. Jacobs, Charles, Jacobs, Weinstein, and Mann (1972) studied the effects of a brief, preinterview orientation to psychotherapy offered to clients, paired with an orientation for psychiatric residents focusing on class-related cultural awareness. Their findings demonstrated that when client and resident were prepared or when the resident only was prepared, lower-income clients were seen for longer periods of time than they were without preparation. Support was also found for the efficacy of pretherapy interventions with poor clients in studies by Heitler (1973) and Strupp and Bloxom (1973); these studies did not, however, include a component addressing therapist awareness or preparation. Padfield (1976) examined the efficacy of two treatment approaches offered to poor rural women diagnosed with depression, one that added goal-setting strategies to the foundation of a supportive, empathic therapeutic alliance and one that was based on the therapeutic alliance itself. The women in the lowest income group showed the most improvement regardless of treatment model, prompting the researcher to comment, "The evidence from this study should help to dispel the old myth that lower-class women are nonverbal and need a behavioral model" (Padfield, 1976, p. 213).

Shifting Attentions

The 1970s, then, had seen a relative surge of support for a perspective summed up by Karon and VandenBos (1977): When therapists have the skills and awareness needed to understand class-related attitudes and issues, then "psychotherapy with the poor patient is no different from good psychotherapy with anyone" (p. 169). Shortly thereafter, however, came what Albee (1996) described as "the counterrevolution" (p. 1132). During the 1980s, psychologists' attention shifted away from concern with the psychological consequences of poverty and other forms of inequality and toward the biology, neurology, and genetics of mental disorders. While this so-called medical model was gaining in prominence, federal support for the CMHC movement waned as the Reagan administration began to scale back funding for CMHCs in the 1980s, Of the 2,000 CMHCs planned for construction, only 750 had been established, and they were now struggling for their economic survival (Humphreys & Rappaport, 1993). Nevertheless, during the 1980s and 1990s, a degree of attention to the issue of psychotherapeutic services for the poor was maintained among specific groups of psychologists.

Feminist psychology. By the early 1980s, feminist thinkers and social critics such as Davis (1983), hooks (1981, 1984), and Lorde (1984) were effectively challenging mainstream feminism on its claims that it represented the experiences of all women—rather, they argued, it was concerned primarily with the experiences of middle-class, White, heterosexual women. As part of this movement, feminist psychology began its own process of self-examination and, in so doing, became a source of advocacy for services to poor clients and the development of class-related cultural competence among therapists. Denny (1986) asked whether poor women could "benefit from, or even survive feminist therapy" (p. 51) as she systematically explored classist bias in feminist psychotherapeutic theory and practice. In the coming years, this effort would be advanced by psychologists such as Brown (1990) and Reid (1995), the latter stating that poor women had been "shut up and shut out" (p. 184) of mainstream psychology as a whole. Other feminist psychologists addressed such issues as classist psychotherapeutic bias (Leeder, 1996) and the improvement of therapists' cultural awareness with regard to class (Chalifoux, 1996).

Family systems therapy. Family therapists and others who work from a systems or structural perspective, who attempt to "view families within a larger social, economic, and political framework" (Mirkin, 1990, p. xiii), use an approach that, by definition, affords an opportunity to consider poverty as it affects psychotherapeutic treatment. Family systems therapists, accordingly, have helped to bring attention to the issue of psychological practice with poor clients. Presenting systems theory as providing a basis for more meaningful treatment formulations for poor clients, Inclan and Ferran (1990) proposed a conceptualization of the problems associated with poverty that uses clients' relationships with the mainstream work world as a starting point. Brown and Parnell (1990), Minuchin (1995), and Boyd-Franklin and Bry (2000) have all described applications of a family systems approach to psychotherapeutic work with clients living in poverty; Aponte (1994) and Minuchin, Colapinto, and Minuchin (1998) contributed books entirely devoted to the topic. Among these authors, Aponte is notable in emphasizing the importance of therapists' own awareness and preparation with regard to their work with the poor.

Psychoanalysis. Given their "reputation for elitism" (Altman, 1995, p. xiii), psychoanalysts might not be expected to figure in a discussion of psychotherapeutic treatment for poor clients; nevertheless, a number of analysts have challenged the field of psychoanalysis to broaden its scope (e.g., Moskowitz, 1996; Siassi & Messer, 1976; Thompson, 1989; Trevithick, 1998). Pérez Foster (1996) wrote of psychoanalysis's "secret shame" (p. 3): clinicians who claim to prize the value of all human life yet have virtually excluded poor and culturally different people from treatment. Altman's (1995) comprehensive explication addressed the classism and racism that are embedded in psychoanalytic theory and practice and described the use of a three-person model for psychoanalytic practice that incorporates the influence of social systems. Focusing on countertransferential issues, Javier and Herron (2002) suggested that not only do psychotherapists have trouble relating to poor people, they also resist such connection defensively. Highlighting the social and political dimensions of poverty, the authors explained that

> most therapists are middle class, so it might be argued that they are too separated from upper class patients to understand them sufficiently, but that is unlikely. Middle-class people frequently wish for more, and often try to achieve it. . . . In contrast, therapists have no interest in being poor, and despite social conscience, do not seek to identify with the poor. In essence . . . the potential for disruptive countertransference is high and prone to override egalitarian and altruistic desires as well. (¶ 9)

Multicultural psychology. Multicultural psychologists have contributed invaluably toward psychotherapists' understanding of the critical importance of cultural difference and, in so doing, have supported discourse regarding psychotherapeutic attitudes toward the poor. However, their consideration of poor clients specifically has been sporadic. Multiculturalists frequently acknowledge poverty when they include class as an aspect of diversity, but their attention is more precisely focused elsewhere: Poor people, after all, are not an ethnocultural group. Some multicultural specialists exclude class intentionally, warning that "concepts of multiculturalism can become diluted to the point of uselessness if the definition is expanded to include more than race and ethnicity" (D. W. Sue et al., 1998. p. 3). In a similar move to disentangle class from culture, the most recent editor of *Cultural and Ethnic Minority Psychology* encouraged a shift in focus among researchers, stating his opinion that "there has been a disproportionate amount of research on socioeconomically disadvantaged ethnic minority persons" (Hall, 2004, p. 4).

2000 and Beyond

Psychology today seems to present two faces regarding the poor. On the one hand, recent contributions to the psychological literature suggest that poor people have again receded into the background of psychological concern. Saris and Johnston-Robledo (2000) summarized the results of their PsycLIT content analysis in the title of their article, "Poor Women Are Still Shut Out of Mainstream Psychology." Similarly, Lott (2002) identified "the near invisibility of the poor in psychology" (¶ 6), Javier and Herron (2002) interpreted a "fear of the poor" (¶ 26) among therapists, and Furnham (2003) observed that "the most important topics in poverty research have been almost totally neglected by psychologists" (p. 164). Moreira (2003) deplored the growing tendency worldwide to relegate mental health treatment for the poor to hospitals and psychiatrists, a trend that she called "the medicalization of poverty" (p. 81). S. Sue and Lam (2002) included social class in their review of psychotherapeutic treatment outcomes for diverse cultural and demographic groups. With regard to poor clients, they observed that "despite the important influence of socioeconomic status on an individual's life, this variable has been widely ignored" (p. 414), and that the most that can be reliably gleaned from the literature is that poor clients are likely to drop out of treatment prematurely. "It seems that there are still biases and stereotypes that psychologists have with regard to this population," the authors concluded (S. Sue & Lam, 2002, p. 414).

Juxtaposed with these findings are the better intentions that are articulated within the field of psychology. The American Psychological Association (APA) recently adopted the Resolution on Poverty and Socioeconomic Status, in which the APA stated that "poverty is detrimental to psychological well-being" and charged psychologists with the responsibility to "treat and address the needs of low-income individuals and families" (APA, 2000, ¶ 23). The proposition's 17 resolutions challenge psychologists to address poverty, classism, practitioner competence and training, and public policy, clearly portraying a field in service to all segments of society. What barriers prevent psychologists from acting more consistently on this charge? Researchers of the 1960s had already established that poor clients terminate treatment prematurely—why, four decades later, does that still constitute the sum of psychology's knowledge about them? And after recurrent calls for attention to therapists' awareness and attitudes regarding the poor—and after multicultural competence has become a mainstay of practitioner training with regard to other aspects of difference—why has there been virtually no advancement in their preparation to work with poor clients?

One answer is offered by Lott's (2002) article, referenced earlier, which outlined psychology's exclusion of working-class and poor people from its research and theorization. Lott described this phenomenon as "distancing from the poor" and presented psychology as only one of many fields and institutions that devalue, discount, or otherwise fail to acknowledge the poor. With regard to practitioners, Lott observed that most psychologists have attained middle-class lifestyles, even when they may have begun life in low-income families. The stigma and isolation associated with poverty, then, might be less salient for psychologists than other aspects of difference that could still be experienced and thus the presence of classism in the field more elusive. In other words, Lott identified the same dynamic in the field at large that Javier and Herron (2002) described in the therapist-client dyad: Unconscious distancing from the poor overrides the better intentions that clearly exist among psychologists, with the result that the poor are "disappeared" from many psychologists' professional and personal worlds.

More specifically, I suggest that classism among psychotherapists manifests itself in distinct attitudinal barriers that deter advocacy for the funding and development of psychological services for poor people and that also compromise the delivery of such services. These barriers play out in tenacious subconscious pretexts and experiences of discomfort among practitioners that, when unexamined, encourage evasion of the underlying issues. If practitioners are to play their part in bringing the APA Resolution on Poverty and Socioeconomic Status (APA, 2000) to life, they must follow its prescription to develop this aspect of their cultural competence. However, unlike many other aspects of difference, there is little in the way of focused training experiences or scholarship to facilitate awareness of classism. I hope to encourage discussion of cultural competence around social class by describing encounters with my own classism, to which I turn now.

Classist Attitudinal Barriers: Four Examples

What awareness-related barriers can a middle-class psychologist expect to encounter during the course of his or her work with poor clients? As a psychologist in a community center located in one of the nation's poorest urban neighborhoods, I have experienced such barriers repeatedly. They come in the form of blind spots, classist stereotyping, and feeling overwhelmed. I should note that not only am I a middle-class psychologist in a poor neighborhood, I am also a White psychologist in a mostly Latino and African American neighborhood, so my attention to cultural competence around race and ethnicity is equally vital, as is the necessity to identify personal and professional barriers that relate to my own racism. Fortunately, supervision and guidance are available to me with regard to those issues: Since graduate school, I have benefited from the rich multicultural counseling literature (e.g., Carter, 1995; Constantine & Sue, 2005: Ivey, D'Andrea, Ivey, & Simek-Morgan, 2002; Ponterotto, Casas, Suzuki, & Alexander, 2001); from explications of Whiteness as an identity (e.g., Helms, 1990; McIntosh, 1988); and from countless workshops, seminars, and focused supervisory experiences. In the community center, staff members attended training sessions on racism, and we have weekly meetings for the sole purpose of enacting antiracist principles in our work. Analogous opportunities for training and professional development with regard to classism are not readily identifiable.

More specifically, the class-related attitudinal barriers that I have encountered organize themselves roughly according to four overlapping themes:

1. *Poor people are forced to contend with so many overwhelming day-to-day problems that they have no use for what a psychologist can offer; what they need is assistance with identifying important basic resources and problem solving.*

This attitudinal barrier, which was one of the earliest that I encountered in myself, is essentially classist while containing a grain of truth. The truth is that the poorest clients withstand existences that are so tumultuous, precarious, and bleak that discussions of concrete survival strategies must indeed be a part of the work. For example, a young man from the community had fallen behind on the rent he paid for a single unheated room and, having hidden from his landlord for months, now had to decide where to go. We discussed such grim alternatives as the notoriously unlivable Emergency Assistance Unit (the first stage in the shelter system) or living in his friend's parked car, which he had done the last time he was homeless. We spent many hours following the trail of phone calls, office visits, lost faxes, and missing files that eventually led to temporary public rent assistance, a meaningful outcome that brought profound relief. Yet, when the young man spontaneously assessed the usefulness of his counseling experience months later, what he emphasized was the opportunity to talk about loneliness, relationships, and the problems in his family and their impact on him—the same sorts of issues, obviously, that people everywhere in society explore. Space and time in which to introspect, analyze obstacles, and consider alternatives were not available in his life. "I needed something like this," he said. (Loneliness, by the way, is an issue that I have heard mentioned frequently; the first individual client I ever had in this community was a 23-year-old man who sat down, looked at me, and said, "Nobody knows me, miss.")

Do I imply that having someone to talk to compares with the importance of having a roof over one's head or takes the place of advocating for the policy changes that will put roofs over more people's heads? Absolutely not. My point is that, time after time, I have been thrown back on my own implicit assumptions about the poor. I have realized that, knowing their lives are difficult, I had effectively reduced their existences to the surmounting of those difficulties, dehumanizing them in the process. I would never have given credence to the more blatant misperception held among some service providers that poor people are incapable of insight (Lott, 2002), but I would have said (and have said) that what poor and working-class people need is economic opportunity and social justice. Given the enormity of that need, what does a psychotherapist have to offer? The answer is that, along with a commitment to "support public policy and programs that ensure adequate income . . . for poor people and all working families" (APA, 2000, Resolution 10), psychotherapists can offer poor people what they offer everyone else: an opportunity to become differently and more fully conscious of their feelings and actions, to be more aware of the societal forces at work in their lives, to imagine and reach for new goals, and to do so within the parameters of a safe interpersonal alliance. When I have been willing to learn and be clinically flexible, I have seen again and again that poor people make the same use of such opportunities that middle-class and wealthy clients do; the difference is that they are otherwise forced to devote much more of their energies toward securing the basics of existence. In the words of a well-known quote attributed to suffrage and labor activist Rose Schneiderman, "The worker must have bread, but she must have roses, too."

2. *Poor people contend with so many overwhelming day-to-day problems that psychologists who work with them can experience their own interventions, even when helpful, as diminished in significance.*

This barrier overlaps with or perhaps underlies the one described above. My first misperception had been that poor people would have little capacity to use psychological services because the circumstances of their lives are so difficult and taxing. As that assumption was discredited through experience, I noticed a disquieting new doubt creeping into my awareness—that my services did not seem quite as valuable or potent as they had before. When I had a mostly middle-class and wealthy clientele, I was working with people whose distress, relatively speaking, was proportionately more available to my interventions. When people have reasonably comfortable lives in which the basics—food, shelter, health care, personal safety—are in place, the relief of psychological conflicts or symptoms can leave them feeling quite well. Life cannot be perfect for any client, of course, and it is the clients themselves who actualize the changes that produce relief—the psychologist does not take credit for that. Nevertheless, a psychologist treating a middle-class client has the opportunity to facilitate a therapeutic effort that returns the client to a largely satisfactory life. This, in turn, leaves the psychologist feeling efficacious, and all parties are suitably gratified. This moment is experienced differently when one's client lives in poverty. Even when they have made the best possible use of psychological services, poor clients frequently depart the office to resume a difficult life of sobering obstacles that a psychologist cannot touch. Against the backdrop of these obstacles, I found myself arriving at session's end feeling unproductive and disoriented, even when the work seemed to help with a client's particular emotional concern.

A conversation with a 65-year-old community member helped me make sense of this impasse. This senior citizen had been a participant in the center's internship program, which included a focus on interpersonal and cultural awareness, so we had shared many discussions of such topics. As we talked about psychology's lack of service to poor people and my work in the center, he observed that, indeed, what poor people require for survival are major changes such as the institution of a living wage and improvements in public education. However, he also believed that to conclude that psychological services were therefore not worthwhile in poor communities was classist and that my feelings of diminished importance in the face of poor clients' unremitting struggles were "[my] issue." As I thought about it, I realized that the issue was that my sense of my own effectiveness and worth as a professional was shaken by the persistent presence of pervasive, elemental, and often dire systemic problems that my clients and I could not alter in the course of our work together. Some portion of this confusion, I believe, comes from disappointment and frustration related to our good intentions to be helpful; some of it comes from the jolt to our professional self-concept that occurs when we repeatedly fail to see clients return to lives that are largely satisfactory. A third factor is that these encounters force psychologists to confront the different positions that they and their clients occupy in society, a barrier in and of itself, as I will describe next.

3. *Working in a poor community takes away the comfort of not knowing how poor people live.*

Most of us who are middle class or wealthy only occasionally brush up against the reality of poverty in this country. For me, this was usually an indirect encounter: I might, for example, feel sincerely moved by a book or news account, by the sight of a homeless person on the street, or by an afternoon spent volunteering in a soup kitchen. Feeling genuine sadness for the deprivation I had seen, I could return to the relative comfort of my existence. The poor, of course, were still all around me, busing tables, cleaning offices, unpacking truckloads of flowers outside florists' shops, and delivering take-out food, but now they melted into the familiar structures of my life. I was free to pay the delivery man and have dinner without necessarily giving much thought to the world he went home to.

Working in a poor community undermines the ignorance that contributes to this bliss. Aponte (1994) observed that one can be "dragged down by the emotional and family devastation, the educational failures, criminal convictions, and domestic violence that so often pervade poor families that are losing or have lost hope, meaning, and purpose" (p. 10). Not all poor families have lost hope: Daily, I meet community members who remain courageous, spirited, and loving in the face of tremendous hardship. I also see, daily, people being crushed beneath the weight of society's ills and failed systems: racism; persistent involuntary unemployment; jobs that do not pay a hardworking adult enough to live on; emergency rooms bursting with people who have no place else to turn for health care; deteriorating public housing; overcrowded, underresourced schools; unpredictable eruptions of violence among both acquaintances and strangers; inconsistent police presence and protection; streets where gang members openly sell drugs but there are few places to buy groceries or clothes. These people see us every day, when they turn on their televisions or come to our neighborhoods to wait tables or clean homes. We rarely see them—and we do not want to.

I do not imply that this avoidance is conscious. Like the authors cited earlier, who suggested that this distancing is the result of unconscious fear of identification with the poor and negative stereotyping, I believe that we avert our gaze from the poor as an unconscious way of preserving our ability to enjoy our relative good fortune amid an unequal distribution of resources. When we from the middle class go into poor neighborhoods to work, we must admit into consciousness a vivid comprehension of the disparity between our lives and theirs. Once we have done so, it is difficult to conjure up the oblivion that previously sheltered us from this awareness, and any unexamined assumptions that may have reassured us—that the poor lead contented, uncomplicated lives or that people are poor because they do not wish to work or that each of us has what we deserve—are suddenly exposed to daylight and lose their power. It becomes impossible not to know that a few subway stops away from cafés full of smiling middle-class faces is what amounts to a third-world country.

The parallels between class privilege and skin color privilege and the pressures to avoid awareness of them are clear. As McIntosh (1988) wrote,

> For me, white privilege has turned out to be an elusive and fugitive subject. The pressure to avoid it is great, for in facing it I must give up the myth of meritocracy. If these things are true, this is not such a free country; one's life is not what one makes it; many doors open for certain people through no virtues of their own. These perceptions mean also that my moral condition is not what I had been led to believe. (p. 9)

Psychologists are, of course, not immune to such pressures, and psychology as a field does not stand apart from the sociopolitical power structure: Cushman (1990); Prilleltensky (1994), and Sampson (1993), among others, have written about professional and academic psychology as both products of and bolsters to the status quo. Such pressures make their influence felt on psychologists as individuals and collectively as a discipline and can be understood as hindrances to service to the poor.

4. *Conventional psychological services are neither familiar to nor widely accepted in the cultures of many poor and working-class communities, so that even poor people who could benefit will not be likely to use them.*

This is another barrier with a basis in reality that demands conceptual, technical, and clinical flexibility in psychologists who face it. In my career, I have been an unquestioning supporter of the importance of multicultural competence, and, in this community, my theoretical stance was put to the test: It quickly became apparent that I would need to be flexible, culturally competent, and innovative all day, every day. Community members who met me were friendly and welcoming; none, however, were rushing to claim any of the week's worth of 50-minute hours that I made available. My schedule book, which had filled so quickly in independent practice and counseling centers, lay empty on the receptionist's desk. I had expected this on an intellectual level, yet now I felt uncertain about how to proceed. I had never realized the extent to which the conventional parameters of mainstream psychological practice reassured me of my competence and professional identity; now, as I began tentatively to reshape the way that I worked with people to better fit their needs, the ghosts of old supervisors whispered dangerously in my ear.

The comfort and confidence that my former supervisors and I derived from these parameters should not have surprised me; as Javier and Herron (2002) have indicated, the culture of the psychologist's office is the culture of Whiteness and class privilege. Operating within the confines of that culture, I felt at home, and using the techniques, guidelines, and customs that my clients and I had tacitly agreed on assured me of my professional fitness. Outside that culture, I initially felt unanchored and a bit directionless, as my new clients did not seem to be playing by the rules that I was used to. They were politely uninterested in speaking with me on the basis of my being an impersonal professional stranger with expertise that related to mental dysfunction. However, the more I participated in center events, the more participation I received in my own interventions, which increasingly included programmatic offerings. I presented workshops and classroom discussion groups on topics like peer pressure, the "holiday blues," and the interface between societal stereotyping and emotional well-being. Gradually, people began to drop by my office to talk, and then they began to schedule times to follow up. Some clients scheduled appointments weekly; most came less frequently than that; a few stopped by to touch base almost daily during weeks of crisis. Others suggested the initiation of new interventions: After five months of individual meetings, one woman ventured, "I know now that I would like to be able to talk to other people like me, people who have been mentally ill and homeless." Many community members had contact with me through center programming exclusively. The unclaimed time in my schedule began to disappear.

As I mentioned earlier, I offer community members essentially the same opportunities that I offered clients in middle-class settings. I am not doing conventional psychotherapy, however. A number of descriptors represent my current professional functions: counseling, psychoeducation, prevention psychology, community psychology. This effort feels integrative rather than directionless; it is also in good accord with multicultural psychologists, who have long contended that the conventional roles and behaviors of psychological practice are "culture bound and potentially unhelpful and oppressive to culturally different clients" (D. W. Sue et al., 1998, p. 81).

Completing the Circle

My attempt to bring a focus to the psychotherapeutic implications of classist distancing does not represent an assertion that classist attitudes, conscious or not, stand in isolation as the causative factor of psychotherapy's relative inattention to poor people. Indeed, those psychotherapists who would like to extend their services to poor clients face significant systemic and procedural deterrents to the realization of their good intentions. As described earlier, the promise of the CMHC movement was never fulfilled, and, in its aftermath, cost cutting in public mental health settings has resulted in few positions for doctoral-level psychologists. Moreover, Medicare and Medicaid reimburse psychologists in some but not all 50 states, and psychologists who can be reimbursed face "historical disincentives" (Sullivan, 1995, ¶ 4) in the form of complex eligibility and claims-processing requirements. These undeniable obstacles are artifacts of the current configuration of health care in this society, and their impact increases the likelihood that many psychotherapists will work with few, if any, poor clients during their careers. These obstacles do not, however, negate the value of exploring classist attitudes as a part of psychotherapeutic preparation: An analogous claim would be that psychotherapists practicing in predominantly White communities have no need for training in cultural competence around race.

In fact, the continuing existence of systemic obstacles to psychological services for poor clients may simply underscore the need for exploration of attitudes toward the poor. The presence of these obstacles is, after all, no secret within the profession—the call for psychologists to become more broadly involved in public health issues generally and in Medicaid policy specifically has been presented repeatedly over the years (Conger. 1988; DeLeon, Frank, & Wedding, 1995; DeLeon, Wedding, Wakefield, & VandenBos, 1992; Shigaki, Hagglund, Clark, Frank, & Checkett, 1999; Sullivan, 1995). "Where are the voices of dissent?" asked Sluzki (2004, ¶ 5), noting that "scores of professionals are [being] pushed out of the Medicaid/Medicare market" (¶ 4) and new proposals are being developed for increased federal restrictions on Medicaid funding. If graduate programs addressed the psychotherapeutic needs of poor clients as part of the clinical training experience, one could reasonably suppose that the next generation of psychotherapists might be more attuned to public policy questions such as these, that such voices might more clearly be heard, and that the dismantling of these systemic disincentives might be undertaken.

This last point brings me back to the sorts of questions with which I began this discussion: Are psychologists content to allow the most vulnerable members of society to he largely excluded from the circle of their services? What steps can be taken to prepare psychotherapists to address the practice- and policy-related issues that would facilitate poor clients' access to their services? I have implied that such preparation might logically begin in the context of clinical training pertaining to other aspects of diversity. Existing models of cultural competence that emphasize such dimensions as awareness, knowledge, and skills could conceivably be adapted for this purpose. Graduate-level teaching and training experiences, then, would constitute an essential first step. Not only would this training extend practitioners' skills, but it also could lay the foundation for new scientific contributions in the form of current empirical data regarding the psychotherapeutic experiences of poor clients and for objective explorations of classism itself.

Closing Comments

Responding to the Resolution on Poverty and Socioeconomic Status (APA, 2000) will require first that psychologists develop cultural awareness and competence around classism, thereby admitting the possibility that psychologists will eventually be prepared to offer poor people the full complement of their skills. In so doing, psychologists must "serve, not colonize" (Aponte, 1994, p. 11) by working in partnership with existing communities from a framework that emphasizes the resilience and autonomy of its members. There is much to learn as APA's 17 resolutions are enacted, which direct psychologists to research classist attitudes, classist public policies, indigenous prosocial movements among poor people, and practitioner competence and training, as well as to advocate and support policies that would ensure poor people's access to basic resources such as adequate income, housing, education, child care, and health care. Embracing this challenge is both a professional and a moral imperative, in that "psychologists who are not participating in some manner in support of these movements may be, in the final analysis, part of the problem" (Sloan, 2003, p. 312).

References

Affleck, D. C., & Garfield, S. L. (1961). Predictive judgment of therapists and duration of stay in psychotherapy. *Journal of Clinical Psychology, 17,* 134–137.

Albee, G. W. (1996). Revolutions and counterrevolutions in prevention. *American Psychologist, 51,* 1130–1133.

Albee, G. W., & Gulotta, T. P. (1997). Primary prevention's evolution. In G. Albee & T. Gulotta (Eds.), *Primary prevention works* (pp. 3–22). Thousand Oaks, CA: Sage.

Altman, N. (1995). *The analyst in the inner city.* Hillsdale, NJ: Analytic Press.

American Psychological Association. (2000). *Resolution on poverty and socioeconomic status.* Retrieved August 12, 2005, from http://www.apa.org/pi/urban/povres.html

Aponte, H. J. (1994). *Bread and spirit: Therapy with the new poor.* New York: Norton.

Azocar, F., Miranda, J., & Dwyer, E. V. (1996). Treatment of depression in disadvantaged women. In M. Hill & E. D. Rothblum (Eds.), *Classism and feminist therapy: Counting costs* (pp. 91–106). New York: Harrington Park.

Baker, N. L. (1996). Class as a construct in a "classless" society. In M. Hill & E. D. Rothblum (Eds.), *Classism and feminist therapy: Counting costs* (pp. 13–24). New York: Harrington Park.

Baum, O. E., Felzer, S. B., D'Zmura, T. L., & Shumaker, E. (1966). Psychotherapy, dropouts, and lower socioeconomic patients. *American Journal of Orthopsychiatry, 36,* 629–635.

Bowen, D. J., Tomoyasu, N., & Cauce, A. M. (1999). The triple threat: A discussion of gender, class, and race differences in weight. In L A. Peplau, S. C. DeBro, R. C. Veniegas, & P. L. Taylor (Eds.). *Gender, culture, and ethnicity* (pp. 291–306). Mountain View, CA: Mayfield.

Boyd-Franklin, N., & Bry, B. H. (2000). *Reaching out in family therapy.* New York: Guilford Press.

Brown, D. B., & Parnell, M. (1990). Mental health services for the urban poor: A systems approach. In M. P. Mirkin (Ed.), *The social and political contexts of family therapy* (pp. 215–236). Boston: Allyn & Bacon.

Brown, L. S. (1990). The meaning of a multicultural perspective for theory-building in feminist therapy. *Women & Therapy, 9*(1–2), 1–21.

Carter, R. T. (1995). *The influence of race and racial identity in psychotherapy: Toward a racially inclusive model.* New York: Wiley.

Chalifoux, B. (1996). Speaking up: White, working class women in therapy. In M. Hill & E. D. Rothblum (Eds.), *Classism and feminist therapy: Counting costs* (pp. 25–34). New York: Harrington Park.

Conger, J. J. (1988). Hostages to fortune: Youth, values, and the public interest. *American Psychologist, 43,* 291–300.

Constantine, C. G., & Sue, D. W. (Eds.). (2005). *Strategies for building multicultural competence in mental health and educational settings.* New York: Wiley.

Cushman, P. (1990). Why the self is empty. *American Psychologist, 45,* 599–611.

Davis, A. (1983). *Women, race, and class.* New York: Vintage.

DeLeon, P. H., Frank, R. G., & Wedding, D. (1995). Health psychology and public policy: The political process. *Health Psychology, 14,* 493–499.

DeLeon, P. H., Wedding, D., Wakefield, M. K., & VandenBos, G. R. (1992). Medicaid policy: Psychology's overlooked agenda. *Professional Psychology: Research and Practice, 23,* 96–107.

Denny, P. A. (1986). Women and poverty: A challenge to the intellectual and therapeutic integrity of feminist therapy. *Women & Therapy, 5*(4), 51–64.

Espin, O. M. (1997). *Latina realities.* Boulder, CO: Westview Press.

Furnham, A. (2003). Poverty and wealth. In S. C. Carr & T. S. Sloan (Eds.), *Poverty and psychology* (pp. 163–183). New York: Kluwer Academic/Plenum Press.

Graff, H., Kenig, L., & Radoff, G. (1971). Prejudice of upper class therapists against lower class patients. *Psychiatric Quarterly, 45,* 475–489.

Griffin, P. (1997). Introductory module for single issue courses. In M. Adams, L. A. Bell, & P. Griffin (Eds.), *Teaching for diversity and social justice* (pp. 61–81). New York: Routledge.

Hall, G. C. N. (2004). Editorial. *Cultural Diversity and Ethnic Minority Psychology, 10,* 3–4.

Hardiman, R., & Jackson, B. (1997). Conceptual foundations for social justice courses. In M. Adams, L. A. Bell, & P. Griffin (Eds.), *Teaching for diversity and social justice* (pp. 16–29). New York: Routledge.

Heitler, J. B. (1973). Preparation of lower-class patients for expressive group psychotherapy. *Journal of Consulting and Clinical Psychology, 41,* 251–260.

Helms, J. (Ed.). (1990). *Black and white racial identity: Theory, research, and practice.* Westport, CT: Greenwood.

Hollingshead, A. B., & Redlich, R. C. (1958). *Social class and mental illness.* New York: Wiley.

hooks, b. (1981). *Ain't I a woman: Black women and feminism.* Boston: South End.

hooks, b. (1984). *Feminist theory: From margin to center.* Boston: South End.

Humphreys, K., & Rappaport, J. (1993). From the community mental health movement to the war on drugs: A study in the definition of social problems. *American Psychologist, 48,* 892–901.

Inelan, J., & Ferran, E. (1990). Poverty, politics, and family therapy: A role for systems theory. In M. P. Mirkin (Ed.), *The social and political contexts of family therapy* (pp. 193–214). Boston: Allyn & Bacon.

lvey, A. E., D'Andrea, M., Ivey, M. B., & Simek-Morgan, L. (2002). *Counseling and psychotherapy: A multicultural perspective* (5th ed.). Boston: Allyn & Bacon.

Jacobs, D., Charles, E., Jacobs, T., Weinstein, H., & Mann, D. (1972). Preparation for treatment of the disadvantaged patient: Effects on disposition and outcome. *American Journal of Orthopsychiatry, 42,* 666–674.

Javier, R. A., & Herron, W. G. (2002). Psychoanalysis and the disenfranchised: Countertransference issues. *Psychoanalytic Psychology, 19,* 149–166. Article retrieved July 2004 from the PsycARTICLES database.

Jones, E. (1974). Social class and psychotherapy: A critical review of research. *Psychiatry, 37,* 307–320.

Karon, B. P., & VandenBos, G. R. (1977). Psychotherapeutic technique and the economically poor patient. *Psychotherapy: Theory, Research and Practice, 14,* 169–180.

Leeder, E. (1996). Speaking rich people's words: Implications of a feminist class analysis and psychotherapy. In M. Hill & E. D. Rothblum (Eds.), *Classism and feminist therapy: Counting costs* (pp. 45–58). New York: Harrington Park.

Liu, W. M., Ali, S. R., Soleck, G., Hopps, J., Dunston, K., & Pickett, T. (2004). Using social class in counseling psychology research. *Journal of Counseling Psychology, 51,* 3–18.

Lorde, A. (1984). *Sister outsider: Essays and speeches.* Trumansburg, NY: Crossing Press.

Lorion, R. P. (1973). Socioeconomic status and traditional treatment approaches reconsidered. *Psychological Bulletin, 79,* 263–270.

Lorion, R. P. (1974). Patient and therapist variables in the treatment of low-income patients. *Psychological Bulletin, 81,* 344–354.

Lott, B. (2002). Cognitive and behavioral distancing from the poor. *American Psychologist, 57,* 100–110. Retrieved July 2004 from the PsycARTICLES database.

McIntosh, P. (1988). *White privilege and male privilege: A personal account of coming to see correspondences through work in women's studies* (Working Paper Series No. 189). Wellesley, MA: Wellesley College. (Available from the Wellesley Centers for Women, Wellesley College, 106 Central Street, Wellesley, MA 02481).

Minkler, M., & Stone, R. (1985). The feminization of poverty and older women. *The Gerontologist, 25,* 351–357.

Minuchin, P. (1995). Children and family therapy: Mainstream approaches and the special case of the multicrisis poor. In R. H. Mikesell, D. Lusterman. & S. H. McDaniel (Eds.), *Integrating family therapy* (pp. 113–124). Washington, DC: American Psychological Association.

Minuchin, P., Colapinto, J., & Minuchin, S. (1998). *Working with families of the poor.* New York: Guilford Press.

Mirkin, M. P. (1990). *The social and political contexts of family therapy.* Boston: Allyn & Bacon.

Moreira, V. (2003). Poverty and psychopathology. In S. C. Carr & T. S. Sloan (Eds.), *Poverty and psychology* (pp. 69–86). New York: Kluwer Academic/Plenum Press.

Moskowitz, M. (1996). The social conscience of psychoanalysis. In R. M. Pérez Foster, M. Moskowitz, & R. A. Javier (Eds.), *Reaching across boundaries of culture and class* (pp. 21–46). Northvale, NJ: Aronson.

Padfield, M. (1976). The comparative effects of two counseling approaches on the intensity of depression among rural women of low socioeconomic status. *Journal of Counseling Psychology, 23,* 209–214.

Pérez Foster, R. M. (1996). What is a multicultural perspective for psychoanalysis? In R. M. Pérez Foster, M. Moskowitz, & R. A. Javier (Eds.), *Reaching across boundaries of culture and class* (pp. 3–20). Northvale, NJ: Aronson.

Ponterotto, J. G., Casas, J. M., Suzuki, L. A., & Alexander, C. M. (2001). *Handbook of multicultural counseling.* Thousand Oaks. CA: Sage.

Prilleltensky, I. (1994). *The morals and politics of psychology.* Albany: State University of New York Press.

Reid, P. T. (1995). Poor women in psychological research: Shut up and shut out. In N. R. Goldberger & J. B. Veroff (Eds.), *The culture and psychology reader* (pp. 184–204). New York: New York University Press.

Sampson, E. (1993). Identity politics: Challenges to psychology's understanding. *American Psychologist, 48,* 1219–1230.

Saris, R. N., & Johnston-Robledo, I. (2000). Poor women are still shut out of mainstream psychology. *Psychology of Women Quarterly, 24,* 233–235.

Shigaki, C. L., Hagglund, K. J., Clark, M., Frank, R. G., & Checkett, D. (1999). Medicaid's not-so-"quiet revolution": A call to action for psychologists. *Professional Psychology: Research and Practice, 30,* 488–494.

Siassi, I., & Messer, S. B. (1976). Psychotherapy with patients from lower socioeconomic groups. *American Journal of Psychotherapy, 30,* 29–40.

Sloan, T. S. (2003). *Poverty and psychology: A call to arms.* In S. C. Carr & T. S. Sloan (Eds.), *Poverty and psychology* (pp. 301–314). New York: Kluwer Academic/Plenum Press.

Sluzki, C. E. (2004). May 1968 revisited. *American Journal of Orthopsychiatry, 74,* 3–4. Retrieved June 2005 from the PsycARTICLES database.

Smith, M., & Dejoie-Smith, M. (1984). Behavioral therapy for non-White, non-YAVIS clients: Myth or panacea? *Psychotherapy, 21,* 524–529.

Strupp, H. H., & Bloxom, A. L. (1973). Preparing lower-class patients for group psychotherapy. *Journal of Consulting and Clinical Psychology, 41,* 373–384.

Sue, D. W., Carter. R. T., Casas. J. M., Fouad, N. A., Ivey, A. E., Jensen, M., et al. (1998). *Multicultural counseling competencies.* Thousand Oaks CA: Sage.

Sue, S., & Lam, A. G. (2002). Cultural and demographic diversity. In J. C. Norcross (Ed.) *Psychotherapy relationships that work: Therapist contributions and responsiveness to patients* (pp. 401–422). New York: Oxford University Press.

Sullivan, M. J. (1995). Medicaid's quiet revolution: Merging the public and private sectors of care. *Professional Psychology: Research and Practice, 26,* 229–234. Retrieved June 2005 from the PsycARTICLES database.

Thompson, C. L. (1989). Psychoanalytic psychotherapy with inner city patients. *Journal of Contemporary Psychotherapy, 19,* 137–148.

Trevithick, P. (1998). Psychotherapy and working-class women. In I. B. Seu & M. C. Heenan (Eds.), *Feminism and psychotherapy* (pp. 115–134). Thousand Oaks, CA: Sage.

28

Working for Social Justice From Within the Health Care System

The Role of Social Class in Psychology

Joshua A. Hopps

William M. Liu

Social class is an enduring cultural phenomenon that has only recently begun to receive attention as a psychological variable (Frable, 1997; Liu, Ali, et al., 2004; Ostrove & Cole, 2003). All of the constructs comprising social class (e.g., income, education, occupation, wealth) are intertwined with central components of life, such as (a) the physical environment and exposure to environmental hazards; (b) the social environment and exposure to violence or support; (c) socialization of personality, mood, and affect management; and (d) health behaviors (Adler et al., 1994). To this list can be added institutions with which individuals must interact to function in society, such as local, state, and federal government agencies, law enforcement officers, and health care systems. These institutions must be considered because they participate in constructing an individual's experience of society and his or her situation within that society. Understanding the interface between individuals and societal institutions can provide an instructive paradigm for exploring the impact these institutions can and do have, thereby providing an intervention point for a social justice–oriented systemic change. In order to achieve a more acute focus, we examine one specific type of institution that plays an indisputably vital role in the life of every individual: the health care system. This is a fruitful area because there has been a great deal of research in the area of health care and demographic variables in general, whereas individuals' interactions with governments and law enforcement have been examined less extensively.

To build the case for the utility of the interface between systems and individuals as a fruitful area of social justice–minded intervention, we will first provide an overview of social class as a psychological construct and the need for psychologists to integrate social class into practice. Second, we will present trends in the literature on the relationship between health and social class. It will be argued that the relationship in question can be discussed by focusing on two areas: individual and systemic contributions. There is an extensive literature on the former, whereas the latter is just beginning to be acknowledged by social science researchers. The data on individual factors will be reviewed, followed by an examination of systemic factors. This is a useful distinction because it is important to account for the variance in health that is contributed by each party. Because the purpose of the chapter is to scrutinize the interface between individuals and systems, it is important to attempt to gauge what each contributes to the equation. What results will allow the isolation of the systemic factors that can impede access to health care or differential health outcomes for different social class groups?

Social Class as a Psychological Construct

Social class permeates virtually all aspects of our lives. Yet for psychologists, it is one of the most difficult cultural constructs to understand and integrate into practice (Frable, 1997). Usually, social class is considered the amalgamation of one's income, education, and occupation (Liu, Ali, et al., 2004; Liu, Soleck, Hopps, Pickett, & Dunston, 2004). Based on these three criteria, it is not clear how social class is derived. That is to say, if a psychologist were given the income, education, and occupation of an individual, how is social class constructed? Furthermore, how do psychologists make sense of a person's income, education, and occupation as pertinent experiences or characteristics of the client? Current explanations fall far too short to be helpful in clinical practice.

Typically, individuals are stratified into preexisting categories of lower, middle, and upper social class, to name a few. Using various levels of the three objective indicators, a social class position is created. Several problems and assumptions arise from this procedure. First, it is assumed that once a person is placed in the "social class," the individual is similar to others in the same social class (i.e., perceives the world similarly). The extant research literature, which is far too extensive to review fully in this chapter, suggests vast subjectivity (i.e., intragroup variation) even among those in the same or similar objective social class (Bullock & Limbert, 2003; Kuriloff & Reichert, 2003; Ostrove & Cole, 2003). Second, there has not been any agreed-on formula for how to place a person in a social class, or on the social class structure (Oakes & Rossi, 2003). Therefore, without consensus on how social class should be operationalized, classification into any stratification system might be problematic for psychologists.

One issue that plagues a psychological understanding of social class is the confusion between social class and socioeconomic status (SES). Oakes and Rossi (2003) posit that the difference between the two constructs has not been clearly defined, and there is conceptual overlap between the two. Power, privilege, income, education, life opportunities, and occupation, for instance, are used in both social class and SES. Regardless of the terminology used, the construct should be linked to some theoretical understanding of how social class functions, and more important, it should be linked with classism (Liu & Pope-Davis, 2003; Liu, Ali, et al., 2004; Liu, Soleck, et al., 2004). This last point, although conceptually simple, has not been done consistently in psychology (Lott, 2002; Ostrove & Cole, 2003). Even though research suggests that classism is related to how people perceive themselves, their experiences, and their psychological well-being (Carter, 2003; Croizet & Claire, 1998; Grella, 1990; Liu, 2002), psychologists have infrequently examined both social class and classism as codependent constructs (Liu, Ali, et al., 2004). Throughout this chapter, we will use the term *social class* because it is conceptually easier to link it with classism. For us, social class represents a person's self-perceived social standing, and the individual's recognition that some people are higher, similar, and lower than the individual is currently. Because of the differences in perceived social class, it is likely that the individual will experience classism from others but also enact classism as a means to maintain his or her social class (Liu, Ali, et al., 2004; Liu, Soleck, et al., 2004).

Currently, several authors have suggested the need for psychologists to address classism (Liu, Ali, et al., 2004; Lott, 2002), examine the subjective experiences of social class (Adler, Epel, Castellazzo, & Ickovics, 2000; Liu, Soleck, et al., 2004; Ostrove & Cole, 2003), and connect social class with various experiences and psychological constructs (Ostrove & Cole, 2003) rather than treating it as a nuisance variable or demographic characteristic. Research has begun to explore the intersections of people's lives in areas such as schooling (Kuriloff & Reichert, 2003), work (Liu, 2002), and different racial groups (Clark, Anderson, Clark, & Williams, 1999; Cole & Omari, 2003). Just as important, research has examined how social class, access to health care, and self-perception are associated with health behaviors and help-seeking attitudes (Boyle & Lipman, 2002; Chen, Matthews, & Boyce, 2002; Cockerham, 1990; Cooper, 2002; Gallo & Matthews, 2003; Krieger, Willains, & Moss, 1997).

Background: Foundational Literature

In the past 30 years, research in the area of health and social class has blossomed into an expansive literature. Several approaches have been taken: (a) examination of the impact of living below the poverty line (e.g., Haan, Kaplan, & Camacho, 1987); (b) the graded effects of social class across the stratification range (e.g., Logue & Jarjoura, 1990); and (c) biopsychosocial mechanisms and pathways (e.g., Lantz et al., 2001). Research initially relied a great deal on longitudinal correlational data, mainly drawing associations between morbidity, mortality, and SES (we will use SES when necessary to accurately represent the original research). Several prominent examples warrant brief exploration. Kitagawa and Hauser (1973) linked death records with education and occupation information for the 1960 U.S. census and found that although mortality rates were dropping for the entire population, higher SES groups enjoyed a mortality decrease that was 60% greater than that of the lower groups. A strong inverse relationship was found between mortality and SES, a finding that has been echoed repeatedly. A full 5-year difference in life expectancy was found between the most and the least educated, and a strong link was found between heart disease and SES (Kitagawa & Hauser, 1973). Silver (1972) sampled all states in the United States from 1959 to 1961 and gathered data on median income in the area, household income, marital status, smoking, psychological stress, climate, air pollution, public health expenditures, and physician distribution. His conclusions reinforced those of Kitigawa and Hauser, finding a negative correlation with mortality for several variables: income, education, stress, and smoking.

In the United Kingdom, the Black Report (Townsend, Davidson, & Whitehead, 1988) and the Whitehall Studies (Marmot, Shipley, & Rose, 1984; Marmot et al., 1991) examined inequalities in the six SES stratifications in the United Kingdom. Mortality was twice as high for the lowest group as for the highest, even after controlling for race and age. On parallel with findings in the United States, there was evidence that the gap was expanding because of a more rapid decline in mortality among those in the upper classifications. As health care improves in quality and accessibility, the disparities between social class groups widen, because these benefits accrue differentially for upper- and middle-class groups, whereas those less privileged continue to be left behind. Similar evidence has been found in other western and eastern nations (e.g., Scandinavia, France, Japan) (Feinstein, 1993). Back in the United States, researchers added to the evidence for an expanding gap in mortality rates between SES groups (Feldman, Makuc, Kleinman, & Cornoni-Huntly, 1989). For White men aged 65–74, the difference between highest and lowest SES groups (measured by education) increased from 10% in 1960 to 100% in 1971–1984. This was mostly attributed to a sharp decline in heart disease among the most educated, whereas rates remained steady for the least educated. Among European American women, the gap between mortality of the highest and lowest educational groups was more pronounced than for their male counterparts. Logue and Jarjoura (1990) added to the complexity of the picture by increasing the focus on the middle of the social class range. In their U.S. sample, when compared with the upper middle class, the lower middle class had twice the mortality rate, and the working class had four times the mortality rate.

The U.S. Department of Health and Human Services (USDHHS, 2003) recently released a comprehensive report detailing disparities in health care in the United States. The National Healthcare Disparities Report details inequalities for members of racial and ethnic minority groups and lower social class groups across the entire health care system. These include limited access to primary care and specialized referrals, different recommendations for tests and interventions, disparate exposure to preventative efforts, and many similar findings, although the scope of the report cannot be encapsulated here. The Department of Health and Human Services has made an important step in making the commitment to annually compile data on health care disparities and track changes over time.

The inverse relationship between health and social class has been replicated across the life span: Neonatal adjustment has been shown to relate to social class (Field et al., 2002), as has adolescent physical and emotional well-being (Brady & Matthews, 2002; Goodman, 1999; Starfield, Riley, Witt, & Robertson, 2002). Adult health risk behaviors are consistently related to poor socioeconomic conditions in childhood (Lynch, Kaplan, & Salonen, 1997). Among seniors, morbidity, mortality, poor quality of life, and cognitive functioning have shown to be inversely related to social class (Bassuk, Berkman, & Amick, 2002; Long, Ickovics, Gill, & Horowitz, 2001; Martikainen, Stansfeld, Hemingway, & Marmot, 1999; Turrell et al., 2002). Furthermore, there is evidence that social class hardship can accumulate across the life span, affecting health, psychological adjustment, self-care ability, and cognitive functioning (Lynch, Kaplan, & Shema, 1997; Turrell et al., 2002).

Not surprisingly, race is highly conflated with social class because of the history of oppression of people of color and continued economic disadvantage. In one study, Williams and Rucker (1996) found that one third of African Americans and 29% of Latinos were below the poverty line compared to 12% of European Americans. African Americans have higher rates of mortality, disease, and disability than do European Americans (Hayward, Crimmins, Miles, & Yang, 2000). Latinos and African Americans are more likely than European Americans to label their health as poor and more likely to report a compromise in the ability to perform activities of daily living (Ren & Amick, 1996). Hayward et al. (2000) found that socioeconomic conditions primarily accounted for the racial gap in health to the exclusion of health behaviors. However, these constructs remain difficult to separate. The Health Disparities Report of the USDHHS analyzed economic disadvantage and race separately and found that when disparities were found, they frequently co-occurred for both of these groups, although there are exceptions to this (e.g., findings of effect of race on health care). Factors such as limited proficiency in English and cultural differences from the provider specifically affect individuals from minority groups, whereas these are much less likely to be the case for majority group members of lower social class groups. Research that could directly address this question by targeting middle-class members of racial and ethnic minority groups is lacking.

Because of the social and methodological complexity of the constructs involved, no single factor is likely to account for all of the variance in the relationship between health and social class. Several theories have emerged about the social class–health relationship with varying amounts of explanatory power. One theory that has fallen out of favor is the drift hypothesis, which states that rather than social class causing poor health outcomes, the opposite is true. Because of poor health and concomitant economic and psychosocial repercussions, individuals slide down the social class scale. However, support never emerged from data, and this explanation has generally fallen from favor (Adler et al., 1994; Haan, Kaplan, & Syme, 1989). Adler and co-workers (1994) have proffered an alternative theory: "SES affects biological functions that in turn influence health status" (p. 17). Because of difficulty operationalizing and conceptualizing social class, we know little about the pathways that affect this relationship. In the next section, a distinction is made in etiology, function, and level of effect that may serve to clarify this matter.

Definitional Issues

An important distinction will be made when discussing the literature from this point forward: Putative causal mechanisms and pathways for the inverse relationship between social class and health will be divided into macro and micro levels. This will be done for two reasons: (a) because of different etiology for macro and micro pathways, these two pathways cannot be assumed to be unitary (Feinstein, 1993); and (b) the potential for different types of interventions to occur on a macro (i.e., community, societal) or micro (individual) level (Seeman & Crimmins, 2001). Macro-level mechanisms are defined as extrinsic, systemic factors outside the control of the individual that play a role in determining their socioeconomic and cultural milieu. Some examples of this are the structure of the health care system, attributes of the community, and racial and social class segregation. Micro mechanisms are those that are intrapsychic, psychosocial, or behavioral in origin. These are intrinsic personal attributes or are purportedly under the control of the individual. Although it can be argued that aspects of personality are determined by one's surroundings, especially during formative years, in order to present a cogent description, personality variables will be placed in the micro or individual domain. However, data on the psychological concomitants of low social class and economic hardship will be presented below. Examples of micro-level variables include health risk behaviors such as smoking, and psychological variables such as locus of control. Although the literature on the contributions of micro-level variables is quite robust, the conceptualization and condensation of macro-level variables as systemic in origin is relatively new (Seeman & Crimmins, 2001).

A number of pathways have emerged from literature as mediating the relationship between health and social class across the social class continuum (Goldman, 2001). The most prominent of these are (a) patterns of health risk behaviors; (b) feelings of control, security, and ability to cope; (c) social support; (d) access to stress-mediating resources; (e) exposure to stress; (f) access to preventive and curative medical care; (g) exposure to poor environmental conditions; and (h) access to health risk and health care information/ education opportunities. These pathways can be divided into micro (individual) and macro (systemic) factors with the first four categorized as micro; the fifth straddling micro and macro; and the sixth, seventh, and eighth categorized as macro. Because exposure to stress can come from both systemic (e.g., classism, racism, economic deprivation) and individual (e.g., risk taking, poor life decisions, relationship discord) factors, the fifth pathway straddles the division between macro and micro causal pathways. These pathways will be expanded upon in the next two sections.

Micro Pathways

Research has, in part, turned from describing societal patterns to describing individual effects and risk factors, focusing on investigations of diseases and health conditions. This allows inferences to be made about the impact of these conditions on resiliency, morbidity, and mortality on an individual, or micro, level.

Potential Mechanisms: Causes and Contributors

Many health conditions have shown a now familiar inverse relationship with social class, such as obesity (Everson, Maty, Lynch, & Kaplan, 2002; Wardle, Waller, & Jarvis, 2002), cardiovascular disease (Singh & Siahpush, 2002; Smith & Hart, 2002; USDHHS, 2003), diabetes (Everson et al., 2002; USDHHS, 2003), fetal development (Field et al., 2002), poor traumatic brain injury prognosis (Hoofien, Vakil, Gilboa, Donovick, & Barak, 2002), subjective health rating (Cohen, Kaplan, & Salonen, 1999; Franks, Clancy, Gold, & Nutting, 1993), subjective life expectancy (Mirowsky & Ross, 2000), and difficulty with activities of daily living (Lynch, Kaplan, & Shema, 1997). Health behaviors have also received a great deal of focus over the past 30 years, but especially so in the past decade. Although behaviors such as smoking, lack of physical activity, alcohol consumption, and poor diet are associated with poor health outcomes (Lantz et al., 1998; Lantz et al., 2001; Logue & Jarjoura, 1990; Lynch, Kaplan, & Salonen, 1997; Marmot et al., 1984; Simon, van de Mheen, van der Meer, & Mackenbach, 2000), they account for only a portion of the variance in the relationship between SES and health, leaving questions about what is the dominating explanation for differences (Lantz et al., 2001). Many behaviors classified as a health risk are often intractable and difficult to change, and even if remediation occurred, the social class imbalance would remain (Lantz et al., 1998). This is not to say that focusing on remediation of health risk behaviors is fruitless. On the contrary, it is the intervention of choice on an individual, micro level. However, broader changes are necessary in order to address all of the factors involved.

Furthermore, psychological factors have been shown to play a role in differential resiliency, adjustment, and coping. Malatu and

Schooler (2002) conclude that general psychological distress accounts for a notable amount of the variance in the inverse relationship between SES and health. Higher social class individuals experience relatively fewer life stressors and rate events as less stressful than do lower-class groups (Adler et al., 1994; Carroll, Bennett, & Davey-Smith, 1993; Stronks, van de Mheen, Looman, & Mackenbach, 1998). Upper-class individuals experience less stress and are better able to cope with what stress they do experience. Exposure to higher levels of stress results in increased activation of the physiological stress response. Chronic elevation in levels of stress hormones and neurotransmitters, such as cortisol and catecholamines, can result in higher levels of chronic stress, poorer response to acute stressors, and poorer health status. Less privileged groups have been found to be higher than their upper-class counterparts in depression (Adler et al., 1994), hostility (Ranchor, Bouma, & Sanderman, 1996), cynicism and trait anger (Haukkala, 2002), poor self-esteem (Twenge & Campbell, 2002), poor sense of mastery (Williams & Rucker, 1996), and mental status decline (Long et al., 2001).

Social support has proven to be a complicated factor because of graded effects across the scope of SES. Social networks of lower-class individuals may be less supportive than those with relatively more social status, or if supportive, they are more likely to be a significant source of stress as well (Williams & Rucker, 1996). Among married couples, low SES was highly associated with joint experience of health problems (Wilson, 2001).

Macro-Level Factors

Access to health care is determined by several factors (Feinstein, 1993): (a) existence and quality of health insurance coverage, (b) provider/treatment variables, and (c) ability to navigate the system. Those at the lower end of SES are less likely to have health insurance and more likely to have poor subjective health status and medical conditions, a particularly difficult combination (Franks et al., 1993). Insurance plans are likely to be restricted for type of pharmaceutical treatment and physician (Feinstein, 1993; USDHHS, 2003). Shi and Starfield (2001) found an inverse relationship between primary care physician supply, income inequality, and mortality. Lower-income individuals may be more likely to use primary care under a universal health care system, but after controlling for health need, these individuals visited specialists less than their middle- and high-income counterparts (Dunlop, Coyte, & McIsaac, 2000). In an investigation of the influence of physician attributes on clinical decisions, McKinlay, Lin, Freund, and Moskowitz (2002) found that while patient demographic variables had no impact on treatment decisions, provider characteristics did. That is, extraneous attributes of the physician influenced health care decisions. Van Ryn and Burke (2000) found that physicians perceived lower- and middle-class individuals more negatively than upper-class individuals on variables such as personality, abilities, and behavioral tendencies. The USDHHS report found that individuals from lower-income and ethnic/racial minority groups were more likely to report poor communication and problems in their relationship with their primary care physician. These individuals were also less likely to receive referrals to specialists as well as certain interventions and diagnostic procedures.

Health literacy, or the ability to achieve a level of comprehension about health care to allow knowledgeable participation in decision making and treatment, has gained currency as a way to draw attention to the importance of full participation of the individual receiving treatment. It is conceived as part of what the treated individual brings to the interaction with the health care system. Therefore, if an individual is somewhat less than assertive in verifying understanding, or has difficulty conceptualizing medical problems, his or her health literacy can be a liability. One third of elderly patients and 80% of patients at public hospitals had poor or marginal health literacy, and this is related to poorer health status, higher hospitalization rates and costs, and reduced use of prevention efforts (Andrus & Roth, 2002; Williams, Davis, Parker, & Weiss, 2002). According to current measures of health literacy, 48% of Americans fall below adequate levels (Andrus & Roth, 2002). Because this is an astoundingly high number, the shortcoming appears to be on the part of the health care industry rather than individuals. Any failure on that scale should be remediated at the source, which is failure to communicate and check that those individuals receiving treatment understand their treatment. Using the example of individuals with diabetes, Schillinger and colleagues (2003) found that even though almost half of the information conveyed by physicians is not retained after a visit, understanding was assessed in only 20% of visits and about 12% of new concepts. Those individuals whose physicians did perform this type of assessment had better markers of adherence with the health care regimen in laboratory results. Schillinger and colleagues recommend that physicians assess for levels of understanding of treatment concepts and tailor subsequent information to the individual's level of health literacy. This is especially important for those from lower social class groups as they appear to have particular difficulty with access to and understanding of health care information (USDHHS, 2003).

There is extensive evidence that lower social class groups have poorer experiences at all levels of health care: preventive, diagnosis and entry, treatment efficacy, and follow-up and readmission. These poor experiences include later diagnosis and admission, poorer prognosis following diagnosis, lower levels of compliance, and more difficulty navigating HMOs and finding nursing home care (Feinstein, 1993; USDHHS, 2003). Individuals from the lower end of the SES hierarchy are more likely to be passive when it comes to managing their own health care, and place the responsibility on the health care system (Cockerham, Lueschen, Kunz, & Spaeth, 1986).

Additionally, access to health risk information and health care educational opportunities can have a significant influence on health outcomes. In an examination of the interaction of social class and racial factors with cancer, limited knowledge, misinformation about cancer, and mistrust of the health care system were related to poorer adjustment and health care behaviors (Matthews, Sellergren, Manfredi, & Williams, 2002). O'Malley et al. (2001) found that women from lower social class groups were significantly less likely to receive a provider recommendation for a mammogram, which reduces the likelihood of receiving this type of preventive care. It is vital that health care providers engage in education and communication across the gamut of social class groups.

Exposure to poor environmental conditions beginning in childhood can also cause disadvantages to accumulate across the life span. Because housing options are restricted as social class decreases, those in lower social class groups are more likely to live in areas with higher crime and violence rates; pollution problems (e.g., hazardous waste, pesticides, industrial chemicals, air pollutants) (Evans, 2004; Seeman & Crimmins, 2001); and poorer drinking water (Anderson & Armstead, 1995; Ewart & Suchday, 2002; Lantz et al., 1998). Lower-class individuals are also more likely to have jobs that increase exposure to dangerous situations or hazardous materials (Feinstein, 1993), and prolonged exposure to poor material conditions is related to poor perceived health (Stronks et al., 1998). Living in areas in which there is a lack of investment in social capital (fewer resources spent on education, transportation, etc.) can have an erosive effect on health and social class advancement (Seeman & Crimmins, 2001). In a study of a large urban area, Haan et al. (1987) found that living in a poverty area was predictive of mortality even after controlling for SES and health factors. In other words, living in inner-city poverty conditions adds additional hardship to an already disadvantaged social class group.

As mentioned above, none of these factors in isolation will be sufficient to fully explain the gradient relationship between social class and health. Examining factors by the macro and micro etiologies allows for parsimonious exploration of a sizeable literature and opening a discussion of interventions on a macro level to supplement the micro-level interventions used on individual factors, such as psychotherapy and education.

Social Justice Intervention

A contradiction exists in the literature in the discussion of the meaning of the above findings for designing and delivering interventions. For example, Lantz et al. (1998), citing the inability of health risk behaviors to account for more than a modest amount of the variance in SES and health, cautioned that public health policies aimed at reducing health risk behaviors, although still indicated, would not eradicate the socioeconomic disparities in health. Designing a mass remediation program for intransigent health risk behaviors would indeed be shortsighted, but community-level preventive and educational initiatives have different goals. The difficulty arises when the sole point of intervention or prevention activity occurs in the sphere of the individual. This ignores the contribution of health care systems and places the onus on people, who may not be facile at operating within an often overwhelming system. It is our contention that although interventions at the individual level must be conducted, and are indeed essential in many cases, a system that is inflexible to the needs of consumers and unaware of its own shortcomings will inevitably fail. Systems must include sufficient flexibility to adapt to the needs of individuals in order to achieve equivalent levels of treatment across social class groups. This flexibility can occur at a policy level within institutions, but, perhaps most important for our purposes here, can also be implemented at the level of the health care provider.

Several of the studies reviewed above give indications not only about where the system fails those within it but also about how those failures can be averted or remediated. In general, lower social classification is related to poorer experiences at all levels of health care, leading to later diagnosis and admission, poorer prognosis, and poor compliance. However, two specific findings will be discussed from the perspective of mental health care providers interested in social justice interventions that are feasible even while working from within, or from without, the system.

First, social class can be predictive of poor knowledge and understanding of, and even misinformation about, medical conditions. Lack of understanding can be an important ingredient in poor compliance with the recommendations of health care professionals. If an individual does not grasp the importance of the health care regimen, he or she may be somewhat less than conscientious about adhering to each aspect. Also, if patients are not informed of the potential pitfalls of adhering to the prescribed treatment, they may be unprepared when the inevitable challenge arises, and compromise their compliance (Rapoff, 1999). Treatment goals may conflict between the provider and the patient (e.g., a different focus on pain, quality of life, etc.), and in such cases, adherence to treatment regimens is vulnerable (Clay & Hopps, 2003). These concerns can be addressed by health care providers by asking questions about specifics of what an individual understands about his or her condition, hopes to gain from treatment, and can reasonably adhere to without undue distress. Prescribing a treatment that is effective but beyond the scope of the individual's behavioral resources is tantamount to no treatment at all. A quick assessment can give the provider an idea of a feasible treatment plan. (For further discussion of treatment adherence related to individual and systemic factors and accommodation of treatment to an individual's lifestyle, see Clay & Hopps, 2003.) A lack of knowledge of preventive medicine can also be a problem. The illustrative example mentioned above was fewer mammograms for women from lower social class groups. This is disturbing because this was due to not only a lack of awareness of the usefulness of breast cancer screening, but also an apparent reluctance among physicians to make this referral.

Health literacy research focused on this issue has found that nearly half of individuals operating within the health system have inadequate understanding of their health care. With such a deficit, individuals cannot fully participate in their own health care, in decision making or in adherence to their prescribed treatment. This doubtless affects their health outcomes, and is at a level that clearly implicates a failure of the health care system to communicate effectively with its consumers. This is an important distinction to maintain, because it shifts the burden onto the entity providing the care, rather than those receiving care. Health care providers should check for understanding of concepts as they are introduced. They should also assess understanding across visits to minimize drift in treatment adherence. Open-ended questions such as, "Do you understand?" may not be useful because the patient may feel overwhelmed or may not want to appear uninformed. Specific probing questions about information conveyed should target key concepts and should serve to check for comprehension and provide a repetition of vital points from the visit. These can easily be phrased to avoid a paternalistic stance: "I've thrown a lot of information your way today and want to make sure we're on the same page about some important points. What do you remember about . . . ?"

Although mental health providers are infrequently able to make direct referrals within health care systems, they can take steps to facilitate their clients'/patients' access to care. Psychoeducation should be a holistic endeavor that not only emphasizes mental health, but also acknowledges the mind-body relationship. Once individuals are more familiar with this relationship, mental health providers can discuss important steps, preventive and remediative alike, that their clients/patients should consider, such as mammograms and prostate exams. Psychotherapy, and virtually every other psychological intervention, involves a great deal of education, and the concepts discussed above apply equally. Checking for memory of material across contacts can give practitioners an idea of what the individual views as important from sessions and also highlight areas that may not be addressed at a deeper level. Education is an inherently empowering endeavor, and its importance should never be underestimated. Aiding an individual in increasing his or her agency within the health care system, or in any setting, can empower a person to operate more competently within a system that may have objectives not entirely compatible with his or her own.

Second, passivity in managing health care is a common way of coping among lower social class groups, and these individuals find it increasingly difficult to navigate HMOs and find nursing home care. Indeed, there is a tendency to place the responsibility of health care on the health care system, a dangerous prospect in a system geared to lower costs rather than advocate for individuals. It is at this point when individuals slip through the cracks, an all too common phrase among those employed in health care.

Again, when direct referrals are not possible, mental health care providers still have options to pursue in advocating for their clients/patients. It is important to reemphasize a biopsychosocial focus on mental and physical health with clients and patients. This should include an assessment of physical well-being and encouraging a visit to a primary care physician when possible. If an individual has known health problems, these should not be seen as beyond the purview of the mental health provider. These problems should be tracked across client contacts, and signs of slipping through the cracks should be noted and addressed with the client. If possible, the mental health provider can request the client's permission to consult with the health care provider. The information available to different providers can often benefit all parties in treatment planning and implementation. In addition, the consultation can include diplomatically worded education of physicians, nurses, and other health care providers about social class issues as they relate to health and health care in general and specifically relate to the client or patient. Consultation may reveal or convey that the individual receiving treatment is not as aware of his or her treatment as desired, and strategies across providers can be designed to boost adherence to medical and psychological treatment. Given the evidence that health care providers' attributes, such as job satisfaction (DiMatteo et al., 1993) and perception of their patients (van Ryn, 2002; van Ryn & Burke, 2000), can influence their decision making and patient outcome, education of providers within the system is vital for systemic change. To achieve a social justice orientation, it is vital that the mental health provider construe his or her helping influence as extending beyond the traditional boundaries of the 50-minute session within the four walls of the consultation room.

Interventions at the Community Level

Social justice interventions at the community level have been shown to be effective in reducing social class disparities in health. In fact, Seeman and Crimmins (2001) cite community efforts to change unhealthy living conditions as some of the most successful public health interventions to date. For example, Syme (1978) conducted a study that made use of community resources for education by training community members to deliver educational information, rather than using standard health care outlets. Community members supplied direct assistance, support, and referrals, and overall compliance with medical regimens was boosted. However, there has been a lack of communication between research and practice in the area of community-level intervention. A more recent example is a program in Houston, Texas (Holleman, Bray, Davis, & Holleman, 2004), developed primarily for homeless individuals and families, most of whom had never had a primary care physician. All individuals beginning the program received an hour with a physician who collaborated closely with psychologists and family therapists to make appropriate physical and mental health referrals. Psychoeducation of the participants was highly emphasized in programs on medication management, and it was highly integrated into support groups and individual psychotherapy, as well as career and family building skills. The emphasis on collaboration—both interdisciplinary and patient-provider—was especially salient for all involved because it allowed for relatively seamless care of the biopsychosocial needs of the participants.

Health promotion theory has focused on both primary and secondary prevention efforts. These preventive steps occur at different points of access, one at the community level and another at the level of an individual health care professional and his or her client. Secondary prevention, or preventive medicine, occurs at the individual level and focuses on screening, educating, and counseling individuals about risky behaviors. There has been a disconnection between these two types of preventive efforts, with conflicting research findings and recommendations to health care providers (Dibble, 2003). This may have resulted in diminished referrals to community organizations focused on primary prevention and less of a focus on social and behavioral issues. Moreover, economically disadvantaged individuals are less likely to have a relationship with a primary care physician, thereby missing both primary and secondary prevention (USDHHS, 2003).

In their review of health promotion theory, Best and colleagues (2003) also noted a disjointed approach and classified current theories as focusing on one of the following, to the exclusion of the others: empowerment, reduction of risk behavior, or structural organization. Each of these theories is grounded in a wealth of theoretical and empirical scholarship in public health; but each contains only a segment of the issue of health disparities within its purview and alone is limited in its ability to comprehensively address current concerns. Best and colleagues argue that to optimize effective implementation of the research, it is vital that all of these be addressed. They propose community partnering as such a model because it allows for empowerment of the community by incorporating its members and establishing a structure that involves local practitioners in multiple disciplines as well as large state, provincial, and local organizations. It also facilitates interventions at the various levels where barriers exist: policy, systemic, and individual. In designing these interventions, it is vital that there be practical and theoretical rapprochement among researchers and practitioners from multiple disciplines. Diversity in theory and discipline is important in order to promote collaboration and maximize theoretical breadth, and to integrate separate but parallel knowledge bases from literature in different disciplines: public health, preventive medicine, nursing, health psychology, social work, and more. The program for homeless individuals described above (Holleman et al., 2004) is an example of an intervention with both breadth and depth at the community and individual levels, focusing on empowerment, education, behavior modification, and training on how to negotiate the health care system.

Communities often have organizations focused on concerns that are specific to their neighborhood, such as social class, race, crime, environmental conditions, and so on. Neighborhood associations are relatively common structural manifestations of a consensus of concern, and thus are often the conduit for political action that communities take about social issues. Although there is a wide degree of variability in the form and activity level of these groups, it is essential that this resource be accessed when designing and implementing interventions at the community level. In fact, neighborhood associations may be more active and more likely to focus on political issues in disadvantaged neighborhoods than in middle-class communities (Lenk, Toomey, Wagenaar, Bosma, & Vessey, 2002). However, the voice generated by these disadvantaged communities may have less clout than those with more resources (Mesch & Schwirian, 1996). By aligning with poorer neighborhoods, researchers and practitioners may directly affect the efficacy of neighborhood associations by providing additional attention to vital issues and improving social and policy-related networks. When professionals work with disadvantaged individuals, there should be a commitment to the community with concrete, planned results to avoid the appearance of exploitation for a research or policy agenda (Sue & Sue, 2002).

Specific Interventions

Making an intervention on a systemic level can strengthen ties and increase individual members' investment in the community. When health risk behaviors occur on such a wide scale, both macro- and micro-level interventions are necessary to address the scope and depth of the problem. Grzywacz, McMahan, Hurley, Stokols, and Phillips (2004) argue that the next era in rectifying health disparities involves intervention at these different levels using empirically derived "promising strategies" (p. 8). At the public policy level, some of the known examples of appropriate starting points for the systemic aspect of health risk behavior prevention and intervention are housing; environmental conditions; and the availability of alcohol, cigarettes, and fatty foods (especially to adolescents). At the level of the health care system, it is important to extinguish unnecessary barriers to health care access, including improving access to transportation; evaluate the cultural competence of all those within the health care system, including administrative staff; and eliminate institutional policies that may be inadvertently racist and/or classist. At the community level, working through established neighborhood associations not only improves the credibility of health care workers, but also can serve to strengthen community networks and establish more accessible care for hard-to-reach individuals. At the individual level, it is important that the targeted audience is known and that all outreach materials are appropriately designed. A biopsychosocial approach is important at the individual level because health status has ramifications for all aspects of human experience. Incorporation of research findings on patient education, like those mentioned above, on an individual and a systemic level is vital if those less skilled in operating within a daunting system are to be incorporated. Further investigation of how providers can facilitate this process is also warranted.

Research would do well to begin to test interventions that navigate at the policy level, the systemic (community and health care system) level, and the individual level. Although such programs are massive undertakings, it is vital that there be an integration of data and experience across disciplines. Continued research on microlevel contributions to the health/social class gradient is necessary, but neglecting the exploration of systemic contributions is tantamount to blaming the victim.

Although the interrelationship between social class and race has thus far proven elusive, it is an important question that should be addressed. An examination of health status and experiences within the health care system of middle- and upper-class racial/ethnic minorities will be an important step.

Conclusion

Social justice is clearly an aspirational goal for mental health providers. We have argued that systemic social justice interventions are possible at the individual level if practitioners extend beyond the comfort zone of the office and face-to-face client contact, and reconceptualize their helping role in a broader fashion. We chose the health care system as an example for such attempts because of the extant disparities in social class and health, and we emphasized a focus on clients' health, education of clients and other providers, and advocacy of clients who are all but invisible on the systemic level. This is certainly beyond what is required and probably what is asked. Overwhelmed with droves of needful patients and their own struggle for autonomy and a helping role within a complex system, many providers may be disinterested in either making or receiving such attempts. To persevere in reaching these providers, exactly those we would like to reach, is easy to ask when preaching to the choir.

References

Adler, N. E., Boyce, T., Chesney, M. A., Cohen, S., Folkman, S., Kahn, R. L., & Syme, S. L. (1994). Socioeconomic status and health: The challenge of the gradient. *American Psychologist, 49*(1), 15–24.

Adler, N. E., Epel, E. S., Castellazzo, G., & Ickovics, J. R. (2000). Relationship of subjective and objective social status with psychological functioning: Preliminary data in healthy White women. *Health Psychology, 19,* 586–592.

Anderson, N. B., & Armstead, C. A. (1995). Toward understanding the association of socioeconomic status and health: A new challenge for the biopsychosocial approach. *Psychosomatic Medicine, 57*(3), 213–225.

Andrus, M., & Roth, M. (2002). Health literacy: A review. *Pharmacotherapy, 22(3),* 282–302. Bassuk, S. S., Berkman, L. F., & Amick, B. C., III. (2002). Socioeconomic status and mortality among the elderly: Findings from four U.S. communities. *American Journal of Epidemiology, 155*(6), 520–533.

Best, A., Stokols, D., Green, L. W., Leischow, S., Holmes, B., & Buchholz, K. (2003). An integrative framework for community partnering to translate theory into effective health promotion strategy. *American Journal of Health Promotion, 18*(2), 168–176.

Boyle, M. H., & Lipman, E. L. (2002). Do places matter? Socioeconomic disadvantage and behavioral problems of children in Canada. *Journal of Consulting and Clinical Psychology, 70,* 378–389.

Brady, S. S., & Matthews, K. A. (2002). The influence of socioeconomic status and ethnicity on adolescents' exposure to stressful life events. *Journal of Pediatric Psychology, 27*(7), 575–583.

Bullock, H. E., & Limbert, W. M. (2003). Scaling the socioeconomic ladder: Low-income women's perceptions of class status and opportunity. *Journal of Social Issues, 59,* 693–710.

Carroll, D., Bennett, P., & Davey-Smith, G. (1993). Socio-economic health inequalities: Their origins and implications. *Psychology & Health, 8*(5), 295–316.

Carter, P. L. (2003). "Black" cultural capital, status positioning, and schooling conflicts for low income African American youth. *Social Problems, 50*(1), 136–155.

Chen, E., Matthews, K. A., & Boyce, W. T. (2002). Socioeconomic differences in children's health: How and why do these relationships change with age? *Psychological Bulletin, 128,* 295–329.

Clark, R., Anderson, N. B., Clark, V. R., & Williams, D. R. (1999). Racism as a stressor for African Americans: A biopsychosocial model. *American Psychologist, 54,* 805–816.

Clay, D., & Hopps, J. (2003). Treatment adherence in rehabilitation: The role of treatment accommodation. *Rehabilitation Psychology, 48*(3), 215–219.

Cockerham, W. C. (1990). A test of the relationship between race, socioeconomic status, and psychological distress. *Social Science and Medicine, 31,* 1321–1326.

Cockerham, W. C., Lueschen, G., Kunz, G., & Spaeth, J. L. (1986). Social stratification and self-management of health. *Journal of Health & Social Behavior, 27*(1), 1–14.

Cohen, S., Kaplan, G. A., & Salonen, J. T. (1999). The role of psychological characteristics in the relation between socioeconomic status and perceived health. *Journal of Applied Social Psychology, 29*(3), 445–468.

Cole, E. R., & Omari, S. R. (2003). Race, class and the dilemmas of upward mobility for African Americans. *Journal of Social Issues, 59,* 785–802.

Cooper, H. (2002). Investigating socio-economic explanations for gender and ethnic inequalities in health. *Social Science & Medicine, 54,* 693–706.

Croizet, J. C., & Claire, T. (1998). Extending the concept of stereotype threat to social class: The intellectual underperformance of students from low socioeconomic backgrounds. *Personality and Social Psychology Bulletin, 24,* 588–594.

Dibble, R. (2003). Eliminating disparities: Empowering health promotion within preventive medicine. *American Journal of Health Promotion, 18*(2), 195–199.

DiMatteo, M. R., Sherbourne, C. D., Hays, R. D., Ordway, L., Kravitz, R., McGlynn, E., Kaplan, S., & Rogers, W. (1993). Physicians' characteristics influence patients' adherence to medical treatment: Results from the Medical Outcomes Study. *Health Psychology, 12*(2), 93–102.

Dunlop, S., Coyte, P. C., & McIsaac, W. (2000). Socioeconomic status and the utilization of physicians' services: Results from the Canadian National Population Health Survey. *Social Science & Medicine, 51*(1), 123–133.

Evans, G. (2004). The environment of childhood poverty. *American Psychologist, 59(2),* 77–92.

Everson, S. A., Maty, S. C., Lynch, J. W., & Kaplan, G. A. (2002). Epidemiologic evidence for the relation between socioeconomic status and depression, obesity, and diabetes. *Journal of Psychosomatic Research, 53*(4), 891–895.

Ewart, C. K., & Suchday, S. (2002). Discovering how urban poverty and violence affect health: Development and validation of a neighborhood stress index. *Health Psychology, 21(3),* 254–262.

Feinstein, J. S. (1993). The relationship between socioeconomic status and health: A review of the literature. *Milbank Quarterly, 71*(2), 279–322.

Feldman, J., Makuc, D., Kleinman, J., & Cornoni-Huntly, J. (1989). National trends in educational differentials in mortality. *American Journal of Epidemiology, 129,* 919–933.

Field, T., Diego, M., Hernandez-Reif, M., Schanberg, S., Kuhn, C., Yando, R., & Bendell, D. (2002). Prenatal depression effects on the foetus and neonate in different ethnic and socio-economic status groups. *Journal of Reproductive & Infant Psychology, 20*(3), 149–157.

Frable, D. E. S. (1997). Gender, racial, ethnic, sexual, and class identities. *Annual Review of Psychology, 48,* 139–162.

Franks, P., Clancy, C. M., Gold, M. R., & Nutting, P. A. (1993). Health insurance and subjective health status: Data from the 1987 National Medical Expenditure Survey. *American Journal of Public Health, 83*(9), 1295–1299.

Gallo, L. C., & Matthews, K. A. (2003). Understanding the association between socioeconomic status and physical health: Do negative emotions play a role? *Psychological Bulletin, 129,* 10–51.

Goldman, N. (2001). Social inequalities in health: Disentangling the underlying mechanisms. In M. Weinstein & A. I. Hermalin (Eds.), *Annals of the New York Academy of Sciences: Vol. 954. Population health and aging: Strengthening the dialogue between epidemiology and demography* (pp. 88–117). New York: New York Academy of Sciences.

Goodman, E. (1999). The role of socioeconomic status gradients in explaining differences in U.S. adolescents' health. *American Journal of Public Health, 89*(10), 1522–1528.

Grella, C. E. (1990). Irreconcilable differences: Women defining class after divorce and downward mobility. *Gender & Society, 4,* 41–55.

Grzywacz, J., McMahan, S., Hurley, J., Stokols, D., & Phillips, M. (2004). Serving racial and ethnic minority populations with health promotion. *American Journal of Health Promotion, 18*(5), 8–12.

Haan, M., Kaplan, G. A., & Camacho, T. (1987). Poverty and health: Prospective evidence from the Alameda County study. *American Journal of Epidemiology, 125,* 989–998.

Haan, M., Kaplan, G. A., & Syme, S. L. (1989). Socioeconomic status and health: Old observations and new thoughts. In J. T. Bunker, T. S. Gomby, & B. H. Kehrer (Eds.), *Pathways to health* (pp. 76–135). Menlo Park, CA: The Henry J. Kaiser Family Foundation.

Haukkala, A. (2002). Socio-economic differences in hostility measures: A population-based study. *Psychology & Health, 17*(2), 191–202.

Hayward, M. D., Crimmins, E. M., Miles, T. P., & Yang, Y. (2000). The significance of socioeconomic status in explaining the racial gap in chronic health conditions. *American Sociological Review, 65*(6), 910–930.

Holleman, W. L., Bray, J. H., Davis, L., & Holleman, M. C. (2004). Innovative ways to address the mental health and medical needs of marginalized patients: Collaborations between family physicians, family therapists, and family psychologists. *American Journal of Orthopsychiatry, 74*(3), 242–252.

Hoofien, D., Vakil, E., Gilboa, A., Donovick, P. J., & Barak, O. (2002). Comparison of the predictive power of socioeconomic variables, severity of injury and age on long-term outcome of traumatic brain injury: Sample-specific variables versus factors as predictors. *Brain Injury, 16*(1), 9–27.

Kitagawa, E. M., & Hauser, P. M. (Eds.). (1973). *Differential mortality in the United States: A study in socioeconomic epidemiology.* Cambridge, MA: Harvard University Press.

Krieger, N., Willains, D. R., & Moss, N. E. (1997). Measuring social class in public health research: Concepts, methodologies, and guidelines. *Annual Review of Public Health, 18,* 341–378.

Kuriloff, P., & Reichert, M. C. (2003). Boys of class, boys of color: Negotiating the academic and social geography of an elite independent school. *Journal of Social Issues, 59,* 751–770.

Lantz, P. M., House, J. S., Lepkowski, J. M., Williams, D. R., Mero, R. P., & Chen, J. (1998). Socioeconomic factors, health behaviors, and mortality: Results from a nationally representative prospective study of U.S. adults. *Journal of the American Medical Association, 279*(21), 1703–1708.

Lantz, P. M., Lynch, J. W., House, J. S., Lepkowski, J. M., Mero, R. P., Musick, M. A., & Williams, D. R. (2001). Socioeconomic disparities in health change in a longitudinal study of U.S. adults: The role of health-risk behaviors. *Social Science & Medicine, 53*(1), 29–40.

Lenk, K., Toomey, T., Wagenaar, A., Bosma, L., & Vessey, J. (2002). Can neighborhood associations be allies in health policy efforts? Political activity among neighborhood associations. *Journal of Community Psychology, 30*(1), 57–68.

Liu, W. M. (2002). The social class–related experiences of men: Integrating theory and practice. *Professional Psychology: Research and Practice, 33,* 355–360.

Liu, W. M., & Pope-Davis, D. B. (2003). Understanding classism to effect personal change. In T. B. Smith (Ed.), *Practicing multiculturalism: Internalizing and affirming diversity in counseling and psychology* (pp. 294–310). New York: Allyn & Bacon.

Liu, W. M., Ali, S. R., Soleck, G., Hopps, J., Dunston, K., & Pickett, T., Jr. (2004). Using social class in counseling psychology research. *Journal of Counseling Psychology, 51,* 3–18.

Liu, W. M., Soleck, G., Hopps, J. A., Pickett, T., & Dunston, K. (2004). A new framework to understand social class in counseling: The social class worldview and modern classism theory. *Journal of Multicultural Counseling and Development, 32*(2), 95–122.

Logue, E. E., & Jarjoura, D. (1990). Modeling heart disease mortality with census tract rates and social class mixtures. *Social Science & Medicine, 31,* 545–550.

Long, J. A., Ickovics, J. R., Gill, T. M., & Horowitz, R. I. (2001). The cumulative effects of social class on mental status decline. *Journal of the American Geriatrics Society, 49*(7), 1005–1007.

Lott, B. (2002). Cognitive and behavioral distancing from the poor. *American Psychologist, 57,* 100–110.

Lynch, J. W., Kaplan, G. A., & Salonen, J. T. (1997). Why do poor people behave poorly? Variation in adult health behaviours and psychosocial characteristics by stages of the socioeconomic lifecourse. *Social Science & Medicine, 44*(6), 809–819.

Lynch, J. W., Kaplan, G. A., & Shema, S. J. (1997). Cumulative impact of sustained economic hardship on physical, cognitive, psychological, and social functioning. *New England Journal of Medicine, 337*(26), 1889–1895.

Malatu, M. S., & Schooler, C. (2002). Causal connections between socio-economic status and health: Reciprocal effects and mediating mechanisms. *Journal of Health & Social Behavior, 43*(1), 22–41.

Marmot, M. G., Shipley, M. J., & Rose, G. (1984). Inequalities in death: Specific explanations of a general pattern. *Lancet, 331,* 1003–1006.

Marmot, M. G., Smith, G. D., Stansfeld, S., Patel, C., North, F., Head, J., White, I., Brunner, E., & Feeney, A. (1991). Health inequalities among British civil servants: The Whitehall II study. *Lancet, 337,* 1387–1393.

Martikainen, P., Stansfeld, S., Hemingway, H., & Marmot, M. (1999). Determinants of socioeconomic differences in change in physical and mental functioning. *Social Science & Medicine, 49*(4), 499–507.

Matthews, A. K., Sellergren, S. A., Manfredi, C., & Williams, M. (2002). Factors influencing medical information seeking among African-American cancer patients. *Journal of Health Communication, 7*(3), 205–219.

McKinlay, J. B., Lin, T., Freund, K., & Moskowitz, M. (2002). The unexpected influence of physician attributes on clinical decisions: Results of an experiment. *Journal of Health & Social Behavior, 43*(1), 92–106.

Mesch, G., & Schwirian, K. (1996). The effectiveness of neighborhood coalition action. *Social Problems, 43,* 467–483.

Mirowsky, J., & Ross, C. E. (2000). Socioeconomic status and subjective life expectancy. *Social Psychology Quarterly, 63*(2), 133–151.

Oakes, J. M., & Rossi, P. H. (2003). The measurement of SES in health research: Current practice and steps toward a new approach. *Social Science & Medicine, 56,* 769–784.

O'Malley, M. S., Earp, A. L., Hawley, S. T., Schell, M. J., Mathews, H. F., & Mitchell, J. (2001). The association of race/ethnicity, socioeconomic status, and physician recommendation for mammography: Who gets the message about breast cancer screening? *American Journal of Public Health, 91*(1), 49–54.

Ostrove, J. M., & Cole, E. R. (2003). Privileging class: Toward a critical psychology of social class in the context of education. *Journal of Social Issues, 59,* 677–692.

Ranchor, A. V., Bouma, J., & Sanderman, R. (1996). Vulnerability and social class: Differential patterns of personality and social support over the social class. *Personality & Individual Differences, 20*(2), 229–237.

Rapoff, M. A. (1999). *Adherence to pediatric medical regimens.* New York: Kluwer.

Ren, X. S., & Amick, B. C., III. (1996). Race and self-assessed health status: The role of socioeconomic factors in the USA. *Journal of Epidemiology & Community Health, 50*(3), 269–273.

Schillinger, D., Piette, J., Grumbach, K., Wang, F., Wilson, C., Daher, C., Leong-Grotz, K., Castro, C., & Bindman, A. B. (2003). Closing the loop: Physician communication with diabetic patients who have low health literacy. *Archives of Internal Medicine, 163,* 83–90.

Seeman, T. E., & Crimmins, E. (2001). Social environment effects on health and aging: Integrating epidemiologic and demographic approaches and perspectives. In M. Weinstein & A. I. Hermalin (Eds.), *Annals of the New York Academy of Sciences: Vol. 954. Population health and aging: Strengthening the dialogue between epidemiology and demography* (pp. 88–117). New York: New York Academy of Sciences.

Shi, L., & Starfield, B. (2001). The effect of primary care physician supply and income inequality on mortality among Blacks and Whites in U.S. metropolitan areas. *American Journal of Public Health, 91*(8), 1246–1250.

Silver, M. (1972). An econometric analysis of spatial variations in mortality rated by age and sex. In V. Fuchs (Ed.), *Essays in the economics of health and medical care* (pp. 161–227). New York: Columbia University Press.

Simon, J. G., van de Mheen, H., van der Meer, J. B., & Mackenbach, J. P. (2000). Socioeconomic differences in self-assessed health in a chronically ill population: The role of different health aspects. *Journal of Behavioral Medicine, 23*(5), 399–420.

Singh, G. K., & Siahpush, M. (2002). Increasing inequalities in all-cause and cardiovascular mortality among U.S. adults aged 25–64 years by area socioeconomic status, 1969–1998. *International Journal of Epidemiology, 31*(3), 600–613.

Smith, G. D., & Hart, C. (2002). Life-course socioeconomic and behavioral influences on cardiovascular disease mortality: The collaborative study. *American Journal of Public Health, 92*(8), 1295–1298.

Starfield, B., Riley, A. W., Witt, W. P., & Robertson, J. (2002). Social class gradients in health during adolescence. *Journal of Epidemiology & Community Health, 56(5),* 354–361.

Stronks, K., van de Mheen, H., Looman, C. W., & Mackenbach, J. P. (1998). The importance of psychosocial stressors for socio-economic inequalities in perceived health. *Social Science & Medicine, 46*(4–5), 611–623.

Sue, D. W., & Sue, D. (2002). *Counseling the culturally diverse: Theory and practice.* New York: Wiley.

Syme, S. L. (1978). Drug treatment of mild hypertension: Social and psychological considerations. *Annals of the New York Academy of Sciences, 304,* 99–106.

Townsend, P., Davidson, N., & Whitehead, M. (1988). *Inequalities in health.* London: Penguin.

Turrell, G., Lynch, J. W., Kaplan, G. A., Everson, S. A., Helkala, E., Kauhanen, J., & Salonen, J. T. (2002). Socioeconomic position across the lifecourse and cognitive function in late middle age. *Journal of Gerontology Series B: Psychological Sciences & Social Sciences, 57B*(1), S43–S51.

Twenge, J. M., & Campbell, W. K. (2002). Self-esteem and socioeconomic status: A meta-analytic review. *Personality & Social Psychology Review, 6*(1), 59–71.

U.S. Department of Health and Human Services, Agency for Healthcare Research and Quality. (2003). *National healthcare disparities report.* Rockville, MD: Author.

van Ryn, M. (2002). Research on the provider contribution to race/ethnicity disparities in medical care. *Medical Care, 40*(Suppl.), I140–I151.

van Ryn, M., & Burke, J. (2000). The effect of patient race and socio-economic status on physicians' perceptions of patients. *Social Science & Medicine, 50*(6), 813–828.

Wardle, J., Waller, J., & Jarvis, M. J. (2002). Sex differences in the association of socioeconomic status with obesity. *American Journal of Public Health, 92*(8), 1299–1304.

Williams, D., & Rucker, T. (1996). Socioeconomic status and the health of racial minority populations. In P. M. Kato & T. Mann (Eds.), *Handbook of diversity issues in health psychology* (pp. 407–423). New York: Plenum.

Williams, M., Davis, T., Parker, R., & Weiss, B. (2002). The role of health literacy in patient physician communication. *Family Medicine, 34*(5), 383–389.

Wilson, S. E. (2001). Socioeconomic status and the prevalence of health problems among married couples in late midlife. *American Journal of Public Health, 91*(1), 131–135.

29

Culture and the Disability Services

Paula Sotnik

Mary Ann Jezewski

Introduction

This chapter presents basic information about key concepts related to cultural diversity among foreign-born persons. Examples relevant to the practice of disability service providers are provided in each section. These concepts will assist the reader in understanding the culture-brokering model. Also included in this chapter is a discussion of concepts related to foreign-born consumers and rehabilitation services.

This chapter should be viewed as a starting point for understanding and providing culturally sensitive services to foreign-born consumers. It is beyond the scope of this chapter to include all the information necessary to provide services to persons from different cultures, but it does provide some generic information necessary to move toward that goal. To truly reach the goal of providing culturally responsive services, one must take the time, despite heavy caseloads and busy schedules, to understand the people we are supporting.

Discussion of Key Concepts

Several concepts are important to understand when providing services to consumers whose culture is different from that of the provider. Knowing the meanings of the following concepts helps service providers reflect on their values and their role in providing services to consumers. A discussion of key concepts also provides the basis for understanding the culture-brokering role and the role of rehabilitation service providers as culture brokers. The terms disability, rehabilitation, and activities of daily living will be discussed within a cross-cultural context. The key concepts in understanding cultural diversity in rehabilitation are listed in Table 1.

Authors' Note: The authors would like to acknowledge Rooshey Hasnain, EdD, for her contribution to this chapter.

Table 1 Key Concepts in Understanding Cultural Diversity in Rehabilitation

Foreign-born	Activities of daily living
Refugees/immigrants	Diversity
Culture	Stereotyping
Worldview	Acculturation
Disability	Cultural competence
Rehabilitation	

Who Are the Foreign-Born?

The Commerce Department's Census Bureau estimates that the foreign-born population of the United States numbered 32.5 million in 2002 (U.S. Census Bureau, 2003). This was the largest number of foreign-born persons in U.S. history and accounted for 11.5% of the total population. In 1970, persons who were foreign-born were only 4.7% of the U.S. population. The rapid increase in the foreign-born population has had an impact on all sectors of U.S. society, including rehabilitation services. Among the foreign-born population in the 2003 census, 52% were born in Latin America, 26% in Asia, 14% in Europe, and the remaining 8% in other regions of the world, such as Africa and Oceania. The rapid growth in the foreign-born population in the past generation has been due primarily to large-scale immigration from Latin America and Asia. According to the 2002 census, the largest foreign-born groups, by country of birth, included persons from Mexico, China, India, Korea, the Philippines, Cuba, Vietnam, the Dominican Republic, and El Salvador.

Persons who are foreign-born include (a) "immigrants," or nonresident aliens admitted for permanent residence; (b) "refugees" admitted to the United States outside normal quota restrictions, based on a well-founded fear of persecution; (c) "asylum seekers" applying to the United States for refugee status; and (d) "undocumented persons" entering the United States without the documents required to reside there legally (Lipson, Dibble, & Minarik, 1996). The foreign-born are those who were not U.S. citizens at birth. Native-born are those who were born in the United States or in a U.S. territory such as Puerto Rico or were born abroad of at least one parent who was a U.S. citizen (Schmidley, 2003).

According to Schmidley (2003), the foreign-born are a diverse group, with variable demographic, social, and economic characteristics depending on the region of birth. The following characteristics are important for understanding the culture-brokering model. Each factor can expedite or hinder the brokering process and affect the success of service provision. In 2002, 25.5% of the family households with a foreign-born householder included five or more people. In contrast, only 12.5% of the family households with a native householder were this large. Educational attainment among the foreign-born varies by region of birth. The highest percentages of high school graduates among the foreign-born were from Asia and Europe (86.8% and 84.0%, respectively). In sharp contrast, the proportion of high school graduates from Latin America was much lower, at 49.1%.

The foreign-born are more likely than the native-born to be unemployed, are more likely to live in poverty, and generally earn less. Data from the March 2002 survey by the U.S. Census Bureau (Schmidley, 2003) show that 31.1% of foreign-born, full-time, year-round workers earned less than $20,000, compared with 17.4% of native workers. High proportions of foreign-born individuals are employed in labor, farming, and service jobs rather than technical or professional specialties.

Estimating the number of foreign-born individuals with disabilities is an extremely difficult task. One reason is that there are many different definitions of disability, both within and between cultures and groups. Smart and Smart (1997) point out that there is no uniform definition of disability in the United States, and different government agencies define disability differently. The National Institute on Disability and Rehabilitation Research, Office of Special Education and Rehabilitative Services (1993) compared three national surveys sponsored by three different federal agencies: the National Center on Health Statistics, the Bureau of the Census, and the Bureau of Labor Statistics. The report shows that each agency uses definitions that address its specific purpose, such as employment, health care, or social security benefits. Particular agencies define the term according to their own limited concerns. Disability rights advocates often use broader definitions.

Individuals, families, and communities also perceive and respond to disabilities differently. A person with a hearing loss, for example, may not consider it to be a disability, and some Southeast Asian groups view a person with blindness as one who possesses a certain valued insight, not a disability. Such great variances in the definition of disability present difficult challenges in measuring the rate of disability in a group. Additionally, changes in terms over time may affect these rates. For example, when the American Association on Mental Deficiency revised its definition of mental retardation to set the IQ cutoff at 70 instead of 85, the population defined as mentally retarded decreased by 13% (Harry, 1992).

According to the National Council on Disability (1993), "Due to a disturbing lack of hard data on minority populations with disabilities, it is not certain precisely how many members of minority groups have disabilities or how fast this population is growing" (p. 3). Furthermore, the National Council on Disability (1999) indicates that virtually every federal estimate of the incidence of disability among people from minority cultures in the United States is likely to be low. This report further indicates that these low estimates appear to have substantially affected the effectiveness of service delivery. Culturally and linguistically inappropriate assessment tools and the stigma associated in identifying oneself as a person with a disability are also among the reasons for a lack of data or inaccurate data on disability rates in certain groups. Because disability involves not only medical considerations but also social, economic, and cultural factors, estimates of the prevalence of disability can vary significantly from one segment of society to another.

However, data compiled by the U.S. Census Bureau have revealed significant differences in disability rates among Americans belonging to various racial and ethnic groups. According to the 2000 Census Bureau's brief on disability status (U.S. Census Bureau, 2003), the overall rate of disability in the U.S. population is 19.3%. The rate is highest for Native Americans and Blacks/African Americans (each at 24.3%), Native Hawaiians and other Pacific Islanders (20%), and whites (19.7%), while those of Hispanic origin have a significantly lower rate (15.3%). Unfortunately, this report does not identify the specific subsets of foreign-born individuals, within a larger ethnic population, who have disabilities (e.g., a Cambodian subgroup within the Southeast Asian population, in which posttraumatic stress syndrome affects a high percentage of adults). Such factors make it nearly impossible to extrapolate the number of individuals with disabilities from specific foreign-born groups.

Refugees and Immigrants

Also important to understand are the reasons foreign-born individuals leave their countries of birth and how the factors behind the decision might influence their lives in the United States. Refugees and immigrants arrive in the United States for many reasons. Some come voluntarily, whereas others are forced to migrate as a result of political volatility or persecution in their homelands. The need or choice to immigrate is often influenced by a number of complex and interwoven political, social, and economic factors that can change over time.

Immigrants, as defined by the Immigration and Naturalization Service, are persons admitted to the United States for lawful permanent residence. The general term *immigrant* can refer to individuals who are granted permission to reside permanently in the United States for a variety of reasons. For example, many immigrants who came voluntarily to the United States between 1820 and 1960 were Europeans wanting to attain the *American dream.* Conversely, *forced immigrants* who migrate to the United States because of persecution or fear of death are termed *refugees.* That group is defined by U.S. and international law as persons outside their own countries who are unwilling or unable to return because of persecution, or a well-founded fear of persecution, based on religion, nationality, social group membership, or political opinion. To illustrate, groups of special concern include the Bosnians who were given priority for refugee status by the United States in 1997 because they were being persecuted by their government because of ethnicity or political opinion. Since 1975, more than two million refugees have been offered permanent resettlement in the United States (U.S. Department of State, 2000).

As mentioned, some immigrant groups who were motivated by the hope of freedom and economic opportunity have voluntarily relocated to the United States. The impetus to move was the desire for access to education, good wages, property ownership, and financial assets. Thus, some individuals decide that a new country is a better option for them than their native country, positively anticipate a move, and plan accordingly. One can surmise that this group and others that share similar migration characteristics might embrace adjustment and acceptance of mainstream America more readily than individuals forced to flee their countries because of force or persecution.

Refugees abandon their countries and their former patterns of existence to relocate to a very different, sometimes unwelcoming new world in which language, culture, social structures, and community resources may be totally unfamiliar. This type of move, referred to as *displacement,* can be characterized by the loss of most of one's belongings; lack of personal, emotional, and physical preparation; and no choice of one's next destination. Frequently, this move, although necessary to escape harm or death, is not a planned or chosen option for refugees. Acceptance and adjustment can be more difficult for refugee groups than for other immigrants. This is particularly true for older refugees, who leave rooted memories, achievements, and, oftentimes, love for their abandoned homeland. It is not unusual for elders to cling to traditions and beliefs because of a strong desire to return someday to the old country.

As an illustration of the plight of one refugee group, consider the recent migration of the Somalis to the United States. Somalis are mostly Sunni Muslims with traditional Islamic values including a strong family base (usually extended family), respect for the elderly, and an ethic of caring for children, the indigent, and individuals in poor health. Many recent arrivals are widows with children who lost their husbands to war. They are both mother and father, without the support of an extended family. Many women have no prior academic or employment skills. The language difference is a major barrier, and their situation can be further aggravated by illiteracy in their own language. Children often serve as interpreters, which can result in a role reversal that diminishes the mother's influence as a revered parent.

Of special significance to disability service providers is understanding the challenge that accessing institutions and services can pose for refugees and immigrants. This challenge, coupled with the sometimes unfavorable perception of disability held by refugees and immigrants, exacerbates the lack of access to needed supports. In addition to facing language and cultural barriers, many individuals are not familiar with the existence, range, and purpose of services for individuals with disabilities. Often, similar services and programs did not exist for individuals with disabilities in their country of birth. Even if refugee groups are made aware of relevant programs, the documentation and processes required by bureaucracies further impede an individual's access to services. Additionally, some groups who fled countries that were ruled by brutal systems might be fearful of any services that might be associated with government, even indirectly, particularly those that request the identification of a physical or emotional disability. Finally, therapies and services might be contrary to the values and beliefs of some groups. Consider our system's advocacy of independence through the use of assistive technology in cases when a family believes its role is to provide total care for an individual. Also consider a mainstream culture that directs an individual to comfortably and proudly divulge his or her disability, contrasted with cultures that believe disability represents dishonor because it is caused by ancestral sins.

This snapshot of many refugees and immigrants is intended to provide the reader with the perspective of recent arrivals and the potential implications for their understanding and acceptance of our service systems. Getting to know newcomer populations by researching and visiting community refugee and immigrant organizations—for example, mutual assistance associations—is a valuable means by which to acquire understanding of the past and current experiences of these groups.

Culture

Hundreds of definitions of culture can be found in the anthropology literature. In this chapter, culture is broadly defined as a system of learned and shared standards for perceiving, interpreting, and behaving in interactions with others and with the environment (Jezewski, 1990). Two key components in this definition are that culture is learned and that it is shared. Human beings learn culture from those with whom they interact, beginning at the moment of birth (and some would say before birth). Family, as well as any others who cared for us as young children, are the formidable teachers of cultural values, beliefs, and behaviors. Values are ideas about what is normal and abnormal, proper and improper, desirable and undesirable, right and wrong. Values form the basis for our beliefs and behaviors. Some of the values held by the majority of Caucasian, middle-class Americans—often referred to as dominant U.S. values—are listed in Table 2.

Table 2 Dominant U.S. Values

Democracy	Achieving/doing
Individualism	Working
Privacy	Materialism
Change	Cleanliness
Progress	Time
Optimal health	Directness/assertiveness
Informality	

For example, many Americans believe it is important to work hard because they value *achieving and doing;* that is, it is important to accomplish tasks. This is not a universal value: Not all cultures value *doing* to this degree. In some cultures, who you are in relation to your family or community is valued more than what you do as an individual.

Culture should be viewed as a system; that is, culture is made up of discrete but interconnected components. A culture system consists of the following elements:

- Normative codes (ways of behaving) such as food practices, religious practices, child-rearing practices
- Communication codes (both verbal and nonverbal)

- Knowledge (information necessary to function as a member of a culture group)
- Problem-solving strategies (how everyday problems are resolved)
- Relationships (family and social)
- Methods of transmitting culture to the young or to new members of the culture group

Underlying and shaping these elements are the basic values and beliefs of the group. These elements function as a whole. A change in one component, or the introduction of new or unfamiliar elements, can affect other components as well as the system as a whole. For example, a recently immigrated elderly Vietnamese woman who develops a disability, and for whom an assisted living environment has been recommended, may have a difficult time adjusting to this environment because she is no longer a part of her family's household. Feelings of abandonment may be strong as a result of the culture from which she comes. The traditional Vietnamese culture is highly family oriented. Two or three generations may be living in the same household. Elders are highly respected, and adults within the family are expected to assume full responsibility for them. Traditionally, elders with disabilities are cared for at home. Institutionalizing an elder member of the family is believed to be disrespectful. The Vietnamese family may feel that it is abandoning the family member and not fulfilling its role as a good and loyal family if it institutionalizes that member. This disruption changes the configuration of the family and, in turn, violates many of the values of Vietnamese culture. In all likelihood, this recently immigrated Vietnamese family will not easily resolve the value conflict that has arisen as a result of the family member's disability. In turn, the life of the person with disabilities is vastly disrupted because of changes in her cultural system. The changes may involve inability to continue some religious practices or the loss of ability to communicate with others. Communication, because of the inability to speak English, and dietary practices are some of the components of the cultural system that could be affected by moving the member with disabilities out of the Vietnamese family. Cultural values and beliefs are continually changing, but at the same time they resist change because they serve the purpose of defining who we are within a group.

It is useful to distinguish between the terms *culture, ethnicity,* and *race.* Although these terms are sometimes used interchangeably in the literature, they are not the same and should not be used interchangeably.

Ethnicity refers to groups of people who are united socially, politically, and geographically and possess a common pattern of values, beliefs, and behaviors (culture) as well as language. Examples of ethnic groups are Irish, Iranian, German, Italian, and Ethiopian. *Culture* is a principal force in shaping an ethnic group.

Race, on the other hand, has to do with the biological component of being human. However, the term *race,* as it has evolved, does not help in understanding the biological component of humans. Historically, the term *race* has evolved into political, emotional, and social situations and constructs that, very often, create dissension and bias between human groups. For the purpose of understanding the diversity of culture, race has little relevance. Essentially, race does not form our values, beliefs, and behaviors, but our values and beliefs *do* influence our views on racial differences and mold our behavior toward people of different races.

Worldview

A fundamental component of culture is an individual's worldview, which includes beliefs about religion, humanity, nature, and one's existence. Worldview relates to the philosophical ideas of being (Jandt, 1995). To effectively support individuals with disabilities who are foreign-born, rehabilitation service providers should have an appreciation of the varied perceptions of one's existence in the world.

Samovar, Porter, and Jain (1981) defined three components of worldview: the individual's perception of himself or herself in relationship to nature, the individual's perceptions of science and its ability to explain the world, and attitudes toward material goods. Differing interpretations are paired with these components in the framework presented in Table 3.

Table 3 Samovar's Components of Worldview

Component	*Different Views*
Individual and nature	Human life is more important than nature OR Humans are part of nature; nature cannot be modified
Science and technology	Individuals can discover an explanation and solution to problems by scientific method OR Problems are predetermined by fate and cannot be solved by human intervention
Materialism	The acquisition of material goods is important OR Self-sacrifice is valued; tangible assets are not

One's worldview takes into account many beliefs that guide behavior and may have particular implications for the perceptions of disability and related services held by some foreign-born groups. One facet of worldview is an individual's relationship to science and technology (Samovar et al., 1981). People who abide by mainstream U.S. culture believe that a scientific strategy can solve problems and that technology can help in this effort. Applying this concept to rehabilitation, an individual with a disability could successfully use a communication device that was developed based on rigorous research. This example is considered commonplace in our rehabilitation service world and culture. In some cultures, however, challenges posed by a disability are conditions that should not be altered; an individual's disability is predetermined by fate and thus cannot be modified by an adaptive device. To further illustrate, some religions are said to be fatalistic because they require submission to the will of God, which some would argue contradicts practices for preventing or remediating disabilities (Miles, 1995).

Another major dimension to the manner in which people perceive their world and behave is an adherence to a collectivist or individualistic value system. The framework shown in Table 4 indicates several examples of diverse cultural values and potential implications for understanding disability and accepting disability-related supports.

Implicit in the U.S. rehabilitation system are *individualistic* values that uphold and encourage self-sufficiency, along with the use of technology or other adaptations to complete daily living tasks independently. Rehabilitation policies and practices including assessments, programs, supports, and success criteria are based on meeting these standards of independence.

For some individuals who embrace strong family interdependence rather than individual independence, these standards will most likely pose conflict with the theory and practice of rehabilitation. Many persons with disabilities want assistive technology, vocational rehabilitation, and other disability services, but—depending on their cultural values—they may want them for different reasons. For example, persons with an individualistic worldview may want assistive technology so that they will be able to live independently in their own homes

Table 4 Collectivist and Individualistic Value Systems

Cultural Orientation	*Personal Characteristics*	*Behavioral Indicators*
Individualism	• Self-expression • Assertiveness • Self-advocacy • Self-realization	• Communicating dissatisfaction with services • Holding a view of services different from that of the family unit or community • Focusing on the individual's unique set of talents and potential
Collectivism	• An individual's existence is inseparable from the family and community • Self-interests are those of the family or larger group • Group activities are dominant	• An individual may not accept transportation and work outside his or her community • Supports to achieve self-sufficiency are not welcomed.

and be economically self-supporting. Persons who abide by collectivist values may want assistive technology in order to continue living with their family and participating in family tasks and recreation. Thus, diverse views guide one's choice of values and goals. Before discussing possible interventions, the service provider should be aware of the consumer's values and goals. Whatever interventions are discussed should be presented in the context of the consumer's preferences as a means of meeting those goals. Consider the following scenario.

A middle-aged Chinese man, Mr. Chen, attended a demonstration of assistive technology products with his wife and two adolescent children. Mr. Chen became blind, as a result of illness, about 5 years ago. Following Mr. Chen's acquired visual disability, his wife shaved him daily. However, being assisted by a female in completing such a personal and masculine task was perceived as devaluing according to his cultural beliefs. Throughout the demonstration, Mr. Chen appeared to disregard the description of products to assist individuals with disabilities. However, he became interested as the presenter explained the functions of a buzzing shaver that beeped when it touched facial stubble. This product enabled effective shaving without the need to see facial hair. He anticipated an opportunity to once again shave himself, and he became very interested in this particular device. Although he did not value many assistive technology products designed to increase overall independence, this particular device was appealing because it supported Mr. Chen's cultural values and beliefs about personal care tasks and masculinity.

Disability

To understand how other cultures understand and define disability, one should begin by examining how disability is seen and understood in the United States. Legislation signed into law to provide equal access for individuals with disabilities in the United States demonstrates an example of how disability is interpreted by Western culture. For example, the Americans with Disabilities Act (ADA) defines the term *disability* as follows:

> With respect to an individual, the term "disability" means (A) a physical or mental impairment that substantially limits one or more of the major life activities of such individual; (B) a record of such an impairment; or (C) being regarded as having such an impairment.
> A person must meet the requirements of at least one of these three criteria to be an individual with a disability under the Act. (Equal Employment Opportunity Commission and the U.S. Department of Justice, 1991)

The ADA stipulates various modalities of supports and accommodations, including products and environmental modifications. Self-sufficiency is often based on nonhuman assistance—for example, assistive technology or environmental interventions—although personal care assistants are also part of the equation.

Analysis of the language and intent of the law reveals significant underlying characteristics that frame the Western definition of disability. Harry (1992) describes these suppositions.

> First, it is assumed that the occurrence of the condition is located within the individual, and only in certain cases of clear genetic or biological etiology would other family members be implicated. Second, it is assumed that the condition should be treated by objectively verifiable interventions, conceived within the parameters of the scientific method. Third, the Western faith in science has tended to result in the belief that, wherever possible, biological anomalies should be corrected; there is little tolerance for deviation from the norm. (p. 22)

What constitutes having a disability in the United States often varies considerably among government agencies, public and private institutions, and consumer groups. Thus, the definition and significance of disability are contingent on the differing perceptions of individuals, communities, and institutions.

The National Institute on Disability and Rehabilitation Research (1999) has identified a new paradigm of disability that

> maintains that disability is a product of an interaction between characteristics (e.g., conditions or impairments, functional status, or personal and social qualities) of the individual and characteristics of the natural, built, cultural and social environments. The construct of disability is located on a continuum from enablement to disablement. Personal characteristics, as well as environmental ones, may be enabling or disabling, and the relative degree fluctuates, depending on condition, time and setting. Disability is a contextual variable, dynamic over time and circumstance. (p. 68578)

The meaning of disability is influenced by the cultural beliefs and values of consumers and service providers. Euro-American values of equality and individual ability as a source of social identity shape a concept of disability that may not be applicable in other groups (Ingstad & Whyte, 1995). Foreign-born populations may view a disabling condition, causal factors, and related services differently than does mainstream America. For Euro-Americans, causation may be attributed to factors such as disease or genetic disorders. Acknowledgment of having a disability is acceptable, and outside intervention is thought to be desirable in American mainstream culture. Individuals who are foreign-born may not hold these opinions about disability. Descriptions of traditional beliefs in some Latino and Asian groups have shown how differential interpretations of the meanings of a disability can become a source of dissonance between professionals and culturally different families (Chan, 1986; Harry, 1992; Leung, 1989; Sotnik & Hasnain, 1998).

For example, Southeast Asian beliefs related to disability and its causation range from those that focus on the behavior of the parents, particularly the mother, during pregnancy to sins committed by extended family members and reincarnation. Disability is sometimes attributed to the sins of the parents or ancestors. A Southeast Asian individual with a disability may be segregated from the community because the disability represents a wrongdoing by the parents or ancestors and is considered a source of disgrace. Generally, disability from birth is stigmatizing for the individual and family because of these traditional beliefs. Acquired disabilities are less stigmatizing (Sotnik & Hasnain, 1998).

The experience of an assistive technology public awareness project illustrates the miscommunication surrounding the term *disability* when used with persons from other cultures. The project disseminated multiple copies of a flyer that publicized the availability of products for people with disabilities. The project's efforts to attract individuals from diverse linguistic, ethnic, and cultural backgrounds to inquire about an assistive device strategy proved unsuccessful. Project staff inquired about the lack of interest and made significant discoveries. Most individuals did not define themselves as persons with a disability because they did not know what the word implied or because disability was considered as a condition that rendered a person helpless. Thus, a person who could not hear was not considered an individual with a disability because he could otherwise function very well at activities that did not require auditory ability. Better success was achieved when outreach materials deleted the term *disability* and described specific conditions, such as "if you have difficulty walking, hearing, seeing, etc."

A collectivist view, inherent in many foreign-born cultures, prescribes that disability reflects the totality of the family rather than just the member with the disability. Harry (1992) also indicates that families who believe that the source of a disability lies in spiritual rather than physical phenomena may be committed to spiritual rather than medical interventions. Harry further states that this finding has been documented among Mexican Americans (Adkins & Young, 1976), Native Americans (Locust, 1988), and some Southeast Asian groups (Chan, 1986).

In the Southeast Asian community, Buddhism is the predominant religion. The principles of Buddhism stipulate that each person is responsible for his or her actions. A belief in Buddhism may establish a precedent wherein Southeast Asians adhere to the concept of *karma,* a belief that one's present life is determined by what one has done, right or wrong, in a previous existence. Thus, followers will accept a perceived misfortune, such as a disability, as predestined.

Disability Service Systems

Disability service systems can be considered as entities that, similar to a country or ethnic enclave, embody a philosophy, values, policies, and practices. The United States Vocational Rehabilitation (VR) system is one example. Although each state's and region's VR program will reflect some divergence in practices, the systems share similar dominant cultural aspects. A brief review of the origin of VR will enable an understanding of the system's cultural foundation. The VR system was created in 1918 with the passage of the Soldier Rehabilitation Smith Sears Act to enable veterans with war-related disabilities to become self-sufficient through employment. Amendments to the 1973 Rehabilitation Act launched a growing increase in consumer self-sufficiency and advocacy by initiating Individual Written Rehabilitation Plans, the independent living program concept, consumer involvement in state agency policy, and increased access by consumers to federally funded programs. A review of contemporary VR legislative content, funding processes, policies, and programmatic practices confirms the incorporation of individualism and independence. Within the last two decades, vocational rehabilitation legislation (Pub. L. No. 95–607 and Pub. L. No. 102–569) reflects the increased emphasis on consumer empowerment and overall independence. Recall our earlier discussion of individualism and collectivism. Table 5 provides some examples of the effects that the values of individualism have on vocational rehabilitation principles.

In a focus group conducted by this author, vocational rehabilitation counselors were asked about the culture of the rehabilitation system. The participants characterized the rehabilitation system as institutionalized and linear. They pointed out that vocational rehabilitation is regulated by legislation, so services are regulated by rules and statutes. The system is driven by outcomes, especially job placement. Success is defined as the quickest route to being placed.

Services are very effective for a certain segment of the population that fits into the prescribed model. This segment typically consists of individuals who believe in the same values, can be readily employed, and are English speaking. Furthermore, because of large caseloads, it is usually impossible to develop relationships with an individual and family members. This is directly opposite to the ideals of provision of culturally responsive services to people from some diverse backgrounds.

Table 5 Effects of Values of Individualism on Vocational Rehabilitation Principles

Individualism	*Concepts of Vocational Rehabilitation*
Self-determination: individuals control personal situations	Consumers set their own rehabilitation goals and are self-advocates
Success is defined in terms of professional achievement of the individual	Employment is an outcome that indicates successful rehabilitation
Each person is unique and independent	Self-sufficiency is an ideal outcome

Another focus group was conducted with families of persons with disabilities from the Dominican Republic. Many of these families felt that it would be shameful and exploitative for them to allow their family members with disabilities to work because it is the responsibility of the family to care for its members with disabilities. Clearly, this runs counter to the philosophy of the vocational rehabilitation system and the independent living movement. Working with families that hold such values does not mean accepting such values, nor does it mean scorning them. A culturally competent service provider will use strategies that involve peer families and community organizations in showing newly arrived families the possibilities that exist in the United States for persons with disabilities to improve the quality of their lives.

Activities of Daily Living

Activities of daily living (ADL) can be defined as those tasks necessary to maintain physical well-being, personal appearance, hygiene, safety, and general functioning in one's home and community. These tasks, along with instrumental activities of daily living (IADLs), span many domains of living and include bathing, dressing, eating, household chores, financial management, and cooking. There are three important questions to address about daily living routines implemented by individuals with disabilities who are also members of foreign-born groups:

1. Are there differences in daily living activities in the person's country of origin in comparison to how they are performed in the United States? For example, persons in rural India usually eat with their hands, sitting on the ground, whereas in the United States eating is usually done at a table, using silverware.
2. How are daily living activities performed by persons with disabilities in that culture?
3. How might individuals from another culture respond to assistance in performing these activities?

The importance, type, variety, and frequency of daily routines may differ considerably from one group to another and, moreover, between generations within the same ethnic group. Table 6 offers a sampling of several groups and some selected differing daily living practices.

The value of specific daily living tasks can differ, contingent upon a group's perception of one's role in life. For example, an individual with a cognitive disability cannot budget or read important documents but can serve as a family member and employee. If the latter roles are perceived as more important, financial management activities conducted by this individual may be considered insignificant.

It is important to keep in mind that not all members of an ethnic group will demonstrate

Table 6 Examples of Daily Living Practices in Selected Cultures

Ethnic Group	*ADL-Related Practices*
Cambodian	Men keep the nail of the right little finger longer than other nails
	Young unmarried women wear an article around the waist that should not be removed, to prevent "love magic"
Russian	The gender of the personal assistance provider is not an issue
	Personal care can be provided by a nurse or an aide
Vietnamese	Hair should not be wet at night; going to bed with wet hair causes headaches
	Only a family member of the same sex should help with personal care

identical daily living activities. Any information describing cultural aspects of personal care is intended to serve as a cue to learn the unique characteristics of an individual and family.

Some individuals with disabilities may need the assistance of another person or a product to complete these tasks. Moreover, individuals with disabilities sometimes have added unique activities that the nondisabled population will not experience, such as accessing other forms of transportation and care of adaptive equipment.

The nature of assistance with daily living skills for persons with disabilities can be affected by many individual characteristics including geography, religion, socioeconomic factors, and the type of disability. For example, many Muslim women do not expose any skin, except for the hands and part of the face, to any man, except her husband (*Family Education and Resource Program,* 1998). Issues such as this are particularly important for personal care assistance provided by other individuals.

Worldview, or how one perceives the world and related personal roles, can also affect the nature of how daily living skills are performed. As described in a previous section, people who adhere to the traditional U.S. mainstream culture of individualism might uphold assertiveness and self-advocacy as admirable characteristics. Behavioral indicators might be manifested when an individual with a disability disagrees with family members regarding types of daily living supports. These individuals may prefer the help of paid employees as personal assistance service providers because this relationship promotes independence and self-advocacy, as opposed to relying on family members for personal assistance. Findings indicate that family providers are generally not the ones consumers find the most satisfactory for many reasons, including encouraging continued dependency (Nosek, Fuhrer, Rintala, & Hart, 1993).

Not everyone holds this opinion, for example, groups that abide by collectivistic worldviews. Southeast Asians, Ethiopians, and Haitians may feel strongly that only family members are appropriate personal care assistants. Because family members often assist an individual with a disability to complete daily routines, the family becomes the assistive technology. The suggestion that a device replace traditional family functions may not be regarded positively (Sotnik & Hasnain, 1998).

Diversity

There are many different types of diversity within a society, among them culture, gender, age, and economic. Although the focus of this chapter is cultural diversity, all the different types of diversity within a society are integral to understanding cultural diversity.

Specific values, beliefs, and behaviors are not universal across groups, but all human groups have a set of values and beliefs that guide their behaviors. When we are learning about specific ethnic or culture groups, it is important to keep in mind that there is as much diversity within groups as there is between groups. For example, when we talk about Native Americans, we are talking about more than 400 different tribal groups. Historically, most of these tribes had little contact with each other, spoke different languages, and did not have the same values and beliefs, and therefore could not be considered in the same culture group. It is inappropriate to consider Native Americans as one culture and to assume that all Native Americans have the same values and beliefs. This is a form of stereotyping. Native Americans may have some of the same values, but there is diversity among tribes as well as between members of the same tribe.

Stereotyping

Very often, when we first begin to learn about different culture groups, the tendency is to take the facts we learn and apply them to everyone who is a member of the group. We do this without evaluating the extent to which the individual members adhere to the dominant values and beliefs of the group. This is a form of stereotyping. Stereotyping refers to the assumption that all members of a group share the same characteristics, values, and beliefs. For example, a service provider may have read that in Mexican families, the man is the decision maker and that women in the family will not make service decisions by themselves. Based on this information, the service provider who applies the stereotype will not spend time discussing service decisions with a Mexican woman without her husband or father present. In some Mexican families, the man may be the primary decision maker, but in other families of Mexican origin, women assume autonomy in making decisions that affect them personally. By assuming the woman will not make decisions about the services she needs, the provider may be raising a barrier to effective intercultural communication and may be undermining a positive service outcome for this consumer. People within a culture group adhere to the basic values and beliefs of the group to varying degrees. The degree of adherence depends on many variables, among them gender, age, and exposure to other culture groups.

In another example of stereotyping using the situation just described, a service provider may read about Mexican families and assume that every Hispanic group adheres to the same values as those of Mexican descent. *Hispanic* is an umbrella term that encompasses people from Mexico, Puerto Rico, and some parts of Central and South America as well as Spain. These varied culture groups have a common language but have been separated culturally for many centuries. In addition, even though their common language is Spanish, the nuances of the language have evolved differently over the centuries.

One way to avoid stereotyping is to look at new knowledge about an ethnic group as a generalization, which is a *beginning* point that indicates common trends for beliefs and behaviors that are shared by a group. Stereotyping is viewed as an *end* point; that is, no attempt is made to learn whether the individual in question fits with what is known about the group.

Stereotyping assumes that every member of the group possesses certain characteristics, adheres to the same beliefs, and behaves in the same manner in any given situation. Generalization, as a beginning point, acknowledges that additional information is needed to determine whether the information known about the group applies to a particular individual within the group and to the particular situation in question. For example, one might read that most Mexican people are members of the Roman Catholic religion or that most people from the Middle East are Muslim. For the rehabilitation service provider to assume that every Middle Eastern consumer adheres to Islam and therefore prays five times a day is stereotyping. It could lead the provider to anticipate behaviors that do not exist and to make inappropriate scheduling decisions.

Possessing knowledge about Islam may increase the service provider's ability to give culturally competent care to Middle Eastern consumers. Stereotyping can be avoided by asking questions about their preferences, such as the opportunity to pray at certain times of the day. Galanti (1991) provides a useful discussion of stereotyping versus generalizing as well as discussions of many other basic concepts related to cultural diversity.

Acculturation

The degree to which one assumes the values and beliefs of a new culture is referred to as the degree of acculturation. Acculturation is influenced by language, length of time spent interacting with people in the new culture, and the intensity of contact with the new culture. Immigrants may be influenced by the U.S. culture, and their values, beliefs, and behaviors may change, based on frequency and intensity of contact. For some, this change will occur rapidly, and for others, the change will occur slowly or not at all. Acculturation essentially becomes a melding of a person's primary culture with that of the new culture. We can never assume that someone who has immigrated to the United States from another culture will assume the values and beliefs of the dominant U.S. society. Acculturation is also influenced by education, economic status, gender, and personal choice.

The following example serves as an illustration of how acculturation evolves in the various members of a newly immigrated family. The young children who come to the United States from another culture and who attend public school tend to acculturate faster and more completely than their parents. Daily exposure to U.S. values through the classroom environment, the pressure to learn English, and peer pressure and the desire for peer friendships all contribute to acculturation in the child. In contrast, the children's mother may be in the home most of the time, especially if there are preschool children in the family and she is not working outside the home. Her closest friends may be women who have immigrated from the same geographic location. This woman may not be under any pressure to learn the ways of the U.S. culture or to become fluent in English. Her social world may revolve around her ethnic community, where her primary language, rather than English, is spoken. The child's father and other family members acculturate depending, in part, on their work outside the home and the need to speak English in their work environments. Their degree of acculturation also depends on their need to attend to activities of daily living, such as shopping, accessing transportation, and interacting with various immigration and social service agencies.

Cultural Competence and Sensitivity

Cultural sensitivity is the awareness by one person of the differences in values, beliefs, and behaviors of another, and the understanding that these values, beliefs, and behaviors are the basis for the way people interact with each other. Cultural sensitivity precedes cultural competence, but it is not considered enough for service providers to be culturally sensitive to the diversity in others. Culturally competent service is responsive to issues related to culture, race, gender, and sexual orientation. Culturally competent service is service provided within the cultural context of the consumer (American Academy of Nursing Expert Panel Report, 1993). Randall-David (1989) defines cultural competence as a set of behaviors, attitudes, and policies that enable a system, agency, or individual to function effectively with culturally diverse consumers and communities. In the context of providing disability services, cultural competency requires recognizing and understanding how economic conditions, race, culture, ethnicity, the social context, and environment define health, disability, and the provision of services (Rorie, Paine, & Barger, 1996).

Rorie and colleagues (1996) provide a useful framework describing a continuum from incompetence to competence. On the incompetent end of the continuum is cultural destructiveness (attitudes, policies, and practices are exhibited that can be destructive to a culture). Movement along the continuum proceeds to cultural incapacity (a biased, authoritarian system that lacks capacity to facilitate growth in culturally diverse groups), then on to culture blindness (the "we're all human" approach in which it is thought that culture, ethnicity, and race make no difference in how services are provided). Next on the continuum is cultural pre-competence (cultural sensitivity wherein there is a decision made and attempts are made to deliver services in a manner respectful of cultural diversity). Following along the continuum is cultural competence (an acceptance of and respect for cultural norms, patterns, beliefs, and differences, along with self-assessment regarding cultural competence), and finally, there is cultural proficiency (motivation toward adding to the knowledge base of culturally competent service provision and developing a culturally therapeutic approach). It should be noted that each time a service provider encounters a consumer from an ethnic group with which the provider is not familiar, the provider may have to move through at least part of the competence continuum. Developing competency takes time with each new cultural encounter.

In 1993, an American Academy of Nursing panel of experts on culturally competent health care was convened to outline the major components of providing culturally competent care to diverse groups of patients. Although the panel concluded that there are no well-tested and tried models that can facilitate the provision of culturally competent care, the panel did identify a number of useful and effective models that have been used to enhance both cultural sensitivity and the delivery of culturally competent services. Jezewski's culture-brokering model was identified as one practice model that offered guidance for the delivery of culturally competent care. Although it was originally developed in the context of health care, it has applications in many fields, including rehabilitation services. If culture is such an important influence on human behavior, how can the disability service provider work through, rather than against, the culture of foreign-born consumers?

References

Adkins, P. G., & Young, R. G. (1976). Cultural perceptions in the treatment of handicapped school children of Mexican-American parentage. *Journal of Research and Development in Education, 9(4),* 83–90.

American Academy of Nursing Expert Panel Report. (1993). Culturally competent health care. *Nursing Outlook, 40(6),* 277–283.

Chan, S. (1986). Parents of exceptional Asian children. In M. K. Kitano & P. C. Chinn (Eds.), *Exceptional Asian children and youth* (pp. 36–53). Reston, VA: Council for Exceptional Children.

Equal Employment Opportunity Commission and the U.S. Department of Justice. (1991). *Americans with disability handbook.* Washington, DC: Government Printing Office. Available at ftp://trace.wisc.edu/PUB/TEXT/ADA_INFO/HANDBOOK/FREG1.TXT

Family Education and Resource Program, Cultural Traditions—Saudi Arabia. (1998). Boston: Children's Hospital.

Galanti, G. A. (1991). *Caring for patients from different cultures: Case studies from American hospitals.* Philadelphia: University of Pennsylvania Press.

Harry, B. (1992). *Cultural diversity, families, and the special education system.* New York: Teachers College Press.

Ingstad, B., & Whyte, S. R. (1995). Disability and culture: An overview. In B. Ingstad & S. Whyte (Eds.), *Disability and culture* (pp. 3–32). Berkeley: University of California Press.

Jandt, F. (1995). *Intercultural communication.* Thousand Oaks, CA: Sage.

Jezewski, M. A. (1990). Culture brokering in migrant farmworker health care. *Western Journal of Nursing Research, 12*(4), 497–513.

Leung, E. K. (1989). Cultural and accultural commonalities and diversities among Asian Americans: Identification and programming considerations. In A. A. Ortiz & B. A. Ramirez (Eds.), *Schools and the culturally diverse exceptional student.* Reston, VA: The Council for Exceptional Children.

Lipson, G. L., Dibble, S. L., & Minarik, P. A. (1996). *Culture and nursing care: A pocket guide.* San Francisco: UCSF Nursing Press.

Locust, C. (1988). Wounding the spirit: Discrimination and traditional American Indian belief systems. *Harvard Review, 58*(3), 315–330.

Miles, M. (1995). Disability in an Eastern religious context: Historical perspectives. *Disability & Society, 10,* 49–69.

National Council on Disability. (1993). *Meeting the unique needs of minorities with disabilities: Report to the president and the Congress.* Washington, DC: Author.

National Council on Disability. (1999). *Lift every voice: Modernizing disability policies and programs to serve a diverse nation.* Washington, DC: Author.

National Institute on Disability and Rehabilitation Research, Office of Special Education and Rehabilitative Services. (1993). Disability statistics. *Rehab brief: Bringing research into effective focus, 14*(8). Retrieved December 7, 2003, from http://codi.buffalo.edu/graph_based/.demographics/.disstats

National Institute on Disability and Rehabilitation Research. (1999, December 7). Long-range plan for fiscal years 1999–2004. *Federal Register, 64*(234), 68576–68614.

Nosek, M. A., Fuhrer, M. J., Rintala, D. H., & Hart, K. A. (1993). The use of personal assistance services by persons with spinal cord injury: Policy issues surrounding reliance on family and paid providers. *Journal of Disability Policy Studies, 4*(1), 89–103.

Randall-David, E. (1989). *Strategies for working with culturally diverse communities and clients.* Bethesda, MD: Association for the Care of Children's Health.

Rorie, J., Paine, L., & Barger, M. (1996). Primary care for women: Cultural competence in primary care services. *Journal of Nurse-Midwifery, 41*(2), 92–100.

Samovar, L. A., Porter, R. E., & Jain, N. C. (1981). *Understanding intercultural communication.* Belmont, CA: Wadsworth.

Schmidley, D. (2003). The foreign-born population in the states: March 2002. *Current Population Reports,* (pp. 20–539). Washington, DC: U.S. Census Bureau.

Smart, J. F., & Smart, D. W. (1997). The racial/ethnic demography of disability. *Journal of Rehabilitation, 63*(4), 9–15.

Sotnik, P., & Hasnain, R. (1998). Outreach & service delivery to the Southeast Asian populations in the United States. In T. S. Smith (Ed.), *Rural rehabilitation: A modern perspective* (pp. 228–259). Arnaudville, LA: Bow River Publishing.

U.S. Census Bureau. (2003). *Disability status: 2000—Census 2000 brief.* Retrieved November 13, 2003, from www.census.gov/hhes/www/disable/disabstat2k.html

U.S. Department of State. (2000). *Fact sheet. U.S. refugee admissions and resettlement program.* Retrieved November 13, 2003, from www.state.gov/www/global/prm/2000_admis_reset.pdf

---

Index

About the Editors

Glenn C. Gamst, PhD, is Professor and Chair of the Psychology Department at the University of La Verne, in La Verne, California. His current research has to do with the effects of multicultural variables such as client–therapist ethnic/racial match, client acculturation and ethnic identity, and provider self-reported cultural competence on clinical outcomes for community mental health clients. Additional areas of specialization and research include memory and cognition, conversational memory, and univariate and multivariate statistical and methodological issues. His research focuses on cultural variables that affect clinical outcomes of community mental health consumers. He also teaches the doctoral statistics sequence in the Clinical-Community doctoral program at the University of La Verne. He is the coauthor of *Applied Multivariate Analysis.* He received his PhD in experimental psychology from the University of Arkansas in 1979.

Aghop Der-Karabetian, PhD, is Professor of Psychology and Associate Dean of the College of Arts and Sciences at the University of La Verne, where he has taught for the last 27 years and has served as chair of the psychology department. He has conducted research on multicultural issues, ethnic and multiethnic identity, seeking psychological help, sex roles, world-mindedness, and environmental activism. He has authored or coauthored over 35 refereed publications. He is one of the cofounders of the Armenian American Mental Health Association and speaks five languages. He was a Fulbright scholar (1974–1978) and received the Sears Excellence in Teaching Award (1989) at the University of La Verne. He received a PhD in social psychology from the University of Kansas in 1978.

Richard H. Dana, PhD, is Research Professor (Honorary) at the Regional Research Institute for Human Services, Portland State University. During his teaching career at state universities, Marquette University, and a professional school, he served as Professor, Director of Clinical Training, Psychology Department Chair, and Dean. He is the author of 16 books, 30 book chapters/monographs, 17 reviews, and approximately 200 journal publications. He has a Diplomate in Clinical Psychology (American Board of Professional Psychology, 1960) and has been licensed in seven states. Since retirement as Professor Emeritus, University of Arkansas (1988), his empirical research program developed the Multicultural Assessment-Intervention Process model (MAIP) for practice while an accompanying multicultural research and training context were described in *Multicultural Assessment Perspectives for Professional Psychology* (1993), *Understanding Cultural Identity in Assessment and Intervention* (1998), and *Handbook of Cross-Cultural and*

Multicultural Personality Assessment (2000). His professional recognition includes Sigma Xi Associate and Member (1949, 1960); Society for Personality Assessment, Bruno Klopfer Distinguished Contribution Award (1984) and Mayman Research Award (2004); Oregon Graduate School of Professional Psychology, Walter Klopfer Award (1987) and Student Association Special Merit Award (1987); and Distinguished Psychologist Award, Arkansas Psychological Association (1988). His most recent books are *Multicultural Assessment Principles, Applications, and Examples* (2005); *Tell-Me-A-Story Assessment of Multicultural Populations*, with G. Costantino and R. Malgady (2007); and *Training for Professional Practice in a Global Society*, with J. Allen, which will be published in 2008.